D1384713

NETWORKS
AND
ORGANIZATIONS

NETWORKS AND ORGANIZATIONS:

STRUCTURE, FORM, AND ACTION

Edited by

Nitin Nohria

and

Robert G. Eccles

Harvard Business School Press
Boston, Massachusetts

96 95 94 93   5 4 3 2 1

Library of Congress Cataloging-in-Publication Data

Networks and organizations : structure, form, and action / edited by
  Nitin Nohria and Robert G. Eccles.
        p.   cm.
  Papers originally presented at a conference held in 1990,
sponsored by Harvard Business School.
  Includes bibliographical references and index.
  ISBN 0-87584-324-7 (acid free paper)
  1. Organizational behavior—Congresses.   2. Social networks—
Congresses.   I. Nohria, Nitin, 1962–   .   II. Eccles, Robert G.
HD58.7.N47   1992
302.3'5—dc20   92-11442
                                                        CIP

The recycled paper used in this publication meets the requirements of the American
National Standard for Permanence of Paper for Printed Library Materials
Z39.49-1984.

Contents

Preface   vii

Plan and Summary of the Book   ix

Introduction: Is a Network Perspective a Useful Way of
Studying Organizations?
NITIN NOHRIA   1

Section I: Linking Structure and Action   **23**

1 Problems of Explanation in Economic Sociology
MARK GRANOVETTER   25

2 The Social Structure of Competition
RONALD S. BURT   57

3 Agency as Control in Formal Networks
HARRISON C. WHITE   92

4 Nadel's Paradox Revisited: Relational and Cultural Aspects
of Organizational Structure
PAUL DiMAGGIO   118

5 Doing Your Job *and* Helping Your Friends: Universalistic
Norms about Obligations to Particular Others in Networks
CAROL A. HEIMER   143

6 Structural Alignments, Individual Strategies, and
Managerial Action: Elements Toward a Network
Theory of Getting Things Done
HERMINIA IBARRA   165

Section II: Different Network Ties and Their Implications   **189**

7 Centrality and Power in Organizations
DANIEL J. BRASS AND MARLENE E. BURKHARDT   191

8 The Strength of Strong Ties: The Importance of *Philos*
in Organizations
DAVID KRACKHARDT   216

9 Information and Search in the Creation of New Business
Ventures: The Case of the 128 Venture Group
NITIN NOHRIA   240

10 Complementary Communication Media: A Comparison of
Electronic Mail and Face-to-Face Communication in a
Programming Team
JAMES L. MCKENNEY, MICHAEL H. ZACK, AND
VICTOR S. DOHERTY   262

11 Face-to-Face: Making Network Organizations Work
NITIN NOHRIA AND ROBERT G. ECCLES   288

**Section III: Organizational Environmental Relations as
Interorganizational Networks**   309

12 Strategic Alliances in Commercial Biotechnology
STEPHEN R. BARLEY, JOHN FREEMAN, AND
RALPH C. HYBELS   311

13 The Make-or-Cooperate Decision in the Context of an
Industry Network
BRUCE KOGUT, WEIJIAN SHAN, AND GORDON WALKER   348

14 Competitive Cooperation in Biotechnology: Learning
through Networks?
WALTER W. POWELL AND PETER BRANTLEY   366

Section IV: Network Forms of Organizations   395

15 The Network Organization in Theory and Practice
WAYNE E. BAKER   397

16 Fragments of a Cognitive Theory of Technological
Change and Organizational Structure
MICHAEL J. PIORE   430

17 Small-Firm Networks
CHARLES PERROW   445

18 On the Limits of a Firm-Based Theory to Explain Business
Networks: The Western Bias of Neoclassical Economics
NICOLE WOOLSEY BIGGART AND GARY G. HAMILTON   471

19 The Organization of Business Networks in the
United States and Japan
MICHAEL L. GERLACH AND JAMES R. LINCOLN   491

Conclusion: Making Network Research Relevant to Practice
ROSABETH MOSS KANTER AND ROBERT G. ECCLES   521

Contributors   528

Index   533

Preface

About three years ago, Nitin suggested to Bob that the Harvard Business School sponsor a colloquium on networks and organizations and publish a volume of papers presented at the colloquium. (Later, Harrison White would remember that Bob had a similar idea several years before that, which to this day Bob cannot recall. But maybe that's why he thought Nitin's idea was a good one.) The reason for such a conference was the recent popularity of the term "network" among academics and managers who are interested in organizations. This term had played a prominent role in Nitin's research on the 128 Venture Group and in Bob's work, in collaboration with Dwight Crane, on investment banking. In both of these studies an important underlying issue was whether "network" referred to certain characteristics of any organization or whether it referred to a particular form of organization. We hoped the conference would help resolve this and other related issues.

Having decided to do a conference and after securing the much-appreciated financial support of the Division of Research at the Harvard Business School through the sponsorship of our research directors Professors Jay Lorsch and Warren McFarlan (past and current Senior Associate Deans of Research, respectively), we then had to decide who to invite to the conference and devise a strategy to persuade them to come. Having learned something about how networks work from our own research, our first step was a meeting at Columbia University with Ron Burt, Mark Granovetter, and Harrison White in March 1990. We discussed the idea of the conference with them, got their promise to participate, and developed a list of people to contribute papers and serve as commentators on the sessions. We contacted the people on our list and were pleased at their positive response, despite the fact the colloquium was going to be held in August 1990. Potential participants were told that the purpose of the colloquium was to bring together a number of prominent scholars who had done work in or were interested in the concept of networks for studying organizations, as well as some thoughtful managers. Our objective was to assess the current state of knowledge about networks in order to determine its present and potential future contribution to the study of organizations.

The format of the conference, as suggested by Warren McFarlan, emphasized discussion in small and large groups. Small study groups of five to eight people who discuss a case before the large class discussion are a tradition at Harvard Business School, and we applied this social technology to the conference. Although some of the participants were initially skeptical of this approach, it worked out well. In addition to the obvious benefits of giving people the opportunity to exchange ideas in an informal setting where there is plenty of "air time" for everybody (always a scarce good at a conference of talented and articulate people), we wanted to ensure that the academics had sufficient opportunity to get the views and reactions of the managers who attended. Toward that end, the final session of the conference was devoted to a panel discussion by the managers. And while one of the academic participants left with a grumbling pronouncement that he "had nothing to learn from them and couldn't imagine being interested in what they had to say," we believe that most of the other participants found this valuable. That some did not simply illustrates again the difficulties faced by those who attempt to bring theory and practice together in both body and spirit.

Later than we hoped, and later than we promised the conference participants and our publisher—the fate of so many volume editors—this book is now complete. We believe it is a good representation of the state of knowledge about networks as applied to the study of organizations at the present time.

We would like to thank all the participants at the conference for writing papers and for providing feedback and commentary on the papers. Special thanks are due to Peter Marsden, Jeff Pfeffer, Richard Scott, and Art Stinchcombe, who played the role of discussants at the conference and provided valuable feedback to the authors of the papers. The timely revisions we received reflect the quality of this feedback and the thoughtfulness of the authors in incorporating it. We would also like to thank our editor, Carol Franco, for her enduring patience and good humor as she watched several deadlines quietly slip away. Many thanks also to Ani Kharajian and Jennifer Wilson, who helped organize the conference. But it was Rita Perloff's perseverance and grit that eventually enabled us to put this volume together. Finally, for the readers of this volume who are more interested in the product than in the process that produced it, we hope that it will stimulate their own thinking in the study and use of networks in organizations.

Plan and Summary of the Book

The chapters in this book are organized in four sections. Section I, Linking Structure and Action, brings together theoretical contributions that deal with the relationship between structure and action. In Chapter 1, Mark Granovetter lays out a paradigmatic orientation to explanation that is shared by most of the authors in this book. His main assertions are that (1) economic action (like all action) is properly seen as embedded in ongoing network of relationships; (2) economic goals are typically pursued alongside such noneconomic goals as sociability, approval, status, and power; and (3) economic institutions (like all institutions) arise from and are maintained by ongoing processes of social construction.

In Chapter 2, Ron Burt develops a more formal model of the social structure of competitive arenas. He argues that social capital—an actor's relationship with other players—is as, if not more, important than the financial and human capital the actor brings to the competitive arena. This is because social relations are conduits for access to information and can generate information benefits. They can also be the source of control benefits obtained by taking advantage of competition between contacts or negotiating between disorganized contacts. Competitive advantage, therefore, obtains to those players with structural autonomy or a network optimized for what Burt calls "structural holes" (gaps between nonredundant contacts).

While Ron Burt views networks as a stable social topology, Harrison White, in Chapter 3, looks at networks as process—being continually generated as actors "control and manoeuver in and around" organizations. If the image of social networks in Burt's model is a crystalline grid, in White's it is a repeating polymer, wherein new strings and ties are constantly formed and broken. Therefore control, according to Harrison, consists "principally in achieving constant changing of the scene for others. Any ongoing organization that is not changing is a battlefield monument, a monument to the successful overturn of control." This notion of control is not inconsistent with that offered by Burt. In both cases, control lies in keeping others from getting organized, in maintaining the disorganization of one's contacts, thereby always keeping open one's choices. The difference lies in the more active use of agency and delegation outlined by White as means of getting control. In Burt's arena it is not clear where structural holes come from or why they persist; in White's arena the gamings and countergamings by which holes are created and filled is seen more clearly.

In Burt's (and implicitly in White's) view, the attributes or attitudes of actors contributes little or nothing in explaining their actions. Indeed, these factors lead to spurious causal explanations. What matters is the structural location of the actors. In Chapter 4, Paul DiMaggio takes exception with this view. He argues that explanations of action can never be purely structural. This is because in orienting themselves towards one another and the world, actors rely on typifications (based on attributes) and accounting systems (based on attitudes). Practical action, therefore, is always guided by structural constraints as well as by cognitive (or normative) orientations that are built up on attributes and attitudes. This, DiMaggio argues, is especially true when action must take place in a fluid, dynamic, and emergent context in which the structure of network relations is unstable, and hence a less reliable guide for action than the situations in Burt's models, where the structure of relations is fairly stable, and hence tightly constrains action. To illustrate his point, DiMaggio analyzes the manner in which individuals were recruited to help form and manage the Museum of Modern Art. He shows how the identification and selection of individuals to join that risky and innovative project was guided by both structural and cognitive considerations. In a separate analysis, DiMaggio shows how much about organizations can be understood as a consequence of the interaction of three factors: the organization's relational network, the distribution of its member's attributes, and its formal structure.

The extent to which the action of individuals is guided by universal norms of role performance or by the structure of one's ties to particular others—a crucial question raised by DiMaggio—is the focus of Carol Heimer's thesis in Chapter 5. She argues that obligations to act are always "simultaneously obligations to perform tasks in a universalistic way as well as obligations to behave responsibly in one's relations to particular network partners." This simultaneity can be the source of considerable tension. As Heimer points out, "whenever we think about organizational members developing ties to particular others, we then worry about universalistic standards being undermined by nepotism, friendship, old-boy ties, and the like. At the same time, though, we recognize that in some instances ties to particular others are part and parcel of a person's job [as in doctor-client and mentoring relationships]." Bureaucracies, according to Heimer, attempt to resolve this tension by mandating universalistic norms, but that is a poor solution since it is "only by helping friends that anyone can ever do business." To be effective, indeed for networks to work, they must be able to combine the virtues of universalism with those of particularism. This can be accomplished if networks are governed by a care orientation (not to turn away from your responsibility to someone) as much as they are governed by a justice orientation (not to treat someone unfairly).

In Chapter 6, Herminia Ibarra elaborates on another issue raised by DiMaggio in Chapter 4. She underscores DiMaggio's view that understanding the alignment between the formal and emergent patterns of interaction in an organization is of considerable importance in predicting its tone and style. She goes further to assert that the nature of this alignment shapes both the constraints as well as the opportunities for actors trying to get things done. Thus, she suggests, the appropriate strategy for action is contingent on the nature of the alignment between the prescribed and emergent networks in which the actor is embedded, as well as on what it is that the actor is specifically trying to accomplish. For instance, innovative and critical action in "integrative" organizational settings where there is little overlap between the prescribed and emergent networks may depend on a strategy that maximizes the kind of structural autonomy outlined by Burt, whereas to accomplish routine actions in a bureaucratic organizational setting where there is considerable overlap between the prescribed and emergent networks may depend on a strategy that maximizes cohesive relations. This contingency perspective on the relation between structure and effective action is Ibarra's key contribution.

Whereas Section I sidesteps the issue of the implications of different types of ties for action in networks, Section II, Different Network Ties and Their Implications, confronts this issue head-on. Its chapters address several dimensions along which ties can vary: (1) their basis—that is, whether they are based on affect, advice, task, or talk; (2) their intensity—whether they are strong or weak, occasional or frequent; (3) their unit of reference—whether they are defined by boundaries drawn around the primary subunit, the department of which the subunit is a part, the organization of which the department is a part, and so on; and (4) the media through which the interaction occurs—whether the interaction is face-to-face or via other telecommunication media.

In Chapter 7, Daniel Brass and Marlene Burkhardt investigate the relationship between the centrality of individuals in different social networks in an organization and their power. They examine centrality with respect to four different units of reference (subunit, department, organization, and dominant coalition) and three networks (workflow, communication, and friendship). Their results indicate that an actor's centrality in the department and dominant coalition, especially in the communication network, most strongly contribute to his or her power. Brass and Burkhardt's analysis highlights many of the complexities involved in network analysis.

Chapters 8 and 9 deal respectively with strong and weak ties and their role in different organizing efforts. David Krackhardt, in Chapter 8, attempts to explain the failure of an effort to organize a union in a small entrepreneurial firm in Silicon Valley. In his view, the unionization effort failed primarily because the leaders of the union effort failed to take into account the network of strong ties based on affect and friendship among the members of the firm. While the union concentrated on and was able to persuade employees who were central in the firm's advice network, they ignored others who were more central in the firm's friendship network. This, in the final analysis, led to their failure. Based on this case, Krackhardt argues that centrality in a network of strong ties can in some organizing efforts—particularly those that require a significant commitment of trust—be just as important, if not more important, than the well-known advantages of being central in networks of weak ties.

In Chapter 9, Nitin Nohria examines the organizing efforts of actors involved in trying to create, manage, and profit from new entrepreneurial ventures in the Route 128 area. A central aspect of these organizing efforts is the search for various kinds of information. Nohria describes an innovative institution—the 128 Venture Group—that acts as a generator of bridging ties, thus facilitating the search objectives of its participants. His analysis adds another example to the long list of previous studies that document the importance of weak or bridging ties in the search for information. In addition, he supports DiMaggio's assertion that actors use typifications and accounting schemes to orient themselves toward one another and to identify and select others during their organizing efforts. Finally, Nohria shows how the network of relations in any social system result from unique historical processes, which explains why there are so few regions like Route 128 and why institutions such as the 128 Venture Group are not more prevalent nor universally successful.

The concluding chapters in Section II deal with an increasingly important issue in contemporary organizations—to what extent can ties based on face-to-face interaction be replaced by ties based on electronically mediated interaction? Advances in telecommunications and information technologies have created new possibilities for interaction that circumvent the time-space barriers of face-to-face communication. This has led to the creation of global electronic networks and utopian visions of network organizations that are based entirely on electronically mediated interactions. Both chapters warn against taking this utopian vision too seriously. In Chapter 10, James McKenney, Michael Zack, and Victor Doherty relate how their study of the communication patterns of a software development team revealed that electronic mail and face-to-face interaction served as complementary channels of communication. While electronic mail was used by the members of the team to monitor the status of projects, send alerts, broadcast information, and invoke specific actions, face-to-face was used to define and discuss solutions to problems and to maintain context by alerting the group to changing task and environmental circumstances. Electronic and face-to-face interaction also tended to be sequenced over time in a manner that expedited task performance while maintaining shared definitions of the context. Thus McKenney et al. conclude that face-to-face is vital to the creation of a shared context and that effective electronic mail relies upon the existence of such a context.

Nitin Nohria and Robert Eccles, in Chapter 11, build on this and other theoretical and empirical studies comparing face-to-face and electronic interaction, to make the even stronger claim that as the amount of electronic interaction in any organization increases, the amount of face-to-face interaction will also have to increase (though not in the same proportion). Otherwise, they argue, the network will lose its robustness and become ineffective. Network organizations, in their view, are neither synonymous with, nor can they be built upon electronic networks.

Section III, Organizations and Their Environments as Interorganizational Networks, contains three chapters that examine the relation between organizations and their environment in the biotechnology industry. All three analyze the pattern of interlinkages among the various organizations involved in this emerging industry.

In Chapter 12, Stephen Barley, John Freeman, and Ralph Hybels study the ecology of the biotechnology industry. They examine the distribution of various types of organizations in the industry and the various types of alliances among them. They investigate which firms are more central in the network and find those positions occupied by publicly held dedicated biotechnology firms and diversified corporations, especially those from Western Europe. They also find well-developed niches in the industry based on distinct forms of participation in the network. Firms in each niche exhibit similar patterns of involvement in strategic alliances as well as similar patterns of engagement in different markets. Thus "niche as defined by market constraint corresponds, in part, to niche as defined by characteristic patterns of interorganizational ties." This duality, according to Barley, Freeman, and Hybels, suggests that "networks of interorganizational relations are maps both of and for strategic action."

Bruce Kogut, Weijian Shan, and Gordon Walker examine this proposition more closely in Chapter 13 by studying the dynamics of alliance formation in the industry. They find that the decision to cooperate is "nested within the changing structure of the network as determined by the prior history of cooperation." Furthermore, they find that over time the decision to cooperate depends less on the attributes of the firm and more on the firm's previous cooperative history. Kogut, Shan, and Walker conclude that structural position strongly influences the strategic behavior of organizations, but that individual firm attributes do matter.

Both Barley et al. and Kogut et al. ignore the question of what motivates firms in the biotechnology industry to cooperate with one another and whether the dense pattern of alliances in the industry represents a stable state or a transitory phase prior to an eventual consolidation. In Chapter 14, Walter Powell and Peter Brantley try to address these questions. In their view, the pattern of alliances in the industry cannot be understood in terms of the dynamics of niche formation or in terms of economizing on transactions costs. Instead, these alliances develop "because the range of relevant skills needed to compete in biotechnology cannot easily be brought under one roof." The evolution of the network of relationships in the biotechnology (and other knowledge- and innovation-intensive) industries must therefore be understood as the evolution of a learning through networks system. This learning perspective suggests that the network structure of the biotechnology industry is not necessarily a transitory phase, but may have properties that make it viable and robust over time.

Section IV, Network Forms of Organization, consists of five chapters that deal with different forms of network organization—the entrepreneurial network firm, small-firm networks such as those found in several industrial districts in Italy, and network-like economies such as those found in Japan, Korea, and Taiwan. These forms of organization have recently received enormous attention because they are seen as being more competitive alternatives to the usual bureaucratic and market modes of organization.

In Chapter 15, Wayne Baker tries to clarify some of the semantic ambiguity surrounding the term *network organization* (since all organizations can, in principle, be conceived of as networks) by offering a precise definition of this specific organizational type: "an organization *integrated* across formal groups created by vertical, horizontal, and spatial differentiation for any type of relation." Observing that previously known network organizations have typically evolved unplanned or resulted from the redesign of a non-network organization, Baker studies a real estate service firm that was explicitly designed ex-ante to have a network form. Baker found that although the firm was not completely integrated, it came close to the ideal definition of a network organization since none of the dimensions of formal differentiation were barriers to interaction for the firm as a whole or for the operating core of dealmakers. Though Baker does not tell us how the firm built or maintains this network form, he does highlight its comparative advantage: "as a flexible and self-adapting organization, it is well-suited to unique customized projects, close customer and supplier involvement in the production process, and complex, turbulent environments."

These are also the widely acclaimed advantages of small-firm networks—a form of organization that is the subject of Chapters 16 and 17. One of the earliest observers and advocates of small-firm networks, Michael Piore tries, in Chapter 16, to outline the economic logic of their growth and development. Using the logic of mass production as a comparative benchmark, he suggests that if the economics of mass production was based on a detailed division of labor limited only by the extent of the market for the goods produced, the economics of small-firm networks is based on a general division of labor that enables growth through the generation of new combinations.

If Piore strives to understand the economic logic of small-firm networks, Charles Perrow strives to understand their organizational logic. In Chapter 17, Perrow who had previously argued that "small is trivial in a world of giants," now tries to argue why "small will not be trivial if many small organizations form a *network.*" He addresses several questions about the scope and viability of small-firm networks (SFNs), such as their product range, their ability to develop new products, their skill set, the extent to which they exploit labor, the reasons for their appearance, and the prospects for their permanence. He develops further propositions for how small-firm networks affect hierarchy, costs, power among organizations and power in the community, the distribution of authority and the distribution of wealth, the production of trust, and the location of infrastructures. Perrow ends up admiring SFNs, though he is quick to caution that in some circumstances these networks can be stifling and pernicious to change.

The final two chapters in Section IV look at network forms of organization at an even higher level of analysis, the structure of national economies. Both these chapters contrast the organization of Asian and Western economic systems—the former being characterized as "network" or "alliance" capitalism and the latter as "market" capitalism. In Chapter 18, Nicole Biggart and Gary Hamilton argue that the network organization of Asian economies—and their remarkable success—cannot be understood easily from the perspective of neoclassical economics. From the neoclassical point of view, the dense relations that link the institutions in these economies into a network would be seen merely as imperfections that would impede their efficiency, instead of properly being seen as ties that bind and give these economies their particular character and economic vitality. Biggart and Hamilton therefore advocate abandoning the neoclassical perspective in favor of a network perspective, not because the former is wrong, but because it is ethnocentric and applies well only to the Western economies on the basis of which it was constructed. Moreover, they show how a network perspective yields much sharper insights into the emergence and success of the Asian economies.

In Chapter 19, Michael Gerlach and James Lincoln describe an ambitious research project they are conducting that attempts to document the organizational differences between the Japanese and U.S. economies. They argue that networks among financial, commercial, and industrial firms in an economy determine significant features of that economy's overall organization and its resulting performance. They go on to offer a series of propositions regarding differences in the structure of the U.S. and Japanese economies, differences in the strategic behavior of U.S. and Japanese firms, and—given these differences—how the network position of firms in the United States and Japan would influence their performance. Though Gerlach and Lincoln do not provide any empirical evidence to support their propositions, they clearly show how network theories and methods can provide "powerful tools in advancing our understanding of such network economies and their competitive advantages relative to the United States."

In the concluding chapter of this book, Rosabeth Moss Kanter and Robert G. Eccles discuss how network research can be made more relevant to practitioners. Their main conclusion is that even though there are important lessons for managers in each of the papers in this book, the papers have been written in a manner that most managers would not find easy or compelling to read. In order to make the important contributions that research on networks and organizations has to offer more accessible and useful to practitioners, they suggest that future research in this area must recognize that managers are more interested in how networks can be created and used than in understanding the characteristics, properties, and consequences of networks. To advance this more active stance toward networks, they highlight several key issues that academics must take into account in conducting their research. The agenda outlined by Kanter and Eccles is a challenging one and holds great promise for bridging the gap between theory and practice.

We believe that the papers in this volume, though not directly written for practitioners, make important contributions in each of the areas Kanter and Eccles outline. Clearly, more needs to be done to make this research more relevant and accessible to practitioners.

Is a Network Perspective a Useful Way of Studying Organizations?

NITIN NOHRIA

The term "network" has become the vogue in describing contemporary organizations. From large multinationals to small entrepreneurial firms, from manufacturing to service firms, from emerging industries such as biotechnology to traditional industries such as automobiles, from regional districts such as Silicon Valley and Italy's Prato district to national economies such as those of Japan and Korea, more and more organizations are being described as networks.[1] Typically, the term "network" is used to describe the observed pattern of organization. But just as often it is used normatively: to advocate what organizations must become if they are to be competitive in today's business environment.

The concept of networking has also become a popular theme at the individual level of analysis: Individuals are alerted to the importance of their so-called "connections" in getting things done or moving ahead in life and are therefore urged to network more—to build relationships that they can use to their advantage.[2] A growing number of networking organizations that help people make all sorts of contacts—from finding dates to finding a venture partner—have sprung up to capitalize on the interest in networks. Many firms (aided by willing consultants) have also joined the bandwagon, offering in-house training programs that help their employees learn about the importance of networks and how to go about building and using them.[3]

What accounts for this enormous contemporary interest in networks? After all, the idea itself is not new. At least since the 1950s, the concept of networks has occupied a prominent place in such diverse fields as anthropology, psychology, sociology, mental health, and molecular biology. In the field of organizational behavior, the concept dates back even further. As early as the 1930s, Roethlisberger and Dickson (1939) described and emphasized the importance of informal networks of relations in organizations.

I believe that there are three major reasons for the increased interest in the concept of networks among those interested in organizational phenomena. The first is the emergence over the last two decades of what Best (1990) has labeled "the New Competition." This is the competitive rise over the last two decades of small entrepreneurial firms, of regional districts such as Silicon Valley in California and Prato and Modena in Italy, of new industries such as computers and biotechnology, and of Asian economies such as those of Japan, Korea, and Taiwan. This New Competition has been contrasted with the old in one important way. If the old model of organization was the large hierarchical firm, the model of organization that is considered characteristic of the New Competition is a network, of lateral and horizontal interlinkages within and among firms.

The competitive success of the New Competition has thus led to an increased interest in networks, particularly as the old seeks to become more like the new. Established firms are trying to restructure their internal organizations along the line of networks.[4] They are also trying to redefine their relationships with vendors, customers, and even competitors; instead of arm's-length, competitive relations, they are seeking more collaborative relations that will bind them together into a network.[5] Several regions have launched initiatives to grow their own version of the entrepreneurial network district.[6] Even at the level of national economic and legislative policy, we hear discussions about the feasibility of adopting Japanese kieretsu-type network structures and about relaxing traditional antitrust policies that forbid collaboration among the firms in an industry.[7]

In addition to the interest in the New Competition, a second reason for the increased interest in networks has to do with recent technological developments. New information technologies have made possible an entirely new set of more disaggregated, distributed, and flexible production arrangements, as well as new ways for firms to organize their internal operations and their ties to firms with which they transact. The rise of such manufacturing and telecommunications networks has led to a concomitant interest in the organizational networks that these new technological developments may spawn.[8]

The maturing of network analysis as an academic discipline over the same period is a third reason for the increased trend toward viewing organizations as networks. Network analysis has grown from the esoteric interest of a few mathematically inclined sociologists to a legitimate mainstream perspective. This development was spearheaded in the 1970s by Harrison White and his affiliates, who developed a formal apparatus for thinking about and analyzing social structure as networks.[9] White's work attracted and spurred several other scholars to produce a richer network approach to studying social structure, including theoretical and methodological tools that could be applied to several substantive areas.[10] It also led to the founding of a new journal on social networks, the publication of several edited volumes and books on network and structural analysis, and the network perspective's adoption and dissemination through articles in leading journals of sociology and organizational behavior.[11] Today, interest in the concept of networks is no longer restricted to a small group of sociologists. It has expanded to include students of organizations in such applied, interdisciplinary settings as business schools.[12]

As a consequence, the network concept "has indeed become fashionable and trendy," which, according to Sarason and Lorentz (1979:3), "of course is a mixed blessing." For those who have been advocates of a network perspective, this period may well be their day in the sun. On the other hand, the faddish popularity of the network concept has created a situation where an observation made by Barnes in 1972, and reiterated a decade later by Burt (1982), is more probably more on target than ever: Anyone reading through what purports to be network literature will readily perceive the analogy between it and a "terminological jungle in which any newcomer may plant a tree." This indiscriminate proliferation of the network concept threatens to relegate it to the status of an evocative metaphor, applied so loosely that it ceases to mean anything.

If this were to happen, it would be most unfortunate, because there is a great deal to learn about organizations (and how to act in them) from a properly applied network perspective. It was in the hope of preventing the network concept from becoming another tired metaphor (as the concept of culture became some time ago), that Bob Eccles and I organized this conference and edited this volume. Our hope was that by bringing together scholars who were in various ways using a network perspective and showing how it could be applied to study organizational phenomena, we would be able to provide some focus and coherence to this mode of enquiry.

My purpose in this introduction, therefore, is to outline the main precepts of a network perspective for the study of organizations and to illustrate some of the main advantages of adopting such a perspective. Fritz Roethlisberger (1977) believed that organizations and behavior in them were such "elusive phenomena" that one could never hope for a definitive theory in the field. All that one could expect was the benefit of a perspective or a framework that could be used like a "walking stick" to support and navigate one's inquiry through the treacherous terrain of organizations. Sustaining Roethlisberger's metaphor, let me suggest that a network perspective is a particularly sturdy walking stick that is likely to hold up well in our intellectual inquiry of organizations. Of course, individuals are likely to have their own trusted walking sticks that they are loathe to relinquish in favor of the network perspective. To persuade them to try is the aim of this introduction and this book.

First, though, a word about the primary audience for whom this book is written: academics who are interested in organizations and organizational behavior. For those already familiar with a network perspective, this book provides a collection of some of the leading-edge ideas and research in this area. For those unfamiliar with this perspective, this book is an invitation to adopt a network perspective. By focusing on organizations and organizational behavior, this book differentiates itself from books that have been written to show how a network perspective may be employed to study social structures in general and from books that have elaborated on network methodology.[13] Though we focus on organizations, this book deals with an extremely broad range of organizational issues from a theoretical as well as an empirical standpoint. It is thereby intended to appeal to a wide audience in the field of organization studies.

Let me also say a word about the audience for whom this book has not been written. Though the concept of networks has certainly been taken up with considerable vigor by managers and other practitioners in organizational settings, this book is not directly written for them. The papers in this volume, as almost all the practitioners who attended our colloquium gently told us, belong to the genre of academics writing for other academics. But the intrepid practitioner who is willing to struggle through obtuse references, dense prose, and statistical analyses, may well find several nuggets of genuine insight, as did some of the practitioners who attended our colloquium.

This is not to say that we are not interested in the relevance of the network perspective for practice. Since the majority of the contributors to this book are professors at business schools (and often consultants to organizations), the applicability of these ideas to the practical concerns of managers is of considerable import and something that we will inevitably have to address. In order to do that effectively, though, it is important first to build a coherent academic platform on the basis of which a network perspective can be applied usefully to study organizational phenomena.

Therefore let me now turn to the issue of what it means to study organizations from a network perspective.

STUDYING ORGANIZATIONS FROM A NETWORK PERSPECTIVE

At the risk of imposing a greater unity of perspective than might be reflected in the subsequent chapters of this book, let me suggest that five basic premises underlie a network perspective on organizations.

1. *All organizations are in important respects social networks and need to be addressed and analyzed as such.* A social network, following Laumann et al. (1978:458) can be defined as "a set of nodes (e.g., persons, organizations) linked by a set of social relationships (e.g., friendship, transfer of funds, overlapping membership) of a specified type." As Lincoln (1982:26) points out, "To assert that an organization is not a network is to strip of it that quality in terms of which it is best defined: the pattern of recurring linkages among its parts." The premise that organizations are networks of recurring relationships applies to organizations at any level of analysis— small and large groups, subunits of organizations, entire organizations, regions, industries, national economies, and even the organization of the world system.

Equally important to note is that formal or prescribed relations (such as those that show up on organizational charts or on input-output tables) do not entirely capture the network of relationships that shape an organization. Informal or "emergent" relationships, to use a phrase suggested by Ibarra (Chapter 6, this volume), are just as important in understanding networks in organizations. These relations can be of many different types. Among other things, they may be based on friendship, advice, or conversational relationships within and across an organization's formal boundaries.[14] Identifying and analyzing these "hidden" networks can be of great significance in understanding organizations.

From a network perspective, then, the structure of any organization must be understood and analyzed in terms of the multiple networks of relationships in the organization (both prescribed and emergent) and how they are patterned, singly and in various combinations.

2. *An organization's environment is properly seen as a network of other organizations.* Ever since organizations were recognized as open systems, the critical significance that an organization's environment plays in shaping its activities has been a principal tenet in organization theory. But just as organization theorists have accused other social scientists (particularly economists) of treating the organization like a black box, they can be accused of treating the environment as a black box surrounding the organization. While organizational theorists talk a great deal about an organization's environment in such terms as the degree of uncertainty or resource scarcity it presents for the organization, they have tended to be vague about the source of these pressures.[15]

Building on the work of such earlier organizational theorists as Dill (1958), Evan (1966), and Warren (1967), proponents of a network perspective argue that the most significant elements of an organization's environment are the other organizations with which it must transact. Moreover, mere identification of those other organizations is insufficient; it is equally important to know the pattern of relationships among them. As Barley et al. (Chapter 12, this volume) so graphically put it, "Not only are organizations suspended in multiple, complex, and overlapping webs of relationships, the webs are likely to exhibit structural patterns that are invisible from the standpoint of a single organization caught in the tangle. To detect overarching structures, one has to rise above the individual firm and analyze the system as a whole."

From a network perspective, then, the environment consists of a field of relationships that bind organizations together. Also called an "interorganizational field" (DiMaggio and Powell 1983:148), these organizations include "key suppliers, resource and product consumers, regulatory agencies, and other organizations that produce similar services or products."

To those familiar with Michael Porter's (1980) framework for analyzing industries, this conception of the environment might appear remarkably similar. In many respects it is, except that greater attention is paid in the network perspective to the overall pattern of relationships among the firms in the industry, an issue that receives short shrift in Porter's framework.

In sum, a network perspective on organization-environment relations pushes beyond abstract notions of environmental uncertainty, resource dependencies, and institutional pressures. It seeks to locate the precise source of these environmental forces by analyzing the pattern of relationships among the organizations that make up the environment.

3. *The actions (attitudes and behaviors) of actors in organizations can be best explained in terms of their position in networks of relationships.* From a network perspective, variations in the actions of actors (and the success or failure of these actions) can be better explained by knowing the position of actors relative to others in various networks of relationships, than by knowing how their attributes differ from one another. For instance, knowing attributes like the relative size and technological capabilities of an organization may be less predictive of its conduct and performance than knowing the structural autonomy it enjoys in its transaction networks.[16]

To borrow a sorting scheme proposed by Ronald Burt, network analysts typically use five different principles—cohesion, equivalence, prominence, range, and brokerage—to analyze an actor's network position and to explain how it influences the actor's actions. Cohesion and equivalence are principles for sorting actors into common groups. Cohesion models group actors together if they share strong common relationships with one another; equivalence models group actors together if they have similar relations with other actors in the organization (even though they may not be directly linked to each other). Both cohesion and equivalence models are used to explain similarities in the attitudes and behaviors of the actors in an organization. Similarities by cohesion are argued to arise from actors discussing opinions in strong, socializing relations, whereas similarities by equivalence are argued to arise from actors playing similar roles with regard to others in the organization and so coming to a shared opinion.[17]

Prominence, range, and brokerage models are used to explain the extent to which an actor is advantageously positioned relative to others in an organization. Prominence models differentiate individuals according to who is in more or less demand. An actor's prominence increases as the actor is the object of relations from many others who are in turn the object of many relations. Actors can use their prominence to push others into doing things that further their own interests.[18]

Range and brokerage models tap a different action potential. They measure the extent to which actors can get away with pursuing their own interests. The simplest range measure is network size, a sum of an actor's relations—the more you have, the more access you have to social resources. More sophisticated range models highlight the importance of the bridging ties that an actor has.[19] Finally, brokerage models are based on the principle that actors are freer to pursue their own interests to the extent that their relations connect them with others who are disorganized and so can be played off against one another. The causal mechanism here is contact with disorganized others.[20]

While network analysts favor explanations based on an actor's location in various networks, they do, of course, recognize that actors also belong to categories based on similarities in their attributes (e.g., ethnicity, gender, etc.). While some, such as Burt (Chapter 2, this volume), argue that categories can be translated into network positions and are hence largely relevant to explanations, others (and I'm in this camp) don't take such an extreme position. As Blau (1982) concludes, an actor's network position and attributes offer complementary insights that taken together offer a fuller explanation of the actor's actions.

4. *Networks constrain actions, and in turn are shaped by them.* While a network perspective, as I have indicated, emphasizes how the network positions of actors constrain or enable their actions, it does not rule out the possibility that actors can change their network positions. Networks are constantly being socially constructed, reproduced, and altered as the result of the actions of actors. While network analysts would maintain that the patterns of relationships in any organization are to a large extent fairly stable and recurring, they recognize that new network ties are being constantly formed and that over time these new ties can change old network patterns in quite dramatic ways.

Thus actors in network models are not seen as atoms locked in a crystalline grid, their every action determined by their structural location. They are, as Harrison White suggests, active, purposeful agents who are constantly trying to wrest control for themselves or blocking others from taking control. This dynamic of actors wrestling for control and seeking advantage is, as White notes, "constantly throwing up fresh hunks of network" (Chapter 3, this volume). Therefore networks are as much process as they are structure, being continually shaped and reshaped by the actions of actors who are in turn constrained by the structural positions in which they find themselves.

5. *The comparative analysis of organizations must take into account their network characteristics.* Traditionally, as Nelson complains (1986:75), most comparative research "does not deal directly with the networks of relationships which make up organization structure. Rather researchers establish variables that are generalizations about these relationships. . . . The major problem with such variables is that they do not reveal the actual configurations of relations which comprise structure."

Centralization, for instance, in comparative studies such as those conducted by the Aston group (Pugh et al. 1968), is usually measured as the average degree of asymmetry in relationships in the organization and by the extent to which decision rights are concentrated among few individuals. What such a measure does not tell us is who the elites or dominant coalitions are in each of the organizations being compared, and what the precise structure of their relationship is with the other groups of actors in the organization. By not capturing the actual configuration of relations, traditional measures of centralization can tell us little about whether the dominant coalition in one organization is more vulnerable than that in another or if there is another group of actors in the organization that is really making the key decisions, the dominant coalition merely being a puppet coalition. By focusing directly on the patterns of relationships through such analytic techniques as graph analysis or block modeling, a network perspective offers a much sharper set of tools to address such questions in comparative analyses.[21]

To take another case, the structure of competition in markets is typically compared using a variable such as concentration ratios; but as White (1981) has shown in his analysis of various forms of markets, such a measure misses the very stuff of competition in markets, which can be understood only by directly modeling the pattern of interaction among market players.

A network perspective, therefore, pushes for comparisons in terms of variables and measures that reflect the overall structure of relationships in the organization, eschewing variables and measures that are generalizations of the pattern of dyadic interactions in the organization.

Taken together, the five basic premises described here define the core features of a network perspective on organizations. It should be readily apparent from the preceding discussion that adopting a network perspective is not merely adopting a new metaphysical image of organizations or bolting a few network variables onto traditional analytical perspectives. If we are to take a network perspective seriously, it means adopting a different intellectual lens and discipline, gathering different kinds of data, learning new analytical and methodological techniques, and seeking explanations that are quite different from conventional ones. This is a tall order and must therefore answer the skeptic's favorite questions—"Why bother?" and "Is it worth it?"

WHAT IS TO BE GAINED BY ADOPTING A NETWORK PERSPECTIVE?

To fully appreciate the advantages of adopting a network perspective, one must read this entire book. It is hard to do adequate justice to any substantive theme within the space constraints of a brief introduction. But in an attempt to demonstrate that it would be worthwhile to read the rest of the book—and thus motivate the reader to do so—I shall briefly discuss four substantive themes that are dealt with more fully in several of the chapters. These four themes span several levels of analysis and have been the subject of considerable attention in organizational literature.

1. What explains differences in the power and influence of individuals in organizational settings? Or put differently, where does power come from?

2. What explains the recruitment patterns that result from different organizing efforts, such as the effort to create a new organization or to mobilize change in an existing organization?

3. What explains the strategic conduct of firms, in particular their choice to enter into strategic alliances? Are these alliances viable long-term organizational arrangements?

4. What distinguishes the organizational characteristics of the so-called New Competition from that of the old. Does the mode of "network" organization characteristic of the New Competition represent the new model of the organization?

1. Power and Influence in Organizations

Questions about what accounts for the distribution of power in organizations have long occupied a central place in organizational theory. Explanations for what gives an individual power in an organization have usually focused, among other things, on the individual's personal characteristics (such as charisma and expertise); socioeconomic profile (including things like gender, race, educational attainments, and social class); formal position in the organization (including place in both the horizontal and vertical differentiation of labor); attitudes and values (such as the extent to which the individual exemplifies the norms and culture of the organization); control over critical resources (including capital, social approval and other rewards, and information); and control over critical contingencies (including task interdependencies and gatekeeping functions).[22]

These explanations have not been fruitless—much of what we currently know about the distribution of power and influence in organizations is based on these ideas. However, it has always been recognized that these factors are not sufficient from an explanatory standpoint, and that an individual's position in various networks of relationships can be a source of power quite independent of other factors. We have long known, for instance, that being central in communication networks is a source of power.[23] What the network perspective provides is a more systematic way of understanding this classic intuition.

As Brass and Burkhardt (Chapter 7, this volume) contend, there are many different ways in which one can be central in a network. One can be central in the sense of degree (being the object of many relations), betweenness (being in the middle of paths that connect others), or closeness (having immediate access to others who are connected). Each provides a different basis of power. To fully understand an individual's power, it is just as important to know which of the various kinds of organizational networks (e.g., advice, work flow, friendship) she is central in, as it is to know the relevant network boundaries within which she is more or less central (e.g., the network demarcated by the immediate subunit, the department in which the subunit is located, the entire organization, or the dominant coalition).

Moreover, as Burt (Chapter 2, this volume) argues, centrality in networks is not the only (or necessarily the most important) source of an individual's power. He suggests that the extent to which individuals can surround themselves with "structural holes" (i.e., sit in the middle of disorganized contacts), the more autonomy and power they are likely to have. Indeed, he would argue that this is a more important indicator of power and influence than centrality is.

As these chapters demonstrate, adopting a network perspective offers some very rich and interesting insights on where power comes from.[24] A network perspective can also shed light on what strategies individuals should employ to try to gain power or seize control, an issue on which the traditional literature is relatively silent. As Harrison White (Chapter 3, this volume) and Herminia Ibarra (Chapter 6, this volume) elaborate, there are some fairly specific propositions that can be derived from a network perspective on the strategies and actions that individuals should take under different situations to increase their power and be able to pursue their own interests.

2. Organizing Efforts

Organizational theorists have always been interested in explaining the factors that facilitate or impede organizing efforts leading to the creation of a new venture or those that involve mobilizing collective action, such as a unionization drive. Their explanations have typically hinged on the role and function of entrepreneurs or leaders—individuals with unusual organizing skills who can mobilize action by sheer dint of persuasion and an unyielding drive. Thus they have devoted considerable effort to understanding the psychological attributes of entrepreneurs and leaders and the conditions that are most conducive for them to flourish. Individual attributes such as achievement orientation and risk-taking propensity, and contextual conditions such as autonomy and slack resources have all been seen to facilitate organizing efforts.[25]

It is also recognized that organizing efforts involve identifying, persuading, and recruiting others to contribute to the objectives the organizing agents have in mind, and that the outcomes (in terms of who joins and who does not) can have a critical bearing on the success of the organizing effort. Organizational theorists such as Kanter (1983) have explicitly directed attention to the importance of the network of relations in which the organizing agents are embedded.

Several of the papers in this volume show more clearly just how critical these networks of relationships can be in shaping the outcomes of organizing efforts. Paul DiMaggio (Chapter 4, this volume), for instance, describes how the founders of New York's Museum of Modern Art (MOMA) used their networks of relationships to recruit key individuals to commit resources to fund the museum and how they recruited others to manage the museum and confer it with legitimacy. As DiMaggio shows, the success of the museum—a very risky idea at the time—could in large part be attributed to the pattern of recruitment that resulted from the way the founders tapped their networks.

David Krackhardt (Chapter 8, this volume) shows how, in contrast to the success of the MOMA organizers, the recruitment strategy of the organizers of a unionization drive led to the eventual failure of their effort. In this case, the organizers did not pay enough attention to an individual who was very central in the firm's friendship network and instead concentrated their recruitment efforts on those individuals who were central in the more visible work-flow networks of the firm. This proved to be their undoing, because in the final analysis the ambivalence of the individual who was central in the friendship network swayed his friends into not supporting the certification drive.

In another chapter, Nohria (Chapter 9, this volume) shows how crucial networks of relations (especially bridging ties) are to the entrepreneur's search for information in the creation of new ventures. Based on this analysis, he suggests that to understand the contextual conditions that facilitate entrepreneurial organizing efforts, one must pay careful attention to the pattern of relationships that exist in a social system, because it is these relations that serve as the pathways for information flows that not only facilitate search but also enable the production of trust and the governability of the system.[26]

3. Strategic Alliances

Organizational theorists typically have explained the strategic conduct of organizational actors, such as the creation of alliances among them as being strategic responses to mitigate and manage competitive uncertainties and resource interdependencies.[27] Those who take a more transaction-cost perspective explain alliances as an effective response to conditions where transactions cannot be easily conducted through market contracts, but the transaction costs involved are not so high as to mandate internal organization.[28] These explanations pay scant attention to how these alliances interconnect to bind the firms into a network of relationships. They also ignore how the network of relationships that emerges over time as a result of alliances between firms shapes and constrains the strategic conduct of firms involved in them.

As the chapters in this volume that analyze the pattern of strategic alliances among firms in the biotechnology industry argue, it is insufficient (and probably erroneous) to explain the strategic behavior of firms in this industry without paying explicit attention to the network of relationships among them. As Barley et al. (Chapter 12, this volume) show, firms in the industry can be partitioned into different niches based on commonalities in their alliancing strategy. These niches also reflect the participation of the firm in different market segments. While the causal direction of this link between alliance and market segmentation strategies is hard to establish, it is clear that the actions of firms are shaped by their position in the overall network.[29]

Moreover, as Kogut et al. (Chapter 13, this volume) demonstrate, the particular alliances that firms establish over time are a function of their position in the network of relationships in previous periods. Thus the decision to cooperate is shaped by, and in turn shapes, the network of relationships in the industry.

Finally, Powell and Brantley (Chapter 14, this volume), raise the interesting possibility that the overall network defines a stable ecology that operates as a learning system; hence the conduct of firms in the biotechnology industry must be understood within this framework.

While the authors in this volume have focused on a particular form of strategic conduct—strategic alliances—other scholars have shown how a network perspective can explain differences in firm conduct on issues such as pricing, philanthropy, and political contributions, and can also predict outcomes such as firm profitability and return on investment.[30]

4. The New Competition

The emergence of the New Competition is often seen by organizational theorists as an adaptive response to changing business and technological conditions that require and enable more "open" and "network" forms of organization. The same logic offered by Burns and Stalker (1961) to explain why firms that were successful in more dynamic environments had an "organic" character, is used to explain the success of new organizational forms such as small entrepreneurial firms, regional districts, and large network-like organizations such as the Japanese kieretsu. Because of historical circumstances, these firms are seen to have organizational characteristics that make them more like networks or organic organizations, and are hence better suited to the dynamic contemporary environment.[31]

It is here that the failure to adopt a coherent network perspective becomes most problematic. It is precisely the lack of a clear understanding of a network perspective that has led to the rampant and indiscriminate use of the network metaphor to describe these new organizational forms. In some cases, this tendency has gone even further and the network organization has been reified as a new ideal type of organization—one that will replace the bureaucracy as the basic model that all organizations, in due course, will adopt if they are to survive and flourish.

From a network perspective, all organizations can be characterized as networks and indeed are properly understood only in these terms. So to say an organization has a network form is a tautology. Nevertheless, there are some proponents of a network perspective who have not rejected outright the idea that "it is meaningful to talk about networks as a distinct form of coordinating economic activity" (Powell 1990:301). The notion that it is meaningful to think of network organization as a distinct form should, in my view, be understood as a rhetorical strategy that is being employed by some theorists to get beyond the markets-and-hierarchies distinction that has become the dominant frame for the comparative analysis of organizations. The rhetoric of networks as a form of organization is an attempt to center attention fully on the distinctive "logic of collective action [in networks] that enables cooperation to be sustained over the long run" (Powell 1990:301). By treating networks as a distinct *form* of organization, those who advocate this perspective deliberately direct attention to *particular network characteristics* that are to some degree relevant to any organization but are especially salient in so-called network organizations, such as dense horizontal linkages across formal organizational boundaries (e.g., Baker, Chapter 15, this volume), reciprocal relationships between small firms in a regional economy (e.g., Perrow, Chapter 17, this volume), or interlocking relationships among economic institutions in Asian economies (e.g., Biggart and Hamilton, Chapter 18, this volume; and Gerlach and Lincoln, Chapter 19, this volume). This rhetorical framing of network as form forces the analyst to attend to what it is that makes these new arrangements efficient, governable, and flexible compared with traditional modes of organizing. It pushes for analysis in network terms and directs attention to key features of these organizations that can be understood only from a network perspective, like the role of linking-pin institutions (such as the banks in the Japanese system and the "impannatore" in the regional districts of Prato and Modena) in the governance of these organizations, and the role of ties that create trust (such as shared ethnic, geographic, ideological, or professional background).

Adopting a network-as-form perspective forces us to understand these new organizations on their own terms (and in terms of those characteristics that best define them) instead of viewing them as merely the amorphous middle in the traditional markets-and-hierarchies continuum.[32]

AN AGENDA FOR FURTHER DEVELOPING
THE NETWORK PERSPECTIVE

The preceding discussion was designed to persuade skeptics that a network perspective can provide insights that other perspectives cannot. In this section, I offer some suggestions for those who already believe in the analytical power offered by the network perspective, by highlighting five fronts on which the network perspective must advance for it to flourish as a way of studying organizations:

1. A Theory of Action

Network analysts share a model of action that treats actors as purposeful, intentional agents. Most would agree with Granovetter (Chapter 1, this volume) that it is important to avoid both undersocialized and oversocialized models of action, and recognize that actors have social as well as economic motives and that their actions are influenced by the networks of relationships in which they are embedded.

Beyond that, though, there are several points of divergence. Some, such as Burt (1982) (Chapter 2, this volume) emphasize the rational, utility-maximizing side of actors, even though their actions are highly constrained by their structural positions. Others, such as DiMaggio (Chapter 4, this volume) emphasize the everyday practical considerations that shape the actions of actors, such as their boundedly rational, institutionally guided cognitive orientations. I will not even pretend to try to resolve this debate. It is one that has persistently dogged the social sciences. Instead, let me further muddy the waters by offering yet another model of action that in my view warrants careful consideration. The motor of action in this model is the actor's pursuit of identity.

This model builds on the work of philosophers such as Arendt (1958) and has been taken up in the social sciences by such sociologists as White (forthcoming) and economists such as Sen (1985:348), who offers a succinct summary: Action is motivated by the

> identity of a person, that is, how the person sees himself or herself. We all have many identities, and being "just me" is not the only way we see ourselves. Community, nationality, class, race, sex, union membership, the fellowship of oligopolists, revolutionary solidarity, and so on, can all provide identities that can be, depending on the context, crucial to our view of ourselves, and thus to the way we view our welfare, goals, or behavioral obligations. A person's concept of his or her own welfare may go well beyond "sympathizing" with them. Similarly, in arriving at goals, a person's sense of identity may be quite central. And, the pursuit of private goals may well be compromised by the consideration of the goals of others in the group with whom the person has some sense of identity.

2. Different Types of Ties and Their Implications

Organizations are composed of ties of a myriad nature. Ties can differ according to whether they are based on friendship, advice, or work; whether what flows through them is resources, information, or affection; whether they are strong or weak ties, unitary or multiplex ties, face-to-face or electronic ties; and so on. Though the complex nature of ties is recognized by everyone who takes a network perspective, there has been, as Wellman (1988:25) has observed, a tendency to "concentrate on the form of network patterns rather than their content . . . a Simmelian sensibility that similar patterns of ties may have similar behavioral consequences, no matter what the substantive context. Pushed to its extreme, [the] argument has been that the pattern of relationships is substantially the same as the content."

As several of the papers in this book reveal, the substance and type of ties in a network can have important implications for action. While there is a growing recognition about the importance of different types of network ties, we are nowhere near having a systematic framework or theory for predicting what kinds of ties matter under what kinds of circumstances in what ways. This is an area that must be given considerable attention in order for the network perspective to make more substantive progress.

3. The Etiology and Dynamics of Networks

Most network analysts treat the network of relations in any organization as a given. The question of what leads to the formation of different network patterns has bedeviled the network perspective for some time now. Competing theories abound. Some have tried to explain the formation of networks on the basis of exchange theory; others have focused on homophily and balance theory, with its emphasis on triad closure; still others have argued that networks are shaped by the control processes of agency, delegation, and specialization.[33] Resolving these debates by pitting them against one another in substantive settings is essential if we are to ever resolve this crucial issue.

In addition to theories of how networks are formed, we need better theories of how networks evolve and change over time. The dynamics of networks are beginning to receive considerable attention, and the findings of these studies will be of considerable interest.[34]

4. Methodological Advances

Though tools for the analysis of networks are now quite freely available, there has continued to be insufficient concern for the methodological limitations of network analysis, particularly in terms of the demanding data requirements to comprehensively analyze even a single organization, let alone being able to conduct large sample comparative studies of organizations. Advances in sampling technologies as well as collaborative large-scale data-gathering projects are necessary for progress on this front.[35]

5. Problem-Centered Research Relevant to Practitioners

There has been a healthy trend in the network literature towards more applied, substantively oriented research. I believe that trend should be pushed with greater vigor so that the network perspective can be employed to address issues that are of direct concern to practitioners. This will require not only a continuing emphasis on problem-centered research but also a conscious effort to make the language and discourse of the network perspective more accessible to managers. As Kanter and Eccles (Chapter 20, this volume) conclude, network research can provide practitioners with the means to define and classify the properties of networks, assess outcomes associated with particular types of networks, and describe the dynamics of network formation and evolution. In this way, a network perspective can help practitioners identify the importance of networks to organizational activities and outcomes, diagnose their current state, and proactively change networks to improve their own performance and the effectiveness of their organizations.

If the network perspective makes rapid progress along the five fronts I have outlined here, I believe that it can have a greater impact than it has had on our understanding of organizations. A decade ago, in a review of the state of organization theory, Pfeffer (1982:276–277) offered the following assessment of the network perspective:

> Social network analysis remains more of a paradigm and framework than a theory, and more promise than fulfilled potential . . . But the importance of the findings of the network studies performed to date and the fundamentally structural nature of organizations argue for the additional development of theories and research on organizations using network properties both in hypotheses describing and explaining the development of networks and in relating network characteristics to other organizational properties.

While I firmly believe that this book demonstrates that the network perspective has made important strides in fulfilling the potential that Pfeffer saw a decade ago, there is still much to be done. Moreover, as Paul DiMaggio remarked at our conference, "The moment for those who come from a network perspective to be the head priests of organizational analysis is now." More than anything else, this book is a call to seize the moment and capitalize on this opportunity.

Notes

1. For a discussion of multinationals as networks, see Bartlett and Ghoshal (1989) and Nohria and Ghoshal (1991); for entrepreneurial firms, see Gilder (1989) and Sengenberger et al. (1990); for manufacturing, see Jaikumar (1986) and Hayes et al. (1988); for professional services, see Eccles and Crane (1988); for biotechnology, see Kenney (1986); for automobiles, see Nohria and Garcia-Pont (1991); for regional districts, see Saxenian (1990) and Piore and Sabel (1984); and for the economies of Japan, Korea, and Taiwan, see Hamilton and Biggart (1988).
2. See, for instance, Maguire (1983), Lipnack and Stamps (1982), and Sarason and Lorentz (1979).
3. See, for instance, Mueller (1986).
4. See, for instance, Mills (1990) for several examples of large firms undergoing such a transformation.
5. See, for instance, Cash and Konsynski (1985), Miles and Snow (1986), and Powell (1987).
6. See Miller and Cote (1985).
7. See Gerlach (1991) and Kotz (1978) for a more detailed comparison of the Japanese and U.S. systems, and several papers in Hirst and Zeitlin (1989) for a discussion of how the adoption of network structures can potentially stem industrial decline.
8. See, for instance, Applegate, Cash, and Mills (1988); Child (1987); Drucker (1988, 1990); Malone and Rockart (1991); Nolan, Pollock, and Ware (1988, 1989); and Hiltz and Torhoff (1978).
9. See White (1970); Lorrain and White (1971); White, Boorman, and Breiger (1976); and Boorman and White (1976) for some of the seminal papers of this period.
10. See Alba (1981), and Burt (1980, 1982) for comprehensive reviews of the work done in the 1970s.

11. The evolution of the field of network analysis is discussed in detail by Wellman (1988).
12. This volume is testimony to this increasingly broad interest in networks.
13. For a collection of essays that deal with the applicability of network analysis to studying social structures generally, see Marsden and Lin (1982) and Wellman and Berkowitz (1988). For more methodologically oriented collections, see Burt and Minor (1983) and a review by Marsden (1990).
14. For discussion of the various types of network relations, see Mitchell (1969, 1974) and Tichy (1981).
15. See Scott (1987) for a detailed discussion of different ways in which organization-environment relations have been conceptualized by organizational theorists.
16. See, for example, Burt (1980a, 1983).
17. See Burt (1980a and b, 1982, 1987) for the distinctions and relative merits of studying similarities by cohesion and equivalence. In organizational behavior, Nelson (1989) provides a good example of how similarities develop by cohesion and how they can be the basis for intergroup conflict. Walker (1985), on the other hand, shows how similarities in attitudes can be based on equivalence.
18. See, for example, Coleman (1988), Bonacich (1987), and Marsden (1983) for prominence-based models of power and social influence.
19. See Granovetter (1973, 1982) and Lin et al. (1981) for examples of models of influence based on range.
20. See Freeman (1977), Cook and Emerson (1978), and Burt (1980a, 1983, and Chapter 2, this volume) for examples of models of power based on brokerage.
21. See Barney (1985) for a good example of a network perspective applied to the comparative analysis of organizations.
22. See Pfeffer (1980, 1992) for an exhaustive review of the literature on power in organizations.
23. See, for example, the early work of Guetzkow and Simon (1955) on the impact of an actor's position in various types of communication networks.
24. Also see Bonacich (1987) and Krackhardt (1990).
25. See, for example, Zaltman et al. (1973), Drucker (1985), and Stevenson and Gumpert (1985).
26. The importance of networks in mobilizing efforts has been brilliantly documented by Faulkner (1983) for the music industry, and by Jenkins (1983) for social movements.
27. See, for example, Pfeffer (1972) and Pfeffer and Nowak (1976).
28. See, for example, Williamson (1985, 1991).
29. Similar results are shown for the automobile industry by Nohria and Garcia-Pont (1991).
30. See, for example, Baker (1984), Burt (1983), and Mizruchi (1989a, 1989b).
31. See Miles and Snow (1986), who exemplify this argument.
32. See Thorelli (1986) and Powell (1987) for earlier framings in which networks were viewed as hybrid arrangements between markets and hierarchies, and Powell (1990) for the revised framing in which networks are seen as a distinctive form of organization.
33. For the exchange theoretic arguments, see Cook (1987); for the triad closure argument, see Leinhardt (1977); and for the control and identity argument, see White (forthcoming).
34. See, for example, Delany (1988) and Levine and Spadaro (1988) for dynamic models of labor market mobility.

35. See Marsden (1990) for a more exhaustive review of the state of network methodology.

References

Alba, Richard D. 1981. "Taking Stock of Network Analysis: A Decade's Results." In S. Bacharach, ed., *Perspectives in Organizational Research*. Greenwich, CT: JAI Press, pp. 39–74.

Arendt, Hannah. 1958. *The Human Condition*. Chicago: University of Chicago Press.

Baker, Wayne. 1984. "The Social Structure of a National Securities Market." *American Journal of Sociology* 89:775–811.

Barnes, J. A. 1972. *Social Networks*. Reading, MA: Addison-Wesley.

Barney, Jay. 1985. "Dimensions of Informal Social Network Structure." *Social Networks* 7:1–46.

Bartlett, Christopher A., and Sumantra Ghoshal. 1989. *Managing Across Borders: The Transnational Solution*. Boston: Harvard Business School Press.

Best, Michael. 1990. *The New Competition*. Cambridge, MA: Harvard University Press.

Blau, Peter M. 1982. "Structural Sociology and Network Analysis: An Overview." In Peter V. Marsden and Nan Lin, eds., *Social Structure and Network Analysis*. Beverly Hills: Sage, pp. 273–280.

Bonacich, Philip. 1987. "Power and Centrality: A Family of Measures." *American Journal of Sociology* 92:1170–1182.

Burns, Tom, and Gerald M. Stalker. 1961. *The Management of Innovation*. London: Tavistock.

Burt, Ronald S. 1980a. "Autonomy in a Social Topology." *American Journal of Sociology*, 85:892–925.

———. 1980b. "Models of Network Structure." *Annual Review of Sociology* 6:79–141.

———. 1982. *Toward a Structural Theory of Action*. New York: Academic Press.

———. 1983. *Corporate Profits and Cooptation: Networks of Market Constraint and Directorate Ties in the American Economy*. New York: Academic Press.

———. 1987. "Social Contagion and Innovation: Cohesion Versus Structural Equivalence." *American Journal of Sociology* 92:1287–1335.

Burt, Ronald S., and Michael J. Minor, eds. 1983. *Applied Network Analysis*. Beverly Hills: Sage.

Cash, James I., and Benn R. Konsynski. 1985. "IS Redraws Competitive Boundaries." *Harvard Business Review* 63(2) (Mar./Apr.): 134–142.

Child, John. 1987. "Information Technology, Organization, and the Response to Strategic Challenges." *California Management Review* (Fall): 33–50.

Coleman, James S. 1988. "Social Capital in the Creation of Human Capital." *American Journal of Sociology* 94:S95–S120.

Cook, Karen S., ed. 1987. *Social Exchange Theory*. Beverly Hills: Sage.

Cook, Karen S., and Richard M. Emerson. 1978. "Power, Equity, and Commitment in Exchange Networks." *American Sociological Review* 43:721–739.

Delany, John. 1988. "Social Networks and Efficient Resource Allocation: Computer Models of Job Vacancy Allocation Through Contacts." In Barry Wellman and S.D. Berkowitz, eds., *Social Structures: A Network Approach*. New York: Cambridge University Press, pp. 430–451.

Dill, William, R. 1958. "Environment as an Influence on Managerial Autonomy." *Administrative Science Quarterly* 2 (Mar.): 409–443.

DiMaggio, Paul, and Walter W. Powell. 1983. "The Iron Cage Revisited: Institutional Isomorphism and Collective Rationality in Organizational Fields." *American Sociological Review* 48:147–160.

Drucker, Peter F. 1985. *Innovation and Entrepreneurship: Practice and Principles*. New York: Harper and Row.

———. 1988. "The Coming of the New Organization." *Harvard Business Review* 66 (Jan.–Feb.): 35–53.

———. 1990. *The New Realities*. New York: Harper and Row.

Eccles, Robert G., and Dwight B. Crane. 1988. *Doing Deals: Investment Banks at Work*. Boston: Harvard Business School Press.

Evan, William M. 1966. "The Organization-set: Toward a Theory of Interorganizational Relations." In James D. Thompson, ed., *Approaches to Organizational Design*. Pittsburgh: University of Pittsburgh Press, pp. 173–188.

Faulkner, Robert R. 1983. *Music on Demand*. New Brunswick, NJ: Transaction.

Freeman, Linton C. 1977. "A Set of Measures of Centrality Based on Betweenness." *Sociometry* 40:35–41.

Gerlach, Michael L., 1991. *Alliance Capitalism: The Social Organization of Japanese Business*. Berkeley: University of California Press.

Gilder, George. 1989. *Microcosm: The Quantum Revolution in Economics and Technology*. New York: Simon and Schuster.

Granovetter, Mark S. 1973. "The Strength of Weak Ties." *American Journal of Sociology* 78:1360–1380.

———. 1982. "The Strength of Weak Ties: A Network Theory Revisited." In P. V. Marsden and N. Lin, eds., *Social Structure and Network Analysis*. Beverly Hills: Sage, pp. 105–130.

Guetzkow, Harold, and Herbert A. Simon. 1955. "The Impact of Certain Communication Nets upon Organization and Performance in Certain Task-oriented Groups." *Management Science* 1 (Apr.–July): 233–250.

Hamilton, Gary G., and Nicole W. Biggart. 1988. "Market, Culture, and Authority: A Comparative Analysis of Management and Organization in the Far East." *American Journal of Sociology* 94 (supplement): S52–S94.

Hayes, Robert H., Steven C. Wheelwright, and Kim B. Clark. 1988. *Dynamic Manufacturing: Creating the Learning Organization*. New York: Free Press.

Hiltz, Roxanne S., and Murray Torhoff. 1978. *Network Nation: Human Communication Via Computers*. Reading, MA: Addison-Wesley.

Hirst, Paul, and Jonathan Zeitlin, eds., 1989. *Reversing Industrial Decline*. New York: St. Martin's Press.

Jaikumar, Ramachandran. 1986. "Post-Industrial Manufacturing." *Harvard Business Review* 64(6) (Nov.–Dec.): 69–76.

Jenkins, Craig J. 1983. "Resource Mobilization and the Study of Social Movements." *Annual Review of Sociology* 9:527–553.

Kanter, Rosabeth M. 1983. *The Change Masters*. New York: Simon and Schuster.

Kenney, Martin. 1986. *Biotechnology: The University-Industrial Complex*. New Haven: Yale University Press.

Kotz, David M. 1978. *Bank Control of Large Corporations in the United States*. Berkeley: University of California Press.

Krackhardt, David. 1990. "Assessing the Political Landscape: Structure, Cognition, and Power in Networks." *Administrative Science Quarterly* 35(2):342–369.

Laumann, Edward O., L. Galskeiwicz, and P.V. Marsden. 1978. "Community Structure as Interorganizational Linkages." *Annual Review of Sociology* 4:455–484.

Leinhardt, S., ed., 1977. *Social Networks: A Developing Paradigm*. New York: Academic Press.

Levine, Joel H., and John Spadaro. 1988. "Occupational Mobility: A Structural Model." In Barry Wellman and S. D. Berkowitz, eds., *Social Structure: A Network Approach*. New York: Cambridge University Press, pp. 452–476.

Lin, Nan, Walter M. Ensel, and John C. Vaughn. 1981. "Social Resources and Strength of Ties." *American Sociological Review* 37:202–212.

Lincoln, James R. 1982. "Intra- (and Inter-) Organizational Networks." In Samuel B. Bacharach, ed., *Research in the Sociology of Organizations*, Vol. 1. Greenwich, CT: JAI Press.

Lipnack, Jessica, and Jeffrey Stamps. 1982. *Networking: The First Report and Directory*. Garden City: Doubleday.

Lorrain, Francois P., and Harrson C. White. 1971. "Structural Equivalence of Individuals in Social Networks." *Journal of Mathematical Sociology* 1:49–80.

Maguire, Lambert. 1983. *Understanding Social Networks*. Beverly Hills: Sage.

Malone, Thomas W., and John F. Rockart. 1991. "Computers, Networks, and the Corporation." *Scientific American* 265(3):128–137.

Marsden, Peter V. 1983. "Restricted Access in Networks and Models of Power." *American Journal of Sociology* 88:686–717.

———. 1990. "Network Data and Measurement." *Annual Review of Sociology* 16:435–463.

Marsden, Peter V., and Nan Lin, eds. 1982. *Social Structure and Network Analysis*. Beverly Hills: Sage.

Miles, Raymond E., and Charles C. Snow. 1986. "Network Organizations: New Concepts for New Forms." *California Management Review* 28:62–73.

Miller, Roger, and Marcel Cote. 1985. "Growing the Next Silicon Valley." *Harvard Business Review* 63(4) (July–Aug.): 114–123.

Mills, Quinn. 1990. *The Rebirth of the Corporation*. New York: Wiley.

Mitchell, J. C. 1969. "The Concept and Use of Social Networks." In J. C. Mitchell, ed., *Social Networks in Urban Situations*. Manchester, U.K.: Manchester University Press, pp. 1–50.

———. 1974. "Social Networks." *Annual Review of Anthropology* 3:279–299.

Mizruchi, Mark S. 1989a. "Similarity of Political Behavior Among Large American Corporations." *American Journal of Sociology* 95(2):401–424.

———. 1989b. "Cohesion, Structural Equivalence, and Similarity of Behavior: An Approach to the Study of Corporate Political Power." Working paper, Center for the Social Sciences at Columbia University.

Mueller, Robert K. 1986. *Corporate Networking: Building Channels for Information and Influence*. New York: Free Press.

Nelson, Reed E. 1986. "The Use of Blockmodeling in the Study of Organization Structure: A Methodological Proposal." *Organization Studies* 7(1):75–85.

———. 1989. "The Strength of Strong Ties: Social Networks and Intergroup Conflict in Organizations." *Academy of Management Journal* 32:377–401.

Nohria, Nitin, and Carlos Garcia-Pont. 1991. "Global Strategic Linkages and Industry Structure." *Strategic Management Journal* 12:105–124.

Nohria, Nitin, and Sumantra Ghoshal. 1991. "Distributed Innovation in the 'Differentiated Network' Multinational." Working paper, Harvard Business School.

Nolan, Richard L., Alex J. Pollock, and James P. Ware. 1988. "Creating the 21st Century Organization." *Stage-by-Stage* 8(4):1–11.

———. 1989. "Toward the Design of the Network Organization." *Stage-by-Stage* 9(1):1–12.

Pfeffer, Jeffrey. 1972. "Merger as a Response to Organizational Interdependence." *Administrative Science Quarterly* 17:218–28.

——. 1980. *Power in Organizations.* Boston: Pitman.

——. 1982. *Organizations and Organization Theory.* Boston: Pitman.

——. 1992. *Managing with Power.* Boston: Harvard Business School Press.

Pfeffer, Jeffrey, and Phillip Nowak. 1976. "Joint Ventures and Interorganizational Dependence." *Administrative Science Quarterly* 21:398–418.

Piore, Michael J., and Charles F. Sabel. 1984. *The Second Industrial Divide.* New York: Basic Books.

Porter, Michael. 1980. *Competitive Strategy.* New York: Free Press.

Powell, Walter W. 1987. "Hybrid Organizational Arrangements." *California Management Review* 30:67–87.

——. 1990. "Neither Market Nor Hierarchy: Network Forms of Organization." In B. Staw, ed., *Research in Organizational Behavior* Vol. 12. Greenwich, CT: JAI Press, pp. 295–336.

Pugh, D. S., D. J. Dickson, C. R. Hinings, and C. Turner. 1968. "Dimensions of Organization Structure." *Administrative Science Quarterly* 13:65–91.

Roethlisberger, Fritz J. 1977. *The Elusive Phenomena.* Boston: Harvard Business School Press.

Roethlisberger, Fritz J., and W. J. Dickson. 1939. *Management and the Worker.* Cambridge, MA: Harvard University Press.

Rogers, Everett M., and Judith K. Larsen. 1984. *Silicon Valley Fever: Growth of High Technology Culture.* New York: Basic Books.

Sarason, Seymour B., and Elizabeth Lorentz. 1979. *The Challenge of the Resource Exchange Network.* San Francisco: Jossey-Bass.

Saxenian, AnnaLee. 1990. "Regional Networks and the Resurgence of Silicon Valley." *California Management Review* 33(1):89–112.

Scott, Richard M. 1987. *Organizations: Rational, Natural, and Open Systems* 2d ed. Englewood Cliffs, NJ: Prentice-Hall.

Sen, Amartya. 1985. "Goals, commitment, and identity." *Journal of Law, Economics, and Organization* 1(2):341–355.

Sengenberger, Werner, Gary Loveman, and Michael Piore, eds. 1990. *The Reemergence of Small Enterprise: Industrial Restructuring in Industrialized Economies.* Geneva, Switz: International Labor Organization.

Stevenson, Howard H., and David E. Gumpert. 1985. "The Heart of Entrepreneurship." *Harvard Business Review* 63(2) (Mar.–Apr.): 85–94.

Thorelli, Hans B. "Networks: between Markets and Hierarchies." *Strategic Management Journal* 7:37–51.

Tichy, Noel. 1981. "Networks in Organizations." In P. C. Nystrom and W. G. Starbuck, eds., *Handbook of Organization Design,* Vol. 2. New York: Oxford University Press, pp. 225–248.

Tichy, Noel, and Charles Fombrun. 1979. "Network Analysis in Organizational Settings." *Human Relations* 32:923–965.

Walker, Gordon. 1985. "Network Position and Cognition in a Computer Software Firm." *Administrative Science Quarterly* 30:103–130.

Warren, Roland L. 1967. "The Interorganizational Field as a Focus for Investigation." *Administrative Science Quarterly* 12:396–419.

Wellman, Barry. 1988. "Structural Analysis: From Method and Metaphor to Theory and Substance." In Barry Wellman and S. D. Berkowitz, eds., *Social Structures: A Network Approach.* New York: Cambridge University Press, pp. 19–61.

Wellman, Barry, and S. D. Berkowitz, eds. 1988. *Social Structures: A Network Approach.* New York: Cambridge University Press.

White, Harrison C. 1970. *Chains of Opportunity*. Cambridge: Harvard University Press.

————. 1981. "Where Do Markets Come From?" *American Journal of Sociology* 87:517–547.

————. (forthcoming). *Identity and Control*. Princeton: Princeton University Press.

White, Harrison C., Scott A. Boorman, and Ronald L. Brieger. 1976. "Social Structures from Multiple Networks I: Blockmodels of Roles and Positions." *American Journal of Sociology* 81:730–780.

Williamson, Oliver. 1985. *The Economic Institutions of Capitalism*. New York: Free Press.

————. 1991. "Comparative Economic Organization: The Analysis of Discrete Structural Alternatives." *Administrative Science Quarterly* 36(2):269–296.

Zaltman, G., R. Duncan, and J. Holbek. 1973. *Innovation and Organization*. New York: Wiley.

LINKING STRUCTURE AND ACTION

1

Problems of Explanation in Economic Sociology

MARK GRANOVETTER

I argue in this paper that a well-conceived economic sociology can, under certain circumstances, improve on the explanations of economic action and institutions typically offered by neoclassical economics. First I want to discuss in a general way why such improvements are possible.

I see three fundamental reasons, each of which identifies a characteristic deficiency in economic explanation: (1) The pursuit of economic goals is typically accompanied by that of such noneconomic ones as sociability, approval, status, and power. Analyses that abstract away from the latter as a matter of principle are handicapped at the outset. (2) Economic action (like all action) is socially situated and cannot be explained by reference to individual motives alone. It is embedded in ongoing networks of personal relationships rather than carried out by atomized actors. (3) Economic institutions (like all institutions) do not arise automatically in some form made inevitable by external circumstances; rather, they are "socially constructed" (Berger and Luckmann 1966). An understanding of this process requires that both theory and empirical research pay attention to dynamics. Limitation of theory to the comparative statics of equilibrium states encourages elliptical accounts of the origins of institutions, such as reliance on functionalist or culturalist explanation.

The qualifying phrases "under certain circumstances" and "*characteristic* deficiency" refer to the two logical cases where economic sociology will not lead to improved explanation: (1) where economic explanation does not display the deficiencies named and (2) where these characteristics are not in fact deficiencies. Thus some economists take account of noneconomic motives, embeddedness, and the processes by which economic institutions

This paper is drawn from draft chapters of my book manuscript, *Society and Economy: The Social Construction of Economic Institutions,* to be published by Harvard University Press.

are constructed, though it is rare to see all three in a single analysis, and all are discouraged by the present theoretical synthesis. Rather, most economists who discuss the issue claim that the economic sphere is sufficiently disentangled and autonomous from other social spheres that noneconomic motives, social relations, and detailed historical processes can be set aside. Part of the contribution of a theoretically vital economic sociology should be a specification of the circumstances under which such claims are correct, rather than a blanket insistence that they can never be.

1. NONECONOMIC MOTIVES, EMBEDDEDNESS, AND ATOMIZATION IN SOCIAL THOUGHT

The first two reasons are analytically separable but empirically related. One reason why people can and do seek such noneconomic goals as sociability, approval, status, and power in the course of their economic activity is that this activity occurs in networks of personal relations. If economic activity were impersonal and atomized, it would be much harder to do so. People could then still seek such goals *indirectly*, in that accumulation of economic resources might be the royal road to power and prestige. But these goals would then be analytically separable from the economic ones, and you would not need to worry about trade-offs among economic and noneconomic motives in the course of economic activity itself, as where corporate executives must balance their interest in profit maximization against their desire to be respected in their upper-class social circle (cf. Useem 1983).

Conversely, one (though not the only) reason why people *conduct* their economic activity through networks of known personal acquaintances is that sociability, approval, status, and power are central human motives; since economic activity is a large part of the lives of many actors, they could hardly be expected to play out that large part in an arena utterly cut off from the chance to achieve those motives, as would be the case in an impersonal, atomized economic life. It is thus common for economic relations that begin in a neutral, impersonal way to develop noneconomic content as people try actively to *prevent* economic and noneconomic aspects of their lives from being separated. This progression was already clear to Durkheim and is a central theme in his *Division of Labor in Society:*

> [E]ven where society rests wholly upon the division of labor, it does not resolve itself into a myriad of atoms juxtaposed together, between which only external and transitory contact can be established. The members are linked by ties that extend well beyond the very brief moment when the act of exchange is being accomplished ([1893] 1984:173).

That people have noneconomic as well as economic motives is hardly news. The issue is whether economic analysis can in fact be segregated from such motives. There are obvious gains in simplification from doing so. But the intellectual history of such segregation is more complex. Albert Hirschman (1977) has traced over several centuries the distinction between the "passions" and the "interests," in which the latter, referring to economic motivations, came to be assumed the province of calm, rational, and benevolent behavior. Noneconomic motives were gradually subsumed to the category of "passions" with the accompanying assumption that their pursuit was not a matter of rational action and therefore not suitable for economic analysis. By the time of Adam Smith this distinction was firmly fixed; it is so clear in the writing of Pareto that his economics and his sociology are so utterly separate that one could read one without suspecting the existence of the other.[1]

Influenced by Pareto, Paul Samuelson (1947) thus commented in his *Foundations of Economic Analysis* that "many economists would separate economics from sociology upon the basis of rational or irrational behavior" (90).[2] It has been extraordinarily difficult for a discipline whose very conception of itself involves an analysis of rational action to contemplate the inclusion of supposedly irrational motives in its arguments.[3]

I attempt no extended analysis of the nature and texture of noneconomic motives here, as this would require a treatise on human motivation. Rather, I argue that the social nature of motives such as sociability, approval, prestige, and power leads immediately to the problem of embeddedness, since only in networks of ongoing social relations are such motives achievable.

The assertion that *economic* action is embedded in networks of personal relations among actors ties into the classic question in social theory of just how *any* behavior and institutions are affected by social relations. Since such relations are in fact always present, the situation occasioned by their absence can be imagined only through a thought experiment like Thomas Hobbes's "state of nature" or John Rawls's "original position." In assuming rational, self-interested behavior affected minimally by social relations, modern economics assumes an idealized state not far from that of these thought experiments. At the other extreme lies what I will call the "strong embeddedness argument": that economic action and institutions are so constrained by ongoing social relations that to construe them as independent is a grievous misunderstanding; and further, that in precapitalist societies, the economizing motives taken as given by classical and neoclassical economic theory cannot be assumed, and the theory thus gives us no insight whatsoever into such action and institutions.

Most sociologists, anthropologists, and historians have taken the strong embeddedness position for economic action in "primitive" or "nonmarket" societies: that such action was heavily embedded there but has become much more autonomous with modernization; that in modern society the economy is more a separate sphere, where economic transactions are no longer determined mainly by the social or kinship obligations of transactors but by rational pursuit of individual gain. It is sometimes further argued that the traditional situation is even reversed: Instead of economic life being submerged in social relations, these relations become an epiphenomenon of the market. The strong embeddedness position is associated with the "substantivist" school in anthropology, identified especially with Karl Polanyi (1944; Polanyi, Arensberg, and Pearson 1957) and with the idea of "moral economy" in history and political science (Thompson 1971; Scott 1976), with neoevolutionism in sociology (Parsons 1937) and with many traditional theories of economic development. It has also some obvious affinity to Marxist thought.

Few economists have accepted this conception of a break in embeddedness with modernization; most assert instead that embeddedness in earlier societies was not substantially greater than the low level they attribute to modern markets. Adam Smith set the tone, postulating a "certain propensity in human nature . . . to truck, barter and exchange one thing for another" ([1776] 1976, Book 1, Ch. 2) and assuming that in primitive society, with labor the only factor of production, people must have exchanged goods in proportion to their labor costs, as in the general classical theory of rational exchange ([1776] 1976, Book 1, Ch. 6). From the 1920s on, certain anthropologists took a similar position, which came to be called the "formalist" one: that even in tribal societies, economic behavior was sufficiently independent of social relations for standard neoclassical analysis to be useful. This position has recently received a new infusion as economists and fellow travelers in history and political science have developed a new interest in the economic analysis of social institutions—much of which falls into what is called the "new institutional economics"—and have argued that behavior and institutions previously interpreted as embedded in earlier societies, as well as our own, can be better understood as resulting from the pursuit of self-interest by rational, more or less atomized individuals (e.g., North and Thomas 1973; Williamson 1975).

My own view, which I will characterize as the "weak embeddedness position," diverges from both schools of thought.[4] While I agree with the economists (and their fellow travelers) that the transition to modernity did not much change the level of embeddedness, I also argue that it has always been and remains substantial: less all-encompassing in the earlier period than claimed in the "strong embeddedness position" of substantivists, development theorists, and evolutionists, but more so in the later period than supposed by them or by economists.

2. OVER- AND UNDERSOCIALIZED CONCEPTIONS OF ACTION IN SOCIOLOGY AND ECONOMICS

I begin the argument by recalling Dennis Wrong's (1961) complaint about an "oversocialized conception of man in modern sociology," a conception of people as overwhelmingly sensitive to the opinions of others and hence obedient to the dictates of consensually developed norms and values, internalized through socialization so that obedience is not perceived as a burden.

Wrong approved the attack on an atomized conception of human action and the emphasis on actors' embeddedness in social context, the crucial factor absent from Hobbes's thinking, but warned of exaggerating the degree of this embeddedness and the extent to which it might eliminate conflict:

> It is frequently the task of the sociologist to call attention to the intensity with which men desire and strive for the good opinion of their immediate associates in a variety of situations, particularly those where received theories or ideologies have unduly emphasized other motives. . . . Thus sociologists have shown that factory workers are more sensitive to the attitudes of their fellow workers than to purely economic incentives. . . . It is certainly not my intention to criticize the findings of such studies. My objection is that . . . [al]though sociologists have criticized past efforts to single out one fundamental motive in human conduct, the desire to achieve a favorable self-image by winning approval from others frequently occupies such a position in their own thinking (1961:188–189).

To the extent that such a conception was prominent in 1961, it resulted in large part from Talcott Parsons's attempt in *The Structure of Social Action* (1937:89–94) to transcend the problem of order as posed by Thomas Hobbes by emphasizing commonly held societal values. Parsons classified Hobbes in what he called the "utilitarian" tradition, which he attacked for treating individual action as atomized, isolated from the influence of others or from any broad cultural or social traditions. But a close reading of such utilitarians as Hume, Smith, Bentham, and John Stuart Mill does not support such a depiction. Rather, they do show considerable interest in how social institutions, norms, and interaction modify and shape individual action (see Camic 1979).

Nevertheless, most of what Parsons alleged to be the case for the "utilitarian" and "positivistic" tradition does seem an appropriate account of the stance of classical—and especially neoclassical—economics on human economic action.[5] In contrast to the oversocialized view pilloried by Wrong (1961), classical and especially neoclassical economics operate with an atomized, *undersocialized* conception of human action. The theoretical arguments disallow by hypothesis any impact of social structure or relations on production, distribution, or consumption. In competitive markets, no producer or consumer noticeably influences aggregate supply or demand or, therefore, prices or other terms of trade. As Albert Hirschman has noted, such idealized markets, involving as they do

> large numbers of price-taking anonymous buyers and sellers supplied with perfect information . . . function without any prolonged human or social contact between the parties. Under perfect competition there is no room for bargaining, negotiation, remonstration, or mutual adjustment and the various operators that contract together need not enter into recurrent or continuing relationships as a result of which they would get to know each other well (1982:1473).

When the classical writers treated traders' social relations at all it was as a drag on the competitive character of markets. In a much-quoted line,

Adam Smith complained that "people of the same trade seldom meet together, even for merriment and diversion, but the conversation ends in a conspiracy against the public or in some contrivance to raise prices." His laissez-faire politics did not permit him to recommend antitrust action, but he did suggest repeal of regulations requiring all those in the same trade to sign a public register, since "the public existence of such information connects individuals who might never otherwise be known to one another and gives every man of the trade a direction where to find every other man of it" ([1776] 1979:232–233). Noteworthy here is not the rather lame policy prescription but the tacit recognition that *social atomization is prerequisite to perfect competition.*

Though some economists in the main line of classical work (e.g., John Stuart Mill) and others in what came to fall outside the main line (such as Marx and the German historical school) were interested in the general social conditions of economic action, a more rigorous and quantitative tradition beginning with David Ricardo (1816) increasingly narrowed the focus in a way that excluded noneconomic matters.[6] This exclusion was extended by the triumph of the neoclassical "marginalists" over the German historical school in the *Methodenstreit* conducted from the 1870s through the early twentieth century. The marginalist approach of Menger, Walras, and Jevons, especially as codified by Marshall, "solved" the classical problem of value by reducing it to the determination of market prices by supply and demand, which was to be understood by the mathematics of maximization.

Twentieth-century economists have continued this line, identifying social influences as involving nonrational action, as in the preceding quotation from Paul Samuelson. In recent years some economists have begun to take social influences more seriously, as more than just frictional drag; but even they continue to interpret them as divergent from rational action. Instead, they conceive social influences as processes in which actors acquire customs, habits, or norms that they follow mechanically and automatically, irrespective of their bearing on rational choice. This view, close to Wrong's "oversocialized conception," is reflected in James Duesenberry's quip that "economics is all about how people make choices; sociology is all about how they don't have any choices to make" (1960:233) and in Ernest Phelps Brown's description of the "sociologists' approach to pay determination" as deriving from the assumption that people act in "certain ways because to do so is customary, or an obligation, or the 'natural thing to do,' or right and proper, or just and fair" (1977:17).

But the apparent contrast between under- and oversocialized views, masks an irony of great theoretical importance: *Both share a conception of action and decision carried out by atomized actors.* In the undersocialized account, atomization results from narrow utilitarian pursuit of self-interest; in the oversocialized one, from the fact that behavioral patterns have been internalized and are thus affected only peripherally by ongoing social relations. That the internalized rules of behavior are social in origin does not differentiate this argument decisively from a utilitarian one, in which the source of utility functions is left open, allowing room for behavior guided entirely by consensually determined norms and values, as in the oversocialized view.[7] Under- and oversocialized resolutions of the problem of order thus merge in their atomization of actors from imr ediate social context. This ironic merger is already visible in Hobbes's *Leviathan*, in which the unfortunate denizens of the state of nature, overwhelmed by the disorder consequent to their atomization, cheerfully surrender all their rights to an authoritarian power and subsequently behave in a docile and honorable manner; by the artifice of a social contract, they lurch directly from an undersocialized to an oversocialized state.

This convergence of under- and oversocialized views helps explain why those modern economists who do attempt to take account of social influences typically represent them in an oversocialized manner. In the theory of segmented labor markets, for example, Michael Piore (1975) has argued that members of each labor market segment have different styles of decision making and that the making of decisions by rational choice, custom, or command in upper-primary, lower-primary, and secondary labor markets, respectively, corresponds to the origins of workers in middle-, working-, and lower-class subcultures. Similarly, Samuel Bowles and Herbert Gintis (1976), in their account of the consequences of American education, argue that different social classes display different cognitive processes because of differences in the education provided to each. Those destined for lower-level jobs are trained to be dependable followers of rules, while those who will be channeled into elite positions attend "elite four-year colleges" that "emphasize social relationships conformable with the higher levels in the production hierarchy. . . . As they 'master' one type of behavioral regulation they are either allowed to progress to the next or are channeled into the corresponding level in the hierarchy of production" (132).

But these oversocialized conceptions of how society influences individual behavior are rather mechanical: once we know individuals' social class or labor-market sector, everything else in behavior is automatic, because they are so well socialized. Social influence is seen here as an external force that, like the Deists' God, sets things in motion and has no further effects, a force that insinuates itself into the minds and bodies of individuals (as in the movie *Invasion of the Body Snatchers*), altering their way of making decisions. Once we know in just what way one has been affected, ongoing social relations and structures are irrelevant. Social influence is all contained inside an individual's head, so in actual decision situations he or she can be as atomized as any *homo economicus*, but with different rules for decisions. More sophisticated (and thus less oversocialized) analyses of cultural influences (e.g., Fine and Kleinman 1979; Cole 1979, Ch. 1) make it clear that culture is not a once-and-for-all influence but an ongoing process, continuously constructed and reconstructed during interaction. It not only shapes its members, but also is shaped by them, in part for their own strategic reasons.

Even when economists do take social relationships seriously, as do such diverse figures as Harvey Leibenstein (1976) and Gary Becker (1976), they invariably abstract away from the history of relations and their position with respect to other relations. The interpersonal ties they describe are stylized, average, and "typical"; devoid of specific content, history, or structural location. Actors' behavior results from their named role positions and role sets; thus we have arguments about how workers and supervisors, husbands and wives, criminals and law enforcers will interact with one another, but these relations are not assumed to have individualized content beyond that given by the obligations and interests inherent in the named roles. This procedure is exactly what structural sociologists have criticized in Parsonian sociology, the relegation of the *specifics* of individual relations to a minor role in the overall conceptual scheme, epiphenomenal in comparison with enduring structures of normative role prescriptions deriving from ultimate value orientations.

A fruitful analysis of any human action—including economic action, my subject here—requires us to avoid the atomization implicit in the theoretical extremes of under- and oversocialized views. Actors do not behave or decide as atoms outside a social context, nor do they adhere slavishly to a script written for them by the particular intersection of sociocultural categories they happen to occupy. Their attempts at purposive action are instead embedded in concrete, ongoing systems of social relations.

3. EMBEDDEDNESS AND ITS EFFECTS ON ECONOMIC ACTION

3.1 The Concepts and the Agenda

I distinguish three levels of economic phenomena to be explained. The first is individual economic action, for which I take Max Weber's definition ([1921] 1968:339):

> Contrary to an unsuitable usage, we shall not consider every instrumental action as economic. Thus, praying for a spiritual good is not an economic act, even though it may have a definite purpose according to some religious doctrine. We also shall not include every economizing activity, neither intellectual economizing in concept formation nor an esthetic "economy of means." . . . We shall speak of economic action only if the satisfaction of a need depends, in the actor's judgment, upon some relatively *scarce* resources and a *limited* number of possible actions, and if this state of affairs evokes specific reactions. Decisive for such rational action is, of course, the fact that this scarcity is *subjectively* presumed and that action is oriented to it.

Weber goes on to note that "needs . . . may be of any conceivable kind, ranging from food to religious edification, if there is a scarcity of goods and services in relation to demand." This is similar to economist Lionel Robbins's classic definition of economics as "the science which studies human behavior as a relationship between ends and scarce means which have alternative uses" ([1932] 1984:15), differing only in Weber's insistence on the importance of the actor's subjective orientation to the means-end situation.[8]

Having adopted this broad definition of economic action, I could then logically go on to discuss a wide range of subjects, including those that constitute recent incursions by economists into domains previously studied only by sociologists—for example, marriage, divorce, crime, and the allocation of time. Instead I confine my attention to examples that are "economic" in the usual sense of having to do with the provision of goods and services, what we might call the "hard core" of economics. I do so mainly for a polemical reason: Even if successful in showing that typically sociological subjects are vitally affected by their embeddedness in webs of social relations, I would at best only restore the *status quo ante bellum*, the intellectual situation before economists began applying their concepts to the sociological realm. I mean to engage in a more radical critique than this, to argue that neoclassical arguments have difficulties even in their most familiar terrain. A successful demonstration of this assertion would carry over *a fortiori* to the more peripheral subjects of recent "economic imperialism."

I also want to explain patterns *beyond* the actions of individuals, what I call "economic outcomes" and "economic institutions." Examples of "outcomes" would be the formation of stable prices for a commodity or of wage differentials between certain classes of workers. So these "outcomes" are *regular patterns* of individual action. What we call "institutions" are different from these outcomes in that they typically involve larger complexes of action and take on a sense that this is how things *should* be done. Institutions also convey, as is well captured in the sociology of knowledge literature, an impression of solidity, what the Germans call "massive facticity"; that is, they become reified, experienced as external and objective aspects of the world rather than as the products of social construction that they really are (see, e.g., Berger and Luckmann 1966).

This social-constructionist perspective is rarely applied to *economic* institutions but is highly relevant there. Examples of economic institutions include entire systems of economic organization, such as capitalism, and—at less macro levels—the way particular organizations, industries, or professions are constituted and carry out their affairs.

Before sketching how one can use the idea of embeddedness to explain economic action, outcomes, and institutions, I must say more about that idea. "Embeddedness" refers to the fact that economic action and outcomes, like all social action and outcomes, are affected by actors' dyadic (pairwise) relations *and* by the structure of the overall network of relations. As a shorthand, I will refer to these as the relational and the structural aspects of embeddedness. The structural aspect is especially crucial to keep in mind because it is easy to slip into "dyadic atomization," a type of reductionism. Thus when such economists as Harvey Leibenstein (1976) and Gary Becker (1976, 1981) treat dyadic activity as structured by the norms and interests entailed in the roles of husband and wife or employer and supervisor, this treatment of social relations has the paradoxical effect of preserving atomized decision making even when decisions are seen to involve more than one individual: Because the analyzed pair of individuals is abstracted out of social context, it is atomized in its behavior from that of other actors and from the history of its own relations. *Atomization has not been eliminated, merely transferred to the dyadic level of analysis.* Note here the use of an oversocialized conception— that of actors behaving exclusively in accord with their prescribed roles— to implement an atomized, undersocialized view.

It is also important to avoid what might be called "temporal reductionism": treating relations and structures of relations as if they had no history that shapes the present situation. In ongoing relations, human beings do not start fresh each day, but carry the baggage of previous interactions into each new one. Built into human cognitive equipment is a remarkable capacity, depressingly little studied, to file away the details and especially the emotional tone of past relations for long periods of time, so that even when one has not had dealings with a certain person for many years, a re-activation of the relationship does not start from scratch but from some set of previously attained common understandings and feelings.

Structures of relations also result from processes over time and can rarely be understood except as accretions of these processes. Thus talking about strikes in factories with large numbers of rural and "guest workers," such as those at German automobile plants, Sabel (1982) notes that

> strikes by peasant workers . . . usually remain episodes, isolated from the rest of the life of the factory and further isolating the peasant workers themselves from other workers. Still, . . . they bring some few peasant workers into contact with the outside society in the person of a union militant, a sympathetic native worker, or a representative of management. . . . To the extent that some of these contacts endure, they can shape the course of later conflict (136).

By tracing out such relations, Sabel is able to make a new interpretation of the turbulent industrial relations in 1970s Italy (Ch. 4). A good cross-sectional account might note the importance of these contacts as liaisons between the two groups but would be unable to contribute to any general argument about the circumstances under which such a structure arose. Without such an account, analysts slip into cultural or functionalist explanations, both of which usually make their appearance when historical dynamics have been neglected.

3.2 The Effects of Embeddedness on Individual Economic Action and on Economic Outcomes

Relational embeddedness typically has quite direct effects on individual economic action. How a worker and supervisor interact is determined not only by the meaning of these categories in a technical division of labor, but also by the kind of personal relationship they have, which is determined largely by a history of interactions. This is partially captured by economists' use of interdependent utility functions, where the utility of another becomes an argument of your own utility function; in plainer language, their welfare becomes part of your own. But this does not really capture the fact that our behavior toward others depends on a structure of mutual expectations that has become a constitutive part of the relationship.

Not only particular relations may affect your behavior, but also the aggregated impact of all such relations. The mere *fact* of attachment to others may modify economic action. Thus you may want to stay in a certain firm despite economic advantages available elsewhere because you are attached to so many fellow workers. And the noneconomic value of such attachments partly explains the tendency of employers to recruit from among those they know, even in the absence of purely economic advantages to doing so.

Structural embeddedness typically has more subtle and less direct effects on economic action. A worker can more easily maintain a good relationship with a supervisor who has good relations with most other workers as well. If the supervisor is at odds with the others, and especially if those others are friendly with *one another*, they will be able to make life very difficult for the one worker who is close to the supervisor; pressures will be strong to edge away from this closeness. If the other workers do not form a cohesive group, such pressures can be mounted only with difficulty.

In saying this I draw on the principle that to the extent that a dyad's mutual contacts are connected to one another, there is more efficient information spread about what members of the pair are doing, and thus better ability to shape that behavior. Such cohesive groups are better not only at spreading information, but also at generating normative, symbolic, and cultural structures that affect our behavior. Thus, in this situation of what has been called "high network density," a worker may have absorbed from the group a set of behavioral principles—norms, if you like—that would make a close relationship with the supervisor literally unthinkable.

While utility functions may be able to handle the case where people care about the welfare of others, they do not seem well suited for interpreting behavior that becomes part and parcel of a longstanding relationship, nor for handling structural effects of the sort I describe here. I argue that utility functions cannot be stretched much beyond the dyadic setting because the technical difficulties implied by the embeddedness of dyadic relations in complex networks of relations would be insuperable. This is not because networks of relations cannot be modeled technically, but because the machinery of utility functions was designed for a different purpose, and the adjustments required for *them* to accommodate networks of interdependent utilities, not to mention structural effects on normative and symbolic structures, would be not only technically difficult, but clumsy and inefficient.

Structural embeddedness also affects the behavior of individuals by its impact on what information is available when decisions are made. Thus whether you leave your job depends not only on your social attachments, but also on whether information on alternative opportunities comes to you. Whether you buy a certain brand of soap can be determined in part by the structure of your social network and the information and influences that reach you through it (Katz and Lazarsfeld 1955). Whether workers believe that their wages are fair depends on how they construct their comparison group—a matter that depends not only on their position in a technical division of labor, but also in noneconomically determined social networks that cut across workplaces (Gartrell 1982).

The economic action of individuals may at times accumulate in ways that result in larger outcomes or what we call "institutions." Whether this occurs, and what shape the outcomes or institutions take when it does, is strongly channeled by the structure of relations in which the actions are embedded. A simple example is the attainment of equilibrium price, which is not an institutional matter in the sense of taking on a normative aspect (except in situations where ideas of "just price" become important), but which does result from an aggregation of individual actions that is only poorly specified in the usual comparative static treatment. In the usual formulation, markets become more competitive and prices more stable as the number of traders increases (e.g., Arrow and Hahn 1971). But Baker (1984) found, in his empirical study of floor trading of stock options, that price volatility increased strongly with the size of the trading group. This occurs because as group size increases, the number of trading relations that the average trader can sustain does not. Thus in a larger group it is harder to know about all trades; information flow is reduced by the size and resulting fragmentation of the trading network, and convergence to a single equilibrium price becomes problematic. The imperfect movement of information that causes this results from fundamental cognitive limitations of human actors in conjunction with the necessary embeddedness of trading in networks of social relations.

Here we rely again on the general principle that fragmentation of network structure will reduce the homogeneity of behavior, a principle that applies to the formation of norms as well as to uniformities with less normative content, such as the gravitation to a particular price. The principle is purely structural, and does not in itself predict which prices different group fragments will approach. Similarly, social psychological studies show that cohesive groups are in agreement on norms, without being able to explain by cohesion alone which norms are developed (cf. Festinger, Schachter, and Back 1948; Seashore 1954).

More generally, market prices are often affected by the fact that trade is carried out not in spot markets but between traders of long acquaintance. Anthropologists report that peasant and tribal markets are typically clientelized—that is, buyers and sellers have long-term continuing relations. This typically leads to sticky prices, as buyers and sellers are unresponsive to price inducements to trade with unfamiliar partners. This stickiness, and the result that adjustments must then be made in quantities so the market is not cleared, is not only important in tribal and peasant settings; macroeconomist Arthur Okun in his book *Prices and Quantities* (1981) argued for a similar impact in modern markets, where most trades are carried out not in auction markets but in what he called "customer markets" with continuing relationships.

Another example of the impact of embeddedness on prices comes from labor markets and involves the "skill differential": the extent of pay differences between skilled and unskilled blue-collar workers. Economist Melvin Reder (1955) wanted to explain why it typically diminishes in times of economic boom. Standard theory suggests that a surge in aggregate demand would increase the demand for skilled and unskilled workers alike, bidding up wages for both. Reder suggested that what happens instead is that rather than raise skilled workers' wages, employers promote workers from the next-to-highest skill level. Pursued vigorously, this strategy leaves a shortage in this next-to-highest level, which is met by substitution from the group below, and so on. When finally a shortage appears in the lowest skill category, and no new labor is available from outside the work force, the wages there must be bid up in relation to higher grades, reducing the skill differential.

I suggest a generalization of this interesting argument: *any* set of jobs where chains of substitutions of this sort are possible may have wage differentials compressed in this way. How do we identify such sets? Reder's argument suggests a simple progression from skilled down to unskilled. But I argue that in practice, which workers *appear* available to employers for upgrading into a particular type of job actually depends heavily on the history and structure of communications networks of the employers and workers *in* this job. Purely technical considerations are unlikely to be primary, since the question is not whether a worker can perform work *previously* done, but how adaptable he or she would be to a different, more complex set of tasks. We know that when making hiring decisions, employers rely on personal contacts even to assess a worker's *previous* productivity (Granovetter 1974); it seems all the more likely that they would do so where the productivity question is inherently more ambiguous.

This implies that where networks of contacts cross firm boundaries rather than being contained within firms, wage differentials might be especially widely affected. Whether such interfirm links exist depends in part on the previous mobility history of current workers, since one's pool of work contacts results directly from these histories. This in turn determines how widespread such effects will be. Thus the embeddedness of economic action may be structured in such a way as to blunt and contain individual actions, so they never do accumulate into larger outcomes—as, for example, when all networks are contained within firms—or may amplify and concatenate such actions, as where networks cross the boundaries of individual firms.

4. EMBEDDEDNESS AND ITS EFFECTS ON TRUST AND MALFEASANCE

4.1 The Problem of Trust and Malfeasance

A central theme in economic sociology is the necessity of trust and trustworthy behavior for the normal functioning of economic action and institutions. Because of this centrality, and because it further illustrates and amplifies my argument, I pause in the general discussion of explanatory strategy to treat the embeddedness of trust and malfeasance in economic life.

As McPherson observes, "any transaction in which the performance of the two parties is separated by time involves an element of trust" (1984:74). But the tendency in economics to treat individuals as atomized self-seekers permits no reasonable account of how trust could develop, and encourages instead various intellectual devices that skirt the issue with mixtures of over- and undersocialized assumptions. In classical philosophy and economics, one such set of arguments asserts that the need for trust is obviated by institutions that structure incentives so as to make the cost of malfeasance prohibitively high. Hobbes's *Leviathan* was the earliest systematic effort of this kind, where the institutional structure is that of autocratic authority. Classical liberalism and its derivatives, classical and neoclassical economics, decisively reject this solution to the problem of trust, adopting instead several implicit and complementary assumptions. One is a quite different argument about how institutions structure incentives: that truly competitive markets render force or fraud unavailing. Competition determines terms of trade that individual traders, as price takers, cannot manipulate. If traders encounter complex or difficult relationships characterized by mistrust or malfeasance, they can simply move on to the legion of others willing to do business on market terms. The force of competition will sweep the unscrupulous from the market. The details of traders' social relations thus become frictional matters. (For a version of this argument see Williamson 1975:27.)

Whether it is autocratic authority or the whip of competition that makes malfeasance too costly to engage in, the argument is similarly undersocialized in assuming that one deals fairly with others only to the extent one's self-interest dictates it. Such unadorned appeal to self-interest to explain the absence of force and fraud has never been entirely persuasive. In the classical period it was supplemented by postulating the existence of a general standard of moral behavior such as the principle John Locke derived from natural law, that "reason" teaches men not to harm one another or to appropriate property beyond what they can usefully develop: what Parsons calls the doctrine of the "natural identity of interests," the "device by which it has been possible for utilitarian thought . . . for two hundred years to evade the Hobbesian problem" (1937:97). Closely allied to this is the divergence in treatment between the "passions" and the "interests" (Hirschman 1977) in which economic motivations came to be assumed the province of calm, rational, and benevolent behavior. This distinction had the effect of watering down Hobbes's problem of order by arguing that certain human motivations, economic ones in particular, kept other less-controllable ones at bay. This implies that one's economic interest is pursued only by comparatively gentlemanly means. Hobbes's inquiry as to why those who pursue their own interest do not use force and fraud, since nothing in the meaning of self-interest excludes this, is finessed by this assumption.

These conceptions do not rely on self-interest but argue in effect that individuals act morally whatever the incentives. Because this moral action is asserted in so unconditional a way, the argument has a rather over-socialized quality. In fact, we see here a striking example of how under- and oversocialized conceptions complement one another: atomized actors in competitive markets are imagined to have so thoroughly internalized certain normative standards of behavior in economic transactions as to eliminate malfeasance.

In neoclassical economics, both institutional and normative assumptions about force and fraud remained very much in the background until two related developments during the past twenty years stimulated a resurgence of interest in such problems. One was increased attention to the micro-level details of imperfectly competitive markets, peopled by small numbers of traders with sunk costs and "specific human capital" investments. In such settings the alleged discipline of competitive markets cannot be called on to mitigate deceit. The other was the wave of interest in the economics of information, which included a realization of the difficulties that arise when information is asymmetric. The informational basis of trust was already apparent to Simmel, who, taking "confidence" as "evidently . . . one of the most important synthetic forces within society," pointed out that it is "intermediate between knowledge and ignorance about a man. The person who knows completely need not trust; while the person who knows nothing can, on no rational grounds, afford even confidence" ([1923], 1950:318). Asymmetric information was first of special interest in insurance markets, where the insured faces a problem of "moral hazard": insurance reduces the motivation to avoid the danger insured against; but insurers cannot know, without large search costs, whether claims result from this kind of negligence. More generally, any complex contingent contract that specifies obligations of each party as depending on what has occurred faces difficulties when the parties differ in their knowledge of the relevant information, as is often the case (Williamson 1975:31–37).

In modern economic literature I see two fundamental answers to the classical problem of how it can be that daily economic life is not riddled with mistrust and malfeasance, and these two link closely to the classical under- and oversocialized accounts. The modern undersocialized account, like the classical one, sees malfeasance as averted because clever institutional arrangements make it too costly to engage in. But rather than attributing this structuring of incentives to the state or to the force of competition, these accounts, found in the "new institutional economics," often interpret arrangements previously supposed to have no economic function, as having "evolved" to discourage wrongdoing. The main such arrangements are elaborate explicit and implicit contracts (Okun 1981), including deferred compensation plans and mandatory retirement, seen to reduce the incentives for "shirking" on the job or absconding with proprietary secrets (Lazear 1979; Pakes and Nitzan 1982), and authority structures that deflect opportunism by making potentially divisive decisions by fiat (Williamson 1975), an updated version of the Hobbesian argument. Sociologists have stressed the use of various institutional devices such as insurance, neutral intermediaries with fiduciary responsibility, professionals whose sole function is to monitor business relations, rating services, and the like, that make possible transactions where individuals have no personal connections to exchange partners and would otherwise avoid the transaction altogether (Zucker 1986; Shapiro 1984). To say, as do Zucker and Shapiro, that such devices produce "trust" seems to me to stretch the word too far, where it applies to all situations where individuals are willing to enter a transaction. I would rather specialize the word to refer to circumstances where one enters a transaction believing that transaction partners will behave properly for reasons that transcend pure self-interest. Where no such expectation can be held we have returned to the Hobbesian situation, and any rational individual would be motivated to develop clever ways to evade the institutional arrangements that mean to structure incentives in ways to avoid malfeasance. It is then hard to imagine that everyday economic life would not be poisoned by ever more ingenious and subtle attempts at deceit.

Some economists have recognized that institutional arrangements and the way they structure incentives could not alone stem force and fraud. After discussing implicit contract arguments that he interprets as stemming distrust, Arthur Okun concedes that while such arrangements may help, they cannot eliminate distrust, which is "a pervasive fact of economic life that extends far beyond the career labor market. Enormous resource costs could be saved in a perfectly honest and open world that would permit do-it-yourself cash registers and communal lawn mowers" (1981:86). Such awareness leads economists to consider the role of morality in economic life. McPherson, for example, dryly describes the "neutral" position on whether self-interest motivates action with no influence from moral standards as being tantamount to supposing "that it is just as natural to help an old lady across the street as to shove her in an alley and take her purse" (1984:72) and observes that the "self-interest hypothesis looks false as a general explanation of behavior. There are too many subtle opportunities to cheat and too few police officers, to make it plausible that the only effective motives supporting moral behavior are the prospects of financial or criminal penalties for immorality" (77). In a study that emphasizes how the structure of incentives determines the presence or absence of political corruption, Rose Ackerman nevertheless begins with the disclaimer that "the widespread delegation of authority to agents in large organizations presupposes that most economic actors are unwilling to milk their positions to the limits of possibility. . . . the continuing operation of familiar institutions would be inexplicable in the absence of widespread personal commitments to honesty and democratic ideals" (1978:5).

Indeed, economists have come to argue, as Okun has implied, that morality is economically valuable, that "the moral character of a society's population is a valuable economic resource" (McPherson 1984:76). Arrow observes that trust "is an important lubricant of a social system. It is extremely efficient; it saves a lot of trouble to have a fair degree of reliance on other people's word" (1974:23). How then does moral behavior arise? Appeal is sometimes made to a "generalized morality." Thus Arrow suggests that societies "in their evolution have developed implicit agreements to certain kinds of regard for others, agreements which are essential to the survival of the society or at least contribute greatly to the efficiency of its working" (1974:26; see also Akerlof 1983 on the origins of honesty).

Now one can hardly doubt the existence of some such generalized morality; without it, you would be afraid to give the gas station attendant a twenty-dollar bill when you bought five dollars' worth of gas. But this conception, in common with the Lockean "natural identity of interests" and the idea of economic action as a gentle, civilized activity, has the oversocialized characteristic of calling on a generalized, automatic response, even though moral action in economic life is hardly automatic or universal (as is well known by gas stations that demand exact change after dark).

Consider a case where "generalized morality" appears to be at work: the patron who, against all economic rationality, leaves a tip in a roadside restaurant far from home. This example has the character of a throwaway line in an introductory economics course because of three characteristics that make it atypical: (1) the transactors are previously unacquainted; (2) they are unlikely to transact again; and (3) information about the transaction is unlikely to reach others they will transact with in the future. Only in such situations can the absence of force or fraud mainly be explained by generalized morality; even then, one might wonder how effective such morality would be if costs of moral action were large.

4.2 The Embeddedness Approach to Trust and Malfeasance

I begin an embeddedness approach to problems of trust and malfeasance in economic life at the individual-level question of when individual economic actors will trust one another and act in trustworthy ways. I see three reasons why individuals might act in economic transactions as they are supposed to. One is because it is in their (social or economic) interest to do so. Another is that they believe it is morally right. These are, of course, the two reasons called on by the under- and oversocialized accounts, respectively; I would be a fool to ignore them, simply for having argued they cannot be the whole story. A third reason is that the actors see doing so as a part of the regularized expectations that characterize their personal relation with their transaction partner. In making an embeddedness argument about trust and malfeasance, I want to stress the importance of this third mechanism, neglected in under- and over-socialized accounts; but it is also crucial to see that institutional arrangements and moral principles, which certainly do play an important role, are themselves embedded in social structure in systematic and predictable ways; that is, such arrangements and principles are also socially constructed, rather than being *alternatives* to a social constructionist account.

I want also to avoid two extremes typical of this discussion: the pessimistic assumption about human nature implicit in the question "how is it that all transactions are not carried out by force and fraud?" and the Panglossian functionalism that searches indefatigably for some mechanism, be it institutional arrangements or generalized morality, to explain why order is indeed sustained, and in so doing overstates the extent of that order. The embeddedness position does not solve "the problem of order," but rather subsumes it to the more general question of under what social structural circumstances one may expect to see trust and trustworthy behavior or mistrust and malfeasance. Such a formulation makes more sense given what we know about economic life: that distrust, opportunism, and disorder are neither absent nor ubiquitous.

That trustworthy behavior may be a regularized part of a personal relationship reflects one of the typically direct effects of relational embeddedness and explains the widespread preference of all economic actors to deal with those they have dealt with before. Our information about such partners is cheap, richly detailed, and probably accurate. The fact of a continuing relation offers incentive to be trustworthy so as to encourage future transactions. But continuing economic relations become overlaid with social content that, apart from economic self-interest, carries strong expectations of trust and abstention from opportunism. That is, I may deal fairly with you not only because it is in my interest, or because I have assimilated your interest to my own (the approach of interdependent utility functions), but because we have been close for so long that we expect this of one another, and I would be mortified and distressed to have cheated you *even if you did not find out* (though all the more so if you did).

That continuing relations make behavior predictable and close off some of the fears that create difficulties among strangers is most obvious in intimate relations. Consider why individuals in burning theaters panic and stampede to the door, leading to desperate results. Roger Brown (1965) has pointed out that far from being the prototypically irrational behavior long assumed by analysts of collective action, this reflects the exigencies of an n-person Prisoners' Dilemma: each stampeder acts rationally given the absence of assurance that anyone else will exit calmly, even though all would be better off if everyone did (Ch. 14). But in the burning houses featured on the eleven-o'clock news we never do hear that everyone stampeded out and that family members trampled one another.

In the family, there is no Prisoners' Dilemma because each is committed to act on behalf of the welfare of the others and is correspondingly confident that the others can be counted on to act selflessly. (If the bank robbers in the Prisoners' Dilemma story were Bonnie and Clyde, could we not expect the famous paradox to be transcended?)

In business relations of long standing, the degree of confidence must be more variable than within families; but Prisoners' Dilemmas are nevertheless often obviated by the strength of personal relations, and this strength is a property not of the transactors but of their concrete relations. Standard economic analysis neglects the identity and past relations of individual transactors, but rational individuals know better, relying on their knowledge of these relations. They are less interested in *general* reputations than in whether a particular other may be expected to deal honestly with *them*, which they infer from their own past dealings with the other. One sees this pattern even in situations that appear, at first glance, to approximate the classic haggling of a competitive market, as in the Moroccan bazaar analyzed by Geertz (1979).

But my account thus far is too rosy, neglecting that the trust engendered by personal relations presents, by its very existence, enhanced opportunity for malfeasance. In personal relations it is common knowledge that, as the old song tells us, "you always hurt the one you love"; that a person's trust in you makes that person far more vulnerable than a stranger. In the Prisoners' Dilemma, knowledge that one's co-conspirator is certain to deny the crime presents all the more rational motive to confess, and personal relations that abrogate this dilemma may be less symmetrical than is believed by the party to be deceived. This elementary fact of social life is the bread and butter of "confidence" rackets that simulate personal relationships, sometimes for long periods, for concealed purposes. Certain business crimes, such as embezzling, are simply impossible for those who have not built up relationships of trust that permit the opportunity to manipulate accounts. The greater the trust, the more the potential gain from malfeasance. That such instances are infrequent is a tribute to the force of personal relations; that they do occur shows the limits of this force.

Correspondingly, in her random sample of 526 investigations taken from the files of the Securities and Exchange Commission over the period 1948–1972, Shapiro "found the degree of intimacy of prior victim-offender relationships surprising. There are indeed more cases in the sample in which at least some of the victims and offenders were acquainted . . . than those in which they were strangers. . . . This . . . conflicts with stereotypes of white-collar crime in which a chasm of interpersonal distance, disembodied transactions, cover-up techniques, middlemen, records, papers, documents and computerization are thought to permanently separate victim and offender" (1984:35).

Whether I cheat my friend depends then, in part, on the nature of my relation with him. It also depends on the structure of incentives and on those moral principles I apply to the situation, and both of these are affected by this relation. To the extent it is important to me socially or economically, I have incentive to avoid cheating; and to the extent my friend and I discuss and influence one another on moral principles, the relationship may affect such principles. But incentives and moral principles are also determined by *structural* embeddedness, the structure of relations in which my relation with my friend is located. My mortification at cheating a friend of long standing may be substantial even when undiscovered. It may increase when the friend becomes aware of it. But it may become even more unbearable when our mutual friends uncover the deceit and tell one another. Whether they do so will depend on the structure of the network of relations—roughly speaking, on the extent to which the mutual friends of the dyad in question are connected to one another. When these connections are many, what is called "high network density," the news will spread quickly; when they are isolated from one another, much less so. So we can expect greater pressure against such cheating in the denser network; such pressures are an important part of incentives and relate directly to economic and social costs of developing a bad reputation. But the pressure against cheating arises not only because of direct sanctions that group members would apply to me, but also because cohesive groups are more efficient than those with sparse relational networks at generating normative, symbolic, or cultural structures that affect our behavior. Thus, in such a group, it may never even occur to me to cheat my friend since I have absorbed a set of standards from the group that literally makes it unthinkable, at least in the group setting. It is a commonplace from studies of intergroup relations, however, that the most scrupulously adhered to norms within a well-defined group may be considered irrelevant when dealing with those outside its pale. This situational aspect of normative influences on behavior results from the structural embeddedness of social action.

Striking levels of both trustworthy behavior and malfeasance, then, may result from structures of personal relations. In the functionalist style of the new institutional economics (see section 5), Ben-Porath emphasizes the positive side, noting that "continuity of relationships can generate behavior on the part of shrewd, self-seeking, or even unscrupulous individuals that could otherwise be interpreted as foolish or purely altruistic. Valuable diamonds change hands on the diamond exchange, and the deals are sealed by a handshake" (1980:6). But this takes into account only relational, not structural, embeddedness. This transaction is surely possible in part because it is not atomized from other transactions but embedded in a close-knit community of diamond merchants who monitor one another's behavior closely and generate clearly defined standards of behavior easily policed by the quick spread of information about instances of malfeasance. The temptations posed by this level of trust are considerable, however, and the existence of *separate* cohesive groups may bound the reach of trust and moral action. Thus the diamond trade has also been the scene of numerous well-publicized "insider" thefts and of the notorious "CBS murders" in New York in 1982.[9]

Now I move beyond the level of individual action to inquire how embeddedness leads to outcomes and institutions relevant to trust and malfeasance. The first observation is that force and fraud are most efficiently pursued by teams, and the structure of these teams requires a level of internal trust—"honor among thieves"—that typically follows preexisting lines of relationship. Elaborate schemes for kickbacks and bid rigging, for example, can hardly be executed by individuals working alone, and when such activity is exposed it is often remarkable that it could have been kept secret given the large numbers of people involved. Law-enforcement efforts consist of finding an entry point to the network of malfeasance, an individual whose confession implicates others who will, in snowball-sample fashion, "finger" still others until the entire picture is fitted together. Because malefactors are intuitively aware of this, they often attempt to structure a network of malfeasance in as decoupled a way as possible. Thus, in the massive OPM leasing fraud, parts of the patterns of fraudulent activity were perceived by investment bankers, banks, insurance companies, pension funds, equity participants, auditors, accountants, lawyers, and employees. But "each of these specialist organizations concentrated on a set of narrow concerns. . . . Because of this division of responsibility, information about OPM was diffused among a number of actors. . . . Few professionals were in a position to piece all the evidence together; no one saw the big picture" (Gandossy 1985:10). The two principals of the company, who were instrumental in organizing the fraud, did their best to maintain this fragmentation and to inhibit communication among these parties.[10]

Illegal activities can take on an aura of normality among those engaged in them, through cultural and linguistic techniques of "neutralization" (cf. Sykes and Matza 1957) that are more likely to develop the more dense the network of malfeasance. In the OPM case, such obviously illegal techniques as pledging the same collateral for several loans came to be designated by such neutral-sounding terms as "double discounts" in the company's central group (Gandossy 1985), and Hirsch (1986) notes the evolution of metaphors describing unfriendly takeovers, which redefined what was initially considered malfeasance as acceptable, even heroic, behavior. Such social structurally mediated use of symbols must help explain why even the most elaborate and blatant schemes of political corruption take on the solidity of established institutions, so that those public officials finally brought to account for their actions invariably defend themselves by explaining that they only participated in the system as they found it, as if it could not have been otherwise.

How widely force, fraud, and consequent disorder spread depends very much on how the network of social relations is structured. Hobbes exaggerated the extent of disorder likely in his atomized state of nature where, in the absence of sustained social relations, one could expect only desultory dyadic conflicts. More extended and large-scale disorder results from coalitions of combatants, impossible without prior relations. We do not speak of "war" unless actors have arranged themselves into two "sides" as the end result of various coalitions. This occurs only if there are insufficient crosscutting ties held by actors with enough links to both main potential groups of combatants to have a strong interest in forestalling conflict. This principle carries over to the business world, where conflicts are tame unless each side can escalate by calling on substantial numbers of allies in other firms, as happens in attempts to implement or block takeovers.

Thus frauds as well as legitimate business enterprises attempt to tap into existing networks in the hope of wide diffusion, more difficult if attempted through impersonal channels. In her study of SEC investigations, Shapiro (1984) reports that in only 39% of the offenses where victim data were available were all victims strangers to one another.

> More frequently, offenses touch victim populations containing groups of associates or portions of various social networks. The sample contains cases with victim pools composed of members of particular church congregations or ethnic associations, officers at several military bases, members of political or social clubs or recreational associations, members of a professional athletic team, a textbook editor and a network of social science professors, members of investment clubs, and networks of political conservatives (36).

Some such networks are brought into the fraud by the use of "bird dogs," enthusiastic investors who are aware of the fraud and convince others to invest; the use of celebrities or community leaders, usually innocent of the fraudulent nature of the scheme, is common as an incentive for others to participate (Shapiro 1984:36–37).

Also relevant to this discussion is the general literature on how groups promote their own private interests at the expense of some putative larger general interest. Whether this is seen as malfeasance depends on one's differential valuation of interests. Adam Smith's denunciation of traders who engaged in price fixing even at social occasions was motivated by his sense that the outcomes given by competitive markets had some quality of natural law about them that should not be disrupted. This baseline of a freely competitive, atomized, impersonal market leads one to see group activities in pursuit of private interests as malfeasance against the common weal. Colander (1984) comments that not only "does the invisible hand guide people toward activities beneficial to society, it also has an underside; individuals following their own self-interest continually attempt to see that the invisible hand does not work" (2). When groups mobilize to gain the support of government on behalf of their interests, analysts of laissez-faire persuasion are particularly outraged, and a recent stream of literature denounces such efforts as "rent-seeking" (see the symposium reported in Colander 1984). In a more balanced treatment, but one similar in spirit to the rent-seeking literature, Mancur Olson (1982) argues that the economic growth of nations is inhibited mainly by what he calls "distributional coalitions" that try to divert productive resources from their most productive use to their own private benefit (see the critique in Tilly 1984). All such arguments use a baseline that cannot exist in the world as we know it, one that assumes there is something unnatural and remediable about the pursuit of self-interest through group structures rather than by isolated individuals. Only when the structure of connections by which groups of individuals actually function, and the way such efforts concatenate into larger efforts or fail to connect with other groups and thereby die out, is taken as the natural starting point for analysis, can we expect to understand outcomes at the societal level.

5. THE SOCIAL CONSTRUCTION OF ECONOMIC INSTITUTIONS AND THE PITFALLS OF FUNCTIONALISM AND CULTURALISM

More so than for individual economic action or economic outcomes, the arguments about how economic institutions originate are sufficiently complex that it would not be useful to sketch them here. But I will make some comments about my general explanatory strategy. I will be arguing that economic institutions are socially constructed, they result from actions taken by socially situated individuals embedded in networks of personal relations with noneconomic as well as economic aims. An adequate understanding of why institutions look as they do requires detailed attention to this process of construction.

Little economic work on the explanation of institutions does this. As in many branches of economics, the emphasis is not on dynamics but on the comparative statics of equilibrium states. But without dynamic argument, we have the ironic outcome that the discipline most devoted to methodological individualism finds itself with no ready way to explain institutions as the outgrowth of individual action and so must resort to accounts that derive them from gross features of the environment. There are two main such accounts: the culturalist and the functionalist positions.

The culturalist position does not derive at all from economic logic, but rather says that some economic outcome or institution has turned out as it has because the group that produced it has some set of cultural beliefs or traits that predisposes it to the observed behavior. Those characterized by a "Protestant ethic" will work harder and produce more successful firms or other outcomes; those with a culture oriented toward cooperation in a hierarchical setting where individuals are subordinated to the society will develop smoothly functioning industrial enterprises (as is claimed for Japan; see, among others, Ouchi 1981). Particular organizations are said to have distinct cultures that resist merger or at least put obstacles in its way.

If groups really did behave in ways so closely determined by their cultures, it would indeed not be necessary to pay attention to the evolution of institutions over time; there would be little such evolution so long as the culture remained stable. But to assume so thorough a domination of action by cultural "principles" is to fall into the oversocialized mode of argument I have criticized here, not to mention that such an argument hovers uncomfortably close to circularity, since the causal tie between cultural beliefs and observed patterns is usually inferred from behavior rather than shown explicitly.

Functionalist accounts cause economists less discomfort, though they are no more distant from circularity than are culturalist ones. This is because the "problems" that observed institutions are said to have originated in order to solve are *economic* problems: hence one can call the explanatory activity "efficiency analysis."

The functionalist strategy characteristic of the new institutional economics, is, like that of culturalist accounts, static rather than dynamic; it is to argue backward from the characteristics of an institution to the reason why it must be present. In *The Economic Theory of Social Institutions*, Andrew Schotter (1981) states this principle in unusually candid form, arguing that to understand any social institution requires that we "infer the evolutionary problem that must have existed for the institution as we see it to have developed. Every evolutionary economic problem requires a social institution to solve it" (2). Such a procedure implicitly assumes a system in equilibrium, since a still-evolving institution might not reveal by inspection what problem it had evolved to solve.[11]

This reflexive avoidance of dynamics rests in part, of course, on the technical difficulty of explicit dynamic accounts (see, e.g., Baumol 1970), but derives more fundamentally, I believe, from the arbitrariness, within a purely neoclassical economic perspective, of accounts of behavior out of equilibrium, when prices are not known to be stable and therefore reliable sources of information. Dynamic models of economic institutions must typically make assumptions about behavior that require knowledge of social affiliations and noneconomic motives, and there is no guidance from purely economic argument about what these assumptions should be. It is thus more comfortable to avoid what is seen as arbitrary.

The assumption that existing institutions are well matched to economic problems is sometimes grounded in a quasi-Darwinian argument that natural selection should weed out inefficient solutions to those problems (the *locus classicus* of this assertion is Friedman 1953:16–22). Unsolved problems present the possibility of profit to those who can solve them, and under suitable assumptions any opportunity for profit will be taken. Inefficiencies will in effect be arbitraged away, or in a more common phrase, part of the rhetoric of modern economics (see McCloskey 1983), "you will not find dollar bills lying in the street."

But such an argument can be sustained only under rather rigorous competitive conditions that provide appropriate selection pressures (see Nelson and Winter 1982 for a discussion of the requirements for an evolutionist argument in economics). The embeddedness of economic activity in networks of personal relations creates systematic structuring of information flows and of the possibility of establishing new institutions that cannot be captured as simple selection pressures; and the pursuit of noneconomic motives alongside economic ones means that actors do not typically strive to maximize economic efficiency alone, but rather make trade-offs among their goals. The upshot of all this is that any observed institution may be the product of a mixture of aims implemented by complex networks of actors. Without an understanding of the historical process by which it arose, the institution can easily be misinterpreted.

The pitfalls, Panglossian and others, of functionalist explanations have been catalogued many times (e.g., Merton 1947; Hempel 1965; Nagel 1961; Stinchcombe 1968; Elster 1983), and rigorous accounts have been given of the requirements that must be met for an *explanandum* to be properly explained by reference to problems it is claimed to solve. Rather than recapitulating these accounts I want to suggest some practical questions one must be able to answer about a functionalist explanation before it can be accepted.

1. Is the problem a problem? If the problem a pattern is alleged to solve is in fact no problem at all, the explanation surely fails immediately.

2. Is the solution a solution? Even if the problem is admitted to be genuine, the institution under scrutiny had better really solve it, otherwise the functionalist account would not be persuasive.

3. Do we understand the process by which this solution has arisen? To avoid this question is to assume that all problems that arise are solved, a proposition that hardly anyone would endorse in this bald form. Part of a functional explanation should be to account for why and how the stipulated problem was indeed solved, rather than falling into the class of problems for which solutions are not found. But once we have an account of just how this solution can arise, we will also understand under what circumstances it cannot. In practice, I argue, this means that the solution will *not* arise in all instances where the problem does, but only in some. The explanation of the pattern will require us to know more than just the problem it solves, but also the auxiliary conditions that are required for this solution to emerge.

4. Why this *particular* solution? What is the range of solutions for this problem, and under what circumstances do others arise? Like the answers to question 3, a response to this question distances us from crude functionalist accounts and reduces the distance between a functionalist explanation and one based on historical sequences.

A functionalist explanation that satisfactorily responds to these four questions would pass muster. The reader may suspect already that, by my lights, very few do. Part of the reason for this is that institutions do not typically arise in any simple way as solutions to problems presented by the environment. Rather, ways of doing things begin for reasons that relate to the various purposes of the actors involved and to the structures of relations they are embedded in.

Further, economic institutions may seem well matched to their economic environment precisely because they have modified that environment to *make* it more suitable. Static analysis could not reveal such a process, but would instead see only the good match and jump to the functionalist conclusion that the institution was created by the environmental characteristics. While there are certainly limits placed by economic environments on how given institutions may be organized, those limits are wider than we typically imagine; and depending on how the institutions are configured initially, there may be several different possible stable configurations. I see the usual situation in effect as a problem in economic dynamics with multiple stable equilibria, a situation in which the historical trajectory of a system determines which equilibrium point will be reached.

Arguments of this kind have been made to good effect for technology. Economic historian Paul David, for example, has shown (1986) how the highly inefficient QWERTY typewriter keyboard became the standard of the industry by the 1890s, despite the existence of many more efficient designs, in which the most frequently typed letters are on the home row. The QWERTY design was developed originally because the first typewriters were built in such a way that the lines you were typing did not come into view until many lines of type later; consequently, key jams could not be detected until many lines consisting of a single letter had already been typed. The QWERTY keyboard minimized such jams, an important feature in this period. Meanwhile, typing schools began to teach this keyboard, so that a cadre of typists who carried this arrangement in their heads became an important consideration for businesses deciding which keyboard to purchase, just as the installed base of QWERTY machines had to be taken into account by those deciding which keyboard to learn. As a result of these feedback effects, QWERTY became established as the technical standard, and was locked in by the large base of existing machines and users. By the 1890s, when this lock-in had occurred, the original rationale for QWERTY had disappeared because each line could be seen as it was typed; but the process could not be, and has not since been, reversed.

This type of argument has been made in full generality by economist Brian Arthur (1989), in a stochastic model of how random events in the early stage of a process can fix an outcome independent of its overall efficiency. In these path-dependent processes, one sees increasing returns to scale because once one of several competing technologies has a temporary lead in the number of users, this lead makes it profitable for various actors to improve it and to modify the environment in ways that facilitate further use. This further use again spurs improvements and reduces the profitability of improving competing but less-adopted technologies. Eventually, less efficient technologies may be locked in by this train of events.

To the extent this is the case, only historical analysis can explain outcomes. If, by contrast, we could assume diminishing returns to adoption of a technology, then

> static analysis is sufficient; the outcome is unique, insensitive to the order in which choices are made, and insensitive to small events that occur during the formation of the market. Under increasing returns, however, . . . [m]ultiple outcomes are possible, and to understand how one outcome is selected we

need to follow step by step the process by which small events cumulate to cause the system to gravitate toward that outcome rather than the others (Arthur 1985:12).

The work of David and Arthur concerns technologies and technological standards. But I argue that many other economic outcomes and institutions are also locked in by processes that need not be confined to random "small events," but rather can be analyzed as evolving from purposive networks of action mounted by interested actors. And what appear to be "random" events from an economic frame of reference can often be systematically treated in a sociological account. Where institutions are at issue, the technical concept of "lock-in" should be linked to the sociological idea of "institutionalization." Just as the technical developments that never took hold are forgotten or dismissed as technically inferior, institutional alternatives that did not occur are forgotten, and stories are told about how the existing form was inevitable given the environment. A central question for a sociology of economic institutions is under what circumstances such stories might be correct.

Notes

1. That economists came to see this separation was only part of a general process by which intellectuals, government officials, and parts of the general public came to envision economic activity as involving only economic motivation. This is the process that Dumont (1977) calls the "triumph of economic ideology," and Reddy (1984) calls the "rise of market culture." Reddy's account of French textile markets in the eighteenth and nineteenth centuries is particularly illuminating in showing how public officials revised data-collection procedures to conform to their assumption that the textile industry followed market principles, despite ample evidence that workers and owners were still strongly influenced by traditional noneconomic motives. These motives were greatly obscured by the new forms of economic data.
2. In personal correspondence with Richard Swedberg, Samuelson acknowledges that this comment reflected Pareto's influence.
3. It is not literally true, of course, that modern economics neglects noneconomic motives. In principle, any motives can enter as arguments of a utility function. In practice this is avoided because there is no theoretical structure within economics that shows how nonpecuniary motives in such functions are to be analyzed. There are a small number of economic arguments where noneconomic motives figure prominently, such as in the labor-market theory of compensating differentials, which derives from Adam Smith. But the intention of this argument is not at all to give noneconomic motives a central explanatory position, or to analyze their role; it is rather to deny that wages can ever fail to have been set by a competitive market process. Far from leading to detailed analysis of noneconomic motives, this argument usually treats such motives as a residual category that need only be vaguely invoked in cases where there appears no other way to save the hypothesis of efficient markets.
4. The terms "weak" and "strong" embeddedness are a clumsy device. But they seem necessary because the term "embeddedness," which I want to use, was brought into common usage by Karl Polanyi (1947), and given what I think of as the errors and rigidities of Polanyi's argument I must make it clear that my own is rather different. In fact, in what follows, to avoid a clumsy usage,

I will usually omit the adjective "weak" from the expression "embeddedness," and ask the reader to keep in mind the distinction I draw here between my view and the "strong embeddedness position."

5. I would speculate that since Parsons had been thoroughly trained as an economist, and was thus conversant with the classical and neoclassical literature, but had not been as well trained in the utilitarian tradition, he took the philosophical stance he found in economics to have necessarily resulted from its roots in the utilitarian tradition, and thus projected that stance back into that tradition.

6. Thus Ricardo's *Principles* is relentlessly stylized, like much twentieth-century neoclassical writing. The single place where he makes room for the influence of social relations is in his treatment of international trade. Faced with the necessity of explaining how countries might differ in efficiency of production of the same good, impossible if capital and labor were perfectly mobile, as he otherwise assumes, he comments:

    Experience shows that the fancied or real insecurity of capital, when not under the immediate control of its owner, together with the natural disinclination which every man has to quit the country of his birth and connexions, and intrust himself with all his habits fixed, to a strange government and new laws, check the emigration of capital. These feelings, which I should be sorry to see weakened, induce most men of property to be satisfied with a low rate of profits in their own country, rather than seek a more advantageous employment for their wealth in foreign nations (1816:136–137).

    It seems clear here that Ricardo allows this exception into his theoretical system because he approves of its consequences; a perfectly competitive market in international trade implies the absence of patriotism or attachments to home, family, and country, the desire for which falls well beyond the orbit of classical liberalism.

7. This implies that the solution offered by Parsons (1937) to the failings he attributed to utilitarian thought is not nearly as radical a break from the position he attacked as he supposed it to be.

8. I take no position on how important subjective orientation is. Modern economics follows Robbins in abstracting away from this, frequently arguing that actors with economic motives act "as if" making a rational calculation, even when no such subjective state can be attributed to them. I will have several occasions to address these issues and will be especially interested in what justifications may be given for this "as if" stance, and under what circumstances it degenerates into a ritualistic affirmation of the universality of neoclassical arguments. For the time being, I simply adopt the general stance that "individual economic action" consists of action oriented to the provision of "needs" as defined by individual actors, in situations of scarcity, without taking any position on the actor's subjective understanding of the economic situation or his degree of calculation. This is a mixture of Weber's and Robbins's stances that will serve for heuristic purposes. Left out of the account for now is the important issue of whether the implication of this stance, that action should be studied in a means-end framework, may not have important limitations.

9. In this case, the owner of a diamond company was defrauding a factoring concern by submitting invoices from fictitious sales. The scheme required cooperation from his accounting personnel, one of whom was approached by investigators and turned state's evidence. The owner then contracted for the murder of the disloyal employee and her assistant; three CBS technicians who came to their aid in the parking garage where the murders took place were also gunned down (Shenon 1984).

10. As Shapiro (1984:84) points out, the strategy of keeping secrets by decoupling

an organization's network structure is generic to all sorts of secrets, as was recognized by Simmel in his discussion of the "secret society."

11. It is interesting to note that the intellectual history of institutional economics in the twentieth century is a replay of that in social anthropology from about 1890 to 1940. Functionalist explanation has been adopted in the new institutional economics in the process of rejecting the explanatory style of the "old" (early twentieth-century) institutionalists who relied on historical accounts of institutions and did not seek to determine what economic functions they served. Structural functional anthropologists of the 1930s and 1940s attacked earlier anthropological accounts grounded in (sometimes rather speculative) history and defended static functional analysis on the ground that one needed to explain any social pattern as part of the coherent social whole, to develop a full and sophisticated understanding of how the social system fit together. Thus Malinowski attacked the notion that some social patterns were "survivals" of earlier periods. "Take any example of 'survival,'" he challenged. "You will find first and foremost that the survival nature of the alleged cultural 'hangover' is due primarily to an incomplete analysis of the facts. . . . The real harm done by this concept was to retard effective fieldwork. Instead of searching for the present-day function of any cultural fact, the observer was merely satisfied in reaching a rigid, self-contained entity" (1944:30–31).

Few current anthropologists would dispute that the functionalism of the 1940s went too far in its disdain for historical accounts and its attempt to display all institutions as part of a coherent whole. As in sociology, wholehearted commitment to structural-functionalism in anthropology did not survive the intellectual (and political) turmoil of the 1960s. It may be that functionalism in institutional economics had as strong a hold as it did in the 1980s on account of its origins in the 1970s, when the political and intellectual climate had cooled again.

References

Akerlof, George. 1983. "Loyalty Filters." *American Economic Review* 73(1):54–63.

Arrow, Kenneth. 1974. *The Limits of Organization.* New York: W.W. Norton.

Arrow, Kenneth, and Frank Hahn. 1971. *General Competitive Analysis.* San Francisco: Holden-Day.

Arthur, W. Brian. 1989. "Competing Technologies and Lock-In by Historical Events." *Economic Journal* 99 (394) (March): 116–131.

Baker, Wayne. 1984. "The Social Structure of a National Securities Market." *American Journal of Sociology* 89(4):775–811.

Baumol, William. 1970. *Economic Dynamics: An Introduction.* 3d ed. New York: Macmillan.

Becker, Gary. 1976. *The Economic Approach to Human Behavior.* Chicago: University of Chicago Press.

———. 1981. *Treatise on the Family.* Cambridge, MA: Harvard University Press.

Ben-Porath, Yoram. 1980. "The F-Connection: Families, Friends and Firms in the Organization of Exchange." *Population and Development Review* 6(1):1–30.

Berger, Peter, and Thomas Luckmann. 1966. *The Social Construction of Reality.* Garden City: Doubleday.

Bowles, Samuel, and Herbert Gintis. 1976. *Schooling in Capitalist America.* New York: Basic.

Brown, Roger. 1965. *Social Psychology.* New York: Free Press.

Camic, Charles. 1979. "The Utilitarians Revisited." *American Journal of Sociology* 85(3):516–550.

Colander, David, ed. 1984. *Neoclassical Political Economy: The Analysis of Rent-Seeking and DUP Activities.* Cambridge, MA: Ballinger.

Cole, Robert. 1979. *Work, Mobility and Participation: A Comparative Study of American and Japanese Industry.* Berkeley: University of California Press.

David, Paul A. 1986. "Understanding the Economics of QWERTY: The Necessity of History." In N. N. Parker, ed., *Economic History and the Modern Economist.* New York: Basil Blackwell.

Duesenberry, James. 1960. Comment on "An Economic Analysis of Fertility." In Universities-National Bureau Committee for Economic Research, eds., *Demographic and Economic Change in Developed Countries.* Princeton: Princeton University Press.

Dumont, Louis. 1977. *From Mandeville to Marx: The Genesis and Triumph of Economic Ideology.* Chicago: University of Chicago Press.

Durkheim, Emile. [1893] 1984. *The Division of Labor in Society*, W. D. Halls, tr. New York: Free Press.

Elster, Jon. 1983. *Explaining Technical Change: A Case Study in the Philosophy of Science.* New York: Cambridge University Press.

Festinger, Leon, Stanley Schachter, and Kurt Back. 1948. *Social Pressures in Informal Groups.* Cambridge: MIT Press.

Fine, Gary, and Sherryl Kleinman. 1979. "Rethinking Subculture: An Interactionist Analysis." *American Journal of Sociology* 85(1):1–20.

Friedman, Milton. 1953. *Essays in Positive Economics.* Chicago: University of Chicago Press.

Gandossy, Robert. 1985. *Bad Business: The OPM Scandal and the Seduction of the Establishment.* New York: Basic Books.

Gartrell, C. David. 1982. "On The Visibility of Wage Referents." *Canadian Journal of Sociology* 7(2):117–143.

Geertz, Clifford. 1979. "The Moroccan Bazaar." In C. Geertz, H. Geertz, and L. Rosen, eds., *Meaning and Order in Moroccan Society: Three Essays in Cultural Analysis.* Cambridge: Cambridge University Press.

Granovetter, Mark. 1973. "The Strength of Weak Ties." *American Journal of Sociology* 78(6):1360–1380.

———. 1974. *Getting a Job: A Study of Contacts and Careers.* Cambridge, MA: Harvard University Press.

———. 1976. "Network Sampling: Some First Steps." *American Journal of Sociology* 81 (May):1287–1303.

———. 1986. "Labor Mobility, Internal Markets and Job-Matching: A Comparison of the Sociological and the Economic Approaches." *Research in Social Stratification and Mobility* 5:3–39.

Hempel, Carl. 1965. *Aspects of Scientific Explanation.* New York: Free Press.

Hirsch, Paul. 1986. "From Ambushes to Golden Parachutes: Corporate Takeovers as an Instance of Cultural Framing and Institutional Integration." *American Journal of Sociology* 91(4):800–837.

Hirschman, Albert. 1977. *The Passions and the Interests.* Princeton: Princeton University Press.

———. 1982. "Rival Interpretations of Market Society: Civilizing, Destructive or Feeble?" *Journal of Economic Literature* 20(4):1463–1484.

Hobbes, T. [1651] 1968. *Leviathan.* New York: Penguin.

Katz, Elihu, and Paul Lazarsfeld. 1955. *Personal Influence.* Glencoe, IL: Free Press.

Lazear, Edward. 1979. "Why Is There Mandatory Retirement?" *Journal of Political Economy* 87(6):1261–1284.

Leibenstein, Harvey. 1976. *Beyond Economic Man.* Cambridge, MA: Harvard University Press.

McCloskey, Donald. 1983. "The Rhetoric of Economics." *Journal of Economic Literature* 21 (June):481–517.

McPherson, Michael. 1984. "Limits on Self-Seeking: The Role of Morality in Economic Life." In David Colander, ed., *Neoclassical Political Economy: The Analysis of Rent-Seeking and DUP Activities*. Cambridge, MA: Ballinger, pp. 71–85.

Merton, Robert. 1947. *Social Theory and Social Structure*. New York: Free Press.

Nagel, Ernest. 1961. *The Structure of Science*. New York: McGraw-Hill.

Nelson, Richard, and Sidney Winter. 1982. *An Evolutionary Theory of Economic Change*. Cambridge, MA: Harvard University Press.

North, Douglass, and Robert Thomas. 1973. *The Rise of the Western World: A New Economic History*. New York: Cambridge University Press.

Okun, Arthur. 1981. *Prices and Quantities*. Washington, D.C.: Brookings Institution.

Olson, Mancur. 1982. *The Rise and Decline of Nations: Economic Growth, Stagflation, and Social Rigidities*. New Haven: Yale University Press.

Ouchi, William. 1981. *Theory Z*. Reading, MA: Addison-Wesley.

Pakes, Ariel, and Shmuel Nitzan. 1982. "Optimum Contracts for Research Personnel, Research Employment and the Establishment of 'Rival' Enterprises." Working Paper No. 871, National Bureau of Economic Research, Cambridge, MA.

Parsons, Talcott. 1937. *The Structure of Social Action*. New York: McGraw-Hill.

Phelps Brown, Ernest Henry. 1977. *The Inequality of Pay*. Berkeley: University of California Press.

Piore, Michael. 1975. "Notes for a Theory of Labor Market Stratification." In R. Edwards, M. Reich, and D. Gordon, eds., *Labor Market Segmentation*. Lexington, MA: D.C. Heath, pp. 125–150.

Polanyi, Karl. 1944. *The Great Transformation*. Boston: Beacon Press.

Polanyi, Karl, Conrad Arensberg, and Harry Pearson, eds. 1957. *Trade and Market in the Early Empires*. New York: Free Press.

Reddy, William. 1984. *The Rise of Market Culture: The Textile Trade and French Society, 1750–1900*. Cambridge: Cambridge University Press.

Reder, Melvin. 1955. "The Theory of Occupational Wage Differentials." *American Economic Review* 45 (December): 833–852.

Ricardo, D. [1816] 1951. *On the Principles of Political Economy and Taxation*. Cambridge: Cambridge University Press.

Robbins, Lionel. [1932] 1984. *An Essay on the Nature and Significance of Economic Science*. New York: New York University Press.

Rose-Ackerman, Susan. 1978. *Corruption: A Study in Political Economy*. New York: Academic Press.

Sabel, Charles. 1982. *Work and Politics: The Division of Labor in Industry*. New York: Cambridge University Press.

Samuelson, Paul. 1947. *Foundations of Economic Analysis*. Cambridge, MA: Harvard University Press.

Schotter, Andrew. 1981. *The Economic Theory of Social Institutions*. New York: Cambridge University Press.

Seashore, Stanley. 1954. *Group Cohesiveness in the Industrial Work Group*. Ann Arbor: Survey Research Center, Institute for Social Research.

Shapiro, Susan. 1984. *Wayward Capitalists: Target of the Securities and Exchange Commission*. New Haven: Yale University Press.

Shenon, Philip. 1984. "Margolies Is Found Guilty of Murdering Two Women." *New York Times* (June 1).

Simmel, Georg. [1923] 1950. *The Sociology of Georg Simmel*, Kurt Wolff, ed. and tr. New York: Free Press.

Smith, Adam. [1776] 1976. *The Wealth of Nations*. Chicago: University of Chicago Press.

Stigler, George, and Gary Becker. 1977. "De Gustibus Non Est Disputandum." *American Economic Review* 67(1):76–90.

Stinchcombe, Arthur. 1968. *Constructing Social Theories*. New York: Harcourt, Brace & World.

Sykes, Gresham, and David Matza. 1957. "Techniques of Neutralization: A Theory of Delinquency." *American Sociological Review* 22 (December): 664–669.

Tilly, Charles. 1984. "Sludge in the Growth Machine" (Review of M. Olson's *The Rise and Decline of Nations*). *American Journal of Sociology* 89(5):1214–1218.

Useem, Michael. 1983. *The Inner Circle: Large Corporations and Business Politics in the U.S. and the U.K.* New York: Oxford University Press.

Weber, Max. [1921] 1968. *Economy and Society*. Guenther Roth and Claus Wittich, ed. and tr. New York: Bedminster Press.

Williamson, Oliver. 1975. *Markets and Hierarchies*. New York: Free Press.

Wrong, Dennis. 1961. "The Oversocialized Conception of Man in Modern Sociology." *American Sociological Review* 26(2):183–196.

Zucker, Lynne. 1986. "Production of Trust: Institutional Sources of Economic Structure, 1840 to 1920." In L. L. Cummings and Barry Stein, eds., *Research in Organizational Behavior*, vol. 8. Greenwich, CT: JAI Press, pp. 53–112.

2

The Social Structure of Competition

RONALD S. BURT

My starting point is this: A player brings capital to the competitive arena and walks away with profit determined by the rate of return where the capital was invested. The market production equation predicts profit: Invested capital, multiplied by the going rate of return, equals the profit to be expected from the investment. Investments create an ability to produce a competitive product. For example, capital is invested to build and operate a factory. Rate of return is an opportunity to profit from the investment.

Rate of return is keyed to the social structure of the competitive arena and is the focus here. Each player has a network of contacts in the arena. Certain players are connected to certain others, trusting certain others, obligated to support certain others, dependent on exchange with certain others. Something about the structure of the player's network and the location of the player's contacts in the social structure of the arena create a competitive advantage in getting higher rates of return on investment. This chapter is about that advantage. It is a description of the way in which social structure renders competition imperfect by creating entrepreneurial opportunities for certain players and not for others.[1]

1. OPPORTUNITY AND SOCIAL CAPITAL

A player brings three kinds of capital to the competitive arena. There are more, but three are sufficient here. First, the player has financial capital: cash in hand, reserves in the bank, investments coming due, lines of credit. Second, the player has human capital: natural abilities—charm,

This material is taken from a book entitled *Structural Holes*, which will be published in 1992 by Harvard University Press. Permission to reproduce the material is gratefully acknowledged. My thanks also to Professor Richard Swedburg, who condensed the original chapter to a size suitable for this anthology.

health, intelligence, and looks—combine with skills acquired in formal education and job experience to equal the ability to excel at certain tasks. Third, the player's relationships with other players are social capital: through friends, colleagues, and general contacts the player receives opportunities to use his or her financial and human capital. I refer to opportunities broadly, but I certainly mean to include the obvious examples of job promotions, participation in significant projects, influential access to important decisions, and so on. The social capital of people aggregates into the social capital of organizations. In a firm that provides services—for example, advertising, brokerage, or consulting—there are people valued for their ability to deliver a quality product. Then there are the "rainmakers," valued for their ability to deliver clients. The former do the work and the latter make it possible for all to profit from the work. The former represent the financial and human capital of the firm; the latter represent its social capital. More generally, property and human assets define the firm's production capabilities. Relations within and beyond the firm are social capital.

1.1 Distinguishing Social Capital

Financial and human capital are distinct in two ways from social capital. First, they are the property of individuals. They are owned in whole or in part by a single individual defined in law as capable of ownership, typically a person or corporation. Second, they concern the investment term in the market production equation. Whether held by a person or the fictive person of a firm, financial and human capital gets invested to create production capabilities. Investments in supplies, facilities, and people serve to build and operate a factory. Investments of money, time, and energy produce a skilled manager. Financial capital is needed for raw materials and production facilities. Human capital is needed to craft the raw materials into a competitive product.

Social capital is different on both counts. First, it is a thing owned jointly by the parties to a relationship. No one player has exclusive ownership rights to social capital. If you or your partner in a relationship withdraws, the connection dissolves with whatever social capital it contained. If a firm treats a cluster of customers poorly and they leave, the social capital represented by the firm-cluster relationship is lost. Second, social capital concerns rate of return in the market production equation. Through relations with colleagues, friends, and clients come the opportunities to transform financial and human capital into profit.

Social capital is the final arbiter of competitive success. The capital invested to bring your organization to the point of producing a superb product is as rewarding as the opportunities to sell the product at a profit. The investment to make you a skilled manager is as valuable as the opportunities and the leadership positions in which you get to apply your managerial skills. The investment to make you a skilled scientist with state-of-the-art research facilities is as valuable as the opportunities and the projects in which you get to apply those skills and facilities.

More accurately, social capital is as important as competition is imperfect and investment capital is abundant. Under perfect competition, social capital is a constant in the production equation. There is a single rate of return because capital moves freely from low-yield to high-yield investments until rates of return are homogeneous across alternative investments. Where competition is imperfect, capital is less mobile and plays a more complex role in the production equation. There are financial, social, and legal impediments to moving cash between investments. There are impediments to reallocating human capital, both in terms of changing the people to whom you have a commitment and in terms of replacing those people with new. Rate of return depends on the relations in which capital is invested. Social capital is a critical variable. This is all the more true where financial and human capital are abundant—which in essence reduces the investment term in the production equation to an unproblematic constant.

These conditions are generic to the competitive arena, making social capital a factor as routinely critical as financial and human capital. Competition is never perfect. The rules of trade are ambiguous in the aggregate and everywhere negotiable in the particular. The allocation of opportunities is rarely made with respect to a single dimension of abilities needed for a task. Within an acceptable range of needed abilities, there are many people with financial and human capital comparable to your own. Whatever you bring to a production task, there are other people who could do the same job; perhaps not as well in every detail, but probably as well within the tolerances of the people for whom the job is done. Criteria other than financial and human capital are used to narrow the pool down to the individual who gets the opportunity. Those other criteria are social capital. New life is given to the proverb of success being determined less by what you know than by who you know. As a senior colleague once remarked, "Publishing high quality work is important for getting university resources, but friends are essential." Only a select few of equally qualified people get the most rewarding opportunities. Only some of comparably high quality products come to dominate their markets. So the question is how.

1.2 The Who and the How

The competitive arena has a social structure: players trusting certain others, obligated to support certain others, dependent on exchange with certain others, and so on. Against this backdrop, each player has a network of contacts: everyone you now know, everyone you have ever known, and everyone who knows you even though you don't know them. Something about the structure of the player's network and the location of the player's contacts in the social structure of the arena adds up to a competitive advantage in getting higher rates of return on investment.

There are two routes into the social capital question. The first describes a network as your access to people with specific resources, creating a correlation between theirs and yours; the second describes social structure as capital in its own right. The idea for the first approach has circulated as power, prestige, social resources, and—more recently—social capital. Nan Lin and his colleagues provide an exemplar for this line of work, showing how the occupational prestige of a person's job is contingent on the occupational prestige of a personal contact leading to the job (Lin 1982; Lin, Ensel, and Vaughn 1981; Lin and Dumin 1986). Related empirical results appear in Campbell, Marsden, and Hurlbert (1986), De Graaf and Flap (1988), Flap and De Graaf (1989), and Marsden and Hurlbert (1988). Coleman (1988) discusses the transmission of human capital across generations. Flap and Tazelaar (1989) provide a thorough review with special attention to social network analysis.

Empirical questions in this line of work concern the magnitude of association between contact resources and your own resources, and variation in the association across kinds of relationships. Granovetter's (1973) weak-tie metaphor, discussed in detail shortly, is often invoked to distinguish kinds of relationships.

Network analysts will recognize this as an example of social contagion analysis. Network structure doesn't predict attitudes or behaviors directly. It predicts similarity between attitudes and behaviors. The research tradition is tied to the Columbia Sociology survey studies of social influence conducted during the 1940s and 1950s. In one of the first well-known studies, for example, Lazarsfeld, Berelson, and Gaudet (1944) show how a person's vote is associated with the party affiliations of friends. Persons claiming to have voted for the presidential candidate of a specific political party tend to have friends affiliated with that party. Social capital theory developed from this line of work describes the manner in which resources available to any one person in a population are contingent on the resources available to individuals socially proximate to the person.

Empirical evidence is readily available. People develop relations with people like themselves (for example, Fischer 1982; Marsden 1987; Burt 1990). Wealthy people develop ties with other wealthy people. Educated people develop ties with one another. Young people develop ties with one another. There are reasons for this. Socially similar people, even in the pursuit of independent interests, spend time in the same places. Relationships emerge. Socially similar people have more shared interests. Relationships are maintained. Further, we are sufficiently egocentric to find people with similar tastes attractive. Whatever the etiology for strong relations between socially similar people, it is to be expected that the resources and opinions of any one individual will be correlated with the resources and opinions of their close contacts.

A second line of work describes social structure as capital in its own right. Where the first line describes the network as a conduit, the second line describes how networks are themselves a form of social capital. This line of work is much less developed than the first. Indeed, it is little developed beyond intuitions in empirical research on social capital. Network range, indicated by size, is the primary measure. For example, Boxman, De Graaf, and Flap (1991) show that people with larger contact networks obtain higher paying positions than people with small networks. A similar finding in social support research shows that persons with larger networks tend to live longer (Berkman and Syme 1979).

Both lines of work are essential to a general definition of social capital. Social capital is at once the structure of contacts in a network and resources they each hold. The first term describes how you reach. The second describes who you reach.

For two reasons, however, I ignore the question of "who" to concentrate on "how." The first is generality. The question of "who" elicits a more idiographic class of answers. Predicting rate of return depends on knowing the resources of a player's contacts. There will be interesting empirical variation from one kind of activity to another, say job searches versus mobilizing support for a charity, but the empirical generalization is obvious: Doing business with wealthy clients, however wealth is defined, has a higher margin than doing business with poor clients. I want to identify parameters of social capital that generalize beyond the specific individuals connected by a relationship.

The second reason is correlation. The two components in social capital should be so strongly correlated that I could reconstruct much of the phenomenon from whichever component more easily yields a general explanation. To the extent that people play an active role in shaping their relationships, then a player who knows how to structure a network to provide high opportunity knows who to include in the network. Even if networks are passively inherited, the manner in which a player is connected within social structure says much about contact resources. *I will show that players with well-structured networks obtain higher rates of return.* Resources accumulate in their hands. People develop relations with people like themselves. Therefore how a player is connected in the social structure indicates the volume of resources held by the player and the volume to which the player is connected.

The nub of the matter is to describe network benefits in competition so as to be able to describe how certain structures enhance those benefits. The benefits are of two kinds, information and control. First I'll describe information benefits because they are more familiar; then I'll examine control benefits, showing how both kinds of benefits are enhanced by the same element of social structure.

2. INFORMATION

Opportunities spring up everywhere; new institutions and projects that need leadership, new funding initiatives looking for proposals, new jobs for which you know of a good candidate, valuable items entering the market for which you know interested buyers. The information benefits of a network define who knows about these opportunities, when they know, and who gets to participate in them. Players with a network optimally structured to provide these benefits enjoy higher rates of return to their investments because such players know about, and have a hand in, more rewarding opportunities.

2.1 Access, Timing, and Referrals

Information benefits occur in three forms: access, timing, and referrals. Access refers to receiving a valuable piece of information and knowing who can use it. Information doesn't spread evenly through the competitive arena. It isn't that players are secretive, although that too can be an issue. The issue is that players are unevenly connected with one another, are attentive to the information pertinent to themselves and their friends, and are all overwhelmed by the flow of information. There are limits to the volume of information you can use intelligently. You can keep up with only so many books, articles, memos, and news services. Given a limit to the volume of information that anyone can process, the network becomes an important screening device. It is an army of people processing information who can call your attention to key bits—keeping you up to date on developing opportunities, warning you of impending disasters. This second-hand information is often fuzzy or inaccurate, but it serves to signal something to be looked into more carefully.

Related to knowing about an opportunity is knowing who to bring into it. Given a limit to the financing and skills that we possess individually, most complex projects will require coordination with other people as staff, colleagues, or clients. The manager asks, "Who do I know with the skills to do a good job with that part of the project?" The capitalist asks, "Who do I know who would be interested in acquiring this product or a piece of the project?" The department head asks, "Who are the key players needed to strengthen the department's position?" Add to each of these the more common question, "Who do I know who is most likely to know the kind of person I need?"

Timing is a significant feature of the information received by the network. Beyond making sure that you are informed, personal contacts can make you one of the people informed early. It is one thing to find out that the stock market is crashing today. It is another to discover that the price of your stocks will plummet tomorrow. It is one thing to learn the names of the two people referred to the board for the new vice-presidency. It is another to discover that the job will be created and your credentials could make you a serious candidate for the position. Personal contacts get significant information to you before the average person receives it. That early warning is an opportunity to act on the information yourself or invest it back into the network by passing it on to a friend who could benefit from it.

These benefits involve information flowing from contacts. There are also benefits in the opposite flow. The network that filters information coming to you also directs, concentrates, and legitimates information about you going to others.

In part, this does no more than alleviate a logistics problem. You can be in only a limited number of places within a limited amount of time. Personal contacts get your name mentioned at the right time in the right place so opportunities are presented to you. Their referrals are a positive force for future opportunities. They are the motor expanding the third category of people in your network, the players whom you don't know but who are aware of you. I'm thinking of that remark so often heard in recruitment deliberations: "I don't know her personally, but several people whose opinion I trust have spoken well of her."

Beyond logistics, there is an issue of legitimacy. Even if you know about an opportunity and could present a solid case for why you should get it, you are a suspect source of information. The same information has more legitimacy when it comes from someone inside the decision-making process who can speak to your virtues. Speaking about my own line of work, which I expect in this regard is typical, candidates offered the university positions with the greatest opportunity are people who have a strong personal advocate in the decision-making process, a person in touch with the candidate to ensure that all favorable information, and responses to any negative information, gets distributed during the decision.

2.2 Benefit-Rich Networks

A player with a network rich in information benefits has (1) contacts established in the places where useful bits of information are likely to air, (2) providing a reliable flow of information to and from those places.

The second criterion is as ambiguous as it is critical. It is a matter of trust, of confidence in the information passed and the care with which contacts look out for your interests. Trust is critical precisely because competition is imperfect. The question is not whether to trust, but who to trust. In a perfectly competitive arena, you can trust the system to provide a fair return on your investments. In the imperfectly competitive arena, you have only your personal contacts. The matter comes down to a question of interpersonal debt. If I do for her, will she for me? There is no general answer. The answer lies in the match between specific people. If a contact feels that he is somehow better than you—a sexist male dealing with a woman, a racist white dealing with a black, an old-money matron dealing with an upwardly mobile ethnic—your investment in the relationship will be taken as your proper obeisance to a superior. No debt is incurred. We use whatever cues can be found for a continuing evaluation of the trust in a relation, but really don't know until the trusted person helps when you need it. With this kind of uncertainty, players are cautious about extending themselves for people whose reputation for honoring interpersonal debt is unknown. The importance of this point is illustrated by the political boundary around senior management for outsider managers trying to break through the boundary (Burt 1992, Ch. 4).

We do know from social science research that strong relations and mutual relations tend to develop between people with similar social attributes such as education, income, occupation, and age (for example, Fischer 1982; Burt 1986, 1990; Marsden 1987; see also note 2). Whether egocentrism, cues from presumed shared background and interests, or confidence in mutual acquaintances to enforce interpersonal debt, the operational guide to the formation of close, trusting relationships seems to be that a person more like me is less likely to betray me. For the purposes here, I put the whole issue to one side as person-specific and presumed resolved by the able player.

That leaves the first criterion, establishing contacts where useful bits of information are likely to air. Everything else constant, a large, diverse network is the best guarantee of having a contact present where useful information is aired.

Size is the more familiar criterion. Bigger is better. Acting on this understanding, people can expand their networks by adding more and more contacts. They make more cold calls, affiliate with more clubs, attend more social functions. Numerous books and self-help groups can assist you in "networking" your way to success by putting you in contact with a large number of potentially useful, or helpful, or like-minded people. The process is illustrated by the networks at the top of Figure 2-1. The four-contact network at the left expands to sixteen contacts at the right. Relations are developed with a friend of each contact in network A, doubling the contacts to eight in network B. Snowballing through friends of friends, there are sixteen contacts in network C, and so on.

Size is a mixed blessing. More contacts can mean more exposure to valuable information, more likely early exposure, and more referrals. But increasing network size without considering diversity can cripple the network in significant ways. What matters is the number of nonredundant

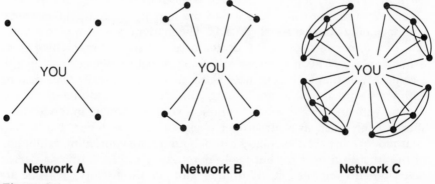

Network A   Network B   Network C

Figure 2-1
Network Expansion

contacts. Contacts are redundant to the extent that they lead to the same people and so provide the same information benefits.

Consider two four-contact networks, one sparse and the other dense. There are no relations between the contacts in the sparse network, and strong relations between every contact in the dense network. Both networks cost whatever time and energy is required to maintain four relationships. The sparse network provides four nonredundant contacts, one for each relationship. No one of the contacts gets you to the same people reached by the other contacts. In the dense network, each relationship puts you in contact with the same people you reach through the other relationships. The dense network contains only one nonredundant contact. Any three are redundant with the fourth.

The sparse network provides more information benefits. It reaches information in four separate areas of social activity. The dense network is a virtually worthless monitoring device because the strong relations between people in the network means that each person knows what the other people know, so they'll discover the same opportunities at the same time.

The issue is opportunity costs. At minimum, the dense network is inefficient in the sense that it returns less diverse information for the same cost as the sparse network. A solution is to put more time and energy into adding nonredundant contacts to the dense network. But time and energy are limited, which means that inefficiency translates into opportunity costs. Taking four relationships has an illustrative limit on the number of strong relations that a player can maintain, the player in the dense network is cut off from three-fourths of the information provided by the sparse network.

3. STRUCTURAL HOLES

It will be convenient to have a term for the separation between nonredundant contacts. I use the term "structural hole." Nonredundant contacts are connected by a structural hole. A structural hole is a relationship of nonredundancy between two contacts. The hole is a buffer, like an insulator in an electric circuit. As a result of the hole between them, the two contacts provide network benefits that are in some degree additive rather than overlapping.

3.1 Empirical Indicators

Nonredundant contacts are disconnected in some way—either directly in the sense of no direct contact with one another, or indirectly in the sense of one having contacts that exclude the others. The respective empirical conditions that indicate a structural hole are cohesion and structural equivalence. Both conditions define holes by indicating where they are absent.

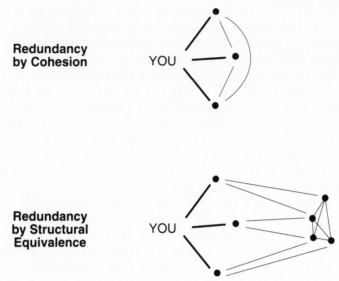

Figure 2-2
Structural Indicators of Redundancy

Under the cohesion criterion, two contacts are redundant to the extent that they are connected by a strong relationship. A strong relationship indicates the absence of a structural hole. Examples would be father and son, brother and sister, husband and wife, close friends, people who have been partners for a long time, people who frequently get together for social occasions, and so on. You have easy access to both people if either is a contact. Redundancy by cohesion is illustrated at the top of Figure 2-2. The three contacts are connected to one another, and so provide the same network benefits. The presumption here—routine in network analysis since Festinger, Schachter, and Back's (1950) analysis of information flowing through personal relations and Homans' (1950) theory of social groups—is that the likelihood of information moving from one person to another is proportional to the strength of their relationship. Empirically, strength has two independent dimensions: frequent contact and emotional closeness (see Marsden and Hurlbert 1988; Burt 1990).

Structural equivalence is a useful second indicator for detecting structural holes. Two people are structurally equivalent to the extent that they have the same contacts. Regardless of the relation between structurally equivalent people, they lead to the same sources of information and so are redundant. Where cohesion concerns direct connection, structural equivalence concerns indirect connection by mutual contact. Redundancy by structural equivalence is illustrated at the bottom of Figure 2-2. The three contacts have no direct ties with one another. They are nonredundant by cohesion. But each leads you to the same cluster of more distant players. The information that comes to them, and the people to whom they send information, are redundant. Both networks in Figure 2-2 provide one nonredundant contact at a cost of maintaining three.

The indicators are neither absolute nor independent. Relations deemed strong are only strong relative to others. They are our strongest relations. Structural equivalence rarely reaches the extreme of complete equivalence. People are more or less structurally equivalent. Also, the criteria are correlated. People who spend a lot of time with the same other people often get to know one another. The mutual contacts responsible for structural equivalence set a stage for the direct connection of cohesion. The empirical conditions between two players will be a messy combination of cohesion and structural equivalence, present to varying degrees, at varying levels of correlation.

Cohesion is the more certain indicator. If two people are connected with the same people in a player's network (making them redundant by structural equivalence), they can still be connected with different people beyond the network (making them nonredundant). But if they meet frequently and feel close to one another, then they are likely to communicate and probably have contacts in common. More generally, and especially for fieldwork informed by attention to network benefits, the general guide is the definition of a structural hole. There is a structural hole between two people who provide nonredundant network benefits. Taking the cohesion and structural equivalence conditions together, redundancy is most likely between structurally equivalent people connected by a strong relationship. Redundancy is unlikely, indicating a structural hole, between total strangers in distant groups. After control benefits have been introduced, I'll return to this issue to discuss the depth of a hole.

3.2 The Efficient-Effective Network

Balancing network size and diversity is a question of optimizing structural holes. The number of structural holes can be expected to increase with network size, but the holes are the key to information benefits. The optimized network has two design principles: efficiency and effectiveness.

3.2.1 Efficiency The first principle concerns efficiency, and it says that you should maximize the number of nonredundant contacts in the network to maximize the yield in structural holes per contact. Given two networks of equal size, the one with more nonredundant contacts provides more benefits. There is little gain from a new contact redundant with existing contacts. Time and energy would be better spent cultivating a new contact to unreached people.[2] Maximizing the nonredundancy of contacts maximizes the structural holes obtained per contact.[3]

Efficiency is illustrated by the networks in Figure 2-3. These reach the same people reached by the networks in Figure 2-1, but in a different way. What expands in Figure 2-1 is not the benefits, but the cost of maintaining the network. Network *A* provides four nonredundant contacts.

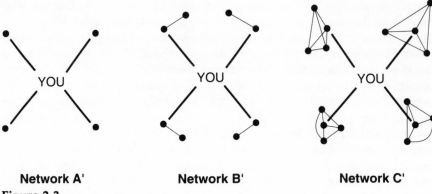

Network A'   **Network B'**   **Network C'**

Figure 2-3
Strategic Network Expansion

Network *B* provides the same number. The information benefits provided by the initial four contacts are redundant with benefits provided by their close friends. All that has changed is the doubled number of relationships maintained in the network. The situation deteriorates even further with the sixteen contacts in network *C*. There are still only four nonredundant contacts in the network, but their benefits are now obtained at a cost of maintaining sixteen relationships.

With a little network surgery, the sixteen contacts can be maintained at one-fourth of the cost. As illustrated in Figure 2-3, select one contact in each cluster to be a primary link to the cluster. Concentrate on maintaining the primary contact, and allow direct relationships with others in the cluster to weaken into indirect relations through the primary contact. These players reached indirectly are secondary contacts. Among the redundant contacts in a cluster, the primary contact should be the one most easily maintained and most likely to honor an interpersonal debt to you in particular. The secondary contacts are less easily maintained or less likely to work for you (even if they might work well for someone else). The critical decision obviously lies in selecting the right person to be a primary contact. That is the subject of trust discussed earlier. With a good primary contact, there is little loss in information benefits from the cluster and a gain in the reduced effort needed to maintain the cluster in the network.

Repeating this operation for each cluster in the network recovers effort that would otherwise be spent maintaining redundant contacts. By reinvesting that saved time and effort in developing primary contacts to new clusters, the network expands to include an exponentially larger number of contacts while expanding contact diversity. The sixteen contacts in network *C* of Figure 2-1, for example, are maintained at a cost of four primary contacts in network *C'* of Figure 2-3. Some portion of the time spent maintaining the redundant other twelve contacts can be reallocated to expanding the network to include new clusters.

3.2.2 Effectiveness The second principle for the optimized network requires a further shift in perspective. Distinguish primary from secondary contacts and focus resources on preserving the primary contacts. Here contacts are not people on the other end of your relations; they are ports of access to clusters of people beyond. Guided by the first principle, these ports should be nonredundant so as to reach separate, and therefore more diverse, social worlds of network benefits. Instead of the player maintaining relations with all contacts, the task of maintaining the total network is delegated to primary contacts. The player at the center of the network is then free to focus on properly supporting relations with primary contacts and expanding the network to include new clusters. Where the first principle concerns the average number of people reached with a primary contact, the second concerns the total number of people reached with all primary contacts. The first principle concerns the yield per primary contact. The second concerns the total yield of the network. More concretely, the first principle moves from the networks in Figure 2-1 to the corresponding networks in Figure 2-3. The second principle moves from left to right in Figure 2-3. The target is network C′ in Figure 2-3; a network of few primary contacts, each a port of access to a cluster of many secondary contacts.

Figure 2-4 illustrates some complexities in unpacking a network to maximize structural holes. The BEFORE network contains five primary contacts and reaches a total of fifteen people. However, there are only two clusters of nonredundant contacts in the network. Contacts 2 and 3 are redundant in the sense of being connected with each other and reaching the same people (cohesion and structural equivalence criteria). The same is true of contacts 4 and 5. Contact 1 is not connected directly to contact 2 but reaches the same secondary contacts, so contacts 1 and 2 provide redundant network benefits (structural equivalence criterion). Illustrating the other extreme, contacts 3 and 5 are connected directly, but they are nonredundant because they reach separate clusters of secondary contacts (structural equivalence criterion). In the AFTER network, contact 2 is used to reach the first cluster in the BEFORE network, and contact 4 is used to reach the second cluster. The time and energy saved by withdrawing from relations with the other three primary contacts are reallocated to primary contacts in new clusters. The BEFORE and AFTER networks are both maintained at a cost of five primary relationships, but the AFTER network is dramatically richer in structural holes, and so network benefits.

Network benefits are enhanced in several ways. There is a higher volume of benefits because more contacts are included in the network. Beyond volume, diversity enhances the quality of benefits. Nonredundant contacts ensure exposure to diverse sources of information. Each cluster of contacts is an independent source of information. One cluster, no matter how numerous its members, is one source of information because people connected to one another tend to know about the same things at about the same time. The information screen provided by multiple clus-

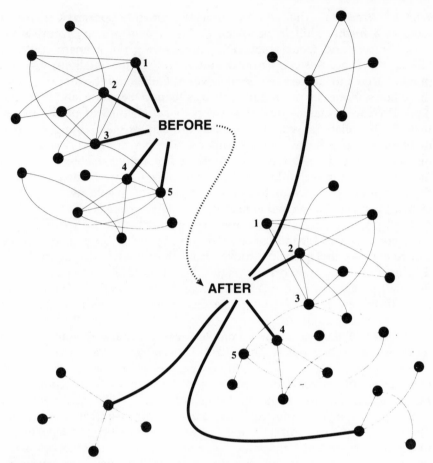

Figure 2-4
Optimizing for Structural Holes

ters of contacts is broader, providing better assurance of the player being informed of opportunities and impending disasters. Further, since non-redundant contacts are linked only through the central player, you are assured of being the first to see new opportunities created by needs in one group that could be served by skills in another group. You become the person who first brings together people, giving you the opportunity to coordinate their activities. These benefits are compounded by the fact that having a network that yields such benefits makes you even more attractive as a network contact to other people, easing the task of expanding the network to best serve your interests.

3.2.3 Growth Patterns A more general sense of efficiency and effective-ness is illustrated with network growth. In Figure 2-5, the number of con-tacts in a player's network increases from left to right on the horizontal axis. The number who are nonredundant increases up the vertical axis.

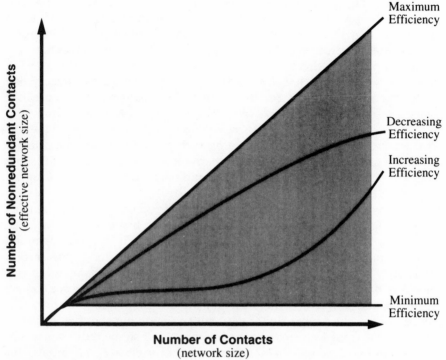

Figure 2-5
Efficiency and Effectiveness

Observed network size increases on the horizontal; effective size increases up the vertical. Networks can be anywhere in the gray area. The maximum efficiency line describes networks in which each new contact is completely nonredundant with other contacts. Effective size equals actual size. Efficient-effective networks are in the upper right portion of the graph. The minimum efficiency line describes networks in which each new contact is completely redundant with other contacts; effective size equals one regardless of multiple contacts in the network.

The two lines between the extremes illustrate more probable growth patterns. The decreasing-efficiency line shows players building good information benefits into their initial network, then relaxing to allow increasing redundancy as the network gets large. Friends of friends begin to be included. Comparisons across networks of different sizes suggest that this is the growth pattern among senior managers (Burt 1992, Ch. 4).

The increasing efficiency line illustrates a different growth pattern. Initial contacts are redundant with one another. A foundation is established with multiple contacts in the same cluster. After the foundation is established, the player's network expands to include contacts in other clusters and effective size begins to increase. There are two kinds of clusters in which optimizing for saturation is wiser than optimizing for

efficiency. The first is obvious. Leisure and domestic clusters are a con-
genial environment of low-maintenance, redundant contacts. Efficiency
mixes poorly with friendship. Judging friends for efficiency is an interpersonal flatulence from which friends will flee. The second exception is a
cluster of contacts where resources are dense. For the CEO, the board of
directors would be such a cluster. The university provost is similarly tied
to the board of trustees. For the more typical manager, the immediate
work group is such a cluster, especially with respect to funding authority
within the group. These clusters are so important to the vitality of the rest
of the network that it is worth treating each person in them as a primary
contact regardless of redundancy. Saturation minimizes the risk of losing
effective contact with the cluster and minimizes the risk of missing an
important opportunity anywhere in the cluster.

The general point is that the probability of receiving network benefits
from a cluster has two components: the probability that a contact will
transmit information to you and the probability that it will be transmitted
to the contact. I count on dense ties within a cluster to set the second
probability to one. The probability of having a benefit transmitted to you
therefore depends only on the strength of your relationship with a contact
in the cluster. However, where the density of ties in an opportunity-rich
cluster lowers the probability of your contact knowing about an opportunity, there is value in increasing the number—and so the redundancy—of
contacts in the cluster so that total coverage of the cluster compensates for
imperfect transmission within it.

3.3 Structural Holes and Weak Ties

In 1973, Mark Granovetter published his now famous article "The
Strength of Weak Ties." The weak-tie argument is elegantly simple. The
stage is set with results familiar from the social psychology of Festinger
and Homans circa 1950, the results I discussed in section 3.1 with respect
to cohesion indicators of structural holes. People live in a cluster of others
with whom they have strong relations. Information circulates at a high
velocity within these clusters. Each person tends to know what the other
people know. Therefore, and this is the insight of the argument, the
spread of information on new ideas and opportunities must come through
the weak ties that connect people in separate clusters. The weak ties so
often ignored by social scientists are in fact a critical element of social
structure. Hence the strength of weak ties. Weak ties are essential to the
flow of information that integrates otherwise disconnected social clusters
into a broader society.

The idea and its connection with structural holes is illustrated in
Figure 2-6. There are three clusters of players. Strong ties, indicated by
solid lines, connect players within clusters. Dashed lines indicate two
weak ties between players in separate clusters. You, as one of the players,
have a unique pattern of four ties: two strong ties within your cluster and
a weak tie to a contact in each in the other clusters. There are three classes

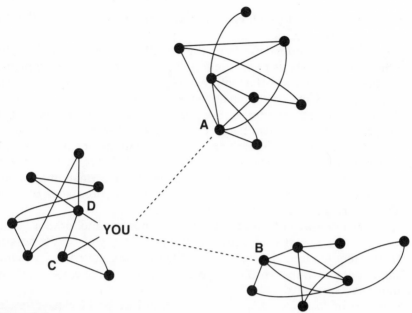

Figure 2-6
Structural Holes and Weak Ties

of structural holes in your network: (1) holes between the cluster around contact *A* and everyone in your own cluster—for example, the hole between contacts *A* and *C*; (2) holes between the cluster around contact *B* and everyone in your own cluster—for example, the hole between contacts *B* and *C*; and (3) the hole between contacts *A* and *B*.

Weak ties and structural holes seem to describe the same phenomenon. In Figure 2-6, for example, they predict the same ranking of information benefits. You are best positioned for information benefits, contacts *A* and *B* are next, followed by everyone else. You have two weak ties, contacts *A* and *B* have one each, and everyone else has none. You have the largest volume of structural holes between your contacts, contacts *A* and *B* have fewer, and everyone else has few or none.

The weak-tie argument is simpler than my argument and already well known. Why complicate the situation with the structural-hole argument?

There are two reasons. First, the causal agent in the phenomenon is not the weakness of a tie but the structural hole it spans. Tie weakness is a correlate, not a cause. The structural-hole argument captures the causal agent directly, providing a stronger foundation for theory and a clearer guide for empirical research. Second, by shifting attention away from the structural hole responsible for information benefits to the strength of the tie providing them, the weak-tie argument obscures the control benefits of structural holes. Control benefits augment, and in some ways are more important than, the information benefits of structural holes. Building both benefits into the argument more clearly speaks to the generality of the phenomenon under study. I'll elaborate the first point, then move to the second in the next section.

The weak-tie argument is about the strength of relationships at the same time that it is about their location. The two dashed lines in Figure 2-6 are bridges. They are the only connection between two otherwise separate clusters of strongly interconnected players (compare Granovetter 1973:1065 on weak ties as bridges). A bridge is at once two things. It is a chasm spanned and the span itself. By title and subsequent application, the weak-tie argument is about the strength of relationships that span the chasm between two social clusters. The structural-hole argument is about the chasm spanned. It is the latter that generates information benefits. Whether a relationship is strong or weak, it generates information benefits when it is a bridge over a structural hole.

Consider a cross-tabulation of ties by their strength and location. Your relationships can be sorted into two categories of strength. Strong ties are your most frequent and close contacts. Weak ties are your less frequent, less close contacts. Between these two categories you have a few strong ties and many weak ties.

Now sort by location, redundant ties within your social cluster versus nonredundant ties to people in other clusters. The nonredundant ties are your bridges to other clusters. From what we know about the natural etiology of relationships, bridges are less likely to develop than ties within clusters. The category of redundant ties includes your strong ties to often-met close friends and colleagues, but it also includes their friends and friends of their friends, whom you meet only occasionally if at all. As you expand your inventory from your closest, most frequent contacts to your more distant ones, contacts tend to be people like yourself before you reach a sufficiently low level of relationship to include people from completely separate social worlds. This tendency varies from one person to the next, but it is in the aggregate the substance of the well-documented tendency already discussed for relations to develop between socially similar people. In the Figure 2-6 illustration, you are one of nine people in your social cluster. You have strong ties to two people. Through those two, you have weak ties to the other six people in the cluster. To keep the sociogram simple, I deleted the dashed lines for those ties and their equivalent inside the other clusters. The other six people in your cluster are friends of friends, people whom you know and sometimes meet but don't have the time or energy to include among your closest contacts. The cluster is clearly held together by strong ties. Everyone has two to five strong ties to others within the cluster. All nine people are likely to know about the same opportunities as expected in a cohesive cluster. Of the thirty-six possible connections among the nine people in the cluster, however, only twelve are solid-line strong ties. The remaining two-thirds are weak ties between redundant friends of friends.

Now cross-tabulate the two classifications and take expected values. The result is given in Table 2-1. Information benefits vary across the columns of the table, higher through nonredundant ties. This is accurately

Table 2-1

The Natural Distribution of Relationships

	LOCATION IN SOCIAL STRUCTURE		
	Redundant Tie Within Cluster	Nonredundant Tie Beyond Cluster	Total
Strength			
Weak Tie	many	some	more
Strong Tie	some	rare	less
Total	more	less	

represented in both the weak-tie and the structural-hole argument. But quick reading of the weak-tie argument, with its emphasis on the strength of a relationship, has led some to test the idea that information benefits covary inversely with the strength of ties. This is a correlation between the rows and columns of Table 2-1, which is no correlation at all. In fact, the typical tie in Table 2-1 is weak and provides redundant information. The correlation in a study population depends on the distribution of ties in the table, but there is no theoretical reason to expect a strong correlation between the strength of a relationship and the information benefits it provides.

The weak-tie argument is about the two cells in the second column of the table. It predicts that nonredundant ties, the bridges that provide information benefits, are more likely weak than strong. In the second column of Table 2-1, weak-tie bridges are more likely than strong-tie bridges. To simplify his argument, Granovetter (1973:1063) makes this tendency absolute by ruling out strong-tie bridges (the "rare" cell in Table 2-1, the "forbidden triad" in Granovetter's argument). As Granovetter puts it: "A strong tie can be a bridge, therefore, only if neither party to it has any other strong ties, unlikely in a social network of any size (though possible in a small group). Weak ties suffer no such restriction, though they are certainly not automatically bridges. What is important, rather, is that all bridges are weak ties" (1064).

Bridge strength is an aside in the structural-hole argument. Information benefits are expected to travel over all bridges, strong or weak. Benefits vary between redundant and nonredundant ties, the columns of Table 2-1. Thus structural holes capture the condition directly responsible for the above-described information benefits. The task for a strategic player building an efficient-effective network is to focus resources on the maintenance of bridge ties. Otherwise, and this is the correlative substance of the weak-tie argument, bridges will fall into their natural state of being weak ties.

4. CONTROL AND THE *TERTIUS GAUDENS*

I've described how structural holes can determine who knows about opportunities, when they know, and who gets to participate in them. Players with a network optimized for structural holes enjoy higher rates of return on their investments because they know about, and have a hand in, more rewarding opportunities.

They are also more likely to secure favorable terms in the opportunities they choose to pursue. The structural holes that generate information benefits also generate control benefits, giving certain players an advantage in negotiating their relationships. To describe how this is so, I break the negotiation into structural, motivational, and outcome components. The social structure of the competitive arena defines opportunities; a player decides to pursue an opportunity and is sometimes successful.

4.1 *Tertius Gaudens*

Beginning with the outcome, sometimes you will emerge successful from negotiation as the *tertius gaudens*. Taken from the work of Georg Simmel, the *tertius* role is useful here because it defines successful negotiation in terms of the social structure of the situation in which negotiation is successful. The role is the heart of Simmel's (1922) later analysis of the freedom an individual derives from conflicting group affiliations (see Coser 1975 for elaboration).[4] The *tertius gaudens* is "the third who benefits" (Simmel 1923:154, 232).[5] The phrase survives in what I am told is a well-known Italian proverb: *Far i due litiganti, il terzo gode* (Between two fighters, the third benefits). It has moved north to a more jovial Dutch phrase: *de lachende derde* (the laughing third).[6] *Tertius, terzo,* or *derde*—the phrase describes an individual who profits from the disunion of others.

There are two *tertius* strategies: being the third between two or more players after the same relationship, and being the third between players in two or more relations with conflicting demands. The first, and simpler, strategy is the familiar economic bargaining between buyer and seller. Where two or more players want to buy something, the seller can play their bids against one another to get a higher price. The strategy extends directly to social commodities: a woman with multiple suitors, or a professor with simultaneous offers of positions in rival institutions.

The control benefits of having a choice between players after the same relationship extends directly to choice between the simultaneous demands of players in separate relationships. The strategy can be seen between hierarchical statuses in the enterprising subordinate under the authority of two or more superiors—for example, the student who strikes her own balance between the simultaneous demands of imperious faculty advisers.[7] The bargaining isn't limited to situations of explicit competition. In some situations, emerging as the *tertius* depends on creating competition. In proposing the concept of a role-set, for example, Merton (1968:393–394) identifies this as a strategy to resolve conflicting role demands. Make simultaneous, contradictory demands explicit to the people posing them, and ask them to resolve their—now explicit—conflict. Even where it doesn't exist, competition can be produced by defining issues such that contact demands become contradictory and must be resolved before you can meet their requests. Failure is possible. You might provide too little incentive for the contacts to resolve their differences. Contacts drawn from different social strata need not perceive one another's demands as carrying equal weight. Or you might provide too much incentive. Now aware of one another, the contacts could discover sufficient reason to cooperate in forcing you to meet their mutually agreed-on demands (Simmel 1902:176, 180–181 calls attention to such failures). But if the strategy is successful, the pressure on you is alleviated and replaced with an element of control over the negotiation. Merton states the situation succinctly: the player at the center of the network, ". . . originally at the focus of the conflict, virtually becomes a more or less influential bystander whose function it is to high-light the conflicting demands by members of his role-set and to make it a problem for them, rather than for him, to resolve *their* contradictory demands" (1968:430).

The strategy holds equally well with large groups. Under the rubric "divide and rule," Simmel (1902:185–186) describes institutional mechanisms through which the Incan and Venetian governments obtained advantage by creating conflict between subjects. The same point is illustrated more richly in Barkey's (1990) comparative description of state control in early seventeenth-century France and Turkey. After establishing the similar conditions in the two states at the time, Barkey asks why peasant-noble alliances developed in France against the central state while no analogous or substitutable alliances developed in Turkey. The two empires were comparable in many respects that scholars have cited to account for peasant revolt. They differed in one significant respect correlated with revolt—not in the structure of centralized state control, but in control strategy. In France, the king sent trusted representatives as agents to collect taxes and affect military decisions in provincial populations. The intrusion by these outside agents, *intendants*, affecting fundamental local decisions was resented by the established local nobility. Local nobility formed alliances with the peasantry against the central state. In Turkey, the sultan capitalized on conflict between leaders in the provinces. When a bandit became a serious threat to the recognized governor, a deal was struck with the bandit making him the legitimate governor. As Barkey puts it, "At its most extreme, the state could render a dangerous rebel legitimate overnight. This was accomplished by the striking of a bargain which ensured new sources of revenue for the rebel and momentary relief from internal warfare and perhaps, an army or two for the state" (1990:18). The two empires differed in their use of structural holes. The French king ignored them, assuming he had absolute authority. The Turkish sultan strategically exploited them, promoting competition between alternative leaders. Conflict within the Turkish empire remained in the province, rather than being directed against the central state. As is characteristic of the control obtained via structural holes, the resulting Turkish control was more negotiated than the absolute control exercised in France. It was also more effective.

4.2 The Essential Tension

There is a presumption of tension here. Control emerges from *tertius* brokering tension between other players. No tension, no *tertius*.

It is easy to infer that the tension presumed is one of combatants. Certainly there is a *tertius*-rich tension between combatants. Governors and bandits in the Turkish game played for life-or-death stakes. Illustrating this inference, a corporate executive listening to my argument expressed skepticism. Her colleagues, she explained, took pride in working together in a spirit of partnership and goodwill. The *tertius* imagery rang true to her knowledge of many firms, but not her own.

The reasoning is good, but the conclusion is wrong. I referred the skeptical executive to an analysis of hole effects that by coincidence was an analysis of managers at her level, in her firm (Burt 1992, Ch. 4). Promotions are strongly correlated, and illuminatingly so for women, with the structural holes in a manager's network.

The tension essential to the *tertius* is merely uncertainty. Separate the uncertainty of control from its consequences. The consequences of the control negotiation can be life or death in the extreme of combatants, or merely a question of embarrassment. Everyone knows you made an effort to get that job, but it went to someone else. The *tertius* strategies can be applied to control with severe consequences or to control of little consequence. What is essential is that control is uncertain, that no one can act as if they have absolute authority. Where there is any uncertainty about whose preferences should dominate a relationship, there is an opportunity for the *tertius* to broker the negotiation for control by playing demands against one another. There is no long-term contract that keeps a relationship strong, no legal binding that can secure the trust necessary to a productive relationship. Your network is a pulsing swirl of mixed, conflicting demands. Each contact wants your exclusive attention, your immediate response when a concern arises. Each, to warrant their continued confidence in you, wants to see you measure up to the values against which they judge themselves. Within this preference webwork, where no demands have absolute authority, the *tertius* negotiates for favorable terms.

4.3 The Connection with Information Benefits

This brings me back to information benefits. Structural holes are the setting for *tertius* strategies. Information is the substance. Accurate, ambiguous, or distorted information is moved between contacts by the *tertius*. One bidder is informed of a competitive offer in the first *tertius* strategy. A player in one relationship is informed of demands from other relationships in the second *tertius* strategy.

The two kinds of benefits augment and depend on each other. Application of the *tertius* strategies elicits additional information from contacts interested in resolving the negotiation in favor of their own preferences.

The information benefits of access, timing, and referrals enhance the application of strategy. Successful application of the *tertius* strategies involves bringing together players who are willing to negotiate, have sufficiently comparable resources to view one another's preferences as valid, but won't negotiate with one another directly to the exclusion of the *tertius*. Having access to information means being able to identify where there is an advantage to bringing contacts together and is the key to understanding the resources and preferences being played against one another. Having that information early is the difference between being the one who brings together contacts versus being just another person who hears about the negotiation. Referrals further enhance strategy. It is one thing to distribute information between two contacts during negotiation, another thing to have people close to each contact endorsing the legitimacy of the information you distribute.

5. ENTREPRENEURS

Behavior of a specific kind converts opportunity into higher rates of return. Information benefits of structural holes might come to a passive player, but control benefits require an active hand in the distribution of information. Motivation is now an issue. The *tertius* plays conflicting demands and preferences against one another, building value from their disunion. You enter the structural hole between two players to broker the relationship between them. Such behavior is not to everyone's taste. A player can respond in ways ranging from fully developing the opportunity to ignoring it. When you take the opportunity to be the *tertius*, you are an entrepreneur in the literal sense of the word—a person who generates profit from being between others. Both terms will be useful in these precise meanings; entrepreneur refers to a kind of behavior, the *tertius* is a successful entrepreneur.[8]

Motivation is often traced to cultural beliefs and psychological need. For example, in *The Protestant Ethic and the Spirit of Capitalism*, Weber describes the seventeenth-century bourgeois Protestant as an individual seeking—in religious duty, in Calvinist "calling"—the profit of sober, thrifty, diligent exploitation of opportunities for usury and trade (1905: especially 166ff). Psychological need is another motive. McClelland (1961) describes the formation of a need to achieve in childhood as critical to later entrepreneurial behavior (a need that can be cultivated later if desired: McClelland 1975). Schumpeter (1912) stresses nonutilitarian motives:

> First of all, there is the dream and the will to found a private kingdom, usually, though not necessarily, also a dynasty. . . . Then there is the will to conquer: the impulse to fight, to prove oneself superior to others, to succeed for the sake, not of the fruits of success, but of the success itself. . . . Finally, there is the joy of creating, of getting things done, or simply of exercising one's energy and ingenuity (93).[9]

5.1 Opportunity and Motivation

These are powerful frameworks for understanding competition, but I don't wish to detour into the beliefs behind entrepreneurial behavior. I propose to leap over the motivation issue by taking, for three reasons, a player's network as simultaneously an indicator of entrepreneurial opportunity and motivation.

First, there is the clarity of an opportunity. Players can be pulled to entrepreneurial action by the promise of success. I do not mean that players are rational creatures expected to calculate accurately and act in their own interest. Nor do I mean to limit the scope of the argument to situations in which players act as if they were rational in that way. I mean simply that between two opportunities, any player is more likely to act on the one with the clearer path to success. The clarity of opportunity is its own motivation. As the number of entrepreneurial opportunities in a network increases, the odds of some being clearly defined by deep structural holes increases, so the odds of entrepreneurial behavior increase. To be sure, a person whose abilities or values proscribe entrepreneurial behavior is unlikely to act, and someone inclined to entrepreneurial behavior is more likely to act, even taking the initiative to create opportunities. Regardless of ability or values, however, within the broad range of acceptable behaviors a person is unlikely to take entrepreneurial action if the probability of success is low. You might question the propriety of a scholar negotiating between two universities that offer a position, but the question is not an issue for the player with one offer.

There are also network analogues to the psychological and cultural explanations of motive. Beginning with psychological need, a person with a taste for entrepreneurial behavior is prone to building a network configured around such behavior. If I find a player with a network rich in the structural holes that make entrepreneurial behavior possible, I have a player willing and able to act entrepreneurially. But it is the rare person who is the sole author of her or his network. Networks are more often built in the course of doing something else. Your work, for example, involves meeting people from very different walks of life, so your network ends up composed of contacts who without you have no contact with one another. Even so, the network is its own explanation of motive. As the volume of structural holes in a player's network increases—regardless of the process that created them—the entrepreneurial behavior of making and negotiating relations between others becomes a way of life. This is a network analogue to the cultural explanation of motive. If all you know is entrepreneurial relationships, the motivation question is a nonissue. Being willing and able to act entrepreneurially is how you understand social life.

I will treat motivation and opportunity as one and the same. For reasons of a clear path to success, or the tastes of the player as the network's author, or the nature of the player's environment as author of the network, a network rich in entrepreneurial opportunity surrounds a player motivated to be entrepreneurial. At the other extreme, a player innocent of entrepreneurial motive lives in a network devoid of entrepreneurial opportunity.

5.2 Measurement Implications

Entrepreneurial motivation highlights a complexity that might otherwise obscure the association between structural holes and rates of return. Consider the graph in Figure 2-7. Players are defined by their rate of return on investments (vertical axis) and the entrepreneurial opportunities of structural holes in their networks (horizontal axis).

The sloping line in the graph describes the hole effect of players rich in structural holes (horizontal axis) getting higher rates of return on investments (vertical axis). The increasingly positive slope of the line captures the increasing likelihood of *tertius* profit. A player invests in certain relationships. They need not all be high-yield relationships. The higher the proportion of relationships enhanced by structural holes, the more likely and able the entrepreneurial player, and so the more likely that the

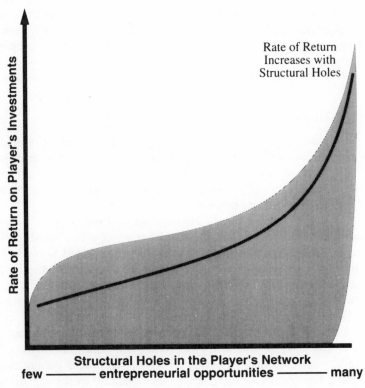

Figure 2-7
Rate of Return and Structural Holes

player's investments are in high-yield relationships. The result is a higher aggregate rate of return on investments.

I have shaded the area in the graph to indicate how I expect data to be distributed around the line of association. There is no imperative that says players have to take advantage of the benefits provided by structural holes. Players rich in entrepreneurial opportunity may choose to develop opportunities (and so appear in the upper right corner of the graph) or ignore them (and so appear in the lower right corner of the graph). Some players in Figure 2-7 are above the line. Some are below. If players were perfectly rational, observations would be clustered around the line. Players would take advantage of any entrepreneurial opportunity presented to them. A control for differences in player motivation, such as a McClelland measure of need for achievement, would have the same effect. The point is not the degree of deviation from the line of association; it is the greater deviation below the line. Variable motivation creates deviations below the true hole effect on rate of return.

This emphasizes the relative importance for empirical research of deviations above and below the line of association. Observations in the lower right corner of the graph, players under-utilizing their entrepreneurial opportunities, might be due to variation in motivation. Observations in the upper left corner are a severe test of the argument. Players who have opportunities can choose whether to develop them. Players without opportunities don't have that choice. Within the limits of measurement error, there should be no observations in the upper left corner of the graph.

6. STRUCTURAL AUTONOMY

I can now summarize the argument with a concept defining the extent to which a player's network is rich in structural holes, and so entrepreneurial opportunity, and so information and control benefits. That concept is structural autonomy. I will present the concept in a general way here (see Burt 1992, Ch. 2, for formal details).

I began with a generic production equation. Profit equals an investment multiplied by a rate of return. The benefits of a relationship can be expressed in an analogous form: time and energy invested to reach a contact multiplied by a rate of return. A player's entrepreneurial opportunities are enhanced by a relationship to the extent that (1) the player has invested substantial time and energy to secure a connection with the contact, and (2) there are many structural holes around the contact ensuring a high rate of return on the investment. More specifically, rate of return concerns how and who you reach with the relationship. Time and energy invested to reach a player with more resources generates more social capital. For the sake of argument, as explained in the discussion of social capital, I assume that a player with a network optimized for structural holes can identify suitably endowed contacts such that I don't have to carry the issue of who as another variable in the analysis. My concern is the how of a relationship, defined by the structure of a network and its connection with the social structure of the competitive arena. Thus the rate of return keyed to structural holes is a product of the extent to which there are (1) many primary structural holes between the contact and others in the player's network, and (2) many secondary structural holes between the contact and others outside the network who could replace the contact.

There is also the issue of structural holes around the player. As the holes around contacts provide information and control benefits to the player, holes around the player can be developed by contacts for their benefit. Developing entrepreneurial opportunities depends on having numerous structural holes around your contacts and none attached to yourself.

These considerations come together in the concept of structural autonomy. Players with relationships free of structural holes at their own end and rich in structural holes at the other end are structurally autonomous. These are the players best positioned for the information and control benefits that a network can provide. These are the players to the far right of the graph in Figure 2-7. Structural autonomy summarizes the action potential of the *tertius's* network. The budget equation for optimizing structural autonomy has an upper limit set by the *tertius's* time and energy, and a trade-off between the structural holes a new contact provides versus the time and energy required to maintain a productive relationship with the contact.[10] The summary conclusion is that players with networks optimized for structural holes—that is to say, players with networks providing high structural autonomy—enjoy higher rates of return on their investments because they know about, have a hand in, and exercise control over, more rewarding opportunities.

7. THE BROADER CONTEXT

The structural-hole argument has four signature qualities:

1. Competition is a matter of relations, not player attributes.

2. Competition is a relation emergent, not observed.

3. Competition is a process, not just a result.

4. Imperfect competition is a matter of freedom, not just power.

These qualities are not individually unique to the structural-hole argument. They are jointly characteristic of it.

First, competition is a matter of relationships, not player attributes. The structural-hole argument escapes the debilitating social science practice of using player attributes for explanation. The unit of analysis in which structural holes have their causal effect is the network of relations that intersect in a player. The intersection is known by various names as a role, a market, or a position in social structure. The players in which relations intersect are physical and legal entities; a person, an organization, or a broader aggregation of physical and legal entities. The attributes of the players in whom the relations intersect—black, white, female, male, old, young, rich, poor—are an empirical curiosity irrelevant to the explanation. Competition is not about being a player with certain physical attributes; it is about securing productive relationships. Physical attributes are a correlate, not a cause, of competitive success. Causation resides in the intersection of relations. Holes can have different effects for people with different attributes or for organizations of different kinds, but that is because the attributes and organizational forms are correlated with different positions in social structure. The manner in which a structural hole is an entrepreneurial opportunity for information and control benefits is the bedrock explanation that carries across player attributes, populations, and time. The task for the analyst is to cut past the spurious correlation between attributes and outcomes to reach the underlying social structural factors that cause the outcome. This point is developed at length elsewhere (Burt 1992, Ch. 5).

Second, competition is a relation emergent, not observed. The structural holes in which competition develops are invisible relations of nonredundancy, relations visible only by their absence. Consider the atavistic driver experiment. You're on the freeway. There is a car ahead of you going 65 MPH. Pull up so your front wheels are parallel to his. Stay there. This won't take long. If he speeds up, speed up. If he slows down, slow down. You feel the tension in yourself as you know it's building in the next car. He looks over. Is this a sexual come-on or a threat? Deciding against sex, he may slow down, hoping you'll go away. If that doesn't work, and he doesn't feel that his car can escape yours, his anger will be apparent only on his face. If he is more confident, he'll accelerate to get away from you. Let him.

For the moment when you two stood in common time and place, you were competitors. Break the parallelism, and the competition is gone. There is no behavioral relationship between the drivers that is competition. Competition is an intense, intimate, transitory, invisible relationship created between players by their visible relations with others. It's the cheek-by-jowl with respect to the passing environment that makes the drivers competitors.

The task of analyzing competition is made more difficult by the fact that the structural holes in which competition thrives don't connect the players we see. They connect invisible pieces of players; the pieces we see in any one of the many roles and markets in which the person or firm is a player. I see one piece of you in the office, another on the street, another at home. Each piece has an attendant network of relations with relevant others. The causal force of structural holes resides in the pattern of relations that intersect in each network. That intersection happens in players, but where it occurs is distinct from the causal force released by its occurrence. This is another view of my first point, people and organizations are not the source of action so much as they are the vehicles for structurally induced action.

These qualities make it very difficult to capture competition without having the conceptual and research tools to represent the social structure of the competitive arena. Understanding competition will be one of the important returns from the work invested during the 1970s and 1980s in network analysis. The social structure of competition is not about the structure of competitive relations. It is about the social structure of the relations for which players compete. The structural-hole argument is not a theory about competitive relationships. It is a theory about competition for the benefits of relationships. To explain variation in competitive success, I have to look beyond the competitors themselves to the circumstances of the relations for which they compete. The terrain on which competition plays out lies beyond the competitors themselves. It lies in their efforts to negotiate relations with other players. Where those relations are positioned in social structure such that there is little room to negotiate, the margin between success and failure is slim. The social structure of competition is about the negotiability of the relationships on which competitors survive. That is the essence of the structural autonomy concept.

Third, competition is a process, not just a result. With important exceptions, most competition theories are about what is left when competition is over. They are an aside in efforts to answer the practical question of how to maximize producer profit. Answering the question requires a definition of how price varies with output. It is convenient to assume that there is a condition of "competition" such that price is constant with output. The presumed competition exists when (1) there are an infinite number of buyers and sellers known to one another, (2) goods can be divided for sale to any number of buyers, and (3) buyers and sellers are free to exchange without interference froma third parties. When goods are exchanged under these conditions, conditions of "perfect" competition, equilibrium prices can be derived that will clear the market. An architecture of powerful economic theory about price and production follows.[11]

The alternative is to start with the process of competition and work toward its results. This is a less elegant route for theory, but one that veers closer to the reality of competition as we experience it. The structural-hole argument is not about the flow of goods. No mechanism is proposed to define the prices that "clear" the imperfectly competitive market. Such a mechanism could be proposed, but not here. This chapter is about the competitive process by which the price and occurrence of transactions is decided. If you will, it is about the players who form the deal, not the lawyers who write the contracts. The social structure of competition is about negotiating the relationships on which competitors survive. Structural holes determine the extent to which, and manner in which, certain players have a competitive advantage in that negotiation.

Fourth, imperfect competition is a matter of freedom, not just power.

The structural-hole argument is a theory of competition made imperfect by the freedom of individuals to be entrepreneurs. In this, the theory cuts across the usual axis of imperfect competition.

In the perfectly competitive arena, any party to a transaction has unlimited choice between alternative partners. Numerous alternatives exist and players are free to choose. The fact of that choice drives price to a minimum. The significance of any one player as an entrepreneur is zero. The structural image is one of relational chaos. Players are free to withdraw from existing relations to join with anyone who better serves their interests. Obligation stops with the execution of the transaction.

Deviations from this image measure imperfect competition, usually defined by the extent to which choice is concentrated in the hands of the strongest player. As Stigler (1957:262) concludes his historical review: "If we were free to redefine competition at this late date, a persuasive case could be made that it should be restricted to meaning the absence of monopoly power in a market." At the extreme of perfect competition, every player has unlimited choice among alternative relationships. At the other extreme, choice is concentrated in the hands of a dominant player. Everyone else is assigned to relations by the cominant player. Familiar images are monopoly, cults, village kinship systems, political machines, fascist bureaucracies. The structural image is one of a completely and rigidly interconnected system of people and establishments within a market. High obligation relations, with obligation enforced by authority or convention, allow neither negotiation nor the strategic replacement of partners.

Observed behavior lies between these extremes. Control is never absolute; it is negotiated—whether exercised through competitive price, bureaucratic authority, or some other social norm. In the most regulated arena, there are special relationships through which certain players move to get around the dicta of the governing mechanism. In the most competitive of arenas, there are relations between certain players that provide them special advantages. Competition is omnipresent and everywhere imperfect.

The extremes of perfect and regulated competition are more similar on a critical point than either is to the reality of observed behavior between them. They are both images of dominance. Players are homogeneously trivial under competitive market pricing and, at the other extreme, homogeneously trivial under the dicta of the dominant player. The dominant player defines fair exchange in the regulated market. Buyer and seller are locked into exchange relations by the dicta of the dominant player. The press of numbers defines fair exchange in the perfectly competitive market. Competition between countless buyers and sellers involves negotiation between alternative relations, not within a relationship. Any one partner in a relationship is a faceless cog, readily replaced with someone else. At either extreme, the lack of negotiation within a relationship denies the individuality of buyer and seller.

But their individuality is the key to understanding competition. The substantive richness of competition lies in its imperfections, the jostling of specific players against one another looking for a way to make a difference. In the substantive details of imperfect competition lie the defining parameters of competition. They are the parameters of player individuality. Competition is imperfect to the extent that any player can affect the terms of any particular relationship. Oligopoly, the extent to which multiple players together constitute a monopoly, is an insufficient answer. The central question for imperfect competition is how players escape domination either by the market or by another player.

That is the focus of the structural-hole argument—a theory of freedom instead of power, of negotiated control instead of absolute control. It is a description of the extent to which the social structure of a competitive arena contains entrepreneurial opportunities for individual players to affect the terms of their relationships.

Notes

1. This chapter is approximately two-thirds of a chapter by the same name in a book, *Structural Holes,* to be published in 1992 by Harvard University Press. Professor Richard Swedberg, who skillfully condensed the original material for the purposes of this anthology, called my attention to an assumption implicit in my argument. I refer to people and organizations in the competitive arena as "players." Professor Swedberg felt I used the term to denote a very active actor, seeking out contacts and opportunities. He gently suggested that the term had a touch of frivolity and that I might do well to substitute with a more neutral term such as "actor." In earlier writing I have used the more neutral term for general discussion (Burt 1982), but for the topic of competition I prefer to use player. It better fits my felt-reality of the phenomenon. More than implying activity, it is a term of peer recognition: "Yes, he's a player." He's a presence in the game. If you have the motivation, resources, and skills to compete, you're a player; otherwise, you're scenery. Everyone is a player in some arenas, scenery in most. This chapter is about the social structural conditions that give certain players a competitive advantage.

2. This point is significant because it contradicts the natural growth of contact networks. Left to the natural course of events, a network will accumulate redundant contacts. Friends introduce you to their friends and expect you to like them. Business contacts introduce you to their colleagues. You will like the people you meet in this way. The factors that make your friends attractive make their friends attractive because like seeks out like. Your network grows to include more and more people. These relations come easily, they are comfortable, and they are easy to maintain. But these easily accumulated contacts do not expand the network so much as they fatten it, weakening its efficiency and effectiveness by increasing contact redundancy and tying up time. The process is amplified by spending time in a single place—in your family, in your neighborhood, or in the office. The more time you spend with any specific primary contact, the more likely you will be introduced to their friends. Evidence of these processes can be found in studies of balance and transitivity in social relations (see Burt 1982:55–60 for review) and in studies of the tendency for redundant relations to develop among physically proximate people (for example, the suggestively detailed work of Festinger, Schachter, and Back 1950; or the work with more definitive data on social contexts by Fischer 1982, and on social foci by Feld 1981, 1982). For the purposes here, I ignore the many day-to-day tactical issues critical to maintaining

a network. Thorough treatment requires considerable discussion and didactic devices. This is the function of the seminars offered by the Denver firm, Strategic Connections. I discuss tactical issues in a short book, *The Network Entrepreneur*, written in 1987 for distribution from the firm.

3. The number of structural holes is not increased directly but is likely to increase. The presumption through all this is that the time and energy to maintain relationships is limited and the constant pressure to include new contacts will use all time and energy available (as in the preceding footnote). Although structural holes are not increased directly by maximizing nonredundant contacts, they can be expected to increase indirectly from the reallocation of time and energy from maintaining redundant contacts to acquiring new nonredundant contacts (as illustrated in Figure 2-4).

4. This theme is often grouped with Durkheim's (1893) argument for the liberating effect of a division of labor, but it is useful to distinguish the two arguments for the present purposes. Simmel focuses on the liberating quality of competition between multiple affiliations, which is the concern here. Durkheim focuses on the liberating quality of interdependent affiliations. Integration, rather than competition, is Durkheim's theme. That theme continues in Blau's (1977) analysis of cross-cutting social circles, in which he argues that conflict between strata becomes increasingly difficult as affiliations provide people with alternative stratification hierarchies. Flap (1988) provides a network-oriented review of such work, building from anthropology and political science, to study the "crisscross" effect inhibiting violence.

5. Georg Simmel introduced this phrase in papers on the importance of group size, translated and published by Albion Small in the *American Journal of Sociology* (Simmel 1896:393–394, 1902:174–189). A later version was translated by K. H. Wolff (Simmel 1923:154–169, 232–234).

6. I am grateful to Anna DiLellio for calling my attention to the Italian proverb and to Hein Schreuder for calling my attention to the Dutch expression. The idea of exploiting a structural hole is viscerally familiar to all audiences, but interestingly varied across cultures in phrasing the profit obtained (an interesting site for a Zelizer-1989 kind of analysis).

7. This point is nicely exemplified in Simmel's (1896:394) discussion of subordination comparing the freedom of two medieval subordinate positions: the bondsman ("unfree") and the vassal:

An essential difference between the medieval "unfree" men and the vassals consisted in the fact that the former had and could have only one master, while the latter could accept land from different lords and could take the oath of fealty to each. By reason of the possibility of placing themselves in the feudal relation to several persons the vassals won strong security and independence against the individual lords. The inferiority of the position of vassalage was thereby to a considerable degree equalized.

8. A substantial block of material was deleted between here and the next section on (1) the literal meaning of entrepreneurs, (2) the importance of structural holes within the clusters of secondary contacts, (3) market boundaries, and (4) a more careful discussion of holes defined by cohesion versus structural equivalence. If the leap to structural autonomy seems awkward here, consider looking at the full discussion (Burt 1992, Ch. 1).

9. I am grateful to Richard Swedberg for giving me the benefit of his careful study of Schumpeter in calling my attention to these passages. Their broader scope and context are engagingly laid out in his biography of Schumpeter (Swedberg 1991). The passages can also be found in the Schumpeter selection included in Parsons et al., *Theories of Society* (1961:513).

10. This sentence is the starting point for an optimization model in which the benefits of a contact are weighed against the cost of maintaining a relation

with the contact, subject to a time and energy budget constraint on the aggregate of contacts in a network. The work is beyond the scope of this discussion, but I want to remove an ostensible barrier to such work, and in the process highlight a scope limitation to my argument. Marks (1977) provides a cogent argument against the energy scarcity metaphor so often used to justify discussions of role negotiations. Instead of viewing roles as energy debilitating, Marks argues for an "expansion" view in which energy is created by performing roles (compare Sieber 1974). Marks and Sieber discuss the advantages of performing multiple roles. Both are responding to the energy-scarcity arguments used to motivate discussions of mechanisms by which people manage role strain (most notably, Merton 1957; Goode 1960). To quote Goode (1960:485), a person ". . . cannot meet all these demands to the satisfaction of all the persons who are part of his total role network. Role strain—difficulty in meeting given role demands—is therefore normal. In general, the person's total role obligations are overdemanding." I have borrowed the theme of overdemanding role obligations. The *tertius* budget constraint concerns both the time and energy cost of maintaining existing relations and the opportunity costs of contacts lost because of redundancy. However, my argument only concerns negotiations within a single role. The mechanisms used to manage role strain, such as segregating role relations in time and space, could also be used by the *tertius* to manage conflict to his or her own advantage, but I am ignoring that possibility, and so limiting the scope of my argument, to focus on the situation in which *tertius* negotiates conflicting demands that have to be met simultaneously.

11. This paragraph owes much to Stigler's (1957) review of the evolution of competition in economic theory. He provides the simple profit question that calls for an assumption of competition. The three conditions for perfect competition are adapted from Edgeworth (1881:17–19), but I appreciated their evolutionary significance only in the context of alternatives laid out in Stigler's (1957) review. Beyond providing context, the clarity of Stigler's presentation, here and with respect to Edgeworth on marginal utility, offers a great improvement over the original. At the same time, as always, the original has value. Edgeworth's characterization of free choice in terms of no intrusive third parties is the key to the social structure of competition. Structural holes are the variable determining the extent to which there are no intrusive third parties to a relationship. Stigler's (1957:247) recoding of that to be the "complete absence of limitations upon individual self-seeking behavior" states the original thought in terms more compatible with subsequent developments in economic theory, but obscures the social structural insight in the original.

References

Barkey, Karen. 1990. "Rebellious Alliances: The State and Peasant Unrest in Early Seventeenth Century France and the Ottoman Empire." Paper presented at the 1989 annual meetings of the American Sociological Association.

Berkman, Lisa. F., and S. Leonard Syme. 1979. "Social Networks, Host Resistance, and Mortality: A Nine-Year Follow-Up Study of Alameda County Residents." *American Journal of Epidemiology* 109:186–204.

Blau, Peter M. 1977. *Heterogeneity and Inequality.* New York: Free Press.

Boxman, Ed A. W., Paul M. De Graaf, and Hendrik D. Flap. 1991. "The Impact of Social and Human Capital on the Income Attainment of Dutch Managers." *Social Networks* 13:in press.

Burt, Ronald S. 1982. *Toward a Structural Theory of Action.* New York: Academic Press.

————. 1986. "A Note on Sociometric Order in the General Social Survey Network Data." *Social Networks* 8:149–174.

————. 1990. "Kinds of Relations in American Discussion Networks." In C. Calhoun, M. W. Meyer, and W. R. Scott, eds., *Structures of Power and Constraint*. New York: Cambridge University Press, pp. 411–451.

————. 1992. *Structural Holes*. Cambridge: Harvard University Press.

Campbell, Karen E., Peter V. Marsden, and Jeanne S. Hurlbert. 1986. "Social Resources and Socioeconomic Status." *Social Networks* 8:97–117.

Coleman, James S. 1988. "Social Capital in the Creation of Human Capital." *American Journal of Sociology* 94, supplement: S95–120.

Coser, Rose Laub. 1975. "The Complexity of Roles as a Seedbed of Individual Autonomy." In L. A. Coser, ed., *The Idea of Social Structure*. New York: Harcourt, Brace, Jovanovich.

De Graaf, Nan D., and Hendrik D. Flap. 1988. "With a Little Help from My Friends." *Social Forces* 67: 453–472.

Durkheim, Émile [1893] 1933. *The Division of Labor in Society*, G. Simpson, tr. New York: Free Press.

Edgeworth, F. Y. 1881. *Mathematical Psychics*. London: C. Kegan Paul.

Feld, Scott. L. 1981. "The Focused Organization of Social Ties." *American Journal of Sociology* 86:1015–1035.

————. 1982. "Social Structural Determinants of Similarity." *American Sociological Review* 47:797–801.

Festinger, Leon, Stanley Schachter, and Kurt W. Back. 1950. *Social Pressures in Informal Groups*. Stanford: Stanford University Press.

Fischer, Claude S. 1982. *To Dwell Among Friends*. Chicago: University of Chicago Press.

Flap, Hendrik D. 1988. *Conflict, Loyalty, and Violence*. New York: Verlag Peter Lang.

Flap, Hendrik D., and Nan D. De Graaf. 1989. "Social Capital and Attained Occupational Status." *Netherlands' Journal of Sociology* 22:145–161.

Flap, Hendrik D., and F. Tazelaar. 1989. "The Role of Informal Social Networks on the Labor Market: Flexibilization and Closure." In H. Flap, ed., *Flexibilization of the Labor Market*. Utrecht, Holland: ISOR, University of Utrecht, pp. 99–118.

Goode, William J. 1960. "A Theory of Role Strain." *American Sociological Review* 25:483–496.

Granovetter, Mark S. 1973. "The Strength of Weak Ties." *American Journal of Sociology* 78:1360–1380.

Homans, George C. 1950. *The Human Group*. New York: Harcourt, Brace and World.

Lazarsfeld, Paul F., Bernard Berelson, and Hazel Gaudet. 1944. *The People's Choice*. New York: Columbia University Press.

Lin, Nan. 1982. "Social Resources and Instrumental Action." In P. V. Marsden and Nan Lin, eds., *Social Structure and Network Analysis*. Beverly Hills: Sage.

Lin, Nan, and Mary Dumin. 1986. "Access to Occupations Through Social Ties." *Social Networks* 8:365–385.

Lin, Nan, Walter M. Ensel, and John C. Vaughn. 1981. "Social Resources and Strength of Ties." *American Sociological Review* 46:393–405.

Marks, Stephen R. 1977. "Multiple Roles and Role Strain: Some Notes on Human Energy, Time and Commitment." *American Sociological Review* 42:921–936.

Marsden, Peter V. 1987. "Core Discussion Networks of Americans." *American Sociological Review* 52:122–131.

Marsden, Peter V., and Jeanne S. Hurlbert. 1988. "Social Resources and Mobility Outcomes: A Replication and Extension." *Social Forces* 67:1038–1059.

McClelland, David C. 1961. *The Achieving Society*. Princeton: Van Nostrand.

————. 1975. *Power*. New York: Irvington.

Merton, Robert K. [1957] 1968. "Continuities in the Theory of Reference Group

Behavior." In Robert K. Merton, ed., *Social Theory and Social Structure*. New York: Free Press, pp. 335–440.

Parsons, Talcott, Edward Shils, Kaspar D. Naegele, and Jesse R. Pitts. 1961. *Theories of Society*. New York: Free Press.

Schumpeter, Joseph A. [1912] 1961. *The Theory of Economic Development*, R. Opie, tr. Cambridge, MA: Harvard University Press.

Sieber, Sam D. 1974. "Toward a Theory of Role Accumulation." *American Sociological Review* 39:567–578.

Simmel, Georg. 1896. "Superiority and Subordination as Subject-Matter of Sociology, II," A. Small, tr. *American Journal of Sociology* 2:392–415.

———. 1902. "The Number of Members as Determining the Sociological Form of the Group, II," A. Small. tr. *American Journal of Sociology* 8:158–196.

———. [1922] 1955. *Conflict and Web of Group Affiliations*, K. H. Wolff and R. Bendix, trs. New York: Free Press.

———. [1923] 1950. *The Sociology of Georg Simmel*, K. H. Wolff, tr. New York: Free Press.

Stigler, George J. [1957] 1965. "Perfect Competition, Historically Contemplated." In G. J. Stigler, ed., *Essays in the History of Economics*. Chicago: University of Chicago Press, pp. 234–267.

Swedberg, Richard. 1991. *Schumpeter—A Biography*. Princeton: Princeton University Press.

Weber, Max. [1904–1905] 1930. *The Protestant Ethic and the Spirit of Capitalism*, T. Parsons, tr. New York: Charles Scribner's Sons.

Zelizer, Viviana A. 1989. "The Social Meaning of Money: 'Special Monies.'" *American Journal of Sociology* 95:342–377.

CHAPTER

3

Agency as Control in Formal Networks

HARRISON C. WHITE

CONTROL IN NETWORKS

Agency is the root of management process. To manage is to make use of ties. To gain and maintain control requires attending to networks of ties. Most managers resort to folk wisdom on ties. Some managers sometimes have the wit to allow for others' use of such knowledge—and so on at further removes. Reality reflects networks into management process. The cumulative impact of networks on management as process is the topic of the present chapter.

Influences and acts among actors run through ties, and how they cumulate into significant actions is heavily influenced by shape and connectivity in the networks of those ties. Seeking, or observing, effective control thus requires making use of and understanding how networks operate, and how a network both is shaped and can be further shaped through the very actions on which it impacts. Discussion and application often focus on using personal contacts in general social and professional life, but rational administration and considered policies also are subject to network mediation. Maneuvers for control in and around formal organizations realize themselves in, and are prime generators of, social networks.

For ideas, leads, and enlightening discussions I am grateful to Peter Bearman, Jeff Bradach, Ken Dauber, Robert G. Eccles, Tom Ertman, Roberto Fernandez, Martin Gargiulo, Roger Gould, Shin-Kap Han, Richard Lachmann, Eric Leifer, John Lie, Marvin M. Reiss, Jae Soon Rhee, Ilan Talmud, Ronan Van Rossem, and Yuki Yasuda. Earlier versions of the paper from which this chapter derives were given at the American Sociological Meetings in 1987 and 1990, and I am indebted to Mayer Zald and John F. Padgett for their comments. I am indebted to Holly Raider for a detailed critique of the previous draft.

Network Background

The challenge is to reconstruct, from a network perspective, the theory of management for firms and other organizations. This challenge has several facets. First, geography and chance in the physical world and other social worlds interact via general social networks with any organization and thereby shape its claims to authority. One example is the phenomenon of the tipping point, the abrupt segregation brought on from apparently innocent bias in desired neighbors cumulated via mobility along networks. This long has been modeled explicitly both in residential segregation by race (Schelling 1978) and in crowd panics (Granovetter 1978, Granovetter and Soong 1983); a related phenomenon is the sudden onset of congestion from queuing in traffic networks (Kleinrock 1975–1976). Analogous happenings in business firms can be modeled similarly.

A second aspect of the challenge comes from a paradoxical inverse relation. Intensity and reliability of ties considered individually, on the one hand, are related inversely to the scope and reach possible through the resulting network of ties, on the other hand. The early works of Bott (1957) and Rapoport (Foster et al. 1963) suggested this, and confirmation came in Milgram's Small World work (cf. Kochen 1989). Important qualitative implications for control were later derived by Granovetter (1973, 1974, 1982, 1985; cf. Wellman and Berkowitz 1988), as the importance of "weak ties" in the Small World. Explicit quantitative and combinatorial models of networks are due to Boorman (1975) and Delaney (1988).

A third aspect of the challenge for network analysis is allowing for how management, as process, itself builds on understanding of folk wisdom on networks, together with allowances for geography and chance. Tracing this out completely is a challenge for a next generation. Many of the earlier findings on social networks as informal organization will be reconfirmed as by-products, and much of formal organization will come to be seen as formed in a dialectic with social networks.

Formal Networks

Coin the term "formal network" to distinguish network generation and use in and around formal organization.[1] Gamings are played out within bureaucracy in and through formal networks. Policy has built the bureaucracy out of agency ties. A principal finding of organization studies has been that announced boundaries can be rhetorical counters in gamings around identities.[2] Identities of actors as units are supplanted as the focus turns to identities of relations, which are manifest through process style within formal networks.

Perceiving, much less understanding, the operation of formal networks requires depth of context. Such depth must be in levels of identity and of time as well as of hierarchy. Such depth can be built only in a case study, and analysis will rest on an assortment of them. For a recent appreciation of the case study see Becker and Ragin (1992).

Esoteric context can be a positive advantage to such case studies. Mechanisms of attempted control and its counterings may be hardest to spot in just those situations with which we are most familiar. So in a search for cogent case studies, canvass different institutional realms and different periods and societies. The French monarchy and the early Christian missionary movement will be included along with current studies of American medical institutions.

Application will focus on modern American business. The wide canvass of network studies on agency as control will frame a set of propositions on reclaiming managerial prerogatives in the present day.[3]

MANAGEMENT AS PROCESS

In reaction to, as well as realization of, agency, individual ties are continuously added to and subtracted from formal networks. Management is a continuing process that involves throwing up fresh network and changing existing networks in order to extend and reinforce agency. Whole hunks of networks are added or rearranged in concert. Reorganization never ends because struggles for control never end.

Always, as part of attempts at rationality and efficiency and legitimacy, some further specialization and/or hierarchy in organization is being propounded. But then, as sure as barnacles grow on hulls, local interests capture the results exactly via networks of specialization and specialization of networks. Some professional, guild, or regional specialization may have been laid down initially by a management plan. Immediately thereafter new ties will spring up, previously existing ties will be enriched, and usually there will emerge some distinct enclaves.[4]

Control struggles thence breed a partition into distinct enclaves. Various enclaves have languages different from one another as well as from any central authority. Therefore these enclaves are difficult for external authority to penetrate. Specialization seeks to evade control; specialization becomes counterorganization.

How can one counter a process that itself is an expression of countering? Any continuing specialized organization has become recalcitrant and refractory to effective control by management. Propositions on effective means of intervention are as much a challenge to analysts to develop, as to managers—or others—to exploit. How management evolved originally is obviously intertwined with such propositions.

Control

To achieve control is to change what would otherwise have happened. A common alternative definition is exemplified by Zald's words about control being "the ability of a person or group, for whatever reason, to affect another person's or group's ability to achieve its goals (personal or collective)" (1970:238). When applied to formal organizations, the two definitions are not so far apart, but Zald's is less useful. The argument presented here is that control can emerge only from interaction between particular organizational schema and spontaneous responses. It follows that effective efforts at control cannot have "goals" in any straightforward sense. Goals may regulate, or at least decorate, the activities of persons and of guilds within the organization, but goals are for that very reason an impediment to effective control on the organization. It is others' goals at the point of interface that may be important for achieving control.

Control may invoke and evoke asymmetry. This is no simple matter. An asymmetric tie requires and implies a whole larger structure; asymmetry is no matter of a pair relation. An apparent case of isolated dominance, for example, will be found on closer inspection to lock into a larger structure. Time distortion is a less focused but more efficient way to achieve some effect of asymmetry as a precursor to control. One can argue that control consists principally in achieving constant changing of the scene for others. Any organization that is not changing is a battlefield monument, a monument to the successful overturn of control.

Zald's definition of control, in terms of manipulating others' goals, presupposes modern Western contexts where everyone has been socialized into the necessary ubiquity of having goals (cf. Agnew 1986; MacPherson 1962). However, the basic analysis should be transposable to times outside the ideology of individualism. We shall begin with observation and analysis made by the intellectual and lawyer Jean Bodin in the West in the 1500s.[5]

In any period and context, control must dispense with the luxury of goals. This is true despite the necessity of reading actions for all the idioms then current in the landscape for control, and especially for goals. What control at the level of general management is about is getting action, getting movement in social formation that otherwise locks up.

Agency

The use of agency augments the scope of action. Agency provides one standard path to control which can build up into organization and formal network. Agency is primordial, however; it is not just an aspect of management in formal organization.[6] Elites, including what today we call executives, spend much of their efforts second-guessing and heading off cumulative effects of agency mechanisms in social networks at large. "Rationality" comes to be understood, at least by elites, as a rhetorical weapon, a device for getting agencies lined up enough to be more readily manipulated.[7] Much of the literature on problems of management can be reframed as networking puzzles of agency and thereby boiled down and made more tangible.

Agency presupposes an identity and its at least partial reproduction elsewhere, so the enactment of agency entails sharing and diluting identity. Between the identity and agent, both mutual trust and authoritative differences are assumed. Agency induces additional agency in a chain reaction, emerging as further levels of social organization.

Within economics there is a vogue for "agency theory," but it is construed in such fashion as to be yet another avenue for economists' retreat from the complexities of embedding (Granovetter 1989, and in this volume): Jensen and Meckling (1976), for example, boast that neither markets nor firms need be distinguished, since economic reality is simply a nexus of contractual relations—a field of pair ties!—as opposed to being networks embedded in social organization. Such a nexus is easier to make fade away than are articulated contexts like the Cyert firm, the Chamberlin market or even the Walrasian auction (see Smith 1989; White 1981, 1989; Leifer 1985). As Powell shows (1990), even business organized in loose collegial and coalitional network forms—itself a resurgence from earlier times (Kriedte et al. 1981)—is not at all a mere aggregation of various sorts of ties. The new agency theory in economics outdoes even the neoclassical synthesis of microeconomics in its retreat from institutional reality.[8] The historic term "agency" should not be surrendered to this vogue; certainly the use here is closer to the established legal uses in business (see Macneil 1978; White 1985:187–188).

Agency and Delegation

Agency is to be mapped in terms of social networks. The mapping is of connections that imply still other connections in ways that are only partially and differentially understood within that population. Agency proper involves one person to do something on behalf of another person vis-à-vis third person(s). Delegation, a special case of agency, requires another person to require yet another—and still more—to carry out the intentions of principal(s). Through its sheer familiarity, delegation makes a comfortable explanation, but conceptualizing how delegation works is difficult. Agency proper, being about specific, less diffuse ties, is easier to theorize. They differ in realization and visibility as network.

Within the management process, delegation is a key constituent in which a tie to an actor predicates further ties established by and through that actor as an intermediary. Thus, along with an authoritative difference, some degree of trust is assumed and granted across an individual tie of delegation. Over time, with its repetition and spread of ties into strings, delegation induces intricate levels of social organization and strata of prestige.

These further levels and strata, these further embeddings, need not continue to be transparent to initial delegations. Ultimate agents may have little visibility. Delegation is not a self-similar process.[9] Effective control is oblique to the public and heralded processes of delegation, and getting control may be a self-similar process.

Efforts to extend control underlie both agency and delegation. Agency as a construct is more neutral with respect to status and more focused than delegation. Agency is more concerned with behavior—and less concerned with stories about behavior.[10]

Agency and delegation may be explicitly construed in network terms. An agent has a relatively discrete tie with a principal, who need not take entire responsibility for—or the whole attention of—the agent. An agent is not in the exclusive domain of one principal, but is also available for other principals. Each tie, however, will concern a domain of particular specialized matters. Thus the agent can become a funnel of access from assorted principals to elsewhere and thereby can gain considerable measure of control; this control may be only in a specialized line, but the control will multiply to the extent the agent holds many principals over many specialized lines. Conversely, principals may have many distinct specialized concerns, and each principal may call on different agents to serve these concerns. A pattern of agency specialization results and may even become formalized in distinct units. This can be called horizontal specialization.

Delegation, by contrast, implies and evokes a string or chain of ties. In such a chain, each subsequent intervening node receives agency in a subordinate mode and then sends agency in a dominant mode, with each successive link having as its concern increasingly more specialized matters. Delegation will thereby tend to include a range of subject matters in various configurations. Each tie will be multiplex. A subordinate tends to be touched by a chain longer than that reaching a person at the top. Call this vertical specialization.

The sequential order in which agency and delegation are concatenated will turn out to be crucial for control outcomes. Academics should be able to illustrate this with some examples from higher administration in their own university: Say a melding of separate faculties is bruited. Existing deans and faculties struggle against it. The president tells one story, the provost tells a different story about implementation. One story is told to an incoming super-dean, the other to a key new dean of an existing faculty. A mess results. Delay and more delay intrudes. The result is simply adding the bruited reorganization on top of the existing partition. Control from the top echelon is enhanced, and within that so is the president's control. But control is not a zero-sum game, and there is a further increment in corporatist strength of an overall faculty heretofore partitioned. A dual hierarchy will result for now. The order of agency and delegation was the key.

Specialization and Centralization

A degree of centralization is one outcome of struggles for control.[11] Centralization implies specialization in the background behind the hierarchy of ranks. Specialization induces some sort of centralization for coherent action, and together they induce larger scale of organization. One must deal with successively larger organizations, as the embedding levels within which agency by delegation continue to be affected. Thus specialization enters as another partially independent input to organization as process. Because the general argument is about varieties of organization, it must deal anyway with identity formations, which include specializations. Alternative specializations, like alternative delegations, become turf in contests for control among managers.

Specialization and centralization can be seen as alternating strategies for achieving external control via boxing-in networks of agency seeking autonomy. But strategies always can be read and adapted by their objects. So specialization and centralization as a pair also are used in efforts at corporatism and departmentalism, which are concerted efforts to evade external control.

For example, the history of Renaissance Florence (cf. Najemy 1982) was an alternation between efforts by middling men to partition the civic life[12] by guilds and thus obviate external control, and countering efforts by elites using their more extensive and varied circles. The elites, as Najemy's title informs us, invoke the idiom of consensus, their counterpart to present-day management's idiom of order. In our own day, Chandler's account (1969) of the rise of the multidivisional form is a parallel to Najemy's account of Florentine politics. Chandler traces a thrust toward functional departments by middling specialists and then illustrates how that thrust was followed by a riposte from corporate elites, who tore up an opaque partition by specialty in favor of arbitrary, parallel divisions.

Agency proper, leading to subsequent delegation, is what generates involute specialization. The delegation thereupon evolves and closes up on itself. By contrast, delegation made first, with efforts to oversee dependent agencies resulting, is the path to retaining centrality of control and dual hierarchies.

Interpretive Aspects

There are three independent interpretive moments of organization phenomena. The first is a control perspective, already initiated. The other two are rational interpretation and identity formation, which bracket specialization. Rationality and identity are so much about perception and interaction that we can turn for additional help to interpretive techniques such as discourse analysis (Cicourel 1970).

There is a logical and elocutionary aspect to specialization as social discourse, but accurate interpretation requires expansion of the ostensible meanings through their embeddings.[13] Discourse can be understood competently only when allowance is made for the strategies—as well as the less explicit schemas—that actors bring to the situation. These realities of everyday social life are also realities of organizational specialization and of delegation, both of which are easily obfuscated by hierarchic formulas.[14]

Organizational process is slippery, and when it looks as if in the midst of so much untidiness there can be no control, this very slipperiness offers the means by which real control can be momentarily grasped. Within organizations, control is subject to special reflexive difficulties. In both formal and informal perceptions of organization, the actors involved must remain mystified about some aspects of control for it to be effective.[15]

Bodin marks a turning point, an explicit recognition of organization achieved, by asking a new question: "What is a state and how is it constructed?" Bodin thus displaced older questions about who are the rulers and what are their powers. But uncovering underlying control processes must be effected afresh, time after time, by each executive as his own Bodin. Progress in the theory of organization requires that control be reconstrued in order to reduce the mystifications behind which it hides. Struggles for control are the sources of organization, including the formal organization in all its guises. Effective management is more a matter of riposte than of repetition.

PROPOSITIONS AND CASE STUDIES

The general argument can be restated briefly. It is that agency and delegation lead to specialization via mechanisms that in part become constructions of corporatism that escape management control.[16] Control in formal networks is attempted through a proper mesh of agency with delegation. Control is escaped exactly during the public proclamation of hierarchies of delegation.

The present chapter examines particular ways to achieve effective management both during and after the emergence of countering patterns of corporatism.[17] This section lays out propositions, the next section takes an action perspective on them, and the subsequent section takes an institutional perspective through the phenomena with which the propositions deal.

Some nuances of the definitions need be specified before they can be used to make explicit computations. Eventually, explicit modeling of endemic struggles over control among formal network contexts will be required.[18] Such modeling is beyond the scope of this reconnaissance, which can only partially fill in the general argument, illustrate it with cases, and then conjecture a set of propositions.

The propositions concern management efforts to regain or enhance control, given existing patterns of agency and delegation that reproduce some partition in specializations that counters control despite permitting a degree of centralization:

1. Delegation always plays off pre-existing delegations—the historicity of organization.
2. Use of agency for control requires direct intervention.
3. Within this direct intervention, specialization is shunned.
4. Direct intervention is coupled with subdelegation.
5. Public secrecy goes with internal openness.
6. The resulting patterns are self-concealing; in particular, any lasting significance is discounted publicly.

These propositions are consistent with some social science theories of "power" in organization (see Clegg 1979), but they are closer to operational, and to the sophistication of elites. Together the propositions mean that contextualization must be joined to contingency effects (Pfeffer and Salancik 1978) for sound analysis of the struggle for control via agency and delegation. Another way to put it is that transactional analysis (Williamson 1975) can be effective only when specified within relations, relations that embed across levels.[19]

Case Study as Probe

It is all too easy to view the preceding six propositions in cross-sectional terms. Case studies, besides providing evidence, can induce sequential interpretation by providing depth in time.[20] Also vital is the fact that a case study can provide sufficiently varied material to permit the development of images not brought to the scene by the observer.

The eventual aim is models of control, and timings are as much part of network control as are topology and interpretation. More than a generation ago, Jacques (1956) singled out time span in his studies of control, but he missed the asymmetry in timing as seen from two sides, controller and controlled. Furthermore, he missed how actual social scales of time are not synchronous between contexts. They are not synchronous between one and another corporatist cell, much less among them and higher administration fractions.

On the present view of control, the case study format is indispensable to capturing and correlating the timing weft and the structural-context warp for weaving control. Robert Alford's plaints about chaos, in his field study of the New York City medical smorgasbord (1975), triggered the original version of this paper. He captured the complexities of delegation and agency in this vast professional sprawl. But Alford was offended by what seem to me to be exactly the prerequisites to gaining any control: namely, shake-ups and some chaos and consequential jumblings of senses of time. Some organization glorying in order seemed a fit setting for a principal case study. Alford's study triggered the present paper, but there is no achievement in uncovering chaos in his case! At this same time there came to hand the commentary by Otto Hintze (1919) on Jean Bodin's pioneering of administrative history,[21] of the Absolutist State of France, which surely fit as a principal case.

Bodin was the first to notice the importance of the commissary, the "off-chart" agent of higher authority.[22] It is from this prototype bureaucracy that we can trace out how managing the large organization evolves and makes wide use of apparently special, temporary, ad hoc, irregular, or anachronistic delegation by agency. Bodin was the first to conceptualize the distinctiveness and usefulness of such commissions at an operative or action level.

Hintze, in seeing analogies in Bodin to Prussian War commissary roles, wove a broader institutional tapestry. Hintze showed how agent commissioners served as a lever for the evolution of whole institutional systems into new forms. Modern parallels both to Hintze's and to Bodin's approaches have been developed in the theory of business management by Chandler (1969) and by Vancil (1979), respectively, and it is no fluke that both authors rely principally on case studies.

A variety of other case studies can confirm and add nuances to the prototype cases of commissaries in Absolutist regimes. Katz (1988) follows up Chandler (1969) but for a later seizure of control within Sears, where a chief executive seems to consciously follow the six propositions. Consider Cuff (1973) on the intertwining efforts at control via agency by Bernard Baruch, by industry statesmen, and by professional military in the World War I War Production Board. A broad historical spectrum of studies, government as well as business, is appropriate to guard tests of the propositions against the parochialism possible in case studies.

HOW TO MANAGE AGENCY

The question is how to manage agency in order to enhance control. The six propositions are offered as an answer. As they become established and further specified, it should be possible to begin unraveling familiar puzzles about management practice.

The first argument is for the nonspecialization of agency (proposition 3 in the preceding section). A core task of agents from central authority— and a major occasion of exerting influence and control—is responding to jurisdictional disputes. This is responding exactly to other orders' problems of specialization, and such response tends to confound incipient specialization in the agents. Argument for the nonspecialization of agency fits Bodin's account. And subsequent to Bodin's time, the rapid evolution of agents for French royal absolutism illustrates the endless pressures that conspire to keep agents generalist in their concerns despite recurrent attempts to tidy them up via specialization of tasks (Anderson 1974:114).

In the parallel Prussian case, "The military commissary appeared simultaneously with the emergence of new mercenary armies as the supreme commander's appointed watchdog over his interests in all their varied forms. . . . Thus, military administration became inseparably entangled with civilian and police administration" (Hintze 1919:281). In France, officers with the title *intendant* early became attached to particular provinces, each of the scope of the whole early Prussian polity, but the same generality of delegation was evident. The whole congeries (cf. Moote 1971) of existing orders of offices, both provincial and central, fought against these extraordinary commissions. The fight was intense not least because of the latter's generality, because they did not pay specific fees to specific bodies for each of their specific actions. In Prussia, "The general institution of the commissaries developed as bearer of extraordinary powers of government, which broke through the established hierarchy of the old administrative system. . . . The actual war commissary is merely an important special type" (Moote 1971). A special type, yes, but exactly not specialized in a substantive bureaucratic sense.

Venality of office (open sale of salaried positions) spread through the Prussian and especially the French governments during these periods (Swart 1949). It is noteworthy that venality never touched the commissary-like agency, which, even though it was committed to delegation, stayed within commissaries themselves. A role that is not specialized cannot be demarcated, and thus it is not easily made fungible.[23]

Now take up two further features of agency operation, direct intervention and subdelegation, propositions 2 and 4. Both are central features by which to identify central agency amidst the welter of obscuring forms and claims for delegation of control. In addition to supervising, intendants intervened at will. Intendants could and did claim the chair of, and vote in, any agency or court on any matter at any time, and the activities of commissaries tended toward the same scope. I argue that this exercised power of direct intervention goes with and presupposes subdelegation.[24]

Pause to consider the contrast with the normal reproduction of hierarchical affairs, where "delegation" means little more than recognition of already institutionalized ties with their attendant rights and duties. Seen from within a resulting enclave, the ties are mutually generalized and disciplined. Seen from the center, the ties are specialized: this contradicts proposition 3 and is delegation as mere celebration; it amounts to abdication of control in deference to corporatist rights. Effective control from some center is always thrusting further delegation in through fresh enlistment of agents, so as to avoid specialization of agents.

Turn to a puzzle about current large business organizations, which case studies have shown likely to become more recalcitrant and refractory to executive control the longer they've been established.

   Puzzle: Should an executive, in getting action, seek out and follow along "corridors of indifference" among managers? Or must the executive, on the contrary, plunge into fields of conflict in order to harness the energies being released and to leverage from the positions taken there?

A lead to the solution may be in proposition 5, on convolutions of privacy in agency. Specialization is public. Control is private. Agency is for delegation of control to cut through and across specialization, exactly because of the endless pressures from below to specialize. And, beginning with Bodin as first theorist, the importance and distinctiveness of privacy for effective agency has been noted. The privacy, of course, goes hand in hand with subdelegation, as well as with lack of specialization. Together they are essential to the flexibility of agency for delegation.

This privacy is in sharp contrast with the public character of the mass of ongoing, intentional, and systematic organization that agency attempts to control. A public character is necessary to the mass of organization, government, business, and so on, because jurisdiction is exactly concerned with public claim (cf. Abbott 1988). These are claims of rights and of obligations versus other such claiming groups. These are claims of fee and of service vis-à-vis the broader society as well. One can even say that exactly in Bodin's Absolutist setting there was an obsession about jurisdiction among all fractions—guilds, corporate *parlements*, tax boards, and so on—although analogues continue within both business and government of France today (Crozier and Thoenig 1976; Suleiman 1987).

An ironic contrast obtains between organization, in its ordinary corporatist mode and ethos of jurisdictional claim, and agency for control taken together with delegation. The contrast is in their respective correlations of public/private with external/internal. Within the mass of organization there is much preoccupation with secrecy against peers. This is secrecy against one's own colleagues within a corporatist enclave. This internal secrecy goes hand in hand with the ostentatiously public character of claims to fee and jurisdiction against other corporate groups, against all comers, that epitomizes corporatist ethos.

On the other hand, it is exactly *within* the lines of agentry from a center asserting control that unusual frankness and openness of shared information is maintained. Lack of openness is the one unforgivable sin there. This internal openness accompanies the strict keeping of privacy vis-à-vis the mass of organization to be controlled. This pairing remains true in the modern era and in business contexts; see, for example, Corey (1978) on procurement agents.[25]

Counteragency

Management via agency is countered not only in detail, and not only through encrusted custom, but also more broadly in attempts at countermanagement. A vivid historical example of reaction-process against agency is the Frondé. This French "revolution" of the 1600s, in the century after Bodin, was made to an unusual degree by middling sorts, as distinct from noble and peasant.

Moote (1971) has shown definitively how the premier corporatist officialdom, the *parlements*, tried to overcome agency of the sorts described above, intendants and the like: "The greatest [paradox of the Frondé] being the fact that a body of royal officials dedicated to the enforcement of law and the principle of royal absolutism could rebel against the king's administration" (vii, xi). The singular article is inapt: even "the" *Parlement* of Paris was a complex of ten chambers that might only rarely meet together in plenary sessions. And it was meaningful only because it was part of a formal network of other regional, local, and specialized *parlements*, which in the modern idiom combined law with registration and legislation.

This *parlement* lattice itself was resilient to being rooted out because it was contraposed to other lattices that were more directly fiscal in operation. And each of these lattices also was intent on operationalizing meaning for its turfs and its members, as against even a "sun god" king. This king was invoked in their halls only to preside over their magisterial concordance of rights with rites.

Similar phenomena of counteragency can be seen in other old regimes in which reassertion of effective control is being attempted. Consider for example Ottoman Turkey, for which Findley (1980) has traced the process in detail over centuries. The broader context of agency and counteragency there concerns agriculture and the provinces.

The same logics of agency and counteragency play out in current large business organizations, which indeed is prime motivation for including these otherwise arcane cases from remote centuries and contexts. Pettigrew's study (1985) of the atrophy and attempted rebirth of Imperial Chemical Industries is such an example. Others are the Katz (1988) and Chandler (1969) case studies introduced earlier.

INSTITUTIONS AS CONTEXTS

Control can be achieved only by use of agency in some particular context. The operation of agency and delegation always have to be seen against a context, a context that is stable enough to be recognizable as an institution, yet is broader than formal organization. Conjectures about agency and delegation versus specialization are incomplete until they also cover how one or another context that can reproduce itself comes about.

Broader social formations are thereby invoked. This reintroduces issues of informal networks, such as the Small World. A scan of very diverse institutional realms and historical periods is even more apposite than before.

Key aspects of control by agency, interpreted in the six propositions, were first uncovered as operational truths within one special type of context. This is the dual hierarchy of commissariats versus regular military organizations. It exhibited itself first in France and later in Germany. A subsequent, rebellious phase of dual hierarchy in France, the Frondé, was discussed earlier.

Qualitative works on dual hierarchy in modern times also abound (e.g., Davis and Lawrence 1977; Schurmann 1968; Simirenko 1982). And it is possible to model such structures in quantitative and formal terms. For example, patterns of conflicts within dual hierarchies have been modeled by semilattices (Evans 1977, Friedell 1967, and see Boyd 1991). Dual hierarchy can be distinguished as an institution in its own right.

Delegation is essentially concerned with relationships and their continuity. Agency initially, and management in general, must be especially concerned with the limits and contents of transactions. Differences in patterns of delegation distinguish one institution from another and specify the context for agency and control.

For them to be found valid as operational principles, the six propositions must of course be consistent with a wide variety of larger institutional contexts. Dual or multiple hierarchies as an institution exhibit the many rigidities of delegation. Remote from them seem to be organizations demonstrating "garbage-can" process (Cohen and March 1974), which exhibits looseness in delegation, in timing, in issues, in short in all aspects of structure.

But garbage-can process is an aspect of any observable formal organization, for a rhetoric of orderly structure is one of the chief concerns in formal organization. Contexts in which garbage-can process is especially common may generate and also presuppose the same six propositions on agency and delegation as were found in dual hierarchies. One can see this, for example, from Padgett's (1980) empirical descriptions and models of federal government budgetary processes. It may be true also in the new institution emerging in international business.[26]

The basic proposition about institutions as contexts can be rephrased as a familiar metaphor. Governance as delegation is primarily a matter of peeling existing onions rather than of planning and growing new layers. Layering does not come from attempts at control. On the contrary, the piling up of layers and induction of embedded levels with distinct identities amounting to the growth of an institution, are vertical products of competing horizontal thrusts among corporatist claims to jurisdiction and fee (cf. Kellett 1958 as an example from the Bodin era).

The Propositions in Context

The first claim, proposition 1, may be a tautology. Historicity is the central feature of formal organization. This is no statement about societies, but rather about workaday organizations in state, business, commerce, and the like (Hannah 1983). It is also a claim that the ultimate reality of bureaucracy is that it is never "created" (Fligstein 1985, 1990). All organizing is the attempted weaving together of bits and hunks of preexisting organization, preexisting not only to disappear into a merged form. There are continuing overlays of guild/craft forms and other local jurisdictions, as in modern profession with bureaucracy. Organization is a matter of population and predecessors and cross-cutting forms (Di-Maggio and Powell 1983; Stinchcombe and Heimer 1985).

Management through agency has the business of dehistoricizing.[27] To supply some control, agency must neutralize the overwhelmingly tangible historical concreteness of organization. Agency is built up and invoked to pierce into some refractory mass of "organizationing" (Mitnick 1980).

Agency darts from this level here to that level there just because stratification evolves on grounds other than control of the congeries (Schwartz 1976). The contrast is clearest in the most corporatist form of organization, seen nowhere so perspicuously as in the *ancien regime* of France, especially when seen in a formation under maximum stress. Consider also in modern times our court system, a fossil remnant of *parlements*, centered around fee and transaction and yet famous for rigidity of delegation.

Other claims can be made about institutions as contexts for delegation that on a broader scale parallel those made in the previous section about managing via agency across delegation to control specialization. The six propositions apply again, but as seen from an external perspective.

Rather than continuing with these propositions on counters to counterorganizing, let us turn to conjectures about dynamics in initial organizing. The order in which delegation and agency devolve once again becomes central. Just as the French Absolutist State is a fitting principal study for tactical analysis, so is the largest and oldest organization in the West a fitting principal subject for strategic analysis.[28]

Missionary Outreach

Christianity emerged out of a process begun by encounters between preexisting Judaic sects, baptismal and Pharisaic (cf., e.g., Flusser 1988; Schoeps 1969; Segal 1986). The doctrinal aspects were of great importance, but there was another side, a nuts-and-bolts of building organization. I argue that doctrine, its existence, and its change as a structure of values, is intertwined always both with formal networks and with ranks as formed among localities.[29] Early leaders, from Paul through the Church Fathers, could be eminently practical organizers while at the same time deeply concerned with doctrine.

Study of conflicts in this eruption of missionary Christianity, like my earlier examination of conflicts in the French Absolutist monarchy, is a guide to current organizational realities. The embedding reemphasized is not unlike that for current business organization seen as the solution to a problem in marketing as much as of one in production, as Chamberlin (1933) urged in a now-neglected classic. Then, as now, the population being marketed was mobile, yet contained strong fissures and a complex locale for formal networks.[30]

The Pauline mission style permitted feedback between doctrine and the pattern of network and ranking. There could be a spiral of intensification leading to relapse and split. Such a formation invites attempts by organizational entrepreneurs to contrive further explicit social pattern, what we call formal organization. The early church was the result.

I conjecture a correlation between value changes and changes in formal organization. Heresies are where there is a serious divergence in explicit doctrine, which reflects the structure of values. Schism, on the other hand, comes from *agreement* on values. Analogous distinctions should be drawn in current organization marketing.

Heresies engender new organizational devices, and indeed the list of early Christian heresies—Gnosticism (Grant 1966), Arianism (Newman 1876), Priscillianism, and so on—is also a list of successive organizational devices installed, from apostolic succession and bishoprics on through the first Council of the whole Church. When doctrinal disagreement is sufficiently reduced, on the other hand, ethnic and political control and agency attempts may coalesce in such a way as to blow the social formation into separate fragments. Schism results, a clear pattern in the early Church.[31]

Focus now, quite apart from religious values, on how delegation, agency, and specialization played out. Christianity spread principally and normally, though not exclusively, through the planting of congregations, which are local groups that evolved into what we call churches. Control over the missionary movement was in tension with self-reproduction of local congregations.

Here are assessments of three successive periods of development. First:

> Wandering charismatics were the decisive spiritual authorities in the local communities, and local communities were the indispensable social and material basis for the wandering charismatics. Both owed their legitimation and existence to their relationship to the transcendental bearer of revelation. It was the homeless wandering charismatics who handed on what was later to take independent form as Christianity . . . the local groups of sympathizers remained within the framework of Judaism . . . entangled in the old situation. . . . Wandering prophets and teachers were still the decisive authorities at the time of the Didache (in the first half of the second century). . . . Their superiors were still the "apostles," who were allowed to stay no more than three days in one place. All these wandering charismatics had a higher reputation than local ministers . . . (Theissen 1982:7).

Then an intermediate period:

> The pre-Nicene bishop is, indeed, in a singular sense "the man" of his own Church—its priest, offering its corporate sacrifice . . . and the minister, in person or by delegation, of all sacraments to all its members. . . . He is the creator of lesser ministers; its representative to other Churches; the administrator of its charity; the officer of its discipline; the centre of its unity; the hub of its whole many-sided life, spiritual and temporal, inward and outward. There were then no retired bishops . . . no translations from see to see . . . [the latter] was denounced by a long series of councils (including Nicaea) as a sin, often actually classed with adultery. . . . This insistence upon God's choice and empowering of the bishop is found at its strongest in just those authors who emphasize most strongly the necessity for his election by his own church. . . . Until 315, presbyter is rooted for life in his (city) Church; but then rapid growth splits City into parishes. And against all declamations the clergy become in fact moveable. . . . Thus become "priests," and sacerdotally like the bishop. But it kills their corporate power as a presbytery. Whereas the bishop, who had been almost purely sacerdotal, now is deciding policy in *his* corporate group, the synod (Dix 1947:198).

Finally, with the beginning of a recognizably Catholic Church:

> Thus the way was opened to the reckoning of the bishop's "succession" not through his episcopal predecessors but through his episcopal consecrators. It was only a novelty in that it emphasized a different set of pre-existing facts: . . . The episcopate has become not a function in the Church but something personal to a man, received simply by the laying on of the hands of others who personally possess it . . . Augustine's theology . . . conceives of a (priestly) order almost exclusively with reference to the individual who exercises it. . . . The idea that the various "orders" were a series of "promotions," each "order" containing within itself, so to speak, the powers of all those "below" it, begins to come only in the second half of the fourth century. . . . This introduction of the principle of "hierarchy" in place of that of an "organ-

ism" is important in its effects . . . it completes the destruction of the idea of the ministry of each local Church as an organic whole . . . it opens the possibility of a clerical "career" by a regular succession of "promotions." . . . Such a view would have been impossible to hold but for the virtual breakdown of the old, jealously corporate notion of the local Church and its local ministry during the two preceding generations (Dix 1947:212–213, 284, 286).

Thus the evolution of the bishop can provide a tracer for probing the evolution of organization that eventuated in the Catholic Church. The bishop at first was merely what we call today the priest, but this was already a revolution for the Pauline missionary formation. In the latter, sacerdotal authority was with the traveling apostle, not in the locally rooted authority. The bishop-priest rolled the two authorities into one. That was key in helping to contain, as well as generate, doctrinal disagreement and confusion. The bishop could define purity and holiness, and yet he was rooted.[32]

There is a basic split between appointment to office, a Greek and Roman concept of public service, and ordination (laying of hands) needed for performance of worship, that is strictly Judaic. This interacts with a second split, between rooted local and mobile general, which impacted the specification of authority. For example, in Dix's words: "James of Jerusalem also seems to have exercised apostolic authority over a whole region, Palestine, and not over the church of the holy city alone . . . [whereas] in the earlier epistles of St. Paul, . . . apparently any apostle can exercise authority in any Church" (1947:230).

What we see is a playing out of agency and delegation. The order in which the two are carried out has major implications for control possibilities. As of 400 A.D. the product became a compromise between predominance of one or the other. As we found earlier, specialization was the key intervening counteraction: in this case, specialization into localities, into congregations. The resulting church proved labile under later strong searches for Papal control (see Berman 1983).

> It is the final result of the adjustment to one another of two originally distinct institutions, the *shaliach* with his personal commission from our Lord himself of a quite undefined scope, and the *zequenin* with a collegiate not a personal authority, for specific purposes with a local society. . . . In the second century they are roughly adjusted by the "localization" of an apostolate within each presbytery . . . into the fourth century, when. . . . The apostolate in turn reacts upon the local presbytery within which it has been functioning for two centuries. . . . It is this fourth century church which has perpetuated itself in Catholic Christendom (Dix 1947:286).

There can be self-similarity over time scope (Abbott 1983) as well as over organization scope. The profile of centuries of church evolution can be seen in the evolution of decentralization of firm and market over some decades.

CONCLUSION

Specific organization, bureaucracy, is meaningless without context, which consists in an institution structured by formal networks. Hintze avoided saying what his editor Gilbert glibly asserts: "It is evident that Hintze's study tried to understand and explain the genesis of a strictly hierarchical centralized administration, independent of popular representation, without self-government" (1919:267). Strictly hierarchical central administration is buncombe. There never was such a thing. The actuality underlying such rhetoric is always embeddings of organization. Nor are commissary—and agency in general—temporary expedients on the way to some tidy, centralized order. On the contrary, they are endemic within any system of organization.

Institutions are hard to change. The very mechanisms of agency and delegation on which one seeks to draw will turn into serpents beneath one's hand. One must expect and allow for that if one is to have some impact, if one is to achieve control through agency.

Agency as control is an endless process of end-running in formal networks. Using agency means cutting into and around the sprawling congeries of bits and pieces that is what real organizations are, everywhere and whenever (Chandler and Daems 1980). The six propositions can be gathered together in several ways to suggest overall operational claims. The principal one is that control by agency, far from seeking orderly hierarchy, seeks and glories in mix-ups and shake-ups (Eccles 1985; Hawley 1969; Vancil 1979).

Return to the case study that triggered this chapter, Alford's (1975) account of New York City health politics. He describes a reality that is part of a new, nonprofit order of organization (cf. Powell and Friedkin 1987) in this society. But then, after this excellent description, Alford misses the main point, at least according to my analysis. He is blinded to efficiency and the like by the rhetoric of tidy organization.

Alford says there has been an endless procession of special commissions and investigations and partial reorganizations among the hospitals and related health providers of the city, enmeshed as they are with federal and state interventions to a variety of private networks of control and fundings on top of a city network. Indeed altogether a "formal network" in my sense. Alford just assumes that the outcome of this mess is nothing much. But those in control, who may be a shifting posse hard to identify, have proceeded in reasonably effective fashion—if their animus was to shake up an ossified medical system.

The existing medical satrapies may be under the impression that "reform" has been stymied by their efforts. But that will occur exactly when reform may in fact have begun to succeed. Whereas if efforts at change had all been made out front, tidily and in public, then for sure there would have been only cosmetic change.

In New York we see just an endless succession of "commissaries" being sent out in ways that are confusing from the public's perspective.

These commissaries are delegated to tweak and poke and hop around among the existing congeries of organizations. Some taxing and fiscal practices are in fact changed. If Alford's study had been repeated a decade later, it would have dawned on the higher-ups that their system really had moved some, despite apparent chaos and blocking. The system has moved in ways they did not want, ways they probably thought they had stalled and stonewalled.

Control by agency, far from requiring order, presupposes and induces some stripe of disorder. This is disorder with respect to the autochthonous corporatist forms that endlessly spin and respin themselves in a context of continuing fraternal strife (Leifer and White 1986). Delegation through active agency does not fight such disorder, but rather presupposes and operates on it, partly by exacerbating it (cf. Ashford 1982:376; Padgett 1980). Control by agency in formal networks does not generate tables of organization; rather, it induces crescive forms.[33]

Words can deceive us. We speak aptly of "organizing" as an ever-fresh process when applied to social movements and community activism. But "organizing" somehow has tended to become frozen in aspic when we consider "serious" organization, when we turn to business and government. Then the terms used shift toward passive mode and architectural tone, toward hierarchy, except in the most acute studies, such as Brady's (1933) realistic portrayal of prewar German industrial ordering in cartels.

Organizations involve complex layerings and embeddings, true, but we need to remind ourselves how fresh and slippery organizations really are as processes, beneath even the most staid exteriors. Organization consists not in a structure but in some minimal rate of change of structure. Show me a fixed network structure of organization and I'll demonstrate to you that it is slipping out of the rational control set up by the initial scheme.

Notes

1. Eccles and Crane (1988) write of the "network nature" of "self-designing organizations"; Powell (1990) surveys a variety of analyses for "emerging network" forms of organization.
2. See the chapters on networks in biotechnology in this volume.
3. Similar and related canvasses have been reported elsewhere (Abbott 1988; Alford 1975; Anderson 1974; Ashford 1982; Brady 1933; Eccles 1981, 1985; Eccles and Crane 1988; Eccles and White 1987, 1988; Leifer and White 1986; Stinchcombe and Heimer 1985; White 1985, 1992a, 1992b).
4. Udy (1970) gives a vivid characterization of this as a general process in work organizations, and he supplies extensive evidence.
5. Bodin was a man of affairs who, consonant with the social infrastructure of his times, began as a monk but, after narrowly escaping being burned at the stake, in 1547 moved to the law and later to parliamentary activity (Tooley 1967:viii).
6. Agency is a term of ordinary discourse about which the dictionary can instruct us: "**agency** . . . 3. the business of any person, firm, etc., empowered to act for another." See White (1985) for historical development of this construct.

7. Pareto long ago insisted on this basic truth (see, e.g., Finer 1966).
8. A great deal *can* be achieved within the neoclassical synthesis from precise dissection of contingencies for incentives in pair ties (cf. Spence and Zeckhauser 1971): such detailed level is where neoclassical notions can be effective.
9. Abbott (1990) explicates and applies this term for social science. If rocks have the same size distribution as do pebbles, and as in turn does sand, we have a self-similar process in nature.
10. Theory for this is laid out elsewhere (White 1992b). The processes of delegation and their conundrums are construed as interaction effects of identity with agency. Identities are emergents that are induced from fluctuations and mismatches in physical and social flows among already existing social actors. Identity and agency interact to generate delegation, with its whole rationalist train of sets of stories available for argument and explanation. Krackhardt (in this volume) can be interpreted in these terms.
11. Brass and Burkardt, in this volume, survey a number of alternative measures of centralization.
12. It would be an anachronism to impose our differentiation of civic into political, economic, and social realms.
13. These embeddings can be developed as expansions into role interpretations (cf., e.g., Gross, Mason, and McEachern 1958), such as are routinely made in ordinary live interaction.
14. Najemy is lucid on the role of stratagems in his study of Florence, Chandler less so. Hamilton and Biggart (1985) comment on the modern situation.
15. Under the heading Agency and Delegation, getting control was argued to be a self-similar process. This suggests using homely experiences—even of childhood and nuclear family—to explore conjectures on control in the large. In what dual hierarchies were you embedded as a child? How do you, or your parents, catenate agency and delegation in ordering your children's lives?
16. The term "corporatism" is currently discussed primarily in political science (e.g., Chalmers 1985, Goldthorpe 1984, Lehmbruch and Schmitter 1982), but when applied to business organization it encapsulates the ideas of Udy (1970) and Vancil (1979).
17. Apparently quite distinct from management is elite control amidst the interaction of social classes across a whole social formation. Ideology plays a greater role, as do devices of insulation. Najemy gives a marvelous dissection of one such situation, Renaissance Florence, which has been particularly well studied.
18. Such approaches include "blockmodels" of multiple networks—see Boyd (1991), Romo (1992), and White, Boorman and Breiger (1976) for theory and see Baker (1987), Krackhardt (1988), and Walker (1985) for recent business application. Wellman and Berkowitz (1988) survey other models of structural equivalence—see Burt 1992—as well as blockmodels, and models of network manipulation—see Burt in this volume.
19. These propositions do contradict much of the theory of agency in existing textbooks that propound a mythical "organization tree" of delegation. Fayol (1916) originated this myth and seduced others to it. The origin was part of a flurry of efforts to bring engineering to bear on social organization. This flurry, which spread as far as the Soviet Union (Bailes 1978), became known as the technocratic movement.
20. Becker and Ragin (1992) provide a survey of the case study form.
21. Forget the Bodin who was the grand theorist of sovereignty. See Franklin (1973).
22. See Book III, 1606 English translation (1962), Chapter 2. As he went on to develop the theory of magistrature in general, Bodin made it out that the

commissary was a crude remnant of an even cruder past, soon to disappear. Little did he know!

23. In the next section this is argued as crucial also for the institutional effectiveness of agency.

24. For further evidence on Prussia, see Rosenberg (1958:47). For evidence from analogous contexts see Bearman (1985) on Tudor administration. For the institutional realm of business, consult Eccles (1981) on the modern construction business and Vancil (1979) on manufacturing.

25. In Asia, idioms of privacy may differ enough to vitiate this statement, but the Lincoln and McBride (1987) survey of networks in Japanese organizations finds considerable comparability with Western organizations: and see, in this volume, Biggart and Hamilton as well as Gerlach and Lincoln.

26. See, for example, Nohria and Ghoshal (1991) on segregation of new specialized networks.

27. See Stinchcombe (1965) on the depth of this challenge.

28. Whether strategic or tactical, the analysis remains focused on network realizations dealing with social classes so that it does not reach sociopolitical policy on a macro level. Such policy may allow for and subsume agency considerations: an example is Bismarck's encysting of the German working class, as elucidated by Roth (1963).

29. Elsewhere (White 1992b, 1993) I label these intertwinings "styles," and argue that each style is so locked in that styles can change only through turbulent overlay of one upon another.

30. Turbulent overlays of persons and groups were characteristic of the network of cities that constituted Asia Minor and the Syriac region for these evolving sects. In modern terms we would refer to the people involved as lower middle class, often artisans, become strangers to peasant life and tribal contexts. For centuries there had been a diaspora of an older form of religion among Hebrews across these cities. Associated on the fringes were God-fearing Gentiles, who did not fully partake of the behavior proscriptions and prescriptions or the orientation to a single central site in Jerusalem. Christianity retained its motivation by balancing its inclusiveness with a powerful exclusivism generated by the covenant conception. Like Judaism, Christianity booked no competitors, even the Jews.

31. It is one which continues through the Donatist schism (Frend 1952) down through the last great schism, between Orthodox and Roman (Meyendorff 1966).

32. Two fixed points of the emerging Church doctrine were one bishop for one city, and anathema on the translation of a bishop from one city to another (Lebretton and Zeiler 1944).

33. "Crescive," Professor Nohria suggests, "is a geological metaphor, of new formations being thrown up by the collision of tectonic plates beneath the surface. New visible structures are thus shaped by subterranean forces. The parallel in social organization are networks and control, the former visible, the latter hidden. It is such a dynamic that I visualize when I read the term "crescive" (editorial communication, November 13, 1990).

References

Abbott, Andrew. 1983. "Sequences of Social Events: Concepts and Methods for the Analysis of Order in Social Processes". *Historical Methods* 16:129–147.

———. 1988. *The System of Professions.* Chicago: University of Chicago Press.

———. 1990. "Self-similar Social Structures." Working paper, Department of Sociology, Rutgers University.

Agnew, Jean-Christophe. 1986. *Worlds Apart: The Market and the Theater in Anglo-American Thought, 1550–1750.* New York: Cambridge University Press.

Alford, Robert R. 1975. *Health Care Politics*. Chicago: University of Chicago Press.

Anderson, Perry. 1974. *Lineages of the Absolutist State*. London: New Left Books.

Ashford, Douglas E. 1982. *British Dogmatism and French Pragmatism*. London/ Boston: Allen & Unwin.

Bailes, Kendall E. 1978. *Technology and Society Under Lenin and Stalin*. Princeton: Princeton University Press.

Baker, Wayne. 1987. "What Is Money? A Social Structural Interpretation." In Mark Mizruchi and Michael Schwartz, eds., *Intercorporate Relations: The Structural Analysis of Business*. New York: Cambridge University Press.

———. 1990. "Market Networks and Corporate Behavior." *American Journal of Sociology* 96:589–625.

Bearman, Peter. 1985. "The Eclipse of Localism and the Formation of a National Gentry Elite in England, 1540–1640." Ph.D. thesis, Department of Sociology, Harvard University.

Becker, Howard, and Charles Ragin, eds. 1992. *What Is a Case? The Logic of Social Inquiry*. New York: Cambridge University Press.

Berman, Harold J. 1983. *Law and Revolution: The Formation of the Western Legal Tradition*. Cambridge, MA: Harvard University Press.

Bodin, Jean. [1606] 1962. *The Six Books of a Commonweale*, Kenneth McRae, ed. Cambridge, MA: Harvard University Press.

Boorman, Scott A. 1975. "A Combinatorial Optimization Model for Transmission of Job Information through Contact Networks." *Bell Journal of Economics* 6:216–249.

Bott, Elizabeth. 1957. *Family and Social Network*. London: Tavistock.

Boyd, John P. 1991. *Social Semigroups: A Unified Theory of Scaling and Blockmodelling as Applied to Social Networks*. Fairfax, VA: George Mason University Press.

Brady, Robert A. 1933. *The Rationalization Movement in German Industry*. Berkeley: University of California Press.

Burt, Ronald S. 1992. *Structural Holes: The Social Structure of Competition*. Cambridge, MA: Harvard University Press.

Calabresi, Guido. 1970. *The Costs of Accidents: A Legal and Economic Analysis*. New Haven: Yale University Press.

Chalmers, Douglas A. 1985. "Corporatism and Comparative Politics." In Howard J. Wiarda, ed., *New Directions in Comparative Politics*. Boulder, CO: Westview, Ch. 4.

Chandler, Alfred. 1969. *Strategy and Structure*. Cambridge, MA: MIT Press.

Chandler, A. D., and Herman Daems, eds. 1980. *Managerial Hierarchies*. Cambridge, MA: Harvard University Press.

Cicourel, Aaron V. 1980. "Three Models of Discourse Analysis." *Discourse Processes* 3:101–132.

Clegg, Stewart. 1979. *The Theory of Power and Organization*. London: Routledge & Kegan Paul.

Cohen, Michael D., and J. G. March. 1974. *Leadership and Ambiguity: The American College President*. New York: McGraw-Hill.

Corey, E. Raymond. 1978. *Procurement Management*. Boston: CBI.

Crozier, Michel, and J. C. Thoenig. 1976. "The Regulation of Complex Organized Systems." *Administrative Science Quarterly* 21:547–570.

Cuff, Robert D. 1973. *The War Industries Board*. Baltimore: Johns Hopkins University Press.

Davis, Stanley, and Paul Lawrence. 1977. *Matrix*. Reading, MA: Addison-Wesley.

Delaney, John. 1988. "Social Networks and Efficient Resource Allocation: Job Vacancy Allocation Through Contacts." In Barry Wellman and S. D. Berkowitz, eds., *Social Structures: A Network Approach*. New York: Cambridge University Press, Ch. 16.

DiMaggio, Paul, and Walter W. Powell. 1983. "The Iron Cage Revisited: Institutional Isomorphism and Collective Rationality in Organizational Fields." *American Sociological Review* 48:147–160.

Dix, G. 1947. "The Ministry in the Early Church." In K. E. Kirk, ed., *The Apostolic Ministry*. New York: Morehouse-Gorham.

Eccles, Robert G. 1981. "The Quasifirm in the Construction Industry." *Journal of Economic Behavior and Organization* 2:335–57.

———. 1985. *The Transfer Pricing Problem: A Theory for Practice*. Lexington, MA: Lexington Books.

Eccles, Robert G., and Dwight B. Crane. 1988. *Doing Deals: Investment Banks at Work*. Boston: Harvard Business School Press.

Eccles, Robert G., and Harrison C. White. 1987. "Concentration for Control? Political and Business Evidence." *Sociological Forum* 1:131–158.

———. 1988. "Price and Authority in Inter-profit Center Transactions." *American Journal of Sociology* 94 (Supplement): S17–S51.

Edgerton, Robert B. 1985. *Rules, Exceptions and Social Order*. Berkeley: University of California Press.

Evans, Peter. 1977. "Multiple Hierarchies and Organization Control." *Administrative Science Quarterly* 11:364–385.

Fayol, Henri. [1916] 1984. *General and Industrial Management*. New York: IEEE Press.

Findley, Carter D. 1980. *Bureaucratic Reform in the Ottoman Empire*. Princeton: Princeton University Press.

Finer, S. E., ed. 1966. *Vilfredo Pareto: Sociological Writings*. New York: Praeger.

Fligstein, Neil. 1985. "The Multidivisional Form." *American Sociological Review* 50:377–391.

———. 1990. *The Transformation of Corporate Control*. Cambridge, MA: Harvard University Press.

Flusser, David. 1988. *Judaism and the Origins of Christianity*. Jerusalem: Magnes Press.

Foster, C. C., A. Rapoport, and C. Orwant. 1963. "A Study of a Large Sociogram." *Behavioral Science* 8:56–66.

Franklin, Julian. 1973. *Jean Bodin and the Rise of Absolutist Theory*. New York: Cambridge University Press.

Frend, W. H. C. 1952. *The Donatist Church*. Oxford: Oxford University Press.

Friedell, Morris. 1967. "Organizations as Semilattices." *American Sociological Review* 32:46–54.

Goldthorpe, John H. 1984. "The End of Convergence: Corporatist and Dualist Tendencies in Modern Western Societies." In J. Goldthorpe, ed., *Order and Conflict in Contemporary Capitalism*. New York: Oxford University Press.

Granovetter, Mark. 1973. "The Strength of Weak Ties." *American Journal of Sociology* 78:1360–1380.

———. 1974. *Getting a Job: A Study of Contacts and Careers*. Cambridge, MA: Harvard University Press.

———. 1978. "Threshold Models of Collective Behavior." *American Journal of Sociology* 78:1420–1443

———. 1982. "A Network Theory Revisited." *Sociological Theory* 1.

———. 1985. "Economic Action and Social Structure: The Problem of Embeddedness." *American Journal of Sociology* 91:481–510.

———. 1989. In Richard Swedberg, ed., *Economics and Sociology*. Princeton: Princeton University Press.

Granovetter, Mark, and Roland Soong. 1983. "Threshold Models of Diffusion and Collective Behavior." *Journal of Mathematical Sociology* 9:165–179.

Grant, R. M. 1966. *Gnosticism and Early Christianity*. New York: Columbia University Press.

Gross, Neal W., S. Mason, and A. W. McEachern. 1958. *Explanations in Role Analysis*. New York: Wiley.

Hamilton, Gary G., and Nicole W. Biggart. 1985. "Why People Obey." *Sociological Perspectives* 28:3–28.

Hannah, Leslie. 1983. *The Rise of the Corporate Economy: The British Experience*. Baltimore: Johns Hopkins University Press.

Hawley, Ellis W. 1969. *The New Deal; and the Problem of Monopoly*. Princeton: Princeton University Press.

Hintze, Otto. [1919] 1975. *The Historical Essays of Otto Hintze 1919*, Felix Gilbert, ed. New York: Oxford University Press.

Jacques, E. 1956. *Measurement of Responsibility*. London: Tavistock.

Jensen, Michael C., and W. H. Meckling. 1976. "Theory of the Firm: Managerial Behavior, Agency Costs, and Ownership Structure." *Journal of Financial Economics* 3:305–360.

Katz, Donald R. 1988. *The Big Store: Inside the Crisis and Revolution at Sears*. New York: Penguin.

Kellett, J. R. 1958. "The Breakdown of Gild and Corporation Control over the Handicraft and Retail Trade in London." *Economic History Review* X:381–394.

Kleinrock, Leonard. 1975–1976. *Queuing Systems*, Vol. 1 and 2. New York: Wiley.

Kochen, Manfred, ed. 1989. *The Small World*. Norwood, NJ: Ablex.

Krackhardt, David. 1988. "Predicting with Networks: Nonparametric Multiple Regression Analysis of Dyadic Data." *Social Networks* 10:359–381.

Kriedte, Peter, Hans Medick, and Jurgen Shlumbohm. 1981. *Industrialization before Industrialisation*. New York: Cambridge University Press.

Lebreton, Jules, and Jacques Zeiller. 1944. *A History of the Primitive Church*. London: Burns, Oates & Washbourne.

Leifer, Eric M. 1985. "Markets as Mechanisms: Using a Role Structure." *Social Forces* 64(2):442–472.

———, and Harrison C. White. 1986. "Wheeling and Annealing: Federal and Multidivisional Control." In James F. Short, ed., *The Social Fabric: Issues and Dimensions*. Beverly Hills: Sage.

Lehmbruch, G., and P. C. Schmitter, eds. 1982. *Patterns of Corporatist Policy-Making*. Beverly Hills: Sage.

Lincoln, James R., and Kerry McBride. 1987. "Japanese Industrial Organization in Comparative Perspective." In W. Richard Scott and James F. Short, eds., *Annual Review of Sociology* 13:289–313.

Macneil, Ian R. 1978. "Contracts: adjustment of long-term economic relations under classical, neo-classical and relational contract law." *Northwestern Law Review* 72:854–906.

MacPherson, C. P. 1962. *The Political Theory of Possessive Individualism*. London: Oxford University Press.

Meyendorff, John. 1966. *Orthodoxy and Catholicity*. New York: Sheed and Ward.

Mitnick, B. M. 1980. *The Political Economy of Regulation*. New York: Columbia University Press.

Mizruchi, Mark, and Michael Schwartz, eds. 1987. *Intercorporate Relations: The Structural Analysis of Business*. New York: Cambridge University Press.

Moote, A. Lloyd. 1971. *The Revolt of the Judges: The Parlement of Paris and the Frondé 1643–52*. Princeton: Princeton University Press.

Najemy, John M. 1982. *Corporations and Consensus in Florentine Electoral Politics, 1280–1420*. Chapel Hill: University of North Carolina Press.

Newman, John Henry. 1876. *The Arians of the Fourth Century*. London: Pickering.

Padgett, John F. 1980. "Managing Garbage Can Hierarchies." *Administrative Science Quarterly* 14:583–604.

Perrow, Charles. 1984. *Normal Accidents: Living with High-Risk Technology*. New York: Basic Books.

Pettigrew, Andrew. 1985. *The Awakening Giant: Continuity and Change in Imperial Chemical Industries*. Oxford: Basil Blackwell.

Pfeffer, Jeffrey, and Gerald Salancik. 1978. *The External Control of Organizations*. New York: Harper.

Powell, Walter W. 1990. "Neither Market nor Hierarchy: Network Forms of Organization." *Research in Organizational Behavior* 12:295–336.

Powell, Walter, and R. Friedkin, eds. 1987. *The Non-Profit Sector: A Research Handbook*. New Haven: Yale University Press.

Pratt, John W., and Richard Zeckhauser, eds. 1985. *Principals and Agents: The Structure of Business.* Boston: Harvard Business School Press.

Romo, Frank. 1992. *Moral Dynamics.* New York: Cambridge University Press.

Rosenberg, Hans. 1958. *Bureaucracy, Aristocracy and Autocracy: The Prussian Experience 1660–1815.* Cambridge, MA: Harvard University Press.

Roth, Guenther. 1963. *The Social Democrats in Imperial Germany: A Study in Working-Class Isolation and National Integration.* Totowa, NJ: Bedminster Press.

Schelling, Thomas C. 1978. *Micromotives and Macrobehavior.* New York: Norton.

Schoeps, Hans-Joachim. 1969. *Jewish Christianity: Factional Disputes in the Early Church,* D. R. A. Hare, tr. Philadelphia: Fortress Press.

Schurmann, F. 1968. *Ideology and Organization in Communist China,* 2d ed. Berkeley: University of California Press.

Schwartz, Michael. 1976. *Radical Protest and Social Structure.* New York: Academic Press.

Segal, Alan F. 1986. *Rebecca's Children: Judaism and Christianity in the Roman World.* Cambridge, MA: Harvard University Press.

Simirenko, Alex. 1982. *Professionalization of Soviet Society.* New Brunswick, NJ: Transaction Books.

Smith, Charles W. 1989. *Auctions: The Social Construction of Value.* New York: Free Press/Macmillan.

Spence, A. Michael, and R. Zeckhauser. 1971. "Insurance, Information and Individual Action." *American Economic Review* 61:380–387.

Stinchcombe, Arthur L. 1965. "Social Structure and Organization." In J. G. March, ed., *Handbook of Organizations.* Chicago: Rand-McNally.

Stinchombe, A., and C. Heimer. 1985. *Organization Theory and Project Management.* Bergen, Norway: Norwegian U. Press.

Suleiman, Ezra N. 1987. *The Notaries and the State.* Princeton: Princeton University Press.

Swart, Koenraad W. 1949. *Sale of Offices in the 17th Century.* The Hague: Nijhoff.

Theissen, Gerd. 1982. *The Social Setting of Pauline Christianity,* John Schutz, tr. Philadelphia: Fortress Press.

Tooley, M. J., ed. 1967. *Six Books of the Commonwealth, by Jean Bodin.* London: Oxford University Press.

Udy, Stanley. 1970. *Work in Traditional and Modern Society.* Englewood Cliffs, NJ: Prentice-Hall.

Vancil, Richard F. 1979. *Decentralization: Managerial Ambiguity by Design.* Homewood, IL: Dow Jones-Irwin.

Walker, Gordon. 1985. "Network Position and Cognition in a Computer Software Firm." *Administrative Science Quarterly* 30:103–130.

Wellman, Barry, and S. D. Berkowitz, eds. 1988. *Social Structures: A Network Approach.* New York: Cambridge University Press.

White, Harrison C. 1981. "Where do Markets Come From?" *American Journal of Sociology* 87:517–547.

———. 1985. "Agency as Control." In John W. Pratt and Richard Zeckhauser, eds., *Principals and Agents: The Structure of Business.* Boston: Harvard Business School Press, Ch. 8.

———. 1989. In Richard Swedberg, ed., *Economics and Sociology.* Princeton: Princeton University Press.

———. 1992a. "Cases are for Identity, for Explanation, and/or for Control." In Howard Becker and Charles Ragin, eds., *What Is a Case? The Logic of Social Inquiry.* New York: Cambridge University Press.

———. 1992b. *Identity and Control: A Structural Theory of Social Action.* Princeton: Princeton University Press.

———. 1993. "Values Come in Styles, Which Must Mate to Change." In M. Hechter and L. Nadel, eds., *Toward a Scientific Analysis of Values.,* New York: Cambridge University Press.

White, Harrison C., Scott A. Boorman, and Ronald L. Breiger. 1976. "Social Struc-
    ture from Multiple Networks: Part I. Blockmodels of Roles and Positions."
    American Journal of Sociology 81:730–780.
Williamson, Oliver E. 1975. *Markets and Hierarchies: Analysis and Antitrust Implica-
    tions.* New York: Macmillan.
Zald, Mayer, ed. 1970. *Power in Organizations.* Nashville, TN: Vanderbilt Univer-
    sity Press.

4

Nadel's Paradox Revisited: Relational and Cultural Aspects of Organizational Structure

PAUL DiMAGGIO

Social theory is all about relations among persons and groups, whereas sociological research usually depends on measures of persons' attributes and attitudes. Network analysis offers a structural alternative to standard research operating procedures, substituting direct measurement of the stuff of social interaction for reliance on problematic proxies.

Network analysis's structural emphasis is its great advantage. But I shall argue that, no matter how it tries, network analysis cannot, for two related reasons, be *purely* structural, if, by that, one refers to explanation based solely on formal modeling of social relations without reference to cultural and subjective aspects of action. First, it cannot do without a theory of action, a set of guiding assumptions about situated actors' orientations toward one another and the world. Second, because it must take account of the substance of cognition (role definitions, action-scripts, typifications, and so on, all of which I shall refer to loosely and interchangeably as "cultural," "cognitive," or "institutional" aspects of networks and role systems), it cannot dispense with data on actor attributes and attitudes.

The network tradition has been critical of data on attributes and attitudes for the right reasons, viewing the former as poor proxies for interaction patterns and the latter as weak and dubious indicators of people's internal states. I will argue that it may be more useful to look at them in a different way, treating *attributes as typifications* that may shape

For thoughtful comments on an earlier draft, I am grateful to Peggy Evans, Emmanuel Lazega, David Krackhardt, Nitin Nohria, the members of Yale's Complex Organization Workshop, and participants in the Harvard Graduate School of Business Symposium on Networks and Organizations.

the evolution of network structures, and treating *attitudes* and other cognitive elements (as revealed in interaction) *as accounting systems* that people use in deciding whether particular relations are worth starting up or maintaining.

After making a case for integrating cultural and relational analysis in the first two sections, I discuss the relevance of the argument to two research problems, one interorganizational (organizing under conditions of uncertainty) and one intraorganizational (the relationship between formal and informal organizational structures).

NADEL'S PARADOX AND THE PROBLEM OF CULTURE

The notion of roles—or, more precisely, status/role systems consisting of social positions (statuses) and stereotyped patterns of relations (roles) associated with those positions—looms large in the recent history of network analysis. Contemporary structural analysis has depicted statuses and roles as emerging out of patterned relations. By contrast, prior accounts of role systems emphasized *both* relational *and* cultural aspects. For Parsons, role relations comprise "classificatory criteria . . . which orient the actor to the object by virtue of the fact that it belongs to a universalistically defined *class*" and "relational criteria . . . by which the object as a particular object is placed in a specific significant *relation* to ego and thus to other significant objects" (1951:89).[1] Indeed, it is precisely because roles are the nexus at which culture (which Parsons in effect reduces to values and norms) and social relations intersect that they are central to Parsons' solution to the "problem of order."

Parsons usually wrote as if normative and relational aspects of role systems meshed rather easily. By contrast, his contemporary, S. F. Nadel (1957) found the duality of roles—the fact that they are simultaneously cultural typifications and patterns of concrete relationships—more troubling. Although Nadel is best known for pointing to the possibility of a formal mathematical approach to analyzing social relations as a basis for characterizing and comparing role systems, he also called attention to the cultural aspect of roles as "class concepts," including norms that exist in "bits of knowledge . . . or perhaps only in an image that people carry in their heads" (28). In order to compare role systems, Nadel believed, it is necessary to reduce role relations to a common metric. Yet roles "include qualities, and hence *differentiae* of an irreducible nature. . . . Each relationship contains unique features which render it incomparable to the others, offering nothing in the way of a common criterion or dimension." How then "can we extract . . . any embracing order while still paying attention to these qualitative characteristics?" (28).

This is *Nadel's Paradox*: A satisfactory approach to social structure requires simultaneous attention to both cultural and relational aspects of role-related behavior. Yet cultural aspects are qualitative and particular, pushing researchers toward taxonomic specificity, whereas concrete social relations lend themselves to analysis by formal and highly abstract methods.

Rather than pursue the problem Parsons sidestepped and Nadel identified, scholars influenced by each of the two focused on just one aspect of the duality. Functionalist role analysis hewed to the cultural and descriptive, enumerating roles and describing the norms that "governed" them. In describing roles, they tended to reify them: in practice, as Nadel pointed out, roles have core features and broad penumbras, the latter of which are neither unique nor required for "appropriate role performance." Descriptive role analysis rarely captured local variation in institutionalized patterns, or the improvised quality of performance that intrigued social constructionists. And, as Nadel argued, cultural analysis could not by itself move from description to comparison: functionalists provided many accounts, but few explanations.

By contrast, following Nadel, Harrison White and his colleagues introduced a formal mathematical approach to role systems in their classic papers on blockmodeling, developing methods for identifying statuses and the relations associated with them out of data on multiple relations among members of a population (White, Boorman, and Breiger 1976) and for comparing social structures (Boorman and White 1976). There is no question that, of the two approaches (normative and relational) to roles, the relational has been the more fruitful (DiMaggio 1986).

What I should like to focus on in that early work is the effort to create a structural sociology that is culture free, the implication that relational aspects of social structures can be studied formally in isolation from subjective or cultural understandings of the actors who populate them.[2] My inference from reading the early blockmodeling work is that the emphasis on relations to the exclusion of culture was in part tactical. That social structures—groups and positions and their relations—should be identified and characterized on the basis of social relations rather than cultural labels (categories or attributes) is the central insight. But the analytic utility of culturally embedded categories is left ambiguous. In an early blockmodeling paper, White (1973) noted that although affective ties are emphasized, "the approach encompasses impersonal and cognitive aspects of social structure." And White et al. (1976:733) acknowledged Nadel's paradox explicitly, but bracketed it for the purposes of that paper. However, claims were made for the purely structural character of blockmodeling: "The cultural and social-psychological meanings of actual ties are largely bypassed in the development" (White et al. 1976:734), to be "inferred from the pattern, in a given population, of all ties of that type" (740).

In other words, in addition to the indisputable insight that one should use relational data to operationalize concepts (statuses and roles) that are, by their nature, relational, one finds two rather different positions coexisting in the early work. The first calls for a pragmatic use of structural analysis, in combination with other kinds of data, as an indispensable means of capturing a global perspective on relational networks. The second contains a much more radical suggestion that structural analysis offers a self-sufficient means of analyzing social systems without recourse to meaning systems or culturally embedded categories.

It is this latter suggestion that is problematic for two reasons. First, culture could not be banished even from static, descriptive analyses of social structure: tossed out the front door, it returns through the back. Cultural understandings enter into blockmodeling in at least four respects (all illustrated in White et al. 1976): (1) the choice of ties on which to base blockmodels; (2) the use of vivid, highly connotative language to denote blocks ("hangers-on," "losers"); (3) the interpretation of blockmodels (on the basis of ethnographic accounts provided in research reports); and (4) the models' validation (including "assessing the homogeneity of persons in a position with regard to suitable characteristics") (770–771). Second, once one shifts—as much recent work has done—from comparative statics to microprocesses (e.g., networks as sources of constraint on behavior, origins of, or change in networks, etc.), one needs a framework of behavioral assumptions.

In fact, the early blockmodeling work—and a continuing tradition in network analysis—*does* have implicitly such a framework; or, at least, it bears an affinity to a perspective on action, associated with cognitive psychology and ethnomethodology, that is distinct both from rational-choice approaches and the Parsonsian tradition (with its voluntaristic emphasis on values and norms and its "as-if" depiction of discursively reasoning, although not instrumentally rational, actors).[3] In contrast to Parsonsianism, blockmodeling shares with ethnomethodology a radical realism (and an equation of the real with concrete social relations, although it conceives of these differently), and a view of culture (rules, attitudes, typifications, etc.) as a mystifying system of post hoc accounts used by actors to normalize or explain interaction rather than to shape it. In contrast to rational-choice models, blockmodeling, ethnomethodology, and cognitive psychology share a view of behavior as situated, frequently unreflective, and usually oriented reflexively to immediate local concerns rather than to long-range strategies.[4] To put it differently, if the cultural vocabulary of Parsonsian functionalism is one of values, norms, and attitudes, and of rational-choice models, interests, and strategies, the cultural vocabulary appropriate to the blockmodeling tradition in network analysis is one of typifications, scripts, systems of classification, and accounts.

The quest for a purely structural sociology inhibited both the development of explicit models of action based on such intuitions and the explicit theorizing of cultural dimensions of behavior. In the absence of an explicit approach to action, it was inevitable that something else would fill the void, and perhaps equally inevitable that the "something" would be rational-actor models, which are the most well-developed and tractable models of action that social scientists possess.

The most explicit and sophisticated effort to address this problem is

Ronald Burt's *Toward a Structural Theory of Action* (1982). Burt treats actors as rational, goal-oriented, utility maximizers, but brings in norms as interdependent utility functions reflecting actors' positions in social networks.[5] Social relations, then, place constraints on purely individualistic optimizing. Variants of this approach are evident as well in experimental work and simulation modeling (Marsden 1982; Cook et al. 1983).

Such models often treat network membership and the access of each member to relations with others as fixed, actors as having a keen sense of their utility functions, and information as either abundant or a resource to which access is constrained by existing relational networks (Burt 1982). Such assumptions permit the development of well-specified behavioral models, many of which have had substantial predictive success. Their greatest applicability is to stable networks under conditions of relatively high certainty. The assumptions may be approximated in market systems in which roles and interests are well institutionalized, rational organization widespread, and environmental change gradual (Burt 1983).

Such models may be least applicable to emergent systems in which the absence of culturally embedded statuses, roles, and norms makes actors particularly dependent upon informal networks, and the structure of such networks particularly consequential for the development of the field. In emergent organizational fields, or fields responding to rapid environmental or technological change, many of the assumptions of rational network models seem less applicable: the population of engaged actors is not fixed (although the population of potential actors may be); actors improvise to create new relations or modify old ones; actors have more or less free access to one another; uncertainty is high; and actors may have numerous objectives, or, where they do possess something like a working utility function, be so uncertain about how to maximize utility as to find goals poor guides to action.

To understand such uncertain, dynamic, and fluid systems, I suspect that one needs to substitute what one might call "practical-actor" for "rational-actor" models. The presuppositions of practical-actor models, which I have argued bear an affinity to those of one tradition in network analysis, derive from a mix of cognitive psychology, ethnomethodology, social constructionism, and contemporary theory (Bourdieu 1990; Collins 1981; Giddens 1984). In organizational sociology, the notion bears an affinity to (and has been influenced by) work in the Carnegie tradition and neoinstitutional theory (March and Simon 1958; Cyert and March 1963; Cohen and March 1974; Meyer and Rowan 1977; Zucker 1977, 1987).

Consistent with Parsonsian action theory, the practical-actor approach views rationality as only one, and rarely the principal, orientation to action, and takes much behavior to be highly conventional. It diverges from Parsonsian action theory in according less importance to the normative aspect of action, and more to the purely cognitive (which, following Garfinkel 1967, is regarded as more problematic) and affective dimensions. And whereas Parsons, with his normative focus, treated the affective dimension in terms of cathectic attachments that were often generalized to abstractions (including norms and values) rather than to concrete persons, practical-action theory emphasizes affiliative ties among actors.[6]

Walter Powell and I have argued elsewhere that much of social and organizational theory is converging on the presuppositions of the practical-action approach, and we have attempted to identify commonalities in such work (DiMaggio and Powell 1991). What I should like to do in the following section of this chapter is speculate about the implications of this perspective for the study of social networks, with the ultimate goal (no more than an aspiration here) of developing behavioral practical-actor models that may serve as alternatives to their rational-actor counterparts.

Problems of organizing have been brought to the fore by recent advances in both organizational ecology and institutional theory, but scholars associated with neither approach regard the issues as settled. Work in organizational ecology has called attention to the pivotal role of new organizations (as opposed to adaptation by existing organizations) in effecting organizational change and has recently focused on the problem of identifying population boundaries and on the emergence of new organizational forms (Hannan and Freeman 1989; Singh and Lumsden 1990). Recent work in neoinstitutional theory has called attention to the emergence and structuration of organizational fields as logically precedent to the institutional isomorphic processes that much research in this tradition has emphasized (DiMaggio 1991b; DiMaggio and Powell 1991; Scott and Meyer 1991). In the section that follows, I will consider the problem of organizing under conditions of uncertainty, suggesting elements of a model of recruitment to new projects.

ORGANIZING NETWORKS: RECRUITMENT IN INTERORGANIZATIONAL ANARCHIES

In November 1929, the Museum of Modern Art opened its doors. MOMA was the first United States museum devoted to modern art—that is, to contemporary art and the art of the previous half-century.[7] At the time, the work of such now-exalted painters as Van Gogh, Cezanne, and Monet, not to mention modernists like Picasso and Duchamp, was ignored by most American museums and devalued by conventional critics. The notion that the work of the present could be as significant as the best culled from the past was still radical; the idea that art develops progressively and that an avant-garde leads the way was positively revolutionary. By valorizing contemporary art in the modern style, MOMA provided stimulus to dealers and collectors, launched movements, affected the collecting policies of established museums, and effaced the boundaries between the high arts of painting and sculpture and such forms as design and advertising art, film, and photography.[8]

MOMA was the brainchild of three wealthy New York women, Abby Aldrich Rockefeller (the wife of John D. Rockefeller, Jr.), Lilly Bliss, and

Mary Sullivan, all active collectors. They recruited an upstate industrialist, A. Conger Goodyear, to head the campaign and created an organizing committee of six men and two women, all of them independently wealthy collectors. With the help of Paul Sachs, a Harvard professor of fine arts, they identified the country's leading museum professionals, sought their support, and embarked on a nationwide fund-raising effort. As the museum's first director, they hired Alfred H. Barr, Jr., a young Wellesley instructor who had taught that college's first seminar in modern art.

Because MOMA was the first museum of modern art in the United States, its founders operated under conditions of uncertainty, with few models. There were still relatively few U.S. collectors of contemporary art, few college or university courses or academic specialists, and no cadre of experienced museum workers in that field. In order to create a museum, the founders of MOMA had to work with what was available to them: some money, some art, and a formidable set of acquaintances.[9]

How did they do it? Given the conventions of the time, which made it necessary for the three ladies who conceived of MOMA to find male sponsorship, why did they choose Goodyear, whom none had met previously, to head the operation? Why was Paul Sachs so important? How did they go about choosing the organizing committee (the members of which would constitute the museum's first board of trustees)? How did they find Alfred Barr, Jr.?

Confident answers to these questions would require substantial archival research. I use the case speculatively here, drawing on the secondary literature, to illustrate the problems of organizing in a new field. At one level, the problem the organizers faced was to acquire resources: money, pictures, and a place to hang them. The organizers were reasonably well equipped by their own wealth and collections to succeed at this level. More important, however, they were impelled by a broadly propagandistic mission, a desire to valorize their tastes and popularize the work of the artists they presented. To achieve this broader goal, the founders needed something more important than money: legitimacy. As champions of unestablished genres, they first had to avoid being cast as rich dilettantes. To legitimate their own efforts, they needed to attract the visible support of legitimate actors and institutions. To create the museum they had in mind, however, they needed supporters who were trustworthy as well as legitimate, individuals who would not take the project over and turn it to their own ends.

These two imperatives—*legitimacy* and *control*—characterize many, if not most, forms of organizing under conditions of uncertainty.[10] Because of this, the most formidable problems of organizing (aside from acquiring resources) have to do with assessing networks to determine which partners will be perceived as most legitimate and which will be reliable, either because they are constrained from staging a coup or because they share the orientations and goals of the organizers.

Organizers, then, must choose partners (of different kinds) from the population of potentially available participants. This occurs in two stages.

First, organizers become *aware of* a subset of potential participants *with resources* to contribute to the project. These resources may consist of material capital (paintings or money in the MOMA case), social capital (i.e., positions in networks that would permit persons to contribute legitimacy to the project), or human capital (i.e., proven competence). In any organizing venture there will be some role specialization such that different mixes of capital are salient for the evaluation of different categories of participant: for example, social capital for providers of public endorsements, material capital for trustees, human capital for paid staff, and so on (Nohria 1990).

Second, they deal with the agency problem, the problem of control, by assessing the *reliability* of those who survive the resource test. There are at least three bases for determining reliability: (1) *reputation* (whether someone is known for his or her probity); (2) *power* (whether the organizers can exercise effective constraint over that person); and (3) *sympathy* (whether the person is inclined to do what the organizers want, independent of prior track record or susceptibility to direct control).

In a world of full information, this would be a relatively simple process. The first stage would drop out, for organizers would be aware already of potential participants. (In a perfectly predictable world, reliability would drop out as well because contingencies could be covered by contract, but this seems too much to ask even hypothetically.) Extensive information about reliability would permit them to winnow the list considerably, until they arrived at a population of persons varying with respect to the resources they could contribute and their position in the network constituted by relations among members of the population. If information about potential participants' resources and reliability were perfect, decisions would be more or less automatic: organizers would merely choose reliable participants (differentiated by role) with the capacity to maximize legitimacy and other needed resources.

In another kind of world, the quality of information about resources and reliability could be viewed as a function of proximity in a social network. In such a system, organizers are likely to weight evaluations by proximity and display a strong preference for those with whom they are closely tied (and thus better informed) and with whom they share close mutual ties (which represent a source of potential control). This seems to characterize the process by which MOMA's organizers chose some members of the organizing committee (e.g., Mrs. Rockefeller's brother, William Aldrich), but does not explain how they chose their president (Goodyear), their staff head (Barr), or other persons from whom they sought public and private support.

Under conditions of uncertainty or resource scarcity, organizers are forced beyond their immediate networks. Identification and assessment processes are influenced not just by networks but by actors' folk conceptions of networks, which brings us to culture. First, potential participants' *attributes* (including biographical information) enter into this process as guidelines that enable organizers to make snap judgments about their suitability; that is, they are important less because they *are* proxies for particular resources or behavioral patterns than because they *are taken as proxies* by organizers. In the case of MOMA, for example, although some members of the organizing committee were close to the founders, others were more distant members of classes—collectors, philanthropists, industrialists—that attracted the organizers' attention. Such categorical judgments enter into organizing at three stages: in attracting attention to potential candidates; in screening candidates; and in allocating acceptable candidates to categories that organizers hope to fill (often as public signals). At the screening stage, I would hypothesize that they function both as disqualifiers, and in an additive process of task-related impression formation of the kind described by status-expectation-states models developed from laboratory experiments (see Webster and Foschi 1989 for summary and illustrations).

Second, *cognitions* (or, more accurately, their observable expressions) enter into the process by which organizers assess reliability. Here I refer to the ways in which people express themselves—the values, norms, or attitudes that can be read into their utterances and more elusive aspects of style. Such aspects of interaction are most important in establishing sympathy as a ground for believing that others are reliable. In other words, consider attitudes (or tastes or expressive styles) as accounting systems by which actors assess their compatibility with one another in the absence of credible information on salient dimensions of performance or ability (see Nohria and Eccles, this volume).

Why emphasize sympathy, as opposed to reputation or power, as a basis for determining reliability? The weight of the three no doubt varies from case to case. In the MOMA case (and, more generally perhaps, in elite philanthropic ventures), sympathy appears to have loomed particularly large. Two factors required the organizers to go beyond their immediate ties to search for allies. For one thing, the legitimacy imperative required them to gain support from participants who were not identified with any particular clique or element of New York social structure. For another, members of the New York elite already had mixed commitments: Many were supporters of the conservative Metropolitan Museum and, presumably, were uneasy about a competing institution built on artistic principles of which they did not approve; and some potential allies (Gertrude Vanderbilt Whitney, Solomon Guggenheim) were making other commitments.

Given the organizers' need to go beyond immediate strong ties, power and reputation for probity became less useful bases of assessment. In such ventures, power often flows out of dense network relations: social constraint stems from the unwillingness of participants to involve themselves in altercations that would ramify widely across their ego nets and subject them to disapproval or other forms of social control. The further afield the organizers went for allies, the less confident they could be of their ability to control them.

Reputation for probity, like contract, is a dubious guide under conditions of uncertainty and, especially, ambiguity of purpose. In the case of

MOMA, some key matters—relative emphases in collecting, the disposition of aging parts of the collection, the museum's relationship with other institutions—were very ambiguous in the beginning and for some time thereafter. Insofar as decisions are left open, they become matters of judgment rather than probity, and the most honorable of persons can disagree. (Indeed, this appears to have been the case at MOMA during the brief but rather conservative reign of Stephen Clark as chairman.)

Under these conditions, organizers are thrown back on sympathy as an assessment criterion. And sympathy is constructed in part out of categories (like us/not like us) and in part out of ongoing interactions in which participants form strong impressions (confidence, distrust) on the basis of the form and content of utterances, as well as less tangible aspects of interaction (timing, dress, patterns of bodily movement) (Collins 1981; Bourdieu 1990; and see White, this volume, on "identity"). The key to such assessment of reliability is the assessor's belief that the assessed is not only honorable (in the sense that one can believe his or her representations and promises) but that he or she is also sympathetic (in the sense that he or she is likely to respond to unforeseeable events in an appropriate manner, and to be perceived as sympathetic and diplomatic by others on whom the success of the project depends). One can conceive of the assessment of sympathy as a cultural *matching process*, in which actors rely subliminally on verbal and nonverbal cues to estimate cultural overlap, experienced as comfort/discomfort and confidence/unease.

In other words, organizing consists of a process by which organizers first use categories or typifications (roles as classificatory concepts, in Nadel's sense) to identify a set of potential participants; and second use interactional criteria (including expressed attitudes) to form an assessment of the reliability of those who survive the initial test. Goodyear, for example, was known to MOMA's founding trio as a wealthy industrialist and a collector of modern art. His name may well have been salient to them because he had been deposed shortly before as president of Buffalo's Albright-Knox Gallery for purchasing a small Picasso. It also seems likely that, because he was an upstater, he lacked entangling ties to other New York interests. Having passed the categorical test, Goodyear was interviewed over a meal. He apparently passed the interactional test, as well, and was recruited to the project.

In selecting the organizing committee, the founders appear to have divided the at-risk population into categories: although all were collectors, some were particularly active in this sphere. One, a trustee of the Chicago Art Institute, provided a comfortably distant liaison to the art museum establishment; one served as a bridge to the German-Jewish segment of New York's elite; one, a magazine publisher, provided a link to media and literary circles; several seem most notable for their wealth.

How do such organizers make selections once they have decided on categories? Consider two matrices, one consisting of evaluations (ranging from a minimum of -1 to a maximum of $+1$) and one representing salience (the degree of confidence ego has in his or her evaluation of alter—from 0, if ego is unaware of alter, to 1, where confidence in the evaluation is complete). For purposes of nominating, truncate evaluations from 0 to 1, and simplify further by taking "salience" as a distance measure from ego to alter based on networks of appropriate ties. Treat the product of the evaluation cell times the salience cell as the probability that an organizer will nominate any other member of the population. The probability that any member of the population will be nominated (and the probability of any number of nominations) can then be calculated from data on the organizers' networks, combined with direct measures of evaluations or proxies of factors likely to influence them. Such proxies might be measures of salient resources that candidates possess (in the MOMA case, wealth or art collections), centrality to relevant social networks (perhaps tapped by affiliations to clubs or formal organizations), and human capital, e.g., measures of educational attainment and career experience.

Such a procedure yields a list of candidates (those members of the population with the highest probabilities of the highest numbers of mentions). In the next stage, organizers apply four screens, eliminating persons who are known not to be available, who are believed to lack sufficient resources, who have attributes taken to be disqualifying, and to whom organizers have direct negative ties. (The first screen presents a difficulty for purposes of modeling; the second can be treated as a decision rule, if one has data on the resources commanded by candidates; the third requires direct or indirect data on categorical decisions rules; the fourth can be inferred from network data.)

Those who remain are ranked on the basis of their reputation-salience score and interviewed. Those who pass the interactional test (i.e., those who exhibit the highest degree of cultural fit with the organizers) will be allocated among the categories the organizers are trying to fill. (Measuring cultural fit properly would require observation of face-to-face interaction; but, as a rough proxy, data on attitudes might be of some use. In order to predict allocation among categories, one would need direct evidence as to the category scheme the organizers employed.)

I have suggested the elements of a means of modeling participation in organizing processes: data on organizers' networks and data on (or predictive models of) evaluations; assumptions combining cumulation of probabilities (that any organizer will nominate a candidate) with a blackballing rule (whereby a single negative assessment excludes a candidate); and a four-stage process: (1) creating a list of candidates; (2) trimming the list; (3) establishing reliability in face-to-face interaction; and (4) allocating survivors among categories.

The legitimacy imperative complicates this sketch (and makes population network data necessary) in two ways. First, insofar as legitimacy is a consideration, organizers will seek advice at two junctures: in compiling lists of candidates for participation and in evaluating the finalists. Given a plausible decision rule for choosing advisors (and data on their relations with others in the population), one could still estimate nomination probabilities in much the same way as suggested here, by treating each organizer's probability of nominating someone as the sum of his or her independent probability and the probabilities of those to whom he or she turns for advice. To factor in the effects of advice at the selection stage, one would similarly treat each organizer's view of the finalists as a composite function of his or her own view and that of the advisors to whom he or she turns (perhaps with a blackballing rule for negative evaluations).

Second, although social capital can be treated with proxy variables as a component of evaluation, it is sufficiently important to try to measure more directly. If one is willing to make the heroic assumption that organizers have an accurate view of the overall network, then one might use weighted centrality scores (Bonacich 1987) as a measure of social capital.

There are two problems with this suggestion, however. First, as Krackhardt (1990) has argued, cognitive networks and actual networks are two different things: organizers concerned with legitimacy may try to recruit participants whom they believe to be central, but whether or not they do so will depend on the accuracy of their information about the network.[11]

Second, even if one is willing to assume that organizers know who is most central, this information is relevant only insofar as the population before which legitimacy is sought is the same as the population of potential participants. In some cases this may be the case (e.g., when entrepreneurs working with a new technology are most concerned about their legitimacy among potential investors or trading partners), but in others it is not. In the case of MOMA, for example, the organizers sought legitimacy in the academic community and the institutional art-museum community. Had they been creating something other than a museum of modern art, they might have turned to local museums for this (as two service organizations, the American Federation of Arts and the American Association of Museums turned to persons active in major art museums, especially the Metropolitan, for key participants in the 1910s and 1920s). But their competitive stance vis à vis other museums, and particularly their controversial view of art, barred this approach to a large degree. Consequently, they relied heavily on a broker with strong ties to the population of academics and professional museum workers they hoped to sustain.

The broker was Paul Sachs of Harvard University. Sachs occupied a unique position in the art-museum world, serving as a liaison among trustees, directors and curators, and academics for almost thirty years. He came to Harvard after a brief but successful career in his family's banking firm, Goldman, Sachs. (He was a product of a marriage between the two families.) A connoisseur of legendary taste, judgment, and tact, he navigated between the worlds of finance and art with tremendous skill, training a generation of museum directors and playing an important role in the politics of the museum world. (Consistent with Burt's argument [this volume], Sachs could employ his talents precisely because his strong ties to sectors that had previously been only weakly connected—museums, universities, and finance—placed him at the center of "structural holes" that were critical to the art world of his time.) Although his own tastes were rather conventional, Sachs actively rallied support for MOMA, providing lists of key museum professionals whose endorsement should be sought, lobbying successfully for a $100,000 grant from the Carnegie Corporation of New York (of symbolic as well as financial value, because Carnegie and its president were close to the leadership of the Metropolitan), and sponsoring his former student, Alfred Barr, Jr., as MOMA's first director.[12]

Such brokers present a special case in organizing efforts that is not easily captured by formal analysis of network data. One problem is methodological: they are important because they are well connected in several networks, rather than extremely central in just one; because their value to organizers is as a bridge to the other networks, data on a single network may not identify them. Another problem is substantive: The most central brokers, like Sachs, experience an escalating accumulation of social capital until they become in effect institutionalized; believed to be central, they are placed at the center of everything, which increases their centrality still more. Persons whose phone calls are always returned, they can be viewed as maintaining on-call linkages with everyone else in the system. Or, to put it another way, they possess a kind of institutionalized power above and beyond that which flows directly from their positions in relational networks.

In any case, this sketch leaves us some distance from a neat model that can predict patterns of recruitment in organizing efforts. For now, let me suggest three reasons why the effort is worth pushing further. First, to the extent that the success of organizing depends on the resources that participants bring to the table, variation in recruitment will influence variation in success, both directly and by influencing legitimacy. Second, insofar as the capacity of organizers to maintain control depends on their recruitment of reliable participants, patterns of recruitment will influence patterns of control. Third, insofar as plans are ambiguous and futures incalculable, recruitment is likely to influence the substantive direction in which an organizing effort evolves (for example, following Selznick [1947] whether the directors of the Tennessee Valley Authority compromise with local farmers to save the public-power initiative, or make other compromises with other groups that sacrifice public power in return for some other part of the Authority's initial mission).

Although I have focused on the micro side in this example, treating the process of organizing from the perspective of the organizers, it seems likely that the overall structure of a network of organizers, potential participants, and advisers influences the recruitment pattern by affecting the probability that organizers can reach into many regions of the network, and the likelihood of generating bandwagons (multiple nominations of the same participants) or stalemates (nominations and vetoes that cancel one another out). Moreover, the results of the recruitment process, by forming new relations, may (or may not) alter the structure of the network as a whole. In the final section of the chapter, we shift to a concern with entire networks, in the context of intraorganizational systems. Here again, the focus is on the interaction of relational and cultural aspects of role systems, the latter represented by actor attributes, treated as typifications.

RETHINKING THE FORMAL/INFORMAL DICHOTOMY: FORMAL ROLES, ATTRIBUTES, AND THE STRUCTURATION OF INTRAORGANIZATIONAL NETWORKS

Organizational researchers have written a great deal about the interaction of formal and informal structures within organizations, and their work falls into two broad traditions. The first has viewed informal structure, based on particularistic homophily, as an impediment to efficient and effective performance (Roethlisberger and Dixon 1961; Dalton 1957). The second has emphasized the ways in which informal structure, based on instrumental and trust relations across formal boundaries (sometimes stimulated by management design), facilitates the pursuit of organizational objectives (Barnard 1938; Kanter 1983; Eccles and Crane 1987).

Although one can interpret these traditions as offering opposing empirical claims, it may be more useful to view each of them as appropriate under different conditions. To return to Nadel's paradox, the extent to which relationally defined roles and shared typifications (both salient attributes of persons and formal roles as described in organization charts and employee manuals) are mutually supportive or inconsistent, and the conditions under which they are, are empirical questions. The central idea in this section is that the degrees of association between three features of organizations—positions in relational networks, positions in the formal role system, and culturally embedded attributes of members outside the formal role system—are variables of potential importance in predicting the tone and style of an organization.

Why do I persist in treating attributes as important, even when one has direct relational measures? Attributes shape interaction in three ways. First, some are proxies for life experiences that generate shared perspectives and potential conversational contents, thus increasing the fit between persons in the "cultural matching" processes described here. Second, shared attributes may induce homophily by leading people to work harder at formative interactions with similar others. In a stunning study of interaction in junior college career-counseling encounters, Erickson and Shultz (1982) discovered that the tenor and outcome of interactions among previously unacquainted students and counselors hinged on the extent to which they were able to "establish co-membership" (i.e., define themselves as members of either a common social network, by finding acquaintances in common, or a common "membership network" [Breiger 1974] by finding some general shared affiliation or interest) in the early stages of the encounter.[13] If we may generalize this, shared attributes are likely to be taken as signals that make it easier for actors to orient themselves to one another (Nohria 1990). Finally, under circumstances of threat and conflict, highly salient attributes may function as banners that short-circuit ongoing network relations by creating almost automatic ties among those who share them. (In contemporary U.S. organizations, race and gender seem particularly notable in this regard, although other labels related to class or professional background may also operate in this way.) The point is *not* that attributes necessarily influence social relations in these ways, for often they do not; rather, tendencies toward homophily vary substantially and consequentially among organizations.

For example, the degree of role clarity within an organization—the extent to which formal roles are good guides to loci of behavioral authority and responsibility—seems likely, other things equal, to be highest when structurally equivalent positions defined by social relations coincide with formal positions in the organizational chart, and lower when structural locations and organizational roles crosscut one another. Thus Barley (1990) found that technological change in a hospital department deinstitutionalized formal roles that had been internally homogeneous with respect to work content—and, there is reason to believe, relational content—thus altering and differentiating the relational aspects of these roles. And Nelson (1989) found higher conflict in organizations with greater discrepancies between relationally defined positions and formal roles.

Following Blau (1977) and research on homophily in friendships within organizations (Marsden 1988, McPherson and Smith-Lovin 1987), the degree of convergence between relationally defined roles (i.e., structurally equivalent positions) and formal roles is likely to be higher the greater the extent to which member attributes are consolidated (i.e., highly correlated with one another, such that homophilic tendencies based on different attributes are mutually reinforcing) and correlated with formal roles. One implication is that the explanatory capacity of conventional models of organization members' sentiments and behavior as a function of member attributes and formal positions will vary depending on the fit of these with patterns emergent from the relational network.

In other words, much about organizations can be understood as a consequence of the interaction of three factors: the organization's relational network, the distribution of attributes, and the formal organizational structure. Of these three aspects, I take relational networks to be the most fundamental for action in two senses. First, at the macro (organizational) level, relational structure (the pattern of structurally equivalent positions and relations among them) either constrains or facilitates the capacity of the organization and its top executives to act. Second, at the micro level, relational patterns represent the actual processes by which influence is exerted and action taken; and thus they mediate the effects of actor attributes and formal positions on organizational outcomes.

Before going further, it is necessary to say a bit more about macrostructure. There is some evidence that relational data, per se, can reveal gross capacities for mobilization at the organizational level. For example, Romo (1986) argues that certain patterns of intraorganizational relations are untenable and lead to substantial conflict. Anheier and Romo (1990) have identified particular relational configurations (identified on the basis of triad censuses and blockmodels) that generate three kinds of inertia: "structural stalemate," "factionalism," and prolonged "organizational failure." Nelson (1989) argues that networks in high-conflict organizations have more unreciprocated ties than do networks in organizations with lower levels of conflict. The key insight—that relational structures can either block or facilitate collective mobilization—is a plausible one (see also White 1961, Sampson 1968) that I ask the reader to accept provisionally.

This will allow us to concentrate on a second problem, which is the effect on organizations of variation in the extent to which relational networks are structured around member attributes and formal organizational roles, respectively. Attributes of persons (culturally embedded informal labels) that influence the formation of social relations (i.e., the probability that cells in a binary sociomatrix will equal 1) represent one *axis of structuration*. Formal organizational roles represent a second. (I will use the term *form of structuration* to refer to four combinations of the role and attribute dichotomies: relations structured by both roles and attributes, by roles alone, by attributes alone, and by neither.) In effect, I propose to complicate the conventional opposition of formal and informal structure with a typology of relational systems based on crude dichotomization of three empirically continuous and analytically independent dimensions: (1) the degree to which member attributes constitute an axis of structuration (a joint product of tendencies toward homophily and structural consolidation); (2) the degree to which formal roles constitute an axis of structuration; and (3) the extent to which relational networks are conducive to collective mobilization versus prone to stalemate.

Taken together, these dichotomies yield eight possibilities, which for want of a better word I call organizational "types" (a term open enough to include structures, informal patterns of interaction, decision-making processes, and aspects of organizational culture). (See Figure 4-1.) I assume a modern society in which formal organizations are bureaucratic— that is, characterized by fixed positions, well-defined formal roles, formal separation of person and office, some version of hierarchical command, formal rules, and long-term employment relations. The discussion that follows brackets causality in order to emphasize affinities.

The two sides of the figure (cells *A–D* and cells *E–H*) mirror one another with respect to forms of structuration and differ only to the extent that the macrostructure is mobilizable or stalemate inducing. On each side of the figure, cells tap each of four forms of network structuration: around roles and attributes (*D* and *H*), around roles alone (*B* and *F*), around attributes alone (*C and G*), and around neither (*A* and *E*).

Traditional accounts that emphasize the negative organizational consequences of informal networks fall into cell *H*, the "clique-based" type,

Relations structured around formal roles?

		No	Yes	No	Yes
Relations structured around attributes?	No	Integrative organization *A*	Weberian bureaucracy *B*	Organized anarchy *E*	Pathological bureaucracy *F*
	Yes	Pseudo-bureaucracy *C*	Strong-culture bureaucracy *D*	Fragmented *G*	Clique based *H*
		Mobilizable		Stalemated	

Figure 4-1

Typology of Organizations According to Variation in Macrorelational Structures, Extent to which Relations are Formal-Structure Based, and Extent to which Relations are Attribute Based

the best example of which comes from Dalton's account of Milo Manufacturing (1959). Accounts that emphasize informal networks' positive contribution to organizational functioning fall into cell *A*, which takes its label, "integrative organization," from Kanter's work or organizations that innovate effectively. Note, however, that what distinguishes the two types of organizations is not simply, or primarily, their capacity for collective action. In contrast to Kanter, I take mobilizing capacity as a function of the overall shape of the network, which is analytically independent of the axes with respect to which relations are structured. In other words, assume for now that networks structured around attributes or around formal roles (or both or neither) can take on stalemated *or* mobilizable structures. It also follows from this that organizations with mobilizable networks can exhibit any of the four forms of structuration.

To elucidate the intuitions on which this typology is based, let us take each of the cells on the left side of the figure, starting with *B* (role-structured/mobilizable) and *C* (attribute-structured/mobilizable). *B* is the most familiar case; its prototype is Weber's model of social relations within a bureaucracy. Social relations adhere to formal role specifications, without attenuation by attributes. In other words, regularities in the relational network are visible on the organization chart; the formal elements of bureaucracy on which Weber concentrated are free to operate unimpeded by social static. Role specifications are clear-cut, rules well defined and universalistically applied, discourse explicit, and record keeping assiduous.

By contrast, cell *C* contains what I call pseudobureaucracy: organizations that are formally bureaucracies but operate instead like bureaucratic cloaks draped over the ongoing life of a status group. Straightforward illustrations in the organizational literature are rare (perhaps Gouldner's gypsum plant under the old management [1957] and Powell's traditional publishing house [1983] fit in some respects); work by historians offers more examples: Story's history of Harvard (1981) and Tomkins' history of the Metropolitan Museum (1973), for two. Pseudobureaucracy may be characteristic of organizations that depend on a single status group for most or all of their key resources, a condition that in the United States has been the case for certain philanthropic and charitable organizations, especially in the cultural sphere. Pseudobureaucracy may also characterize some family firms or specialty-product companies with elite clientele. Social relations in pseudobureaucracies follow the grooves of established patterns, with members of an elite dominating interaction and influence flows. Formal roles are unimportant; executives may be figureheads or recruited on the basis of in-group affiliations. Organizational participants are aware of and accept the categorical allocation of interaction rights and influence, but characteristically do not talk about it. Discourse in such organizations thus tends to be implicit and takes much for granted; rules are poorly formalized, or else admit to many exceptions; record keeping is often loose.

Cell D is more complicated, because formal roles and attributes both structure concrete social relations among organization members. For this to work, an organization requires a strong culture in the Japanese sense— a heavy overlay of symbolism—in order to avoid disruptive tensions between the formal and informal authority systems (Dore 1973). (This might not be the case if statuses were highly consolidated, but under those conditions organizations are more likely to move towards cell C.) Formal aspects of structure are especially important with respect to ritual interactions; attributes may provide a firmer basis for much instrumental work. (Hierarchical position may itself be attached to some master status such as age.) Rules are explicit but relatively few; symbolic hierarchy is strong, but informal ties facilitate its circumvention; discourse may tend to the implicit. Control is exerted through career incentives, which are likely to be constrained by attribute-based relational networks toward what Kanter (1977) has called "homosocial reproduction."

By contrast, in cell A neither attributes nor formal roles structure informal relations markedly. Indeed, Kanter's "integrative organization" (at the managerial levels, a restriction that ought to be applied to my discussion of all of these types) is notable for the fluidity of its networks, the absence of constraints (either roles or attributes) to interaction. Indeed, Kanter's emphasis on management is particularly appropriate because of the relatively unstructured quality of the integrative organization: whereas in role-based structures the organization to some degree runs itself, and in pseudobureaucracies it emerges out of the ongoing informal relations of the dominant status group, integrative organizations require more continual fine tuning. As Kanter describes them, roles are sketchily defined, rules are few and unconstraining, ritual is limited and discourse explicit, all of which contributes to a suppleness that facilitates innovation and change.

Types A–D are viable and capable of high performance, although this depends on the environment that they face. Each of these types has a flip side that shares its form of structuration but is less viable due to a stalemate-inducing macrostructure. Cell F is a stalemated version of the

Weberian bureaucracy: with nothing to fall back on but a formal role, and a relational structure that is not conducive to task-oriented affiliations, the bureaucrat defensively adheres to a narrow definition of his or her task and exhibits slavish obedience to formal rules. (Note that this reaction inheres not in bureaucracy, per se, but in an organization in which keen competition among departments and ranks, in the absence of either mobilizable coalitions or crosscutting bases of affiliation, leads to energetic fault-finding and attendant concern with "tail-covering.") The prototype for cell F is Merton's pathological bureaucracy (1940).

The stalemated version of cell C (pseudobureaucracy) is organizational fragmentation under which the hegemony of a dominant status group breaks down, leading to endemic conflict that, in the absence of legitimate formal authority, is difficult to contain. Again, this type is less well documented (perhaps see Perrow 1963), but it is evident in journalistic narratives of investment banks in the 1980s (Lewis 1989) and in numerous anecdotal accounts of organizational "crisis" in charitable organizations as they grow dependent on actors outside a once-dominant status group. Whether cell C organizations fragment under externally induced crisis may depend on the extent to which status consolidation characterizes the organization (outside of the top group), with relations based on intersecting statuses more conducive to mobilization than those based on consolidated ones.

The stalemated counterpart of strong-culture bureaucracy is what might be called a "clique-based" organization. Here relational structures based on formal roles and attributes encompass groups with both departmental affiliations and social attributes in common (Dalton's cliques are the prototype) that enter into conflict. Finally, the stalemated version of the integrative organization is the "organizational anarchy" (Cohen and March 1974). Although the fit with the prototype is inexact, intuitively it seems possible that social relations guided neither by formal roles nor by patterned attributes are likely, under conditions of blocked mobilization, to generate an aimless, inconsistent, unpredictable quality in organizational action that can be structured neither by effective fiat (as in systems where formal roles structure relational networks) nor by behind-the-scenes status-group mobilization (as in attribute-driven systems).

This rough sketch will require five kinds of specification and elaboration in order to generate clear-cut predictions. First, what critical dimensions of the ideal types bear an affinity to forms of structuration? Here I have mentioned role clarity, number and bindingness of rules, discourse style (explicit vs. implicit), and a few others, but have been neither systematic nor synoptic. Second, what processes account for the posited connections between forms of network structuration and organizational-level characteristics? Again, I have offered some suggestions, but these have been rather rough rationales, and the behavioral assumptions that underlie them require unpacking.

Third, does this typology, which I have described in terms of affinities, bear the seeds of a causal model? If so, what might it look like? Are forms of structuration causally independent, or are certain combinations of axes of structuration more likely to occur than others? Given a mobilizable or stalemated macrostructure, to what extent do forms of structuration influence organizational-level outcomes independent of technology or environmental constraint, and to what extent do they mediate technological and environmental effects? To what extent are there feedbacks between organizational-level features and informal relational structures, and to what extent are the latter susceptible to design?

Fourth, what are the relationships between the forms of structuration and what I call the "macrorelational structure" of the organization? Although I have treated them as analytically independent, it is possible that certain forms of structuration (in combination with environmental and technological factors) may themselves tend to facilitate either mobilizability or stalemate, leaving certain cells in the typology empirically underpopulated. To the extent that the research on which I relied to bolster the argument that different macrostructures are differentially prone to stalemate or conducive to mobilization provides adequate examples of such structures, there are interesting possibilities for modeling. Relatively simple assumptions, for example, about distributions of salient attributes among persons and persons among formal organizational roles, combined with probabilistic assumptions about status consolidation, attribute homophily, and formal-role homophily would permit one to generate networks that could be tested (against macrostructural baselines from the research described earlier—White 1961; Romo 1986; Anheier and Romo 1990; and Nelson 1989) for tendencies towards mobilizability or stalemate.

Finally, what are the implications of this framework for understanding organizational performance? We must be careful not to confuse mobilizability with high organizational performance; because performance is so environmentally dependent, it cannot be deduced from organizational factors alone. In stable environments, organizations with stalemated nets may do well or at least persist over long periods. When environmental change is sufficiently volatile, even organizations with mobilizable nets may not meet challenges adequately. Within the category of organizations with mobilizable nets, it seems likely that each type is best suited to certain kinds of environmental challenges. As Kanter (1983) suggests, the suppleness of integrative organizations equips them particularly well to adjust to rapid environmental change, whereas strong-culture bureaucracies may be more adept at responding to gradual environmental change. Weberian bureaucracies are probably especially good at generating rational appearances required by regulatory agencies (following the argument of Meyer and Rowan 1977), whereas pseudobureaucracies, while excellent at infighting in local environments, do poorly in response to regulatory pressure.

CONCLUSIONS

Neither of these two discussions—about organizing under conditions of uncertainty or about forms of structuration of relational networks within organizations—resolves Nadel's paradox; but each, I hope, illustrates the utility of confronting it. In the MOMA example, we saw that the development of entrepreneurial projects required organizers not only to use existing social relations, but also to construct new ones; further, we saw that the latter process was driven not only by interests, but by culturally embedded typifications of other actors, appropriate strategies, and social structure. The discussion of intraorganizational networks likewise called attention to the extent to which informal networks are structured around typifications (and the typifications around which they are structured) as variables of substantial importance.

The proposed strategy is to treat normatively and relationally defined roles not as analytic alternatives between which researchers may choose, but as disjunctive aspects of actors' social and cognitive environments. Such a strategy highlights the extent to which action is driven concomitantly by social relations and social typifications: by the empirical dispersion of concrete ties, which rarely conform neatly to well-defined role labels, and by the scripts and schema that people employ in ordering the social world.

This view leads away from rational-actor to what I have called practical-actor conceptions of action; it emphasizes what actors do *not* know about social structure and the shortcuts they use to operate under uncertainty. It also leads toward a concern with process, away from the analysis of networks frozen in time and toward identifying the ways in which actors construct new relations. To be sure, existing relational structures play an important role in this, as do strategic interests. All but the most constraining social structures, however, provide opportunities for choice; and strategies that make sense to given actors are shaped by the culturally embedded categories and decision rules they use in devising them. And even when strategy formation approaches the norm of synoptic rationality, culture shapes the tactics actors use to navigate through social space.

Insofar as this perspective points to a solution to Nadel's paradox, it lies in reconceptualizing role systems as operating at two levels—the cultural and social—simultaneously, and in treating this not as a problem, but as an opportunity to examine empirical consequences of variation in the relationship between the two. This solution points not to a rejection of structural analysis, but to its extension to the cultural realm, and to the ways in which structures of culture and structures of relations interpenetrate and interact.

Notes

1. Parsons' theory is discussed at greater length in DiMaggio and Powell (1991) and DiMaggio (1991a).

2. In a recent paper, White (1990) deals directly with the interaction of cultural and relational aspects of social systems. His framework is similar to that presented here in its social-constructionist presuppositions and its description of values as "accounting systems" (although White uses the term somewhat differently). White's approach is different, but complementary, in that it focuses on the middle range of analysis, posits a limited set of archetypes and styles, and relates these to large structural patterns. This chapter emphasizes microprocesses from the perspective of organizers, and brackets the questions of where cultural categories come from and their fit with macrostructures.

3. For the suggestion of a parallel between blockmodeling and ethnomethodology, I am grateful to Chris Winship (personal communication, c. 1976).

4. On ethnomethodology, see Cicourel 1974 and Heritage 1984; for a view of Garfinkel's work that emphasizes change in his perspective over the course of his career, see Alexander 1987.

5. Because economists tend to portray the domain assumptions of rational-actor models as universal elements of the human condition, it may seem odd to treat them as "cultural"; but they are as culturally specific as any others, constituting actors as individual optimizers with independent utility functions and a rational, calculating orientation to exchange (see Etzioni 1987; Granovetter 1985; Friedland and Robertson 1990). Burt acknowledges this on the first page of *Toward a Structural Theory of Action*, describing the notion of purposive action as "more a social norm than an explanation."

6. Interpreting Parsons is tricky because he rarely spelled out the behavioral implications of his theory, he was not always entirely consistent, and for describing cognitive processes he was dependent on a vocabulary that predates the cognitive revolution. Indeed, the argument can be made that his "theory of action" is consistent with the practical-actor theory I describe, and that the two differ not in content but in level of analysis—Parsons operating at the analytic level, and the research and theory on which I draw operating at the level of behavior. My own reading of Parsons suggests that much of what he wrote about the normative grounding of action is sensible only if one has in mind discursively reasoning actors with a reasonably clear sense of their own norms and values.

7. Katherine Dreier's *Societé Anonyme* was a precursor, but lacked such characteristics of the museum form as a permanent gallery and a collection (McCarthy 1991).

8. This discussion relies primarily on Lynes 1973, Marquis 1989, and McCarthy 1991 for material about MOMA. The discussion of MOMA's context draws on "The Diffusion of High Culture," Chapter 3 of my work in progress on the social organization of the high-culture arts in the United States.

9. Although Mrs. Rockefeller was wedded to a man of extraordinary wealth, as McCarthy (1991) points out, he contributed little to MOMA and she herself controlled limited funds.

10. I would include in this not only efforts to create new organizational forms— whether these are museums of modern art, high-tech ventures (Nohria 1990), or novel types of government agencies—but also radical change in the structures and strategies of existing organizations, which, as Hannan and Freeman (1984) have argued, bear many of the characteristics of organizational births.

11. It may be possible to estimate actors' cognitive networks from data on their own ties, if one assumes that people know something about the nets of people to whom they are connected and generalize about overall structures from the parts that they know—but that is a topic for a different paper.

12. I am grateful to Mrs. Richard Stillwell for permission to consult the Paul Sachs oral history at Columbia University; for the specifics of his role in support of MOMA, which Lynes (1973) and Marquis (1990) treat more generally, I have relied on correspondence that is part of that collection. Although Mrs.

Rockefeller and Frank Crowninshield, another member of the organizing committee, had supported Barr's exhibitions of contemporary art in Cambridge several years before, Sachs's support for Barr appears to have been decisive in his selection.

13. Indeed, the effects of counselor and student race or ethnicity, a key concern of the researchers, were mediated almost entirely by the effectiveness of attempts to discover "co-membership" statuses. White counselors and African-American students were somewhat less successful in establishing co-membership than white counselors and students of similar ethnic background, but once they did, the outcomes of the interactions were similar to others in terms of measures of special help, encouragement, and interactional comfort.

References

Alexander, Jeffrey C. 1987. *Twenty Lectures: Sociological Theory Since World War II.* New York: Columbia University Press.

Anheier, Helmut K., and Frank P. Romo. 1990. "Structural Stalemate: Elements of a Theory of Structural Failures." Unpublished manuscript.

Barley, Stephen R. 1990. "The Alignment of Technology and Structure through Roles and Networks." *Administrative Science Quarterly* 35:61–103.

Barnard, Chester. 1938. *The Function of the Executive.* Cambridge, MA: Harvard University Press.

Blau, Peter. 1977. *Inequality and Heterogeneity.* New York: Free Press.

Bonacich, Philip. 1987. "Power and Centrality: A Family of Measures." *American Journal of Sociology* 5:1170–1182.

Boorman, Scott A., and Harrison C. White. 1976. "Social Structure from Multiple Networks, II: Role Structure." *American Journal of Sociology* 81:1384–1446.

Bourdieu, Pierre. 1990. *The Logic of Practice.* Stanford, CA: Stanford University Press.

Breiger, Ronald L. 1974. "The Duality of Persons and Groups." *Social Forces* 53:181–190.

Burt, Ronald S. 1982. *Toward a Structural Theory of Action.* New York: Academic Press.

———. 1983. *Corporate Profits and Co-Optation.* New York: Academic Press.

Cicourel, Aaron V. 1974. *Cognitive Sociology.* New York: Free Press.

Cohen, Michael, and James G. March. 1974. *Leadership and Ambiguity.* New York: McGraw-Hill.

Cohen, Michael, James G. March, and Johan Olsen. 1972. "A Garbage-Can Model of Organizational Choice." *Administrative Science Quarterly* 17:1–25.

Collins, Randall. 1981. "On the Microfoundations of Macrosociology." *American Journal of Sociology* 86:984–1014.

Cook, Karen S., Richard Emerson, Mary R. Gilmore, and Toshio Yamagishi. 1983. "The Distribution of Power in Exchange Networks: Theory and Experimental Results." *American Journal of Sociology* 89:275–305.

Cyert, Richard, and James G. March. 1963. *A Behavioral Theory of the Firm.* Englewood Cliffs, NJ: Prentice-Hall.

Dalton, Melville. 1959. *Men Who Manage.* New York: Wiley.

DiMaggio, Paul. 1986. "Structural Analysis of Organizational Fields." In Barry Staw and L. L. Cummings, eds., *Research in Organizational Behavior* Vol. 8. Greenwich, CT: JAI Press, pp. 335–370.

———. 1991a. "The Micro/Macro Dilemma in Organizational Research: Implications of Role-Systems Theory." In Joan Huber, ed., *Macro-Micro Relationships.* Newbury Park, CA: Sage.

———. 1991b. "Constructing an Organizational Field as a Professional Project: U.S. Art Museums, 1920–1940." In Walter Powell and Paul DiMaggio, eds.,

The New Institutionalism in Organizational Analysis. Chicago: University of Chicago Press.

DiMaggio, Paul, and Walter W. Powell. 1991. "Introduction." In Walter Powell and Paul DiMaggio, eds., *The New Institutionalism in Organizational Analysis.* Chicago: University of Chicago Press.

Dore, Ronald. 1973. *British Factory—Japanese Factory: The Origins of Diversity in Industrial Relations.* Berkeley: University of California Press.

Eccles, Robert G., and Dwight B. Crane. 1987. "Managing Through Networks in Investment Banking." *California Management Review* 30:176–195.

Erickson, Fred, and Jeffrey Shultz. 1982. *The Counselor as Gatekeeper.* New York: Academic Books.

Etzioni, Amitai. 1987. *The Moral Dimension.* New York: Free Press.

Friedland, Roger, and A. F. Robertson, eds. 1990. *Beyond the Marketplace.* Chicago: Aldine.

Garfinkel, Harold. 1967. *Studies in Ethnomethodology.* Englewood Cliffs, NJ: Prentice-Hall.

Giddens, Anthony. 1984. *The Constitution of Society.* Berkeley: University of California Press.

Gouldner, Alvin W. 1957. *Patterns of Industrial Bureaucracy.* New York: Free Press.

Granovetter, Mark. 1985. "Economic Action, Social Structure, and Embeddedness." *American Journal of Sociology* 91:481–510.

Hannan, Michael T., and John Freeman. 1984. "Structural Inertia and Organizational Change." *American Sociological Review* 49:149–165.

Heritage, John C. 1984. *Garfinkel and Ethnomethodology.* Cambridge: Polity Press.

Ibarra, Herminia. 1989. *Network Location and Participation in Innovations.* Ph.D. dissertation, Yale University.

Kanter, Rosabeth Moss. 1977. *Men and Women of the Corporation.* New York: Basic Books.

———. 1983. *The Changemasters.* New York: Simon & Schuster.

Krackhardt, David. 1990. "Assessing the Political Landscape: Structure, Cognition, and Power in Organizations." *Administrative Science Quarterly* 35:342–369.

Lewis, Michael. 1989. *Liar's Poker.* New York: Penguin.

Lynes, Russell. 1973. *Good Old Modern: An Intimate Portrait of the Museum of Modern Art.* New York: Atheneum.

March, James G., and Herbert Simon. 1958. *Organizations.* New York: Wiley.

Marquis, Alice G. 1989. *Alfred H. Barr, Jr.: Missionary for the Modern.* Chicago: Contemporary Books.

Marsden, Peter V. 1982. "Brokerage Behavior in Restricted Exchange Networks." In Peter V. Marsden and Nan Lin, eds., *Social Structure and Network Analysis.* Beverly Hills, CA: Sage, pp. 201–218.

———. 1988. "Homogeneity in Confiding Relations." *Social Networks* 10:57–76.

McCarthy, Kathleen D. 1991. *Women's Culture: Philanthropy, Art and Power, 1830–1930.* Chicago: University of Chicago Press.

McPherson, J. Miller, and Lynn Smith-Lovin. 1987. "Homophily in Voluntary Organizations." *American Sociological Review* 52:370–379.

Merton, Robert K. 1940. "Bureaucratic Structure and Personality." *Social Forces* 17:560–568.

Meyer, John W., and Brian Rowan. 1977. "Institutionalized Organizations: Formal Structure as Myth and Ceremony." *American Journal of Sociology* 83:341–363.

Nadel, S. F. 1957. *Theory of Social Structure.* London: Cohen and West.

Nelson, Reed E. 1989. "The Strength of Strong Ties: Social Networks and Intergroup Conflict in Organizations." *Academy of Management Journal* 32:377–401.

Nohria, Nitin. 1990. "Information and Search in the Creation of New Business Ventures: The Case of the 128 Venture Group." Chapter 9, this volume.

Parsons, Talcott. 1937. *The Social System.* Glencoe, IL: Free Press.

Perrow, Charles. 1963. "Goals and Power Structures: A Historical Case Study." In

Eliot Freidson, ed., *The Hospital in Modern Society*. New York: Macmillan, pp. 112–146.

Powell, Walter W. 1983. *Getting into Print: Decision-Making in Academic Publishing.* Chicago: University of Chicago Press.

Roethlisberger, F. J., and William J. Dickson. 1961. *Management and the Worker.* Cambridge: Harvard University Press.

Romo, Frank P. 1986. *Moral Dynamics: A Blockmodeling Study of Conflict in a Mental Hospital.* Ph.D. dissertation, Yale University.

Sampson, S. F. 1968. *A Novitiate in a Period of Change: An Experimental and Case Study of Social Relationship.* Doctoral dissertation, Cornell University.

Selznick, Philip. 1947. *TVA and the Grass Roots*. New York: Harper & Row.

Story, Ronald. 1981. *The Forging of an Aristocracy*. Middletown, CT: Wesleyan University Press.

Tomkins, Calvin. 1973. *Merchants and Masterpieces: The Story of the Metropolitan Museum of Art.* New York: Dutton.

Walker, Gordon. 1985. "Network Position and Cognition in a Computer Software Firm." *Administrative Science Quarterly* 30:103–130.

Webster, Murray, Jr., and Martha Foschi, eds. 1989. *Status Generalization: New Theory and Research.* Stanford, CA: Stanford University Press.

White, Harrison C. 1961. "Management Conflict and Sociometric Structure." *American Journal of Sociology* 67:185–199.

———. 1973. "Equations, Patterns and Chains in Social Structure: Some Calculus of Networks and Categories." Working draft. Revised and published as "Models for Interrelated Roles from Multiple Networks in Small Populations." In P. J. Knopp and G. H. Meyer, eds., *Proceedings of the Conference on the Application of Undergraduate Mathematics in the Engineering, Life, and Managerial and Social Sciences.* Atlanta: Georgia Institute of Technology. 1974.

———. 1990. "Values as Network Dimensions: Of Styles which Mate to Change." Paper presented at the Interdisciplinary Conference, "Toward a Scientific Analysis of Values," Feb. 1–4, 1989, Tucson, AZ. Third revision.

White, Harrison C., Scott A. Boorman, and Ronald L. Breiger. 1976. "Social Structure from Multiple Networks, I: Blockmodels of Roles and Positions." *American Journal of Sociology* 81:730–780.

Zucker, Lynne G. 1977. "The Role of Institutionalization in Cultural Persistence." *American Sociological Review* 42:726–743.

———. 1987. "Institutional Theories of Organization." *Annual Review of Sociology* 13:443–464.

Doing Your Job *and* Helping Your Friends: Universalistic Norms about Obligations to Particular Others in Networks

CAROL A. HEIMER

UNIVERSALISM AND PARTICULARISM

I have heard it said of Talcott Parsons that he was "so universalistic that he wouldn't help a friend." Despite sociologists' views that organizations are built on the norm of universalism, I will argue that actually, organizational life is as much about helping your friends as about behaving universalistically. The point is that if members of an organization are to serve their clients well, they must in some cases become their friends (this is probably a bit of an overstatement) in order to know what the clients need; if members of an organization are to decide whom they can trust as coworkers, they have to become friends with the coworkers; and if members of an organization are to develop skills that are crucial to an organization, they must be confident of the organization's loyalty to them.[1] Relations are among named individuals who know one another as particular others and not just as generalized actors playing broadly defined roles. When actors play out their general roles, these roles are meaningful only in the context of the loyalty they feel to one another and the knowledge they have of one another's needs, quirks, and whims. In short, my argument is that Parsons has left us with a false dichotomy since only by "helping friends" can anyone ever do business. To formulate it with less paradox, almost every relation to a category of people such as fellow

I would like to thank Wendy Espeland, Jane Mansbridge, and Arthur Stinchcombe for insightful written commentaries, useful references, and supportive discussions. Nitin Nohria, Robert Eccles, Richard Scott, Harrison White, and other conference participants also provided helpful comments.

workers or clients actually consists of a series of actions that at any particular time and place are directed to a particular named individual. The universalistic norms then require that one do what a series of particular individuals need or want, as well as deserve, at a given time.

But often the peculiarities of the individuals figure prominently in each interaction, and as a consequence of those interactions ties develop between named individuals. Through these networks built on particularistic ties, organizations reach their universalistic ends. For example, scholars serve the universalism of science by hearing or reading and commenting on a paper by a particular person at a particular time. Their obligations under the norms are to that person and his or her scholarly work. If they discharge their obligations well, a link in a scientific network is formed, tying them all together.

In this paper I discuss when universalism without network ties to particular others is counterproductive for organizations. I argue first that the work of Parsons and Shils (1951) falls short as a *description* of what goes on in organizations, and especially in their relations with network partners, largely because networks are structured less by universalistism than by the obligations of network partners to one another. These obligations are simultaneously obligations to perform tasks in a universalistic way and obligations to behave responsibly in one's relations to particular network partners. By asking who is responsible for what and to whom, what organizations and individuals do to increase the likelihood of responsible behavior, and where pressures for universalism and for particularism come from, we can address this paradox that norms simultaneously require universalistic and particularistic behavior and uncover some of the strategies network partners use for meeting these theoretically conflicting but actually often mutually supportive demands.

Mark Granovetter (this volume) argues that "economic activity . . . occurs in networks of personal relations" and that people "try actively to *prevent* economic and noneconomic aspects of their lives from being separated." My argument parallels his, though we start from different places and have different aims. Granovetter's quarrel is primarily with economists and sociologists studying economic life. Granovetter aims to show that economic life is not really distinct from family life (or religious life or whatever); because it is embedded in the rest of social life, economic life is never governed solely by economic motives or universalistic rules. My quarrel is with theorists writing about normative systems. My argument is that those who contend that organizations are (and should be) governed by universalistic rules are wrong because life in organizations and networks necessarily entails obligations to concrete others that can be met responsibly only by adopting a particularistic orientation. At the core of both arguments, then, is Granovetter's claim that "the mere *fact* of attachment to others may modify economic action" (Chapter 1, this volume).

Finally, I argue that Carol Gilligan's (1982) work on the contrast between an ethic of care and an ethic of rights fits neatly the distinction between universalism and particularism, and enriches the argument here because it is in essence an argument about the kind of morality that really governs network relations. An ethic of care is often demanded in organizations. The key to all of these arguments is that universalistic norms generate responsibilities to particular others as named nodes in a functioning network.

This paper is concerned with the general question of the conditions under which the fundamental opposition between universalism and particularism breaks down, the roles in which the requirement to be universalistic is at odds with responsible behavior, and how the tension between those two requirements is resolved. At least six issues are of interest here:

1.   The rules that grow up in bureaucracies tend to be rules about universalism, about how to deal with categories of people or types of relationships rather than about the need to take account of individual differences, idiosyncratic characteristics, or unusual circumstances. Why do we tend to have such an imbalance, with explicit rules about universalism but silence about particularism?

2.   We recognize that it is sometimes *irresponsible* to be too universalistic and that when the circumstances of a job require particularism, that particularism may well not be of the suspect sort of favoring one's friends and family. Can we say anything about the conditions under which responsible particularism will be especially important?

3.   It is hard to distinguish between "bad" and "good" particularism, and so difficult to legislate particularism. In contrast, it is easy to tell the difference between universalism and particularism and so to legislate that people should behave universalistically. Because of this there may be a tendency for organizations concerned with justice to err on the side of universalism.

4.   Particularism is an expensive virtue compared with universalism because it requires tracking individuals rather than categories and requires long relationships, extensive record keeping, and the like, all of which are expensive.

5.   We can say *where* tensions about particularism will be located (teaching, any kind of people processing, any place where adjustments to individual specifications are required and so where condensed communication born of repeat interactions is important, situations in which there are ombudsmen), and what kinds of occupations will be ones in which techniques for being universalistically particularistic will grow up.

6.   Some of the central debates about careers in modern organizations revolve around the question of how to be particularistic and how *not* to be particularistic (mentorship, which many value, is about particularism, but so are some forms of sexual harassment, and those anxious to avoid sexual harassment may avoid the close relationships that are required for effective mentoring).

The classic statements about the contrast between universalism and particularism come from Max Weber's (1978) writings about legal formalism, the process of rationalization, and the driving forces behind the codification of law,[2] and from Talcott Parsons' work on the pattern variables.[3] Parsons and Shils argue:

> In confronting any situation, the actor faces the dilemma whether to treat the objects in the situation in accordance with a general norm covering *all* objects in that class or whether to treat them in accordance with their standing in some particular relationship to him or his collectivity, independently of the objects' subsumibility under a general norm (1951:81).

Though Parsons and Shils here emphasize the relationship between two actors, I would argue that particularism need not entail judgments made in the light of what kind of relationship one actor has with another, but only information that one actor has about another as a result of a joint history. That is, the distinction I have in mind has as much to do with considering the other's biography, whether or not one figures prominently in that biography, as with considering one's relation to the other. So particularism involves two things: considering a person "in the round" rather than just as a member of a category, and considering a person in the context of his or her relationships to oneself and to others in a network. These two aspects of particularism are not entirely separable, of course, since the information need to evaluate a person in the round typically comes from having a tie to that person.

My argument will be that all universalistic category systems must have a distinction analogous to the distinction between rating and underwriting in insurance. Rating tells how a category of risks is to be treated. Underwriting classifies individual risks into those categories by evaluating the risk in the round. Just as in insurance the treatment of an individual is modified over time as the insurer's experience with him or her accumulates ("experience rating"), eventually placing the individual into his or her unique category, so network partners start with a general rule about how to treat one another and modify that rule in the light of their developing understanding of each other. Only the most rigid bureaucracies treat their interaction partners truly universalistically, and even in those situations only a few unimportant or powerless interaction partners are treated that way.

UNIVERSALISM AND BUREAUCRACY

One virtue of bureaucracies is that they create order and predictability by producing rules that regulate the treatment of particular categories of people.[4] The rules tell members of categories how they should conduct themselves and how they can expect to be treated if they conduct themselves according to the rules. Rules give people obligations—to come to work on a fixed schedule, to perform various tasks, to treat all customers equally, not to judge family members by more relaxed standards, for a few examples. But rules also give people rights—to expect that other people will do their own work, for example, and to anticipate advances in salary and rank if they meet certain criteria. Most bureaucratic rules are also universalistic; all persons occupying a particular category have the same or similar obligations, will be judged by the same standards, and have the same rights. The universalistic orientation of bureaucratic rules is not accidental. Without universalism it would be difficult to form the categories to which rules apply, and the rules would not do nearly as much to increase the predictability of organizational life.

When organizations and occupations are not governed by universalistic orientations, we find two characteristic difficulties, one associated with obligations and the other with rights. When, for instance, workers' obligations to customers are not defined universalistically, workers may treat customers erratically. And when workers' rights are not defined universalistically, workers may have difficulty claiming promotions that they deserve (see Kanter 1977 and Heimer 1986 on careers of clerical workers). Without some standard against which to chart their progress, an assumption that anyone who meets a standard should be rewarded accordingly, and some way to demonstrate that they have the skills and experience required for a higher-level position, employees who have lower-status characteristics or who occupy lower-status positions may find it especially difficult to claim that they should receive promotions. Neckerman and Kirshenman (1991) make a similar point about the hiring of minority workers. They find that black applicants are more likely to be hired by employers who use (universalistic) skills tests as part of their recruitment process rather than by those who rely only on more subjective assessments.

But the predictability and order associated with universalism have their down side, of course. One difficulty is that job descriptions, a hallmark of the universalism of bureaucracy, go hand in hand with people insisting, "That's not my job!" Precise job descriptions often are too narrow, either because they do not include the full range of tasks associated with a given occupation or because they fail to take into account the full range of variation in customers and clients. Because clients vary, precise job descriptions are hard to write for occupations that entail interactions with other people. Thus it is difficult to write job descriptions for, or to "script" (scripts are really a form of job description) what Leidner (1988) calls "interactive service work." Leidner argues that employers of interactive service workers may try to transform their workers by teaching them appropriate attitudes and interactional styles when the work itself cannot be scripted because of variations in the customers. That is, employers try to reduce variation by standardizing their employees, as they cannot standardize their customers or clients. When interactive service work can be scripted (e.g., at McDonald's), some customers are irritated at being treated too universalistically. "Suggestive selling" is one example. Being asked if they want apple pie after stating clearly that all they want are french fries causes anger in some.

The second difficulty with universalism comes when organizations fail to accommodate the variation in those who have careers in the organization. All workers do not learn at the same pace, so a year of experience may make one worker ready to move on to more complex tasks while another worker needs an additional year of apprenticeship. Although one might write a general norm about "merit" at the end of an apprenticeship in that job, in the practical case that norm comes down to treating Wendy differently from Nicki. How the advantages of universalistic treatment of workers will need to be traded off against particularism will depend on how narrow the specifications are in any given line of work, and whether the "true" requirements (e.g., being able to perform some task rather than "having a year of experience") can be written in an easily administered universalistic rule. Educational programs that require students to proceed lockstep through them entail considerable cost to students who are too dull or too bright for the program. Loosely coupled educational organizations (Weick 1976) may sacrifice fewer students even though they must sacrifice the efficiency of universalism. Organizations that process people (especially, perhaps, those that process minds and personalities rather than bodies) necessarily deal in unstandardized parts and therefore need to relax their universalism.

MAKING RULES: WHY IS IT EASIER TO LEGISLATE UNIVERSALISM THAN PARTICULARISM?

I have argued that most of the rules in bureaucracies are universalistic rules. But it is certainly possible to construct particularistic rules instead (though one would probably need many more of them). In this section I explore some of the reasons why organizations have tended to write universalistic rather than particularistic rules.

Universalism is cheap for the same reason that standardization is. If all bolts of a particular size will work interchangeably with all nuts of that same size, then it is easier to find a match. If all students have to take the same courses to get a degree, then it is easier to check their transcripts. If admissions criteria are based on standardized test scores rather than a reading of work submitted with the application form, then the admission committee will have less work and an easier time defending its decisions. If all customers are willing to buy the same model of car, then an assembly line can produce large batches and benefit from economies of scale. If all customers are charged the same price and given the same payment schedule, then the accounting department will have less work. If the health of all potential plasma donors can be assessed in a standardized way, then the work of plasma center employees can be streamlined and also can be inspected easily by the FDA (Espeland 1984).[5]

The point is not that one cannot make particularistic rules, but rather that in comparison to universalistic rules, particularistic rules are more complex (they have to take account of more variations), more difficult to formulate (someone has to decide which variations are important enough to be explicitly covered by the rule), more difficult to administer (someone will have to determine which rule applies, and the rules typically have to be treated as guidelines or rules of thumb rather than laws), and more difficult to evaluate (partly because one must evaluate relationships rather than individuals).[6]

Particularistic Rules Are More Complex

Universalism and particularism are the two poles of a continuum. Universalism requires that one treat *all* objects in a particular class the same way. Particularism, in contrast, requires that a person treat objects "in accordance with their standing in some particular relationship to him or his collectivity" (Parsons and Shils 1951:81). But members of a collectivity are, of course, members of a class. Thus one can move from treating *all* objects alike to treating them according to their membership in some large category, to treating them according to membership in some subcategory, to treating them according to their relationship with oneself. What varies here is the size of the category (all humans, all citizens of the United States, all members of my immediate family, all my husbands) and the degree to which one has an interest (either positive or negative) in a person by virtue of his or her membership in some category. The more particularistic the rule, the more one has to keep track of individuals and their biographies rather than keeping records on a small number of traits of those individuals. As co-citizens, we keep track of few traits of our fellow citizens; as coworkers, we keep track of more because our relationships with coworkers are more complex than our relationships with co-citizens; and at some points in the life cycle, at least, we are concerned with more facts about family members than about coworkers. Particularism is thus an expensive virtue because the more particularistic the rule, the more it requires tracking individuals rather than categories. Thus "all my husbands should do their share of the dishes" has to be adapted to all the responsibilities of the partners that determine their shares of the work this week.

Particularistic Rules Are More Difficult to Formulate

The difficulty with formulating more particularistic rules is that someone has to have the imagination to dream up which variations are likely to be relevant and likely to occur often enough that they should be explicitly included in the rule. The more universalistic the rule, the fewer the categories and situations that need to be distinguished. A completely universalistic rule is one that says that *everyone* is to be treated the same way. But as a rule shades toward particularism, then distinctions have to be made, and the legislator has to anticipate which distinctions will be relevant, frequently occurring, and politically legitimate. The development and subsequent refinement of rules about salary or benefits might be a good example here. Ultimately, as I will argue, a rule about responsibilities or rights in a network has to be justified on universalistic grounds by a claim that it is a rule that applies to a category even if there is currently only one object in that category. Considerable ingenuity is required to figure out what class an object is a member of, and to convince others that the classification system that one proposes is truly the optimal one.

Two quite different responses are possible when one confronts a situation in which the empirical world is more complex than the world imagined by most rule systems. Earlier I implicitly suggested that the solution is to develop more flexible or more detailed rules. Rule makers would attempt to imagine what contingencies will arise and to formulate rules appropriate to them. Alternatively, flexibility can be built in at a different point. Rigidity in rules can be compensated for by flexibility in the application of those rules. Sometimes this flexibility is approved by the authorities, sometimes not. Johnson (1972), for instance, argues that gundecking[7] is a response to "contingencies that could not possibly be adequately covered by any set of formal rules and procedures" (243).

Of course, all rules are problematic and require adaptation and improvisation to specific situations. Thus the application of rules is a process of making universal dicta apply to particular individuals in particular situations. As Comaroff and Roberts (1981) argue, though, the relationship between rules and reality is a dialectical one in which rules have to be interpreted in the light of real situations, while those real situations simultaneously lead to further elaboration of the rules themselves:

> . . . *mekgwa le melao* [norms and customs] represent a symbolic grammar in terms of which reality is continually constructed and managed in the course of everyday interaction and confrontation. Far from constituting an "ideal" order, as distinct from the "real" world, the culturally inscribed normative repertoire is constantly appropriated by Tswana in the contrivance of social activity, just as the latter provides the context in which the value of specific *mekgwa* may be realized or transformed. In short, notwithstanding the classical opposition drawn between them, norm and reality exist in a *necessary* dialectical relationship, a relationship that gives form to the manner in which Tswana experience and navigate their universe (247).

The less segregated the legislative, executive, and judicial processes, the more one would expect adjustment to reality to occur as modification and elaboration of rules rather than as evasion of rules, creative interpretation, or gundecking. My argument is that among the kinds of reality to which universalistic rules stand in a dialectical relation is the reality that all organizational work is done in a network of relations among named individuals.

Particularistic Rules Are More Difficult to Administer

The more particularistic the rule, the more difficult the task of determining which category a person falls into and therefore which rule applies. Those who administer the rules will need to know the system of rules and the details of individual biographies. Further, particularistic rules are likely to have to be treated as guidelines or rules of thumb rather than laws. Not all individual situations will be explicitly covered by the rules; individual situations may change and then it will be unclear whether the old or the new rules apply. Such situations are especially likely to arise as groups not previously part of an organization become members. For instance, rules about the timing of major career decisions, formulated when almost all the employees were male, have had to be modified in law firms and academic institutions to take account of the family responsibilities of some women (and, increasingly, of some men). One would expect further modification of rules if the new laws abolishing mandatory retirement at 70 lead older employees to remain in the work force.

Particularistic Rules Are More Difficult to Justify and Evaluate

Particularistic rules tend to be difficult to justify in a universalistic environment.[8] The ideology of organizations is a universalistic one, and our routines for evaluating outcomes tend to be geared around notions of fairness in the application of rules (Did everyone get the same thing as everyone else? Did everyone have an equal chance? Did people get what they paid for?) rather than around evaluating outcomes in the light of biography. Part of the problem is that our standards of evaluation are better adapted to judging individuals in isolation than to judging them in the context of their biographies and relationships. Our standards of evaluation also are geared to providing justifications to third parties, including regulatory agencies. The involvement of third parties and the desire to appear legitimate should intensify the pressure to provide universalistic explanations for behavior, but I do not take up that issue here.

When issues of fairness surface, particularistic rules are considerably harder to defend than universalistic ones. But when issues of responsibility arise, particularism is easier to defend than universalism. When clients believe that they are buying a standardized product or service, universalistic rules will work, but when they believe that they are instead buying the services of an agent, then they will not be satisfied with a universalistic answer to their complaints.

Good and bad particularism are hard to tell apart. Particularism has a bad name, especially when it occurs in the context of public life or business relations. In those contexts, particularism means treating people unfairly, giving undeserved advantages, not giving everyone an equal chance. But many tasks have to be done particularistically if they are to be done well. As students get further along in their educations, we expect them to be judged particularistically in the sense that we expect to evaluate the success of a dissertation project in the light of the intellectual objectives of the doctoral student.[9]

Similarly, we would be appalled if a physician tried to treat a patient without taking a medical history. The point here is that particularism need not be the particularism of the family that Parsons argued was balanced by a universalistic school system. Considering each individual in the round is not just something that parents do with their small children; it is something that other systems do as their components become more dissimilar—for instance, in the later stages of careers. In university systems, for example, distinguished professors are rarely treated as if they are interchangeable universal parts, whereas assistant professors often are. Senior professors negotiate for salaries when they enter a new organization; assistant professors commonly accept a predetermined sum.

One of the interesting questions here is whether it is possible to distinguish "good" particularism from "bad" particularism. When is a particularistic relationship between a superior and a subordinate one of healthy mentorship, when is it sponsorship, and when is it a case of the boss favoring his blue-eyed boy? Should faculty members discuss only intellectual issues with their students, or should they engage in (even initiate?) discussions of career plans, of career and family plans, or of the difficulties of working out personal relationships in a professional context? The standard held in public life is that public officials should not act in ways that might *look* unethical, even if their actions are in fact innocent. A salient example: elected officials should not accept campaign contributions from corporations that will be affected significantly by legislation or other decision making in which they participate. The problem with this standard is that many things that *look* wrong are not wrong; there is a heavy price attached to avoiding all acts that look wrong. Counseling, which most would agree is part of a faculty member's job, often goes on behind closed doors, and closed doors look wrong to some. Mentorship, sponsorship, and favoritism cannot be distinguished from one another by whether or not they entail closed-door sessions between superior and subordinate, long and intense discussions (sometimes over drinks and dinner), and contact outside the main work setting; all three tend to involve contacts that "look bad," and all three are particularistic in the sense that they entail the collection and use of detailed information about the subordinate and an attempt to help the subordinate prepare for and find good positions in the future.

My point here is that to avoid the charge of particularism, we may instead choose an irresponsible universalism based on equal ignorance of all those whose fates we might affect. We do not actually want faculty members to refuse to counsel students (particularly students of the opposite sex) merely because others might accuse them of giving better grades to those they have counseled. Can we not collect information sufficient to consider individuals in the round while still retaining some objectivity in our deliberations about how they should fare compared with others?

I believe that we can answer this question by invoking the particularistic standard that Charles Tilly proposes for the evaluation of scholarly work. Tilly (1989) praises Stinchcombe for writing (what I would call) particularistic book reviews and suggests how a book reviewer can "reconcile empathy and firmness": "[by] separating the value of the enterprise from the quality of its execution, judging both, but concentrating on the rigorous application of standards that belong to the enterprise at hand, rather than some other project the [reviewer] may prefer" (435).

Tilly does not actually mean that a reviewer should not compare one book with another, but instead that part of the evaluation of a book should be based on the standards that are derived from the author's own purpose (presuming, of course, that that purpose itself meets certain "outside" standards), on the particular features of the intellectual problem and body of evidence that the author is working with. Tilly also clearly does not mean that one should evaluate a project mainly in the light of the history of one's own relationship to it; but he does mean that one should develop enough of a relationship to a piece of work to be able to tell what its goal is, what standards are appropriate to it.

This, then, is particularism with a stress on the particular features of the object *itself*, rather than on one's *own* particular characteristics or of the object's standing (as Parsons and Shils put it) in its relation to oneself. But typically we do not collect sufficient information to develop that particularistic standard unless we first develop a relationship with the object or person. It is here, I believe, that Parsons and Shils went wrong. In order to have "good" particularism, one needs to be familiar with many features of an object or person. One needs detailed information. But such information is collected only in the context of a relationship. So though one can analytically distinguish a dimension having to do with quantity of information from one having to do with the existence of a relationship, I would argue that some cells of this table are empty because the two dimensions are conflated empirically.

In addition, "good" particularism entails skill in seeing the general in the particular. The task is to make up the classification system and a standard of judgment by starting with the object that is to be classified and evaluated. If there were a class to which this object belonged, what would it be, and how would this member of the class compare with others? For instance, a great judge can make a rhetorically convincing case turning the particular instance into a universal principle even though he or she knows of only one instance of this principle. "Good" particularism, then, can be justified to a third party by showing what potentially universalistic category the object belongs to. One has to know the object in the round but justify the evaluation or decision by arguing that all objects in the same universalistic category would merit this treatment, if there should ever happen to be any others.

One might label these two kinds of particularism *disinterested* and *self-interested* particularism. Disinterested particularism is usually normatively acceptable because it can be justified as potentially universalistic; self-interested particularism usually cannot be justified in this way and so is not ethically acceptable.

From the preceding discussion we should conclude that if a person were really to be so universalistic that he or she wouldn't help a friend, this could only mean that he or she did not know the "friends" well enough to be able to judge what categories they might fit into and there-fore what treatment (other than that given to everyone else) would be appropriate. As Benhabib (1987) puts it,

> While every procedure of universalizability presupposes that "like cases ought to be treated alike" or that I should act in such a way I should also be willing that all others in a like situation act like me, the most difficult aspect of any such procedure is to know what constitutes a "like" situation or what it would mean for another to be exactly in a situation like mine.
> . . . Without assuming the standpoint of the concrete other, no coherent universalizability test can be carried out, for we lack the necessary epistemic information to judge my moral situation to be "like" or "unlike" yours (90, 91).[10]

I have argued that particularism is about one's relationship with the other party and especially about the knowledge of the other party's idiosyncrasies that one comes to possess through the relationship. I would guess, though, that there are some sources of particularism that tend to be particularly suspect. Relationships that are central to one's identity, that have been developed in identity-forming experiences, tend to make it harder to disentangle the part of particularism that has to do with addi-tional knowledge from the part that has to do with attachment and vic-arious (or direct) participation in the other party's welfare. When two people have grown up together, gone through a religious conversion together, or been deeply in love, these experiences tend to color their perceptions permanently and to make it impossible to disentangle the knowledge component of joint biography from the emotional investment component. If one wants the benefits of particularism without the costs, one should be suspicious when someone says with too much feeling that "she and I go back a long time."[11] I am arguing, then, that "good" par-ticularism, because it is information intensive, tends to occur only in the context of relationships, but that we can still distinguish between relation-ships according to the extent to which they are so central to the identities of both parties that neither one is likely to be able to evaluate the other in a disinterested way.[12] We would expect, for example, that kinship net-works would generally be less universalistic than networks among profes-sional colleagues in a teaching hospital.

WHERE IS PARTICULARISM IMPORTANT IN ORGANIZATIONS?

Particularism in Relations with Customers and Clients

Some kinds of customers and clients will need or want to be treated par-ticularistically, while for others universalism will do just fine. Whenever individual biography features prominently in the service being provided to a client, then we would expect that a particularistic orientation would be more satisfactory than a universalistic one. Whenever the product being supplied to a client is unique rather than prefabricated, custom-designed rather than built entirely by preexisting pattern, we would expect a particularistic relation between customer and service provider. Whenever the service entails a long-term contract between customer and service provider and especially when it entails adjustment of the service as the needs of the client change, we would expect particularism. Particularism should be especially important whenever the fit between the service and the client is likely to affect how well the client functions (e.g., we would expect more particularism in relations between legal counsel and clients than between caterers and clients).

What mechanisms facilitate particularism? Custom design (when it is not fake), variations in size, collection of details about an individual before making decisions about what course of treatment is appropriate (e.g., counseling in schools, medical histories in HMOs and hospitals), job ladders and rules about how to decide what experiences and training prepare a person for a particular occupation, and diagnostic tests (both for skills and in medicine) are all designed to make it easier for organizations to accommodate variations in needs, tastes, and abilities. In relations between customers and suppliers of products or services, all of the mechanisms that move a relation in the direction of hierarchy (that is, away from a strictly market relation in which a customer buys a ready-made product off the shelf, away from rigid contracts toward contracts that incorporate elements of hierarchy) facilitate particularism in the sense of shaping the relation and what is supplied to the needs of the two parties (Stinchcombe 1985). Boilerplate is universalistic; the less a contract is composed of boilerplate, the more particularistic it is.

Stewart Macaulay (1963) noted that contracts are considerably more likely to contain details about the definition of performance than about the effect of contingencies, still less likely to contain explicit discussion of the effect of defective performances, and quite unlikely to contain discussion of legal sanctions. My argument would be that these details are hard to write in a way that is both flexible and legally binding, and that this is partly for the reasons I have specified here: that particularistic rules are more complex, more difficult to formulate, more difficult to administer, more difficult to justify and evaluate. In the early stages of a relationship, when the contract is written and signed, it is just easier to design a contract around the more universalistic elements and to skip the more particularistic ones. One does not want to be bound by inappropriate particularism; one wants to be able to work particularism out in the context of the relationship between the organizations and their agents rather than in the courts.

Particularism in Career Development

Organizations need to be able to combine the virtues of universalism with those of particularism in the way that they arrange careers. One could argue that from the point of view of employees, universalistic systems would be valuable at career stages (or in careers) in which the employees have relatively little power and so will need to be able to assert their rights or claim contested benefits. Thus particularism seems not to be especially beneficial to clerical workers who then cannot claim rewards as their *due* but instead get rewards that depend on their relationships with particular others and the support that those particular others are willing to give their claims (if they make them). In contrast, particularism tends to be an advantage to powerful employees who can claim that they should be treated better than other employees, that their relationship to an organization (as a founder, as a leader of a crucial team, or as someone who gave his or her "best years" to the organization—all potentially universalistic categories) should be respected.

One could also argue that universalism is an advantage in earlier stages in which employees or others who have careers in an organization are acquiring a foundation, and that particularistic treatment is more appropriate at later stages when diversification is taking place.[13] Particularism may become increasingly important the longer people stay in organizations simply because there is more of a relationship to be particularistic about. One cannot really be a "company man" after a week on the job.[14]

If the existence of a relationship is what determines whether employees are treated universalistically or particularistically, then one would expect that anything that increases the strength of the relationship between the organization and an employee will make it more likely that the organization will treat the employee particularistically. Among the things that might increase the strength of the relationship between an employee and an organization are the following:

- Tenure (employees who have been in an organization longer should have a stronger relationship than those who have been with an organization only briefly).

- A position that gives one a tie with "important" people. ("Important" people are more likely to be thought of as representatives of the organization; thus a tie with such people is more likely to be a tie to the organization.)

- A position that gives one a tie with people who are making decisions about the employee's career. (See Heimer 1984 for a discussion of how location in an organization affects both one's access to information and the likelihood that one's interests are taken into account in the formulation of company policies.)

- Company policies that disseminate information about people (e.g., through newsletters, announcements of awards, company picnics, etc.) so that ties between individual workers are more likely to be multistranded. Some of these factors explain variations between individuals within a single organization; others explain variations between organizations.

Particularism, Biography, and Trust

In trying to explain "homosocial reproduction" in organizations, Rosabeth Kanter (1977) argues that managers have tended to hire others like themselves (white, Protestant, male, Anglo-Saxon backgrounds) because they believed that they could trust such people. Segregated social structures confound the effects of joint biography and the effects of social similarity. Thus when people hire those with whom they "go back a long time," arguing that this allows them to predict their coworkers' behavior, we cannot tell whether the predictability of a friend's behavior is due to having in common gender, religion, social class, educational institution, and ethnicity, or is instead due to the information acquired by a long period of observation. Probably common biography and common characteristics have independent effects.

We would expect, then, to find particularism in parts of an organization where people care about being able to predict reliably that other people will behave reliably, and especially when "reliability" in a job is really "responsibility" for adapting flexibly to changing situations and goals, detailed knowledge of individual predispositions, skills, purposes, and ties to others. We would therefore expect particularism to play an important role whenever judgment and honesty are important to a job—whenever the job description is vague and there is a lot at stake. Managerial positions are obviously an important example of this.

That biography is important when the stakes are high is evident in such common procedures as credit checks (e.g., for mortgages and insurance) and security clearances. When the stakes are high, individuals are of course asked questions about those aspects of their lives that are most obviously related to the stakes (e.g., for a mortgage, they are asked about their incomes and debts); but they are also asked to give permission for extensive "inspection" by the organization with whom they are entering a contract. The point of this inspection is that when no preexisting relationship automatically provides an organization with the details of one's life, the organization needs access to biography through formal investigation. When an organization has access to biography, one is less likely to find extensive formal investigation. Thus in the diamond trade and in organized crime, ethnicity (which means that one leads one's life in the community) substitutes for a formal investigation. Two conditions make a formal investigation superfluous: readily available information, and a situation wherein the person is dependent on a community and because of that dependency is less likely to violate trust.[15]

PARTICULARISM AND ORGANIZATIONAL NETWORKS

While relationships between interaction partners are governed by universalistic rules, one ordinarily expects that over the duration of a relationship those rules will be bent a bit to accommodate the needs of particular interaction partners. This will happen partly through the formation of categories and general rules to take into account the characteristics and needs of those partners, partly through the introduction of modifications of general rules to accommodate interaction partners, and partly by one actor turning a blind eye to a favored partner's minor violations. In networks of interactions, the universalistic rules of the official system are tempered by the particularism that grows up in relationships between organizations and between the members of one organization and the members of another.

A network is distinguished from the yellow pages by the particularism in the ties among the organizations. If long-standing clients of a law firm were treated like strangers walking in off the street, or if the users of IBM computers were given service that failed to take into account the history of their troubles or the goodwill built up over a long relationship, organizations would not succeed in making these clients into long-term members of their networks. The lore surrounding the care and feeding of important network members suggests that particularism plays a fundamental role in organizational networks. That goodwill appears as an accounting category further supports my point, and shows that particularism is considered a legitimate part of organizational life by a group of people who make their living policing the universalism of others' expenditures.[16]

We have previously failed to see that universalism by itself is an unworkable principle, because particularism inevitably enters as category systems are refined and applied to individuals. But this particularism continues to be held in check by the requirement that particularistic treatment be justified on universalistic grounds through the formulation of a general rule showing which one-member category this actor belongs to and how members of that category should in general be treated. In the same way that insurers justify individual rates, particularism in organizational networks is made consistent with the universalistic principles of bureaucracies through demonstrating the connection between individual cases and general categories.

To overstate the point, organizations are islands of universalism in a particularistic sea. Within an organization one must employ the rules of the organization to justify one's claim on universalistic grounds. In relations with outsiders these rules do not apply. One can claim that one's product is superior, that one's students or protégés are the best and most deserving, and that one's organization has the best service record without having to provide a full and balanced consideration of the alternatives. A person giving a reference for a job applicant does not ordinarily ask detailed questions about the competition before giving an evaluation of his or her candidate. The reason for this is that all universalistic treatment has to be delivered ultimately to particular named other people, people with whom we have networks of continuing relations. Ignoring that continuity and particularity of networks in organizations renders universalism impotent.

PARTICULARISM, RESPONSIBILITY, AND THE
ETHIC OF CARE AND RELATIONSHIPS

In this section I discuss the connection between particularism, responsibility, and relationships. My point is that responsible behavior is necessarily partly particularistic and necessarily about relationships.

The difference between a rule- or justice-oriented system of ethics and a care-oriented system has been hotly discussed in social science circles in recent years (Held 1990, Gilligan 1982, Gilligan et al. 1988, Mansbridge 1990a and 1990b, Ruddick 1980). The argument that Gilligan and others make has two parts: first, that there are two distinct orientations to moral dimensions, what they call a "justice orientation" and what they call a "care orientation"; and second, that men are more likely to have a justice orientation, whereas women are more likely to have a care orientation. Gilligan and Attanucci explain the distinction this way:

> The distinction made here between a justice and a care orientation pertains to the ways in which moral problems are conceived and reflects different dimensions of human relationships that give rise to moral concern. A justice perspective draws attention to problems of inequality and oppression and holds up an ideal of reciprocity and equal respect. A care perspective draws attention to problems of detachment or abandonment and holds up an ideal of attention and response to need. Two moral injunctions—not to treat others unfairly and not to turn away from someone in need—capture these different concerns. From a developmental standpoint, inequality and attachment are universal human experiences; all children are born into a situation of inequality and no child survives in the absence of some kind of adult attachment. The two dimensions of equality and attachment characterize all forms of human relationship, and all relationships can be described in both sets of terms—as unequal or equal and as attached or detached. Since everyone has been vulnerable both to oppression and to abandonment, two moral visions—one of justice and one of care—recur in human experience (1988:73–74).

Whether or not there is a connection between gender and this distinction is immaterial here; what is important is that an ethical system in which behavior is judged by a standard of care rather than a standard of justice is one in which judgments are based on the relationships between people, on particularistic grounds, rather than on the application of a single rule to everyone.

Elsewhere I have argued that taking responsibility entails accepting contingency (Heimer 1986). Responsible behavior then entails providing different things under different circumstances, collecting enough information to know what the other party needs and so what one is obliged to supply, and accepting that one's own welfare varies with what one is required to provide or do for the other party. Many contracts are written so that what exactly is required of the parties varies with the circumstances. When the norm or contract says a fiduciary or professional must adapt to what a person needs (or, in some cases, wants), then the contingencies that determine needs give particular individuals, those with bad luck, superior claims; conversely, these same contingencies increase the obligations of those meeting the needs. Thus one is responsible to meet the demands of those who can make legitimate claims under the contingencies of the contract. If one is obliged to care for some person or to supply some good to another organization "come hell or high water," then taking responsibility means adjusting one's tasks so that one can still fulfill one's obligations. Of course responsibility is more onerous when there is a lot of hell and high water.

Mansbridge (1990a and 1990b) argues that there are costs to "gratuitous gendering," to harnessing an idea too tightly to gender, so that for instance one might exaggerate the empirical connection between some phenomenon and gender or neglect the nongendered arguments for an idea. Here I am constructing a nongendered argument for something that has been discussed up to this point mainly in the light of its alleged connection to gender. The ethic of care can be defended by the argument I have been making for particularism. And then much of the argument of this paper can be restated in the following form: Many things cannot get done in organizations without networks governed by an ethic of care. An ethic of care means the creation of particularistic obligations to others in the network. Responsible response to uncertain environments and to the needs they generate often requires such a network tied together by an ethic of care, and so requires disinterested particularistic norms.

Notes

1. When organizational takeovers become common, we would expect workers to be less willing to invest in organization-specific human capital precisely because the particularistic relation between worker and employer is undermined. Workers are treated then as factors of production rather than as friends.

2. Weber argues that the rationalizing tendencies he is describing "were not part of any articulate and unambiguous policy on the part of the wielders of power" (809) but instead came from the need for rational administration (and so were driven more by the administrators) and from pressure from powerful interest groups (such as the bourgeois classes). Law was rationalized on formal rather than substantive grounds, became more universal (that is, the law of the land began to prevail over special laws applying to different status groups), and was increasingly likely to be codified. Codification, Weber argues, was especially likely to be favored by "those who had hitherto suffered most from the lack of an unambiguously fixed and generally accessible set of norms, i.e., of norms that would allow checking up on the administration of justice" (849). This argument that disadvantaged groups such as the peasantry would be eager to have laws codified is especially interesting given contemporary arguments that legal codes necessarily disadvantage the powerless since they are written to take account of the interests and experiences of those in power. Presumably no codes are worse than codes written by the powerful, which in turn are worse than codes written to take full account of difference.

   Weber also discusses anti-formalist tendencies in modern law, including legal decisions made "in the light of concrete evaluations rather than in accordance with formal norms" (886; generally, 882–889).

3. See, especially, Weber 1978:815–819, 848–852, 880–895, and 973–980; Parsons and Shilis 1951:76–88. For a defense of universalism because of its relation to equality, see Berlin 1969.

4. Interestingly, Weber argues that "very recent legal developments have brought

an increasing particularism within the legal system" (1978:880) since though commercial law may not be status group law (and so particularistic on those grounds) it is *class* law (and so particularistic on different grounds). These particularistic laws, he argues, are the result of occupational differentiation and pressure from commercial and industrial groups. Weber also identifies a second cause of this increasing particularism, which is more important for the argument being made here. He argues that commercial and industrial groups have wished to "eliminate the formalities of normal legal procedure for the sake of a settlement that would be both expeditious and better adapted to the concrete case. In practice, this trend signifies a weakening of legal formalism out of considerations of substantive expediency . . ." (882).

5. Espeland notes that plasma center employees "freely improvise on these official rules" both to accommodate healthy donors whose vital signs do not fall within the designated limits (the example she gives is of a long-distance runner whose pulse, temperature, and blood pressure were always too low) and to eliminate potential donors who are deemed undesirable (1984:142–143). In this case, the objective criteria in the rules were sometimes inappropriate and it was necessary to make individual exceptions in order to achieve the goal.

6. One could argue, of course, that all rules are universalistic. But rules vary, as Weber (1978) argued, in whether they apply generally or apply only to particular groups. What I have in mind here is a slightly different distinction, that particularistic rules take account of variations between individuals and say how the general rule is to be modified for various subgroups.

7. Gundecking is the falsification of reports by writing them up as if one has actually carried out the tests or procedures whose results are being reported. One can gundeck all or only part of a report. Johnson's (1972) account is of gundecking reports on a U.S. Navy Destroyer.

8. I should note here that a number of feminist writers have also made a case against universalism, though mostly on different grounds than those I argue here. Minow (1987), for instance, argues eloquently that universal rules, reflecting "choices by those in power about what characteristics should matter" (38), are only facially neutral and tend to favor those who are "normal" over those who are "different." Discussing the dilemma of difference—that negative consequences follow both from ignoring difference and from taking it into account (71–72)—she argues that "[i]nstead of an impartial view, we should strive for the standpoint of someone committed to the moral relevance of contingent particulars" (75).

  While Minow has some sympathy with the need to create simplifying categories and with the impulse to classify (though she would argue that these are not neutral processes—see pp. 35 and 64)), Young (1987) apparently sees no value in such systems of categories. She argues against the notions of universality and of impartiality which, she argues, make moral reason "unable to understand and evaluate particular moral contexts in their particularity" (61). The conception that public life should be blind to sex, age, race, and the like, she argues, has "resulted in the exclusion of persons and aspects of persons from public life" (74). Both Spelman (1988) and Bartlett (1990) argue against the use of analytic categories (in particular "woman") on the grounds that such categories obscure important differences among members of the category (in this case differences in race, class, sexual orientation, and the like, among women) and lead to a consideration of the needs and interests of only the dominant subgroup in the category (in this case white, middle-class, heterosexual women). As Bartlett puts it, "Any category, no matter how narrowly defined, makes assumptions about the remaining characteristics of the group that fail to take account of members of the group who do not have those characteristics" (1990:848). Bartlett goes on to give a limited endorsement to the processes of generalization and abstraction: "Contextualized reasoning is also not . . . the polar opposite of a 'male' model of abstract thinking. All major forms of legal reasoning encompass processes of both contextualization and abstraction. . . . Feminists do not and cannot reject . . . the process of abstraction" (856–857). Bartlett later writes that "Feminist practical reasoning . . . exposes and helps to limit the damage that universalizing rules and assumptions can do; universalizations will always be present, but contextualized reasoning will help to identify those currently useful and eliminate the others" (887). While feminists differ, then, in the extent to which they reject the entire process of categorizing and abstracting, what they do share is a profound skepticism about the fairness and objectivity of purportedly universalistic rules. My argument here is that universalistic rule systems contain within themselves a requirement for contextualizing particularism.

9. I stress here that it is the *intellectual* objectives of the student that set the standard against which the student's project is judged. A doctoral student's broader goals may include getting a degree and a good job. The dissertation adviser is expected to continue to judge universalistically how useful the project is and how well the person has pursued the project. Particularism enters in only in the development of the standard against which the project should be judged.

10. Benhabib argues for what she calls "interactive universalism," drawing on Gilligan's work to make a case against what she calls the "substitutionalist universalism" of moral philosophers.

11. Stouffer (1951) finds that though people generally endorse universalistic principles, they also recognize situations in which they would violate universalistic principles (for instance in refusing to turn in a buddy for violating some rule). It may be that what happens here is that two principles are coming into conflict. One cannot simultaneously follow the universalistic principle that all interaction partners should be treated similarly and the principle of reciprocity which would argue that one should distinguish those with whom one had a relationship (and to whom one therefore owed loyalty) from those with whom one did not. Such normative challenges to universalism may provide some clue about where we are especially likely to find particularism.

12. This fusion of identities and of utility functions may, however, be extremely important in other contexts. But just as particularism necessarily enters into universalistic relations, so universalism plays a part in deeply particularistic ones. See Heimer and Stinchcombe 1980.

13. The exception here is probably in young children who, partly because of low capacity and partly because each month of age is such a large proportion of the biography, cannot be treated universalistically. Mannheim somewhere notes that cohorts in effect increase in size as people age, but our system of categories does not adjust enough for that. If we are going to treat all one-year-olds, two-year-olds, and three-year-olds each as a group, then when people approach age 60, the ground should include people 50–70. Rather than alter the category system that much, it probably makes more sense to consider the case of each three-year-old on its own merits.

14. This is no doubt partly because people have to be taught how—and how not—to be particularistic. New employees are probably not taught the rules of particularism, but instead are socialized into the practice of particularism. Among other things, this means that the practice of particularism is likely to be different in different subgroups, and that there are likely to be clashes along the boundaries of groups about what is legitimate and what is not. Kanter's (1977) discussion of the particularistic relations of secretaries whose careers had been blocked provides some evidence both about socialization to particularism and about variations in particularistic practices within a single organization.

15. For fuller discussions of this connection between trust, availability of information, and interdependence, see Hechter 1987, Heimer 1976, Stinchcombe 1990, and Weber 1946. Boyd and Richerson (1990) discuss the relationship between ethnicity and cooperation.

16. Weber notes that the law tends to be rigorously formalistic "as far as it is required for security to do business," but becomes "informal for the sake of business goodwill where this is required by the logical interpretation of the intention of the parties or by the 'good usage' of business intercourse, interpreted as some 'ethical minimum' " (1978:894).

References

Bartlett, Katharine. 1990. "Feminist Legal Methods." *Harvard Law Review* 103(4):829–888.

Benhabib, Seyla. 1987. "The Generalized Other and the Concrete Other: The Kohlberg-Gilligan Controversy and Feminist Theory." In Seyla Benhabib and Drucilla Cornell, eds., *Feminism as Critique: On the Politics of Gender*. Minneapolis: University of Minnesota Press, pp. 77–95.

Berlin, Isaiah. [1956] 1969. "Equality." In William T. Blackstone, ed., *The Concept of Equality*. Minneapolis: Burgess, pp. 14–34.

Boyd, Robert, and Peter J. Richerson. 1990. "Culture and Cooperation." In Jane J. Mansbridge, ed., *Beyond Self-Interest*. Chicago: University of Chicago Press, pp. 111–132.

Comaroff, John L., and Simon Roberts. 1981. *Rules and Processes: The Cultural Logic of Dispute in an African Context*. Chicago: University of Chicago Press.

Espeland, Wendy N. 1984. "Blood and Money: Exploiting the Embodied Self." In Joseph A. Kotarba and Andrea Fontana, eds., *The Existential Self in Society*. Chicago: University of Chicago Press, pp. 131–155.

Gilligan, Carol. 1982. *In a Different Voice: Psychological Theory and Women's Development*. Cambridge, MA: Harvard University Press.

Gilligan, Carol, and Jane Attanucci. 1988. "Two Moral Orientations." In Carol Gilligan, Janie Victoria Ward, and Jill MacLean Taylor, eds., *Mapping the Moral Domain*. Cambridge, MA: Harvard University Press.

Gilligan, Carol, Janie Victoria Ward, and Jill MacLean Taylor, eds. 1988. *Mapping the Moral Domain*. Cambridge, MA: Harvard University Press.

Granovetter, Mark. 1992. "Problems of Explanation in Economic Sociology." Chapter 1, this volume.

Hechter, Michael. 1987. *Principles of Group Solidarity*. Berkeley: University of California Press.

Heimer, Carol A. 1976. "Uncertainty and Vulnerability in Social Relations." Unpublished M.A. paper, University of Chicago.

———. 1984. "Organizational and Individual Control of Career Development in Engineering Project Work." *Acta Sociologica* 27(4):283–310.

———. 1986. "On Taking Responsibility." Unpublished draft. Department of Sociology, Northwestern University.

———, and Arthur L. Stinchcombe. 1980. "Love and Irrationality: It's Got to be Rational to Love You Because It Makes Me So Happy." *Social Science Information* 19(4/5):697–754.

Held, Virginia. 1990. "Mothering versus Contract." In Jane J. Mansbridge, ed., *Beyond Self-Interest*. Chicago: University of Chicago Press, pp. 287–304.

Johnson, John M. 1972. "The Practical Uses of Rules." In Robert A. Scott and Jack D. Douglas, eds., *Theoretical Perspectives on Deviance*. New York: Basic Books, pp. 215–248.

Kanter, Rosabeth Moss. 1977. *Men and Women of the Corporation*. New York: Basic Books.

Leidner, Robin L. 1988. *Working on People: The Routinization of Interactive Service Work*. Unpublished Ph.D. dissertation, Northwestern University.

Macaulay, Stewart. 1963. "Non-contractual Relations in Business: A Preliminary Study." *American Sociological Review* 28:55–67.

Mannheim, Karl. 1952. "The Problem of Generations." In Karl Mannheim, *Essays in the Sociology of Knowledge*. London: Routledge & Kegan Paul.

Mansbridge, Jane J. 1990a. "Feminism and Democracy." *The American Prospect* 1(1):126–139.

———. 1990b. "'Difference' as a Feminist Political Strategy." Unpublished paper, Northwestern University.

Minow, Martha. 1987. "The Supreme Court 1986 Term. Foreward: Justice Engendered." *Harvard Law Review* 101:10–95.

Neckerman, Kathryn M., and Joleen Kirschenman. 1991. "Hiring Strategies, Racial Bias, and Inner-City Workers." Chicago: Department of Sociology, University of Chicago. (Revision of paper presented at the annual meetings of the American Sociological Association, August 1990.)

Parsons, Talcott, and Edward A. Shils. 1951. "Categories of the Orientation and Organization of Action." In T. Parsons and E. A. Shils eds., *Toward a General Theory of Action*. New York: Harper and Row, pp. 53–109.

Ruddick, Sara. 1980. "Maternal Thinking." *Feminist Studies* 6(3):343–367.

Spelman, Elizabeth V. 1988. *Inessential Woman: Problems of Exclusion in Feminist Thought*. Boston: Beacon Press.

Stinchcombe, Arthur L. 1985. "Contracts as Hierarchical Documents." In A. L. Stinchcombe and C. A. Heimer, *Organization Theory and Project Management: Administering Uncertainty in Norwegian Offshore Oil*. Oslo and London: Norwegian University Press and Oxford University Press, pp. 121–171.

———. 1990. "Consent to be Judged." Paper presented at the annual meetings of the Law and Society Association, June 1, 1990.

Stouffer, Samuel A. 1951. "An Empirical Study of Technical Problems in Analysis of Role Obligation." In T. Parsons and E. A. Shils, eds., *Toward a General Theory of Action*. New York: Harper and Row, pp. 479–496. (Stouffer's chapter includes a reprint of the paper he coauthored with Jackson Toby, "Role Conflict and Personality," which appeared in the March 1951 issue of *American Journal of Sociology*.)

Tilly, Charles. 1989. "Preface." *Sociological Forum* 4(3):435–438.

Weber, Max. 1946. "The Protestant Sects and the Spirit of Capitalism." In H. H. Gerth and C. Wright Mills, eds. and trs., *From Max Weber: Essays in Sociology*. New York: Oxford University Press, pp. 302–322.

———. 1978. *Economy and Society*. Guenther Roth and Claus Wittich, eds. Berkeley: University of California Press.

Weick, Karl. 1976. "Educational Organizations as Loosely Coupled Systems." *Administrative Science Quarterly* 21 (March): 1–19.

Young, Iris Marion. 1987. "Impartiality and the Civic Public: Some Implications of Feminist Critiques of Moral and Political Theory." In Seyla Benhabib and Drucilla Cornell, eds., *Feminism as Critique: On the Politics of Gender*. Minneapolis: University of Minnesota Press, pp. 56–77.

6

Structural Alignments, Individual Strategies, and Managerial Action: Elements Toward a Network Theory of Getting Things Done

HERMINIA IBARRA

STRUCTURAL ALIGNMENTS, INDIVIDUAL STRATEGIES, AND MANAGERIAL ACTION

In recent years there has been a resurgence of interest in the patterns of network relationships that characterize the internal workings of business firms and the behavior of their managers. Based on the observation that much of what occurs in organizations is only vaguely related to top management directives, the organizational chart, and the logic of vertical integration (Powell 1990), many organizational scholars argue that it is informal or emergent networks of relationships that account for regularities in day-to-day work, distinguish effective from ineffective individuals and groups, and generally provide key channels for the business of getting things done. As noted by J. R. Lincoln,

> a continuing theme in organizational study is the extent to which adaptive organizations do in fact operate in terms of official and prescribed internal networks or whether they must regularly mobilize the spontaneous, informal, and interpersonal ties of sentiment and collegiality in order to achieve organizational goals . . . informal networks are indispensable to organizational functioning, and managers must learn to manipulate them for organizational ends (1982:11).

While a wealth of managerial research (e.g., Kanter 1983, 1989; Kotter 1982, 1985) has suggested that patterns of informal network interactions play an important role in facilitating the achievement of desired individual and organizational outcomes, we know very little about what specific kinds of network patterns lead to what particular action outcomes. Managerial research has tended to use the network concept metaphorically, without clear specification of network characteristics such as types of flows and variations in structure (Tichy and Fombrun 1979). Moreover, this body of work has emphasized individuals' behavioral strategies without much attention to the larger structural patterns in which they are embedded. As a result, the image that emerges is one of unconstrained patterns of interaction and discretionary action, and few guidelines are provided concerning optimal strategies for getting things done in any given structural context.

Network-analytic studies, on the other hand, have provided many insights into the macro-level properties and structures of organizational networks, but have remained largely descriptive: Most debates have focused on the nature of structure, rather than on antecedents and consequences of structure (Tichy 1981; Kadushin 1988; Monge and Eisenberg 1987). Moreover, network theorists have for the most part emphasized the ways in which an existing and stable structure limits and constrains human interaction (e.g., Burt 1982), with little discussion of the strategies used by people to form, constantly change, and mobilize their networks of relationships. Overall, the emphasis has been on opportunity and constraint derived from structure, as opposed to actions and strategies that create structure and compensate for structural limits or maximize network resources.

This chapter draws from these two literatures to explore connections between structural context, as defined by the relationship between prescribed and emergent patterns of interaction, and individual strategies for making use of those structures, in an attempt to better understand managerial action.

Prescribed and Emergent Structure

A social network is "a specific set of linkages among a defined set of persons, with the additional property that the characteristics of these linkages as a whole may be used to interpret the social behavior of the persons involved" (Mitchell 1969:2). In organizations, prescribed networks are composed of a set of formally specified relationships between superiors and subordinates and among functionally differentiated groups that must interact to accomplish an organizationally defined task. Prescribed networks also encompass the sets of relationships created by "quasi-structure": committees, task forces, teams, and dotted-line relationships that are formally sanctioned by the firm but more fluid than relationships represented by the organizational chart (Schoonhoven and Jelinek 1990). An emergent network, on the other hand, involves informal, discretionary patterns of interaction where the content of the relationship may be work related, social, or a combination of both. Emergent networks develop out of "the purposive action of social actors who seek to realize their self-interests, and depending on their abilities and interest, will negotiate routinized patterns or relationships that enhance these interests" (Galaskiewicz 1979: 16).

Common to both the managerial and network literature has been a lack of conceptual and empirical focus on the relationship between emergent networks and the prescribed features of an organization (Kadushin 1988; Tichy and Fombrun 1979). As Dalton noted many years ago (1959:222), "multiple relations, with continuous interaction and change, become too dynamic to be handled entirely inside such conceptual walls as 'formal-informal.'" A more realistic approach, he argues, entails attention to the "interconnections between formal and unofficial as they draw apart, collide and/or irregularly perform functions" (226).

Informal networks, however, are still commonly described in contrast, or opposition to, formal organizational structures, although empirical evidence suggests that in many organizations they overlap to a considerable extent (e.g., Krackhardt 1990; Kadushin and Brimm 1990). Lincoln (1982), for example, has argued that formal structure is "at best a highly idealized image of organizational reality. At worst it is pure ideology, bearing little direct relation to internal organizational networks" (8).

The problem with viewing the formal configuration of roles and procedures in opposition to actual patterns of interaction is that it implicitly opposes constraint and agency, instead of focusing on the "interpenetration" or dynamic interaction of the two (Ranson et al. 1980:2). An alternative perspective suggests that the formal or prescribed network provides the ground rules:

> The framework of rules, roles, and authority relations seeks to facilitate prescribed purposes by differentially enabling certain kinds of conduct, conferring support for forms of commitment, as well as constraining and obligating those who reject the claims entailed by the framework. The framework rather than being removed from organizational working, is intrinsically involved in shaping the actual operation of rules and the real working of authority, sustaining the distribution and conception of the division of labor (Benson 1977, quoted in Ranson et al. 1980:3).

In concert with this approach, several researchers have emphasized the interdependence of formal and informal structure (Stevenson 1990; Shrader, Lincoln, and Hoffman 1989; Kadushin and Brimm 1990). Kadushin and Brimm (1990:5), for example, note that "shadow" networks arise from the requirements of the formal organization and are "always pegged to or draped around the scaffolding of the formal arrangements of the organization, and generally do not have an existence separate or away from the organization." Variation in the pegs, therefore, alters the form of emergent networks (Tichy and Fombrun, 1979:929).

In sum, a cogent argument has been made that "formal and emergent networks coexist, and each can be best understood in the context of the other" (Monge and Eisenberg 1987:309). Nevertheless, there has been little guidance provided in the literature concerning factors that govern the relationship between formal and informal structures, the degree and nature of the alignment, and the extent to which resulting patterns affect individual and organizational action possibilities. In defining the organizational context for action, therefore, the common formal/informal dichotomy is discarded in favor of a focus on the interplay, or forms of alignment, between prescribed and emergent networks.

Structure and Strategy

An important, yet often implicit, debate in the network and managerial literatures concerns the tension between purposeful action and structural constraint (Parsons 1964; Coleman 1986; Poole and Van De Ven 1989). Existing structural arrangements, both formal and informal, clearly limit or shape the interaction patterns of individuals: Studies that ignore the total network structure are "methodologically bound to a conclusion which gives explanatory weight to the discretionary strategies and interactions of organizational members" (Ranson et al. 1980:4). Yet these interactions also shape and define the network structure over time. More importantly, individuals may differ in the skills that they apply in using their structurally based resources and in their strategies for maximizing the utility of their networks.

Thus, while individual action must be viewed in the context of existing structural constraints, following Pettigrew (1973), emphasis is given to the role played by those individuals in the structuring of social action over time:

> By their ability to exert power over others, individuals can change or maintain structures as well as the norms and expectations on which these structures rest. An individual's behavior is therefore governed not only by the structure of the situation in which he participates but also by his ability to shape and mold that structure to fit his interests (1973:31).

This chapter proposes that optimal strategies for mobilizing network relationships or augmenting structural resources will differ by organizational context, as defined by prevailing forms of network alignment.

Managerial Action

The notion of contingency has a long history in organizational research (Burns and Stalker 1961; Lawrence and Lorsch 1967): We have long taken for granted the idea that different types of formal organizational structures are differentially suited for different tasks. Little progress, however, has been made in the development of contingency theories of intraorganizational informal structure (Barney 1985), and there has been virtually no academic discourse on the action implications of the relationship between emergent and prescribed networks.

Two key action dimensions are frequently discussed in the literature: innovativeness and criticality. The routine-innovative dimension captures the degree of uncertainty inherent in the task at hand. Innovative tasks require new knowledge, experimentation, flexibility of organizational structure, and often—since it is necessary to be able to mobilize support for ideas quickly and efficiently—very different implementation strategies than do routine tasks (Zaltman, Duncan, and Holbek 1973; Burns and Stalker 1961). The peripheral-critical dimension concerns the extent to which the action or task is central to the organization's livelihood and is associated with the degree of visibility and risk inherent in the action. One would expect different strategies to be efficacious for actions that have a critical bearing on the organization versus those having a more peripheral effect.

This chapter focuses on these two broadly defined action categories to advance the argument that different types of action tend to be facilitated or inhibited by particular modes of alignment between emergent networks and formal structure. Systemic constraints, however, may be mitigated by the use of particular strategies in developing and mobilizing network relationships for collective action.

Overview of Paper

As we have discussed, three general factors independently and in interaction are associated with effectiveness of network use for getting things done: characteristics of the organizational context (alignments), the degree of individual adroitness in managing that context (strategies), and the kind action. The first portion of this chapter describes and contrasts two archetypal forms of network organization: integrative and hierarchical systems. These hypothetical systems provide the context for exploring varying patterns of structural alignment between prescribed and emergent networks, which in turn have strong implications for the action potential of such systems. The second section of the chapter discusses three categories of individual network strategies and assesses their effectiveness in the context of particular forms of alignment and task requirements. The chapter concludes with a model linking structural alignments, individual strategies, and action.

NETWORK FORMS OF ORGANIZATION

A growing body of recent research has documented the emergence of "network organization" as a distinct structural form that is neither market nor hierarchy. Network organizations are described as characterized by lateral or horizontal patterns of exchange, interdependent flows of resources, and reciprocal lines of communication (Powell 1990; Nolan, Pollock, and Ware 1988). According to Powell (1990), networks are more flexible and effective than hierarchies in responsiveness to changing conditions: New information is more easily disseminated, interpreted, and acted on without the constraint of passing information or searching for resources up and down a hierarchy. While some networks may certainly function as such, here it is argued that there is no one generic form of network organization. Multiple forms exist, and the realization of commonly touted benefits of network structure and interaction is in effect contingent on precise properties of the network.

Three properties of network structure, density, connectivity, and hierarchy are associated with flexibility and ease of information exchange (Krackhardt 1989). Density is defined as the ratio of actual to potential ties among actors in a network; connectivity is the degree to which members of a network are linked together through direct or indirect ties (Burt 1982). High density and connectivity imply a high degree of interdependence among different segments of the network and, by corollary, a high degree of intergroup contact in network relationships. Density and connectivity may be used to describe both prescribed and emergent structures: The addition of dotted-line reporting relationships to a simple hierarchy, for example, adds density, connectivity, and intergroup contact. Networks also differ in their degree of hierarchy and centralization, concepts that describe patterns of stratification or inequality in the extent to which actors are involved in relations and which apply to both prescribed and emergent networks.

> A system is centralized to the extent that all relations in it involve a single actor. It has hierarchical structure to the extent that a single actor is the direct or indirect object of relations in it . . . both these models describe the extent to which a dominant elite is defined by networks (Burt 1982:61).

Thus the contrast between networks and hierarchies, traditional and post-bureaucratic organizations, is captured by the network analytic concepts of density, connectivity, and hierarchy:

> mechanistic or bureaucratic structures . . . comprised centralized, structured, single-stranded, and sparse networks of asymmetric communication and control relations. In contrast, the organic organization associated with adaptive firms in turbulent environments was constituted by networks of dense, lateral, diffuse, and reciprocal relations (Shrader, Lincoln, and Hoffman 1989:45).

A contrasting model of organizational systems is offered by researchers who conceptualize organizational structure as a system of political coalitions in which individuals and subgroups vie for power and influence (e.g., Lawler and Bacharach 1983; Pettigrew 1973). Here the focus is on how patterns of links between interest groups structure cliques, coalitions, and cleavages (Wellman 1988). It is assumed that a "network which is partitioned into islands of relations, isolated from one another or bridged by infrequent ties, is structurally very different from one in which relations are evenly or homogeneously distributed" (Shrader, Lincoln, and Hoffman 1989:48). In network-analytic terms this entails specifying how the total network is partitioned through clustering, or patterns of dense areas of interaction (Burt 1982).

Integrative and hierarchical systems also appear to differ in clique structure. A high incidence of cliquing or dense clusters of relations joined by sparse or distant ties, for example, has been hypothesized to be characteristic of mechanistic as opposed to organic organizations (Shrader et al. 1986). Kanter's (1983) notion of segmentalist and integrative firms highlights the same phenomena. Moreover, cliques in hierarchical systems tend to be fairly stable, organized around enduring values, agendas, and characteristics rather than more fluid task-specific goals. By contrast, fluidity is much more characteristic of integrative systems, where coalitions are short term, deal with only one temporally bound issue, and then disband (Kanter 1983).[2] Finally, in hierarchical systems, intraclique relationships tend to be characterized by similarity of personal characteristics, background and experience, and ideologies (Dalton 1959); coalitions in integrative systems evidence greater internal diversity, often as a reflection of task demands.

A political perspective also emphasizes bases of power and influence. Three general factors empower individuals vis-à-vis their network contacts: their reputation, knowledge, and expertise;their formal position and place in the status hierarchy; and their alliances and group memberships. Within integrative systems, power stems primarily from control of information; influence is derived from expertise and is specific to the task at hand (Nolan, Pollock, and Ware 1988). The pecking order of informal groups is based on skill and performance rather than on personal qualities and demographic attributes (Walton and Hackman 1986). In hierarchical systems, by contrast, the most valued commodity is authority or standing within the hierarchy. While alliances are important resources in both types of systems, personal characteristics define their utility to a greater extent than task-relevant skills in hierarchies (Dalton 1959).

Miller and Friesen (1980) have suggested that organizational systems are characterized by a coherence or common orientation of component structural attributes and processes and thus may be considered as exemplars of common archetypes. Extending their work to the realm of network organization, this chapter focuses on two archetypal forms: hierarchical and integrative systems.

Structural Alignments:
Defining the Network Context for Action

A core thesis of this chapter is the notion that the action potential of organizational systems is highly contingent on the degree of overlap or alignment between prescribed and emergent networks. The degree of alignment refers to the extent to which prescribed and emergent networks are tightly or loosely coupled. Loose coupling is defined by a situation in which elements are responsive, but retain evidence of separateness and identity (Weick 1979) or by systems that either have few variables in common or have in common variables that are weak (Orton and Weick 1990). A state of loose coupling, for example, would entail highly disjointed formal and emergent structures, or structures operating to accomplish highly differentiated tasks, sometimes even at cross-purposes.

But as clarified by Orton and Weick (1990), loose coupling is a multidimensional concept: Organizations contain interdependent elements
that vary in the number and strength of their interdependencies. Consequently, these writers argue that rather than portraying systems as
loosely or tightly coupled, researchers should search for simultaneously
occurring patterns of tight and loose coupling:

> To state that an organization is a loosely coupled system is the beginning of
> a discussion, not the end. What elements are loosely coupled? What domains
> are they coupled on? What domains are they decoupled on? What are the
> characteristics of the couplings and decoupling? (1990:219)

I propose that relevant domains for the exploration of patterns of coupling
and decoupling are the relationship-contents of networks. Three types
are frequently distinguished: workflow, influence, and expressive
relationships. Work-flow relationships are the channels of communication
and resource exchange used in getting things done on a daily basis (Brass
1984); these may be formally or informally established. Influence networks
are the systems of favors granted and owed, of mutual benefit and protection, and of connections invoked for the exercise of power. Influence networks may also be of a formal nature, corresponding to hierarchical
authority or informally derived on the basis of reputation, expertise, or
control of critical contingencies (Pfeffer and Salancik 1978). Finally, expressive relations or friendship networks involve the exchange of liking and
social support (Tichy, Tushman, and Fombrun 1974; Fombrun 1982).
While expressive networks are exclusively defined by emergent patterns
of interaction, individuals' friendship, workflow, and influence networks
may overlap to a great extent, or may be highly compartmentalized and
functionally differentiated.

In sum, prescribed and emergent networks may overlap in workflow,
in influence, or in both; expressive networks may overlap to varying
extents with other networks. Moreover, these various types of networks
may perform similar functions in some types of organizational systems,
while in others their usage is highly differentiated. Finally, organizations
differ in relative clarity with respect to occasions on which one network
rather than the other is invoked (Kadushin and Brimm 1990). The degree
and modes of alignment between prescribed and emergent networks
structure the allocation of valued resources, thus regulating opportunity
for action.

Alignments in Hierarchical Systems

It has long been hypothesized that emergent and prescribed networks
within hierarchical systems tend to be loosely coupled, functioning independently and sometimes even at odds with each other (see Tichy 1981
for a review). This is the situation often reported in studies of lower participants, where influence is independent of formal authority, and
informal organization emerges to restrict output, resist change, or

accomplish a parallel set of objectives (Roethlisberger and Dickson 1939; Crozier 1964; Walton and Hackman 1986).

Earlier, however, it was argued that the degree of alignment varies for different types of network relationships. Moreover, the extent of alignment must be established from a total system perspective, rather than within any particular, formally designated group (e.g., nonsupervisory personnel). When these factors are considered, this chapter proposes that a more differentiated pattern of alignment characterizes hierarchical systems.

Empirical evidence suggests that hierarchical systems are characterized by a high degree of overlap between emergent influence networks and formal structures of authority. In a study of three organizations, one organic and two mechanistic, Tichy and Fombrun (1979) found a reasonably high degree of fit between prescribed and emergent networks in the mechanistic firms (hierarchical authority was reinforced by network centrality), while in the organic firm the two sources of power appeared to vary independently. The high correlations between network centrality and hierarchical level reported in most network studies of traditional organizations is consistent with this finding (Brass 1984; Krackhardt 1990). Thus the following proposition:

Proposition 1. *Emergent influence networks and prescribed authority structures are tightly coupled in hierarchical systems.*

As noted by Walton and Hackman (1986), different types of control or compliance systems create different motivations for the development of emergent structures. The coercive control mechanisms characteristic of hierarchical systems lead to the development of networks used for protection against or circumvention of formal rules (Tichy 1981; Walton and Hackman 1986). Keller (1989), for example, in her chronicle of the trials and tribulations of General Motors, describes what appeared to be a loosely coupled system where prescribed and emergent work-flow networks performed entirely different functions:

Over the years, the system had become so paralytic that nothing could happen if they went through the system. What we found out was that the organization worked by an informal network of people. They call this being effective outside the system. The way they got things to work was really through this informal network (118).

Accordingly,

Proposition 2. *Emergent and prescribed work-flow networks are loosely coupled in hierarchical systems.*

It is also often reported that coercive control mechanisms lead to the development of emergent networks that function primarily to fulfill expressive needs, have more affective content than task-relevant information and influence, and are segregated from formal structures, controlling a large sphere of organizational activities (Tichy and Fombrun 1979; Tichy 1981; Etzioni 1961; Walton and Hackman 1986). While a compelling argument has been made that these assertions apply primarily to the friendship networks of lower participants with limited opportunity for advancement (Kanter 1977), friendship networks in hierarchical systems are often segregated by status, which corresponds to formal authority. As a result, friendship networks may not overlap to any considerable extent with the other networks of relationships. Therefore

> Proposition 3. *Expressive and instrumental (work-flow and influence) networks are loosely coupled in hierarchical systems.*

Action in Hierarchical Systems In systems characterized by the previously described patterns of alignment, experimentation and innovation tend to be problematic. The tight coupling of influence and authority networks stands in sharp contrast to commonly reported innovation requirements: access to diverse people and skills; unrestricted communication; and influence based on knowledge, expertise, and ability to contribute to solutions rather than on bureaucratic sources of power (Kanter 1983; Nolan, Pollock, and Ware 1988). The inevitable problems of hierarchy (both formal and informal) include the filtering and distortion of information (Wilensky 1967), a slower pace of decision making, and restricted or highly specified procedures for access to required resources (Kanter 1983). As a result, hierarchies are difficult to mobilize quickly (Powell 1990).

Kadushin and Brimm (1990), for example, report a case where emergent networks operated side by side with the formal organization structure, but remained too far underground or too localized to be capable of carrying out key organizational communication and problem-solving tasks. While prescribed and emergent networks overlapped to a great extent in the structure of influence relations (i.e., members of higher echelons tended to also be prominent in emergent advice networks), they were loosely coupled in workflow and friendship ties, thus hindering innovative action—in this case the implementation of a decentralized, global approach to decision making.

These difficulties are balanced, however, against the unique strengths of this pattern of alignment: the ability to leverage existing knowledge and standardize routine procedures (Burns and Stalker 1961) and the singleness of purpose required for carrying out action in domains that are central to the organization's purpose (Pierce and Delbecq 1977; Zaltman et al. 1973). Tightly coupled systems are more conducive to systemwide change (Firestone 1985; Meyerson and Martin 1987; Orton and Weick 1990). The tight coupling of influence and authority networks, therefore, facilitates continued operations while providing the unity of purpose and centralized coordination required for large-scale change.

Loose coupling, on the other hand, detracts from managers' ability to plan, predict, and control change (Meyerson and Martin 1987; Orton and Weick 1990). The loose coupling of prescribed and emergent workflow networks provides opportunities for the use of alternative pathways for action, as illustrated by the General Motors example cited earlier. The stability of emergent networks in hierarchical systems, in conjunction with the loose coupling of workflow networks, however, may heighten vulnerability to changes in formal structure. As Keller noted in her General Motors study, a major corporate reorganization can render existing informal networks nonoperational, provoking the near collapse of the true operating structure:

> One of the most common things people said to me after the reorganization— both suppliers and people inside GM—was, "I don't know who to go to anymore." Literally, the whole organization had to go fishing for that informal infrastructure. It should have been managed along with the management of the formal structure (1989:119).

Finally, the loose coupling of instrumental and expressive networks in hierarchical systems suggests that innovation may be problematic since contact and coordination across diverse groups is difficult. As noted by Krackhardt and Stern (1988), an organization characterized by friendship ties that cut across departmental boundaries is better suited to adapting to environmental changes and uncertainty. Dysfunctional consequences of these forms of alignment include restricting rather than promoting cross-organizational communication, producing in-group versus out-group dynamics and protective coalition formation (Kadushin and Brimm 1990; Dalton 1959).

Alignments in Integrative Systems

While organizations may differ in the extent to which they approximate integrative or network characteristics as the ideal type is approached, prescribed and emergent networks may be difficult to distinguish. Investment banks are an example of this type of firm; structure is best characterized as a dynamic and flexible network, the network of ties in flux, adapting rapidly to changing market conditions and customer needs (Eccles and Crane 1987).

Most organizations, however, are not pure types, and the degree of alignment must be considered with respect to different relationship contents. In integrative systems, emergent and prescribed work-flow networks are tightly coupled: emergent networks play an important role in the flow of information and influence related to task accomplishment. As noted by Tichy (1981), normative control mechanisms[3] tend to lead to the development of informal structures that are integrated and that overlap with the formal structure. Similarly, Walton and Hackman (1986) have found that in high-commitment (normative control) organizations "the boundaries between organizationally created and self-enacted group phenomena are blurred and difficult to sort out" (183). This may be partially explained by the dynamic or self-designing nature of the organization, where prescribed structure often arises from task-driven emergent networks (Schoonhoven and Jelinek 1990). Thus

Proposition 4. *Emergent and prescribed work-flow networks are tightly coupled in integrative systems.*

By contrast, informal influence networks overlap to a much lesser extent with prescribed authority networks in integrative systems than in hierarchical systems (Tichy and Fombrun, 1979). As noted earlier, influence derives from possession of knowledge and expertise relevant to specific decision domains. As a result, major organizational activities in integrative organizations are frequently initiated, organized, and implemented outside the domain of formal approval processes. This leads to a fifth proposition:

Proposition 5. *Emergent influence networks and prescribed authority structures are loosely coupled in integrative systems.*

Finally, network relationships in integrative systems tend to be multi-stranded (Shrader et al. 1986), producing overlap between expressive and instrumental networks. Tichy, for example, argues:

> In a normative compliance system, many of the participants needs tend to be met within the formal work setting; thus, there is a high degree of overlap for relationships and groups which fulfill both instrumental and expressive needs . . . friendship cliques and work groups show a high degree of overlap (1973:201).

Moreover, friendship ties tend to be structured by common interests rather than personal attributes or formal roles (Kanter 1983; DiMaggio, this volume). Hence the following is proposed:

Proposition 6. *Expressive and instrumental networks are tightly coupled in integrative systems.*

Action in Integrative Systems The tight coupling of emergent and prescribed work-flow networks that define integrative systems facilitates the dissemination and interpretation of new information and allows ideas to be translated into action quickly (Powell 1990). This, in conjunction with loosely coupled influence and authority networks that provide alternative pathways for action, facilitates nonroutine action and flexibility in responsiveness to changing conditions. In addition, the ease with which many diverse individuals can communicate directly through both formal and informal channels promotes autonomy and heightens the extent to which individuals and groups can work on "pet projects" that may not be centrally connected to the principal tasks of the organization. This is reinforced by friendship networks that are equally diverse and are not segregated from work-related activities. Relationships that exchange both information and affect are stronger than relationships with any one type of exchange (Tichy 1981).

A commonly noted innovation dilemma, however, concerns the finding that organizational characteristics that promote the generation of innovative ideas and entrepreneurial action may result in conflict, a lack

Table 6-1

Structural Alignments

ORGANIZA-TIONAL SYSTEM	DEGREE OF ALIGNMENT OF PRESCRIBED AND EMERGENT NETWORKS			ACTION IMPLICATIONS	
	Work-flow Networks	Influence Networks	Expressive Networks	Facilitates	Inhibits
Integrative	tight	loose	tight	innovative peripheral	routine critical
Hierarchical	loose	tight	loose	routine critical	innovative peripheral

of singleness of purpose, and competing diverse values (Pierce and Delbecq 1977; Zaltman, Duncan, and Holbeck 1973; Duncan 1976). The loose coupling of emergent and prescribed influence networks is key to understanding this dilemma: the existence of multiple centers of initiatives that enhance the generation of innovative ideas often results in cumbersome consensus processes at final decision stages. Thus integrative organizations face the problem of chaos, which inhibits efficiency in the domain of critical action, or those tasks central to the organization's livelihood, over the short term.

In sum, organizations characterized by different structural configurations differ in the extent to which emergent networks reinforce or complement prescribed channels or the degree to which they instead provide alternative pathways for action. Table 6-1 provides a summary of the patterns of alignment expected to characterize integrative and hierarchical systems. It is important to note that both archetypal systems are characterized by simultaneous loose-tight coupling, albeit in different domains. In hierarchical systems, workflow and friendship networks provide alternative pathways for actions; in integrative systems, alternative routes are provided by influence networks. A strong argument has been made that simultaneous loose-tight coupling results in greater adaptiveness in the face of changing conditions over the long term (Orton and Weick 1990), thus both types of systems have the potential for adaptability. The following section explores the implications of these patterns of alignment for individual network development and action.

INDIVIDUAL STRATEGIES: DEFINING SOURCES OF ADVANTAGE AND CONSTRAINT

Earlier it was proposed that the ability to "get things done" consists in large part of skill in managing the interplay between prescribed and emergent structures. Thus at an individual level we argue that variance in action outcomes will be accounted for by individuals' strategies for maximizing the utility of their networks. A guiding assumption is that the mobilization of networks for action is contingent "not only on the possession and control of system-relevant resources but also on skillful use of them. The successful use of power is a matter of tactical skill rather than merely of possession" (Pettigrew 1973:230).

The literature is replete with inventories of individual network strategies and influence tactics (e.g., Kotter 1985; Kaplan 1984; Keys and Case 1990; Pettigrew 1975); but again, this is not an area where the notion of contingency has been fully exploited. Little attempt has been made at specifying the conditions under which certain types of strategies may be more effective than others, and scant attention has been focused on the identification of interactions between strategies, context, and action. Here, by contrast, prevailing network alignments are viewed as defining an individual's opportunity structure for action. Structure, therefore, defines the potential for action, while strategies describe its enactment. In terms of Kanter's (1983) framework, structure facilitates or constrains the acquisition of power tools (information, resources, and support), and strategies govern their actual acquisition and deployment.

This section explores the effectiveness of different network strategies in the context of specific forms of alignment and for the accomplishment of particular types of tasks. This requires consideration of two aspects of network strategies: strategies that entail the formation and development of a personal network that is suited to functioning in a particular type of system and strategies involving the selective mobilization or adaptation of a personal network for a specific purpose.[4] The latter aspect emphasizes the identification of task or action requirements, emphasizing Kaplan's assertion that

> networks aren't built to serve some vague global purpose, but to get help on the manager's specific tasks. To reap the full benefit of their networks, managers must excel not only at growing but also at harvesting. Managers get work done by activating their relationships selectively (1984:51).

Three general categories of network development strategies will be discussed, and a discussion of strategies in context will follow.

Network Strategies

At a broad conceptual level, three principal categories of strategic choices affect individual's capacity to get things done: autonomy, diversity, and fluidity. Autonomy refers to the extent to which the individual has membership in, or linkages to, multiple prescribed and emergent groupings (e.g., functional groups, coalitions). The notion of diversity captures the extent to which an individual's network encompasses relationships among diverse individuals within and across various groupings. Fluidity refers to whether the configuration of relationships comprising the network is stable and enduring or in a constant state of flux.

Cohesion versus Autonomy The concept of cohesion versus autonomy refers to the extent to which an individual pursues network strategies that produce near-full encapsulation and tight interdependence within a given network of relationships versus the degree to which the strategic thrust is to preserve autonomy at whatever cost. At the heart of cohesion/autonomy strategies is the negotiation of organizational boundaries: cohesion strategies sharpen the lines or boundaries dividing actors, whereas autonomy strategies blur distinctions among subgroupings. This negotiation determines the extent to which individuals are able to develop relationships and exchange resources among the various formal and informal groupings comprising a system.

Network analytic constructs may also be utilized as indicators of the types of strategies employed by individuals in attempting to negotiate organizational boundaries. The concept of structural autonomy addresses the trade-off between the maximization of potential and the minimization of constraint, defining an actor's ability to pursue and realize interests without constraint from other actors in the system (Burt 1982). Autonomy is "high for actors occupying a position with many conflicting group affiliations and low for those occupying a position affiliated with only one other position" (270). When an individual has diversified relations with members of other groupings, competitive claims can be balanced against one another to limit constraint.

A second indicator of cohesion/autonomy strategies involves the distinction between strong ties, or the relatively dense areas of a personal network, and weak ties, bridging nonoverlapping areas of the network (Granovetter 1973). According to Granovetter, weak ties are

> of importance not only in ego's manipulation of networks, but also in that they are the channels through which ideas, influences, or information socially distant from ego may reach him. The fewer indirect contacts one has the more encapsulated he will be in terms of knowledge of the world beyond his own friendship circle (1973:1370–1371).

Arriving at a similar conclusion, Blau and Alba note that

> high integration, the proliferation of strong ties, does not greatly enhance a unit's influence, even though strong ties usually imply alliances that may be useful. This advantage is properly counterbalanced by the disadvantages that have been suggested for strong ties—the demands they make in time and effort and their encapsulation of the group (1982:376).

As argued by Stinchcombe (1987), however, influence and persuasion are most easily exercised in social relations that are close and intense, particularly under conditions of scarcity. Thus both types of relationships are necessary and their relative balance must be skillfully managed. Pettigrew (1975), for example, found that the ability of staff managers to make effective use of their external network links was contingent on their degree of access to, and quality of, within-group support. Cohesion/autonomy strategies, therefore, may be evidenced in the extent to which an individual establishes a network where most contacts also have strong ties to one another, versus a pattern of network relationships characterized by extragroup boundary spanning.

Autonomy strategies are particularly critical for innovative action, since innovative ideas tend to be interdisciplinary or interfunctional in origin and benefit from a broader perspective (Kanter 1988:171). Furthermore, noted Kanter,

> the ability of managers to get things done depends more on the number of networks in which they centrally involved than on their height in a hierarchy . . . In the emerging organization, managers add value by deal making, by brokering at interfaces, rather than by presiding over their individual empires (1989:89).

On the other hand, while cross-cutting ties between organizational subgroupings provide external loyalties and alternative channels for action, these are also ties that bind, producing greater permeability of boundaries, with concomitant obligations, pressures for isomorphism (DiMaggio and Powell 1983), and potentially reduced autonomy. This tension is most vividly exemplified in mobilizing support for organizational innovations. Innovation champions are often caught in the double bind of needing to rely on extragroup contacts to obtain resources and mobilize support for their ideas, but at the same time struggling to preserve some measure of autonomy over the process, in fear of perverting the innovation to conform to the demands of each previously enlisted constituency (e.g., Walton 1975; Kanter 1988).

Similarity versus Complementarity Network development patterns are shaped according to two basic principles: similarity and complementarity (Laumann et al. 1978). Differences rooted in ascribed attributes and available resources govern most social relationships in organizations (Blau 1982). The interdependencies created by vertical and horizontal differentiation lead to the formation of complementary ties between actors who differ on positions in the division of labor or in access to scarce resources (Lincoln 1982; Laumann et al. 1978). Similarity of goals, tasks, and personal characteristics, on the other hand, produces common interests and world views, and best explains the spontaneous ties of interpersonal attraction (McPherson and Smith-Lovin 1987; Marsden 1988).

While cohesion/autonomy strategies refer to the number of subnetworks to which individuals have access through their direct and indirect network links, similarity/complementarity strategies concern the degree of diversity actors seek out in their contacts. In network analytic terms, these concepts specify an individual's range (Burt 1982) of network relationships, or the degree of diversity (social heterogeneity) contained in those linkages.

Social homogeneity produces cohesion that increases ease of communication, improves predictability of behavior, and fosters relationships of trust and reciprocity (Lincoln and Miller 1979; Kanter 1977). People in the same department or function, for example, tend to share similar ways of viewing the world, and this commonality facilitates interaction (Alderfer 1987). Managers may also have an edge if they share a common work history or similar demographic characteristics with their network contacts:

> When a manager enters an exchange, it is more likely to go well if other things being equal, the demographic characteristics of the other party match up with those of the manager. Similarities of skin color, gender, age, country of origin and socioeconomic status smooth the way for each party to identify with and reach the other (Kaplan 1984:44–45).

Friendship, which often forms on the basis of commonality, in turn smooths the way for the acceptance of proposals and ideas (Strauss 1962). The constraint of restricting interaction to similar others, however, stems from peer's enforcement of norms concerning appropriate behavior (Rogers and Kincaid 1981). Homogeneity inhibits creativity and innovation by restricting diversity (Nystrom 1979). According to Kanter, "contact with those who see the world differently is a logical prerequisite to seeing differently ourselves" (1988:173). In his classic study of social factors related to performance in a research and development laboratory, Peltz (1956) found that the highest-performing scientists were those who had frequent contact with colleagues who were dissimilar to themselves in values and background. Similarly, research groups composed of individuals with diverse academic training and affiliation tend to be more productive than less diverse groups (Birmbaum, in Orton and Weick 1990).

Thus the tension between similarity/complementarity strategies must be skillfully managed, and optimal strategies may vary under differing conditions. In turbulent task environments and under conditions of uncertainty, for example, individuals tend to assume a more defensive posture and are more likely to direct their networking strategies to those they believe they can depend on—often those who are similar in personal attributes such as race and educational background (Galaskiewicz and Shatin 1981). Negative consequences of such an approach, however, include what Kanter (1977) has termed the homosocial reproduction of management.

Stability versus Fluidity   As noted earlier, both prescribed and emergent networks may be composed of relatively enduring, stable relationships and the more fluid constellations of relationships that are rapidly formed and dissolved (or infrequently activated) according to short-term, highly specific demands. Most managers' networks are comprised of both types of contacts, but individuals may differ in the relative balance of fluid and stable relationships.

Effective managers handle the routine intricacies and bureaucratic components of their jobs via a relatively stable set of contacts formed as a function of task interdependencies and requirements. One common tactic, for example, is to develop contacts in each area on which a manager is dependent:

I've worked at building my contacts in other departments so that when I need something done that involves another department, I have someone who will give me a fast, cooperative answer" (Kaplan 1984:40).

Stable network relationships are particularly important for critical action and getting things done under conditions of uncertainty or threat:

> relationships for getting routine things done can sprout almost like weeds. But relationships strong enough to stand up under heavy pressure are another story. Sturdy relationships take time to develop. Executives with many years in the same organization especially value their long-time contacts. An executive . . . asserted . . . "growing up in the company, I have worked with all these guys. I know them; they know me. These relationships help tremendously in a crisis situation or when you need something quickly." History matters. Relationships gain strength as both parties show that they can and will come through for each other (Kaplan 1984:50).

On the other hand, managers are continually in a state of building and extending webs of influence, repairing damaged threads, and building new webs with every career change (Keys and Case 1990). Kaplan (1984) also stresses that networks are dynamic: "[managers] never have the luxury of sitting back and saying 'Now I can relax: I've got all the connections I need'" (50). How much network flexibility and dynamism is desirable is a function of both task requirements and organizational context. Innovative projects, for example, require greater fluidity, putting "a premium on the manager's ability to activate relationships—to define the project and to build a coalition of sponsors and collaborators to implement the project" (Kaplan 1984:51). To the extent that an organization's environment is in flux, "a high degree of organizational fluidity is needed so that internal ties can adapt to changing external patterns" (Eccles and Crane 1987:181).

Fluidity/stability strategies are related to the two other categories of network strategies discussed here. Greater fluidity usually entails heightened diversity and autonomy; stability is associated with cohesion and similarity. The following section considers the implications of structural alignments and action requirements for individual network strategies in more depth.

Network Strategies in Context

As proposed earlier, differing organizational systems, as a result of their network alignments, facilitate different types of action. In integrative systems, autonomy, diversity, and fluidity strategies are predominant and facilitate the types of actions these systems carry out best— innovative and peripheral action; in hierarchical systems, cohesion, similarity, and stability strategies are more common, facilitating routine and critical action. Regardless of structural context, however, some balance of cohesion/autonomy, similarity/complementarity, and fluidity/stability

stability strategies is more likely to be effective than the extremes. This is particularly the case for action that is both innovative and critical. Less careful attention to balancing strategic poles suffices for more routine and peripheral action. Thus

Proposition 7. *Effective managers in all contexts evidence a balance of cohesion/autonomy, similarity/complementarity, and stability/fluidity strategies.*

Proposition 8. *Innovative and critical action requires a more skillful balance of strategic poles.*

Careful management of the balance of network strategies may also allow managers to circumvent factors that inhibit action within their particular operating context, facilitating routine and critical action in integrative systems and innovative and peripheral action in hierarchical systems. For example, in integrative systems critical action may require a tighter or more cohesive network of relationships that provides control in the form of intertwined visions and convergent leadership initiatives (Kotter 1990); routine actions probably require greater network stability to reduce inefficiencies (Nolan, Pollock, and Ware 1988). On the other hand—since the more innovative a task, the more network autonomy, diversity, and fluidity are required—actors in hierarchical systems attempting nonroutine courses of action are better served to broaden their networks.

Structural alignments also impact the effectiveness of individual strategies by defining places in the system where there is most "room for maneuver." These tend to be the relational domains characterized by loose coupling between prescribed and emergent networks. In hierarchical systems, for example, where formal authority and informal influence are practically one and the same, there are fewer "rational" choices for the exercise of influence in attempts to get things done. By contrast, the divergent authority and influence networks of integrative systems allow greater possibilities in forging alternative pathways for action. A second means of circumventing systemic tendencies, therefore, entails working through emergent networks that are loosely coupled with the corresponding prescribed order. This leads to a further proposition:

Proposition 9: *Systemic tendencies may be mitigated by balancing network strategies and by taking advantage of loosely coupled elements of the system.*

A final consideration is whether the task or action requires joint activation of prescribed and emergent channels. Action that is both innovative and critical usually requires joint activation of prescribed and emergent networks. By contrast, it seems reasonable to assume that individuals have most leeway in their choice of channels for carrying out action that is both routine and peripheral. Prescribed networks handle routine-critical action most effectively; innovative-peripheral action relies more on the mobilization of emergent networks. Thus network strategies also entail decisions with respect to when and for what purposes to use prescribed or emergent channels independently or in conjunction. When it is not

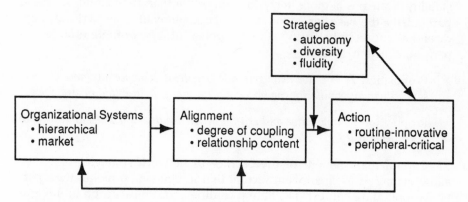

Figure 6-1

Summary Model: Alignments, Strategies, and Action

critical to activate both types of networks jointly, actors create greater "room for maneuver" by working through emergent networks that are loosely coupled with the corresponding prescribed structures. Thus

Proposition 10: *The effectiveness of network strategies is contingent on the extent to which prescribed and emergent networks must be jointly activated.*

CONCLUSION: STRUCTURE, STRATEGY, AND ACTION

Figure 6-1 provides a preliminary model of proposed interactions among alignments, strategies, and action in integrative and hierarchical systems. Structure and strategy, however, must be considered in interaction: Particular strategies produce changes in structure, while structure to some extent determines what strategies for action will be required. Action in turn produces changes in alignments and, through learning processes, in individual strategies. Therefore structure is both the medium and outcome of action; both coexist in a mutual process of production and reproduction (Poole and Van De Ven 1989).

Certain of the concepts and proposed interrelations among concepts comprising the model depicted in Figure 6-1 have a measure of empirical support; others are more speculative. The notion of alignment between composite elements of an organizational system, for example, has gained recent currency (Lawler and Bacharach 1983; Barley 1990), and the literature has witnessed a resurgence of theories of structuration (Ranson et al. 1980) emphasizing the dynamic relationship between structure and individual action. Clearly, conceptual frameworks encompassing structure, strategy, and action must specify the complex interdependencies among them. To a considerable extent, however, the multiple interactions proposed here remain untested and invite research evidence to modify and build network theories of getting things done.

The discussion thus far also points to a number of key issues that require greater conceptual and empirical attention. First, while this paper focused on two archetypal organizational forms and their associated modes of alignment, most business firms contain elements of both integrative and hierarchical systems. Many organizations today, for example, require both routine coordination of multiple specializations (efficiency) and rapid adjustment to a shifting environment (flexibility) (Nolan, Pollock, and Ware 1988; Shoonhoven and Jelineck 1990), and as a result are attempting to structure as hybrid integrative-hierarchical systems. Such hybrids will be characterized by more complex patterns of alignment and require more sophisticated network management strategies than those outlined here. The simple model proposed here, however, may provide a roadmap to guide field research aimed at uncovering the actual complexity of such systems.

Research is also needed on the durability or robustness of network alignments over time. If organizations are constantly changing their formal structures, then alignments are potentially also in constant state of flux. Future research should investigate what happens to these alignments when organizations change their prescribed or emergent structures. Tushman and Romanelli (1985) have argued that cycles of convergence move an organization toward high alignment of structures, systems, controls, and resources, while in periods of reorientation "strategies, power, structure, and systems are fundamentally transformed toward a new basis of alignment" (173). Similar equilibrium models may provide a theoretical basis for exploring the dynamic nature of structural alignments.

Notes

1. Multiple labels commonly used to denote these contrasting forms include the following: mechanistic and organic (Burns and Stalker 1961), bureaucratic and post-bureaucratic, segmentalist and integrative (Kanter 1983). Based on the assumption that all patterns of interaction may be conceptualized as networks, the term "integrative" systems is borrowed from Kanter (1983) as replacement for the more commonly used term, "network" organization.
2. A distinction is often made between coalitions, which are temporary alliances for limited purposes, and cliques, which are long lived and pursue a broad range of purposes (Tichy 1973).
3. Normative control mechanisms are based on the internalization of core values and the allocation of symbolic rewards. Because coercive rules and controls have been forfeited, managers rely on individuals to internalize organizational values.
4. In the previous section the term "network" referred to the patterns of relationships comprising a system; in this section it is used to denote a particular actor's constellation of relationships or what is commonly referred to in the network literature as an "ego network."

References

Alderfer, C. 1987. "An Intergroup Perspective on Group Dynamics." *Handbook of Organizational Behavior.* Englewood Cliffs, NJ: Prentice-Hall.

Barley, S. 1990. "The Alignment of Technology and Structure through Roles and Networks." *Administrative Science Quarterly* 35:61–103.

Barney, J. B. 1985. "Dimensions of Informal Social Network Structure: Towards a Contingency Theory of Informal Relations in Organizations." *Social Networks* 7:1–46.

Blau, J. R., and R. D. Alba. 1982. "Empowering Nets of Participation." *Administrative Science Quarterly* 27:363–379.

Blau, P. 1982. "Structural Sociology and Network Analysis: An Overview." In P. V. Marsden and N. Lin, eds., *Social Structure and Network Analysis.* Beverly Hills: Sage.

Brass, D. J. 1984. "Being in the Right Place: A Structural Analysis of Individual Influence in an Organization." *Administrative Science Quarterly* 29:518–539.

Burns, T., and G. M. Stalker. 1961. *The Management of Innovation.* London: Tavistock.

Burt, R. S. 1982. *Toward a Structural Theory of Action.* New York: Academic Press.

Coleman, J. S. 1986. "Social Theory, Social Research, and a Theory of Action." *American Journal of Sociology* 16:1309–1335.

Crozier, M. 1964. *The Bureaucratic Phenomenon.* Chicago: University of Chicago Press.

Dalton, M. 1959. *Men who Manage—Fusions of Feeling and Theory in Administration.* New York: Wiley.

DiMaggio, P. 1992. "Nadel's Paradox Revisited: Relational and Cultural Aspects of Organizational Structure." Chapter 4, this volume.

DiMaggio, P., and W. W. Powell. 1983. "The Iron Cage Revisited: Institutional Isomorphism and Collective Rationality in Organizational Fields." *American Sociological Review* 48:147–160.

Duncan, R. B. 1976. "The Ambidextrous Organization: Designing Dual Structures for Innovation." In Ralph H. Kilman, Louis R. Pondy, and Dennis P. Slevin, eds., *The Management of Organization Design.* New York: Elsevier North-Holland, 167–188.

Eccles, R. G., and D. B. Crane. 1987. "Managing Through Networks in Investment Banking." *California Management Review* (Fall) 176–195.

Etzioni, A. 1961. *A Comparative Analysis of Complex Organizations.* New York: Macmillan.

Firestone, W. A. 1985. "The Study of Loose Coupling: Problems, Progress, and Prospects." In A. C. Kerckhoff, ed., *Research in Sociology of Education and Socialization* Vol. 5. Greenwich, CT: JAI Press, pp. 3–30.

Fombrun, C. J. 1982. "Strategies for Network Research in Organizations." *Academy of Management Review* 7:280–291.

Galaskiewicz, J. 1979. *Exchange Networks and Community Politics.* Beverly Hills: Sage.

Galaskiewicz, J., and D. Shatin. 1981. "Leadership and Networking Among Neighborhood Human Service Organizations." *Administrative Science Quarterly* 26:343–448.

Granovetter, M. 1973. "The Strength of Weak Ties." *American Journal of Sociology* 6:1360–1380.

Kadushin, C. 1989. "The Next Ten Years." *Connections* 2:12–23.

Kadushin, C., and M. Brimm. 1990. "Why Networking Fails: Double Binds and the Limitations of Shadow Networks." Paper presented at the International Social Network Conference, San Diego.

Kanter, R. M. 1977. *Men and Women of the Corporation.* New York: Basic Books.

———. 1983. *The Change Masters.* New York: Simon & Schuster.

———. 1988. "When a Thousand Flowers Bloom: Structural, Collective, and Social Conditions for Innovation in Organizations." In Barry M. Staw and L. L. Cummings, eds., *Research in Organizational Behavior* Vol. 10. Greenwich, CT: JAI Press, pp. 169–211.

———. 1989. "The New Managerial Work." *Harvard Business Review* 6:85–92.

Kaplan, R. E. 1984. "Trade Routes: The Manager's Network of Relationships." *Organizational Dynamics* (Spring): 37–52.

Keller, M. 1989. *Rude Awakening: The Rise, Fall and Struggle for Recovery of General Motors*. New York: William Morrow.

Keys, B., and T. Case. 1990. "How to Become an Influential Manager." *Academy of Management Executive* 4:38–51.

Krackhardt, D. 1989. "Graph Theoretical Dimensions of Informal Organization." Paper presented at the National Meetings of the Academy of Management, Washington, D.C.

———. 1990. "Assessing the Political Landscape: Structure, Cognition, and Power in Organizations." *Administrative Science Quarterly* 35:342–369.

Krackhardt, D., and R. N. Stern. 1988. "Informal Networks and Organizational Crises: An Experimental Simulation." *Social Psychology Quarterly* 51(2):123–140.

Kotter, J. P. 1982. *The General Managers*. New York: Free Press.

———. 1985. *Power and Influence: Beyond Formal Authority*. New York: Free Press.

———. 1990. *A Force for Change*. New York: Free Press.

Laumann, E. O., J. Galaskiewicz, and P. V. Marsden. 1978. "Community Structure as Interorganizational Linkages." *Annual Review of Sociology* 4:455–484.

Lawler, E. J., and S. B. Bacharach. 1983. "Political Action and Alignments in Organizations." In S. B. Bacharach, ed., *Research in the Sociology of Organizations* Vol. 2. Greenwich, CT: JAI Press, pp. 83–107.

Lawrence, P. R., and J. W. Lorsch. 1967. *Organization and Environment*. Boston: Harvard Business School, Division of Research.

Lincoln, J. R. 1982. "Intra- (and Inter-) Organizational Networks." In S. B. Bacharach, ed., *Research in the Sociology of Organizations* Vol. 1. Greenwich, CT: JAI Press.

Lincoln, J. R., and J. Miller. 1979. "Work and Friendship Ties in Organizations: A Comparative Analysis of Relational Networks." *Administrative Science Quarterly* 24:181–199.

Marsden, P. V. 1988. "Homogeneity in Confiding Relations." *Social Networks* 10:57–76.

McPherson, J. M., and L. Smith-Lovin. 1987. "Homophily in Voluntary Organizations." *American Journal of Sociology* 52:370–379.

Meyerson, D., and J. Martin. 1987. "Cultural Change: An Integration of Three Different Views." *Journal of Management Studies* 24:6.

Miller, D., and P. Friesen. 1980. "Archetypes of Organizational Transitions." *Administrative Science Quarterly* 25:269–299.

Mitchell, J. C. 1969. "The Concept and Use of Social Networks." In J. Clyde Mitchell, ed., *Social Networks in Urban Situations*. Manchester, England: Manchester University Press.

Monge, P. R., and R. M. Eisenberg. 1987. "Emergent Communication Networks." In F. M. Jablin, L. L. Putnam, K. H. Roberts, and L. W. Porter, eds., *Handbook of Organizational Communication: An Interdisciplinary Perspective*. Beverly Hills: Sage.

Nolan, R. L., A. J. Pollock, and J. P. Ware. 1988. "Creating the 21st Century Organization." *Stage by Stage* 8(4)1–17.

Nystrom, H. 1979. *Creativity and Innovation*. Chichester: Wiley.

Orton, J. D., and K. E. Weick. 1990. "Loosely Coupled Systems: A Reconceptualization." *Academy of Management Review* 15(2):203–223.

Parsons, T. 1964. *The Social System*. New York: Free Press.

Peltz, D. C. 1956. "Some Social Factors Related to Performance in a Research Organization." *Administrative Science Quarterly* 1(3):310–325.

Pettigrew, A. 1973. *The Politics of Organizational Decision Making*. London: Tavistock.

———. 1975. "Towards a Political Theory of Organizational Intervention." *Human Relations* 28:191–208.

Pfeffer, J., and G. R. Salancik. 1978. *The External Control of Organizations*. New York: Harper & Row.

Pierce, J. L., and A. L. Delbecq. 1977. "Organization Structure, Individual Attitudes, and Innovation." *Academy of Management Review* 2:27–37.

Poole, M. S., and A. H. Van De Ven. 1989. "Using Paradox to Build Management and Organizational Theories." *Academy of Management Review* 14(4):562–578.

Powell, W. W. 1990. "Neither Market Nor Hierarchy: Network Forms of Organization." In B. Staw and L. L. Cummings, eds., *Research in Organizational Behavior* Vol. 12. Greenwich, CT: JAI Press, pp. 295–336.

Ranson, S., B. Hinings, and R. Greenwood. 1980. "The Structuring of Organizational Structures." *Administrative Science Quarterly* 25:1–17.

Roethlisberger, F. J., and W. J. Dickson. 1939. *Management and the Worker*. Cambridge, MA: Harvard University Press.

Rogers, E. M., and D. L. Kincaid. 1981. *Communication Networks*. New York: Free Press, 1981.

Shoonhoven, C. B., and M. Jelineck. 1990. "Dynamic Tension in Innovative High Technology Firms: Managing Rapid Technological Change Through Organizational Structure." In M. A. Von Glinow and S. A. Mohrman, eds., *Managing Complexity in High Technology Organizations*. New York: Oxford University Press, pp. 90–118.

Shrader, C. B., J. R. Lincoln, and A. N. Hoffman. 1989. "The Network Structures of Organizations: Effects of Task Contingencies and Distributional Form." *Human Relations* 42:43–66.

Stevenson, W. B. 1990. "Formal Structure and Networks of Interaction within Organizations." *Social Science Research* 19:113–131.

Stinchcombe, A. L. 1987. "An Outsider's View of Network Analyses of Power." In R. Perruci and H. R. Potter, eds., *Networks of Power: Organizational Actors at the National, Corporate, and Community Levels*. New York: Aldine, pp. 119–113.

Strauss, G. 1962. "Tactics of Lateral Relationships." *Administrative Science Quarterly* (Sept.): 161–186.

Tichy, N. 1973. "An Analysis of Clique Formation and Structure in Organizations." *Administrative Science Quarterly* 18:194–208.

———. 1981. "Networks in Organizations." In P. C. Nystrom and W. H. Starbuck, eds., *Handbook of Organization Design*, Vol. 2. New York: Oxford University Press, pp. 225–248.

Tichy, N. M., and C. Fombrun. 1979. "Network Analysis in Organizational Settings." *Human Relations* 32:923–965.

Tichy, N. M., M. L. Tushman, and C. Fombrun. 1974. "Social Network Analysis for Organizations." *Academy of Management Review* 4:507–519.

Tushman, M. L., and E. Romanelli. 1985. "Organizational Evolution: A Metamorphosis Model of Convergence and Reorientation." In B. Staw and L. L. Cummings, eds., *Research in Organizational Behavior*, Vol. 7. Greenwich, CT: JAI Press, pp. 171–222.

Walton, R. E. 1975. "The Diffusion of New Work Structures: Explaining Why Success Didn't Take." *Organizational Dynamics* 3:3–22.

Walton, R. E., and J. R. Hackman. 1986. "Groups Under Contrasting Management Strategies." In P. S. Goodman, ed., *Designing Effective Work Groups*. Jossey-Bass, pp. 168–201.

Weick, K. 1979. *The Social Psychology of Organizing*. Reading, MA: Addison-Wesley.

Wellman, B. 1988. "Structural Analysis: From Method and Metaphor to Theory and Substance." In B. Wellman and S. D. Berkowitz, eds., *Social Structures: A Network Approach*. Cambridge: Cambridge University Press, pp. 19–61.

Wilensky, H. L. 1967. *Organizational Intelligence*. New York: Basic Books.

Zaltman, G., R. Duncan, and J. Holbeck. 1973. *Innovations in Organizations*. New York: Wiley.

DIFFERENT NETWORK TIES AND THEIR IMPLICATIONS

7

Centrality and Power in Organizations

DANIEL J. BRASS
AND
MARLENE E. BURKHARDT

One need not be an expert on social networks to predict that the center node in a star configuration (position D in Figure 7-1a) will be the most powerful position. If presented with Figure 7-1a, few people would even ask whether the nodes represented individuals or groups, or whether the lines represented communications, friendship, or buy-sell transactions. Nor would anyone question whether the interaction was restricted, repeated, or symmetric. Most people would simply look at the diagram and declare position D the most powerful.

In addition, few people would be surprised to learn that a common finding in social network studies is that central positions are often associated with power and influence. Results consistent with this power/centrality relationship have been reported in small laboratory work groups (Shaw 1964), within organizations (Brass 1984, 1985; Fombrun 1983; Krackhardt 1990; Burkhardt and Brass 1990), across organizations (Galaskiewicz 1979), in professional communities (Breiger 1976), and community elites (Laumann and Pappi 1976).

However, predicting the most central, powerful position becomes more problematic when the four-person Figure 7-1a network is embedded within a larger network, such as that depicted in Figure 7-1b. For example, Figure 7-1a might represent a work group, and Figure 7-1b might represent that same work group embedded within a department in an organization. Designating the most central position becomes even more complicated if we add further work groups within additional departments to represent an entire organization. The problem becomes one of identifying

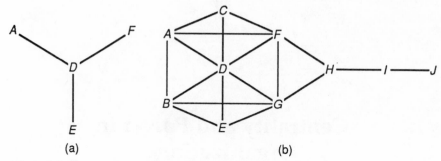

Adapted from Krackhardt (1990).
Figure 7-1

the appropriate unit of reference. In this case, should centrality within the work group, within the department, or within the entire organization be considered?

In addition to determining the unit of reference, determining the centrality of positions by simply looking at the diagrams becomes problematic as various combinations of nodes and links are considered. Even a small five-person network might produce differing opinions as to which position is most central (Freeman 1979). Of course, various remedies to this problem have been suggested in the form of mathematical formulas for calculating centrality. For example, one of the simplest calculations would involve counting the number of links connected to each position. However, this simple degree measure does not account for the system-wide properties of an extended network. Thus other centrality measures, which account for both direct and indirect links, have been offered (Freeman 1979).

The focus on system properties and indirect links led to the development of centrality measures that weight an individual's centrality by the centrality of those to whom he or she is directly connected. That is, one's centrality is increased by virtue of being linked to highly central others. If we assume that centrality and power are highly correlated, we can arrive at the conclusion that one's power is increased via links with powerful others. This proposition leads to consideration of additional units of reference within an organization. For example, direct links with top-level executives or with the dominant coalition in an organization may be positively related to power.

Connections to powerful others, however, may not increase one's power in certain situations. For example, while powerful others may provide useful information in a communications network, negotiating with powerful others in a bargaining network may produce negative results. Recent findings by Cook et al. (1983) suggest that under certain conditions ("negatively connected" networks) conventional measures of centrality do not relate to power. Two relationships in a network are said to be negatively connected when exchange in one diminishes or prohibits exchange in the other. These findings have led to attempts to define new measures of centrality that apply to all types of networks. For example, Bonacich (1987:1170) has added a parameter to his measure that "reflects the degree to which an individual's status is a function of the statuses of those to whom he or she is connected."

The exceptional findings of Cook et al. (1983) point out the importance of considering the type of interaction described by the social network. Various types of networks exist within organizations—workflow, communications, friendship. Whether any "negative" networks exist within organizations is unknown.

This chapter will examine empirically the relationship between power and centrality within an organization. In doing so it will provide some limited evidence concerning the preceding questions. We begin with a theoretical discussion of power and attempt to describe various centrality measures from this theoretical perspective. We consider three measures of centrality (degree, closeness, and betweenness) across four units of reference (work group, department, organization, and dominant coalition) for three different networks (workflow, communications, and friendship). In addition, we consider the possibility of negative networks by relating an individual's power to the power of those with whom he or she is connected. Finally, we discuss the results in terms of the practical benefits of an organizational assessment of centrality and power.

Power

With the resurgent interest in power in organizations, a multitude of theories and approaches have been offered. Common to many of these approaches is a reliance on exchange theory, or a dependency framework such as that offered by Emerson (1962). The power of A over B is typically defined as the extent to which B is dependent on A (Marsden 1983). Building on this framework, the strategic contingencies and resource dependency approaches (Hickson et al. 1971; Salancik and Pfeffer 1977) posit that power (the inverse of dependence) derives from control of relevant resources. Control by one actor implies that another actor in the social relationship has few alternative sources for acquiring the resource. One actor controls or mediates another's access to the outcome or resource. A relevant resource is one that is in demand or in which another actor has a high motivational investment (Emerson 1962). Thus employees who are able to control desired resources increase others' dependence on them and, via the exchange process, are able to acquire the resources or bring about the outcomes they desire (Pfeffer 1981).

In addition to increasing others' dependence on them, actors seeking power must also decrease their dependence on others. This may be done by decreasing one's motivational investment in outcomes controlled by others, or by increasing the number of alternative sources available for acquiring the outcome (Emerson 1962). In other words, one must have access to relevant resources that is independent, not controlled or mediated by others.

The relationship between power and dependence becomes more complex when one considers the multitude or variety of outcomes that may be considered relevant or in demand in organizations. Thus A may control a particular outcome that is relevant to B, but B may control another, different resource that is desired by A. Thus, in order to acquire power in an organization, two conditions are necessary: actors must both decrease their dependence on others and increase others' dependence on them.

We use the terms "resources" and "outcomes" interchangeably and in the broadest sense to include both tangibles and intangibles. In addition, we do not assume that exchange relationships involve only one transaction, or that transactions occur at only one time. Nor do we assume that it is possible for any pair of organizational actors to exchange resources with one another (Marsden 1983). Exchanges are restricted by opportunities for contact, ideological similarity, or "social inertia" (Marsden 1983:690). In organizations, some exchanges are mandated by workflow procedures and the prescribed hierarchy of authority.

Centrality

The concept of centrality has been operationalized and measured in a variety of ways. For example, Freeman (1979) summarized three related measures of centrality (degree, closeness, and betweenness) and attempted to clarify them conceptually.

Degree The degree measure of centrality is calculated by simply counting the number of adjacent links to or from an actor. Based solely on direct connections, Freeman (1979) conceptualized it as a measure of activity. It is infrequently discussed, often entirely ignored, in most social network discussions of power because it does not capture the system-wide properties of the network (Cook et al. 1983). In Figure 7-1, position D has the highest degree centrality in both examples.

However, from our exchange perspective on power, the degree measure of centrality may represent the number of alternatives available to an actor. Increasing one's alternatives increases one's power. Cook and her colleagues (1983:288–289) caution against equating resource availability with number of alternatives, noting that it "makes no difference how many bad sources of supply a position has." However, we cannot logically assume that alternatives are "bad sources" any more than we can assume them to be "good sources." Absent additional information, we must assume that more alternatives, as represented by the degree measure of centrality, are better than fewer alternatives.

The degree measure may also be appropriate for capturing power-enhancing behaviors that occur via direct interaction, such as ingratiation and reciprocation. In addition, Murnighan and Brass (1991) note that coalition formation occurs one person at a time, in direct interaction between the founder and potential members. Direct links also represent the avoidance of relying on mediating positions for indirect access to resources.

Closeness   Closeness measures of centrality account for both direct and indirect links in indicating how "close" a person is to all other persons in the network. It is generally calculated by summing the lengths of the shortest paths (geodesics) from a point to all other points. Direct links are counted as one step, with indirect links given proportionally less weight in the measure. In Figure 7-1a, position *D* is the most central. However, in Figure 7-1b, positions *G* and *F* are most central when using the closeness measure.

This measure can be interpreted to represent efficiency (extent to which an actor can reach all other actors in the shortest number of steps) or independence (being close to all other actors, a person is less dependent on intermediaries) (Freeman 1979). According to Freeman, it indicates the extent to which an actor can avoid the control of others.

In accounting for indirect access to others, the closeness measures allow for the possibility that an actor with only a few direct links may be central by virtue of those few links being to highly central others. For example, an employee who is connected to central employees in the communication network may have access to important information, a vital source of power in most organizations.

Betweenness   Betweenness measures of centrality calculate the extent to which actors fall between pairs of other actors on the shortest paths (geodesics) connecting them (Freeman 1979). Following Freeman, this measure represents potential control over others. Thus, if persons *A* and *C* were connected only through person *B*, *B* would fall "between" *A* and *C* and would mediate the flow of any resources between *A* and *C*. In Figure 7-1a, position *D* mediates the flow between any two of the other positions. However, in Figure 7-1b, position *H* is the most central when calculating the betweenness measure.

Freeman (1979) suggests that this measure is particularly appropriate for assessing power in communication networks; a mediating person may withhold or distort information in transition. Whereas the closeness measure represented avoiding the control of others, the betweenness measure represents controlling, or increasing the dependence of others.

Other Centrality Measures   In addition to the above three, numerous other measures of centrality have been offered. One of the most frequently used in research on interlocking directorates is the measure developed by Bonacich (1987). An actor's centrality is his or her summed connections to others weighted by the centrality of those others. The measure assumes that an actor's centrality is a function of the centralities of those actors with whom the actor has direct ties. Other measures based on similar assumptions include those developed by Hubbell (1965), Coleman (1973), and Burt's measure of prestige (1982).

Stephenson and Zelen (1989) have proposed one of the few measures of centrality that is not based on geodesics, but takes into account multiple shared paths between points. They argue that resources do not always flow along the shortest path, perhaps due to random fluctuations or actors who intentionally attempt to hide or shield the source of the resource, or avoid the flow of the resource through a particular intermediary. Still other measures of centrality have been suggested by Friedkin (1990).

Because it is impractical to include all these measures, we have chosen to consider degree, closeness, and betweenness based on their previously discussed theoretical implications. That is, closeness and betweenness represent the two necessary conditions for acquiring power: decreasing your dependence on others and increasing others' dependence on you. The degree measure most closely corresponds to Emerson's notion of alternatives. Together, these three best capture the dependency framework (Emerson 1962) used by many organizational scholars.

As illustrated in Figure 7-1b, the complexity of embedded relationships within an organization makes it possible for each measure of centrality to contribute unique variance in predicting power. While we expect some overlap among the measures, we hypothesize that each will be positively related to power and that each will add to the variance explained by the other two.

Units of Reference

The appropriate unit of reference for calculating centrality scores is often constrained by the method or level of analysis. For example, in laboratory studies there is only one unit of reference to consider, the small group created in the laboratory. At the group or organizational level of analysis, the small number of other units (departments, organizations, communities, etc.) restricts various combinations of subsets. Hence little attention has been given to unit of reference. However, at the individual level of analysis within an organization it is possible to consider centrality within a person's immediate work group, within departments or divisions, or within the entire organization. Likewise, an employee's power may depend on his or her connections to a particular group of persons, such as top-level executives.

Although theory and one's research questions may designate some units of reference as more important than others, this does not seem to be the case when considering power in organizations. Given the possibility of multiple, different sources of power in organizations (Pfeffer 1981), considering multiple reference units may be important. Following this logic, we calculated centrality measures with regard to subunit (work group with the same immediate supervisor), department (groups of 30 to 50 employees as formally designated by the company), and the entire organization. In addition, we calculated centrality in reference to a small group of top-level executives that we refer to as the dominant coalition.

The utility of this multiple-reference-unit strategy may be limited by the size of the group in combination with the particular centrality measure. Assuming that an average employee may not be able to interact effectively with more than 50 to 60 others, degree centrality scores will probably not be affected much by large size. For a large organization of 1,000 or more employees, the calculation of betweenness measures of centrality may be very time-consuming. In addition, using such a large number of employees may tend to homogenize the scores. For example, closeness scores may lose some meaning when calculated for very large numbers. In an organization of 1,000, every individual will probably receive the same path length for 500 to 600 employees who are not indirectly connected in paths shorter than three links. At the other extreme, everyone may receive the same closeness score within a small work group of five or fewer, provided that interaction is not restricted within the group.

In the organization under investigation, the departmental unit of reference seemed to represent the ideal size (30 to 50 employees) in relation to the preceding discussion. In addition, the five departments in this particular organization were relatively autonomous units, whereas the subunit workflow dependencies tended to cross subunit boundaries. That is, most of the subunits represented functional (homogeneous) groupings of employees whose workflow dependencies extended to other subunits within the department. Thus we hypothesized that centrality within the departmental unit of reference would be more strongly related to power than when using either the subunit or entire organization as the unit of reference. We expected centrality with regard to the dominant coalition to be a relatively strong and unique predictor of power, with little overlap with the other units of reference.

Types of Networks

This study considers the relationship between power and the centrality of organizational employees within three social networks: (1) workflow network, (2) communication network, and (3) friendship network. These networks correspond to three of the basic flows noted by Tichy, Tushman, and Fombrun (1979): (1) exchange of goods, (2) exchange of information or ideas, and (3) affect or liking. From our exchange-theory framework on power, these types of transactions form the bases for interdependencies among employees.

Workflow Network   Although informal or emergent patterns of behavior can, and typically do, occur in a workflow, this network is formally prescribed. Even when accounting for informal modifications, the workflow represents a highly restricted interaction network. Within the workflow network, the basis for interdependencies among workers is established by the division of labor; as the overall organizational task is divided, workers performing parts are dependent on one another. As the work flows through the organization, workers exchange inputs and outputs. The relevant outcome is the performance of one's task, which continues the successful flow of work.

Having many alternative sources for acquiring inputs or distributing outputs decreases a worker's dependence on others, and, conversely, should increase his or her power. Thus we would expect degree centrality to be positively related to power. Likewise, mediating the flow of work (betweenness) may also provide one with control. Because most work-flow transactions are dyadic in nature, closeness centrality may relate to power only to the extent that indirect connections provide other valued resources such as information. In addition, closeness centrality in reference to the entire organization may virtually eliminate any possibility that those on the boundaries of the organization can be considered central. However, boundary-spanning individuals in organizations are thought of as powerful because of their ability to reduce uncertainty for the technical core (Thompson 1967).

Communication Network Interdependencies among people in communication networks are based on the exchange of information. Likewise, the relevant resource is information. Employees who are centrally located in the communication network have potential access to (closeness) and control over (betweenness) information and thus are potentially powerful (Pfeffer 1981; Mechanic 1962; Freeman 1979).

In addition to assessing communication network centrality in a person's subgroup, department, and the entire organization, we also used the dominant coalition in the organization as a unit of reference. We defined this coalition as a small group of high-level individuals who had the most influence and decision-making authority in the organization. Communication connections with this group may provide a person with valuable information and support. Likewise, mediating information to and from this top-executive group may provide control over important information. That is, centrality with regard to the dominant coalition will likely increase others' dependence on the central person with regard to information about "what's going on in the company."

Friendship Network Employees in organizations are also linked together on the basis of social liking, or friendship. In such a network, the relevant resource, friendship, may not be the direct source of power. Rather, friendship may be instrumental in obtaining other relevant resources such as information or rewards. Friendships may also be the bases for forming coalitions, although it is equally likely that coalition partners may develop friendship. Regardless of the direction of this relationship, the overlay of friendship on work relationships may make it difficult for friends to with-hold valuable information or join opposing coalitions. To the extent that friendships are instrumental in acquiring information, we would expect overlaps with the communication network and similar relationships between centrality and power.

Network Connections

Recent research by Cook and colleagues (Cook et al. 1983; Yamagishi, Gillmore, and Cook 1988) has pointed out the importance of considering the concept of network connection—the nature of the link joining two or more dyads. The importance stems from the finding that under certain conditions centrality was not related to power (Cook et al. 1983). Among other things, these conditions include whether the connection is characterized as positive or negative.

In considering two exchange relations, A-B and B-C, they are defined as being connected at B (and forming the network A-B-C) only when the exchange between A and B in some way affects the exchange between B and C, and vice versa (Cook et al. 1983; Yamagishi et al. 1988). If the A-B exchange affects the B-C exchange positively, and vice versa, then the two relations are said to be positively connected at B. For example, B obtains information from A that allows B to help C solve a problem. A communication network is often used as an example of a positively connected network. Two relations are defined as negatively connected when exchanges in one diminish or prohibit exchanges in the other. For example, B's meeting with A forces B to cancel a meeting with C. In the negatively connected network, A-B-C, A and C are in competition for, or in conflict over, resources controlled by B. Competitive economic market structures, friendship networks, and dating relations are often cited as examples of negatively connected networks (Cook et al. 1983; Yamagishi et al. 1988). Yamagishi and colleagues also consider mixed networks—networks in which both positive and negative connections exist.

Do negative networks exist in organizations? Can we expect to find evidence that centrality does not relate to power? Judging from previous studies (Fombrun 1983; Brass 1984; Burkhardt and Brass 1990), the answer is no. However, examples of negative connections are not difficult to find in organizations: A purchasing agent selects one supplier over another; a supervisor decides to promote one subordinate rather than another; a manager goes to lunch with one friend rather than another.

Of the networks studied in this research, the communication network is most often listed as an example of a positively connected network. On the other hand, the friendship network is often cited as an example of a negative network. However, as previously noted, friendship in organizations may be instrumental in acquiring other relevant resources, such as information. Thus the expected overlap between friendship connections and communication connections (people talk with their friends) may cancel out any of the negative connections associated with a friendship network. In addition, it seems intuitive that one person can have several friends without creating competition. Perhaps the negative connections would result only from specific facets of friendship, such as romantic or mentoring relationships.

The workflow network involves the flow of resources, such that B exchanges the resources obtained from A with another partner, C. Obtaining resources (inputs necessary for job performance) from A enhances B's exchange with C (outputs from B become C's inputs). This type of resource flow represents positive connections (Yamagishi et al. 1988). However, B may have alternative sources of inputs other than A. In receiving inputs from A, B may exclude other sources such as D.

Likewise, in distributing his outputs to C, B may exclude other recipients, such as E. Thus the A-B-C network is positively connected, but the A-B-D network and the C-B-E network are negatively connected. The result is that the A-B-C-D-E network is considered "mixed" (Yamagishi et al. 1988).

The analysis of mixed networks and the reasoning behind predictions of centrality/power relationships is somewhat complex, even for small networks (see Yamagishi et al. 1988 for details). We do not attempt it for the large, complex workflow network in the organization studied. However, the practical implications of these laboratory studies is distinctly illustrated by Bonacich (1987). He notes that the advantages or disadvantages of being connected to powerful others may depend on whether the network is positive or negative.

Connections to Powerful Others   Following Bonacich (1987), whether one's centrality or power is increased by connections to high status or powerful others depends on whether the connections are positive or negative. In a positive communication network, the amount of information available to employees is positively related to the amount of information available to those with whom they have contact. Assuming that power derives from information, being connected to powerful central others should be positively related to power in the communication network.

However, in negatively connected bargaining situations, being connected to powerful others—those with many alternatives—puts one at a disadvantage. It is advantageous to bargain with others who have few options—those who are relatively less powerful. In bargaining situations, exchange with one partner precludes exchange with another. Some evidence of avoidance of powerful others is also found in the coalition-formation literature (Murnighan and Brass 1991).

We empirically explored the possibility of negative connections by calculating the power of those with whom an employee is connected. We expect this index to be positively correlated with individual power when considering the communication network. A positive relationship is also expected for the friendship network, to the extent that it overlaps with the communication network. However, the workflow network presents the possibility of a negative relationship. Being connected to powerful others in the work flow may place one in a position of dependence. From such a position it is unlikely that one would be able to place demands on powerful others concerning the acquisition of inputs or the distribution of one's outputs.

We also analyzed the relationship between one's own centrality and the power of those with whom one was connected. This analysis is necessary to the extent that one does not assume that centrality is equivalent to power. Rather, we are interested in the extent to which central employees are connected to powerful others. Because of the voluntary nature of the friendship network, we are also interested in the relative power of those whom one chooses as friends. Do employees choose friends who are more powerful, less powerful, or of similar power to themselves?

METHOD

Participants

One hundred forty nonsupervisory employees of a newspaper publishing company (87.5% response rate) participated in the study by completing a questionnaire administered by the researcher. The immediate supervisors of these employees completed a different questionnaire. In addition, 90% of the higher-level managers (above first-line supervisor) completed the same questionnaire as the nonsupervisors. In all cases, participation was voluntary and respondents were assured that their responses would be seen only by the researchers and be used for research purposes only.

Measures

Networks On the nonsupervisory questionnaire, respondents were asked to list the names of persons (1) who provided them with inputs to their jobs or to whom they distributed outputs from their own work; (2) with whom they talked frequently about work-related activities; and (3) whom they considered to be close friends. These listings provided the raw data for the centrality measures for the three networks: (1) workflow; (2) communication; and (3) friendship. Listings by the higher-level managers on this nonsupervisory questionnaire were used in part to identify the dominant coalition (details follow in this section). Reciprocation rates were 84% for the workflow network, 76% for the communication network, and 87% for the friendship network. Based on follow-up interviews concerning discrepancies, all links were treated as reciprocated.

The workflow network was also assessed via interviews and direct observation by the researcher. This independently derived network was compared with the network generated by the employee listings, and all discrepancies between the two were resolved via interviews following the questionnaire administration.

Centrality Three different measures of centrality (degree, closeness, and betweenness) were calculated for the sample of 140 nonsupervisory employees for each network (workflow, communication, and friendship) using three different units of reference (subunit, department, and entire organization). Subunits included all employees with the same immediate supervisor; departments corresponded to the five formally designated departments. In addition, the three centrality measures were calculated for the communication network using the dominant coalition as a unit of reference.

Following Freeman (1979), the degree measures of centrality were calculated by counting the focal employee's number of direct links. This number was divided by $n - 1$ (n = number of persons in the unit of reference) so that comparisons of degree centrality could be made across subunit and departments of different size.

The closeness measures of centrality were operationalized as the minimum distance between a focal employee and all other persons in the unit of reference (Freeman 1979). The sum of the lengths of the geodesic paths to all other persons in the reference unit was divided by $n - 1$. The closeness centrality measures were transformed by the formula $1 - [(d - 1)/dmax]$, where d equals the path distance and $dmax$ equals the largest observed value of d (Lincoln and Miller 1979; Brass 1984). This transformation does not change the magnitude of the relationship between closeness and other variables, but reverses the sign such that higher scores reflect greater closeness centrality.

The betweenness measures of centrality were calculated using the formula developed by Freeman (1979). To determine betweenness centrality, the probability of a focal person falling on the geodesic (shortest path) connecting any two other persons is summed over all unordered pairs of persons. The value is then divided by $(n^2 - 3n + 2)/2$, the maximum value when n equals the number of persons in the unit of reference. In calculating the betweenness centrality scores in the workflow network, direct connections with persons outside the organization were included. Without including these connections, all boundary-spanning employees would receive scores of zero on the work-flow betweenness measures because their positions represent the first or last link in the organization's workflow network.

Power Two independent reputational measures of power were obtained. Nonsupervisors were asked to "list the names of persons whom you consider to be influential at the newspaper. That is, list persons who seem to have pull, weight, or clout in this company. List as many or as few as you think necessary." The mean number of nominations received by each employee in the nonsupervisory sample was 1.37, with a standard deviation of 1.85.

The second measure of power was obtained by asking the immediate supervisor of each employee to rate that employee on a seven-point Likert type scale (1 = very little influence; 7 = very great amount of influence). Instructions were the same as noted previously, with modifications appropriate to rating rather than listing the names. The mean score was 2.80, with a standard deviation of 1.49. The correlation between supervisors' ratings and number of nominations received from nonsupervisors was .70 ($p < .01$), indicating substantial agreement between supervisors and non-supervisors.

These immediate first-level supervisors were not asked to list work-flow, communication, or friendship interactions in order to avoid the possibility of method-variance contamination in their power ratings. The names of all the immediate subordinates of each supervisor were listed on the rating form so that there would be no bias in the recollection of names.

Dominant Coalition Considered in identifying the dominant coalition were the communication and friendship patterns of the ten persons in the organization who received the most listings as powerful on the nonsupervisory questionnaire. Based on the relative number of listings and the interaction patterns, four of these ten persons were selected as representing the dominant coalition. These four individuals indicated reciprocated communication and friendship connections, and were ranked first, second, third, and fifth in the nonsupervisory listings of power.

Power of Others Each of the nonsupervisory employees was assigned six indices representing the average power of those other persons with whom the focal employee was connected. The six indices represented supervisor ratings of power and nonsupervisors' listings of power for workflow, communication, and friendship connections. For the supervisors' ratings of power, the means and standard deviations were as follows: workflow 2.41, .63; communication 2.92, .95; and friendship 2.61, 1.11. For the nonsupervisory listings, the means and standard deviations were as follows: work flow 1.19, .52; communication 1.79, 1.19; and friendship 1.30, 1.21.

RESULTS

Means, standard deviations, and intercorrelations among the workflow network centrality measures are presented in Table 7-1; Table 7-2 indicates the same for the communication network centrality measures. The intercorrelations between the work flow and communication network measures are presented in Table 7-3.

Due to the large number of variables in this study, the friendship network results were not included in the tables, except in reference to the

Table 7-1
**Means, Standard Deviations, and Intercorrelations
for Workflow Measures**

	MEAN	S.D.	1	2	3	4	5	6	7	8
Subunit										
1. Degree	.61	.61								
2. Closeness	.90	.07	.57							
3. Betweenness	.35	.08	.18	.08						
Department										
4. Degree	.24	.28	.15	.43	−.26					
5. Closeness	.76	.16	.03	.13	−.08	.59				
6. Betweenness	.04	.07	.48	.54	.28	.32	.49			
Organization										
7. Degree	.04	.02	.25	.44	.17	.27	.20	.36		
8. Closeness	.65	.12	−.28	−.29	.09	−.13	.27	.18	−.02	
9. Betweenness	.01	.02	−.01	.14	.15	.06	.16	.15	.32	.27

$p < .05$ for all $r > .14$; $p < .01$ for all $r > .20$

Table 7-2

Means, Standard Deviations, and Intercorrelations for Communication Network Measures

	MEAN	S.D.	1	2	3	4	5	6	7	8	9	10	11
Subunit													
1. Degree	.55	.46											
2. Closeness	.87	.12	.63										
3. Betweenness	.07	.06	.31	.26									
Department													
4. Degree	.19	.18	.22	.34	.04								
5. Closeness	.77	.11	.27	.57	.05	.71							
6. Betweenness	.05	.03	.18	.23	.24	.58	.32						
Organization													
7. Degree	.04	.02	.27	.41	.26	.59	.54	.73					
8. Closeness	.63	.07	.16	.44	.17	.26	.63	.38	.65				
9. Betweenness	.01	.04	.08	.19	.26	.37	.26	.78	.82	.54			
Dominant Coalition													
10. Degree	.16	.40	.11	.19	.27	.44	.28	.44	.44	.23	.51		
11. Closeness	.71	.11	.14	−.11	.13	.51	.12	.34	.48	.12	.36	.59	
12. Betweenness	.03	.07	.09	.16	.25	.36	.22	.68	.69	.40	.85	.71	.49

$p < .05$ for all $r > .14$; $p < .01$ for all $r > .20$

power of others. This was done because preliminary analyses of the correlations between corresponding measures in the communication and friendship networks indicated substantial overlap (*r*s from .60 to .97). Correlations of the friendship network measures with the power measures produced virtually the same results as obtained when using the communication network measures. When controlling for the communication measures, the friendship measures did not add significantly ($p < .05$) to any of the relationships studied. However, in some cases the partial correlations between the communication measures and power measures were significant when controlling for the corresponding friendship measures. Thus including the friendship measures in the tables would have been a redundancy.

As indicated in Table 7-1, the department betweenness measure correlated significantly with all the other workflow centrality measures. The department closeness measure was strongly correlated with the subunit degree and betweenness measures, but was negatively correlated with the subunit betweenness measure and the organization closeness measure. Degree and closeness measures were highly correlated, with the exception of organization measures. Subunit betweenness was negatively related to department degree.

For the communication network measures (Table 7-2), intercorrelations between measures within subunits were highly correlated. The organization degree measure was strongly correlated with all the other measures. In general, the intercorrelations for the communication net-

Table 7-3

Intercorrelations Between Communication and
Workflow Network Measures

	WORKFLOW								
	Subunit			Department			Organization		
	Deg.	Close.	Betw.	Deg.	Close.	Betw.	Deg.	Close.	Betw.
Communication									
Subunit									
1. Degree	.56								
2. Closeness	.24	.19							
3. Betweenness	.07	.05	.09						
Department									
4. Degree	.13	.37	−.19	.49					
5. Closeness	.21	.37	−.17	.28	.21				
6. Betweenness	.04	.21	.08	.12	−.12	.08			
Organization									
7. Degree	.13	.27	.11	.02	−.17	.11	.21		
8. Closeness	.11	.08	.04	−.15	−.06	.09	.20	−.01	
9. Betweenness	.06	.18	.09	.01	−.17	.08	.16	.06	.06
Dominant Coalition									
10. Degree	.26	.39	.01	.38	.02	.25	.21	−.16	−.02
11. Closeness	.22	.28	.02	.21	.04	.24	.27	−.12	.03
12. Betweenness	.12	.26	.11	.09	−.15	.18	.23	.05	.04

$p < .05$ for all $r > .14$; $p < .01$ for all $r > .20$

work measures were higher than those for the workflow network. Correlations across networks (Table 7-3) were moderate to low. The subunit degree measures correlated highly, as did the department degree measures.

Centrality Measures

Table 7-4 presents the zero-order correlations for the centrality measures and the supervisors' ratings of power. All of the degree measures and most of the closeness and betweenness measures correlated significantly with the supervisors' power ratings. In addition, Table 7-4 shows the standardized betas when all the degree, closeness, or betweenness measures were simultaneously entered into a regression equation. The adjusted R^2 for each set of measures is also presented. Two significant negative betas occurred; closeness in the communication network for the entire organization, and betweenness in the workflow for the entire organization. Most of the betas for the workflow measures were not significant. As separate sets, the degree measures and the closeness measures explained the most variance in supervisors' ratings of power.

Table 7-4

Relationships Between Centrality Measures and Supervisors' Ratings of Power

MEASURE	DEGREE		CLOSENESS		BETWEENNESS	
	r	beta	r	beta	r	beta
Communication						
Subunit	.23**	.013	.17*	.167	.06	−.014
Department	.51**	.562**	.35**	.366**	.33**	.358**
Organization	.29**	−.145	.12	−.239*	.22**	−.195
Dominant Coalition	.35**	.183*	.46**	.458**	.26**	.152
Workflow						
Subunit	.25**	.159	.23**	.017	.11	.055
Department	.21**	−.152	.14	.029	.24**	.214**
Organization	.16*	.013	−.08	.103	−.19*	−.223**
Adjusted R^2		.29**		.30**		.17**

$*p < .05; **p < .01$

Table 7-5 presents the zero-order correlations, betas, and adjusted R^2 for the centrality measures and the nonsupervisors' listings of power. Most of the measures were significantly correlated with power. However, as in Table 7-4, the subunit betweenness measures for both networks did not relate significantly to power. The set of degree measures explained the most variance in the nonsupervisors' listings.

Continuing the analyses of the measures of centrality, Table 7-6 presents the results of hierarchical regressions with each set of measures being entered first in the regression equation, followed by each of the

Table 7-5

Relationships Between Centrality Measures and Nonsupervisors' Listings of Power

MEASURE	DEGREE		CLOSENESS		BETWEENNESS	
	r	beta	r	beta	r	beta
Communication						
Subunit	.24**	−.012	.18*	.085	.13	.019
Department	.50**	.358**	.35**	.186	.46**	.444**
Organization	.42**	.066	.25**	.030	.35**	−.246
Dominant Coalition	.49**	.292**	.39**	.323**	.41**	.275**
Workflow						
Subunit	.31**	.214	.39**	.285**	.08	−.039
Department	.22**	−.186	.06	−.049	.33**	.286**
Organization	.15*	−.043	−.06	.127	−.04	−.075
Adjusted R^2		.35**		.28**		.29**

$*p < .05; **p < .01$

Table 7-6

Hierarchical Regression Analyses for Measures of Centrality

	Adjusted R^2 Supervisors' Ratings	Adjusted R^2 Nonsupervisors' Listings
Degree	.29	.35
add closeness	.34*	.36
add betweenness	.30	.37
Closeness	.30	.28
add degree	.34	.36**
add betweenness	.36*	.34**
Betweenness	.17	.29
add degree	.30**	.37**
add closeness	.36**	.34*

*significant ($p < .05$) change in R^2

**significant ($p < .01$) change in R^2

other two sets of measure. Overall, the results in Table 7-6, taken in combination with Tables 7-4 and 7-5, point out the strength of the degree measures of centrality.

Units of Reference

Zero-order correlations, standardized betas, and adjusted R^2 for the four units of reference in relation to supervisors' ratings of power are presented in Table 7-7. Similar analyses for nonsupervisors' listings of power are presented in Table 7-8. For both measures of power, centrality

Table 7-7

Relationships Between Units of Reference and Supervisors' Ratings of Power

MEASURE	SUBUNIT		DEPARTMENT		ORGANIZATION		DOMINANT COALITION	
	r	beta	r	beta	r	beta	r	beta
Communication								
Degree	.23**	.053	.51**	.589**	.29**	.447**	.35**	.181
Closeness	.17*	.091	.35**	−.081	.12	−.044	.46**	.378**
Betweenness	.06	.004	.33**	.012	.22**	−.144	.26**	−.015
Workflow								
Degree	.25**	.115	.21*	−.132	.16*	.201*		
Closeness	.23**	.121	.14*	.032	−.08	.068		
Betweenness	.11	.074	.24**	.187*	−.19*	−.310**		
Adjusted R^2	.05*		.27**		.14**		.22**	

*$p < .05$; **$p < .01$

Table 7-8

**Relationships Between Units of Reference and Nonsupervisors'
Listings of Power**

MEASURE	SUBUNIT		DEPARTMENT		ORGANIZATION		DOMINANT COALITION	
	r	beta	r	beta	r	beta	r	beta
Communication								
Degree	.24**	−.035	.50**	.346**	.42**	.432**	.49**	.316**
Closeness	.18*	.093	.35**	−.005	.25**	−.011	.39**	.193
Betweenness	.13	.091	.46**	.218*	.35**	−.007	.41**	.116
Workflow								
Degree	.31**	.120	.22**	.008	.15*	.107		
Closeness	.39**	.313**	.06	−.142	−.06	.026		
Betweenness	.08	.027	.33**	.326**	−.04	−.135		
Adjusted R^2		.15**		.35**		.16**		.26**

*$p < .05$; **$p < .01$

measures for department and dominant coalition accounted for the most
variance. In particular, the degree measures for the department, organization, and dominant coalition in the communication network were strong.
Negative betas resulted for the organization-wide betweenness measures for
both networks.

Table 7-9

Hierarchical Regression Analyses for Units of Reference

	Adjusted R^2 Supervisors' Ratings	Adjusted R^2 Nonsupervisors' Listings
Subunit	.05	.15
add department	.28**	.34**
add organization	.15**	.24**
add dominant coalition	.25**	.30**
Department	.27	.35
add subunit	.28	.34
add organization	.26	.33
add dominant coalition	.32**	.38**
Organization	.14	.16
add subunit	.15	.24**
add department	.26**	.33**
add dominant coalition	.28**	.29**
Dominant Coalition	.22	.26
add subunit	.25	.30*
add department	.32**	.38**
add organization	.28**	.29

*significant ($p < .05$) change in R^2

**significant ($p < .01$) change in R^2

Results of hierarchical regression analyses (Table 7-9) were consistent with these findings. In Table 7-9, each set of centrality measures for a particular unit of reference was entered into the regression equation first. That set of measures was then followed in the regression equation by the set of centrality measures for one of the other units of reference. Only the set of centrality measures for the dominant coalition added significantly to the variance explained by the centrality measures for department. In all cases the centrality measures for department added significantly to the variance explained in power.

Power of Others

Correlations between individual power and the power of those with whom the individual was connected in the workflow, communication, and friendship networks are presented in Table 7-10. The power of those with whom one was directly connected in the communication and friendship networks was positively and significantly related to one's own power. However, this was not the case for workflow connections. The power of those with whom one was connected in the workflow was not related, or was negatively related to one's own power.

Do employees choose more powerful persons as friends; or, do they prefer affiliation with persons less powerful than themselves? Based on the strong positive correlation between one's own power and the power of friends, the answer is neither. That is, people tend to choose friends who are relatively similar to themselves in terms of power.

Are central employees connected to powerful others? The answer tends to be no. Due to the large number of possible relationships, we

Table 7-10
Correlations Between Individual Power and Power of Others

	INDIVIDUAL POWER	
	Supervisors' Ratings	**Nonsupervisors' Listings**
Power of Others		
Workflow		
Supervisors' Ratings	−.17*	.03
Nonsupervisors' Listings	.01	.11
Communication		
Supervisors' Ratings	.37**	.19*
Nonsupervisors' Listings	.32**	.24**
Friendship		
Supervisors' Ratings	.50**	.35**
Nonsupervisors' Listings	.36**	.31**

$*p < .05; **p < .01$

summarize the results of this analysis rather than present several tables. Of the 180 possible correlations, only 65 were significant at $p < .05$. Of those, 32 were significant at $p < .01$, and only 20 of those were greater than .25, the highest being .41 (departmental workflow betweenness with supervisors' ratings of power of others). In general, the communication and friendship centrality measures were negatively and not significantly related to the power of others in the workflow. Department closeness in both the communication and friendship networks was positively related to power of others in the communication and friendship networks. The closeness measures of friendship were all negatively related to the power of others in the workflow. Also, department measures of degree and closeness in the workflow were positively related to power of others in the workflow. With these few exceptions, the overall results were weak and inconclusive.

DISCUSSION

Overall, the results of this study indicated that centrality was positively and significantly related to power in an organization no matter which measure of centrality or unit of reference was chosen. The exception to this was the betweenness measures of centrality within the subunit and organization for both communication and workflow networks. However, departmental betweenness was strongly related to power. As with the betweenness measures, the departmental measures in general accounted for the most explained variance in power.

Unit of Reference

Thus it appears that the department is the most applicable unit of reference for calculating centrality measures in this organization. This finding emphasizes the importance of accounting for embeddedness in an organization. With a few exceptions, subunit measures of centrality were not highly correlated with department or organization measures. In some workflow cases, the correlations were negative. This may be due to the functional, homogeneous task groupings within many subunits in our sample. That is, employees within the same subunit performed the same task, with primary workflow connections crossing subunit boundaries. With communication and friendship links likely "shadowing" the required workflow links, these connections across subunits may be an important source of power. Results might be different in an organization composed of relatively autonomous product (heterogeneous) subunits.

There may be a size limit on the relevance of embeddedness. Considering a nonsupervisory employee's centrality within the entire organization may effectively homogenize the scores. That is, within a large organization there will be many persons who are far removed from any employee. In relation to these far-removed persons, every focal will receive similar centrality scores, thus decreasing the variance in scores. The standard deviations reported in Tables 7-1 and 7-2 tend to support this notion. With a few exceptions, the organization centrality measures have lower standard deviations than the department or subunit measures.

Another related possibility is that these far-removed persons, outside one's department but in the organization, are of little importance in establishing one's power. That is, one's power reputation may depend primarily on contacts with one's more immediate reference group. This may also suggest that there are power centers within organizations. For example, there may be relatively large clusters or cliques of individuals within which one establishes one's power base.

The appropriate unit of reference with regard to centrality/power relationships may depend on the density, or desired density of connections in an organization. For organizations requiring rapid change to environmental fluctuations, the organizational unit of reference may be of crucial importance. That is, the survival of the organization may depend on communication across departments. To discover that the strongest relationships between centrality and power occur at the departmental unit of reference may suggest that changes are needed. In addition, an organization interested in rapid change might attempt to decrease the mean score for closeness centrality for the entire organization. Thus the assessment of power and centrality in regard to unit of reference can have practical implications for the organization. Discouraging relatively isolated "fiefdoms" and rewarding connections across departments and divisions may be necessary.

Measures

Perhaps the least-expected result of this study was the strength of the degree measures of centrality when compared to the more elaborate closeness and betweenness measures. The degree measures did as well or better than the others in relating to power. It may be that degree reflects alternatives, and increasing alternatives increases one's power in exchange relationships (Emerson 1962). Regarding the communication network, direct contacts avoid the unreliability of information mediated through others. Direct contacts may also be necessary for coalition formation (Murnighan and Brass 1991), and may be the best source of information in learning the network (Krackhardt 1990).

Stronger results for the betweenness measures might have been obtained if supervisory personnel had been included in the sample. Organizations typically structure their hierarchies so that supervisors mediate communication from the top down and vice versa. A manager who does not score well on betweenness, especially in relation to the dominant coalition, may not be performing his or her liaison role effectively. We might also expect managers to score higher than subordinates on centrality within the entire organization, as coordination of activities across departments is often considered a managerial responsibility.

For an organization that prides itself on easy access (an "open-door" policy), a strong correlation between degree measures of centrality and power may provide an indication that the policy is working. However, direct access may not always be the most efficient way to transmit information. If the degree measures totally dominate the closeness measures, or the betweenness measures, it may indicate that designated channels of communication are not being followed or that information obtained through them is unreliable. However, that was not the case in this study. Both the closeness measures and the betweenness measures within the department and in relation to the dominant coalition were strongly related to power.

Networks

Some of the negative correlations and betas for organization-wide work-flow measures may reflect the reliance of the organization studied on organization boundary-spanning personnel. For a newspaper publishing company, advertising, reporting, and circulation tasks are crucial to success. Because of the nature of their tasks, these employees operate on the boundaries of the organization, which effectively prevents them from obtaining high scores on closeness and betweenness within the organization. For these employees, centrality may not be a primary source of power. Rather, they may acquire power by effectively coping with environmental uncertainties (Salancik and Pfeffer 1977).

Likewise, the strong correlations between the communication network measures and power may reflect the importance of information to a newspaper publishing company. In addition, the findings indicated that centrality in the friendship network was not significant when controlling for centrality in the communication network. Contrary results (i.e., dominance of the friendship centrality measures over the workflow or communication measures) would be cause for concern. An organizational assessment that showed that friendship by itself was the primary source of power would signal a need for change.

Network Connections

Although not directly assessed, results of this study indicated some evidence of negative connections within the workflow. Being connected to powerful others in the workflow was not positively related to power, as was the case in the communication and friendship networks. This finding may reflect a greater number of alternative sources, the focal being just one alternative, for the powerful other in the workflow. That is, the power of the person with whom the focal is connected may be the result of his or her having many alternatives to the focal. This would decrease the focal's power while increasing the power of the person to whom the focal is connected. It may also indicate that competition and bargaining, rather than the sharing of information, is occurring in the workflow.

Although the friendship network has often been offered as an example of a negatively connected network, we found no evidence of this. In relation to power, the friendship network apparently operated as a source of information, much the same as the positively connected communication network.

Conclusions

Although this research provides some empirical answers to questions concerning centrality and power in organizations, other questions remain. For example, we did not attempt to measure subunit or departmental power in relation to individual power. Membership in a powerful department may increase individual power, especially when reputational measures of power are used. Brass (1984, 1985) found that departmental membership was significantly related to individual power. More cross-level research is needed to investigate possible interactions between individual, subunit, and departmental power. Relational "frog pond" effects are also possible. That is, does one acquire more power by being a relatively powerful frog in a relatively small pond (powerless department), or by being a relatively powerless frog in a large, powerful pond?

Because of the cross-sectional nature of this study, we cannot determine the causal relationship between power and centrality. Does centrality lead to power? It is equally likely that powerful employees are sought out by others, thus increasing their centrality. In one of the few longitudinal studies of networks and power, Burkhardt and Brass (1990) found evidence supporting the notion that centrality preceded power following a technological change.

The need for longitudinal network studies is also apparent when considering the very practical question of how you change a network. While we have endorsed the utility of an organizational assessment of networks and power, few suggestions for changing the network have been offered. Results have shown changes in communication network patterns and power following the introduction of a new technology (Burkhardt and Brass 1990). Absent a radical jolt, such as a change in technology, Pfeffer (1981) has noted the stability of the distribution of power within an organization. Commitment to previous decisions, institutionalization of attitudes and behaviors (Burkhardt 1991), and the ability of those in power to generate additional power, all contribute to stability. Those in power are unlikely to relinquish their power. Very little is known about how network patterns form, how stable they are, or what is needed to change them.

In addition, more research is needed to determine the interrelationships between personal characteristics, strategies, and tactics, and network positions. While we take the position that network structure will provide constraints on personal strategies, Brass and Burkhardt (1992) found that assertiveness and coalition building were related to degree and closeness measures of centrality. Their results indicate that both network position and behavioral strategies were related to power.

Caution must be exercised in generalizing the results of this study to other organizations. As we have noted in the discussion, characteristics of the sample and the organization may have directly affected the findings. The selection of measures and units of reference, as well as the types of networks addressed, must be guided by theoretical and practical considerations. These measures, units of reference, and networks should be viewed as complementary rather than competing alternatives. Each provides a different theoretical perspective and application. In combination they can provide useful insights for both research and practice in organizations.

References

Bonacich, Phillip. 1987. "Power and Centrality: A Family of Measures." *American Journal of Sociology* 92:1170–1182.

Brass, Daniel J. 1984. "Being in the Right Place: A Structural Analysis of Individual Influence in an Organization." *Administrative Science Quarterly* 29:518–539.

———. 1985. "Men's and Women's Networks: A Study of Interaction Patterns and Influence in an Organization." *Academy of Management Journal* 28:327–343.

Brass, Daniel J., and Marlene E. Burkhardt. 1992. "Potential Power and Power Use: An Investigation of Structure and Action." Working paper, Pennsylvania State University, University Park, PA.

Breiger, Ronald L. 1976. "Career Attributes and Network Structure: A Blockmodel Study of a Biomedical Research Specialty." *American Sociological Review* 41:117–135.

Burkhardt, Marlene E. 1991. "Institutionalization of Technological Change." Working paper, Wharton School, University of Pennsylvania, Philadelphia, PA.

Burkhardt, Marlene E., and Daniel J. Brass. 1990. "Changing Patterns or Patterns of Change: The Effect of a Change in Technology on Social Network Structure and Power." *Administrative Science Quarterly* 35:104–127.

Burt, Ron S. 1982. *Toward a Structural Theory of Action*. New York: Academic Press.

Coleman, James S. 1973. *The Mathematics of Collective Action*. Chicago: Aldine.

Cook, Karen S., Richard M. Emerson, Mary R. Gillmore, and Toshio Yamagishi. 1983. "The Distribution of Power in Exchange Networks: Theory and Experimental Results." *American Journal of Sociology* 89:275–305.

Emerson, Richard M. 1962. "Power-dependence Relations." *American Sociological Review* 27:31–41.

Fombrun, Charles. 1983. "Attributions of Power Across a Social Network." *Human Relations* 36:493–508.

Freeman, Linton C. 1979. "Centrality in Social Networks: Conceptual Clarification." *Social Networks* 1:215–239.

Friedkin, Noah E. 1990. "Theoretical Foundations for Centrality Measures." Department of Education and Sociology, University of California, Santa Barbara.

Galaskiewicz, Joseph. 1979. *Exchange Networks and Community Politics*. Beverly Hills: Sage.

Hickson, David J., Christopher R. Hinings, Charles A. Lee, Rodney E. Schneck, and Johannes M. Pennings. 1971. "A Strategic Contingencies Theory of Intraorganizational Power." *Administrative Science Quarterly* 16:216–229.

Hubbell, Charles H. 1965. "An Input-output Approach to Clique Identification." *Sociometry* 28:377–399.

Krackhardt, David. 1990. "Assessing the Political Landscape: Structure, Cognition, and Power in Organizations." *Administrative Science Quarterly* 35:342–369.

Laumann, Edward O., and Franz U. Pappi. 1976. *Networks of Collective Action: A Perspective on Community Influence Systems*. New York: Academic Press.

Lincoln, James R., and Jon Miller. 1979. "Work and Friendship Ties in Organizations: A Comparative Analysis of Relational Networks." *Administrative Science Quarterly* 24:181–199.

Marsden, Peter V. 1983. "Restricted Access in Networks and Models of Power." *American Journal of Sociology* 88:686–717.

Mechanic, David. 1962. "Sources of Power of Lower Participants in Organizations." *Administrative Science Quarterly* 7:349–364.

Murnighan, J. Keith, and Daniel J. Brass. 1991. "Intraorganizational Coalitions." In Max Bazerman, Blair Sheppard, and Roy Lewicki, eds., *Research on Negotiation in Organizations*, Vol. 3. Greenwich, CT: JAI Press, pp. 283–306.

Pfeffer, Jeffrey. 1981. *Power in Organizations*. Marshfield, MA: Pitman.

Salancik, Gerald R., and Jeffrey Pfeffer. 1977. "Who Gets Power—and How They Hold onto It: A Strategic Contingency Model of Power." *Organizational Dynamics* 5:3–21.

Shaw, Marvin E. 1964. "Communication Networks." In L. Berkowitz, ed., *Advances in Experimental Social Psychology*. New York: Academic Press, pp. 11–147.

Stephenson, Karen, and Marvin Zelen. 1989. "Rethinking Centrality: Methods and Examples." *Social Networks* 11:1–37.

Thompson, James D. 1967. *Organizations in Action*. New York: McGraw-Hill.

Tichy, Noel M., Michael L. Tushman, and Charles Fombrun. 1979. "Social Network Analysis for Organizations." *Academy of Management Review* 4:507–519.

Yamagishi, Toshio, Mary R. Gillmore, and Karen S. Cook. 1988. "Network Connections and the Distribution of Power in Exchange Networks." *American Journal of Sociology* 93:833–851.

8

The Strength of Strong Ties: The Importance of *Philos* in Organizations

DAVID KRACKHARDT

THEORY

In 1973, Mark Granovetter proposed that weak ties are often more important than strong ties in understanding certain network-based phenomena. His argument rests on the assumption that strong ties tend to bond similar people to each other, and these similar people tend to cluster together such that they are all mutually connected. The information obtained through such a network tie is more likely to be redundant, and the network is therefore not a channel for innovation. By contrast, a weak tie more often constitutes a "local bridge" to parts of the social system that are otherwise disconnected, and therefore a weak tie is likely to provide new information from disparate parts of the system, Thus, this theory argues, tie strength is curvilinear with a host of dependent variables: no tie (or an extremely weak tie) is of little consequence; a weak tie provides maximum impact, and a strong tie provides diminished impact.

Subsequent research has generally supported Granovetter's theory (Granovetter 1982), but two issues have been neglected in the research stream. First, there is considerable ambiguity as to what constitutes a strong tie and what constitutes a weak tie. Granovetter laid out four identifying properties of a strong tie: "The strength of a tie is a (probably linear) combination of the amount of time, the emotional intensity, the intimacy (mutual confiding), and the reciprocal services which characterize the tie" (1973:1361). This makes tie strength a linear function of four quasi-independent indicators. At what point is a tie to be considered weak? This is not simply a question for the methodologically curious. It is an important part of the theory itself, since the theory makes a curvilinear prediction. If we happen to be on the very left side of the continuum of tie strength, then increasing the strength of the tie (going from no tie to weak tie) will increase the relevant information access. On the other hand, at some point making the ties stronger will theoretically decrease their impact. How do we know where we are on this theoretical curve? Do all four indicators count equally toward tie strength?

In practice, tie strength has been measured many different ways. Some have measured strong ties as reciprocated nominations, weak ties as unreciprocated nominations, and no ties as no nominations (Friedkin 1980). Other measures have included recency of contact (Lin, Dayton, and Greenwald 1978). Sometimes labels such as "friend," "relative," or "neighbor" are used to identify strong ties (Erickson and Yancey 1980; Lin, Ensel, and Vaughn 1981). Others (Granovetter 1973:1371) have simply used frequency of interaction as a surrogate for tie strength. One may intuitively agree that these strong ties are clearly *stronger* than the set of weak ties as measured. But it is clear that all of these measures capture the essence of what Granovetter meant when he spoke of the category "strong ties."

The Psychology of Strong Ties

The second issue that has been all but ignored since Granovetter's seminal article is the affective character of strong ties. Of the four characteristics of strong ties, two of these—emotional intensity and intimacy—are inherently subjective and interpretive. A third, "reciprocal services," is perhaps behavioral, but one could argue that the equitable exchange implied by this term is also a subjective criterion. Only the first criterion, time spent in the relationship, is clearly objective.

Again, this is not simply a measurement issue. Granovetter's theory draws on the psychological theory of balance (Heider 1958; Newcomb 1961). From this theory, Granovetter notes that given a triad of actors, *A*, *B*, and *C*, if *A* is strongly tied to *B* and to *C*, then it is likely that the triad will be balanced: that is, *B* and *C* will be strongly tied to each other also. There is certainly evidence of this effect (see, for example, Davis 1979). But what has been forgotten in this research effort is that the underlying rationale for balance is psychological.[1] Heider (1958) uses words like "stress," "tension," and "disharmony" to describe what happens to a person who faces an unbalanced situation. These disquieting affective states presumably motivate the individual to resolve the imbalance. Moreover, the tendency to resolve an unbalanced triad is strongest when the strength of affective attachment is strong. Once triads are balanced, no local bridge can exist. In other words, Granovetter's claim that strong ties do not constitute local bridges is dependent on balance, which in turn is influenced by the affective component of those ties. Yet we seldom see affective dimensions captured in the operationalizations of strong ties.

The Strength of Strong Ties

In his review of a decade of research on the strength-of-weak-ties hypothesis, Granovetter (1982) rightly pointed out that strong ties can play an important role, and that role should not be ignored. In fact, he noted: "Weak ties provide people with access to information and resources beyond those available in their own social circles; but strong ties have *greater motivation* to be of assistance and are typically more easily available" (113; emphasis mine). Citing Pool (1980), he further asserted that strong ties are more likely to be useful to the individual when that individual is in an insecure position. Granovetter concluded from his review of the research (1982:113–117) that people in insecure positions are more likely to resort to the development of strong ties for protection and uncertainty reduction. In a parallel argument, Krackhardt and Stern (1988) posited that the pattern of friendship ties within an organization will be critical to an organization's ability to deal with crises. Through a set of organizational simulations, they demonstrated that an organization characterized by friendship ties that cut across departmental boundaries is better suited to adapting to environmental changes and uncertainty.

This chapter will build on that theme: the strength of strong ties in cases of severe change and uncertainty. People resist change and are uncomfortable with uncertainty. Strong ties constitute a base of trust that can reduce resistance and provide comfort in the face of uncertainty. Thus it will be argued that change is not facilitated by weak ties, but rather by a particular type of strong tie. To develop this theme, I will draw from Granovetter's original idea of what constitutes a strong tie and his later ideas about how strong ties are useful. First, I will replace the definition of tie strength as a continuous variable with a set of conditions for a particular type of tie, a tie I will call *philos*, the Greek word for friend. (I will reserve the word "friend" for other uses, to be explained shortly.)

A *Philos* Relationship

Since the concept of strong ties has been clouded with ambiguity and inconsistency, I will use the Greek word *philos* to designate a particular type of tie that, because of its special character, has implications that make it different from other types of ties. Grammatically, I will use *philos* as a noun, and rules governing its use will be similar to that of the word "friend." That is, one may say "*A* is a *philos* to *B*" or, in the symmetrical case, "*A* and *B* are *philos*." I will define a *philos* relationship as one that meets the following three necessary and sufficient conditions:

1. *Interaction.* For *A* and *B* to be *philos*, *A* and *B* must interact with each other. The implication of this component is that there will be a high probability that each will have access to information that the other has, since such frequent interactions will provide opportunities to exchange such information.

2. *Affection.* For *A* to be *philos* of *B*, *A* must like *B*, *A* must feel affection for *B*. This evaluative component allows much of the important balance predictions of Heider and transitive closure predictions of Granovetter to hold. Heider (1958:202) also made predictions about the symmetry of the

"liking" relationship, and one may assume that in most cases such relationships are symmetrical. However, one can imagine occasions when affection is not reciprocated, resulting in an asymmetric relationship.

3. *Time.* A and B, to be *philos*, must have a history of interactions that have lasted over an extended period of time. That is, there is no such thing as instant *philos*. One implication here is that *philos* relationships cannot be studied in laboratory experiments. While one can induce short-term affective states and study "liking" (e.g., Byrne 1971), the study of *philos* is relegated to the field, where relationships have sufficient time to develop.

Note that I have not eliminated the psychological, affective quality of the relationship in defining *philos*. In fact, it is explicitly there, and to remove it destroys the predictions I would like to make from the relationship. While the definition of *philos* is not precisely the same as Granovetter's definition of strong ties, one may safely infer that *philos* relations constitute strong ties as Granovetter saw them.

The combination of these qualities are defined to be *philos*. But they also actively combine to make a theoretical prediction, one of *trust*. Interaction creates *opportunity* for the exchange of information, some of which may be confidential. Affection creates *motivation* to treat the other in positive ways, or at least not to do something that would hurt the person (because to do otherwise would create imbalance and consequent feelings of stress, disharmony, tension). And time creates the *experience* necessary to allow each person to predict how the other will use any shared information. These are the ingredients of trust. Granovetter has argued that the structure of embedded relationships in a social system is a necessary part of sociological inquiry to systematic change: "The embeddedness argument stresses instead the role of concrete personal relations and structures (or 'networks') or such relations in generating trust and discouraging malfeasance" (1985:490). With this article, Granovetter has switched emphasis from the strength of weak ties to the strength of strong *philos* ties. I predict that the *philos* relations will be the critical ones in generating trust and discouraging malfeasance.

The three components are necessary for *philos* because without any one of them the basis for trust falls apart. Without current interaction, there is little opportunity to share critical or confidential information. Without the history, there is no experience to know how the other will use the confidential information or who he or she will share it with. Without the positive affect, there is less motivation to maintain Heiderian balance, to share confidential information or to refrain from malfeasance.

Etic *Philos* versus Emic Friends

The underlying construct here is the well-defined *philos*. The concept most closely associated with this idea in the English language is that of "friend." Unfortunately, as Fischer (1982) has pointed out, the term "friend" is not well defined. In particular, he noted that the term means different things to different people. Based on a set of questionnaire responses about people's acquaintances, Fischer suggested that people use the label "friend" to denote a relationship devoid of any other formal designation (like "father"). However, within the set of coworkers, he found that friends were those with whom one had "sociable interaction" and with whom one would "discuss personal matters," ideas at least consistent with my notion of *philos*.

The correspondence between *philos* and friend can be best related to the anthropological dichotomy between etic and emic definitions. *Philos* is a theoretical construct, an etic concept with precise if abstract meaning. Friend is an emic construct, a word whose true meaning is embedded in the minds of those people in our society who use it frequently. As Fischer notes, we cannot abandon the term "friend" in the pursuit of science simply because the term has an imprecise definition: "It is too important a 'folk concept,' an idea that people use to order their worlds. And, it is too much a part of our own intellectual apparatus" (1982:288).

I will not try to define the folk meaning of friend. Instead, I will assume that the emic word "friend" is an estimate of the etic concept *philos*, just as a sample statistic is an estimate of a population parameter. The extent to which these two constructs match is a question worth exploring. As with all estimates, there will be error; I cannot even assure the reader that the estimate is unbiased. But the face validity of the idea that friends are people who like each other, have known each other for a reasonable time, and frequently interact with each other is at least minimally defensible. I will insist on differentiating between friend and *philos* because it is important to keep the distinction between the etic concept and the emic estimator of that concept.

What follows is a case study of a firm that underwent a union certification campaign. Just prior to this campaign, network data were collected in this firm (see Krackhardt 1990 for a description of the network study). Following the campaign, interviews were conducted with six key informants who provided information about the events that led to the initiation of the union attempt and also to the eventual failure of the campaign itself. I will provide an account of the critical events that occurred and relate these events to two kinds of strong (at least frequent) ties, the friendship and advice networks. These events underscore the importance that *philos* relationships (as measured by friendships) play over and above strong but affectless working relationships, such as the advice relationship, in the course of organizational change.

METHOD

A small entrepreneurial firm, called here Silicon Systems, is located on the West Coast of the United States in an area known for its many small, start-up firms as well as some more established ones. Silicon Systems' business involved the sales, installation, and maintenance of state-of-the-art information systems in client organizations. Its clients ranged from local banks to schools to medium-sized manufacturing firms to research and development (R&D) labs. Until recently its largest competitors, firms such as IBM and AT&T, focused their marketing efforts on the neighboring metropolitan areas. But recently the growth potential of Silicon Systems' market had attracted the attention of these competitors. According to Silicon Systems' top managers, the small firm's competitive edge rested in its ability to respond more efficiently to idiosyncratic customer demands.

Silicon Systems was wholly owned in equal shares by the three top managers. All employees worked in the single-story building owned by the company. They saw one another regularly, although installers worked many days at client sites rather than in the office. Thus Silicon Systems employees were familiar with one another to varying degrees, and each employee had an opinion about every other employee, with the occasional exception of new hires.

The firm had grown from three people to thirty-six in fifteen years. Much of this growth occurred in the five years preceding the study. Most of these years had been profitable, and the owners anticipated no downward trend in their business.

The Networks of Strong Ties

With the exception of a few employees who had just joined the firm, all of the 36 employees knew one another to some degree and conversed occasionally. Granovetter (1973:1371) defined weak ties as those who interact more than once per year and less than twice per week. He operationalized strong ties as those who interacted at least twice per week. By his criteria, all the employees in Silicon Systems would be considered at least weakly tied to one another.

The presence or absence of weak ties, therefore, is not a viable question in this context. Instead, the focus in this case will be on the presence or absence of various types of strong ties. And, in particular, I claim that the affective component of the strong tie is important in understanding the dynamics surrounding crises or changes in organizations. To demonstrate this, I will distinguish between two types of strong (that is, frequent) ties: a network of advice interactions stemming from routine work problems and a network of *philos* relationships in the firm.

Consistent with my cognitive theme, the network information obtained in this case study was based on the actors' own perceptions about who was related to whom in the firm. Each person provided his or her own estimate of the entire structure (Krackhardt 1987) of both a *philos* and an advice network. These maps are represented as "cognitive cubes," or more formally, $R_{i,j,k}$, where i is the sender of the relation, j is the receiver of the relation, and k is the perceiver of the relation. The directions for the "advice" section of the questionnaire were as follows:

In this section, you will find a set of similar questions with a list of people after each question. The question is: "Who would this person go to for help or advice at work?" That is, if this person had a question or ran into a problem at work, who would they likely go to, to ask for advice or help? Please answer the question by placing a check next to the names of all the people the person is likely to go to. . . . Some people may go to several people for help or advice. Some may go only to one person. Some may not go to anyone, in which case do not check anyone's name under that question.

These directions were followed by 36 questions (e.g., "Who would Cindy Stalwart go to for help or advice at work?"), each asking the same question about a different employee. Each of these 36 questions was followed by a list of 35 names, any number of which the respondent could check off in response to the question.

Similarly, another section of the questionnaire asked about friendships. The directions for this section paralleled those in the previous section:

. . . This time the question is: "Who would this person consider to be a personal friend?" Please place a check next to all the names of those people who that person would consider to be a friend of theirs.

Again, the question was repeated 36 times, once for each employee's name (e.g., "Who would Abe consider to be a personal friend?"), and each question was followed by a list of 35 names from which the respondent could check any number.

The three-dimensional data from these questionnaires allow two different types of aggregations to be formed, each represented in a two-dimensional matrix. The first aggregation creates what will be referred to as the "actual network." The second aggregation is a simple slice of the cognitive cube and will be referred to as the "perceived network." Specific definitions follow.

Actual Network   The actual network for both the friendship and advice relations will be identified by an asterisk: $R^*_{i,j}$ (see Krackhardt 1990 for more details). This network is defined as follows:

$$R^*_{i,j} = 1 \quad \text{if } R_{i,j,i} = 1 \text{ and } R_{i,j,j} = 1;$$
$$\phantom{R^*_{i,j} =} 0 \quad \text{otherwise.}$$

That is, both i and j must agree that i goes to j for help and advice before the relation $i \rightarrow j$ in actual advice network is recognized. Similarly, both i and j must agree that i considers j a friend before the $i \rightarrow j$ link is recorded as existing in the actual friendship network.

Perceived Network and Cognitive Accuracy   In the network study prior to the union certification campaign, I found that the individual's ability to accurately reconstruct the advice network predicted that person's reputational power in the organization (Krackhardt 1990). I argue that having an accurate knowledge of the informal organization gave the employee a competitive edge in any political endeavor. In the current case study, I will refer to the accuracy scores of individuals who were critical players in the pre-union activities and in the union drive itself because these scores shed light on the political perspicacity of key employees.

The degree to which a respondent was accurate in his or her perceptions of the networks was simply defined as the correlation between the individual's perceived network and the actual network, as defined earlier. The individual K's perceived network is denoted $R_{ki,j}$, and the correlation with $R^*_{i,j}$ from here on will be referred to as person K's accuracy score.[2]

Centrality

The three most common measures of centrality—degree, closeness, and betweenness—are compared and reviewed by Freeman (1979). I will restrict my discussion to degree and betweenness centrality. Degree centrality is the simplest form of centrality and comes in two forms: indegree and outdegree. The indegree of an actor in the network is the number of other people who choose that actor in the particular relationship. For example, Steve, the president, had an indegree of 19 in the actual advice relationship (see Table 8-1). This meant that 19 employees went to Steve for help and advice at work. Outdegree is the number of people chosen by the actor. For example, Steve had an outdegree of 7 on the actual advice relationship, meaning that he went to seven others for help and advice. The indegree and outdegree of an actor are often good indicators of the informal status that the individual has in the organization. For example, people with high indegrees in the advice relationship are those with experience and know-how to give advice. Those with high outdegrees tend to reach out to others.

Betweenness is somewhat more complicated in its definition. Using Freeman's (1979) notation, betweenness centrality is defined as follows:[3]

$$C_B(k) = \frac{2 \, \Sigma_i^n \, \Sigma_j^n \left(\dfrac{g_{i_j}(k)}{g_{i_j}} \right)}{n^2 - 3n + 2}$$

for all unordered triples i, j, k, where $i < j$, n is the number of nodes in the network, $g_{ij}(k)$ is the number of geodesics (shortest paths) between nodes i and j in the network, and $g_{ij}(k)$ is the number of geodesics from i to j that include k. To the extent that k lies on the shortest paths between each pair (i, j), then k would be said to have high betweenness centrality. Thus a person with high betweenness is in a position to act as gatekeeper for information that flows through the network. Moreover, betweenness is an indication of the nonredundancy of the source of information. To the extent that a person is connected to otherwise disconnected parts of the network, and therefore has access to different, nonredundant sources of information, that person will have a higher betweenness score.

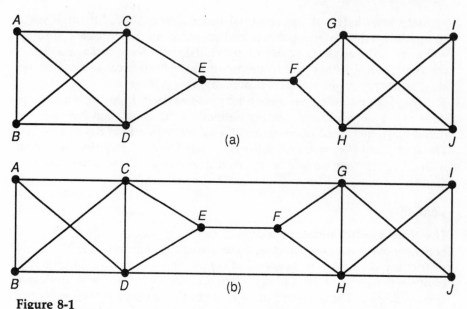

Figure 8-1

Two Sociograms Illustrating Differences in Centrality

The difference between degree and betweenness is illustrated in Figures 8-1a and 8-1b. Each figure describes a set of relationships (indicated with lines) among a set of people (indicated with capital letters). In Figure 8-1a, persons C, D, G, and H have the highest degree centrality, with 4 indegrees and outdegrees each (the choices are assumed to be symmetric in this hypothetical example, so that indegrees and outdegrees are equal). Each of the remaining people has degree centrality of 3. In contrast to these degree measures, betweenness indicators suggest that a different set of people occupy prominent positions in Figure 8-1a. Persons E and F are between 4/9 of other pairs of people, for a betweenness score of .444. Persons C, D, G, and H are between less than 20% of the pairs of people, for a betweenness score of .185. The remaining people have 0 betweenness. It is E and F's position with their access to *separate* groups that gives them such high betweenness scores.

But if we add merely two lines to Figure 8-1a to connect C with G and D with H (see Figure 8-1b), we destroy this advantage that E and F shared. E and F's betweenness drops from .444 to .056; C, D, G, and H's betweenness barely changes from .185 to .190 (the remaining points are still 0). By adding these lines, the groups on each side are no longer dependent on the E–F bridge. In fact, the entire structure is more wedded together so that no point enjoys the particularly central position that E and F did in Figure 8-1a.

It is worth noting the parallel between the betweenness measure of centrality and Granovetter's concept of a local bridge. A local bridge is a property of a tie; the numerical value of a local bridge (referred to as its *degree*) is equal to the shortest alternative path between the two points connected by the bridge (say, *A* and *B*) if that bridge were to be removed. The more that the others around *A* and *B* are tied together by direct or relatively short alternative paths, the lower the value or degree of the local bridge between *A* and *B*. Betweenness is an attribute of a node in the graph; local bridge degree is an attribute of a tie. But both measure the degree to which the actors reach disparate and unconnected parts of the social system. The higher the degree of the local bridges a person is connected to, the higher that person's betweenness score will be. Thus I refer to the betweenness of actors in these networks in my discussion of the union certification campaign at Silicon Systems, keeping in mind this relationship to Granovetter's idea of the importance of such bridges.

THE UNIONIZATION ATTEMPT: A CASE STUDY

Four months after the network data were fed back to the firm, Silicon Systems was confronted with an unexpected dilemma. The National Labor Relations Board (NLRB) called the president of the firm (Steve) to inform him that the NLRB was granting a petition by a national union to hold a certification election at Silicon Systems. This news came as a total surprise to top management. They felt nervous about the outcome and extremely sensitive about what this meant about the future of the firm. Further, they asked me to refrain from talking to anyone at the firm about the union or the union drive.

After the union drive was completed, I approached the top management of the firm for permission to interview some key people about what had happened. At that time, I talked to three people who were involved in the process on the condition that no one's identity be divulged. Subsequently, top management gave me permission to interview three more employees to verify the information obtained in the first set of interviews. The six informants were interviewed at length about their view of the union and the events surrounding the certification drive. The interviews were primarily unstructured, but specific questions were always included: "What were the key events in the certification campaign?" "Who were the main players (both for and against the union)?" "Why do you think the union failed to gain certification?" The six people represented a spectrum of employees in terms of their own support for the union and in terms of their longevity with the firm (one person had been there for over 15 years, one had been there for less than a year). Because of the sensitivity of this issue, none of the information below is attributed to any individual in the firm. All accounts reported here represent a consensus of the informants.

By the time top management found out about the employees' union interests, enough employees had signed union authorization cards that the NLRB granted the union's request to have a certification election in two months' time. The three owners were highly concerned, since they believed that they would lose a distinct advantage they had over their

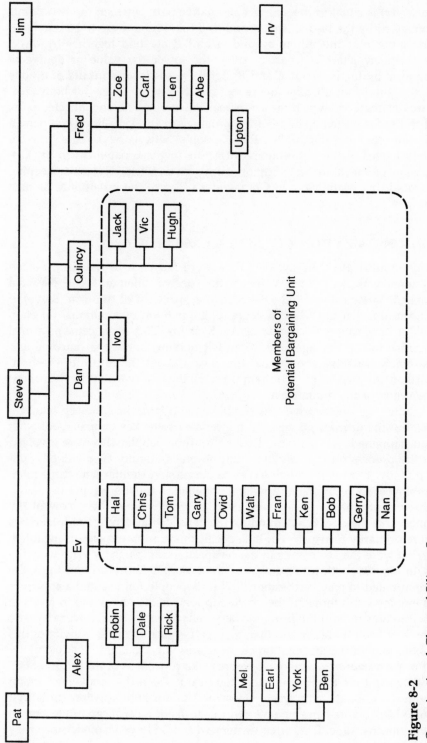

Figure 8-2
Organizational Chart of Silicon Systems

larger competitors if the firm became unionized. They consulted labor lawyers to find out what options they had. Their lawyers informed them that there were legal constraints on what they could do to actively discourage certification without risking an unfair-labor-practices judgment. They decided that they would work within these constraints to provide what information they could to support management's position. However, the fate of the certification campaign depended largely on the dynamic forces between the union officials and the nonmanagement employees, especially those in the bargaining unit itself.

Representatives of neither the union nor the NLRB were willing to divulge what percentage of the bargaining unit had signed authorization cards. But an official of the union did confirm that, as a matter of policy, they do not request an election unless they have at least 55% of the bargaining unit signed up. Moreover, according to this official, the union prided itself on not losing certification elections. The union does not ask the NLRB to conduct an election unless it feels certain it will win. Election campaigns are costly, and the union does not like to lose face.

During the two-month campaign period, the national union held several organizing meetings. Gripes were aired about the firm. As is typical in such cases, debates ensued around the pros and cons of unionization. Feelings strengthened as the vote grew closer.

To understand the dynamics involved, it will be useful to refer to individual employees in the context of their positions in both the formal organization and the informal networks. The pseudonyms for these employees and their respective formal positions in the organizational chart are given in Figure 8-2. The advice network and friendship network are displayed in Figures 8-3 and 8-4, respectively. In the advice network (Figure 8-3), arrows indicate the direction of the advice relationship. For example, the arrow from Bob to Chris (near the top of the figure) indicates that Bob goes to Chris for help and advice. A double-headed arrow, such as the one found between Vic and Rick, indicates that each actor goes to the other for help and advice. The friendship network does not display arrows, because the majority of friendship relations are symmetrical. With the exception of isolates, the placement of the actors in these figures is determined by a multidimensional scaling (MDS) of the graph-theoretic path distances between actors in the network.[4] The MDS solution tends to put the central actors in the middle of the figure and more peripheral actors scattered around the sides.

In addition to these pictoral representations, degree and betweenness centrality scores and accuracy scores are provided in Tables 8-1 and 8-2. Employee names are arranged in the tables in descending order of betweenness centrality. Three employees chose not to fill out the questionnaire, and consequently no accuracy score could be calculated for them. These missing accuracy scores are indicated by an "M" in Tables 8-1 and 8-2. I was able to calculate centralities for those employees even though they did not fill out the questionnaire because I had estimates of their relations based on other employees' perceptions.

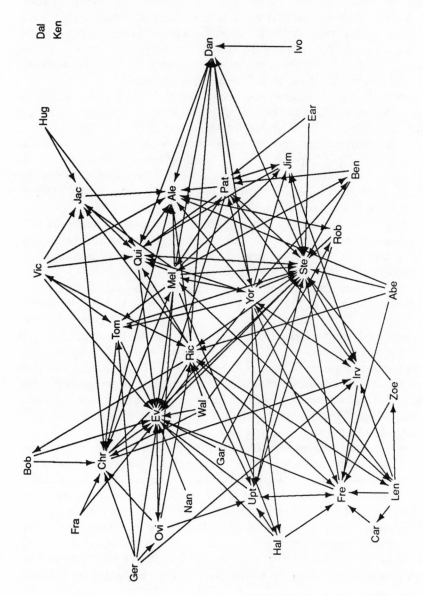

Figure 8-3
Sociogram of Advice Network

Table 8-1

Centralities and Accuracy on the Advice Network

		CENTRALITIES			
ID	Name	Indegree	Outdegree	Betweenness	Accuracy (rank)
5	Ev	19.	1	0.20130	0.485 (3)
19	Steve	19.	7.	0.16405	0.411 (20)
24	Rick	6.	11.	0.08208	M (M)
13	Mel	5.	15.	0.06711	M (M)
6	Fred	9.	3.	0.06249	0.459 (7)
17	Quincy	10.	3.	0.05753	0.514 (1)
25	York	5.	15.	0.05551	0.391 (22)
30	Dan	7.	3.	0.05488	0.430 (10)
29	Chris	7.	6.	0.05263	0.384 (23)
16	Pat	7.	9.	0.03259	0.420 (16)
27	Alex	11.	2.	0.03217	0.397 (21)
12	Len	3.	7.	0.02444	0.212 (33)
35	Irv	6.	5.	0.01912	M (M)
10	Jack	5.	2.	0.01593	0.332 (30)
21	Upton	7.	3.	0.01373	0.413 (19)
20	Tom	4.	3.	0.00834	0.378 (24)
18	Robin	2.	3.	0.00799	0.436 (9)
15	Ovid	2.	4.	0.00469	0.429 (12)
22	Vic	1.	6.	0.00375	0.352 (28)
33	Gerry	0.	5.	0.00274	0.302 (32)
7	Gary	0.	2.	0.00195	0.423 (14)
1	Abe	0.	4.	0.00139	0.482 (4)
36	Jim	5.	4.	0.00111	0.417 (17)
26	Zoe	1.	2.	0.00073	0.475 (5)
8	Hal	2.	3.	0.00067	0.371 (27)
2	Bob	1.	2.	0.00024	0.333 (29)
23	Walt	0.	4.	0.00024	0.417 (18)
28	Ben	2.	4.	0.00000	0.499 (2)
3	Carl	1.	1.	0.00000	0.374 (26)
32	Fran	0.	2.	0.00000	0.378 (25)
31	Earl	0.	2.	0.00000	0.423 (15)
34	Hugh	0.	2.	0.00000	0.470 (6)
9	Ivo	0.	1.	0.00000	0.442 (8)
14	Nan	0.	1.	0.00000	0.314 (31)
11	Ken	0.	0.	0.00000	0.429 (11)
4	Dale	0.	0.	0.00000	0.426 (13)

The Key Players in Management: Steve and Ev

Steve was the founder and president of this company. He knew all of its operations. As noted earlier, in the advice network his indegree was 19 and outdegree was 7 (see Figure 8-3 and Table 8-1). It is no surprise that he was the recipient of so many requests for help and advice. The fact that Steve reached out to seven employees on a regular basis for help and advice underscored his management style: he liked to stay in touch with what was going on in the firm, especially among his management team members, to whom most of his outdegree ties are pointed. He also

Table 8-2

Centralities and Accuracy on the Friendship Network

		CENTRALITIES			
ID	Name	Indegree	Outdegree	Betweenness	Accuracy (rank)
29	Chris	12.	16.	0.16202	0.362 (11)
2	Bob	6.	4.	0.10899	0.344 (15)
24	Rick	11.	9.	0.10573	M (M)
19	Steve	8.	6.	0.10472	0.349 (14)
21	Upton	5.	4.	0.09101	0.356 (12)
6	Fred	4.	2.	0.08981	0.334 (18)
35	Irv	8.	7.	0.07368	M (M)
16	Pat	5.	4.	0.07013	0.323 (23)
13	Mel	6.	7.	0.06695	M (M)
20	Tom	10.	10.	0.06651	0.363 (10)
33	Gerry	8.	7.	0.06615	0.381 (8)
4	Dale	8.	7.	0.05218	0.331 (20)
11	Ken	9.	7.	0.02812	0.384 (7)
14	Nan	5.	7.	0.02504	0.188 (31)
34	Hugh	6.	7.	0.01955	0.407 (3)
3	Carl	2.	4.	0.01792	0.391 (5)
30	Dan	5.	5.	0.01377	0.442 (1)
12	Len	2.	4.	0.00944	0.329 (21)
26	Zoe	3.	2.	0.00695	0.414 (2)
18	Robin	4.	4.	0.00280	0.333 (19)
9	Ivo	3.	2.	0.00268	0.398 (4)
15	Ovid	4.	3.	0.00240	0.302 (25)
27	Alex	3.	3.	0.00230	0.336 (17)
7	Gary	3.	2.	0.00118	0.311 (24)
5	Ev	2.	1.	0.00000	0.292 (26)
22	Vic	1.	3.	0.00000	0.275 (28)
8	Hal	1.	2.	0.00000	0.155 (33)
23	Walt	1.	2.	0.00000	0.352 (13)
36	Jim	1.	1.	0.00000	0.221 (29)
10	Jack	1.	1.	0.00000	0.200 (30)
31	Earl	0.	2.	0.00000	0.380 (9)
28	Ben	0.	1.	0.00000	0.292 (27)
1	Abe	0.	1.	0.00000	0.387 (6)
32	Fran	0.	0.	0.00000	0.325 (22)
17	Quincy	0.	0.	0.00000	0.341 (16)

enjoyed the second-highest betweenness score, indicating that his ties were spread out among various groups within the firm. As indicated by his accuracy score, Steve's knowledge of the advice network was somewhat below the median in the firm. His lack of a better understanding of many of the informal advice ties can be attributed to his lack of attention to the rank and file of the firm.

An interesting contrast to Steve's managerial style was provided by Ev, the technical expert in the firm. Ev supervised the installation of much of the most sophisticated equipment in the field. His critical role in the organization was underscored by the fact that he had the highest betweenness score in the advice network—even higher than that of Steve, the president. Ev's ability to solve problems in the field made him indispensable to a wide variety of people within the firm. His outdegree score, however, was 1 (Steve). His approach was more that of the engineer—the problem solver—than that of the manager. People came to him with problems, and he solved them or told others how to solve them. Ev did not see as part of his job that he had to seek out others' opinions, advice, or help. But by being so close to where the action was, he was in a good position to observe the informal advice network, His accuracy score reflected this good position: he had the third-highest accuracy in the advice network at Silicon Systems.

While no one questioned Ev's technical skills, some of the installers who worked for Ev indicated discontent with his managerial style. In fact, unbeknownst to top management at the time, dissatisfaction with Ev had spawned union interest on the part of several of the installers. As a result, contact was made secretly with a national union to organize the firm.

The installers' feelings toward Ev are illustrated in his position in the friendship network (Figure 8-4). Ev had only two indegrees (two people considered him a personal friend), neither of whom were people who worked with him in the field. His betweenness in the friendship network was zero. Moreover, Ev's accuracy score for the friendship network was the eighth-lowest in the firm. Not only was friendship something he failed to engage in at work; he also paid little attention to it among others who worked for him or around him.

In contrast, Steve had eight indegrees in the friendship network (eight people considered him a personal friend), and those who chose him were reasonably spread out, as he had the fourth-highest betweenness score. Despite his central position, however, his accuracy score was only slightly above the median for the firm, again because he tended to pay more attention to the top of the organization than to the rank and file. His lack of familiarity with the bottom of the organization led to his overwhelming sense of surprise and betrayal when he was informed by the NLRB that a union drive was under way.

Key Members of the Potential Bargaining Unit: Chris, Hal, Ovid, and Jack

The most central person in the friendship network was Chris, with 12 indegrees, 16 outdegrees, and a betweenness score of .162, substantially higher than the next-closest score. He had a more accurate assessment of the friendship network than anyone in management except Dan. Chris had been with the firm for a number of years, and his experience as a veteran installer was appreciated. But because his technical skills were not as strong as Ev's, Chris did not enjoy as central a position in the advice network as Ev did. In the field, however, Chris was often informally put in charge of a group of people to install some computer equipment, and his coworkers preferred working with him to working with Ev.

Before the union was contacted, Chris was very supportive of the union's goals. He was concerned about issues of pay and job security for himself and his fellow installers. While he was not the one who contacted the union, he had discussed with his colleagues the possibility of joining a union.

After the union was contacted, Chris took a back seat to others who were organizing on behalf of the union. He did not lead the organizing meetings, and he said very little publicly. Several fellow employees turned to him for guidance on this issue, but he resisted taking a leadership role. His reticence stemmed from two sources. First, the union made little effort to get him involved. While the union officials spent time with employees at the local bars and other locations, they never approached Chris with plans about his own role in the process. Second, Chris had strong feelings of ambivalence about the union. As noted earlier, he felt positively toward the union issues of pay and fair treatment by supervisors, but he also felt loyalty to the firm itself. He had been with the firm for a number of years, and he had grown to like his job and his coworkers. He did not want to be part of something that he thought might potentially damage the firm. Rather than attempt to lead his colleagues in any particular direction, he chose to remain in the background and did not actively involve himself in the debates at the meetings. As the vote approached, he felt more and more torn. Less than three weeks before the certification vote, he resigned from the firm rather than face the pressures of publicly committing on the union issue. He rejoined the company two days after the certification vote was taken.

Strong prounion positions were held by three key members of the potential bargaining unit: Ovid, Jack, and Hal. All three men had less betweenness centrality than the two antiunion employees, Mel and Robin. All three had a poorer cognitive picture of the friendship network than Robin (Mel did not fill out the questionnaire, so his cognitive accuracy score was not available). Jack and Hal had minimal friendship ties to others in the potential bargaining unit. While Ovid strongly favored the union, he was very quiet about it, to the point that only a few people knew where he actually stood on the issue. It also was known that he was to leave shortly after the vote, so his influence was diminished. Jack was vocal about his dissatisfaction with how the company treated him. But his position on the periphery of the friendship network (see Figure 8-4, on the extreme left) aptly describes his lack of informal influence with most of his colleagues. He was considered someone who had a grudge and who was motivated by his own personal agenda to be prounion.

The most central actor in the union's attempt at organizing everyone was Hal. He was the union's original contact with the firm and he was the instigator for the drive. He was the union's key spokesman at the organizing meetings, many of which he ran personally. He told the union representatives that he could get enough of his coworkers to vote for the union to assure a victory for the union. For the union's part, it obviously and publicly chose Hal to lead the employees in the organization attempt.

As one can see in Figure 8-4 (on the right-hand side), Hal was not a central actor in the friendship network. It was true that Hal was the most enthusiastic supporter of the union, which is largely why the union officials selected him. However, he was not the person who wielded the most informal influence among his colleagues. In fact, he was seen by several members of the potential bargaining unit as a "loose cannon," and not "one of the guys."

Other Key Players: Robin and Mel

There was considerable antiunion feeling in the company, but none of it was located in the bargaining unit being organized. The key nonmanagement company supporters included Robin and Mel. Both were considered "one of the guys" and would often go drinking at local bars with people from the bargaining unit. They were vehemently opposed to the union and told people so. As can be seen in Figure 8-4, Robin and Mel were friends with each other as well as with several of the members of the bargaining unit, including Chris. In fact, their friendship with Chris contributed to Chris's ambivalence toward the union. Thus while they were not formally part of the bargaining unit, they wielded considerable informal influence within that group.

At the start of the two-month campaign, the union had the interest and lukewarm support of a majority of the people in the bargaining unit. In the opinion of several people who were interviewed for this study, the company would have lost the election had it been held on the first day of the campaign. While it is not known exactly how many people were pro-union at the start, according to a union spokesperson interviewed, at least eight of the fifteen members of the potential bargaining unit had signed authorization cards.

Over the two months, the incessant pushing on the part of Hal (and to some extent Jack), instead of rallying support, served only to alienate several coworkers. This, combined with the antiunion position of Mel and Robin, led to a gradual deterioration of support for the union over the campaign period. In the end, the union was defeated in the certification election by a vote of 12 to 3.

DISCUSSION

What this study shows is that the key players in the advice network were not the key actors in the friendship network. Most striking is Ev's relative status in the friendship network. He was connected to the president (Steve) and another, peripheral employee. None of the employees who worked with him in the field were connected to him in the friendship network. By contrast, Chris was the most central actor in the friendship network. Chris was an installer with friendships that cut across functional and hierarchical boundaries. But his position in the advice network was relatively minor.

Chris's ambivalence stemmed from his feelings about the union in conjunction with his feelings about his friends, Mel and Robin. That is, he felt strongly that the union provided important protection for him and his fellow workers. He had been a voice in favor of contacting a union before the certification campaign began. But as his friends started to argue intensively against the union, he experienced the stress and tension that Heider predicted in such an imbalanced situation. Chris and Mel had a strong mutual "advice" tie, also (that is, Chris would go to Mel for advice and vice versa). But, according to his closest associates, this work-based tie was not what contributed to Chris's discomfort in this situation. The informants I talked with would always refer to Chris's friends as influential on his behavior in this case. The only work-based relationship they discussed as influential in Chris's behavior was his relationship with Ev (his supervisor). If anything, this relationship with Ev, who was strongly opposed to the union, prompted Chris to be more inclined to support the union. Again, this is consistent with Heider's prediction: Since Chris's evaluation of Ev was negative and Ev's evaluation of the union was negative, Heider would predict that Chris would be positively disposed toward the union.

Davis (1963) noted that Heider's balance theory could be used to derive predictions about "cross-pressure" responses (Berelson, Lazarsfeld, and Mcphee 1954). Cross-pressure situations arise when people are linked to groups that differ in their evaluations in important ways. Chris was in a prototypical cross-pressure situation. Davis quoted Berelson et al. (1954:284): "An individual who is characterized by any type of cross-pressure is likely to change his mind in the course of the campaign, to make up his mind late, and occasionally, to leave the field and not to vote at all."

Putting this in balance-theory language, Davis himself wrote: "To the extent that *Person* has a positive bond to *Other*$_1$ and also to *Other*$_2$ . . . , it becomes increasingly difficult for him to adopt a stable attitude toward *X*" (1963:205). He further noted that the stronger the bond between *Person* and *Others*, the more difficult it is to resolve his attitude toward *X*. *Philos* bonds are particularly strong, since they involve strong affect and also have been invested in for some time. In Chris's case, it was because of the *history and affection* for his colleagues, some of whom (like Ovid) were strongly in favor of the union and others of whom (like Rob and Mel) were strongly opposed to the union, that Chris felt those cross-pressures and finally decided to withdraw from the decision.

It is impossible to know all the reasons for the union's failure to organize Silicon Systems. But according to the informants, a significant part of the failure was due to the fact that the union selected ineffective, nonpowerful people to represent it in the process. While Hal and Jack were enthusiastic and articulate supporters of the union and its cause, they were not considered influential among their peers. Note that they were connected to their peers through the advice network: Hal to five people and Jack to six (see Figure 8-3). But they were marginal players in the friendship network: Hal had two connections (neither of them to other members of the potential bargaining unit), and Jack had only one (see Figure 8-4). As with Chris, when people spoke of Jack and Hal's roles in the process, they referred to affective qualities of friendship—or lack of it—in discussing how little influence each had in swaying the opinions of his coworkers.

Moreover, the union failed to recognize and address the influence that Robin and Mel had over members of the bargaining unit. In contrast to Hal and Jack, Rob and Mel had several friendship connections to members of the potential bargaining unit, most notably Chris. It is clear from Figure 8-4 that Chris could have played an influential role in the process, if he had chosen to do so. His sympathies were with the union, but his alliances were torn. The union officials chose to ignore Chris. Had they co-opted and convinced him to take an active pro-union role, others in the unit might have followed suit and voted for certification.

The Power of an Outsider

Thus we note that some people *behaved* in ways that indicated support for the union; others behaved in ways that indicated support for the management position. But the fact that the individuals *behaved* in particular ways is not enough. They had to be influential, also, for this behavior to be leveraged into actual support. This influence, this leverage, comes from the actors' positions in the *philos* network vis-à-vis others who were to have the final vote on this issue.

An outsider, such as the union in this instance, does not have either a formal or an informal position of influence from which to change people's thinking. But an outsider can acquire knowledge of such positions that others hold. For an outsider, the friendship network (Figure 8-4) provides a map of potential influence. Knowledge of this map provides the outsider with an increased power base with which to accomplish his or her goals.

These conclusions stem largely from references to the friendship network, not the advice network, for two reasons. First, those people interviewed often referred to friendships in talking about who was influential in the campaign. Second, there are theoretical justifications for expecting friendships to be key in the certification drive. Krackhardt and Stern (1988) suggested that friendship links embody trust and that trust leads to cooperation under times of crises or radical change and uncertainty. When radical change requires trust to implement, affect can play an important role in determining where the power lies. In relatively tranquil times, however, work gets done in an organization by well-practiced and routine procedures. When exceptions to the routine are common, the process by which these exceptions are handled becomes part of the routine. In such times the patterns of daily or weekly interactions over work-flow problems become the building blocks of power in the organization. Those who know how to handle the routine exceptions are the ones who know how to get things done and will assume powerful roles (Crozier 1964).

Second, it was clear that affective evaluations and resulting trust dominated the process because the union drive amounted to a major change for the organization—an organizational crisis, from management's point of view. The advice network reflected technical expertise and routine work-flow knowledge. The proposed change was nonroutine;

advice on this critical issue was sought from those one trusted (as friends), not from technical experts.

I would speculate that had union officials had access to the information in Figure 8-4, they might have revised their strategy in their attempt to organize Silicon Systems. While they did not have access to structural power, they could have developed a more accurate assessment of power by asking the same friendship questions used in this research. Their lack of awareness of the *philos* network, in other words, represented a lost opportunity for gaining power as an outsider.

My earlier study results show that accuracy in assessing the *advice* network, not the friendship network, was significantly related to reputational power of the members of the firm (Krackhardt 1990). In this study, however, I argue that power is enhanced through an understanding of the *philos* network. This seeming contradiction makes sense in light of the theoretical arguments just made. At the time that the network and power data were being collected, the firm had not experienced any tumultuous events or environmental jolts. In answering questions about influence and power, employees were responding according to their experiences in their day-to-day lives in the organization. As in the case of Ev, those people central to the advice network, the experts, are likely to derive power from such routine situations. On the other hand, the certification move was an attempt to introduce a significant change in the organization (from both management's and workers' perspectives). Dealing with this change did not require routine information. It required trust, which is better represented in a *philos* network than in an affectively neutral advice network.

CONCLUSION

We opened this chapter by noting that Granovetter's strength-of-weak-ties hypothesis had found support in the literature, but that the support had left some issues unaddressed. Our study did not set out to test or expand the weak-ties hypothesis but attempted to refocus on the importance of strong ties within an organization. In particular, using Granovetter's own logic, we can see how strong ties may become important in organizations when they are spread out among the players.

But a critical part of networks rests in a forgotten aspect of the strong-ties argument: The affect level of these ties cannot be ignored. Frequent interactions that are not part of the *philos* relations are not going to have the same effect as those that are. Someone, even an outsider, who understands the structure of *philos* ties within an organization will be much more able to anticipate political resistance and facilitate change.

Just as I opened by referring to Mark Granovetter, it is fitting that I close with a reference to his current work. In his keynote speech at the 1990 INSNA conference, Granovetter admitted that he tried to escape the label of a social networker and move on to "more substantive interests in stratification, economic sociology and sociological theory" (Granovetter 1990). But, he went on, no matter which substantive avenue he traveled, a review of the literature in that area led him to rediscover the importance of networks in understanding the social phenomena under scrutiny. Granovetter's current thinking differs especially with that of economists who seek to explain forces toward equilibria: "This means talking seriously about how changes occur. And what happens in such a dynamic account is that you have to look at how people make use of their location in social networks to mobilize resources in order to achieve their economic goals."

If change were simply dependent on new information, then weak ties would be preeminent. But when it comes to major change, change that may threaten the status quo in terms of power and the standard routines of how decisions are made, then resistance to that change must be addressed before predictions can be made about the success of that change effort. A major resource that is required to bring about such change is trust in the propagators of that change. Change is the product of strong, affective, and time-honored relationships. Change is the product of *philos*.

Notes

1. An alternative to the psychological explanation has been offered by Davis (1968:548). He suggests that groups cluster on attributes having less to do with sentiment and more to do with the social categories they belong to or to the fact that organizations are naturally divided into subgroups that facilitate balanced clusters of interaction. This is an interesting conjecture, one that deserves more systematic study. Nonetheless, there is some evidence suggesting that Heider's explanation is at least part of the picture. Krackhardt and Kilduff (1990) explored the friendship patterns within a small firm. The patterns of friendship did not clump into easily identifiable groups, as Davis would have predicted. But, consistent with balance theory, when an individual disagreed with his or her friends about their evaluations of others in the workplace, there was a strong tendency for that person to be relatively disaffected with his or her experience at the organization.
2. Since person k has some input into the definition of $R^*_{i,j}$, that is, when $i = k$ or when $j = k$, these "local ties" were excluded from person k's accuracy score. For a more thorough discussion, see Krackhardt 1990:350.
3. Betweenness is calculated from the underlying graph of the asymmetric relation R^*. That is, the asymmetric relation is made symmetrical first before the betweenness score is computed. See Krackhardt 1990:351, for more details.
4. The program used here was an adaptation of Lingoes and Roskam's (1973) MINISSA package. See Kruskal and Wish's (1978) discussion of MDS and the various packages available.

References

Berelson, B. R., Paul F. Lazarsfeld, and W. N. McPhee. 1954. *Voting: A Study of Opinion Formation in a Presidential Campaign*. Chicago: University of Chicago Press.

Byrne, D. 1971. *The Attraction Paradigm*. New York: Academic Press.

Crozier, M. 1964. *The Bureaucratic Phenomenon*. Chicago: University of Chicago Press.

Davis, James A. 1963. "Structural Balance, Mechanical Solidarity and Interpersonal Relations." *American Journal of Sociology* 68:444–463.

————. 1968. "Social Structures and Cognitive Structures." in R. P. Abelson, E. Anderson, N. J. McGuire, T. M. Newcomb, M. J. Rosenberg, and P. H. Tannenbaum, eds. *Theories of Cognitive Consistency: A Source Book.* Chicago: Rand McNally.

————. 1979. "The Davis/Holland/Lernhardt Studies: An Overview." In Paul W. Holland and Samuel Lernhardt, eds. *Perspectives on Social Network Research.* New York: Academic Press.

Erickson, E., and W. Yancey. 1980. "Class, Sector and Income Determination." Unpublished paper, Department of Sociology, Temple University.

Fischer, Claude S. 1982. "What Do We Mean by 'Friend'? An Inductive Study." *Social Networks* 3:287–306.

Freeman, Linton C. 1979. "Centrality in Social Networks: Conceptional Clarification." *Social Networks* 1:215–239.

Friedkin, N. E. 1980. "A Test of Structural Features of Granovetter's Strength of Weak Ties Theory." *Social Networks* 2:22–41.

Granovetter, M. S. 1973. "The Strength of Weak Ties." *American Journal of Sociology* 78:1360–1380.

————. 1982. "The Strength of Weak Ties: A Network Theory Revisited." In P. V. Marsden and Nan Lin, eds. *Social Structure and Network Analysis.* Beverly Hills: Sage.

————. 1985. "Economic Action and Social Structure: The Problem of Embededness." *American Journal of Sociology* 91(3):481–510.

————. 1990. "The Myth of Social Network Analysis as a Special in the Social Sciences." INSNA Conference, San Diego.

Heider, Fritz. 1958. *The Psychology of Interpersonal Relations.* New York: Wiley.

Krackhardt, David. 1987. "Cognitive Social Structures." *Social Networks* 9:109–134.

————. 1990. "Assessing the Political Landscape: Structure, Cognition, and Power in Organizations." *Administrative Science Quarterly* 35:342–369.

Krackhardt, David, and Martin Kilduff. 1990. "Friendship Patterns and Culture: The Control of Organizational Diversity." *American Anthropologist* 92(1):142–154.

Krackhardt, David, and Robert Stern. 1988. "Informal Networks and Organizational Crisis: An Experimental Simulation." *Social Psychology Quarterly* 51:123–140.

Kruskal, Joseph B., and Myron Wish. 1978. *Multidimensional Scaling.* Beverly Hills: Sage.

Lin, N., P. W. Dayton, and P. Greenwald. 1978. "Analyzing the Instrumental Use of Relations in the Context of Social Structure." *Sociological Methods and Research* 7:149–166.

Lin, N., W. M. Ensel, and J. C. Vaughn. 1981. "Social Resources and Strength of Ties: Structural Factors in Occupational Status Attainment." *American Sociological Review* 46:393–405.

Lingoes, J. C., and Edward E. Roskam. 1973. "A Mathematical and Empirical Analysis of Two Multidimensional Scaling Algorithms." *Psychometrika* 38:93.

Newcomb, J. M. 1961. *The Aquaintance Process.* New York: Holt, Reinhart and Winston.

Pool, I. 1980. "Comment on Mark Granovetter's 'The Strength of Weak Ties': A Network Revisited." Presented at the Annual Meetings of the International Communications Association, Acapulco, May.

9

Information and Search in the Creation of New Business Ventures: The Case of the 128 Venture Group

NITIN NOHRIA

INTRODUCTION

The importance of social relations and institutions in facilitating the search process in situations of imperfect information and uncertainty has been recognized for some time. In a study of job mobility in the labor market for white-collar workers, Granovetter (1974) discovered the central role played by acquaintances or those with whom one had "weak ties" in the search for a new job. Since then, the serendipitous transfer of information through informal social contacts has been found to be a primary mechanism by which search proceeds in many other markets with imperfect information. Of course, there are other, more formal institutions such as job fairs, search firms, and brokers that facilitate search in imperfect markets. And economists such as Kreps (1990) have described the important role that reputation, formal educational qualifications, and professional certification play in facilitating search.

In this chapter, I seek to further our knowledge of the role that various social institutions play in facilitating search under conditions of imperfect information. I discuss an innovative institution, designed to facilitate search, that has received little attention previously. Called the 128 Venture Group, this institution draws its name from its location in the Route 128 high-technology region encircling Boston—a region that has gained prominence as a thriving center for the creation of new high-technology ventures (Piore and Sabel 1984). Described at greater length under its own heading later in the chapter, the 128 Venture Group is a monthly forum where actors interested in creating new high-technology ventures, meet to pursue their complementary interests. These actors include entrepreneurs who seek to start or build a new enterprise, venture capitalists and others who want to invest in such enterprises, managers who aspire to become a part of such an enterprise's management team, and professionals who can provide a variety of services to new firms. The search for information is the principal reason participants come to this forum. The matters investigated range from identifying potential new business opportunities, keeping abreast of present and emerging technology and market trends, seeking out partners with whom one can collectively build a new venture, conducting due diligence to verify the quality of existing leads, to finding out what the competition is doing.

The 128 Venture Group is remarkably successful at facilitating the search efforts of its participants. The purpose of this chapter is to explain the success of the 128 Venture Group. In doing so I hope to add to our theoretical knowledge of how social institutions facilitate search. I also aim to shed light on a matter of considerable practical relevance. The 128 Venture Group, as a part that is evocative of the whole, offers insights into the social organization of high-technology regions such as Route 128 and Silicon Valley.

CREATING NEW BUSINESS VENTURES

In order to grasp the economic significance of the 128 Venture Group, one must start by understanding the process of creating and building high-technology enterprises and the nature of information and search in this situation. The situation here can be analyzed along similar lines as that proposed by DiMaggio (Chapter 4, this volume) based on his study of the founding of the Museum of Modern Art.

The creation of a new business venture requires solving what Baker and Faulkner (1991:283) have called a "combinatorial problem." In the creation of new ventures, as in the Hollywood movie productions they describe, "elements are combined, taken apart, and recombined in a continuous process of organization formation and dissolution." Elements that must be combined in the creation of new ventures generally include someone with an innovative idea for a new venture, a provider of venture capital, candidates for the venture's management team, and providers of professional and other support services. These actors do not come together all at once. Rather, participants confront a dynamic problem in which a changing combination of technical, capital, management, and support-service resources are required at different stages of a venture's development.

The life cycle of the typical venture in the Route 128 area—over which it may progress through three to five stages of development—is about three to five years. As Piore (1986) has observed, at the end of this period, the typical venture will either have failed and gotten dissolved or have succeeded and been reorganized as a stable organization. Even when ventures succeed, the initial elements are often withdrawn: the venture's management team replaced by a more "professional" management group, and the highly speculative venture capital replaced by traditional financing. The technical entrepreneurs, venture capitalists, and management team members who combined to create the venture are often again in search of new opportunities.

Finding others who can provide complementary resources on a timely basis is thus the focal problem confronting participants in the world of high-technology enterprise. But the resources that need to be combined cannot be drawn randomly from four homogeneous categories labeled "technology," "capital," "management," and "services." Specialized expertise and tacit knowledge are the resources that must be brought to bear to create and build a new venture. Every new venture presents a novel organizational challenge: previous or similar experiences are usually of limited use, and events pertinent to the consequences of the venture are few. The existing knowledge of the partners must be applied to untried situations. And the success with which they can apply that knowledge usually determines their gain.

As DiMaggio (Chapter 4, this volume) has pointed out, the novelty associated with new ventures also saddles them with the burden of establishing "legitimacy." Faced with the liability of newness, a new venture must garner institutional support and legitimacy. The social capital that the partners bring to the venture therefore becomes an important factor to consider in putting together the right combinations.

Moreover, as DiMaggio further notes, the uncertainty regarding the evolution and ultimate success of new ventures creates the added problem of "control." It is impossible to write contracts among the partners that take into account all future contingencies a new venture may face. This creates potential problems of moral hazard, especially since the stakes and investments involved are high. Also, commitments made at any stage are not easily reversible and may constrain future options. Moreover, the opportunity costs can be very high, because conflict among the partners can paralyze—and in some cases even destroy—a new venture. The problem of control makes the trustworthiness and integrity of the partners a critical issue.

But even among partners with integrity, there can be room for conflict. Since decisions pertaining to the venture cannot be made with certainty, they become, to quote DiMaggio (Chapter 4, this volume: 127), "matters of judgment rather than probity, and the most honorable of persons can disagree." It is for this reason that great importance is attached to the "chemistry" (or what DiMaggio calls "sympathy") among the actors, that vital invisible lubricant that can help reduce potential friction.

All of these difficulties in forming appropriate combinations result in a situation in which all actors have a mutual interest in finding appropriate matches. As in what are more generally known as matching markets (Sondak and Bazerman 1989), "finding people on the other side of the market whom you like, who also like you, is the heart of the problem facing the participants." As one entrepreneur I interviewed graphically summarized:

> A high-technology venture is like a jig-saw puzzle. Each of the pieces is unique and must fit together perfectly if you want the venture to be a success. So the chase in which everybody is involved,—be it the entrepreneur, the venture capitalist, the management team candidate or whoever else is in the game—is the search for those perfect "matches" that will help put the puzzle together.

But successfully putting these puzzles together is no easy matter, given the incomplete information and uncertainty inherent in the creation of a new enterprise. To start with, it is hard to know where to find partners who can provide complementary resources. Even if one can identify potential options, it is harder yet to get reliable signals of the quality of the resource being sought. There are few unambiguous signals such as price or clear proxies such as education (Spence 1973) for the questions that inevitably come up in the creation of a new venture: Is the technology truly innovative? Is the cost of capital too high? Can this person contribute as a member of the management team? Is this the right patent attorney?

Quality is not the only matter hard to determine. Ascertaining the probity of potential partners is equally difficult. The trustworthiness of partners often reveals itself only after the matches have been made. Knowing whether the team will have the right chemistry involves just as much uncertainty. Intuition and "gut feeling" are often the only guides that one can rely upon.

Ironically, despite the fact that the actors are engaged in economic transactions that are pushing out existing technological frontiers, the information situation they face in the creation of new business ventures in the Route 128 region is remarkably like that confronted by actors in a much more traditional economic setting—the Moroccan bazaar (Geertz, 1978:29–30).

> In the bazaar information is poor, scarce, and maldistributed, inefficiently communicated, and intensely valued. . . . The level of ignorance about everything from product quality and going prices to market possibilities and production costs is very high, and a great deal of the way in which the bazaar is organized and functions can be interpreted as either an attempt to reduce such ignorance for someone, increase it for someone, or defend someone against it.
>
> These ignorances mentioned above are *known* ignorances, not simply matters concerning which information is lacking. Bazaar participants realize how difficult it is to know if the cow is sound or its price right, and they realize it is impossible to prosper without knowing.
>
> [Therefore] the search for information—laborious, uncertain, complex, and irregular is the central experience of life in the bazaar. Every aspect of the bazaar economy reflects the fact that the primary problem facing its participants (that is, "bazaaris") is not balancing options but finding out what they are.

Thus activities that turn on information—searching, monitoring, scouting, evaluating, testing, confirming, deciding—constitute a large part of the everyday life of the participants in both these settings.

It is useful to think about the search efforts of the participants in the venture creation process as being organized along three fronts. The first front is the purposeful search for information that has a direct and immediate bearing on items on one's agenda (Arrow 1970:47–51); the search for a new marketing manager, a source of second-round financing, or some beta-sites to test the prototype version of a new product. These search activities exact the most amount of energy. A great deal of care is also taken to ascertain the quality of the information being collected.

A second front along which search proceeds is continuous monitoring (Arrow 1970). In an information situation characterized by constant flux, every scrap of information—from emerging technologies, to the progress of competing ventures, to the climate of the venture capital market, to who are unhappy in their present jobs—is of potential value. Generally, though, considerably less energy is devoted to monitoring than to active search, and less stringent standards are applied to check the quality of the information gained. This is not to suggest that monitoring is unimportant or inconsequential to the actions taken. Often monitoring yields initial information that is then pursued more vigorously and can ultimately lead to revised expectations and beliefs.

The search for old and new contacts that can serve as sources of information is the third front on which effort is expended. As one venture capitalist pointed out, "the information one gets is only as good as where one sits and whom one knows." Thus networking, or actively building new and maintaining old social relations with a view to creating a vantage position (Useem 1987) in the flow of information, is regarded as being an important activity in its own right.

As in all search situations, participants in the new venturing process are acutely aware that the benefits of collecting additional information have to be traded off against the costs of doing so (Stigler 1968). Beyond the time invested in search, which is a direct cost, another issue that affects the time spent in search is the question of *timing*. It is widely believed by the participants in the venturing process that one of the key factors that determines the success of a venture is its timing. Being too early or too late, it is felt, can have a huge impact on the expected value of the venture. Thus the amount of time spent in search is managed with timing in mind.

It is the search for information along all these fronts that motivates people to attend the meetings of the 128 Venture Group. Thus, to be a viable institution over the long haul, the 128 Venture Group has to offer those who attend its meetings more perceived informational benefits or gains than the effort they feel they have to expend. Let us now turn to a description of the 128 Venture Group to see how it meets this challenge.

THE 128 VENTURE GROUP

The 128 Venture Group was founded in 1983 by Michael Belanger, an entrepreneur, consultant, and venture capitalist. He launched the group at a time when market conditions had produced a surplus of venture capital in the Route 128 region and "old-school investors were seeking young start-ups outside the normal channels." Belanger sensed that the time was ripe to establish a "marketplace" where players could get together to realize their complementary interests. Belanger was also driven by strong personal motives. As an entrepreneur and investor, he intended to use the 128 Venture Group to establish a central and privileged position for himself in the flow of information.

Belanger's model for such a marketplace came from his experience with other venture-capital clubs, in particular the Connecticut Venture Capital Group. In 1982, he asked some well-connected friends in the Boston venture-capital community to endorse his concept in a letter that he mailed to about 500 members of the local entrepreneurial community. The response was very encouraging, and in January 1983, more than 80 people turned out for the first meeting of the 128 Venture Group.

The charter of the 128 Venture Group declares that it will do the following:

> Provide a forum where the technical innovators seeking to start or build a firm can meet informally with the venture community representatives and individual investors who provide seed capital and venture funding as well as potential candidates for their management team.

To this end, the 128 Venture Group regularly convenes for a breakfast meeting on the second Thursday of every month. The venue is the Newton Marriott, a hotel located just off Route 128, the highway that arcs the Boston area and from which the group draws its name and symbolic legitimacy. The meeting starts at 7:30 A.M. and usually lasts for about three hours.

Now in their tenth year, the meetings attract from 80 to 200 people each month. Most of the participants live in the Route 128 area, though a handful of itinerants from neighboring states and even other nations are perhaps the rule rather than the exception. About two-thirds of the participants at a given meeting are newcomers. The other third are regulars, who participate about once every quarter. There is also a small group of people that attends nearly every meeting.

Two weeks prior to each meeting, an announcement is sent to the 800 people on the regular mailing list. This mailing list includes previous participants and names drawn from the mailing lists of other entrepreneurial associations in the region (such as SBANE, BCS).[1] A large number of attendees learn about the group's activities by word of mouth or through the media.

Included in the announcement is a preregistration form that can be returned along with a preregistration fee of $30. The fee covers the cost of renting the hotel, serving breakfast, and the modest administrative expense of running the group. A list of preregistered participants is made available before the breakfast meeting. However, preregistration is not necessary and anyone can register at the door by paying $35 on the morning of the meeting.

Participants are asked to identify themselves at the meeting in terms of four categories: (1) capital, (2) technology, (3) professional services, or (4) management-team candidate. To this end, each is asked to wear an identification tag bearing his or her name and a prominent colored dot that represents the specified category: green for capital, red for technology, yellow for professional services, and blue for management-team candidate. A wide variety of participants attend the meetings; from partners of the largest venture-capital firms in the region to individual investors, from entrepreneurs with well-established high-technology ventures to college students with wild-eyed ideas, from management-team candidates who see themselves as CEOs to engineers looking for a new job, and from lawyers and accountants and headhunters representing established firms to individuals selling expertise in writing business plans.

On the day of the meeting, registration starts at 7:30 A.M., and the breakfast meeting itself at 8:00. Participants start arriving at about 7:00, registering and milling around before the meeting convenes for breakfast. These informal conversations constitute a distinct first phase of the meeting, since they are conduits for information flows.

In the second phase of the meeting, participants sit down for breakfast at tables that accommodate between eight and ten people. After introductory remarks by the chairman of the group, each participant is given 60 seconds to introduce himself or herself and make a "pitch" to the group with the aid of a cordless microphone.[2] The chairman sets the tone by delivering a pro-forma one-minute introduction. He then hands the microphone to a trusted regular to make the first pitch. The time limit on introductions is usually enforced; the long winded speaker is interrupted by the well-known method of the water glass tapped with a metal spoon.

Introductions vary in style, but generally include information about who the person is, a short personal occupational history, current status, and interest in attending the meeting. Participants in the audience listen to the introductions quite carefully.[3] Often they take notes of the people whose messages are of particular interest to them.[4]

After the introductions are over—and sometimes midway through them if the number of participants is very large—an invited speaker presents his or her views on a subject of topical interest to entrepreneurs. The talk is usually short (about 20 minutes) and is followed by an equally short question-answer session. The invited talks are not the focus of the meeting and I met few people who attended merely to listen to the talk.

The conclusion of these activities signals the end of the formal meeting, but interaction among the participants continues. The meeting now enters its third phase, and a flurry of activity ensues. In what is almost a scramble, participants try to establish contact with those whose interests they perceived to be complementary to theirs. Often these conversations lead to the exchange of business cards, a contact or lead established that can be followed up after the meeting. This "networking" continues for about half an hour and then people disperse, usually by 10 or 10:30 A.M., to continue with their regular business day.

The rest of the activity takes place outside the meeting; some leads are pursued, others neglected. The only other direct outcome of the meeting is that a final list of all the participants—their names, addresses, and phone numbers—is mailed to each of them about five days after the meeting.

SEARCH AND THE 128 VENTURE GROUP

While the espoused purpose of the 128 Venture Group is to provide a forum that facilitates the search for resources to create or build a new high-technology enterprise, prima facie one can hardly help being skeptical about its chance for success. The participants of the 128 Venture Group must conduct meaningful search in a complex and imperfect information situation with very limited opportunities for interaction—the brief conversational encounters at the beginning and end of the meeting and the one-minute pitch. The difficulty of the situation is exacerbated by the fact that very few of them know one another prior to the meetings. How then do they go about conducting their search?

Building on the model proposed by DiMaggio (Chapter 4, this volume) actors employ three interrelated criteria to guide their search for partners. The first criterion is the extent to which the other person meets a set of categorical attributes. For instance, venture capitalists have a long checklist of conditions that ventures at different stages need to satisfy, and they screen opportunities based on the extent to which these expectations are fulfilled. Actors in all other categories have their own sets of idealized attributes that they hope to find in a partner. These criteria are not overdetermined—everyone realizes that their wish list is just an idealization, and compromises are always necessary. But there is always a core set of criteria that a partner must meet. Some criteria of this type are the stage, magnitude of financing, and technologies that a venture capitalist is willing to accept. Some venture capitalists, for example, consider only zero-stage ventures in the software industry with financing needs of less than $250,000, whereas others do only final-stage deals and IPOs larger than $1 million.

Categorical judgments are used extensively to screen the one-minute pitches given by the participants at the meeting. To employ a distinction made by Rees (1966), the one-minute pitch economizes on search at the "intensive" margin while it facilitates "extensive" search. It provides an efficient way for the participants to survey all the options with very little cost. It helps participants sort through the options to determine those cases worthy of intensive search. Since search costs are all additive and the total attention that can be devoted is constrained, it is important for most participants to spend their time at the meeting productively. The frenzy of interaction that ensues at the end of the meeting is not a random pattern but one that has definite shape imparted by the one-minute pitches. Most participants seek out specific others whose signals interested them; they can be quite brusque with those who try to engage them in casual conversation (as I quickly learned in my odd role of researcher). Typically, participants find between one and five of the hundred pitches worth pursuing through further conversation. Categorical criteria continue to play an important role through the due diligence process, getting more fine grained and specific as the actors near the decision to make a match.

The second criterion that shapes search is relational. Given the difficulty of ascertaining the quality of information, it becomes essential for actors to determine how reliable a potential partner is and how much they can trust him or her. This problem assumes special significance in the 128 Venture Group, where most participants are strangers. As a result, introductions and the ensuing conversations are far more complex than the casual exchange of names and handshakes. Participants engage in intensive and pointed cross-examination through which they refine their understanding of each other's occupational histories, social affiliations, and references. The purpose of this mutual probing is to try to get a "fix" on each other's social positions. This is accomplished either by searching for a commonly shared contact or experience, or by finding an anchor with which the other interactant is familiar. Mutual exploration of career histories is the device often used to find such a "fix" on the basis of which trust is developed. The following conversation is illustrative:

A: I've been involved in this venture for the last two years.
B: And what were you doing before that?
A: Well, I graduated from MIT, worked in Raytheon for a while, then went on to GTE Labs. During that time I was basically working on defense contracts. Then about five years ago, I joined a friend of mine in this instrumentation venture, but that was soon acquired and that's when I decided to start my own venture.
B: Which part of Raytheon did you work in? I used to know some folks who were also involved in defense contracts there.
A: Mostly I was working in the ultrasonic instruments lab, but I moved around a bit. Who were these folks you knew?
B: A couple of them I knew quite well. One's name was C and the other was D.
A: Sorry, never ran into them.

B: I also knew this guy who was working in GTE. I can't remember his name now, but he was a pretty important person in their dealings with the Defense Department.
A: Was it E, or maybe F?
B: Yes that's it. F. I met him during a seminar we attended together a couple of years ago. If you meet him, do give him my regards.
A: Sure! And what do you do?

This exchange allows participants to define their social positions by establishing a common link via person F. Depending on what each interactant knows about F and how much they value his or her assessments, they attach different quotients of credibility to this interaction. Perceptions of reliability increase with the strength of the tie that the participants have with the common link. The set of social affiliations that an individual has thus serves as an index that is searched by the prospective partner to ascertain reliability.

The third criterion that shapes search is the emotional reaction generated during interaction. Each actor gauges the other in terms of interpersonal "chemistry." DiMaggio (Chapter 4, this volume:127) argues that one can conceive of the assessment of interpersonal chemistry as a "cultural matching process in which actors rely subliminally on verbal and nonverbal cues to estimate cultural overlap experienced as comfort/discomfort, and confidence/unease." The flow of emotional energy shapes the creation of social ties. Positive flows increase the likelihood of further interaction, and negative flows diminish the chances. What determines the flow of emotional energies in an encounter is at once calculative and fuzzy. In an interaction that is conducted in the spirit of mutual sizing up, there is the distinct possibility that one or the other interactant may not "compute" up to the other's expectations. Face-to-face contact is considered crucial to the assessment. Links are often forged because the interactants "hit it off" or destroyed because "the vibes weren't there"— reasons that are entirely subjective.

To summarize, in the case of the 128 Venture Group as in DiMaggio's study of the organization of MOMA, search consists of a matching process in which participants first use categories, typifications or classificatory criteria to identify a set of potential participants; second, they use relational criteria (the index of the other's relations) to establish the trustworthiness of the participant; and third, they use emotional criteria (generated in face-to-face interaction) to decide whether they should pursue the interaction further.

This search procedure works remarkably well in this imperfect-information situation. Based on the experiences of the participants I interviewed, the 128 Venture Group facilitates the search for a broad range of information: Finding "leads" that led to a "match"; establishing a valuable "network contact"; learning of a technological development that had key competitive implications; getting some key "intangible" facts on a "deal" being scouted; "staying on top"; discovering a major flaw in current plans during a "reality check"; and so on. Of course, not all participants found the information they were seeking, nor did any one find all the information desired. However, overall, not one person whom I interviewed (I interviewed over 200) felt that their participation was a total waste of time and effort. At the very minimum, they felt that they had "learned something new."

While information of all types is useful in one way or another for the creation of new business ventures, the 128 Venture Group's performance with respect to the search for "matches" is of particular interest because that is the central concern in the creation of new business ventures. In Table 9-1, I report the results of a more systematic examination of the performance of the 128 Venture Group from this standpoint.

Every month, for a period of six months, I picked twenty participants at random (controlling for the size of the four categories—capital, technology, management, and professional services), telephoned them a day after the meeting, and asked if they would be willing to talk with me at monthly intervals for the next three months. In these interviews (of about one-half hour each), I asked them about developments based on their 128 Venture Group attendance. The results reported in Table 9-1 are based on the 103 participants who agreed to become a part of my study.

It is important to note that a 128 Venture Group meeting is not the place where matches are concluded. It is only a forum that assists in identifying options or leads, some of which after further investigation or "due diligence" may ultimately result in matches. However, since the cost of

Table 9-1

Performance of the 128 Venture Group with Respect to the Search for Complementary Resources

CATEGORY	NUMBER INTERVIEWED	LEADS	MATCHES
Technology	42	15—Capital	3
		7—Management	2
		4—Services	2
		26—Subtotal	7
Capital	29	16—Technology	4
		1—Management	1
		2—Services	1
		19—Subtotal	6
Management	20	6—Technology	2
		1—Services	0
		7—Subtotal	2
Services	12	5—Technology	3
		2—Management	1
		7—Subtotal	4
TOTALS	103	59	19

due diligence is considerable, the quality of "leads" is not taken lightly and has significant economic value.

As reported in Table 9-1, of the 103 participants interviewed, slightly over half (56%) found a total of 59 significant leads via the meetings. A "significant lead" is defined as an opportunity identified at a meeting that was followed up by at least one face-to-face interview between the actors within a month of the meeting.[5] This is to distinguish such leads from the numerous business cards one inevitably collects by the end of a meeting. So, for example, reading Table 9-1 from left to right, of the 42 people I interviewed who identified themselves at the meeting as providers of technology, 15 had met with a potential provider of capital, 7 had met with potential management team candidates, and 4 had met with professional service providers based on the search they had conducted at the meeting. It must be noted that not all these leads were "direct" leads. That is, they didn't necessarily involve a participant one had directly met at the meeting. Some leads (a total of 12 in the overall sample) were "indirect," based on the referral of someone whom the interviewee had met at a meeting.

Of the 59 total leads, 19 led to matches (or "deals") within an additional two months.[6] These matches spanned the full spectrum from zero-stage financing of $50,000 to an acquisition of over $10 million; from management-team candidates who were young marketing executives to those who were CEOs and COOs; and from professional services providers such as lawyers, consultants, and accountants who were affiliated with top firms to those who worked independently. Because I did not track the further evolution of the ventures after matches were made, I have no data on the eventual quality of the matches.

While these findings are thus by no means conclusive proof of the effectiveness of the 128 Venture Group, certain inferences can still be drawn. It is clear from Table 9-1 that this institution actually works. It is evident from the data that the 128 Venture Group can facilitate the search for matches and thereby help in the creation of new business ventures. Further, the different types of matches realized indicates that the 128 Venture Group works in a wide variety of search situations ranging all the way from the placement of a management professional to a major acquisition.

But what explains the success of the 128 Venture Group at facilitating search? The explanation, I contend, lies in understanding the social structure in which the 128 Venture Group is embedded—the Route 128 region—and the structural position that the group occupies in it (Granovetter 1985, Chapter 1, this volume).

THE SOCIAL STRUCTURE OF ROUTE 128

The structure of any social context can be analyzed in terms of the different foci around which individuals organize their social relations and the connections among these foci (Simmel 1950; Feld 1981). A focus is defined as any entity around which joint activities are organized; foci include firms, associations, hangouts, and families. The importance of foci for social structure is that as a consequence of their joint activities associated with any focus, individuals interact with one another and develop positive sentiments for one another; hence they tend to get interpersonally tied and form a cluster.

Membership in different foci not only generates an individual's nexus of social relations, but also shapes the individual's cognitive categories, typifications, and conventional understandings. As we have seen, since both these aspects—the conventional understandings that individuals carry around as well as the set of their social affiliations—play a key role in their search behavior, the underlying social structure can have a profound effect on the success of search.

If the foci in the underlying social system are disconnected, then search will be harder and it will be more difficult to mobilize new ventures. This is because participants affiliated with different foci will not pass through classificatory or relational screens during the search process. On the other hand, if the foci overlap a great deal, there will be a much greater chance of successful search and the creation of new ventures.

The Route 128 region can be characterized as having highly overlapping foci. To see why, one needs to understand the region's history.

The history of high-technology enterprise in the Boston area predates World War II. Rogers and Larsen describe this early period as follows:

> Several spin-offs from MIT research laboratories occurred prior to World War II: Ionics, High Voltage, and EG&G for example. Carl Taylor Compton was president of MIT in this era and he encouraged his engineering faculty and staff to become involved in area private firms. In his view the high-technology start-ups represented an important kind of technology transfer in which innovations coming out of MIT research labs would be commercialized by for-profit companies. The net result was that MIT faculty were not just allowed to engage in consulting with these local firms, they were encouraged to do so. The MIT policy of close industry-university relationships was unique for the 1930s, almost heretical in its day. But to the great advantage of the local economy in the Boston area, it worked. [. . .] Without MIT, there would be no Route 128 complex (1984:236).

President Compton's vision and initiative forged a vital link between the academic research community and high-technology enterprises. But he did more than that. Compton also played a key role in shaping the venture-capital industry that provided the financing for these new enterprises. He played a key role in the 1946 formation of American Research and Development Corporation (ARDC), the nation's first institutional venture fund. Realizing that the new high-technology companies that were being spun off from MIT and elsewhere required startup venture capital, he took the lead in founding ARDC, obtaining the money from

Boston-based insurance companies. The original board of directors of ARDC included four MIT department chairmen in addition to a prominent group of bankers and industrialists. This mix of technical, financial, and industrial expertise was seen as being essential to creating an entity that could effectively finance technology-oriented enterprise. By creating new foci that brought together members in these different spheres, Compton created bridges across social circles that were unconnected historically.

The result was a new model for creating new high-technology ventures, a model that came to be institutionalized in the postwar period and greatly influenced the further evolution of the Route 128 innovation complex.[7] Rogers and Larsen continue their description:

> The first little acorns that were to grow into the Route 128 oak forest were planted by President Compton, but the high-technology complex did not really sprout until massive federal funding for wartime research began in the early 1940s. That is when the basic formula for Route 128 fell into place: Federal government monies went to MIT research laboratories, which spun-off engineer entrepreneurs who took a "hot idea" for a technological innovation from the banks of the Charles River out to Boston's western suburbs on Route 128 in the form of a new company (1984:237).

The most prominent example of this formula at work was the formation of Digital Equipment Corporation (DEC). Kenneth Olsen, an engineer in the MIT Lincoln Laboratory who developed the TX-O computer under a military contract, left MIT in 1956 to found DEC and pursue the commercial development and application of his research at MIT. Financed by venture capital from ARDC, this enterprise ultimately led to the production of the PDP-1, the first commercial minicomputer, an innovation that spawned a whole new industry.

Route 128 shifted into a high-growth phase from 1955 to 1971, a period when the number of firms jumped from 39 to 1,200, primarily a result of defense and aerospace contracts (Rogers and Larsen 1984: 237). Many of these new firms were spin-offs from MIT. In a survey conducted in 1968, Roberts (1968) found that the origin of over 200 firms in the region could be traced to MIT. Other new firms were spin-offs from earlier startups such as DEC, whose family tree numbers more than 30 firms and includes such prominent names as that of its competitor, Data General (Dorfman 1983).

The venture-capital industry also experienced dramatic growth. By the early 1960s, several large Boston financial institutions also became involved in venture capital. First National Bank of Boston formed an SBIC affiliate for providing loans to technology-oriented businesses, and around the same time, Federal Street SBIC was established by a consortium of Boston banks with the same aim (Florida and Kenney, 1987:19–20). The evolution of the venture-capital industry followed a pattern similar to that of new high-technology business enterprises. Proliferation by spin-offs from preceding generations was as prevalent in the venture-capital industry as it was in high-technology enterprises. Some of the prominent cases of this mode of growth by spin-offs are documented by Florida and Kenney:

> ARD, similarly [to DEC], became an incubator for venture capital funds. In 1963, Boston Capital Corp. was founded by ARD alumnus, Joseph Powell. By the 1970s, ARD alumni were instrumental in launching a host of top level partnerships including Palmer, Greylock, Charles River Partnership and Morgan Holland. In 1968, Peter Brooke left his position as manager of First National Bank of Boston's high technology loan program and went on to launch TA Associates which currently manages more than $1.5 billion in capital, making it the largest venture capital fund in the country. As the technology base of the Boston region developed, a host of partnerships were organized by veteran venture capitalists. Both Burr, Egan and Deleage and Claflan Capital Management were formed by former TA Associates employees, while the Venture Capital Fund of New England was established by the managers of First National Bank of Boston's Venture Group (1987b:20–21).

Following this boom a serious decline set in, as the Vietnam War ended, the economy went sour, and government contracts were cut back. The early 1970s were years of considerable economic and social problems. But the institutions built in the earlier period provided a springboard for the region to capitalize on the explosive expansion in commercial computer applications and related demand for industrial equipment and instruments that occurred in the late 1970s.

From 1975 to 1979, the region added 75,000 employees to its high-technology work force. Moreover, as the pioneering research of David Birch (1980) documented, the greater part of this growth came from the creation of new enterprises rather than from the growth of existing firms. Once again, many of the new enterprises were spin-offs from MIT's research labs and earlier generations of high-technology firms. The venture-capital industry took off again in 1978, after the federal capital-gains tax had been reduced to 28% and some of the restrictions on investment by pension-fund managers relaxed.[8] Eventually this growth included increases in the size of existing venture-capital funds, the formation of several new funds, and the opening in the Boston area of branch offices of funds headquartered elsewhere.

Growth in this period was accompanied by increasing specialization of resources necessary for the creation of new ventures. A support-services industry specialized to the needs of high-technology enterprise emerged. Specialization also proceeded along the lines of technologies and stages of an enterprise's development, as experience began to sharpen people's appreciation of how enterprise needs varied along these dimensions. Venture capitalists starting specializing in early-stage, later-stage, or bridge financing, for example, and according to a specific technology such as hardware or software; those who provided management and professional services followed a similar pattern. As a result, not only did the number of economic roles that participants could play in the entrepreneurial process proliferate, but the roles themselves became more progressively specialized and sharply defined.

It is important to note that the Route 128 high-technology network was primarily "home grown." That is, unlike similar networks such as California's Silicon valley, it did not relied on major inflows of technical entrepreneurs, venture capitalists, management talent, and supporting services from other regions.[9] This shared regional affiliation therefore provides an underlying social bond for the region's entrepreneurial network.

The history of the Route 128 region clearly shows the key role played by a small number of focal organizations in shaping the structure of the region's entrepreneurial network. The genealogy of most of its high-technology enterprises may be traced to MIT or DEC, and that of its venture capital organizations to ARD.[10] This pattern of local growth through successive spin-offs has created a richly joined network analogous to those forged by kinship relationships.[11]

A number of formal organizations—professional associations, clubs, societies, and groups—all recognized more or less explicitly as serving a "networking" function, also play a prominent role in the region as foci around which social ties form. Founded in 1938, the oldest such organization is the Small Business Association of New England (SBANE), which organizes numerous workshops, fairs, seminars, and ongoing small group meetings such as Dialog (Kanai 1988). Also prominent is the Massachusetts High Technology Council (MHTC), a political interest group that represents CEOs from some 150 companies that account for more than 50% of the state's high-tech employment (Saxenian 1985). Other notable organizations are the MIT Enterprise Forum (Kanai 1988); the Boston Computer Society (BCS), which has a large membership; The Networking Institute (TNI), a private organization similar to SBANE, that promotes electronic networking; and various networking organizations for special interest groups such as women entrepreneurs, minorities, and so on.[12]

Seen against the backdrop of this network of organizations, the 128 Venture Group is just one focal point for the formation of ties. However, two features of the group distinguish it from other organizing foci in the region's network.

First, the 128 Venture Group is the only institution explicitly geared towards facilitating information flows related to the creation of *new ventures*. In other forums, these flows are the by-product of other activities and not the main purpose. To the extent that the 128 Venture Group brings together participants with a shared purpose to traffic in the exchange of information, it is quintessential of what Goffman (1959) calls a "focused gathering"—a set of persons engrossed in a common flow of activity and relating to each other in terms of that flow. As Goffman argues, even in such temporary and minimal interaction situations, a powerful sense of organizational membership may be created and orderly social behavior may be obtained. This is because focused gatherings such as the 128 Venture Group concentrate, amplify, and crystallize the participants' shared stocks of cultural knowledge around a common interest and experiential base:[13]

> What we have, then, is a kind of interactional modus vivendi. Together the participants contribute to a single overall definition of the situation which involves not so much a real agreement as to what exists, but rather a real agreement as to whose claims in what issues will be temporarily honored—a level of agreement that may be referred to as a working consensus (Goffman 1959).

The group's second distinguishing characteristic is that a disproportionately large number of the social ties created here are weak and therefore potentially bridging ties. This is because a majority of the participants who attend each meeting are strangers to one another. Even among those who may have been present together at previous meetings, or may have met in other organizational contexts, links tend to be weak. The 128 Venture Group thus acts as a "weak-tie generator" where participants with different affiliations within the network may create bridging ties with one another.[14]

The importance of weak ties in facilitating search and transmitting information in fragmented social networks has been well demonstrated. Many of the other strengths of weak ties apply in this situation as well. Since first proposed by Granovetter (1973, 1974) in his study of mobility of technical and professional labor markets, the central role played by weak ties in facilitating search in matching markets has been well established—both empirically (Freidkin 1980; Granovetter 1982) and formally (Boorman 1975; Delaney 1980). Applying these results to the situation at hand, we can readily explain the "leads" and "matches" reported in Table 9-1 to have resulted from information flows over the weak ties created by the 128 Venture Group. Besides the search for matches, the flow of information through the weak ties created by the 128 Venture Group also helps participants in many of their other monitoring and search activities. As Rogers (1983) has documented, weak ties such as those created by the 128 Venture Group also facilitate the diffusion of innovation. Moreover since knowledge in the high-technology industry has increasingly come to be embodied in human beings, the gathering of 80 to 200 new people every month provides invaluable information to an astute participant.

Bridging ties are as efficient in the diffusion of cultural information as they are for economic information; this has been established by previous studies on the creation of youth subcultures (Fine and Kleinman 1979). Personal opinions, prejudices, and reputations spread quickly within a network with many bridging ties. Thus by generating weak ties the 128 Venture Group contributes to the development of norms that keep malfeasance in check. For instance, while leaving a company to pursue a personal idea is a lauded ambition, the opportunist who "jumps ship" once too often is castigated, and the individual who has sold out on a project's secrets is considered reprehensible. The flow of information through such weak ties helps to police and control norm violations by affecting reputations and facilitating their rapid diffusion throughout the network.

Finally, a subtle but important effect of weak ties that has been suggested by Granovetter (1982) is the development of individual cognitive flexibility. An individual who has several weak ties is exposed to a wide variety of viewpoints and activities and develops cognitive flexibility and a cosmopolitan outlook. Such a cosmopolitan cognitive orientation is of great value in the business-venturing process. It permits one to assess a much wider range of options and hence be more effective in searching for complementary resources. Thus attendance at the meetings exposes participants to the bewildering range of talk that must be learned to keep apace with the tumult of the business-venturing process.

CONCLUSIONS AND DISCUSSION

While the manner in which the 128 Venture Group is embedded in the region's entrepreneurial network explains how it enables search, this very aspect also defines its constraints and limits. Options that are outside conventional understandings or are not easy to fix in terms of their social position can be mistakenly rejected. This is evident in the difficulties faced by entrepreneurs who promote technologies alien to the local "code" (Arrow 1970). The following example illustrates the point clearly:

> An engineer with a great idea to increase the efficiency of the Rankine Cycle, a technology with a potentially major impact on thermal energy plants, evoked little interest within the 128 Venture Group, as he was touting a technology that was outside the domain of expertise and experience of most participants. That this bias can sometimes lead to the rejection of perfectly viable ventures was demonstrated when a Canadian thermal plant decided to license the engineer's technology with considerable benefit.

There are also regional constraints on the scope of the markets that the 128 Venture Group can help make. Search is usually restricted to finding a match with someone who is a resident of the Route 128 region. Since trust is largely process based and relies on reputational credibility built on occupational history, certification by mutually known contacts, and the prospect of future exchange—participants from outside the region have a hard time in this market.

As a part that is evocative of the whole, the limits of the 128 Venture Group are also indicative of the limitations of the region as a whole. It raises questions about viability of the region in the event of a major technological discontinuity or in the event of some major shifts in the supply of venture capital. It also raises the practical question of whether regional high-technology districts such as Route 128 and Silicon Valley

(Saxenian 1985) are unique historical exceptions or general models that can be replicated elsewhere.

As the foregoing discussion has shown, a vibrant high-technology district will not automatically emerge from the planned geographic concentration of resources such as a high-technology university, research labs, venture capital, skilled technical and managerial talent, and enterprise-oriented services. Miller and Cote (1985) have documented the cases of Sophia-Antipolis near Nice and Sheridan Park in Toronto, where just such a concentration of resources (Dorfman 1983), did not materialize into a vibrant high-technology center. Instead, the various clusters of resources ossified into respectable research islands artificially maintained at public expense. Similarly, in Houston and Stamford, planned attempts to create market-generating institutions like the 128 Venture Group have also had little success. These cases warn against ignoring the social and historical context in which economic action is embedded.

However, they do not suggest that we despair of making general propositions about the conditions that help to create vibrant high-technology regions. My analysis of this case along with case studies of other successful regional districts such as Silicon Valley in California, Prato and Modena in Italy, Cambridge in England, and Baden-Wuerttemberg in Germany (Piore and Sabel 1984) suggest the following general propositions:

First, it is important for the region to have either an established traditional indigenous technological base such as woolens and textiles in Prato and Modena and machine tools in Baden-Wuerttemberg, or a well-developed innovative technological community such as in microcomputers along Route 128, semiconductors in Silicon Valley, and software technologies in Cambridge, England. This shared technology provides a network for information flows and a framework for the tacit understanding of new technological ideas.

Second, it is important that technical innovation occur within a richly interconnected social structure, a point that has also been made by Aldrich and Zimmer (1986). The ties that bind the structure together may be the result of kinship relations, political ties, common ethnicity, or, as in the case of Route 128, common institutional affiliations. Such a social structure is vital for the ongoing production of trust and the development of social norms. These ties further facilitate the information flows that are so necessary for the creation of new ventures.

Finally, institutions that facilitate search such as the 128 Venture Group are likely to flourish only in a large and somewhat fragmented social structure where traditional groups or cliques do not control the norms and resources of the community. Such an institution would be unlikely to gain hold in regions like Prato or Modena, where the *impannatore* are the traditional coordinating foci of the technological community, or in Baden-Wuerttemberg where the network is dominated by local craft unions. On the other hand, weak tie generating institutions may be viable in regions like Silicon Valley and Cambridge, England.

These are fairly broad propositions. If we are to develop finer-grained and more definitive propositions, we will need to analyze other regions and their institutions in a manner that systematically examines the networks of relations that define their social structure.

Notes

1. Indeed, about once a year the 128 Venture Group may hold its meeting in collaboration with other area groups such as the Boston Computer Society Entrepreneurs and Consultants Group or the entrepreneurship clubs that exist in universities such as MIT, Harvard, and Babson.
2. The "over 100 rule" takes effect when the number of attendees exceeds that number, and the time allowed for introductions is reduced to 40 seconds.
3. I was surprised, for instance, at how many people with whom I spoke later remembered what I had said in my introduction.
4. The note taking is facilitated by the preregistrants list, which is made available to all participants at the beginning of the meeting. This is a further incentive to preregister, because many people like to end their introductions by drawing the audience's attention to the location of their name, address, and telephone number on the preregistration list.
5. Form letters mailed to all the participants are not included as leads.
6. I tracked participants only for a period of three months. This was done by a telephone interview in which I asked them if they had followed up on any lead found via the 128 Venture Group, if an initial meeting had taken place, and if any further commitment had been made pursuant to an initial meeting.
7. This successful model diffused through what DiMaggio and Powell (1983) have called "mimetic isomorphism" and thus had an influential role in shaping the present division of labor and institutional structure of the region.
8. Unleashed after the reduction in the federal capital-gains tax from 42% to 28% in 1978, the venture-capital pool in the United States grew from about $2.5–3 billion in 1978 to over $16 billion in 1986. Of this amount about 12% is concentrated in the New England area. The causal relation between the growth of venture capital and new business activities is somewhat of a chicken/egg problem, because while venture capital was essential to the formation of new enterprises, venture capitalists are attracted only to regions where the number of business opportunities and incidence of startups is high. Venture capital and startups form a symbiotic "circle of goodness" that feeds on—and reinforces—itself.
9. A caveat is in order. This is true to the extent that the region does not have to import people who have finished their education. Because of the area's strong university system, though, it has always attracted some of the best intellectual talent in the world.
10. In a recent study, Dukakis and Kanter (1988) estimated that of the new enterprises established in the Route 128 area since 1975, as many as 72% can trace their origins to some affiliation with MIT.
11. Of course, these spin-offs may also lead to embitterment and cleavages. The most famous spat along Route 128 involved Ken Olsen, founder of DEC, and Ray Stata, founder of Analog Devices, and had fairly serious consequences: Olsen refused to become a part of the Massachusetts High Technology Council, an important regional political interest lobby that was the brainchild of Stata. Aside from the chasm between these individuals, there are many ties among engineers lower down in the corporations who were previously colleagues and for whom this spin-off was a less personal issue.

12. A compendium of networking organizations may be found in Lipnack and Stamps (1986).
13. The idea that shared stocks of knowledge are the wellspring from which social order and organization flow is the central theme in the sociology of Alfred Schutz (1970).
14. It is important to note that ties are created only among *some* of the participants in a meeting. This is because some interactions have minimal significance and create no ties at all. The mere fact that everybody listens to everybody else's one-minute pitch and receives a list of all the participants names, addresses, phone numbers, and interests are not sufficient to constitute a weak tie, because nothing may flow through the tie.

References

Aldrich, Howard, and Catherine Zimmer. 1986. "Entrepreneurship through Social Networks." In D. Sexton and J. Kasarda, eds., *The Art and Science of Entrepreneurship*. Cambridge, MA: Ballinger.

Arrow, Kenneth J. 1970. *The Limits of Organization*. New York: Norton.

Baker, Wayne E., and Robert R. Faulkner. 1991. "Role as Resource in the Hollywood Film Industry." *American Journal of Sociology* 97(2):279–309.

Birch, David. 1980. *The Job Creation Process*. Cambridge, MA: MIT Program on Neighborhood and Regional Change.

Boorman, Scott. 1975. "A Combinatorial Optimization Model for Transmission of Job Information Through Contact Networks." *Bell Journal of Economics* 6(1):216–249.

Delaney, John. 1980. "Aspects of Donative Resource Allocation and the Efficiency of Social Networks: Simulation Models of Job Vacancy Information Transfers Through Personal Contacts." Ph.D. dissertation, Yale University, New Haven, CT.

DiMaggio, Paul J. 1992. "Nadel's Paradox Revisited: Relational and Cultural Aspects of Organizational Structure." Chapter 4, this volume.

DiMaggio, Paul J., and Walter W. Powell. 1983. "The Iron Cage Revisited: Institutional Isomorphism and Collective Rationality in Organizational Fields." *American Sociological Review* 48:147–160.

Dorfman, Nancy S. 1983. "Route 128: The Development of a Regional High Technology Economy." *Research Policy* 12:299–316.

Dukakis, Michael S., and Rosabeth M. Kanter. 1988. *Creating the Future*. New York: Summit Books.

Feld, Scott L. 1981. "The Focused Organization of Social Ties." *American Journal of Sociology* 86(5):1015–1035.

Fine, Gary Alan, and Sherryl Kleinman. 1979. "Rethinking Subculture: An Interactionist Analysis." *American Journal of Sociology* 85(1):1–20.

Florida, Richard L., and Martin Kenney. 1987. "Venture Capital and High Technology Entrepreneurship." *Journal of Business Venturing* 3:301–319.

Friedkin, Noah. 1980. "A Test for Structural Features of Granovetter's Strength of Weak Ties Theory." *Social Networks* 2:411–422.

Geertz, Clifford. 1978. "The Bazaar Economy: Information and Search in Peasant Marketing." *American Economic Review* 68(2):28–32.

Glaser, Barney, and Anslem Strauss. 1967. *The Discovery of Grounded Theory*. Chicago: Aldine.

Goffman, E. 1959. *The Presentation of Self in Everyday Life*. New York: Anchor.

Granovetter, Mark. 1973. "The Strength of Weak Ties." *American Journal of Sociology* 78(6):1360–1380.

———. 1974. *Getting a Job: A Study of Contacts and Careers.* Cambridge, MA: Harvard University Press.

———. 1982. "Strength of Weak Ties: A Network Theory Revisited." In Peter V. Marsden and Nan Lin, eds., *Social Structure and Network Analysis.* Beverly Hills: Sage.

———. 1985. "Economic Action and Social Structure: A Theory of Embeddedness." *American Journal of Sociology* 82:929–964.

Kanai, Toshihiro. 1988. "Entrepreneurial Networks: A Comparative Analysis of Networking Organizations and their Participants in an Entrepreneurial Community." Ph.D. dissertation, MIT, Cambridge, MA.

Kreps, David M. 1990. *A Course in Microeconomic Theory.* Princeton: Princeton University Press.

Lipnack, Jessica, and Jeffrey Stamps. 1986. *The Networking Book: People Connecting with People.* New York: Routledge and Kegan Paul.

Miller, Roger, and Marcel Cote. 1985. "Growing the Next Silicon Valley." *Harvard Business Review* (July–Aug.):114–123.

Piore, Michael J. 1986. "Corporate Reform in American Manufacturing and the Challenge to Economic Theory." Mimeographed. Cambridge, MA: Department of Economics, MIT.

Piore, Michael J., and Charles E. Sabel. 1984. *The Second Industrial Divide: Possibility for Prosperity.* New York: Basic Books.

Roberts, Edward B. 1968. "Entrepreneurship and Technology." *Research Management* (July): 249–266.

Rogers, Everett M. 1983. *The Diffusion of Innovation* 3d ed. New York: Free Press.

Rogers, Everett M., and Judith K. Larsen. 1984. *Silicon Valley Fever: Growth of High-Technology Culture.* New York: Basic Books.

Sahlman, William A., and Howard H. Stevenson. 1985. "Capital Market Myopia." *Journal of Business Venturing* 1:7–30.

Saxenian, Anna Lee. 1985. "In Search of Power: The Organization of Business Interests in Silicon Valley and Route 128." Mimeographed. Cambridge, MA: Department of Political Science, MIT.

Schutz, Alfred. 1970. *On Phenomenology and Social Relations.* Chicago: University of Chicago Press.

Simmel, Georg. 1950. *The Sociology of Georg Simmel.* New York: Free Press.

Sondak, Harris, and Max H. Bazerman. 1989. "Matching and Negotiation Process in Quasi-Markets." *Organizational Behavior and Human Decision Process* 44:261–280.

Spence, A. M. 1973. *Market Signalling: Information Transfer in Hiring and Related Processes.* Cambridge, MA: Harvard University Press.

Stigler, George. 1968. *The Organization of Industry.* Homewood, IL: Richard D. Irwin Co.

Useem, P. 1987. *The Inner Circle.* Cambridge: Harvard University Press.

10

Complementary Communication Media: A Comparison of Electronic Mail and Face-To-Face Communication in a Programming Team

JAMES L. McKENNEY, MICHAEL H. ZACK, AND VICTOR S. DOHERTY

Management work is communication intensive, and managers must establish and maintain complex communication networks for performing their work (Kotter 1982, McCaskey 1982, Mintzberg 1973). Creating and maintaining a system of organizational communication is a key function of the executive (Barnard 1938). While managers' preference for face-to-face (FTF) communication has been documented (Mintzberg 1973, Kurke and Aldrich 1983), little research has been performed to explain that preference or to examine how managers are using the emerging alternatives to the traditional media of FTF, telephone, and written documents.

This study explored the managerial use of electronic mail or messaging (EM) for task-oriented communication. Using an analytical case method, we examined over time the different roles of EM and FTF within the work routines of a computer programming team. Based on an information-processing model of managerial work, we describe how managers' structured use of particular networks and media was appropriate to supporting organizational programs as well as to enacting responses to unusual events.

The information-processing view of an organization focuses on how managers deal with uncertainty or ambiguity. Our study showed that the work of managers fell into two categories: problem solving and organizing. Problem solving tended to reduce or eliminate ambiguity and equivocality[1] and to build a shared interpretive context. Organizing activities functioned within that context to reduce uncertainty.[2] The team's different information-processing needs influenced the use of communication media, with rich face-to-face communication dominant for the problem-solving tasks, and the lean, efficient communication medium of electronic mail (EM) for organizing tasks.

In analyzing communication roles by hourly samples we observed that communication appeared to be dynamic, fluid, and at times chaotic. Yet by increasing the time intervals to reflect more accurately the activities at the group level, a relatively stable, cyclical pattern of communication roles and relations emerged. There was a detectable periodicity during the day, and within that cycle there occurred detectable, regular sequences of communication exchanges.

THE INFORMATION PROCESSING VIEW OF NETWORKS IN ORGANIZATIONS AND IN MANAGEMENT WORK

Our study focused on ways managers use electronic messaging in performing different roles and stages of problem solving and organizing. The literature is flush with taxonomies of what managers "do" (e.g., Barnard 1938; Fayol 1949; Kotter 1982). Hackman and Walton (1986) proposed a simplified description of the functional manager as one who monitors the work group and takes action to provide the most favorable work conditions. Our view of management work builds on an information-processing framework that we will discuss; the behavior will be described in Hackman's and Walton's terms.

From the information-processing perspective, organizations can be described as sets of actors exchanging information to accomplish tasks and build knowledge (Zack and McKenney 1989). These patterns of information exchange can be short lived and created for a particular purpose, or they can be enduring routines or programs (March and Simon 1958) that support the group's ongoing activities. Thus communication exchanges can be described as temporal sequences of communication events (i.e., executing a particular program in a situation) or as networks representing the pattern of communication exchanges of a group over an extended period of time.

Daft and Lengel (1986), building on Weick's (1979) notion of equivocality, further elaborated on the information-processing view by proposing that organizations dealt with two types of information-processing situations. In the first, the problem or issue being addressed could be defined and framed. Perhaps many possible solutions to a complex problem existed, or certain pieces of information were lacking, rendering the situation uncertain; but at least the problem could be defined in a way that was meaningful to all. In the second type of situation, however, the problem itself defied interpretation. Either the situation was so novel or anomalous as to be not meaningful, or there were multiple interpretations, each separately logical but mutually exclusive and not globally meaningful. Thus building a shared understanding of a situation was necessary before action could be taken.

In the information-processing framework, the manager's job is first to determine whether the nature of the task is uncertain or ambiguous, and then to act accordingly. For the uncertain task, the manager must identify who possesses the relevant facts and how they should be accessed. For the ambiguous situation, the manager must involve those relevant persons having potential knowledge to enact an acceptable definition of the situation (be it a customer complaint or a personnel problem). With experience, an organization can turn ambiguous tasks into uncertain tasks. Reducing ambiguity is therefore considered problem solving, and reducing uncertainty is considered organizational work.

Problem solving includes managerial communication for building an understanding of and enacting solutions to equivocal problems, recognizing the need to shift priorities, and drawing on expertise to choose appropriate alternatives for action. These situations often thrust the manager into a role of expert problem solver who must define the problem by creating, enacting, or recalling a potential solution. Definitions of problems and solutions provide a group with an interpretive framework for understanding and addressing their situation (Weick and Bougon 1986).

Organizational work includes managerial communication in support of action within an enacted context, including monitoring performance conditions, taking or invoking appropriate action, communicating priorities, coordinating activities, and motivating employees (Hackman and Walton 1986; Weick 1979). We focused on a group of managers communicating among themselves. As such, they were interactors rather than solitary actors and their activities could be described by their communication programs and networks.

RESEARCH OBJECTIVES AND PROPOSITIONS

Managers typically have several available communication channels. Their options usually include FTF (including meetings and one-on-one encounters), telephone, and written memos or reports. Increasingly, organizations are adding electronic channels such as EM or voice mail. At the study site, telephone and written memos played an insignificant role in day-to-day management activity within the group, as the group members were collocated and were experienced EM users. Thus we limit our analysis to comparing FTF (both one-on-one and meetings) with EM, covering the media spectrum from rich to lean.

Our overall objective was to explore the electronic communication network phenomenon and to raise a set of issues for further investigation. Our immediate purpose was to evaluate three conjectures, which we will describe.

Choice of Medium

Effective managers choose a medium and channel appropriate to the information-processing task (Daft, Lengel, and Trevino 1987). Daft and Wiginton (1979) proposed that communication about ambiguous or ill-defined situations required the use of rich, iterative media. The less ambiguous the issue, the leaner the medium required. Richness was described in terms of complexity of language supported, flexibility of format, number of simultaneous channels of communication, and degree to which the message was personalized. Of the two media we observed, FTF was by far the richer. Weick (1979) proposed that resolving ambiguity and equivocality required interactive cycles of communication and back-and-forth exchange; thus in those situations interactivity is another necessary channel characteristic. EM limits communication patterns to a strict alternating series of messages. That is, one party sends a complete message to another before a reply is sent back. In contrast, FTF is highly interactive, enabling continuous and even simultaneous two-way exchange. By use of an overly lean medium, information may be lost and the message can either be misinterpreted or rendered ambiguous. An overly rich medium, by contrast, may result in more information than is needed being conveyed, making the communication inefficient for both sender and receiver: ambiguity might be introduced into an otherwise well-defined situation.

Therefore our first conjecture was that the proportional use of EM to support organizational work would exceed its use for problem solving. The manager's role involves resolving problem-driven equivocality via FTF early, then relying on structured information to monitor the group, allocate resources, and shift priorities—communication programs that, to be efficient and effective, should be unequivocal. Thus, to the extent that problem solving is relatively equivocal while organizational work as we have defined it is relatively unequivocal, problem solving would rely on rich media and organizational tasks on lean media. As EM is a more efficient medium of communication (Rice and Bair 1984) and fits these managerial communications requirements, managers should rely more on EM for organizational communication and on FTF for problem-solving communication.[3] We will state the preceding as our first proposition:

P1: The proportion of communication via EM will be greater for organizational communication than for problem-solving communication.

Communication Programs

Individual managers must develop a set of communication networks that are effective and efficient. These networks must effectively enable meaningful communication that will in turn facilitate the organization's processes for attaining its goals in a timely and satisfactory manner. They must efficiently communicate the most information with the least investment of time, effort, and resources. Given time demands, managers typically rely on preestablished routines to accomplish these objectives. For example, the implied objective of most routine, periodic operating meetings is to bring people to a common understanding of priorities and relevant issues and to share information to that end. We suggest that this rich FTF communication activity supports the enactment of a shared interpretive context, reducing equivocality and enabling subsequent routine communication of unequivocal information via lean and efficient channels such as EM.

Because programmed behavior is the most efficient means for dealing with routine, recurring situations (March and Simon 1958), we conjectured that the management group would evolve identifiable sequences of actions such as analysis, FTF discussions, and EM exchanges to accomplish particular tasks (McKenney 1988). We expected that programs would evolve from recurring or expected instances of both equivocal and uncertain tasks and that these routines would employ FTF and EM communication in an identifiable, patterned fashion. Where occasions of equivocality were expected or known to arise routinely, rich exchanges would occur via scheduled or habitual forums (e.g., scheduled meetings or morning coffee exchanges). Where exchanges of unequivocal information typically took place, they too would rely on networks using lean channels (e.g., EM). We will state the preceding as our second proposition:

> P2: Communication programs will exist for both problem-solving and organizational activity. Communication networks will employ both FTF and EM channels of communication.

The Overall Pattern of Management Communication

Managerial communication relies on a broad, all-inclusive, and comprehensive network. Its form varies from dyads to large meetings, and its functions range from the simple exchange of facts to enacting relevant frameworks and establishing social and political ties for maintaining the network itself (Tichy 1981). To address particular tasks or situations, managers can build ad hoc communication networks by piecing together face-to-face meetings, one-on-one exchanges, phone, and electronic networks as needed. Some may be standard procedures for the organization; others can be developed as needed. For example, a generalized managerial approach might be to use "expensive" meetings to create the shared understanding that enables subsequent efficient and effective communication via written memos, reports, or EM.

Porter and Roberts (1976) discussed the influence of task on communication patterns. Their work suggested that routines and communication patterns established to perform individual tasks (alluded to in Proposition 2) might add up to an overall macro routine or pattern of communication. Similarly, the blockmodeling technique of White et al. (1976) demonstrates how macro structure emerges from micro interaction. Taken together, the notions that managers create communication networks to address particular tasks and that communication patterns of particular tasks might contribute to an overall pattern of communication suggests that we would expect to observe an overall management communication pattern for the group. We will state the preceding as our third proposition:

> P3: The communication of the management group will exhibit an overall pattern reflecting the work routines of the group.

THE STUDY

We examined the use of electronic messaging within a self-contained team of computer programmers responsible for the ongoing development of the operating-system software for their company's office automation system. The work involved an intellectual process to produce an information-intensive product under deadline. Members of the organization relied to a great extent on routines, but often had to respond to unexpected events. They are experienced users of information-processing technology, and they used that technology to create the product (a computer program) as well as to communicate via electronic messaging.

A series of enhancements, each considered a new product, was under development and planned for release over time. The team had a series of specific release dates and a set of functional specifications for each enhancement. The managers viewed the budget allocation as adequate, but they anticipated difficulty in meeting the deadlines.

Software development is a complex information task that gives rise to many highly equivocal situations as a result of numerous interrelationships, frequently conflicting objectives, and the precise but arbitrary way in which software is created (Walker 1985). In Weick's (1979) sense, the observed situation often required making judgments to enact design information, as there was considerable equivocality as to exactly what the customer desired. Yet the design process required an unambiguous set of specifications or definitions of functions that depended on the existing state of the software and the desired new services for the next version. Therefore many solutions were enacted by experienced systems developers (Walker 1985).

Sources of uncertainty for this project included (1) errors or "bugs" in the existing software; (2) new functional requirements; and (3) the typical problems with scheduling and production. In Tushman and Nadler's (1978) terms, there was both internally and externally generated uncertainty, as well as a high degree of interdependence because all were working simultaneously on parts of the same computer program. The managers dealt with a variety of information, and consequently their job had a high level of complexity and a varied level of analyzability (Perrow 1986).

We used the case-study method, supported by both qualitative and quantitative data. Our intent was to amass multiple sources of evidence to describe the phenomena under study. Our first proposition required measurement of the level of communication activity for organizational *versus* problem-solving communication. Our second proposition required a description of the communication programs for each type of communication. Both propositions were examined by describing the sequential patterns of task-oriented communication (i.e., programs). To do this, we observed the organization over four months, which allowed us to understand its programs and habits for several tasks differing in their information-processing characteristics. We also conducted extensive interviews and administered questionnaires. We traced the flow of information as reported on contemporaneous activity logs maintained by the managers and as implied by computer-generated lists of electronic mail messages. By obtaining data on message topics, time sent, sender, and recipient, we were able to identify particular tasks and their sequence of communication events. We were further able to link the data collected by various methods. Task sequences could be traced through electronic mail listings, activity logs, and observations.

EM data were gathered automatically throughout the period with no effort from the managers and were therefore more accessible to us. Most phone messages were to individuals outside the company and were not tracked in detail. Meetings were usually held for project reviews and either covered a range of topics or focused on a particular task.

We collected data in two phases: an exploratory pilot stage and a more intensive follow-up. During the initial stage we collected a four-week sample of EM, had two observation periods of logged data, and conducted a series of structured interviews with each participant. The bulk of the data in the second phase was gathered in an eight-week period. During that time we captured EM messages; gathered data on phone use, FTF communications, and meetings over the course of *four* days of structured observation and activity logs; and conducted three structured interviews along with nine days of random observations to track particular tasks. The observation and logging were done during periods of intense communication activity. When events were going as planned, not many communication events occurred. Typically, after marketing-review periods or shortly before new product testing, a flurry of activity would occur; we scheduled observation periods for these times to confirm EM activities and specific task-related communications. We asked certain people to keep logs on particular tasks.

We defined a task as a coherent action objective of two or more individuals that involved several communication events with a discernible beginning and end, and that was judged a job-related responsibility by the task initiator. Because a task could be any combination of cognitive steps with an observable output, the definition of a particular task was somewhat arbitrary, and our level of analysis was a function of the objective of the study. The tasks we tracked had managerial and problem-solving components that extended over time periods ranging from an hour to several weeks.

The documented routines were probably a biased sample, since we tracked only those that had an identifiable beginning. Some problems simmered over a long period and were discussed at meetings and in the halls. For those issues, the logs reflected a time slice of a longer-term process.

THE DATA

The project manager organized his 10-person management team, supervising 28 professionals, as shown in Figure 10-1.

At the start of our study the team had been working on the project for over two years and had been active EM users for over a year. All the managers used EM continuously and all but one believed that it was their most efficient means of communicating. Although all worked within 60 feet of one another, most individuals received and sent more than a dozen EM messages a day within the group. They used the phone occasionally to contact individuals outside the group, and they participated in one or two short meetings a day in addition to many one-to-one (FTF) exchanges.

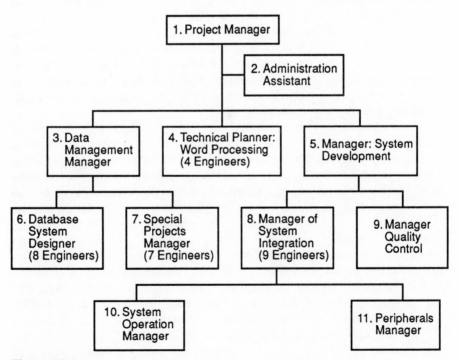

Figure 10-1

Organizational Chart of Project-System Responsibilities

Table 10-1

RESPONDENT NO./JOB DESCRIPTION		AVERAGE NUMBER OF MESSAGES SENT/DAY			
	% EM	Phone	FTF	EM	Total
1. Project Manager	77	3	8	37	48
2. Admin Assistant	20	11	19	13	43
3. Data Management	56	4	14	23	41
4. Word Processing	53	3	23	29	55
5. System Development	48	6	22	26	54
6. Data Base System	45	1	10	9	20
7. Special Projects	74	1	4	14	19
8. Integration	64	3	11	25	39
9. Quality Control	53	1	14	17	32
10. System Operation Mgr	75	1	19	61	81
11. Peripherals	22	3	22	7	32

The overwhelming majority of meetings were one on one, with an occasional third joining. The observed norm was to have short, small meetings when needed, with one scheduled project review meeting per week to review progress and revise plans after the project manager had met with his boss.

The data in Table 10-1 show the average number of messages by channel, the total number of messages per day, and the percentage of messages by EM for the 11 managers. The average number of messages per day varied widely—from 19 for manager 7 (a special projects manager), to 81 for manager 10 (the system operation manager). For all but two individuals, EM accounted for the largest percentage of messages. Nevertheless, there was a wide range: from 22% EM for manager 11 to 77% for manager 1. As discussed below, the nature of their tasks accounted for this large variance.

The entire group communicated across all media using metaphors to identify topics and status; individuals reverted to technical jargon when dealing with problem finding or solving. The metaphors allowed efficient EM use, since they could communicate much information with a few symbols. For example, the development of the word-processing system was code named Purple Dragon; a minor glitch was communicated as "Its claws are dulled," followed by various exchanges or solutions. A major glitch was "Its wing is broken," which prompted a meeting and various interpretations and reinterpretations of how to fix the "wing." The up-to-date meaning of the metaphors seemed to be maintained by impromptu FTF meetings in the hall or at coffee breaks. Most meetings were highlighted by metaphorical discussions followed by technical jargon and by occasional reference to code displayed on a terminal.

The project group relied on media of EM, FTF (one-on-one), and meetings for different purposes in accordance with the equivocality and uncertainty of the task. Yet over all they relied heavily on EM, in large part because of their work habits. They all checked development status via the computer system and were accustomed to working alone for hours on the terminal. EM communication was a natural complement to their work, and they were expert at creating social links via the system. Equivocality often arose due to individuals' different solutions to a problem. These differences of opinion would initiate an FTF discussion to determine the best approach. Once equivocality was reduced, the main challenge was to reach an understanding about how to build the computer program code. Although programmers entered computer code individually on-line, they often communicated by exchanging EM while looking at each other's code on their computer screens.

DATA ANALYSIS

To investigate Proposition 1 (that the proportion of EM would be greater than the proportion of FTF for organizational versus problem-solving media usage) and for Proposition 2 (that programs existed), we developed flow diagrams (shown in Figures 10-2 to 10-5) of four action programs, each initiated by a different manager. These were selected from 11 patterned sets of activities identified in the trial period.

During the observations, we documented organizational and problem-solving activities according to our framework. Organizational communications were typically used for changes in status or priorities, in essence to change context and motivate task-oriented actions. Problem solving usually related to the computer software. The managers tended to categorize problem solving versus organizational work according to the following criteria: if it related to customer problems or designing or developing the system, it was classified as problem solving; everything else was organizational. In general, the classifications were contextual judgments by the observer-analysts, made on the basis of communicated topics and surrounding events.

The flow diagrams articulate a complete program of all steps observed, and a more routinized and abbreviated version denoted by an asterisk for steps executed when a particular situation was unequivocal or certain. Note that as our research was exploratory, the grain of our design (and thus the limits to our subsequent level of analysis) was coarse. Further, although the tasks were rated overall as to equivocality and uncertainty, it proved too intrusive to categorize particular instances as equivocal or uncertain. A universal program was a weekly meeting that focused on status, problems, and shifting priorities. The meeting was a vital context-building enacting activity, but it proved too complex to capture unobtrusively for detailed analysis.

The tasks selected for tracking and analysis had observable organizational and problem-solving components varying in degree of uncertainty and equivocality. After we had a solid description and a tentative program, we discussed the steps with each manager and then observed the group to refine the program definition. As summarized in Table 10-2, the tasks ranged from 12 to 21 steps. A total of 61 steps was broken down

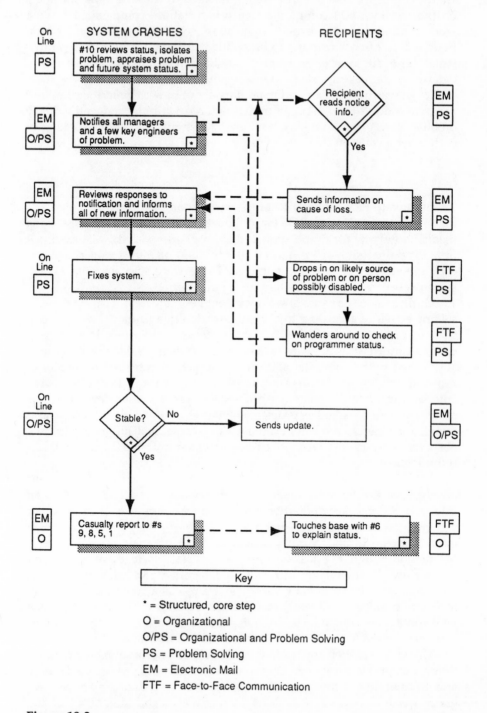

Figure 10-2
System Recovery Procedure

Table 10-2
Number of Steps

TASK	SYSTEM RECOVERY	SYSTEM TROUBLE REPORT	PROBLEM SOLVING	PROBLEM FINDING	TOTAL
Figure	3.1	3.2	3.3	3.4	
Organizational	2	4	5	8	19
Problem Solving	6	9	14	4	33
Org/PS	4	1	2	2	9
TOTAL	12	14	21	14	61

into 19 organizational, 33 problem solving, and 9 that combined organizational and problem solving.

A brief description of the diagrammed tasks follows. Manager 10 initiated the operating system recovery routine (Fig. 10-2) on failure of the main development system. Failures occurred because programmers had inadvertently created computer code that interrupted the operation of the system. Rated an uncertain-unequivocal task, twenty-eight occurrences were observed with five requiring FTF meetings. Manager 2 initiated the system trouble resolution procedure (Fig. 10-3) when she received a system-trouble report from marketing identifying a customer's system problem. Rated an uncertain-unequivocal task, uncertainty about the request was resolved by the manager first contacting a likely expert. Most often she simply forwarded the request immediately to the expert who handled the situation. The procedure became more routinized during the course of the study as the manager learned which individuals handled which problems. Of the twenty-one occurrences, seven required FTF discussions. Manager 8 initiated the system integration problem-solving procedure (Fig. 10-4) most mornings during periods of integrating the various new subsystems into the operating system, when reviewing system test runs for errors. Rated an equivocal and uncertain task, it was the most complex procedure observed and was intended to isolate particular system problems to specific tasks and relevant engineers. Of the eight instances in which these tasks were initiated, only one was finished via EM. Manager 1 initiated the problem-finding procedure (Fig. 10-5), rated equivocal and uncertain, when he sensed a system problem but was not sure of the exact nature and did not think it was being addressed. Of the seven occurrences, only one was completed on the first morning of discussion, when it was decided there was no problem.

The programs showed that EM was used for monitoring status, sending alerts, framing discussion topics, and invoking action; FTF was used for defining and discussing problematic situations. The objective of the FTF discussions varied from informing to intelligence gathering and reducing equivocality. The system operation manager used EM as a broadcast medium alerting all users to the uncertainties of the system crash and then discussing responses with receivers. The system trouble-

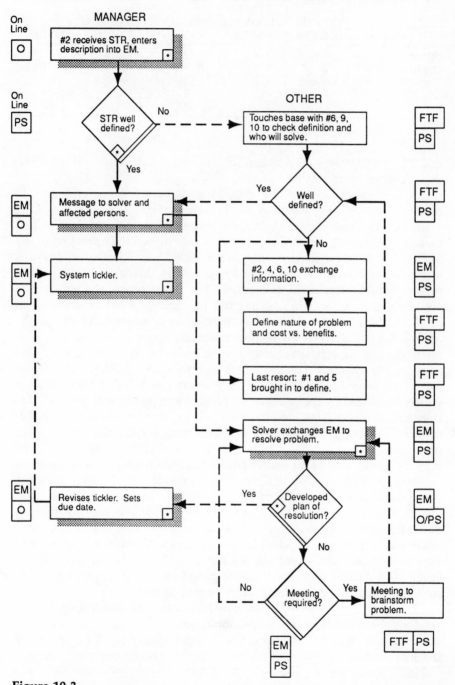

Figure 10-3
STR Resolution Procedure

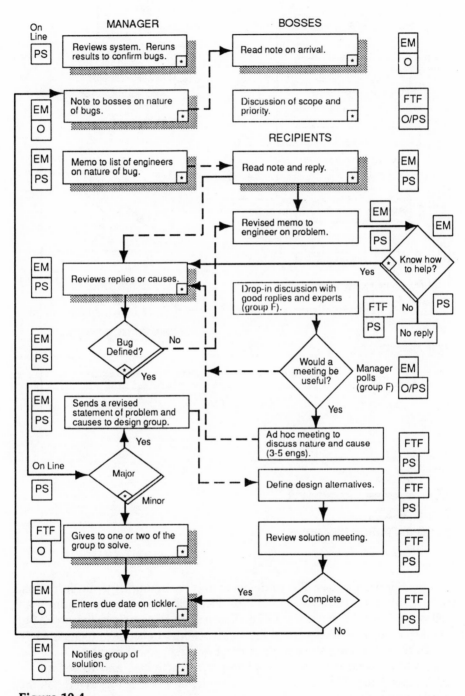

Figure 10-4
Problem-Solving Procedure

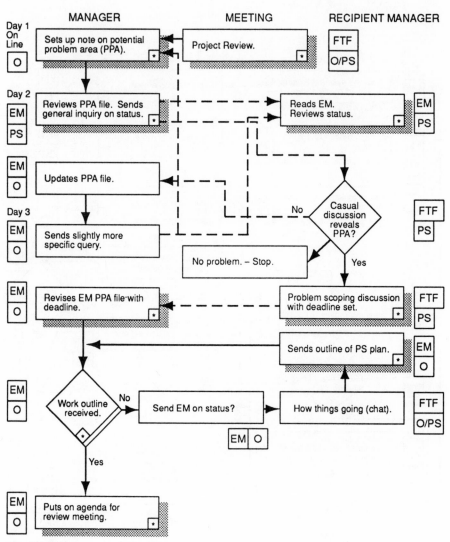

Figure 10-5
Problem-Finding Procedure

report coordinator used EM to delegate known situations to an individual or to notify a range of experts of a problematic situation; she would then follow up with the experts via FTF. The system integrator relied on EM to keep the project team aware of key equivocalities in order to focus his FTF activities and to alert the team to priorities. The project manager used his EM system to keep track of problem-finding activities and to set up his problem-solving FTF contacts. EM recipients were made aware of the specific topic of impending FTF meetings. Thus, even in highly equivocal situations, EM framed a situation for a few experts and created an awareness of the sender's concern. The follow-up FTF discussion then had an implicit agenda.

The programs demonstrated a consistent pattern of communication for the group's problem-solving activities—in essence, a metaroutine to handle nonroutine events (Tuchman 1973). The problem-solving events all started with a meeting or on-line analysis of the system to frame a problem situation, followed by an EM notice to particular members of the group to alert them to the situation, followed by an FTF discussion. Thus EM was used efficiently and effectively because of the shared understanding of the task context. For example, to start the intelligence phase of problem solving (Newell and Simon 1972), the sender could identify by line number a section of the program representing the problem. For fact-finding requests, a shared norm of *not* replying when the recipient had no information (together with a norm of rapid response when the recipient *did* have the information) reduced the level of communication and thus the search effort during the intelligence phase. FTF was used to exchange opinions on the nature of the problem and to propose alternative solutions. Often member of the group would design an alternative and test it during a discussion. The documented programs demonstrated that EM is not an independent medium but carries a set of messages within a consensually known intellectual context.

A numerical comparison of media use for problem solving versus organizational steps for the complete version of the programs showed a higher proportional use of EM for organizational communication. The analysis provides evidence for the general conjecture that EM is used more frequently than FTF for organizational communication, while FTF is important for identifying and resolving ambiguities or for decomposing complexity for problem solving. The proportional use of EM shifted noticeably when compared to FTF for the shortened, low-equivocality/low-uncertainty ("routinized") versions of all tasks, as summarized in Figure 10-6. (For the routinized tasks the number of communication events dropped, as did the number of problem-solving steps.) The proportion of communication for problem solving shifted to EM in general due to low equivocality and uncertainty. The greatest shift was in large reduction of FTF for problem solving as increased routine in the low-equivocality situations rendered the situation less problematic and more amenable to EM. Overall, these results demonstrate that EM can be a useful managerial tool for working in an environment with low equivocality or a strongly shared understanding of the task.

To determine the influence of a task on overall patterns of communication structure (as suggested by Proposition 3), we made a sociometric analysis of EM and FTF use, isolating the dominant patterns of communication for the management group. The patterns were identified on the basis of a blockmodel analysis (Breiger et al. 1975; White et al. 1976). Blockmodeling procedures analyze a set of directional messages from one person to another. The messages are recorded in a relational matrix in which the rows and columns have the same headings. Thus a row shows

		ORG	PS	ORG/PS	TOTAL
Complete	FTF	2	14	3	19
	EM	15	14	5	34
	TOTAL	17	28	8	53
	% EM	88	50	63	64
Routinized	FTF	2	1	2	5
	EM	11	10	3	24
	TOTAL	13	11	5	29
	% EM	85	91	60	83

Figure 10-6

Comparison of Complete Program versus "Routinized" Version

one person's messages to others, while the corresponding column shows all the messages received from others. Analysis yields a permutation of the matrix in which those individuals with similar patterns of sending and receiving messages over similar channels are placed together in a single subgroup (block). We created two separate relational matrices, one for one-on-one FTF and one for EM. These matrices were combined (stacked) and entered to the CONCOR blocking algorithm. The blocking generated from our data is shown in Table 10-3 (numbers identifying individuals refer to the organizational chart given in Figure 10-1).

Density matrices based on this permutation and showing the relative degree of communication at different block intersections for each medium, are shown in Figure 10-7 (1 indicates complete interconnection, with all rows contacting all columns; 0 indicates no interconnection).

Figure 10-8 depicts the major communication flows between the blocks, with arrows where the density of communication is greater than the mean.

Communication patterns were coherent among the four blocks. Each block performed a unique role in the group and focused on different topics and communication functions. The interpretation of these blockmodels was supported by structured interviews as well as by observations and opinions of participants. Block A (project manager, 1; technical planner, 4; system developer, 5; and system integrator, 8) was the coordinating and planning group, which served as gatekeeper to the

Table 10-3

BLOCK	FUNCTION	MEMBERS
A	Organizers and Planners	Nos. 1, 4, 5, 8
B	Coordinators	Nos. 2, 9, 10
C	Specialist Coordinators	Nos. 3, 11
D	Experts	Nos. 6, 7

	EM			
	A	B	C	D
A	1	.67	.25	0
B	.75	.50	.17	.17
C	.50	0	0	.50
D	0	.17	.50	0

$x = 45/110 = .41$

	FTF			
	A	B	C	D
A	.42	.59	.13	.38
B	.34	.34	.50	.17
C	.13	.50	0	.50
D	0	.17	.50	.50

$x = 36/100 = .33$

Figure 10-7

marketing groups and field offices; it included the most senior and experienced software managers in the group, who backed one another up during individual absences. Their communication topics were more organizational than problem solving, although one manager would often initiate a problem by shifting priorities or raising new design requirements. Their messages involved proportionally less problem solving and more enacting of objectives and motivating than did those in the other blocks.

Block A had strong two-way communication ties within itself and with Block B, occasional exchanges with Block C, and no direct links to Block D. In particular, the project manager (1) in Block A relied on the administrative assistant (2) in Block B to follow up and to obtain status reports. The administrative assistant had access to a computer file schedule of action events that the project manager maintained, and she would check with relevant individuals on status and remind them of action items daily. The integrator (8) in Block A served as the general metronome of the group. He was the key link between Blocks A and C as well as with most of the system engineers; he maintained a comprehensive EM status file on the project and on individual work assignments. Individual engineers constantly touched base with him to report status and to confirm design choices.

Block B (administrative assistant, 2; quality control manager, 9; and system operation manager, 10) was the operational group and the key set of status reporters and monitors. Administrative assistant (2) kept in constant touch with managers 9 and 10 and Block A, to keep them informed and to obtain direction. The quality control manager (9) was responsible for documentation and for getting the product through quality assurance, using mainly EM and meetings. He was also responsible for maintaining up-to-date schedules and establishing priorities. To keep track of status he maintained strong EM links to managers 8 and 10. For managers 9 and 10, EM communication was a fact-finding medium used primarily for requesting information on technical issues and problems. For 2, the electronic messages were mostly organizational: checking on status and alerting individuals to changes, or following up for 1.

Block C (data management manager, 3; and peripherals manager, 11) was the specialist block that had strong two-way ties with Blocks B and D. The data base manager (3) was responsible for software that supported

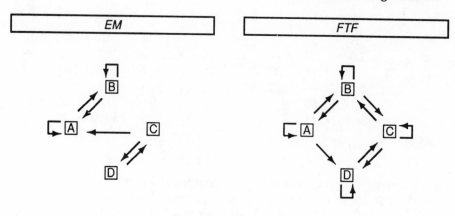

Block	Function	Members
A	Organizers and Planners	Nos. 1, 4, 5, 8
B	Coordinators	Nos. 2, 9, 10
C	Specialist Coordinators	Nos. 3, 11
D	Experts	Nos. 6, 7

Figure 10-8
Basic Communication Block Relations

applications, such as the data base, communications, and peripherals, and dealt with suppliers through 11. Experienced customers dealt directly with both 3 and 11 on particular problems. Those two managers spent the bulk of their time solving problems related to maintaining schedules and handling customer situations. The peripherals manager (11) spent 80% of his time on printer issues and the remainder on screens and keyboards. He occasionally informed 8 via FTF of required system changes. His low EM use was attributed to lack of context; while his colleagues were developing software, he was working with suppliers to connect their peripherals to the system. Because documentation on these problems was obscure, extensive FTF sessions were often necessary to ensure that the development programmers understood exactly what was required. His main functions were problem solving and information exchange, along with status reporting.

Block D included the data base system designer (6) and operating system specialist (7), who communicated with their boss (3) in Block C and received status information from Block B. Their electronic messages had a technical focus and were primarily factual information exchange for resolving problems of all the blocks. They communicated the least and had the narrowest scope.

To evaluate the patterns of communication by media throughout the day, we used the permutation in Table 10-3 to analyze EM and FTF for the four blocks for the five time periods shown in Figure 10-9. These periods reflected the typical behavior of the team. *Period one* early morning log in, read mail, and then touch base with relevant colleagues; *period two* analytical work on-line; *period three* lunch and social activity; *period four* work or meetings; *period five* EM exchanges throughout the organization. The pattern of communication articulated in this series reflects the ongoing software development process of the group.

The members of the management team spent from two to six hours daily on a terminal analyzing the system and using EM to outside and inside groups, particularly to remote sales-service individuals. Each morning the system integrator reviewed the output of the previous day's programming and tested the system on-line. He informed his bosses of this analysis and they briefly discussed priorities; then a set of objectives or questions were forwarded to the team via normal channels. Mid-morning, after this information was digested and work had begun, ambiguities were resolved via FTF. Programming then began in earnest and proceeded until the end of the day when testing began, generating a new flurry of communication. The to-from arrows indicate communication links between blocks or within blocks during the period.

This analysis confirms the general pattern identified in the programs: that early morning exchanges of EM and FTF were followed by task-driven events. The EM messages from Blocks A to C in the early morning were followed up with FTF in mid-morning. The complementarity of EM shows a daily pattern of links and follow-up and emphasizes the job functions and relationships. Block D was composed of the doers who took direction from their boss in Block C, but they contacted Block B for clarification and to answer requests for information. Block B was the operational monitor and had the largest number of active links throughout the day.

The analysis demonstrates that EM communication patterns differed according to the nature of the job, and reflected the nature of roles and the tasks of the individuals vis-à-vis other blocks. The patterns represent a macro view of the programs that serve to set the pace of work in the project. The structure reflects the cyclical and repeating pattern of management work whereby managers engaged in EM early in the day to assess status, sent more directed EM and FTF messages in the middle of the day to monitor progress and to move the process along, and had a more general EM exchange later in the day to assess the current situation and to set priorities for the next cycle. Early morning FTF was organizationally oriented, moving to more directed problem solving in the middle of the day and more patterned FTF late in the afternoon, complementing the pattern of EM communication. This analysis lends additional support

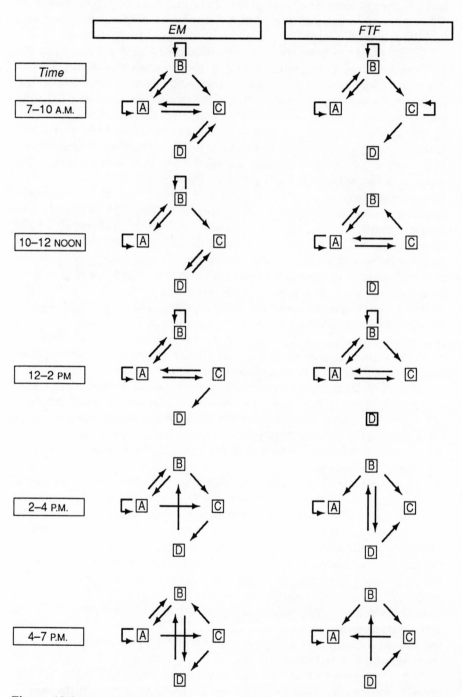

Figure 10-9
Daily Communication Patterns

to the proposition that the pattern of managerial communication is dependent on the group's tasks.

CONCLUSIONS

This study explored the role of EM by a managerial group for task-oriented communication, guided by an information-processing model of managerial work. Our findings indicate that programs make up the bulk of the managers' communication activity on a day-to-day basis. The results support our conjectures that managers communicate according to task- and role-driven programs of behavior, and that those programs include a purposeful choice of communication channel and medium. These programs depend on particular multimedia networks, the use of which changes with the task. Managerial groups form programs for communication about both equivocal issues and problems and well-defined issues requiring the exchange of merely factual information. These routines include the use of FTF and EM. Evidence for a consistent pattern of equivocality-reducing behavior suggests that groups create metaroutines for providing a routine response to novel or undefined events. Once situations are meaningfully defined, mainline task management programs can be invoked.

We specifically proposed that equivocal problem solving would rely on rich FTF exchange while less equivocal but possibly uncertain situations, such as monitoring task status, coordinating efforts, and exchanging needed facts, would rely on lean but efficient EM. Our findings support these conjectures. Managers appear to make purposeful task-driven choices about not only those with whom they communicate, but also the channel and medium they use.

We identified a fundamental trade-off between the efficiency of communication provided by EM in well-defined contexts versus the ability to build a shared understanding and definition of the situation or task via FTF. FTF (both one-on-one and scheduled meetings) provided the richness to support the level of interactivity, immediacy of feedback, and social presence required to resolve equivocal issues or issues requiring a complex set of exchanges, and created a shared understanding in the group so that a focused and structured communication-in-context could occur.

EM and FTF proved to be complementary channels of communication. The primary roles of EM were to monitor status, send alerts, broadcast information, and invoke action. FTF was used to define and discuss solutions to problems, and to maintain context by alerting the group to shifting priorities as a result of external events of improved understanding of the project over time. A weekly meeting served as a routine context-building process. A typical sequence of communication would be the use of EM to broadcast a problem alert or a new priority to the group, or to delegate a task to specific individuals or departments. This would be followed by an FTF discussion to better define the issue and come to an agreement on how to proceed. Finally, EM would be used to coordinate and to monitor the status of further efforts.

The study validated the usefulness of our framework for studying the communication behavior of managers, which divided management work into organizational and problem-solving activities. While not exhaustive of all managerial activities and in need of further refinement, the framework begins to address the essential information-processing roles of the manager: to define and enact meaning for the group or organization, and to marshal the information necessary to take coordinated action toward attaining the organization's goals. The information-processing characteristics of equivocality and uncertainty, directly related to this framework, appeared to influence strongly the communication behavior (including choice of medium) of the management group.

We looked at communication patterns at two levels of granularity: (1) the structure of the overall network, and (2) the particular task-driven communication sequences that operated within that structure. We developed a complementary picture of communication as behavior that occurs in sequence through time in pursuit of task-related goals, and as behavior that operates within and helps to define an overall communication structure for the management group. The duration of our study did not permit us to draw conclusions about how the sum of the particular task routines over time forms structure, or how the underlying structure constrains or influences the evolution of these routines: the "chicken-and-egg" situation addressed by structuration theory.

We can, however, speculate that organizing and problem-solving routines result in interactions that create procedural expectations for future interactions. These expectations include aspects such as topics, timing, channel, medium, and participants. For example, the group we observed exhibited a norm of using EM followed by an FTF meeting for a particular set of topics and participants. At the same time, the sum of the tasks performed by one person and the resulting sum of interactions it requires defines a role set that creates similar expectations about communications. The key mechanism of structuration appears to be the shared expectations people harbor concerning their own and all other group members' communication habits. The notion of expectations suggests a stochastic or probabilistic flavor to the situation. That is, most situations are not fully determined. Managers can't very well predict the incomprehensibly complex set of factors that make up their experiences. This notion is consistent with the interaction patterns we observed within our short-interval time sample, patterns that at times bordered on randomness. In the aggregate, however, these expectations are more often met than not, forming a coherent structure and a constraint on further expectations.

In the sense of Weick's (1979) enactment theory, people *enact* their communication events to conform to their expectations, further constraining and structuring them. For example, while the manager of the group never engaged in small talk about the weather or nonbusiness activities, the technical planners routinely did. Their FTF followed this pattern in all observed FTF events. These communication patterns appeared to change in one of two ways. Either they mutated slowly as the group incrementally learned to perform a task in a new way based on experience; or they changed radically when things were so equivocal or anomalous (i.e., when managers confronted an extreme "problem") that the current order was challenged and new interaction routines were invented. These inventions eventually became institutions, and the cycle repeated.

We offered a way to examine the structuration process at both levels. The overall communication structure comprised a set of purposeful task-oriented communication processes, each of which was invoked depending on the external or internal stimuli to the group and used only a part of the overall structure across any particular period of time. The individual programs showed that media use was a function of the task, while the blockmodels suggested that media use was also a function of the structural role.

Finally, our study raised the issue of context and its role in enabling meaningful and efficient communication. Context was not our main focus, but it was the underlying theme of many of our conclusions. Meaningful communication requires a shared understanding of the background knowledge needed to interpret the information being exchanged. This understanding is often part of the communication event itself, and we observed that much of managerial communication is directed to the creation of this shared understanding. Much communication, however, occurs within a shared context already established. This context can exist on a very general level, such as the culture of the society, organization, or group. For example, computer programmers tend to share a particular culture. More specifically, the context includes the group's shared knowledge of things such as the task, everyone's role within that task, who knows what about what, work and communication habits of group members, and group norms. The programmer team we observed used an elaborate shorthand code based on mythological metaphor to refer efficiently to system problems. The collective memory of the group stored past problems and events that could be recalled in a brief phrase via EM to set an elaborate context for a cryptic message to follow.

In sum, FTF effectively serves as a context-creating medium, while EM is a context-reliant medium. Further study of this conjecture will require a more focused and finer-level "micro analysis" of communication behavior to trace context-building and context-using communication.

Notes

1. Ambiguity occurs when a situation is so unclear or anomalous as to defy interpretation; equivocality occurs when multiple possible interpretations exist. We will use the term "ambiguity" to refer to both types of indeterminacy.

2. We use the term "organizing" as suggested by Weick (1979), meaning activities to set goals, monitor, keep in touch, exchange information, etc.
3. By not explicitly relating this notion of fit to group or managerial effectiveness, we implicitly assume an ecological (or selection) definition of effectiveness (Draizin and Van de Ven 1985). That is, the group, by virtue of its continued existence, must have been effective.

References

Barnard, C. I. 1938. *The Functions of the Executive.* Cambridge, MA: Harvard University Press.

Breiger, R. L., S. A. Boorman, and P. Arabie. 1975. "An algorithm for clustering relational data, with application to social network analysis and comparison with multidimensional scaling." *Journal of Mathematical Psychology* 12 (Aug.): 328–383.

Cyert, R. M., and J. G. March. 1963. *A Behavioral Theory of the Firm.* Englewood Cliffs, NJ: Prentice-Hall.

Daft, R. L., and R. H. Lengel. 1986. "Organizational information requirements, media richness and structural design." *Management Science* 32(5) (May): 554–571.

Daft, R. L., R. H. Lengel, and L. K. Trevino. 1987. "Message equivocality, media selection and manager performance." *MIS Quarterly* 11(3) (Sept.): 355–366.

Daft, R. L., and J. C. Wiginton. 1979. "Language and organization." *Academy of Management Review* 4(2):179–191.

Draizin, Robert, and Andrew H. Van de Ven. 1985. "Alternative forms of fit in contingency theory." *Administrative Science Quarterly* 30:514–539.

Fayol, H. G. 1949. *Industrial Management.* London: Pitman.

Fulk, J., C. W. Steinfield, J. Schmitz, and J. G. Power. 1987. "A social information processing model of media use in organizations." *Communication Research* 14(5) (Oct.): 529–552.

Galbraith, J. K. 1973. *Designing Complex Organizations.* Reading, MA: Addison-Wesley.

Hackman, R. J., and R. E. Walton. 1986. "Leading groups in organizations." In Paul S. Goodman et al., eds., *Designing Effective Work Groups.* San Francisco: Jossey-Bass.

Isenberg, D. J. 1986a. "Thinking and managing: a verbal protocol analysis of managerial problem solving." *Academy of Management Journal* 29(4): 775–788.

———. 1986b. "The structure and process of understanding: implications for managerial action." In Henry P. Sims, Jr. and Dennis A. Gioia, eds., *The Thinking Organization.* San Francisco: Jossey-Bass, pp. 238–262.

Kotter, J. P. *The General Managers.* 1982. New York: The Free Press.

Kurke, L. B., and H. E. Aldrich. 1983. "Mintzberg was right: a replication and extension of *The Nature of Managerial Work.*" *Management Science* 2(8) (Aug.): 975–984.

March, J. G., and H. A. Simon, with H. Guetzkow. 1958. *Organizations.* New York: Wiley.

March, James G., and J. P. Olsen. 1976. Ambiguity and Choice in Organizations. Bergen: Universitetsforlaget.

McCaskey, M. B. 1982. *The Executive Challenge: Managing Change and Ambiguity.* Boston: Pitman.

McGrath, J. E. 1990. "Time matters in groups." In J. Galegher, R. E. Kraut, and C. Egido, eds., *Intellectual Teamwork: Social and Technical Bases of Cooperative Work.* Hillsdale, NJ: Lawrence Earlbaum.

McKenney, J. L. 1988. "How managerial use of electronic mail influences organizational information processing: An explanatory study." Boston: Division of Research, Harvard Business School. Working Paper 88-067.

Mintzberg, H. 1973. *The Nature of Managerial Work*. New York: Harper and Row.
———, D. Raisinghani, and A. Theoret. 1976. "The structure of unstructured decision processes." *Administrative Science Quarterly* 21 (June): 246–275.
Newell, A., and H. A. Simon. 1972. *Human Problem Solving*. Englewood Cliffs, NJ: Prentice-Hall.
Perrow, C. 1986. *Complex Organizations: A Critical Essay*. 3d ed. New York: Random House.
Porter, L., and K. H. Roberts. 1976. "Organizational communication." In M. Dunnette, ed., *Handbook of Industrial and Organizational Psychology*. Chicago: Rand-McNally.
Rice, Ronald E., and James Blair. 1984. "New organizational media and productivity." In Ronald E. Rice, ed., *The New Media*. Beverly Hills: Sage.
Stewart, R. 1985. *The Reality of Management*. London: Pan Books.
Thompson, J. D. 1967. *Organizations in Action*. New York: McGraw-Hill.
Tichy, N. M. 1981. "Networks in organizations." In Paul C. Nystrom and W. H. Starbuck, eds., *Handbook of Organization Design*. New York: Oxford University Press.
Tuchman, Gaye. 1973. "Making news by doing work: routinizing the unexpected." *American Journal of Sociology* 79(1): 110–131.
Tushman, M. L. and D. A. Nadler. 1978. "Information processing as an integrating concept in organizational design." *Academy of Management Review* 3(3) (July): 613–624.
Walker, G. 1985. "Network position and cognition in a computer software firm." *Administrative Science Quarterly* 30:103–130.
Weick, K. E. 1979. *The Social Psychology of Organizing* 2d ed. Reading, MA: Addison-Wesley.
Weick, K. E., and M. G. Bougon. 1986. "Organizations as cognitive maps." In Henry P. Sims, Jr. and Dennis A. Gioia, eds., *The Thinking Organization*. San Francisco: Jossey-Bass.
White, H. C., S. A. Boorman, and R. L. Breiger. 1976. "Social structure from multiple networks. I. Blockmodels of roles and positions." *American Journal of Sociology* 81(4) (Jan.): 730–780.
Zack, M. H., and J. L. McKenney. 1989. "Organizational information processing and work group effectiveness." Working Paper 89-054, Harvard Business School, February.

11

Face-to-Face:
Making Network Organizations Work

NITIN NOHRIA
AND
ROBERT ECCLES

The most general use of the term "network" is for the structure of ties among the actors in a social system. These actors may be roles, individual persons, organizations, industries, or even nation states. Their ties may be based on conversation, affection, friendship, kinship, authority, economic exchange, information exchange, or anything else that forms the basis of a relation. Thus in this broad sense, the structure of any social organization can be thought of as a network (see reviews by Mitchell 1974; Berkowitz 1982; Burt 1982; Lincoln 1982; Wellman and Berkowitz 1988; and Marsden 1990).

However, two narrower conceptions of the term "network" have come to prominence recently. Each occupies a central place in what has been described as a transition in advanced economies from an industrial to a post-industrial society (Touraine 1971; Bell 1974). One use of "network" refers to a new ideal type of organization that is radically different from the Weberian bureaucracy (Baker, this volume; Miles and Snow 1986) and is characterized by relations that are based on neither hierarchical authority nor market transactions (Powell 1990; Thorelli 1986). Those who use the term this way see the emergence of this new network organizational form as the result of accelerating changes in the environment that create greater uncertainty and increased information-processing requirements (Miles and Snow 1986; Child 1987). And while no consensus has emerged about the analytical distinctiveness of *the* "network" organization, or even about the term itself—kindred labels include "post-industrial" (Huber 1984), "heter-

We are grateful to John King for his very helpful comments on an earlier version of this chapter.

archical" (Hedlund 1986), "self-designing" (Eccles and Crane 1988), "post-bureaucratic" (Heydebrand 1989), and "cluster" (Mills 1990)—those who posit the emergence of such a new organizational form commonly emphasize its network properties as consisting of a fluid, flexible, and dense pattern of working relationships that cut across various intra- and interorganizational boundaries.

The other use of the term "network" refers to new modes of organization that are made possible by advances in information and telecommunications technologies such as facsimile machines, electronic mail, voice mail, videoconferencing, teleconferencing, electronic bulletin boards, electronically mediated meetings, computerized data bases, and so on (Forester 1987). Hiltz and Torhoff (1978) exemplify this vision:

> We will become the Network Nation, exchanging vast amounts of both information and socio-emotional communications with colleagues, friends, and "strangers" who share similar interests. . . . we will become a "global village." . . . An individual will, literally, be able to work, shop, or be educated by or with persons anywhere in the nation or in the world (quoted in Poster 1990:121).

The network in Network Nation and similar conceptions is basically an electronic network, which is also presumed to enable a fluid, flexible, and dense pattern of interconnections that cut across various intra- and interorganizational boundaries.

Not surprisingly, because of the similarities in their conception these two uses of the term "network" often—though not always—converge. Network Organization becomes synonymous with Network Nation. As typified by Drucker (1988), the network organization becomes the information-based organization—built up, as it were, on relations of price, authority, and trust (Bradach and Eccles 1989) that are no longer negotiated in face-to-face interaction, but are mediated electronically and enabled by advanced information technology architectures (Nolan et al. 1986, 1988, 1989). The network organization is envisioned as a sprawling and organic electronic network connecting the employees of the firm with one another as well as with their customers, vendors, and strategic partners (Malone and Rockhardt 1991).

In this convergence of these two conceptions of the term "network" lies a dangerous fallacy that we wish to highlight in this chapter. The fallacy is to believe that Network Organization is synonymous with Network Nation. Or, to put it a little differently, *network organizations are not the same as electronic networks, nor can they be built entirely on them.* Undoubtedly, advances in information technology can and will play a key role in shaping the network organization. But because of the efficiency and ease of use of electronically mediated exchange the temptation is that it will replace relationships based on face-to-face interaction. The question is whether these electronically mediated exchanges can be as effective.

Our view is that they cannot. As we argue in greater detail later in the chapter, issues of uncertainty, ambiguity, and risk—the daily fare of a network organization—are difficult to address through electronically mediated exchange. Effective network organizations also require the kind of rich, multidimensional, robust relationships that can be developed only through face-to-face interaction. Thus electronically mediated exchange cannot and should not replace all face-to-face interaction. However, we do not wish to suggest that there is no role for the former in the network organization. Electronically mediated exchange can increase the range, amount, and velocity of information flow in a network organization. But the viability and effectiveness of this electronic network will depend critically on an underlying network of social relationships based on face-to-face interaction. Indeed, there may well be a minimum ratio of face-to-face to electronically mediated exchange that is vital to maintain in order for network organizations to work effectively.

NETWORK ORGANIZATION, INFORMATION TECHNOLOGY, AND ELECTRONIC NETWORKS

The emergence of the network organization, it is argued, is being necessitated by the changing character of industrial economies. Among the most salient of these changes are the increasing globalization of the world economy, the rapid entry and exit of competitors, the unpredictable emergence and obsolescence of new products and technologies, the customization of demand and increasing emphasis on value-added services, the emergence of flexible manufacturing to meet this demand, rapid changes in the political environment, and an increasingly mobile and heterogeneous work force—all of which combine to create conditions of unprecedented knowledge intensity, uncertainty, ambiguity, and risk (Piore and Sabel 1984; Miles and Snow 1986; Child 1987; Drucker 1990; Eccles and Nohria 1991).

In order to respond to these conditions, the argument continues, firms must be fast, flexible, responsive, and knowledge intensive. They must be action-oriented—rapidly bringing people and resources (including the relevant information and expertise) together to address opportunities and threats as they arise. This, the argument concludes, calls for replacing traditional bureaucratic approaches to organization with more adaptive, self-designing, network organizations—leading to a rallying cry that has been embraced by business academics, journalists, and managers themselves. (See, for example, a June 17, 1991, *Fortune* article that author Brian Dumaine felicitously entitled "Bureaucracy Busters.")

Though the notion that the network organization is more appropriate for conditions of uncertainty, ambiguity, and risk has achieved faddish popularity recently, it is actually not new. In a seminal work, Burns and Stalker (1961) argued that in unstable environments, the bureaucratic or "mechanistic" organizational form is ineffective. Instead, they argued, an "organic" organization comprised of a complex network of ties that transcend whatever formal hierarchy exists and form and dissolve as necessary is more effective in such environments.

Thus, while many of those advocating a new approach to organization have merely rediscovered the "organic" organization, what is new is their view that information technology and electronic networks will play a central role in facilitating the emergence of such network organizations, whether from scratch or by transforming existing organizations. By making it easier to collect, analyze, and disseminate information, these technologies are seen to have the potential to transform hierarchies into networks in at least four ways (Child 1984, 1987; Keen 1987; Applegate et al. 1988; Drucker 1988; Zuboff 1988; and Rockhardt and Short 1991).

First, information technology makes it possible to reduce the number of management levels in the hierarchy, especially middle-management ranks, since these people are no longer needed for processing information up and down the organization. Moreover, by providing a dramatically enhanced potential for control, information technology greatly increases the span of control (Beniger 1986). This reduction in the number of management levels reduces the amount of bureaucracy separating senior executives from workers. Empowered with information, the front-line workers become "knowledge workers," acting autonomously to deal with issues and events that they are closest to. Top management's role becomes one of providing broad vision and overall strategic direction (Zuboff 1988; Drucker 1988).

Second, information technology makes it easier for people to communicate directly with one another across time and space through such media as electronic mail (Sproull and Kiesler 1991) and videoconferencing (Fulk and Dutton 1984). Increases in capabilities for communication flows also help to break down existing authority structures and entrenched organizational boundaries that are usually reinforced by determining and controlling access to information.

Third, information technology improves the ability of organizations to communicate with one another through interorganizational systems and other forms of electronic data interchange. This blurs the boundaries of the firm and increases the range of possible relationships between organizations beyond pure market or pure hierarchical exchanges (Cash and Konsynski 1985; Malone and Rockhardt 1991).

Fourth, information technology contributes to flexibility, a prominent feature of the network organization. Work stations, relational data bases, and prototyping systems-development methodologies have made it easier to design and redesign measurement and control systems, which facilitates structural change. Also, storing knowledge in the form of open data bases and expert systems enables organizations to be less dependent on particular employees and more able to respond with greater flexibility to a more diverse and dynamic labor market (Walton 1989).

There is thus no doubt that information technology can and will play a prominent role in the emergence of the network organization. But in their enthusiasm for the new technology and their "technotopian" vision of the Network Nation, the champions of information technology sometimes fail to recognize its limits. One of the main reasons is that they primarily subscribe to an information-processing view of organizations (Galbraith 1973), often ignoring an organization's social dimensions.

The social dimension of organization is especially crucial in the network organization because the type of coordinated action that is required is rarely routine. It has to be novel and imaginative, in tune with the volatile, uncertain, and changing environment confronted by the organization. For this kind of coordinated action, people must act under conditions of great ambiguity of purpose and means to achieve ends. They must negotiate a shared understanding of the context, discover sources of information, decide who can be depended on, distribute work among these people, and develop rules and norms for further action and monitoring progress toward their goals (Hackman and Morris 1978). For accomplishing this, the social structure provided by roles, norms, and status and reinforced by trust and personal engagement with others is critical (Kiesler et al. 1984). It is here that we begin to see the limits of the technotopian vision of the network organization: the structure required for the organization to work effectively under these conditions, we argue, just cannot be built on electronic networks. It crucially depends on face-to-face interaction. To support this proposition, we draw on a substantial literature that compares face-to-face interaction with electronically mediated exchange and examines the relative strengths and weaknesses of each.

FACE-TO-FACE INTERACTION VERSUS ELECTRONICALLY MEDIATED EXCHANGE

A necessary backdrop for comparing the relative efficacy of face-to-face interaction and electronically mediated exchange is a model of human interaction and social organization. We take a moment to sketch quickly a model that draws heavily on the work of Collins (1987). Paraphrasing Collins, the basic building blocks of all social organization are the repeated interactions among two or more members that take place in different settings. These interactions can take various forms—formal or informal, public or private—and can provide the setting for various types of interaction—talk, work, sociability, domination, authority, or exchange. During any interaction, Collins notes, participants reveal to one another and interpret their roles and identities, their intentions, and the meaning of their actions. Moreover, it is important to recognize that these interactions are not isolated events, each independent of the other. They are usually part of a chain of interactions that repeat themselves over time and across space. The actors participating in any interaction bring to it the history of all their previous interactions and carry away from it a new interactional history and repertoire. Each interaction also produces a certain amount of emotional energy that affects the motivation of the participants to engage in future interaction with one another and shapes their future strategies for interacting with one another.

Also, despite their seemingly routine character, every interaction is fraught with uncertainty. Order has to be negotiated in each interaction: about roles and identities, about meaning and action, about feelings and emotions (Cherry 1978). Yet everyday interaction typically proceeds without any difficulty—so much so that we tend to take it for granted (unless, of course, our routine expectations are breached, as Garfinkel 1967 showed). The fact that it does depends principally on the vast store of communicative resources that we all possess, the imprint of all our past experience. With this, we can hear snatches of speech, see vague gestures and grimaces, and from such thin shreds of evidence we are able to make a continual series of inferences and guesses with extraordinary effectiveness. What is even more remarkable is that we can do so given that our communicative resources are not stored as detailed or exact cognitive blueprints for action or interpretation, but as a set of "gists" on which we build and fill in details in situ from the contexts in which we interact (Donnellon 1986). Successful interaction—and therefore effective organization—depends to a great extent upon how well the uncertainty inherent in all interactions can be resolved. As Gronn (1983) has argued, effective administration depends on successful communication. That, in turn, can depend on the media and context in which the interactions are held. Thus it can make a big difference if interaction is face-to-face or electronically mediated.

Face-to-face interaction and electronically mediated exchange differ in three fundamental ways. First, in face-to-face interaction, the participants are always copresent—at the same time and place. In electronically mediated exchange there is no need for, nor is there often the possibility of, such copresence. Interaction usually transcends the barriers of space and time. Thus, while electronically mediated exchange liberates participants from the constraints of space and time, the lack of copresence means that all kinds of social context clues are filtered out. From the most basic issues of the actors' sex, age, and gender to more subtle contextual signals such as which actor has a corner office, a larger desk, an imposing personality, there is a great paucity of cues in electronically mediated exchange (Sproull and Kiesler 1991).

Second, face-to-face captures the entire bandwidth of human interaction. It covers all the senses—sight, hearing, smell, taste, and touch—that provide the equipment through which individuals receive information. Not only does face-to-face interaction capture the full bandwidth of physical sense, it also captures the full range of psychoemotional reactions—such as discomfort, ease, attraction, and so on—that are so important to human interaction. No other communication medium has such a total bandwidth. Thus, to draw on a distinction proposed by Goffman (1963), face-to-face interaction captures not just impressions "given" but those "given-off"; the former refers to all the information that the interactants want to "give" one another (a data transfer, as it were), whereas the latter refers to the emotive signals that the interactants emit, exude, or "give off" for the other(s) to glean.

Third, relative to electronically mediated exchange, the structure of face-to-face interaction offers an unusual capacity for interruption, repair, feedback and learning (Schegloff 1987). In contrast to interactions in other media that are largely sequential, face-to-face interaction makes it possible for two people to be sending and delivering messages simultaneously. The cycle of interruption, feedback, and repair possible in face-to-face interaction is so quick that it is virtually instantaneous. As Goffman (1963:15) notes, "a speaker can see how others are responding to her message even before it is done and alter it midstream to elicit a different response." When interaction takes place in a group setting, the number of "conversations" that can be going on simultaneously when the interactants are face-to-face is even harder to replicate in other media.

All these differences between face-to-face and electronically mediated exchange have several important implications for dyadic and group interaction, and hence for the effectiveness of any social organization. Here we focus on four issues that have a special bearing on the effectiveness of network organizations:

1. How quickly and completely can *roles and identities* be established so that the actors can orient themselves toward one another, especially since new task groupings and teams are constantly being formed in the network organization?

2. How well can the actors resolve issues in the face of *uncertainty and ambiguity*, the prevailing conditions confronted by network organizations?

3. Because quick, coordinated action that can seize opportunities and deflect threats is vital to success of the network organization, how easily and effectively can *collective action be mobilized?*

4. Because their strength and adaptability are key for the ongoing and long-term viability of the network organization, how *robust* is the structure of relationships?

Identity

Face-to-face meetings are essential for forming the precise mental images of others that facilitate the development of our strategy for interacting with them. We all have had the experience of forming mental images of people we have communicated with only through written documents, electronic mail, or over the telephone. These media fail to give us a complete picture of a person to fix in our mind. Using the clues we get from the communications, however, we form images of what someone may look like and be like. These images are based on criteria and categories we use to understand others: gender, race, and age; whether the person is strong or weak, passive or aggressive, conservative or liberal, self-interested or other-interested, competent or incompetent, and so on. Based on these images we create models about the person's motives, their likely responses to actions, and a personal strategy for interacting with them.

Before face-to-face communication occurs, our mental image of a person is incomplete; therefore so is our strategy for interacting with the person. Even if we know the other's role is that of boss, worker, expert, or the like, this is not an image that is given nor is it encoded as a script to which everyone routinely adheres. As Carol Heimer (this volume) points out, these roles are not universal, they are particular. The identity of a boss is not complete until one knows, for example, when and with whom she is considerate or tough; such particular impressions must be filled in for the role to take on real meaning. The strong initial impressions that are formed when meeting someone go a long way toward completing the mental image. In fact, it often takes a great deal of subsequent data and experience to change this image in any substantial way. Strong feelings of like or dislike, trust or distrust, attraction or repulsion, and so forth are often formed in the first face-to-face interaction. The loose but useful term "chemistry" is used to describe the combination of affective reactions two people have to each other, and much of this chemistry is catalyzed in first impressions (Schlenker 1980).

The importance of face-to-face interaction for forming impressions is even more critical when many people are involved. Face-to-face interaction can proceed among several individuals simultaneously. Indeed, this is a characteristic that may be most difficult to replicate in any other medium. Teleconferencing, even videoconferencing, just cannot capture the range of communication that proceeds when people meet face-to-face with one another in a group. The most subtle dynamics, such as how people seat themselves at a meeting, who congregates with whom, and how relative status and group memberships are signaled and established, depend on the resources made available by face-to-face interaction and a shared physical setting. Pairs and groups that gather together construct social membership and identity in multifaceted ways that cannot be duplicated by the same set of people meeting all the others in one-on-one interactions. As Sproull and Kiesler (1986) have observed, role differentiation is diminished and unstable in electronic interaction.

Thus electronically mediated exchange offers only limited impressions with which to construct the meaningful identities that enable people to orient themselves to, and develop strategies for interacting with, one another. This means that so long as the issues requiring communication between people who have never met are such that their identities are not very important, electronically mediated exchange will work fine. But if effective communication depends on a better understanding of the people involved—a knowledge of how much you can trust them, for instance—then you need the richer mental image that can be obtained only through face-to-face interaction.

Negotiating Uncertainty and Ambiguity

A large body of theoretical and empirical evidence holds that electronically mediated exchange is much less effective than face-to-face interaction in conditions of ambiguity and uncertainty (see Trevino et al. 1987 for a review). As Daft and Lengel maintain,

> Managers will turn to rich media when they deal with the difficult, changing, unpredictable dimensions of organizations. Rich media enable them to com-

municate about and make sense of these processes. Face-to-face and tele-phone media enable managers to quickly update their mental maps of the organization. Rich media enable multiple cues and enable rapid feedback. Less rich media might oversimplify complex topics and may not enable the exchange of sufficient information to alter a manager's understanding (1984:200).

It is not just the richness of the medium and its ability for interruption, feedback, and repair that influence the resolution of uncertainty and ambiguity. Poster makes the following important additional observation:

> In face-to-face interaction, so much depends not on what is said, but on who says it, how they make their intervention, what clothes they wear, their body language, facial and oral expressions. All of this is absent in electronically mediated exchange. Without the normal cues and routines of face-to-face speech to guide the interaction, simple procedural issues may raise fundamental difficulties. Problems arise over matters like taking turns and keeping the discussion going. . . . A good portion of the discussion must be devoted to messages about messages, supplementary information to supply what is ordinarily embedded in the context of speech. . . . Because the conventions of speech are so drastically upset, computer conferencing easily becomes talk-about-talk (1990:121–122).

Thus, as experimental results have shown, differences in initial positions held by negotiators converge more rapidly in a face-to-face situation. Also, electronically mediated exchange groups take longer to reach a consensus and exchange fewer remarks in the time allowed them, even controlling for the time it takes to input/type comments (Kiesler et al. 1984). The evidence from field settings is consistent with these experimental findings (McKenney et al., this volume). What this implies is that while electronically mediated exchange may be adequate for routine communication, face-to-face is essential when the issues are uncertain and ambiguous.

Mobilizing Collective Action

Coordinated action in network organizations requires people and resources to come together to address constantly changing opportunities and threats. In this regard, electronically mediated exchange can be very effective in bringing together a diverse and large number of inputs. As Sproull and Kiesler (1991) note, one of the most significant kinds of messages on electronic networks begins with the refrain "Does anybody know . . . ?" These messages solicit all kinds of information and usually receive a good number of responses. For example, in their study of Tandem Computers, a company that employs 10,500 people who are all connected via electronic mail, they found an average of about six does-anybody-know messages broadcast every day and an average of about eight replies to each. The ability of electronic mail to reduce the impediments to communication across space and time, as well as its low cost (in terms of time and effort) and ease of use certainly have a lot to do with this increased information flow (see Crawford 1982, and Nyce and Groppa 1983 for evidence from the experience of Digital Equipment Corporation and Manufacturers Hanover Trust). However, as Poster observes, another important reason is that electronically mediated exchange circumvents the "power relations that govern synchronous speech. Factors such as institutional status, personal charisma, rhetorical skills, gender, and race—all of which may deeply influence the way an utterance is received—have little effect in electronically mediated exchange. Equality of participation is thereby encouraged. . . ." (1990:122). Experiments done by Sproull and Kiesler support this observation: "Using a [electronic] network induced the participants to talk more frankly and more equally. Instead of one or two people doing most of the talking as happens in many face-to-face groups, everyone had more equal say. Furthermore, networked groups generated more proposals for action than did traditional ones" (1991:119).

Thus electronically mediated interaction is certainly more "egalitarian," but it is also more "disorganized" (Williams 1977). It is difficult for people interacting electronically to move beyond generating proposals for action and be decisive in taking action. One reason, discussed earlier, is that ambiguous and uncertain issues are hard to address via electronically mediated exchange. Another reason is that the very democratic character of electronic interaction that makes it so open also makes it hard to resolve conflicts and establish who is in control and who has authority to make critical decisions. A clear leadership structure, which Hackman (1990) and Kotter (1990), among others, consider critical for effective coordinated action, is hard to achieve when the mode of interaction is electronic. Indeed, the anonymity and spatiotemporal distance that electronic interaction provides can lead to open displays of anger and escalating conflict or what is called "flaming" behavior (Kiesler 1986; Solomon 1990). Finally, mobilizing collective action involves "signing up" or motivating others to contribute their best efforts to the task at hand (Kidder 1981). It is hard to get someone to sign up electronically. You expect someone to speak to you face-to-face if they want you to do something with them that is of even modest significance. When issues are interpersonally involving, individuals prefer media with more social presence (Short, Williams, and Christie 1976). To sum up, electronically mediated exchange can help in enabling information flows useful for mobilizing action, but face-to-face interaction is vital to actually taking action.

Robustness

Electronic networks are not very robust because they are highly susceptible to opportunistic behavior. Lying, fraud, sabotage, and other antisocial actions are hard to detect in electronically mediated exchange. Without the full bandwidth of face-to-face communication, how can you tell whether someone is being profoundly sincere or totally deceptive? As a case in point, Stone (1991) tells the story of Julie, a person on an electronic network in New York in 1985:

> Julie was a totally disabled older woman, but she could push the keys of a computer with her headstick. The personality she projected into the "net"—

the vast electronic web that links computers all over the world—was huge. On the net, Julie's disability was invisible and irrelevant. Her standard greeting was a big, expansive "HI!!!!!!" Her heart was as big as her greeting, and in the intimate electronic companionships that can develop during online conferencing between people who may never meet, Julie's women friends shared their deepest troubles, and she offered them advice—advice that changed their lives. Trapped inside her ruined body, Julie "herself" was sharp and perceptive, thoughtful and caring.

After several years, something happened that shook the conference to the core. "Julie" did not exist. "She" was, it turned out, a middle-aged male psychiatrist. . . . He spent weeks developing the right persona. A totally disabled, single, older woman was perfect. He felt that such a person wouldn't be expected to have a social life. Consequently her existence only as a net persona would seem natural. It worked for years, until one of Julie's devoted admirers, bent on finally meeting her in person, tracked "her" down (2–3).

As "Julie's" case shows, such duplicity is easy over electronic networks because the communication channels are narrow and each person has great control over the spin on his or her communications. Though duplicity is certainly possible in face-to-face interaction, it is harder. As John King (1991) wrote us, "Free riders, log-rollers, back-stabbers, and other vermin are much more easily rooted out when subjected to the sensitive noses of the angry wolfpack, *in vivo*." It is hard to trust someone without—as they say—a hard look in the eye. Not only is opportunistic behavior harder to detect in electronic networks, its implications can be more damaging. Consider the recent sabotage by a Cornell graduate student who spread a "virus" through the nation's major electronic networks, paralyzing several critical operations, some of which presumably could have compromised U.S. national security (Hafner and Markoff 1991). Despite sophisticated advances in ways to ensure the security and reliability of electronic networks, they remain vulnerable and fragile.

The difficulty of keeping opportunism in check and generating trust in electronic networks has the related implication that norms and conventions—which, according to Elster (1989), form the "cement" of all social organization—are harder to develop and enforce. Though an increasing number of norms and conventions regulate behavior in electronic networks, they are breached on a frequent basis; hence they tend to be much weaker than their counterparts in networks built on face-to-face interaction (Kiesler 1986).

Not only are face-to-face relations important for the robust everyday functioning of network organizations, they are vital for the robustness of these organizations over time. As the circumstances in which people have to work together change, their relations need to change as well. Changes in each person's responsibilities, skills, interests, and objectives need to be incorporated. Face-to-face interaction is especially effective at making each person aware of changes both in the other and in his or her self as reflected in the other, thereby facilitating necessary adjustments in the relationship. Through repeated face-to-face interactions, both parties have the opportunity to enhance and revise their mental images of each other and to develop and revise strategies of action that enable each to work with the other. As people accumulate experiences working together on a variety of issues in a variety of circumstances, they learn more about how each views the world. They also learn to communicate more effectively by developing a better understanding of how each uses language, the categories that are important to them, the heuristics they employ, and the forms of verbal and nonverbal shorthand and codes they use.

This is not to say that face-to-face communications do not also lead to disagreements, conflicts, and even ruptures. Sometimes these are a result of an insufficient quantity and frequency of face-to-face communication, which leads to the parties drifting apart. When they come together and more effective communication takes place, the differences become apparent and erupt. But even when these fissures occur in the context of frequent face-to-face communication, rarely does the solution lie in reducing the amount of such interaction. Repairing relationships is best done through face-to-face interaction.

Thus face-to-face communication plays an essential role in establishing and maintaining the kind of multidimensional and robust relationships necessary for effective interaction and coordinated action in situations of uncertainty, ambiguity, and risk.

If we admit that some face-to-face interaction is necessary for network organizations to work effectively, the next question is: How much is enough? What is the role of and balance between face-to-face and electronically mediated interaction in the network organization?

FACE-TO-FACE AND ELECTRONICALLY MEDIATED EXCHANGE IN THE NETWORK ORGANIZATION

The champions of advanced information technology—those who see the network organization as built upon and almost synonymous with electronic networks—would argue that the benefits and ease of use of the new technology will result in it replacing face-to-face communications. As electronically mediated interaction increases, they argue, the amount of face-to-face interaction that is necessary will decline sharply and may even become entirely redundant.

The problem with this *substitution hypothesis* is that it is not universal. As we have argued, electronically mediated exchange can substitute for face-to-face interaction only when the identities of the interactants are not very important, when the circumstances at hand are certain and unambiguous, when the actions necessary are standard and routine, and when ongoing interaction does not depend on a robust structure of relationships. There is both theoretical (Allen and Hauptman 1990) and empirical research that supports our view. Studying the circumstances in which people use different communication media and the stated reasons for their choices, Trevino et al. (1987) found that face-to-face interaction was pre-

ferred for difficult, ambiguous communications because of its capacity for
rapid feedback and multiple cues. Symbolic reasons were also given for
choosing face-to-face interaction, suggesting that the additional cues of
caring, building teamwork, showing trust, and informality were important. The telephone was used most frequently for situational reasons,
although both content and symbolic reasons play an important role. The
situational benefits of the telephone emphasized its ease, speed, efficiency, and ability to span long distances, as well as its capacity under the
right conditions to help resolve difficult ambiguous messages and send
symbolic cues such as urgency, personal concern, or deference to the
receiver's status. The use of electronic media, however, was driven most
by situational determinants. Because it is quick, efficient, and provides
access to busy people, electronic mail is appropriate for simple, routine
messages and for reaching many people simultaneously. E-mail is rarely
associated with symbolic reasons other than to signal urgency and get a
quick response.

This leads to the somewhat ironic conclusion that the best circumstances for using electronically mediated exchange to replace face-to-face
interaction are those in which the more traditional market or hierarchical
organization is quite effective. When relations are impersonal, unambiguous, standardized, and atomistic as they are in ideal markets, electronic
exchange can effectively substitute for face-to-face interaction. The success
of the NASDAQ financial securities market in the United States and the
recent transformation of the London Stock Exchange to an electronic
market are cases in point. Equally, when relations are role based, certain,
routine, and unchanging, as they are presumed to be in ideal bureaucracies, electronic interaction can be used to enhance the efficiency of the
organization by reducing unnecessary middle-management layers, clerical
and staff positions, and travel expenses. And so far, as is true for such
celebrated examples as Mrs. Fields Cookies (see Walton 1989 for a detailed
discussion of how information technology is used by this organization),
this is primarily how information technology has been used (Nolan et al.
1989). Even in these situations, face-to-face interaction cannot be replaced
entirely. According to a recent article in the *Economist*, traffic in the financial district's restaurants and meeting places increased greatly after the
London Stock Exchange's electronic conversion, as actors in the market
sought ways to maintain face-to-face contact. And despite being connected to all her stores by various electronic linkages, Debbie Fields, CEO
of Mrs. Fields Cookies flew over 350,000 miles in 1986 alone to meet face-
to-face with her employees.

This suggests that a minimum amount of face-to-face interaction is
necessary for any type of social organization to work effectively. Furthermore, under circumstances where the required form of organization is
neither markets nor hierarchies, but networks, we would hypothesize that
in order to derive the benefits of the increasing capability of electronically
mediated exchange, the amount of face-to-face interaction will actually
have to increase. This is because an extensive, deep, robust social infra-

structure of relationships must exist so that those using the electronic media will truly understand what others are communicating to them. As the proportion of face-to-face communications decreases, this infrastructure deteriorates and the vast quantity of electronically mediated exchanges will at best turn out to be noise (characteristic of most electronic mail from people one does not know very well) and at worst simply add to the confusion. Voluminous and rapid communications that are useless or misinterpreted by people whose relationships are inadequate for processing the information in situations of uncertainty, ambiguity, and risk are more likely to create organizational anarchy than to contribute to the development of an effective network organization. Therefore, as the amount of electronically mediated exchanges increases, there has to be a corresponding increase in the amount of face-to-face interaction.

This increase does not have to be one for one. Electronically mediated exchange has the potential to increase the range and velocity of information flows in a network organization. But the amount of leverage that can be achieved has an upper bound because of the constraint on the total time that can be spent in face-to-face contact. As one approaches the limit on the time that can be spent in face-to-face contact, one also approaches a limit on the amount of electronically mediated exchange. This is because it is vital to maintain a minimum ratio of face-to-face to electronically mediated exchange. We would further hypothesize that this ratio is likely to be greater as the environment of the network organization becomes more uncertain, unusual, ambiguous, or risky.

While not much empirical work has been done that is directly relevant to these hypotheses, it is worth noting that based on a review of a number of field studies, Culnan and Markus (1987) found that the use of electronic media tends to reduce the use of telephones and memos and occasionally reduces the need for meetings, but usually increases face-to-face and written communication. This is also consistent with the experience of organizations such as investment banks (Eccles and Crane 1988) and some high-technology firms we have studied such as Digital Equipment Corporation and Compaq Computer Corporation. These are prime examples of network organizations, and both make extensive use of face-to-face communication, despite the fact that both are also very aggressive about the use of information technology in communications.

Investment banks are particularly revealing because of the attention that is paid in these organizations to creating physical spaces that will facilitate face-to-face interaction. They also emphasize face-to-face contact with issuers and investors despite being linked to them electronically. The notion of an upper bound on the amount of communication that is possible because of limits on the time available for face-to-face interaction is also evident in investment banks. The fast and furious pace of investment banking and the increasing amount of time that has to be spent in front of the computer means that the only way that face-to-face communication can increase is through an expanded workday. Thus investment bankers are well known for extensive meetings, frequent travel, business breakfasts/luncheons/dinners, and socializing in "nonwork hours" through Friday beer parties, outings, and other company events.

Figure 11-1 provides a graphic summary of our propositions regarding the balance between face-to-face and electronically mediated interaction. The vertical axis depicts the amount of face-to-face interaction necessary as the amount of electronically mediated exchange, represented on the horizontal axis, increases. The initial condition is the amount of face-to-face interaction necessary in the absence of any electronically mediated exchange. The graph is divided into two regions. In the shaded region, as the downward-sloping line OC indicates, one can replace face-to-face with electronically mediated interaction. This is possible only for market and hierarchical organizations. Even here, a minimum amount of face-to-face interaction must be maintained. The other region applies to network organization. As the upward-sloping line OA shows, as electronically mediated interactions increase, the amount of face-to-face interaction must correspondingly increase. The slope of this line, which is the ratio of the amount of face-to-face to electronic interaction, is less than one, indicating the potential of information technology to increase the range and velocity of information flows in the organization. The more uncertain, unusual, ambiguous, or risky the environment of the organization, the steeper we would expect the slope of this line to be. Finally, the graph shows the upper bound on the amount of face-to-face interaction because

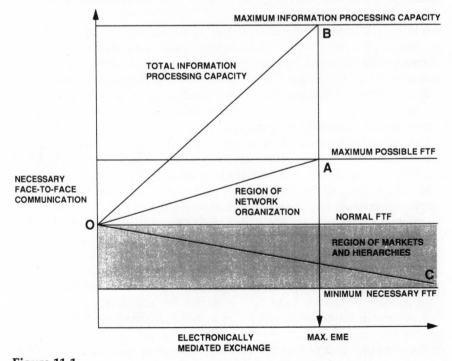

Figure 11-1

The Balance Between Face-to-Face and Electronically Mediated Exchange of time constraints, which correspondingly sets limits on the amount of electronically mediated exchange and the total information-processing capacity (as indicated by the line OB) of the organization.

IMPLICATIONS FOR PRACTICE

The managerial implications of our argument are apparent. While managers can and should take advantage of the emerging information and telecommunications technologies, they should not view them as an easy replacement for face-to-face interaction. As Robert B. Horton, president of British Petroleum, a firm that makes extensive use of information technology, cautions: ". . . [T]echnology is only a support mechanism, not a substitute for in-person contact" (*Fortune,* June 3, 1991:120). This is recognized by successful managers in many industries. Senior executives in geographically dispersed firms spend many days every year "on the road" in order to meet face-to-face with their managers. Although modern communications technologies have made it possible for them to get a great deal of information on a daily basis, they do not view this as a substitute for face-to-face communication. Even the legendary Harold Geneen (1984), who perhaps epitomized management by the numbers, gathered a large group of managers together every month to review each business's results in front of all others. Rice (1991) estimates that the best communicators spend about 40% of their time in face-to-face encounters, and this is a limit because they don't have more time to give.

Managers must also be careful that participants in their organizations' electronic networks spend more time and are more resolute in interacting face-to-face instead of taking the easy route of communicating electronically. There are several stories of organizational ineffectiveness induced by indiscriminately substituting face-to-face communication with other communication media. To counteract this tendency, some firms are devising ingenious strategies. For instance, at a manufacturer of computer disk drives we studied, every time someone wants to send a message electronically, a prompt automatically appears on their computer screen: "Do you really want to send this electronically?" By forcing their employees to make a conscious choice, managers at this firm are hoping to maintain the right balance between face-to-face and electronically mediated interaction.

IMPLICATIONS FOR FUTURE RESEARCH

Our contention that using electronically mediated exchange to help create a network organization requires more, not less, face-to-face communication may appear counterintuitive, but we believe the arguments presented in this chapter make it at least a reasonable hypothesis. We do admit, however, that there is little hard data that support our argument. It is unlikely that the research methodologies typically used in communications research—laboratory experiments, surveys, and limited in-company field studies—will shed much light on whether our hypothesis is true or not. The best way to address it would be through a few in-depth, longitudinal case studies.

An especially rigorous design would be to study two so-called network organizations that were roughly similar on the most salient dimensions, especially performance, and had introduced extensive electronically mediated exchange communications. If the amount of face-to-face communications declined in one and its performance deteriorated relative to the other, which maintained a higher ratio of face-to-face and electronically mediated exchange communications, our hypothesis would gain some support. Such a study has obvious measurement problems—performance, amount of communications using the different media, and establishing a causal relationship between communications patterns and performance—even if two such companies could be identified and the researcher was fortunate enough to have their experiences differ in this way.

Another way of getting at this hypothesis would be to study companies whose experience varied in terms of how extensively electronically mediated exchange was used. While there are a number of causes for differential adoption rates and usage patterns, it would be informative if the companies that were more satisfied with electronically mediated exchange and used it more had also increased the amount of face-to-face communications.

Finally, given our lack of knowledge about the problem and the relative newness of the technologies in most companies, simply directing attention to the question of what is the right balance between electronically mediated exchange and face-to-face communication is useful. Even informal conversations with managers about their experiences would provide insights that could guide future research.

CONCLUSION

The crux of our argument is that you cannot build network organizations on electronic networks alone. At the core, the network organization depends on a network of relationships forged on the basis of face-to-face interaction. This network of relationships serves as the substrate on which the electronic network can float or—to use a wonderful phrase from Granovetter (1985)—be "embedded." What the electronic network can do is accelerate as well as amplify the communication flow, but its viability and effectiveness will depend critically on the robustness of the underlying social structure. This implies that one has to be careful in substituting face-to-face ties with electronic ones. It is vital to maintain a critical ratio of face-to-face to electronic interactions. It may be even more critical to maintain face-to-face relationships with those individuals who can serve as bridging ties (Granovetter 1973) gatekeepers, champions, and so on. These are the relationships that provide the foundation on which the rest of the network depends.

To individuals who envision the world becoming an electronic village, our position may appear overly conservative. They can point to technologies such as the telephone and wireless that over a period of time had dramatic implications for the emergence of new organizational forms—for example, the geographically dispersed organization with central urban headquarters connected to field operations through telecommunications technologies (Pool 1983). It is only a matter of time, they may reason, before network organizations will become synonymous with electronic networks. It is possible that just as blind people develop enhanced sensitivity to sound, users of electronic media may compensate for the limitations in innovative ways. The tale comes to mind of World War II Morse-code operators who recognized one another according to the speed and style of their touch and developed a whole network of relationships on this basis. While nobody can tell what the future holds, we think that face-to-face interaction will remain a necessary basis of all social organization. Perhaps remote, asynchronous, and anonymous communication will produce a different society (see Lyon 1988 and Marvin 1988 for some provocative possibilities). If so, that society will look so unlike the one we inhabit today that we will probably need an entirely new sociology of organizations.

References

Allen, T. J., and O. Hauptman. 1990. "The Substitution of Communication Technologies for Organizational Structure in Research and Development." In J. Fulk and C. Steinfield, eds., *Organizations and Communication Technology.* Beverly Hills: Sage.

Applegate, Lynda, James Cash, and Quinn Mills. 1988. "Information Technology and Tomorrow's Manager." *Harvard Business Review* 66 (Nov.–Dec.): 128–136.

Baker, Wayne. 1992. "The Network Organization in Theory and Practice." Chapter 15, this volume.

Bell, Daniel. 1974. *The Coming of Post-Industrial Society.* London: Heinemann.

Beniger, James R. 1986. *The Control Revolution.* Cambridge, MA: Harvard University Press.

Berkowitz, S. D. 1982. *An Introduction to Structural Analysis.* Toronto: Butterworths.

Bradach, J. L., and R. G. Eccles. 1989. "Price, Authority, and Trust: From Ideal Types to Plural Forms." *Annual Review of Sociology.* 15:97–118.

Burns, Tom, and Gerald M. Stalker. 1961. *The Management of Innovation.* London: Tavistock.

Burt, Ronald S. 1982. *Toward a Structural Theory of Action.* New York: Academic Press.

Cash, James I., and Benn R. Konsynski. 1985. "IS Redraws Competitive Boundaries." *Harvard Business Review* 64 (Mar.–Apr.): 134–142.

Cherry, Colin. 1978. *On Human Communication: A Review, a Survey and a Criticism* 3d ed. Cambridge, MA: MIT Press.

Child, John. 1984. "New Technology and Developments in Management Organization." *Omega* 12(3):211–223.

Child, John. 1987. "Information Technology, Organization, and the Response to Strategic Challenges." *California Management Review* (Fall): 33–50.

Collins, Randall. 1987. "Interaction Ritual Chains, Power and Property: The Micro-Macro Connection as an Empirically Based Theoretical Problem." In J. C. Alexander et al., eds., *The Micro-Macro Link.* Berkeley: University of California Press.

Crawford, Albert M. 1982. "Corporate Electronic Mail—A Communication Intensive Application of Information Technology." *MIS Quarterly* 6:1–14.

Culnan, Mary J., and M. Lynne Markus. 1987. "Information Technologies." In Frederick M. Jablin, Linda L. Putnam, Karlene H. Roberts, and Lyman W. Porter, eds., *Handbook of Organizational Communication.* Beverly Hills: Sage, pp. 420–443.

Daft, Richard L., and Robert H. Lengel. 1984. "Information Richness: A New Approach to Managerial Behavior and Organization Design." *Research in Organizational Behavior* 6:191–233.

Donnellon, Anne. 1986. "Language and Communication in Organizations." In H. P. Sims and Associates, eds., *The Thinking Organization.* San Francisco: Jossey-Bass.

Drucker, Peter. 1988. "The Coming of the New Organization." *Harvard Business Review* 66 (Jan.–Feb.): 35–53.

———. 1990. *The New Realities.* New York: Harper and Row.

Dumaine, Brian. 1991. "Bureaucracy Busters." *Fortune* (June 17): 36–50.

Eccles, Robert G., and Dwight Crane. 1988. *Doing Deals: Investment Banks at Work.* Boston: Harvard Business School Press.

Eccles, Robert G., and Nitin Nohria. 1991. "The Post-Structuralist Organization." Working paper, Harvard Business School.

Elster, Jon. 1989. *The Cement of Society.* New York: Cambridge University Press.

Forester, Tom. 1987. *High-Tech Society: The Story of the Information Technology Revolution.* Cambridge, MA: MIT Press.

Fulk, Janet, and William Dutton. 1984. "Videoconferencing as an Organizational Information Processing System: Assessing the Role of Electronic Meetings." *Systems, Objectives, Solutions* 4:105–118.

Galbraith, Jay. 1973. *Designing Complex Organizations.* Reading, MA: Addison-Wesley.

Garfinkel, Harold. 1967. *Studies in Ethnomethodology.* Englewood Cliffs, NJ: Prentice-Hall.

Geneen, Harold. 1984. *Managing.* Garden City: Doubleday.

Goffman, Erving. 1963. *Behavior in Public Places.* New York: Free Press.

Granovetter, Mark. 1973. "The Strength of Weak Ties." *American Journal of Sociology* 78(6):1360–1380.

Granovetter, Mark S. 1985. "Economic Action and Social Structure: The Problem of Embeddedness." *American Journal of Sociology* 91:481–510.

Gronn, P. C. 1983. "Talk as the Work: The Accomplishment of School Administration." *Administrative Science Quarterly* 28:1–21.

Hackman, J. Richard. 1990. *Groups That Work (and Those That Don't).* San Francisco: Jossey-Bass.

Hackman, J. R., and C. G. Morris. 1978. "Group Tasks, Group Interaction Process, and Group Performance Effectiveness: A Review and Proposed Integration." In L. Berkowitz, ed., *Group Processes.* New York: Academic Press, pp. 1–55.

Hafner, Katie, and John Markoff. 1991. *Cyberpunk: Outlaws and Hackers on the Computer Frontier.* New York: Simon and Schuster.

Hedlund, Gunnar. 1986. "The Hypermodern MNC: A Heterarchy?" *Human Resource Management* (Spring): 9–35.

Heimer, Carol. 1992. "Doing Your Job *and* Helping Your Friends: Universalistic Norms about Obligations to Particular Others in Networks." Chapter 5, this volume.

Heydebrand, W. V. 1989. "New Organizational Forms." *Work and Occupations* 16(3):323–357.

Hiltz, Roxanne S., and Murray Torhoff. 1978. *Network Nation: Human Communication Via Computers.* Reading, MA: Addison-Wesley.

Huber, George P. 1984. "The Nature and Design of Post-Industrial Organization." *Management Science* 30:928–951.

Keen, Peter G. W. 1987. "Telecommunications and Organizational Choice." *Communications Research* 14(5):588–606.

Kidder, Tracy. 1981. *The Soul of a New Machine.* Boston: Atlantic Monthly Press.

Kiesler, Sara. 1986. "The Hidden Messages in Computer Networks." *Harvard Business Review* 64 (Jan.–Feb.): 46–60.

Kiesler, Sara, Jane Seigel, and Timothy W. McGuire. 1984. "Social Psychological Aspects of Computer-Mediated Communication." *American Psychologist* 39(10):1123–1134.

King, John. 1991. Personal communication.

Kotter, John. 1990. *A Force for Change.* New York: Free Press.

Leavitt, Harold J., and Thomas Whisler. 1958. "Management in the 1980s." *Harvard Business Review* 36 (Nov.–Dec.): 41–48.

Lincoln, James R. 1982. "Intra (and Inter-) Organizational Networks." In Samuel B. Bacharach, ed., *Research in the Sociology of Organizations*, Vol. 1. Greenwich, CT: JAI Press.

Lyon, David. 1988. *The Information Society: Issues and Illusions.* Cambridge: Polity.

Malone, Thomas W., and John F. Rockart. 1991. "Computers, Networks, and the Corporation." *Scientific American* 265(3):128–137.

Marsden, Peter V. 1990. "Network Data and Measurement." *Annual Review of Sociology* 16:435–463.

Marvin, Carolyn. 1988. *When Old Technologies Were New: Thinking About Electronic Communication in the Late Nineteenth Century.* New York: Oxford University Press.

McKenney, James L., Michael H. Zack, and Victor S. Doherty. 1992. "Complementary Communication Media: A Comparison of Electronic Mail and Face-to-Face Communication in a Programming Team." Chapter 10, this volume.

Miles, Raymond E., and Charles C. Snow. 1986. "Network Organizations: New Concepts for New Forms." *California Management Review* 28:62–73.

Mills, Quinn. 1990. *The Rebirth of the Corporation.* New York: Wiley.

Mitchell, J. C. 1974. "Social Networks." *Annual Review of Anthropology* 3:279–299.

Nolan, Richard L., and Alex J. Pollock. 1986. "Organization and Architecture, or Architecture and Organization." *Stage by Stage* 6(5):1–10.

Nolan, Richard L., Alex J. Pollock, and James P. Ware. 1988. "Creating the 21st Century Organization." *Stage by Stage* 8(4):1–11.

———. 1989. "Toward the Design of Network Organizations." *Stage by Stage* 9(1):1–12.

Nyce, Edward H., and Richard Groppa. 1983. "Electronic Mail at MHT." *Management Technology* (May): 65–72.

Piore, Michael J., and Charles F. Sabel. 1984. *The Second Industrial Divide.* New York: Basic.

Pool, I. de Sola. 1983. *Forecasting the Telephone: A Retrospective Assessment.* Norwood, NJ: Ablex.

Poster, Mark. 1990. *The Mode of Information.* Chicago: Chicago University Press.

Powell, W. W. 1990. "Neither Market Nor Hierarchy: Network Forms of Organization." *Research in Organizational Behavior* 12:295–336.

Rice, Faye. 1991. "Champions of Communication." *Fortune* (June 3): 111–120.

Rockhart, John F., and James E. Short. 1991. "The Networked Organization and the Management of Interdependence." In Michael Scott-Morton, ed., *The Corporation of the 1990s.* New York: Oxford.

Schegloff, Emanuel A. 1987. "Between Micro and Macro: Contexts and Other

Connections." In J. C. Alexander et al., eds., *The Micro-Macro Link*. Berkeley: University of California Press.

Schlenker, B. 1980. *Impression Management*. Belmont, CA: Wadsworth.

Short, J., E. Williams, and B. Christie. 1976. *The Social Psychology of Telecommunications*. London: Wiley.

Solomon, Jolie. 1990. "As Electronic Mail Loosens Inhibitions, Impetuous Senders Feel Anything Goes." *The Wall Street Journal* (Oct. 12): B1.

Sproull, Lee, and Sara Kiesler. 1986. "Reducing Social Context Cues: Electronic Mail in Organizational Communication." *Management Science* 32(11):1492–1512.

———. 1991. "Computers, Networks, and Work." *Scientific American* 265(3):116–127.

Stone, Rosanne A. 1991. "Will the Real Body Please Stand Up? Boundary Stories about Virtual Cultures." In Michael Benedikt, ed., *Cyberspace: First Steps*. Cambridge, MA: MIT Press.

Thorelli, H. B. 1986. "Networks: Between Markets and Hierarchies." *Strategic Management Journal* 7:37–51.

Touraine, Alain. 1971. *The Post-Industrial Society*. Trans. by Leonard F. X. Mayhew. New York: Random House.

Trevino, L. K., R. H. Lengel, and R. L. Daft. 1987. "Media Symbolism, Media Richness, and Media Choice in Organizations: A Symbolic Interactionist Perspective." *Communication Research* 14(5):553–574.

Walton, Richard E. 1989. *Up and Running: Integrating Information Technology and the Organization*. Boston: Harvard Business School Press.

Wellman, Barry, and S. D. Berkowitz, eds. 1988. *Social Structures: A Network Approach*. New York: Cambridge University Press.

Williams, E. 1977. "Experimental Comparisons of Face-to-Face and Mediated Communications: A Review." *Psychological Bulletin* 84:963–976.

Zuboff, Shoshana. 1988. *In the Age of the Smart Machine: The Future of Work and Power*. New York: Basic Books.

ORGANIZATIONAL-ENVIRONMENTAL RELATIONS AS INTERORGANIZATIONAL NETWORKS

Strategic Alliances in
Commercial Biotechnology

Stephen R. Barley, John Freeman,
and
Ralph C. Hybels

INTRODUCTION

Notions of resource dependence, power, and exchange have long been central to theories of organizations and their environments. Such theories often begin with an ecological premise: all organizations rely on their environment for essential resources. However, unlike biological entities, organizations cannot exploit their environments directly because other organizations usually control the resources they need. Therefore organizations must engage in exchange if they are to survive. An organization may turn to some organizations for financing, to others for personnel, and to still others for information, raw materials, or political support. When exchange relations and their underlying dependencies endure, stratification of influence occurs and a power structure emerges.

Although studies of resource dependence have contributed greatly to our understanding of interorganizational relations, they have traditionally done so by focusing on individual firms and their immediate partners in exchange. Researchers have paid little attention to relations among the partners or to the partners' relations with organizations not tied to the focal firm. The organization-centered perspective of resource dependence has therefore promulgated, however unwittingly, a fragmented view of the system of interorganizational exchange. In reality, the extent to which organizations are constrained by exchange relations is likely to be far

This research was supported by National Science Foundation grant SES-8811489. Computations were supported by the Cornell Supercomputer Center, which is supported by the National Science Foundation and New York State. The authors thank Carol Murphree for her assistance with the research.

greater than even resource-dependence theory implies. Not only are organizations suspended in multiple, complex, and overlapping webs of relations, but the webs are likely to exhibit structural patterns that are invisible from the perspective of a single organization caught in the tangle. To detect overarching structures, one has to rise above the individual firm and analyze the system as a whole.

Aided by faster computers and new analytic tools, researchers have recently begun to explore the systemic structures of "interorganizational networks." In general, the literature on interorganizational networks can be grouped into two streams according to the type of organizations examined. One stream has focused primarily on nonprofit community service organizations (Laumann and Pappi 1976; Laumann, Galaskiewicz, and Marsden 1978; Galaskiewicz 1979; Knoke and Rogers 1979; Boje and Whetten 1981), while the other has centered on profit-making firms (Mariolis 1975; Burt 1979, 1980a, 1983; Galaskiewicz and Wasserman 1981; Gogel and Koenig 1981; Mizruchi 1981; Mintz and Schwartz 1985). Both streams have strengths and weaknesses.

Local community studies are notable for their sensitivity to multiplexity, the fact that organizations may be tied to each other in numerous ways: for instance, by exchanges of money, personnel, client referrals, and political support. Such studies usually portray interorganizational networks as richly connected, stratified systems of dependencies. However, almost by definition, local community studies focus on small sets of relatively heterogenous organizations located in geographically bounded regions. The geographical boundaries of a local community obscure important exchange relations with organizations located elsewhere. A more serious deficiency is that local community studies rarely include multiple representatives of the same population of organizations. Hence it is difficult to determine whether most organizations of a given type typically play similar roles in exchange networks.

In contrast, network studies of profit-making firms generally involve large numbers of organizations as well as multiple representatives of a variety of organizational populations. Their broader scope allows one to more readily grasp the complexity of the network and the roles commonly played by particular types of organizations. For instance, researchers have repeatedly found that banks are the most central actors in networks formed by interlocking directorates (Mariolis 1975; Gogel and Koenig 1981; Mizruchi 1981; Fennema 1982; Mintz and Schwartz 1985). However, network studies of profit-making firms also evidence common limitations, the most important of which has been a failure to examine a sufficiently broad range of relationships. The vast majority of studies have focused exclusively on either equity holdings or overlapping boards of directors. The failure to consider multiple relations undoubtedly generates a distorted view of how influence is structured in a multiorganizational system. For example, highly central actors in a financial network are unlikely to be central in a network of marketing relationships. Our knowledge of relations among profit-making firms would be vastly improved by retaining the local community study's concern with multiplexity, while continuing to sample multiple members of the various populations associated with an organizational community, or what Knoke and Rogers (1979) term an "organizational field." An organizational field can be understood as a community of organizations that have some functional interest in common—for instance, criminal justice, or mental health, or the manufacture and sale of computers. Membership in an organizational field is not limited to organizations directly involved in developing, producing, or distributing the products or services associated with a functional area; fields also include organizations that provide funding, that have regulatory oversight, and that offer ancillary services.

However, investigations of multiplex relations among profit-making firms confront significant difficulties. As local community studies demonstrate so well, many relationships among organizations are informal and undocumented. Corporations often have proprietary and even legal reasons for keeping informal alliances secret. Although publicly held firms are required by the Securities and Exchange Commission to inform investors and regulators of board memberships and major equity holdings, they often do not announce other types of relationships, even to stockholders. Private firms are especially unlikely to divulge information because they face few requirements to make their business activities public. The sheer size of many corporations also complicates the gathering of information about interorganizational relations, as arrangements made by subsidiaries may not be widely known even among top management.

Furthermore, there is reason to believe that formal alliances among corporations were relatively rare until recently (Harrigan 1985; Gomes-Casseres 1988). To be sure, stable structures of supply and distribution have long been common in industry. However, researchers have had easy access to such information only in oligopolistic industries, such as automobile manufacturing, where alliances have functioned as proxies for vertical integration (e.g., Masten, Meehan, and Snyder 1989). In such instances the obvious dominance of a few central firms and the stability of relationships over time have rendered the power structure relatively transparent. Consequently, the limited availability of information and the marginal legality of formal cooperation has traditionally forced researchers to examine and reexamine the few lawful and well-documented types of relations that exist among publicly owned firms.

In recent years new opportunities for research have emerged as alliances among corporations have become more common and more widely publicized. This historical change resulted, in part, from the Reagan administration's more laissez-faire regulatory philosophy (especially with regard to the antitrust laws), the weakening of the Federal Trade Commission, and the passage of legislation designed to further organizational cooperation. In retrospect, the shift in governmental policy and the change in corporate behavior appear to have been associated with increased competition from Japan, whose economic success has been widely attributed to stable organizational alliances.

But while political and economic circumstances may explain the increasing prevalence of organizational alliances, they cannot explain why organizations in certain sectors of the economy have taken greater advantage of the freedom to collaborate. Further insight into the relative propensity to collaborate may be gained by studying industrial sectors where alliances have become especially frequent. In no area of economic endeavor have alliances become more common or crucial than in the recent commercialization of biotechnology.

HISTORY OF THE BIOTECHNOLOGY COMMUNITY

Physics and chemistry have been intimately bound to industrial development since the late nineteenth century, when firms such as Westinghouse and Du Pont established the first industrial research and development labs.[1] But biology played a relatively insignificant role in the economy until the late 1960s. The 1970s witnessed a rapid acceleration of commercial interest in biological research, sparked by two pathbreaking discoveries that revolutionized molecular biology and transformed its standing in the public eye.

In 1973, Herbert Boyer of Stanford and Stanley Cohen of the University of California at San Francisco developed a technique for inserting pieces of frog DNA (via plasmids) into the genes of the bacterium *E. coli*. Not only did the modified *E. coli* produce proteins encoded by the foreign DNA, but even more miraculously, their offspring exhibited the same capacity. Industrialists and investors immediately recognized the potential of the technique now known as recombinant DNA (RDNA): Boyer and Cohen had essentially proven the feasibility of transforming everyday microorganisms into cheap and prolific facilities for manufacturing proteins characteristic of other species. Products that have since been made with recombinant techniques include growth hormone, interferon, and human insulin.

In 1975, Cesar Milstein and Georges Kohler of the British Medical Research Council successfully fused cells from a mouse myeloma with cells derived from mouse B-lymphocytes to create a "hybridoma." Hybridomas are self-replicating cell lines that secrete antibodies and can be grown in vitro[2] or in the peritoneal cavity of a mouse. Because each hybridoma produces one and only one type of antibody, the antibodies were dubbed "monoclonal" (MAbs). Earlier "polyclonal" techniques were by comparison imprecise, as they yielded serums containing multiple antibodies. Milstein and Kohler's work proved to be a boon for the production of vaccines and immunoassays. By creating and propagating an appropriate hybridoma, one could now engineer or clone large quantities of a specific antibody at low cost.

In 1974, a number of scientists involved in RDNA research called for a moratorium on further research until the technology's risks could be more adequately assessed (Berg 1974). The call led to the now-famous

Asilomar Conference of 1975, during which most leading American molecular biologists ratified the notion of a voluntary moratorium as well as the formation of what became the Recombinant DNA Advisory Committee (RAC) (Krimsky 1982). The resulting slowdown in the commercialization of biotechnology was reversed in 1976 when the U.S. Patent Office granted Stanford University and the University of California rights to Boyer and Cohen's technique for using plasmids to transfer foreign DNA to a microorganism.

Almost immediately, alert venture capitalists and management consultants began to search the campuses of major universities for molecular biologists willing to found new enterprises to exploit the commercial potential of RDNA and monoclonal antibodies (Yoxen 1983). In the same year that the RDNA patent was granted, Guy Swanson, an enterprising venture capitalist, encouraged Boyer to found Genentech, which soon became one of the leading firms in biotechnology. Over the next four years, approximately 45 similar firms were formed in the United States to take advantage of the opportunities opened by the new technologies.[3]

On October 14, 1980, Genentech issued its first public stock offering at $35 per share. Within an hour after the market opened, Genentech's stock was trading at $89 per share, a record rise for Wall Street (Teitelman 1989). The event triggered a period of intense speculation in the stocks of new biotechnology companies. The strong market for initial offerings also encouraged venture capitalists to fund a bevy of new startups. Over the next two years, at least 155 dedicated biotechnology firms (DBFs) were founded in the United States alone.

Thus by 1982 recombinant DNA and hybridoma technology were widely viewed as having opened a vast commercial frontier where genetically engineered microorganisms would be used to degrade wastes and manufacture medical and industrial products. Some entrepreneurs even dreamed of directly manipulating the genetic code of higher organisms, including humans. The promise of spectacular profits was particularly acute in the areas of new drugs, new diagnostics, waste treatment, new plants, and even genetically altered livestock. As a result, interest in commercializing the technologies rapidly spanned traditional industries and organizational populations.

By the mid-1980s, over 500 freestanding dedicated biotechnology firms had been established worldwide to pursue some form of genetic engineering. Because many of these firms engage in research applicable to a wide variety of contexts, they cannot easily be assigned to a single industry even though they are typically quite small. Moreover, numerous leading firms in the pharmaceutical, chemical, agricultural, and energy industries have established their own research programs on RDNA and cell fusion technology. Still other firms have been established exclusively to fund biotechnology ventures or to provide necessary equipment and supplies. Taken together, dedicated biotechnology firms, investors, government agencies, universities, suppliers, private research labs, and the large diversified corporations with which all are associated can be viewed as an organizational community: a system held together by commensalistic and symbiotic ties (Hawley 1950, 1986).

Biotechnology and Microelectronics

Many observers have claimed that commercial biotechnology heralds a new industrial era similar to that spawned by microelectronics. At first glance, the biotechnology community does appear to have much in common with the semiconductor and computer industries. Both have been characterized by rapid technical change, small innovative firms, sizable expenditures on R&D, massive infusions of venture capital, and rapid growth (Office of Technology Assessment 1984; Oakey 1984). However, there are important differences between the two technical communities that help explain why strategic alliances have played a more central role in biotechnology.

Whereas most small computer firms have been founded by engineers who previously worked for large companies in the microelectronics industry (Brittain and Freeman 1980; Rogers and Larsen 1984), most biotechnology firms have been established by scientists associated with universities. Although experienced engineers often possess some knowledge of production and marketing as well as R&D, academic scientists typically have little knowledge of either. Most new microelectronics firms have also immediately sought to produce a device whose prototype may have already been developed. In contrast, biotechnology firms have generally been founded to pursue applied and, in some cases, even basic research in molecular biology. Development and production may be the firm's ultimate goal, but because of biotechnology's stage of scientific development, most DBFs do not succeed in producing anything analogous to an engineering prototype for many years. Consequently, not only do many new DBFs lack production facilities as well as products to take into development, but their founders are likely to lack the experience necessary for bringing products to market (Dubinskas 1985).

The nature of R&D and the product life cycle continue to differ even after the biotechnology firm has begun to produce a product. The development phase of a biotechnology product is likely to last much longer than that of a computer or a microelectronic component (Office of Technology Assessment 1984). In part, the difference reflects the fact that biotechnology is more a basic than an applied science. However, the development cycle's length is also exacerbated by the fact that biotechnology's most promising products, therapeutic drugs and diagnostic assays for humans and animals, are subject to stringent regulatory procedures that have no parallel in microelectronics.

Another important difference is that microelectronic devices have commonly been sold as components of more complex systems. Their customers are manufacturing companies. In contrast, most of biotechnology's products are sold directly to end users or to professionals they employ. For instance, agricultural biotechnology companies sell directly to farmers and veterinarians; pharmaceutical firms sell to physicians or their patients; and manufacturers of diagnostics are likely to sell their kits directly to laboratories that perform tests for referring physicians. Marketing to end users is more expensive than marketing to manufacturers.

It is also worth noting that established electronics corporations possess competencies and facilities that allow them to enter quickly markets that smaller firms open. In contrast, established corporations in the pharmaceutical, chemical, and agricultural industries have only recently begun to develop expertise in biotechnology. Command of the science still resides largely with academic scientists and small firms. Furthermore, the markets for many of biotechnology's products are limited and thus not amenable to the economies of scale that have made production factors crucial to competition in the electronics industry.

Finally, unlike microelectronics, biotechnology's fate is linked to an uncertain legal environment and shifting public opinion. Biotechnical research poses hazards that are not present in the development of electronic products. The risk of accidentally releasing a dangerous organism may not be as serious as it is sometimes portrayed (see, e.g., Howard and Rifkin 1977), but the fear of such a possibility has engendered more regulation of research than has ever occurred in other high-tech businesses. Consequently, surprise court rulings, congressional action, and public outcries have all had dramatic implications for the structure of alliances among organizations in the biotechnology community.

Strategic Alliances in Biotechnology

The particular constraints and opportunities surrounding commercial biotechnology appear to have compelled organizations to form an elaborate web of formal alliances. The indeterminate but vibrant link between the science and the technology of molecular biology poses severe uncertainties for corporate activity. Frontiers of knowledge in molecular biology and genetic engineering are changing more rapidly than in most other sciences, basic or applied. Consequently even well-heeled corporations cannot hope to track, much less fully exploit, relevant scientific advances by relying solely on the published literature and their own research operations. Instead, relevant technical knowledge is more efficiently obtained by direct access to research conducted elsewhere. As a result many diversified corporations have sought access to knowledge and skills by forming alliances with DBFs (Teitelman 1989), and DBFs and diversified corporations alike have sought to develop and maintain ties with universities and research institutes where important breakthroughs in molecular biology routinely occur (Kinney 1986).

If established corporations are motivated to ally themselves with dedicated biotechnology companies to gain a window on the technology, DBFs are in turn motivated to form alliances for financial reasons. Small biotechnology companies often require assistance from larger firms to overcome barriers to entry. Faced with the high cost of obtaining government approval for products, many DBFs have chosen to "contract out" their clinical trials. Similarly, many dedicated biotechnology firms have established marketing agreements with larger firms to gain access to established distribution channels and foreign markets. Manufacturing agreements have been attractive to small firms without production facilities, and some DBFs have even been willing to license their technology in order to ease cash flow problems. Thus in commercial biotechnology it has become commonplace for smaller firms to broker scientific and technical expertise in exchange for access to the larger firms' financial resources, manufacturing capabilities, and marketing expertise.

The volatility of financial markets in recent years has been an additional incentive for DBFs to form alliances. During the early 1980s, venture capitalists provided most of the funding for biotechnology startups, in return for a significant proportion of the firms' equity. Largely as a consequence of the extended development cycle, however, even the oldest DBFs have yet to show more than trivial returns on sales (Office of Technology Assessment 1988; Burrill 1989). The high cost of research and development, clinical trials, and marketing have in most cases now exceeded the capacity of venture-capital financing.

Venture-capital firms normally are funded through partnerships, which usually have a fixed date for payback. Venture capitalists are reluctant to fund enterprises when they suspect a low probability of recapturing their investment within a few years (Carleton 1986). The stock market crash in 1987 deflated venture capital's interest in biotechnology, an interest that had already begun to wane (Teitelman 1989), and signaled the end of the mania for initial public offerings. The amount of venture capital available to biotechnology peaked in the early 1980s and has since declined precipitously (Burrill 1989). Moreover, because most dedicated biotechnology firms lack sufficient collateral, most banks have been unwilling to provide loans (Office of Technology Assessment 1984). Consequently, DBFs have experienced increasing pressure to finance research and development by establishing ties to other organizations with commercial interests in biotechnology.

The R&D limited partnership has been an important vehicle for financing commercial biotechnology. Under such an agreement, the DBF usually assumes the role of general partner and therefore all liability. The limited partners, typically wealthy individuals or corporations, buy a share of the future profits or losses from a particular development program. Unlike their counterparts in equity financing agreements, limited partners do not participate in the management of the firm. Limited partners neither sit on the firm's board nor vote as shareholders.

According to the Office of Technology Assessment (1984:270), biotechnology's reliance on contract research has been without parallel in any commercial area, with the possible exception of small defense contractors. Agreements between DBFs and established firms regarding later stages of product development have also been common. Under the typical product-development agreement, an established firm funds the development of a new application and acquires an exclusive license to market the product, while the DBF retains patent rights and receives royalties. In sum, a unique combination of technical, social, political, and economic forces have made commercial biotechnology a hotbed for strategic alliances. As such, it provides an ideal setting for studying interorganizational relations and the social networks they form.

THE STUDY

Since 1988, we have been investigating the networks formed by strategic alliances among organizations in the biotechnology community. Ultimately we aim not only to describe the historical development of the networks, but also to propose a hybrid approach to studying organizations and their environments that synthesizes insights and methods drawn from network analysis and population ecology (Barley and Freeman 1988; Freeman and Barley 1990). In this study, our objectives are more modest. Here we provide a preliminary glimpse at the structure of the biotechnology community and its alliances. Our findings must be regarded as tentative, because data collection and analysis are still very much in progress.[4]

Sources of Data

We compiled our data from a variety of biotechnology-oriented directories, the most important of which was *Bioscan*, an annual directory published by Oryx Press. All information on the alliances reported in this paper are drawn from the 1988 volume of *Bioscan*. Data on alliances are therefore current through 1987. Data on the characteristics of organizations involved in the alliances were drawn from the 1990 as well as the 1988 volumes of *Bioscan*.[5] Several additional directories were used to identify organizations involved in the biotechnology community: (1) *Genetic Engineering and Biotechnology Yearbook, 1985*; (2) *Genetic Engineering and Biotechnology Firms Worldwide Directory, 1985*; (3) *Bioengineering News World Biotech Company Directory: 1985–1986*; (4) *The Biotechnology Directory, 1986: Products, Companies, Research and Organizations*; (5) *Biotechnology Guide, U.S.A.* (Dibner 1988); and (6) *Sixth Annual GEN Guide to Biotechnology Companies* (1987).

Our goal has been to identify all United States-based organizations that have contributed to the commercialization of biotechnology. In addition, we have sought to identify all organizations—both American and foreign—with which these U. S. firms have established formal ties as well as all organizations with which their partners are allied. In short, we have employed a two-step snowball sampling strategy. From the directories we drew information on a number of organizational attributes: each organization's country of origin, whether it was publicly or privately owned, its involvement in specific markets, and its use of particular technologies.

The resulting data base contains information on ten of the most important types of organizations composing the biotechnology community:

- *Dedicated biotechnology firms* established primarily to pursue biotechnological research and development in areas of commercial promise (e.g., Biogen, Genentech, Cetus, Centocor);

- *Universities* that carry on basic or applied research in biotechnology through either their academic departments or through centers dedicated to biotechnical research (e.g., MIT, Stanford, University of California, Davis);

- Private or public *research institutes* that conduct research in one or more areas of biotechnology (e.g., The Whitehead Institute, Fred Hutchins Cancer Research Center);

- *Diversified corporations* in the chemical, pharmaceutical, energy, and agricultural industries that either conduct R&D on biotechnology or that fund research by dedicated biotechnology firms, universities, or research institutes (e.g., Schering-Plough, Monsanto, Shell Oil, Kodak, Corning Glass);

- *Investors* including banks, pension funds, venture capital firms, and other organizations that hold substantial equity in one or more dedicated biotechnology firms (e.g., Biotechnology Investments Ltd., Inco Securities Corporation, Hambrecht & Quist);

- *Government agencies* that have jurisdiction over the products and processes of biotechnical research or that provide grants for genetic research (e.g., the U.S. Food and Drug Administration, the U.S. Department of Agriculture, the National Institutes of Health);

- *Hospitals* involved in clinical trials or the development of new therapeutics and diagnostics based on biotechnological research (e.g., Massachusetts General Hospital, City of Hope);

- *State biotechnology centers* that fund conferences, sponsor research, and disseminate information on genetic engineering (e.g., The North Carolina Biotechnology Center);

- *Suppliers of goods* that provide equipment, chemicals, and biologicals necessary for RDNA and cell fusion research or bioprocess engineering (e.g., Aalto Scientific Ltd., Beckman Instruments, Cambridge Technology, Inc.);

- *Suppliers of services* that consult with other organizations on such topics as bioprocess production and system scale-up (e.g., Bolt, Beranek and Newman, Biotechnology Review Associates).

Whenever possible, organizations were assigned to one of the ten categories based on information contained in the directories. Organizations known to be involved in biotechnology through strategic alliances but about which there was insufficient information to render a classification were coded as *not otherwise classified*.

As of December 1989, we had identified 3,056 organizations that either have or have had some form of involvement in the U.S. biotechnology community. When subsidiaries are subsumed under their parents, the data base contains information on 1,939 organizational families. As can be seen in Table 12-1, when aggregated to the corporate level, 525 (or 27%) of the organizations are dedicated biotechnology firms, nearly three quarters of which are freestanding firms. Diversified corporations that pursue in-house research on biotechnology, that manufacture or market products made by biotechnical processes, or that have strategic alliances with one or more dedicated biotechnology firms account for 13% of the organizations. The 11% that are organizations primarily involved in basic research include 127 universities, 81 research institutes, and 8 research hospitals.

The remainder of the data base consists of (1) venture-capital firms and other investors (12%); (2) firms that supply equipment, reagents, and other materials necessary for biotechnological research and production (11%); (3) other organizations somehow involved in biotechnology, including state biotechnology centers, trade associations, repositories for storage of organisms and cell tissue, suppliers of services, and firms about which we have insufficient information for clear classification but which appear to be dedicated biotechnology firms (11%); and (4) organizations that we have not yet been able to classify (15%).

In addition to collecting data on organizations involved in commercial biotechnology, we studied their formal relationships. Organizational alliances were coded as dyadic ties.[6] As of December 1989, the data base contained information on 3,441 ties distributed among 10 different types of relationships: (1) equity holdings; (2) the provision of research grants; (3) involvement in a joint venture; (4) R&D agreements; (5) product development agreements in which research activity is not involved; (6) research agreements in which product development is not involved;

Table 12-1

Types of Organizations Involved in the U.S. Biotechnology Community

TYPE OF ORGANIZATION	N	%
Dedicated biotechnology firm	525	27
Diversified corporation	257	13
University	127	7
Research institute	81	4
Hospital	8	<1
Government agency	47	2
Investor	229	12
Supplier of goods	208	11
Supplier of services	60	3
State biotechnology center	8	<1
Trade association	2	<1
Repository	2	<1
Potential DBF	95	5
Not otherwise classified	290	15
TOTAL	1939	100

Table 12-2

Frequency of Various Types of Relationships in the U.S. Biotechnology Community

TYPE OF RELATIONSHIP	N	%
Equity holdings	792	23
Marketing agreement	551	16
Licensing agreement	478	14
Development agreement	463	13
Research agreement	266	8
Joint venture	201	6
R&D agreement	200	6
Manufacturing agreement	140	4
Grant	83	2
Supply agreement	75	2
Unspecified agreement	192	6
TOTAL	3441	100

(7) supply agreements; (8) manufacturing agreements; (9) marketing agreements; and (10) licensing agreements. Each tie's record contains information on the type of relation, the dates on which the relation was formed or dissolved, and the identities of the organizations involved.

As Table 12-2 indicates, agreements pertaining to either research or development are the most frequent type of alliance among members of the biotechnology community. Development agreements, research agreements, and R&D agreements together account for 27% of the ties established by organizations of all types. Equity ties are the next most common form of relationship: 23% of the ties denote equity holdings. Another 16% of the alliances are marketing agreements, while licensing agreements account for 14%. Taken together these seven types of agreements account for 80% of the alliances. Grants (2%), joint ventures (6%), supply agreements (2%), and manufacturing agreements (4%) are far less common.

Finally, in building the data base from the directories we recorded instances of ecologically significant events in the form of organizational histories suitable for event-history analysis. The histories include founding dates and the dates of organizational mergers, acquisitions, spin-offs, splits, bankruptcies, and name changes.

ANALYSES

Ecological Findings

An examination of the foundings of dedicated biotechnology firms of various kinds attests to the shifting sources of funding in commercial biotechnology and underscores the increasing importance of diversified corporations. Figure 12-1 plots the percentage of dedicated biotechnology firms founded annually between 1971 and 1987. The figure presents data

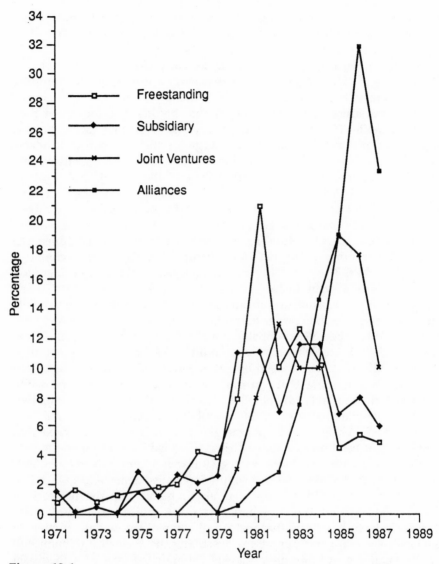

Figure 12-1

Percentage of All Alliances and DBFs Founded Annually by Year of Founding

on three types of DBFs separately: freestanding firms, subsidiaries, and joint ventures. The distribution of foundings clearly differs by type of DBF. Births of freestanding firms peaked in 1981, when 81 organizations or 21% of all freestanding DBF's were founded. Diversified corporations as well as diversifying DBFs began to establish biotechnology subsidiaries earnestly in 1980. The rate of founding subsidiaries remained relatively stable until 1984, after which it declined. The formation of joint ventures peaked in 1985–1986.[7] That the founding of joint ventures in biotechnology is a relatively recent trend can be most clearly seen by noting that 55% of all joint ventures were established after 1984, whereas 75% of all freestanding DBFs were founded before 1984.

These patterns suggest that since the early 1980s there has been a significant shift away from forming freestanding firms toward founding organizations with direct corporate sponsorship. The data are also consistent with the claim that venture capital has become less important than corporate capital. The increasing importance of diversified corporations is further underscored by the recent surge in the number of strategic alliances (see Figure 12-1). In a single year, 1986, 31% of all existing alliances were formed. Even more telling is the fact that 73% of all alliances were formed between 1985 and 1987. As foundings of freestanding and subsidiary biotechnology firms began to decline, the rate of alliance formation markedly increased.

The shift to corporate funding may also be a factor in what appears to be a very uncommon pattern of mortality among dedicated biotechnology firms. Only 54 (9%) of all DBFs in our data base have ceased operation over the entire 15-year history of the biotechnology community's existence.[8] Since the closing of subsidiaries and joint ventures may reflect parental reorganizations rather than market forces, mortality among freestanding DBFs offers a potentially more accurate picture of population dynamics in the biotechnology community. We know of only 24 freestanding DBFs that have ceased operating since 1975. These 24 represent 6% of the freestanding DBFs in our data base. Regardless of how one assesses it, the mortality rate of DBFs is exceptionally low when compared to other populations studied by population ecologists (Hannan and Freeman 1989). Given the recent emergence of DBFs, it is remarkable that they have not been more seriously affected by liabilities of newness.

One explanation for biotechnology's low mortality rate may be that the large number of alliances has simply forestalled a shakeout. Of course a shakeout may still occur, but it is also possible that the network of alliances has altered the ecological dynamics typical of a competitive market. Indeed, it may be that instead of competitive models, models of symbiosis are more appropriate for describing the ecological dynamics of the biotechnology community. Viewed through the lens of a theory of interorganizational symbiosis, it is conceivable that many DBFs now function as low-cost external sources of research and development for larger corporations.

If the symbiotic thesis is warranted, then one might ask which firms have most benefited from the expanding population of dedicated biotechnology firms. Clearly, DBFs have frequently allied themselves with leading firms of the pharmaceutical, chemical, food, energy, and agricultural industries. However, to make such a claim tells us very little about the relative distribution of power because organizations in these industries are precisely those most likely to be affected by biotechnology. A more intriguing answer to the question is suggested by examining the nationalities of organizations involved in commercial biotechnology.

Nationality

An initial assessment of the extent of international involvement in U.S. biotechnology can be made by perusing Table 12-3, which lists the nationality of organizations in our data base. Not surprisingly, the field is overwhelmingly dominated by American firms: 73% of the organizations are domestic. Nonetheless, two foreign countries have a significant presence: 8% of the organizations are Japanese and 4% are located in the United Kingdom. No other country accounts for more than 2% of the population.

Table 12-3

Organizations Involved in the U.S. Biotechnology Community, by Country of Origin

COUNTRY	N	%
United States	1106	73.0
Japan	113	7.5
United Kingdom	65	4.3
France	28	1.8
Canada	33	2.2
West Germany	23	1.5
Sweden	22	1.5
Netherlands	18	1.2
Italy	13	.9
Australia	17	1.1
Israel	9	.6
Switzerland	11	.7
Belgium	13	.9
Denmark	6	.4
Austria	4	.3
China	8	.5
Finland	5	.3
Taiwan	1	.1
Spain	1	.1
Brazil	1	.1
Hungary	2	.1
India	2	.1
Ireland	2	.1
South Korea	1	.1
Malaysia	1	.1
Norway	2	.1
Singapore	2	.1
Czechoslovakia	1	.1
Hong Kong	1	<.1
Kuwait	1	<.1
New Zealand	1	<.1
Saudi Arabia	1	<.1
Subtotal	1514	100.0
Unknown Country	425	
TOTAL	1939	

The figures reported here are for organizations aggregated to the level of parent firms.

Table 12-4

Number of Alliances that U.S. Organizations Have with Organizations from Selected Regions and Countries

REGION	N	%
United States	1488	64
Western Europe	438	19
Japan	308	13
Canada	42	2
Australia/New Zealand	18	1
Asia (besides Japan)	15	<1
Other Countries	14	<1
TOTAL	2323	101

A somewhat different perspective can be gleaned by examining the nationality of the organizations with whom American firms have established formal ties. Table 12-4 provides an overview. Note that 64% of the alliances established by U.S. firms are with U.S. partners, 13% are with Japanese organizations, while 19% are with Western European companies. No other country or region accounts for more than 2% of the alliances in which U.S. firms are involved. At first glance, the distribution of percentages seem very similar to those in Table 12-2. However, the tendency for American firms to join with partners from specific nations varies considerably by type of alliance.

Table 12-5 presents the number of each type of alliance that U.S. organizations have formed with organizations from various countries and regions. The data clearly indicate that sources of direct funding are overwhelmingly American in origin: U.S. organizations are partners in 74% of the equity ties and 99% of the grants. However, U.S. firms have established a majority of their joint ventures (58%) with foreign partners. Firms from specific regions are also chosen more frequently for some types of alliances than they are for others. For instance, even though Japanese firms are involved in only 13% of all alliances, they are partners in roughly a quarter of the manufacturing and marketing agreements. Similarly, Western European companies are more frequently partners in joint ventures (29%) and supply agreements (29%) than one would anticipate from their general involvement in all alliances (19%).

The data in Table 12-5 suggest that U.S. firms gain access to foreign markets primarily through joint ventures or supply, production, and distribution agreements with foreign corporations. Foreign corporations not only offer DBFs a significant source of funding (they account for 35% of all alliances), but because they are frequently engaged in arrangements that involve the transfer of products or information, they are also likely to be privy to much of the intellectual property formed by American biotechnology firms. The relatively high level of Japanese involvement may appear particularly ominous to some, who view it as foreshadowing an experience similar to that of the computer industry. Such suspicions

Table 12-5

Country of Origin of Partners of U.S. Firms, by Type of Strategic Alliance

TYPE OF ALLIANCE

PARTNER'S COUNTRY	Equity N	%	Grant N	%	JV N	%	R&D N	%	Supply N	%	Manuf. N	%	Market N	%	License N	%	TOTAL N	%
United States	275	74	79	99	53	42	465	69	37	64	56	55	198	49	262	67	1425	65
Western Europe	64	17	1	1	36	29	113	17	17	29	19	19	97	24	65	17	412	19
Japan	24	6	—	—	21	17	72	11	2	3	23	23	92	23	53	14	287	13
Canada	4	1	—	—	3	2	16	2	1	2	—	—	9	2	5	1	38	2
Australia/N.Z.	2	1	—	—	1	1	6	1	—	—	1	1	5	1	2	1	17	<1
Asia not Japan	1	<1	—	—	5	4	1	<1	—	—	1	1	3	1	2	1	13	<1
Other Countries	2	1	—	—	6	5	1	<1	1	2	1	1	2	<1	1	<1	14	<1
TOTAL	372		80		125		674		58		101		406		390		2206	

In this table R&D agreements include any agreement listed in *Bioscan* as an R&D agreement, a development agreement, or a research agreement.

have recently been expressed in the business press. However, the mere fact that a country's firms are frequent partners in specific types of alliances is not a sufficient condition for wielding power in an interorganizational network (Burt 1977; Freeman 1979). To become powerful within a network, organizations must also be relatively central to the network's structure.

Centrality in the Network of Strategic Alliances

Broadly speaking, centrality refers to how critical a point (in this case, an organization) is to the network's global structure. Centrality can be measured in several ways, each of which is associated with a different substantive interpretation. An organization's *degree* centrality is simply the number of other organizations to which the focal organization is tied. Degree is typically used as a measure of an actor's *involvement* in a network (Freeman 1979). An organization tied to ten other organizations is said to be twice as involved as an organization with five such alliances. In contrast, *betweenness* centrality is usually interpreted as a measure of an actor's *power*. An organization garners power over any two organizations when it lies on the shortest path between the two in a given network of relations. For example, if organization A is tied directly to organization B, and organization B is tied directly to organization C, but organizations A and C have no direct ties, then the shortest path (the *geodesic*) between A and C is the two-step path through B. B therefore has power over A and C because it is in a position to broker the flow of information and resources between A and C.

In a network of N members, an organization obtains the highest possible betweenness score when all $N - 1$ other organizations are tied only to that organization. In this case the focal organization would lie on all the geodesics in the network and would be called a *star*. Specifically, a star lies on $[(n - 1)(n - 2)]/2$ geodesics. The *relative betweenness* of a point is a ratio that measures the extent to which a point in a network approaches the betweenness score of a star (Freeman 1979). An organization's relative betweenness can vary from a minimum of 0, when it lies on no geodesics, to a maximum of 1, when the organization is in fact a star.

Each specific type of strategic alliance forms a network that can be analyzed on its own. The separate networks also can be combined into an overarching, multiplex network. We calculated the degree and the relative betweenness of each organization in each separate network as well as in the multiplex network. We proceeded as follows:

After folding subsidiaries into their parents and eliminating defunct organizations, 1,809 organizations remained. These organizations constituted the nodes of our networks. We constructed 10 (k = 10) $N \times N$ adjacency matrices in which cell a_{ijk} was set equal to 1 whenever organization I and organization J were bound by at least one strategic alliance of type K. Otherwise, a_{ijk} was set equal to zero. Each matrix was made symmetric by taking the union of a_{ijk} and a_{jik}. In other words, cell a_{ijk} and cell a_{jik}

were both set equal to one whenever either contained a one, otherwise both were set equal to zero. We also constructed an eleventh matrix to represent the multiplex network formed by considering all ten types of alliances simultaneously. In this matrix, a_{ij} was set equal to one whenever organization I and organization J were bound by at least one alliance of any type. If I and J had no alliances whatsoever, a_{ij} was set equal to zero. As with the individual adjacency matrices, the multiplex matrix was made symmetric by union.

The resulting networks were extremely sparse. In any graph of N points, the number of possible ties (or lines) is equal to $N(N - 1)/2$. The density of a network is the ratio of the number of ties that exist to the number of possible ties. The density of the 10 individual networks ranged from .00004 (4 for every 100,000 possible ties) for the grant network to .0005 (5 for every 10,000 possible ties) for the equity network. The density of the multiplex network was .002. Such sparse networks are to be expected given the large number of actors involved.[9]

After we constructed the adjacency matrices, degree and betweenness scores were calculated for each organization for each individual network as well for the multiplex network.[10] We employed regression analysis to determine what organizational attributes might be associated with greater centrality in biotechnology's networks of strategic alliances. Specifically, we regressed an organization's degree and relative betweenness on the following variables: (1) the age of the firm in 1989; (2) five dummy variables indicating whether the organization was a DBF, a diversified corporation, an investor, a basic research organization, or a supplier of goods; (3) three dummy variables indicating whether the organization was located in the United States, Japan, or Western Europe; and (4) a dummy variable indicating whether the organization was publicly or privately held. After deleting all cases with missing values, the sample was reduced to 466 organizations. Because the results for the individual networks generally parallel the results for the multiplex network, we report only the results for the latter.

Table 12-6 displays the regression analysis of degree centrality in the multiplex network. The data indicate that dedicated biotechnology firms and diversified corporations are more involved in the multiplex network than are other types of organizations. That DBFs and diversified corporations should have higher degree centrality is to be expected, because they are precisely the organizations likely to have the greatest interest in forming strategic alliances.

Publicly held organizations also tend to be more involved than privately held organizations. Two explanations are plausible. The Securities and Exchange Commission requires publicly held organizations to disclose information about certain types of alliances, particularly the identity of any organization that holds a significant block of the firm's stock. Privately held organizations are under no such mandate. Consequently, information on alliances involving publicly held firms may simply be more complete.[11] A second explanation for the greater involvement of publicly

Table 12-6

Organizational Determinants of Degree Centrality in the Multiplex
Network of Alliances

FIRM ATTRIBUTE	COEFFICIENT
Intercept	-0.748
Age	0.219
DBF	2.660[a]
DC	3.974[b]
INV	2.733
UNIV/RI	2.256
SG	0.071
American	-0.078
Japanese	-1.740
W. European	6.250[c]
Public	6.246[c]
R^2	.29
N	466

[a]$p <= .10$ [b]$p <= .05$ [c]$p <= .01$

Key to firm attributes:

Age:	Age in 1989
DBF:	Dedicated biotech firm
DC:	Diversified corporation
INV:	Investor
UNIV/RI:	University or research institute
SG:	Supplier of goods
American:	American organization
Japanese:	Japanese organization
W. European:	Western European organization
Public:	Organization is publicly held

held firms is that they tend to be older and therefore have greater visibility
and more resources. The effects of age and visibility are likely to be most
pronounced among dedicated biotechnology firms. Potential suitors may
consider publicly held biotechnology firms to be more attractive and less
risky partners for a strategic alliance. We suspect that both dynamics contribute to the result.

Finally, Western European organizations appear to be more involved
in the multiplex network than do organizations from other regions. An
examination of similar regressions calculated on the networks of specific
alliances indicated that the result largely reflects the fact that Western
European firms have invested in a large number of U.S. biotechnology
firms, either through direct equity holdings or through the formation of
joint ventures.

Table 12-7 displays regression results for relative betweenness in the
multiplex network. As in the analysis of degree centrality, three conditions are seen to significantly increase an organization's relative betweenness in the network of strategic alliances: being a dedicated biotechnology
firm, being publicly owned, or being Western European. Consequently

Table 12-7

Organizational Determinants of Relative Betweenness in Multiplex
Network of Alliances

FIRM ATTRIBUTE	COEFFICIENT
Intercept	−0.001
Age	3E-05
DBF	0.002[a]
DC	0.003
INV	0.002
UNIV/RI	0.001
SG	−2E-04
American	−6E-04
Japanese	−0.003
W. European	0.005[a]
Public	0.006[c]
R^2	.18
N	466

[a]$p <= .10$ [b]$p <= .05$ [c]$p <= .01$

Key to firm attributes:

Age:	Age in 1989
DBF:	Dedicated biotech firm
DC:	Diversified corporation
INV:	Investor
UNIV/RI:	University or research institute
SG:	Supplier of goods
American:	American organization
Japanese:	Japanese organization
W. European:	Western European organization
Public:	Organization is publicly held

one can argue that such organizations are likely to have greater power in
the biotechnology community because they are best positioned to control
the flow of information and technology. Surprisingly, the coefficient for
being a diversified corporation was not significant. One would think that
large firms should occupy a relatively powerful position in the network,
because they are the primary sources of funds. However, analyses of the
individual networks revealed that diversified corporations are significantly
more likely to have high betweenness scores only in the network of marketing agreements. Dedicated biotech firms have been particularly dependent on large established firms for product positioning and distribution.

   In sum, the results for both measures of centrality indicate that dedicated biotechnology firms and publicly held firms are likely to be more
central than other types of organizations. These findings are entirely predictable, of course. The results for nationality are more intriguing.
Western Europeans appear to have greater access and more influence in
the network of alliances than do the Japanese. This finding may point to
an important but frequently overlooked distinction between commercial
biotechnology and commercial microelectronics. Although the Japanese

are known for their engineering and manufacturing skills, their scientific community is less accomplished. In contrast, the scientific community in Western Europe is generally regarded to be as sophisticated as its American counterpart: the European community is simply smaller. Consequently, while the Japanese have emphasized skills that would enable them to compete in industries that pivot on engineering prowess, they may be positioned less well than the Europeans to compete in an industry so closely tied to basic science. However, as commercial biotechnology matures and as bioprocess engineering becomes commercially more important, the relative position of Japanese firms may change.

Analyses of centrality focus attention on a network's global structure and the position of organizations within that structure. A radically different approach would be to examine the properties of ego networks, those sectors of the network that surround each individual organization. (For an elaboration of the distinction see Burt 1980b, 1982.) A more localized approach would enable one to determine whether distinct patterns of involvement exist and whether these patterns are associated with particular classes or populations of firms. Stable patterns associated with specific populations would provide evidence for distinctive ecological and strategic orientations to commercial biotechnology.

For instance, even though dedicated biotechnology firms are generally more central than other organizations in the network of alliances, there is no reason to believe that all DBFs evidence similar patterns of participation. In fact, one might imagine that DBFs with different goals and attributes would seek different kinds of alliances with different kinds of organizations. In other words, differences in the structure and content of firms' ego networks might indicate their involvement in different niches.

The concept of a niche offers an intriguing means for understanding different patterns of involvement in a network of alliances. In population ecology, niches are typically defined as portions of resource gradients that define the survival space of a specific population of plants, animals, or organizations. Market segmentation and technical specialization represent such portions of resource gradients. First we will map niches as structured flows of multiple resources or, more specifically, as distinct forms of participation in a multiplex network. Later we will examine market distinctions as an additional dimension for understanding niche structure.

Niches and Alliance Patterns

We selected the 149 American DBFs that had degree centrality greater than one in at least one of the ten networks. Having more than one alliance of a given type was taken as an indication that the firm emphasized that type of alliance. For each type of alliance we created a dichotomous variable that indicated whether the organization seemed to emphasize that type of relationship. Each variable assumed a value of one when the organization had two or more alliances of the type represented by the variable; otherwise the variable was set equal to zero. The firms'

Table 12-8

Percentage of Dedicated Biotechnology Firms in Each Strategic Cluster Involved in Particular Alliance Networks

CLUSTER			TYPE OF RELATIONSHIP									
Number	Name	Size	Equity	Grant	Jt.Ven.	R&D	Devel.	Resrch	Supply	Manuf.	Market	License
1	Generalists	8	100	38	50	88	88	88	50	100	100	100
2	Aspiring generalists	18	94	—	56	44	100	67	17	—	78	89
3	Marketers	20	50	—	—	—	5	—	—	—	95	20
4	Developers & marketers w/production-	13	69	—	—	7	100	—	—	—	62	—
5	Developers & marketers w/o production	17	7	—	—	21	71	—	—	71	64	50
6	Captives and initial startups	27	100	—	—	—	—	—	—	—	—	—
7	Applied research labs for hire	7	86	—	14	100	43	—	—	—	—	14
8	Licensers	16	56	6	6	—	25	—	6	—	—	100
9	Basic scientists	11	—	55	18	—	36	—	9	—	—	—
10	Basic research labs for hire	12	42	—	—	8	33	100	17	—	8	33

To be classed as being involved in a network, an organization must have degree ≥ 2.

Table 12-9
Attributes of Dedicated Biotechnology Firms in Each Strategic Cluster

CLUSTER NAME	ATTRIBUTES							
	% Jnt Ven.	% Public	Mean Age	Mean Rel. Bet.	Mean Degree	Mean Ties	Mean # Japanese Ties	Mean % Japanese Ties
Generalists	0	100	12	.029	27	51	10.37	19
Aspiring generalists	6	94	9	.018	18	29	1.97	6
Marketers	0	58	10	.004	6	8	.70	6
Developers & marketers w/ production	0	69	6	.004	7	11	.38	5
Developers & marketers w/o production	7	69	7	.003	6	11	1.14	11
Captives and initial startups	33	25	7	.003	5	7	.15	2
Applied research labs for hire	0	86	8	.008	11	15	.71	7
Licensers	13	67	7	.005	7	9	.50	7
Basic scientists	9	46	9	.002	4	5	.36	5
Basic research labs for hire	8	82	8	.005	6	10	.91	9

values on the ten variables were then submitted to Ward's clustering algorithm.[12] If different types of dedicated biotechnology firms evidenced distinct patterns of involvement, then the algorithm should have clustered firms into groups in which attributes and level of activity in the various networks differed in an interpretable manner.

After inspecting the resulting dendogram, the ten-group clustering was chosen for analysis. Table 12-8 indicates the percentage of each cluster that had more than one alliance of each type. Table 12-9 presents descriptive statistics for the firms in each cluster. The data in Tables 12-8 and 12-9 show that the clusters are coherent and meaningful. Each cluster exhibits distinct characteristics and evidences a unique pattern of involvement in the networks of strategic alliances. We suspect that each cluster represents a distinct niche within the biotechnology community or a different organizational strategy for forming alliances. It is important to note, however, that we use the term "strategy" to encompass only realized strategies (Mintzberg 1978). We make no assumption about the role of managerial volition in shaping an organization's strategic profile.

Members of the first cluster appear to be *generalists*. The cluster is composed of eight of the largest biotechnology firms, all of which have received considerable publicity in the popular and business press: Biogen, Chiron, Collaborative Research, Genentech, Genetics Institute, Genex, Genzyme, and Integrated Genetics. These eight firms are the only DBFs that are involved in every type of alliance. They emphasize R&D-oriented agreements as well as market-oriented agreements. They are the only group involved in manufacturing agreements as well as grants. The generalists are all publicly held and are, on average, older than the firms in the other clusters: their mean age is 12 years. Generalists have many more alliances than members of other clusters (mean is 51) and are bound to more organizations (mean is 27). The generalists also have the highest relative betweenness scores in the multiplex network (mean is .029) and hence should be relatively influential within biotechnology community. Finally, the generalists are most heavily allied with the Japanese: on average, 19% of their alliances are with Japanese firms.

The eighteen organizations in the second cluster are perhaps best thought of as *aspiring generalists*. Like the first cluster, the second is composed of well-known firms such as Advanced Genetic Sciences, Amgen, Calgene, California Biotechnology, Centocor, Cetus, and Molecular Genetics. Aside from the generalists, no other group is involved in more types of alliances. When compared to the generalists, however, the aspiring generalists are less heavily vested in all types of alliances with the exception of development agreements. No aspiring generalist receives grants or is involved in a manufacturing agreement. The aspiring generalists rank second in terms of their average number of ties (mean is 29), the number of firms with which they have alliances (mean is 27), and their relative betweenness in the multiplex network (mean is .018). The average member of the second cluster is three years younger than a generalist and has fewer ties to Japanese corporations. In other words, the aspiring generalists appear to be younger and less well-connected versions of the generalists.

The third cluster is composed of twenty dedicated biotechnology firms whose alliance strategy appears to consist primarily of forming marketing agreements. Not only do 95% of these *marketers* have more than two marketing agreements, but they are involved in few other types of alliances with the exceptions of equity and licensing arrangements. Although the marketers are the second-oldest group (10 years), only two clusters have fewer ties per member (mean is 8). Marketers appear to be firms that can produce and manufacture products but have no marketing capability.

Members of the fourth cluster are similar to those of the third except that they are universally involved in development agreements and have no licensing agreements. The pattern of involvement suggests that members of the fourth cluster may take on development agreements in order to produce products that are in turn marketed by, but not licensed to, other firms. Consequently, we categorize these firms as *developers and marketers with production capacities.*

The fifth cluster may represent *developers and marketers without production capacities.* Like those of the fourth cluster, members of the fifth cluster are heavily vested in development and marketing agreements. Unlike members of the fourth cluster, however, they are also involved in manufacturing and licensing agreements. These activities suggest that the firms have no production capacity, because they either license their products to other companies or contract out for the manufacturing of their products. Aside from the generalists, no other cluster has a higher average percentage of alliances with Japanese firms (11%).

The sixth cluster appears to be composed of *captives and initial startups.* These DBFs either exist primarily to serve one or two organizations or are in the very early stages of activity in which external relations are limited to financial ties. Of the firms in this cluster 33% are joint ventures, and all are the recipients of equity investments by other firms. In fact, captives and startups are involved in no alliance network other than the equity network. As a result, they have the second-lowest number of ties (mean is 7) and are the least likely to be involved with the Japanese (mean is 2%). The captive and startup cluster also contains the fewest publicly held firms (25%).

Dedicated biotechnology firms in the seventh cluster appear to operate as *applied research labs for hire.* These firms are universally involved in R&D agreements and frequently in development-only agreements. Their lack of manufacturing, marketing, and licensing agreements indicates that cluster members may not seek to produce their own products. On average, the applied researchers have the third-highest number of alliances (mean is 15). None are joint ventures and most are publicly owned. The cluster's pattern of involvement suggests that members may have chosen to specialize in doing applied R&D for their strategic partners.

Licensers comprise the eighth cluster. The sixteen dedicated biotechnology firms in this group are universally involved in the licensing network and are only marginally involved in other types of alliances. This cluster may be composed of two types of companies: those that obtain licenses *from* other organizations, and those that license patented processes or products *to* other organizations. Indeed, some may be brokers who license technologies from other organizations and then license them to a third party (Freeman and Barley 1990).

The eleven dedicated biotechnology firms in the ninth cluster have no equity ties and are the most heavily involved in the grants network (55%). Moreover, only 46% of the cluster's firms are publicly held. No other cluster has a lower average number of alliances (mean is 5) or is tied to fewer organizations (mean is 4). Aside from receiving grants, members of the cluster are likely to form only development agreements. The cluster's pattern of alliances suggests that this group specializes in acquiring government grants and research contracts. Since grants are most likely to be awarded for basic research, we label this cluster of dedicated biotechnology firms *basic scientists*.

The final cluster of firms appear to be *basic research labs for hire*. These dedicated biotechnology firms are universally involved in research agreements, which are typically established with larger organizations during the earliest stages of research and development. They differ from the basic scientists in that their funding comes from corporate rather than government sources. They differ from applied research labs insofar as they emphasize research rather than development work. Basic research labs also have more licensing agreements than either basic scientists or applied research labs, which suggests that they specialize in producing products and processes that can be licensed to other organizations for further commercialization.

In summary, the cluster analysis suggests not only that American biotechnology firms engage in different patterns of alliances, but also that these different patterns are associated with firms whose attributes differ in a coherent fashion. Particularly encouraging is the fact that clusters are interpretable both as strategic orientations and niches for organizational survival and growth within the biotechnology community. For instance, some firms have apparently diversified their involvement across all types of alliances and have established relationships with many different partners. This generalist strategy may be characteristic of dedicated biotechnology firms that wish to become major players in the pharmaceutical, chemical, or agricultural industries. By diversifying both partners and ties, a firm not only increases its cash flow and avoids a specialist's niche, but remains relatively autonomous with respect to any one of its partners. This was the strategy pursued by Genentech (Teitelman 1989), although ultimately it was insufficient to preclude takeover by Hoffman-La Roche.

Other dedicated biotechnology firms may have sought out specialized niches by engaging only in particular types of strategic alliances. For instance, applied research labs for hire apparently operate as providers of applied R&D services, whereas basic research labs for hire have specialized in performing basic research for other corporations. Licensers have focused on licensing patentable products and processes, whereas developers and marketers license few products but look to larger organizations for either marketing or manufacturing capabilities. A small subset of American DBFs, the basic scientists, concentrate on acquiring government sponsored research grants or contracts and as a result may compete directly with universities. Finally, some DBFs among the captives and initial startups have linked their fates to one or two diversified corporations and may serve their partners almost as if they were research and development subsidiaries.

Niche and Market Orientation

A second approach for assessing whether a firm's position in the network of strategic alliances indicates involvement in a specifiable niche is to determine whether firms in similar markets engage in similar patterns of alliances. The approach follows from the observation that biotechnology firms operating in different markets face different constraints on strategic action. Dedicated biotechnology firms producing human pharmaceuticals or in vivo diagnostics face formidable costs during later stages of product development. The FDA requires extensive clinical trials before new drugs can be approved for human use. Moreover, drugs and diagnostics are often marketed directly to physicians, which requires a large sales force and sophisticated advertising. These constraints encourage firms to form alliances with pharmaceutical companies that have greater expertise in conducting clinical trials and marketing clinical products.

The contrast between DBFs that produce human hormones and those involved in biomass conversion illustrates how market differences influence a firm's organizational alliances. Human hormones are used in the treatment of glandular dysfunctions, while biomass conversion entails producing energy by degrading waste. Whereas licensing agreements account for 17% of the alliances formed by firms specializing in human hormones, they account for only 9% of the alliances formed by firms specializing in biomass conversion. In contrast, equity investments represent 29% of the alliances formed by biomass firms but only 17% of the alliances formed by hormone-producing firms.

To determine whether markets influence a firm's involvement in the network of strategic alliances, we first classified all DBFs by market and then cross-tabulated markets by the types of alliances in which the firms were involved and by the types of organizations with which they were allied. Each DBF was assigned to one of five broad market categories based on the classification system used in the 1990 edition of *Bioscan*.[13] *Agricultural* products constituted the first market class and included not only the breeding of plants, but also the production of bioherbicides, pesticides, and other botanical products. The *Veterinary* market encompassed such products as veterinary therapeutics and diagnostics, feed additives, and embryos. *Human Diagnostics*, both in vitro and in vivo, formed the third market category. The fourth category, *Human Therapeutics*, included drugs, anticancer agents, vaccines, human hormones, and so forth. All other markets, such as cell tissue culture, biomass, specialty chemicals, and bioprocessing were assigned to the miscellaneous category, *Other*.

To simplify the analysis, we also collapsed the ten types of alliances into five categories. *Manufacturing* and *marketing* agreements remained as previously defined. However, development agreements, research contracts, and R&D agreements were combined into a single category, *R&D agreements*. *Funding* agreements included grants, joint ventures, and equity investments. Finally, supply and licensing agreements were collectively termed *transfer agreements*.

Table 12-10 presents the cross-tabulation of market domain by type of alliance. The data in Table 12-10 clearly suggest that markets do affect the type of alliances that biotechnology firms form: the chi-square test for the presence of an association is strong and significant ($X^2 = 93$; $df = 16$; $p < .001$). The row marginals indicate that firms producing human therapeutics or veterinary products engage in many more alliances than do firms in other markets. Dedicated biotechnology firms operating in these markets account for over 80% of all alliances that have been formed. The result reflects not only that a larger number of firms have pursued human therapeutics and veterinary product development, but also that regulatory constraints are more severe in those areas than in any other.

Comparisons among the table's cells also reveal intriguing differences. For instance, funding agreements account for over half (51%) of the alliances formed by DBFs in agricultural markets, but they represent no more than 30% of the alliances formed by firms pursuing human diagnostics, human therapeutics, or veterinary products. Agricultural firms probably rely more heavily on funding agreements than other types of ties because, in general, agricultural products are subject to less stringent regulations: product development therefore requires less collaboration. A further reason is that agricultural products have until recently attracted much less commercial attention than have human and veterinary healthcare products. This interpretation is lent credence by the fact that firms

Table 12-10

The Propensity of Dedicated Biotechnology Firms in Different Markets to Form Types of Alliances

	TYPE OF AGREEMENT					
MARKET AREA	Funding (%)	Manufacture (%)	Market (%)	R&D (%)	Transfer (%)	TOTAL (%)
Agriculture	51	5	4	36	3	118 (100)
Veterinary	28	5	19	31	17	872 (100)
Human diagnostics	27	4	34	19	16	121 (100)
Human therapeutics	30	5	17	19	16	901 (100)
Other	48	3	11	24	15	101 (100)

Chi-square: 93.975; DF: 16

The body of the table reports row percentages.

operating in the smaller markets classified as "other" also rely heavily on funding agreements. Not only are the markets for biomass conversion, bioprocess engineering, and biotechnologically produced specialty chemicals less well developed, but they are nearly devoid of regulation.

Table 12-10 also indicates that firms producing agricultural and veterinary products are more likely to form research and development agreements than are firms in other markets. Precisely why this should be so is currently unclear. However, it is generally held that most agricultural and veterinary applications are technologically less advanced than human applications. For instance, it has historically been more difficult to conduct recombinant DNA experiments on plant cells because, unlike animal cells, they are surrounded by a cell wall that inhibits diffusion across the cell membrane. Finally, marketing agreements appear to be more important to firms specializing in human diagnostics (34%). This result may reflect the fact that within commercial biotechnology the market for human diagnostics is the most mature. In vitro diagnostic kits account for a large proportion of biotechnology's current sales.

Table 12-11 intimates that market domain may also have some influence on with whom dedicated biotechnology firms ally themselves. The chi-square associated with the cross-tabulation of market domain by type of partner indicates the presence of a significant association ($X^2 = 98.8$; $df = 28$; $p < .001$). However, close examination of the table suggests that two facts apparently account for most of the variation. First, as in the previous analysis, the row marginals indicate that firms in the human therapeutics and veterinary markets are far more likely to have partners (i.e., to form alliances). Second, regardless of market, a dedicated biotechnology firm is most likely to ally itself with either a diversified corporation or another DBF.

Nevertheless, the cells of the table do suggest several market-driven differences in the propensity to form alliances with different types of organizations. Compared to dedicated biotechnology firms in all other markets, those in agriculture are least likely to form alliances with other DBFs and most likely to rely on investors. Conversely, firms producing human diagnostics are most likely to ally themselves with other DBFs and least likely to rely on investors. Firms producing human diagnostics are also less bound to diversified corporations. The pattern associated with agricultural firms seems consistent with the type of alliances they form: because agricultural firms rely more heavily on funding arrangements, it follows that they should be more frequently tied to investors. Because the development of in vitro diagnostics requires less capital than the development of therapeutics, and because diagnostics have generated more sales than biotechnology's other products, firms in the diagnostics market may have less need to turn to diversified corporations for support. The diagnostic market's relatively secure financial position may enable firms to not only preserve their autonomy, but also emphasize alliances with biotechnology firms that possess needed technical expertise.

Although the cross-tabulations in Tables 12-10 and 12-11 indicate that

Table 12-11

The Propensity of Dedicated Biotechnology Firms in Different Markets to Ally with Different Types of Partners

	TYPE OF PARTNER								
MARKET AREA	DBF (%)	DC (%)	INV (%)	PDBF (%)	RI (%)	SG (%)	U (%)	Other (%)	TOTAL (%)
Agriculture	13	41	29	0	2	3	8	4	107 (100)
Veterinary	22	44	7	4	6	4	8	6	818 (100)
Human diagnostics	37	29	7	3	4	10	4	6	118 (100)
Human therapeutics	25	38	14	3	5	4	8	4	911 (100)
Other	24	38	15	1	5	7	5	6	85 (100)

Chi-square: 98.801; DF: 28

Key to types of firms:

DBF: Dedicated Biotechnology Firm
DC: Diversified Corporation
INV: Investor
PDBF: Potential Dedicated Biotechnology Firm
RI: Research Institute
SG: Supplier of Goods
U: University

Percentages in the body of the table are row percentages.

markets may influence types of alliances as well as types of partners, they only offer evidence of a bivariate relationship. Would the relation between a firm's market and its involvement in the network of alliances still hold after the effects of other variables were taken into account? To answer this question, we estimated two sets of paired logit models. The first set sought to predict the types of firms with which dedicated biotechnology firms were allied; the second sought to predict the types of alliances they had formed.

Both sets of models used the same control variables, all of which had previously been shown to be related to the formation of alliances. Four groups of control variables were used. The first group consisted of two variables: one indicated whether the DBF was a subsidiary and the other whether the DBF's partner was a subsidiary. The second group of control variables recorded whether either the DBF or its partner was publicly held. The third group of control variables contained nominal codes for the country in which either the DBF or the DBF's partner was located. The final group of control variables indicated the period during which either the DBF or its partner was founded. Three periods of founding were considered: before 1977, between 1977 and 1982, and after 1982.

Table 12-12 displays the results of an analysis of variance (ANOVA) for the nested logit models designed to predict the type of firms with which dedicated biotechnology firms were allied. The first model contains only the control variables. The second model adds a variable representing the markets in which the DBFs operated: agriculture, veterinary products,

Table 12-12

Anova Results for Maximum Likelihood Estimates for Logits Predicting the Type of Partner

	df	Chi-sq	p	df	Chi-sq	p
Intercept	7	66.74	.0001	7	35.07	.0001
Ego is subsid	7	42.72	.0001	7	32.56	.0001
Alter is subsid	7	147.82	.0001	7	110.71	.0001
Ego is public	7	67.85	.0001	7	68.16	.0001
Alter is public	7	146.83	.0001	7	128.32	.0001
Ego country	14	28.04	.0141	14	24.26	.0426
Alter country	14	116.18	.0001	14	88.95	.0001
Ego period	7	48.95	.0001	7	29.77	.0001
Alter period	7	286.13	.0001	7	194.50	.0001
Ego market	—	—	—	28	74.30	.0001
Likelihood ratio	1288	1095.88	1.000	2051	1428.21	1.00

Ego = the focal organization; Alter = the partner.

human diagnostics, human therapeutics, or other. Not only were all variables in both models significant, but the models themselves were significant. More important, however, the second model increased the chi-square by 332.3 while it decreased the degrees of freedom by 28. The improved fit was significant at well beyond the .001 level.

Table 12-13 presents similar ANOVAs for the logit models designed to predict the type of alliances established by each biotechnology firm. Neither the period of founding of either firm nor the nationality of the DBF were significant in the first model. However, after adding market orientation in the second model, the nationality of the DBF became significant ($p < .05$) and the focal firm's founding period became significant at a probability less than .10. Paralleling the previous analysis, a DBF's market

Table 12-13

Anova Results for Maximum Likelihood Estimates of the Type of Alliance

	df	Chi-sq	p	df	Chi-sq	p
Intercept	4	50.56	.0001	4	19.78	.0006
Ego is subsid	4	29.46	.0001	4	21.98	.0002
Alter is subsid	4	70.79	.0001	4	46.64	.0001
Ego is public	4	74.54	.0001	4	51.67	.0001
Alter is public	4	36.45	.0001	4	18.65	.0009
Ego country	8	12.65	.1244	8	15.67	.0473
Alter country	8	75.65	.0001	8	53.80	.0001
Ego period	4	7.58	.1084	4	9.43	.0512
Alter period	4	5.84	.2111	4	4.35	.3602
Ego market	—	—	—	16	60.85	.0001
Likelihood ratio	724	820.71	.0071	1136	1133.35	.5166

Ego = the focal organization; Alter = the partner.

orientation was a significant predictor ($p < .0001$) of the types of ties it formed. Inclusion of market orientation in the second equation added 312.6 to the chi-square while burning 16 degrees of freedom. The improved fit was significant at better than the .001 level.

Together the two analyses indicate that even when other factors are taken into account, a DBF's market orientation continues to influence both the types of ties it establishes and the types of organizations with which it forms alliances. In sum, the logits suggest that the way in which a firm participates in the network is integral to its strategy for survival and growth. Niche as defined by market domain corresponds in part to niche as defined by characteristic patterns of interorganizational ties. However, the ontological status of an interorganizational niche remains ambiguous. Is a niche best understood as strategy or structure? Future analyses may employ longitudinal methods to explore this question further. Ultimately, however, it may not be possible to resolve the duality of structure and strategy. Action sustains structure, and structure sustains action. Networks of interorganizational relations are maps both of and for strategic action.

CONCLUSIONS

Fundamental discoveries in molecular biology regarding the chemical basis for heritability stimulated the rapid development of a new family of technologies. These technologies in turn have spawned numerous new ventures whose founders are interested in a wide variety of commercial applications. In recent years, however, disappointment with the slow pace of product development has soured the financial market's taste for biotechnology investments. After years of dependence on venture capital and public financing, the managers of dedicated biotechnology firms increasingly have turned to formal cooperative relationships for their vital resources. Many such relationships are with the leading firms in their own markets. As a result, networks of interorganizational alliances have become integral to the structure of the biotechnology community.

A majority of the organizations that form alliances with dedicated biotechnology firms are large diversified corporations. Many are among the most powerful actors in the pharmaceutical, chemical, food, energy, and agricultural industries. Nevertheless, there is a general perception that the market shares of these diversified corporations are vulnerable in the long run to innovations based on biotechnology. Although some have established their own biotechnology laboratories, many diversified corporations have formed strategic alliances with small biotechnology firms to obtain access to and leverage over a broad range of research.

Strategic alliances in biotechnology generally involve the exchange of knowledge for money. Often the exchange requires a smaller firm to sacrifice some degree of autonomy (for instance, over determining its goals for research and development) to gain access to markets with high barriers to entry. For many biotechnology firms, the compromise may forestall bankruptcy, merger, or acquisition. As a result, the population of dedicated biotechnology firms as a whole may enjoy reduced liabilities of newness. It is well known that large numbers of dedicated biotechnology firms can no longer secure venture capital and that most have yet to turn a profit. Yet failure rates among biotechnology firms appear to be remarkably low.

The network of alliances transcends national boundaries. Through strategic agreements, European and Japanese multinational corporations have become deeply involved in the U.S. biotechnology community. Ties to foreign corporations may offer U.S. biotechnology firms opportunities to fund long-term research, while perhaps retaining more autonomy than contracts with large domestic corporations would allow. Many of the most important questions regarding the influence of international ties on the structure of commercial biotechnology remain unanswered. What will be the ultimate effects of a large-scale transfer of technical knowledge to the industries of competing nations? Will the Japanese or Western Europeans ultimately usurp America's dominant position in biotechnology through financial and market leverage?

Frankly, we have not begun to explore such weighty issues. This chapter has been no more than a preliminary report on research still under way on a community that is itself still evolving. We have begun to map the structure of niches in the biotechnology community using a variety of classification techniques including empirically derived clusters of firms based on similar postures in the networks of alliances. To push these analyses further, however, we need to learn much more about the conditions under which alliances are negotiated, what benefits parties expect to receive, and what the perceived costs and pitfalls of such relationships may be. We expect to draw more heavily on such knowledge when specifying future analytical models.

Notes

1. Our brief history of commercial biotechnology is culled from a number of sources. We have found Watson and Tooze (1981), Krimsky (1982), Yoxen (1983), Elkington (1985), Kenney (1986), and Teitelman (1989) to be especially informative.
2. "In vitro" is outside the living organism; "in vivo" is within the living organism.
3. This and other frequencies of firms, foundings, and alliances are compiled from our own data bases, which are described later in the chapter.
4. The analyses in this paper were conducted on our data set as it existed in December 1989. Since then, the project has continued and additional data have been collected. Consequently, findings presented in subsequent papers will surely differ in detail, but we strongly suspect that the general patterns will remain unchanged.
5. Future analyses will include data on alliances as well as firms from *Bioscan*, *1990*.
6. Dyadic coding allowed us to compile the network data base in a relatively straightforward manner. However, to use the procedure we had to assume

that alliances involving more than two organizations could be accurately disaggregated into $(n^2 - n)/2$ dyads. Such an assumption would be incorrect if the alliance encoded a tree structure as would occur if firm A licensed a technology to firm B, which in turn licensed it to firm C. However, such structures appear to be relatively rare.

7. Because of possible undersampling in the most recent year, the pattern for joint ventures may be an artifact of *Bioscan 1988*. Future analyses using alliance data from the 1990 edition will resolve this issue.
8. Our definition of mortality was quite liberal. We included not only foldings and bankruptcies, but also acquisitions and mergers.
9. In general, one can expect the density of an adjacency matrix to decline exponentially as the number of nodes increases. That density declines is not particularly troublesome, at least theoretically, although large sparse matrices may pose computational difficulties.
10. Computations were done on Cornell's Supercomputer using modified Fortran programs provided by David Krackhardt.
11. *Bioscan* does, however, gather information from a variety of sources in addition to annual reports and other public documents. In fact, it relies primarily on information gathered directly through a periodic survey of firms.
12. We used PROC CLUSTER in SAS version 5.1.
13. The editors of *Bioscan* assign market and technology codes, called "subject terms," to each firm in the directory. The 86 individual codes are hierarchically arranged under more encompassing codes such as "Human Diagnostics" and "Human Therapeutics." We used these higher-level codes when assigning firms to markets.

References

Aldrich, Howard. 1979. *Organizations and Environments*. Englewood Cliffs, NJ: Prentice Hall.

Barley, Stephen R., and John Freeman. 1988. "Niche and Network: The Evolution of Organizational Fields in the Biotechnology Industry." Proposal submitted to the Sociology Program of the National Science Foundation.

Berg, Paul. 1974. "Potential Biohazards of Recombinant DNA Molecules." *Science* 185:303.

Bioengineering News World Biotech Company Directory. 1985–1986. Oak Harbor, WA: Deborah J. Mysiewicz.

Bioscan. 1988. Phoenix: Oryx Press.

Bioscan. 1990. Phoenix: Oryx Press.

The Biotechnology Directory 1986: Products, Companies, Research and Organizations. 1986. New York: Stockton Press.

Boje, David M., and David A. Whetten. 1981. "Effects of Organizational Strategies and Contextual Constraints on Centrality and Attributions of Influence in Interorganizational Networks." *Administrative Science Quarterly* 26:378–395.

Brittain, Jack W., and John H. Freeman. 1980. "Organizational Proliferation and Density-Dependent Selection." In John Kimberly and Robert Miles, eds., *Organizational Life Cycles*. San Francisco: Jossey-Bass, pp. 291–338.

Burrill, G. Steven. 1989. *Biotech 89: Commercialization*. New York: Mary Ann Liebert.

Burt, Ronald S. 1977. "Power in Social Topology." *Social Science Research* 6:1–83.

———. 1979. "A Structural Theory of Interlocking Corporate Directorates." *Social Networks* 1:415–435.

———. 1980a. "Cooptive Corporate Actor Networks: A Reconsideration of Interlocking Directorates Involving American Manufacturing." *Administrative Science Quarterly* 25:557–582.

————. 1980b. "Models of Network Structure." *Annual Review of Sociology* 6:79–141.

————. 1982. *Toward a Structural Theory of Action: Network Models of Social Structure, Perception, and Action.* New York: Academic Press.

————. 1983. *Corporate Profits and Cooptation: Networks of Market Constraints and Directorate Ties in the American Economy.* New York: Academic Press.

Carleton, Willard T. 1986. "Issues and Questions Involving Venture Capital." In Gary Libecap, ed., *Advances in Entrepreneurship, Innovation, and Economic Growth* Vol. 1. Greenwich, CT: JAI Press.

Dibner, Mark. 1988. *Biotechnology Guide, U.S.A.* New York: Stockton Press.

Dubinskas, Frank A. 1985. "The Culture Chasm: Scientists and Managers in Genetic-Engineering Firms." *Technology Review* 88:24–30.

Elkington, John. 1985. *Inside the Gene Factory: Inside the Genetic and Biotechnology Business Revolution.* New York: Carroll and Graf.

Emery, F. E., and E. L. Trist. 1965. "The Causal Texture of Organizational Environments." *Human Relations* 18:21–32.

Fennema, Meindert. 1982. *International Networks of Banks and Industry.* Boston: Martinus Nijhoff.

Freeman, John, and Stephen R. Barley. 1990. "The Strategic Analysis of Interorganizational Relations in Biotechnology." In Ray Loveridge and Martyn Pitt, eds., *Strategic Management of Technological Innovation.* New York: Wiley.

Freeman, Linton C. 1979. "Centrality in Social Networks: Conceptual Clarification." *Social Networks* 1:215–239.

Galaskiewicz, Joseph. 1979. *Exchange Networks and Community Relations.* Beverly Hills: Sage.

Galaskiewicz, Joseph, and Stanley Wasserman. 1981. "A Dynamic Study of Change in a Regional Corporate Network." *American Sociological Review* 46:475–484.

Genetic Engineering and Biotechnology Firms Worldwide Directory. Kingston, NJ: Sittig and Noyes.

Genetic Engineering and Biotechnology Yearbook. 1985. New York: Elsevier.

Gogel, Robert, and Thomas Koenig. 1981. "Commercial Banks, Interlocking Directorates and Economic Power: An Analysis of the Primary Metals Industry." *Social Problems* 29:117–128.

Gomes-Casseres, Benjamin. 1988. "Joint Venture Cycles: The Evolution of Ownership Strategies of U.S. MNEs, 1945–75." In Farok J. Contractor and Peter Lorange, eds., *Cooperative Strategies in International Business.* Lexington, MA: D.C. Heath.

Hannan, Michael T., and John Freeman. 1989. *Organizational Ecology.* Cambridge, MA: Harvard University Press.

Harrigan, Kathryn Rudie. 1985. *Strategies for Joint Ventures.* Lexington, MA: D.C. Heath.

Hawley, Amos H. 1950. *Human Ecology.* New York: Ronald.

————. 1986. *Human Ecology: A Theoretical Essay.* Chicago: University of Chicago Press.

Howard, Ted, and Jeremy Rifkin. 1977. *Who Should Play God?* New York: Dell.

Kinney, Martin. 1986. *Biotechnology: The University-Industrial Complex.* New Haven: Yale University Press.

Knoke, David, and David L. Rogers. 1979. "A Block Model Analysis of Interorganizational Networks." *Sociology and Social Research* 64:28–52.

Krimsky, Sheldon. 1982. *Genetic Alchemy: The Social History of the Recombinant DNA Controversy.* Cambridge, MA: MIT Press.

Laumann, Edward O., Joseph Galaskiewicz, and Peter V. Marsden. 1978. "Community Structure as Interorganizational Linkages." In Alex Inkeles, ed., *Annual Review of Sociology* Vol. 4. Palo Alto, CA: Annual Reviews, pp. 455–484.

Laumann, Edward O., and Franz Pappi. 1976. *Networks of Collective Action: A Perspective on Community Influence Systems.* New York: Academic Press.

Mariolis, Peter. 1975. "Interlocking Directorates and Control of Corporations: The Theory of Bank Control." *Social Science Quarterly* 56:425–439.

Masten, Scott E., James W. Meehan, and Edward A. Snyder. 1989. "Vertical Integration in the U.S. Auto Industry: A Note on the Influence of Transaction Specific Assets." *Journal of Economic Behavior and Organization* 12:265–273.

Mintz, Beth, and Michael Schwartz. 1985. *The Power Structure of American Business.* Chicago: University of Chicago Press.

Mintzberg, Henry. 1978. "Patterns in Strategy Formation." *Management Science* 24: 934–948.

Mizruchi, Mark S. 1981. *The Structure of the American Corporate Network: 1904–1974.* Beverly Hills: Sage.

Oakey, Ray. 1984. *High Technology Small Firms: Innovation and Regional Development in Britain and the United States.* New York: St. Martin's.

Office of Technology Assessment. 1984. *Commercial Biotechnology: An International Analysis.* Washington, DC: U.S. Government Printing Office.

———. 1988. *New Developments in Biotechnology: U.S. Investment in Biotechnology.* Washington, DC: U.S. Government Printing Office.

Pfeffer, Jeffrey, and Gerald R. Salancik. 1978. *The External Control of Organizations: A Resource Dependence Perspective.* New York: Harper & Row.

Rogers, Everett M., and Judith K. Larsen. 1984. *Silicon Valley Fever: Growth of High-Technology Culture.* New York: Basic Books.

Sixth Annual GEN Guide to Biotechnology Companies. 1987. New York: Genetic Engineering News.

Teitelman, Robert. 1989. *Gene Dreams: Wall Street, Academia, and the Rise of Biotechnology.* New York: Basic Books.

Terreberry, Shirley. 1968. "The Evolution of Organizational Environments." *Administrative Science Quarterly* 12:590–613.

Thompson, James D. 1967. *Organizations in Action.* New York: McGraw-Hill.

Warren, Roland L. 1967. "The Interorganizational Field as a Focus for Investigation." *Administrative Science Quarterly* 12:396–419.

Watson, James D., and John Tooze. 1981. *The DNA Story: A Documentary History of Gene Cloning.* San Francisco: W.H. Freeman.

Yoxen, Edward. 1983. *The Gene Business: Who Should Control Biotechnology?* New York: Harper & Row.

CHAPTER

13

The Make-or-Cooperate Decision in the Context of an Industry Network

BRUCE KOGUT, WEIJIAN SHAN,
AND
GORDON WALKER

One of the most important decisions facing an organization is which activities should be carried out internally and which should be purchased. This question is frequently characterized as "make or buy," and the answers to it determine the boundaries of the firm. A fruitful line of research on this question is transaction cost economics (Williamson 1985), which has sought to determine organizational boundaries by comparing the costs of internal production to the costs of relying on the market for production. These costs are related partly to the size of the firm and to its internal capabilities, as well as to the hazards of relying on the outside market.[1]

The problem of what determines a firm's boundaries has frequently been extended to include cooperative modes of interfirm relationship that are intermediate between market and organization. Such modes include joint ventures, licensing, and other long-term cooperative agreements. "Make or buy" thus becomes "make or cooperate." It is the latter problem that we investigate here.

In the research program to which this chapter belongs, we analyze the decision to make or cooperate as influenced by the structure of relationships in a network of firms. As a way to fix ideas, it is useful to emphasize that in transaction cost studies, the influence of the external network is reduced to a summary variable measuring the degree of supplier market competition in a market; the fewer the suppliers, the greater the risk that prices may be renegotiated, especially if the buyer cannot switch easily to other sources.

This research was supported through a grant from AT&T administered by the Reginald Jones Center, Wharton School, University of Pennsylvania

However, in our analysis, the market cannot be characterized simply by the degree of competition; rather, it is analyzed as a network with an evolving social structure. This structure has two important implications for the behavior of the firms in the network:

1. The structure of cooperative relationships influences the distribution of information available to firms about current and potential partners in the network.
2. Therefore the knowledge of a firm regarding the availability of cooperation with partners in the industry is determined by its position in the network structure.

The make-or-cooperate decision is made in the context of a concrete network as opposed to an abstract market. The network is not, however, simply given, but is itself emergent over time. The decision to cooperate is nested within the changing structure of this network as determined by the history of prior cooperation. Through the accumulation of interfirm ties a cooperative network is gradually formed, and this network defines and constrains the realm of feasible opportunities for the individual companies. Although firms make boundary decisions as individual agents and in response to the information available, the availability of information is influenced by the cumulative pattern of cooperation in the industry represented in the structure of the network.

The linking of the make-and-cooperate relationship to the distribution of information is not inconsistent with a liberal notion of what constitutes a market. Market prices are not given abstractly but are the negotiated outcomes of participating agents (Baker 1984). The discovery of buyers and sellers is influenced by the prevailing cooperative structure. Stated concretely, buyers and sellers must first find one another, and this process of search is influenced by their primary relationships with other firms as well as by the relationships of other firms to one another.

For this reason, the network approach to make or cooperate is essentially historical in nature. Information is conditioned on past decisions, or what we call the cumulative pattern, of cooperation. To understand current practice requires an analysis of the persistence of previous behavior as captured in the structure of the network.

We explore these arguments by studying the history of cooperation among new biotechnology firms (NBFs) and their partners, which are primarily large established corporations. Having suggested how the network may influence firm behavior, we turn to testing a model predicting how many new relationships NBFs establish over time. Because our dependent variable (the number of new cooperative relationships a firm establishes in a time interval) is a count measure, we test our hypotheses using negative binomial regression. This procedure is carried out in two successive periods, with a network measure of NBF information about partners and firm-level characteristics as predictors of new cooperative relationships.

The results of this analysis point in two important directions. First, we show that while the decisions of firms regarding their boundaries are related to conventional attributes (e.g., size), the network effect is consistently a better predictor. Second, the results provide insight into the common claim that firms are slow to change.

EMBEDDEDNESS AND NEW INDUSTRIES

The rise of new industries has generated a literature rife with disagreement over the characterization of new firms and their propensity to cooperate. As White (1981) has noted, markets arise neither from a vacuum nor from yet-to-be-defined consumer preferences, but from the structural relations among existing firms. In the language of Granovetter (1985), social—and thus economic—action is "embedded" in historical structures of relationships among actors. Though changeable, these structures are persistent over time and inform individual choice.

The present study appraises the merits of Granovetter's argument that an individual's (or firm's) actions are neither completely voluntary ("undersocialized") nor normatively prescribed ("oversocialized"). He writes:

> A fruitful analysis of human action requires us to avoid the atomization in the theoretical extremes of under- and oversocialized conceptions. Actors do not behave or decide as atoms outside a social context nor do they adhere slavishly to a script written for them by the particular intersection of social categories that they happen to occupy. Their attempts at purposive action are instead embedded in concrete, ongoing systems of social relations (1985:485).

By analyzing the influence of both individual and network variables on firm behavior, we evaluate empirically the contribution of this perspective.

NETWORK STRUCTURE AND COOPERATION

The issue of how the structure of cooperation influences the behavior of network members is especially important in the case of new industries. Two mechanisms were emphasized by Schumpeter (1934): the willingness of banks to fund venture capital and the departure of entrepreneurs from existing organizations to join or start new firms. More recent studies have confirmed the importance of the latter mechanism; Boeker's (1989) study of founders of semiconductor firms is a good example. Other institutions—such as universities, research centers, and government—may also play a role in the structural evolution of new industries.

Critical for many industries are cooperative relationships between new and incumbent firms. Consider the problems facing new firms in the biotechnology industry, which uniformly begin as research-and-development operations; they lack the means to distribute their products. In Stigler's view, the vertical integration decision facing these firms is equivalent to a theory of functions. If external firms lack the requisite specialized knowledge, forward integration (i.e., a "make" decision) should ensue.

An alternative is to build cooperative relationships with established firms that have the capability to perform these functions (i.e., a "cooperate" decision). At the start of the industry, new entrants face a homogeneous (and atomized) environment in the absence of cooperative relationships. Due to firm-level heterogeneity (e.g., size, product diversity, and unspecified factors), some firms engage in cooperative relationships, either intensely or moderately.

Interfirm variation of this kind has an interesting implication. Whereas economic agents act in the context of a social structure, it by no means follows that they are positioned identically in the structure. Furthermore, firms differ in their capability to influence the structural development of their environments. In fact, the structural heterogeneity of the network is the cumulative product of the observed strategies of individual firms. These strategies have an observable effect: cooperative relationships are either focused within a group of partners or spread across many groups.

We represent network structure by partitioning both startup firms and their established partners separately into groups in which members are structurally equivalent. Structurally equivalent startup firms share the same partners; conversely, structurally equivalent partners share the same startup firms. The intersection of a group of startups and a group of partners contains the relationships they have together. The number of these relationships may be small or large. If it is small, then we can assume the startup group knows little about the group of partners; but if there are many relationships linking the two groups, the startup group knows a great deal about the established firms in the partner group. Thus the more-or-less-dense intersections of structurally equivalent startups and structurally equivalent partners define the industry distribution of information about interfirm cooperation.

We call startup groups that have many linkages with structurally equivalent partners "highly focused." The question we address here is whether increasing focus over time is related to more new cooperative relationships. We argue that *how* potential relationships are located in the network is important for *whether* they will be realized. The distribution of information on potential partners, as represented in the structure of the network, leads startup firms to choose partners that are structurally equivalent. As a startup's focus increases over time, therefore, better information on partners is available and more new relationships should occur. The evolution of network structure thus simultaneously constrains which partners a startup is likely to choose and enables the formation of new relationships with these partners, thereby making the decision to cooperate more frequent than the decision to make.

FIRM ATTRIBUTES AS DETERMINANTS OF
INTERFIRM COOPERATION

To compare the influence of changes in startup focus on cooperative frequency to the influence of firm attributes, we identify a set of firm-level
variables commonly employed in the literature. Past studies of cooperative
relationships in the biotechnology industry have looked at the question of
whether a firm has entered into *any* cooperative relationship. Analyzing
data on individual products for a sample of NBFs, Shan (1990) found that
competitive position, size, and product diversity influenced the cooperative decision. Because Shan's measures for competitive position are at the
product level, they cannot be directly replicated in the present study
because our focus is on the firm's cooperative frequency across products.
A reasonable proxy is age of the NBF, which allows the propensity of
cooperative behavior to vary over its life history. Moreover, following
Shan's reasoning, early entrants may have less need to cooperate due to
first-mover advantages in the market.

Product diversity can also be expected to promote cooperation by presenting more opportunity to cooperate. In addition, as many NBFs are
focused in one area of technical expertise (e.g., a disease group) with
many applications, greater diversity across types of application should
induce cooperation to loosen resource constraints. Thus product diversity
should be related to higher frequency of cooperative agreements.

Size presents a more complicated set of issues. Whereas Shan found
a negative relationship between size and cooperation, Boyles (1969) found
that the frequency of joint ventures more than proportionally rises with
size. Whether this difference arises from a nonlinearity in the size-to-
propensity relationship (i.e., large firms either have no cooperative
relationships, or proportionally more) is addressed partially in the analysis
that follows.

In addition to the variables of age, size, and product diversity, we
also analyze the effect of firms that have been able to raise equity through
secondary markets. As Schumpeter argued, a critical element in the birth
of a new industry is the availability of credit. Through credit, entrepreneurs can purchase and transfer productive assets from traditional industries to themselves. Banks have performed a fundamental role in
achieving this end, but recently their role has been greatly abetted by the
growth of venture-capital markets that permit the raising of financing
through a public offering of equity.

The effect of issuing public equity on the propensity to engage in
cooperative relationships has, however, an ambiguous interpretation.
From the perspective of theories such as population ecology, which see
cooperative relationships as one way of providing resources to the firm,
the public offering of equity provides an alternative source of funding.
Hence it should decrease the need to cooperate and to acquire resources
from a partner.

On the other hand, it could also be argued that the ability to issue

Table 13-1

Predicted Signs to Relationship of Covariates to Number of Agreements

	FIRST PERIOD	SECOND PERIOD
Size	+	+
Age	?	−
Diversity	+	+
Public offering	+/−	+/−
Change in density	*	+
Residual	*	−

*Variable estimated from first period data and used only in second period estimations.

public equity is an indicator of a firm's legitimacy. As Meyer and Rowan (1977) have argued, organizations vary in the extent to which they are granted institutional legitimacy. In this view, only firms with strong product-development portfolios can attract investors to purchase the equity. Public trading of an NBF may therefore signal to potential partners that its future is bright. Thus a positive association between publicly held firms and the frequency of cooperative relationships may be expected.

Table 13-1 summarizes the preceding discussion on the predicted signs of the parameter coefficients to the covariates. The predictions are presented for two periods of network evolution. Age has an ambiguous effect in the first period, as it both proxies the competitive effect (i.e., followers may attempt to leapfrog by cooperative agreements) and a cumulative bias (i.e., older firms have a longer opportunity to cooperate). This cumulative bias should be insignificant for agreements in the second period. Moreover, the possibility that the first-period relationships may have fully exhausted a firm's propensity to cooperate is addressed by incorporating directly a measure of saturation in the second-period model. This measure, labeled "Residual," is described in the section headed "Discussion" at the end of the chapter.

RESEARCH DESIGN

Sample

The commercialization of the new biotechnologies (comprising the techniques of genetic engineering—recombinant DNA—and monoclonal antibodies) in the 1970s and 1980s led to the emergence in the United States of hundreds of startup firms. Though the industry is new in terms of its technology, its techniques are used to develop products in existing industries, especially pharmaceuticals, chemicals, plant and animal agriculture, and pollution and waste control. In addition, the research and manufacturing requirements have instigated the development of new bioinstruments, thereby affecting the capital-good suppliers to biotechnology firms in these industries.

The unit of analysis in this study is the NBF, which we define as an independent firm formed for the specific purpose of commercializing the new biotechnology. The data for the analysis come from two main sources: (1) a commercial directory of biotechnology firms, *Bioscan*, published and updated quarterly by Oryx Press, Inc. and (2) telephone interviews with the sample firms. *Bioscan* provides information on firm attributes as well as a listing and description of cooperative agreements. Cooperative agreements, which are counted to form the dependent variable, include all joint ventures, licensing, and long-term contracts between NBFs and commercial firms.

All firms in the final sample must be *independent* business entities specializing in the commercialization of biotechnology products. In order to select a homogeneous industry, all firms in the sample must have at least one pharmaceutical product in either the therapeutic or the diagnostic area, or both. Excluded from this initial sample are established companies, their subsidiaries and divisions, and joint venture entities. Since only firms that have engaged in at least one agreement can contribute to network structure, NBFs with no agreements are also excluded.[2]

Application of the preceding criteria results in a sample of 114 NBFs. Of the 114, 22 have agreements only with universities and research institutes. Many of these agreements are licensing of the original patents stemming from university research. We dropped these NBFs from the sample in order to retain a homogeneous group engaging only in clearly commercial and ongoing agreements. Although university ties are important—albeit often only for the initial licensing and subsequent consulting service—our focus is on the structuring of relationships among commercial

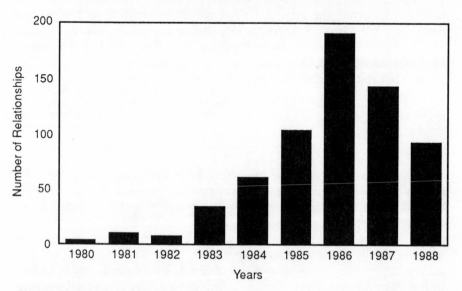

Figure 13-1
Formation of Cooperative Ventures by Sample Firms

Table 13-2

Descriptive Statistics of Number of Agreements

PERIOD FROM 1976 TO	MEAN	STANDARD DEVIATION	MAXIMUM
January 1, 1986	1.84	2.71	15
January 1, 1987	3.47	3.77	20
January 1, 1988	4.68	4.50	25
January 1, 1989	5.38	5.00	26

competitors.[3] Of the remaining 92 NBFs, 5 were missing data. Thus 87 NBFs were used in the sample.

From the beginning of the biotechnology industry, cooperative agreements have played a significant role. In Figure 13-1, the number of relationships is tracked for the 87 firms between the years of 1983 and 1988. Clearly, 1986 represents a watershed year, with the number of agreements falling in 1987 and 1988. This ebb in frequency may reflect structural shifts, but it also raises the possibility of the saturation of the propensity to cooperate, a possibility that we model directly.

The peak in 1986 presents a reasonable cut point in comparing the evolution of network structure. In Table 13-2, means and standard deviations are given for relationships cumulative to 1986, 1987, 1988, and 1989 (the latter representing the total number of relationships up to January 1, 1989). Relationships up to 1986 represent under one-half the total, but those up to 1987 over one-half. For this reason, we divide our samples into two periods. For the purposes of sensitivity analysis, we run the estimates for both January 1, 1986 and January 1, 1987 as the cut points.

Measurement

Bioscan and the telephone survey also provide data to be used as measures of the firm-level attributes. Age is measured as the time from founding. Product diversity is a count of how many of the following sectors a firm participated in: therapeutic drugs, diagnostic drugs, agricultural applications, veterinary drugs, and food and brewery. Size is measured as the number of employees. Both age and size are measured at the end of the period; missing size data for each year were corrected either by interpolation or by regression estimates, depending on the availability of information for other years.

OPERATIONALIZATION OF NETWORK STRUCTURE

We identified the structure of the network of cooperative relationships, and thereby the extent to which NBFs were focused or unfocused, with blockmodeling techniques (White, Boorman, and Breiger 1976; Arabie, Boorman, and Levitt 1978). First we analyzed the asymmetric matrix of

In the graphs below, points on scale represent maximum densities.
The numbers of partner group affiliations (i.e., nonzero blocks) are
in parentheses above maximum density.

(a) CALCOPT Analysis of Relationships up to 1985

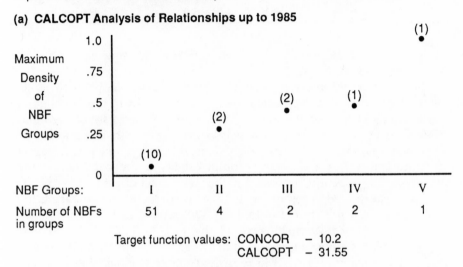

Target function values: CONCOR – 10.2
                         CALCOPT – 31.55

Total number of partner groups: 11.

(b) CALCOPT Analysis of Relationships up to 1986

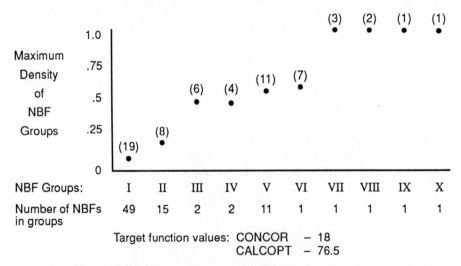

Target function values: CONCOR – 18
                         CALCOPT – 76.5

Total number of partner groups: 24.

Figure 13-2
Maximum Densities of NBF Groups

(c) **CALCOPT Analysis of Relationships up to 1988**

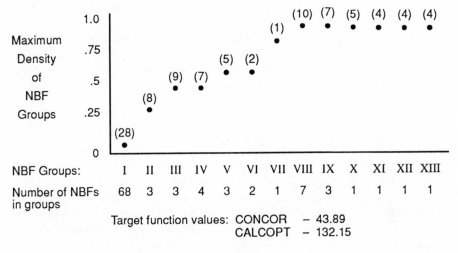

Target function values: CONCOR   − 43.89
CALCOPT   − 132.15

Total number of partner groups: 35.

Figure 13-2 *(Continued)*

cooperative relationships between NBFs and their partners with CON-
COR, a well-known network analysis algorithm (Breiger, Boorman, and
Arabie 1975) that has been used frequently in interorganizational research.
Second, we applied an algorithm called CALCOPT[4] to reallocate network
members from group to group in the partition if the shift in group membership improved a target function based on the dispersion of densities
between structurally equivalent groups of firms. The CALCOPT target
function is thus based on the principle underlying our concept of focus as
a predictor of increased cooperation in the network. CALCOPT evaluates
the CONCOR partition sequentially for possible changes in group membership sequentially until no change improves in the target function.
CALCOPT was applied to the CONCOR partitions of both NBFs and
partners separately.

The results of applying CALCOPT to the CONCOR partitions for
relationships up to 1985, to 1986, and to 1988 are shown in Figure 13-2.
For each year, the figure shows (1) the CALCOPT and CONCOR target
function values, (2) maximum densities of each group of NBFs, and (3)
the number of NBFs in each group. For all three years, the CALCOPT
target function values show strong increases over the CONCOR values,
indicating that the reallocation of network members among groups substantially improves the dispersion of densities in the blockmodel.

Because blocks with one or a few members are distinct in each density
matrix, the density matrices across years share a strikingly similar pattern
that corresponds to our theoretical distinction between focused and unfocused firms. In each network there is a rapid progression in a group's

maximum density from a very large group of NBFs with very low maximum density to groups of NBFs with maximum densities of about .5, to a set of groups with maximum density of 1.0. It should be clear that high maximum density is associated quite strongly with a small number of NBF group members and a small number of partner groups. Thus, as maximum density increases, so does (in our terminology) the focus of the NBF. We therefore use the change in the maximum density of an NBF group as our measure of change in focus.

NEGATIVE BINOMIAL REGRESSION

The dependent variable in our model is the number of cooperative relationships into which an NBF enters within a given year. Because the variable is a count measure (i.e., an integer truncated at 0), we model the probability that the number of relationships will occur n times within an interval. A natural choice of a discrete model is a regression with a Poisson distribution. That is, we specify the underlying distribution as

$$\text{Prob } (Y = y_j) = \frac{e^{-\lambda_j}\lambda_j^{Y_j}}{Y_j!} \ (1),$$

with Y_j being the count of relationships for the jth firm. To incorporate exogenous variables, lambda can be made a function of the covariates:

$$\lambda_j = e^{\Sigma B_i X_{ij}},$$

where B are the coefficients, X are the covariates (with X_1 set to one), i indicates the ith variable, and j is the jth firm. The exponential function ensures nonnegativity.

The Poisson distribution contains the strong assumption that the mean and variance are equal to λ_j. For most social-science data, the variance is likely to exceed the mean, indicating overdispersion, which tends to bias downward the estimated standard errors. The data presented in Table 13-1 points to a likely violation of the Poisson assumption in our data.

We resolve this problem by modeling explicitly the disturbance as firm heterogeneity. A common procedure to correct for overdispersion is to specify a compound distribution (Johnson and Kotz 1970). In the regression model, λ is again set equal to the exponentially weighted sum of the covariates, but with the addition of an error term. A frequent specification of the distribution for the error term is the gamma, so that the now compound Poisson reduces to the negative binomial model. The modeling of heterogeneity not only relaxes the stringent assumption of equal mean and variance in the Poisson model, but also accounts for omitted variable bias, thus providing for a stronger comparison of the contribution of changes in network position against firm-level effects.[5]

RESULTS

Table 13-3 presents descriptive statistics for the covariates. (The last two variables are explained under the Discussion heading that follows the subsequent tables.) The correlations show some association between the dummy variable for public offering and several of the other variables, but the magnitudes do not suggest problems of multicollinearity. The collinearity between the density variables is not a problem, since they are never used in the same regression.

In the estimates that follow, we run the regression for two different cut points: January 1, 1986 and January 1, 1987. The cut point affects the magnitude but never the signs of the parameters and only infrequently their significance levels. We use two-tail significance tests.

As we noted earlier, the negative binomial regression accounts for heterogeneity and generates an estimate (labeled α) of the degree of overdispersion of the variance. It also can be interpreted as representing either intrinsic randomness or omitted variables. This latter interpretation is especially important. Because α picks up firm-level heterogeneity that is not eliminated by the other covariates, it captures unobserved factors that generate across-firm differences in their propensities to cooperate. In the absence of a complete theory describing why firms differ in their coopera-

TABLE 13-3

Descriptive Statistics of Covariates

	MEAN	STANDARD DEVIATION	LOWEST VALUE	HIGHEST VALUE
1. Size	127.48	194.770	5	1200
2. Age	5.163	2.678	0	14
3. Diversity	2.033	0.988	0	5
4. Public offering	0.641	0.482	0	1
5. Change in focus[1]	0.225	0.313	0	1
6. Change in focus[2]	0.224	0.292	0	0.969
7. Residual[1]	−0.143	2.370	−12.5	10.45
8. Residual[2]	−0.048	2.907	−7.984	12.02

PEARSON CORRELATION MATRIX							
	(1)	(2)	(3)	(4)	(5)	(6)	(7)
(1)	1.0000						
(2)	0.2889	1.0000					
(3)	0.2966	0.2388	1.0000				
(4)	0.2132	0.3862	0.3937	1.0000			
(5)	0.0975	0.0120	0.3308	0.3031	1.0000		
(6)	−0.0894	−0.0536	0.2905	0.2291	0.7400	1.0000	
(7)	−0.0875	−0.2259	−0.1761	−0.1005	0.2442	0.2152	1.0000
(8)	−0.0458	−0.0193	−0.0525	−0.0485	0.3175	0.2560	0.7393

[1] Estimated with cut point at January 1, 1986.

[2] Estimated with cut point at January 1, 1987.

Table 13-4

Poisson and Negative Binomial Regression Estimates of Effects of Covariates on the Number of a Firm's Relationships (First-Period Result)

	1986 CUTOFF	1987 CUTOFF
Intercept	−1.356***	−0.060
	(−3.05)	(−0.17)
Size	0.001*	0.001**
	(1.835)	(2.01)
Age	0.124**	0.025
	(2.40)	(0.62)
Diversity	0.396***	0.361**
	(2.50)	(2.82)
Public offering	0.087	0.236
	(0.33)	(1.19)
α	0.570**	0.365**
	(2.54)	(2.85)
Log-likelihood	−142.08	−188.68

(Two-tail test)   (Student T in parentheses)

***p < .01

**p < .05

*p < .10

tive choices, this specification reduces an omitted variable bias, while at the same time provides an estimate of the significance of firm variation.[6]

Table 13-4 presents the negative binomial regression estimates of the firm-level covariates on the count measure of the number of agreements in the first period. Sensitivity analysis around the cut points is included, with the 1987 cut-point results also shown. The estimates show that product diversity and size are significant at .05 level. Omitted firm-level heterogeneity, represented by α, indicates substantial overdispersion of the variance.

Table 13-5 gives the second-period estimates, which contain the same covariates (though the values may have changed for the time-varying variables). In addition, the variable—Change in Focus—is included. The results confirm our central hypothesis that an increase in focus is related to an increase in cooperative agreements. This result is significant at the .001 level.

Public offering is positively signed, indicating that firms that have issued equity on secondary markets also tend to engage in more cooperative agreements. Causality, however, cannot be inferred, as cooperative agreements can provide the legitimacy required for public offering of equity. However, the low significance level discourages any interpretation. Diversity is positively signed and significant in most of the regressions. Size is not significant.

Table 13-5

Poisson and Negative Binomial Regression Estimates of Effects of Covariates of the Number of a Firm's Relationships (Second-Period Result)

	1986 CUTOFF	1987 CUTOFF	1986 CUTOFF	1987 CUTOFF
Intercept	.467	−.194	0.385	−0.360
	(1.27)	(−.421)	(1.12)	(−0.86)
Size	.0004	.0004	0.0003	0.001
	(1.01)	(.646)	(1.00)	(1.12)
Age	−.0567	−.0421	−0.035	−0.022
	(−1.29)	(−.696)	(−0.84)	(−0.39)
Diversity	.279***	.265*	0.228**	0.203
	(2.42)	(1.75)	(2.25)	(1.45)
Public offering	.591*	.549	0.348	0.326
	(1.82)	(1.40)	(1.10)	(0.83)
Change in focus	—	—	0.815***	1.016***
	—	—	(3.15)	(2.64)
α	.288***	.4540**	0.228**	0.370**
	(2.68)	(2.44)	(2.30)	(2.11)
Log-likelihood	−191.32	−154.85	−186.69	−151.30

(Two-tail test)

*** $p < .01$

** $p < .05$

* $p < .10$

DISCUSSION

The results confirm that the number of new cooperative agreements is positively related to shifts in a firm's focus in the network structure. As relationships accumulate over time, previous industry decisions increasingly constrain a firm to cooperate. The relationship between change in a firm's focus and the number of new agreements suggests that movement in the network is possible, but only through extensive relational contracting.

This result is not an artifact of the scaling or of a potential tautology between the densities measuring NBF focus and the number of NBF relationships. A firm could as easily disperse its cooperative efforts across many partner groups as concentrate its relationships within a few. Thus there is no definitional bias toward a correlation between change in focus and cooperation. Also, it is important to underscore that the density measures that form the basis of the variable "Change in focus" are derived from the *cumulative* pattern of relationships in the industry.

It would be interesting and important to have greater insight into the underlying determinants of focused and unfocused firms. Why firms

should differ in this dimension is largely unknown. The significance of
the heterogeneity measure suggests that there is a considerable way to go
before pinning down individual firm variations in the decision to cooperate, regardless whether this cooperation leads to a focused or unfocused
position in the network.

To initiate an inquiry into this unknown variation, two avenues of
reasoning seem appropriate. One is to posit simply that firms differ in
their inherent propensities to cooperate, and leave unsettled for the time
being whether these differences arise from leadership or from other firm
or market-structure influences. A second line of inquiry is to consider a
saturation effect; that is, the second-period variation results from not
incorporating the variation in first-period cooperation. Some firms may
have started period two already saturated in agreements.

We now address both of these issues. From the models estimated in
Table 13-5, residuals were generated from the first-period estimates. A
positive residual indicates that a firm entered into more relationships than
could be predicted by the covariates; a negative residual indicates the con-
verse. An inherent tendency to cooperate suggests that the first-period

Table 13-6

**Poisson and Negative Binomial Regression Estimates of Effects of
Covariates on the Number of a Firm's Relationships
(Second-Period Result)**

	1986 CUTOFF	1987 CUTOFF
Intercept	.041	−.618
	(.098)	(−1.37)
Size	.0004	.0006
	(1.06)	(1.051)
Age	−.022	−.012
	(−.57)	(−.22)
Diversity	.258**	.223
	(2.52)	(1.61)
Public offering	.365	.295
	(1.06)	(.73)
Change in focus	.744***	.864**
	(2.93)	(2.25)
Change in partner scope	.421	.63
	(1.40)	(1.49)
α	0.217**	0.357**
	(2.02)	(2.12)
Log-likelihood	−185.5	150.0

(Two-tail test)   (Student T in parentheses)
***$p < .01$
**$p < .05$
*$p < .10$

Table 13-7

Poisson and Negative Binomial Regression Estimates of Effects of Covariates of the Number of a Firm's Relationships (Second-Period Result)

	1986 CUTOFF	1987 CUTOFF
Intercept	0.402 (1.11)	−0.346 (−0.84)
Size	.0004 (1.01)	.0001 (1.11)
Age	−0.037 (−0.88)	−0.023 (−0.42)
Diversity	0.220* (1.92)	0.209 (1.51)
Public offering	0.359 (1.10)	0.316 (0.82)
Change in focus	0.838*** (3.21)	0.972** (2.46)
Residual	−0.010 (−0.35)	−0.015 (0.32)
α	0.227** (2.25)	0.364** (2.10)
Log-likelihood	−186.64	151.20

(Two-tail test)   (Student T in parentheses)

***$p < .01$

**$p < .05$

*$p < .10$

residual should be positively correlated with the number of relationships in the second period. A negative relationship indicates that a saturation point limits the number of agreements.

The results given in Tables 13-6 and 13-7 show no significant relationship between the residuals (measured at the two different cut points) and the number of period-two relationships. It is possible that these two effects of inherent tendency and saturation cancel any relationship. But these results also increase the plausibility that the omitted causes of cooperation are structural in origin.

CONCLUSION

This study represents an initial inquiry into the effects of structural position on individual organizational choice. Individual firm attributes matter, but so does the degree of the firm's focus in the network. There is apparent merit in taking a middle ground between the atomization of either an under- or oversocialized view of individual action.

Comparing the effects of the network and firm attributes over time is intriguing. While the influence of firm attributes declines, that of network structure remains strong. Cooperative choice appears to be significantly nested within the cumulative pattern of previous decisions by individual actors. It is the structure of the network, rather than the attributes of the firm, that plays an increasingly important role in the choice to cooperate.

The importance of the network effect on individual firm choice suggests why firms may be slow to change what they do. Information regarding with whom to cooperate or with whom to compare one's performance is almost self-evidently structured by the relationships among firms. The knowledge of an organization cannot be separated from the stability and persistence of its relationships with other organizations. Our study suggests that the slowness of firms to change, or what is commonly called inertia, may be properly understood as reflecting the stability of the network and thereby the information set available to the firm.

If history matters in the sense of a structural accumulation of past individual decisions, the consequences are profound. It should be clear that focusing exclusively on the transaction as the unit of analysis is inadequate to capture the structural effects that we have identified. The study of the make-or-cooperate decision requires an analysis of the network context within which it is made.

Notes

1. See Walker and Weber (1984) for an early test.
2. This exclusion should be kept in mind in interpreting the result. Its effect is to bias conservatively the estimated contribution of the variable measuring the influence of changes in network position on the frequency of cooperation, since all firms with no cooperative agreements have no change in their focus in the network.
3. The density of noncommercial ties is, in any event, very low and contributes negligibly to network structure.
4. The version used in our analysis is a revision by Walker (1985) of Scott Boorman's original algorithm.
5. See Hausman, Hall, and Griliches (1984) and Cameron and Trivedi (1986). Greene's statistical package (LIMDEP) provides this test as a standard feature.
6. Of course, omitted variable bias is not entirely eliminated, for the assumed gamma distribution and its parameterization are not completely general. For an unrestricted parameterization of the gamma distribution, see Schmittlein and Kim (1989).

References

Arabie, Phipps, Scott A. Boorman, and Paul R. Levitt. 1978. "Constructing Blockmodels: How and Why." *Journal of Mathematical Psychology* 17:21–63.

Baker, Wayne. 1984. "The Social Structure of a National Securities Market." *American Journal of Sociology* 89:775–811.

Boeker, Warren. 1989. "The Development and Institutionalization of Subunit Power in Organizations." *Administrative Science Quarterly* 34:388–410.

Boorman, Scott, and Paul R. Levitt. 1983. "Blockmodeling Complex Statutes:

Mapping Techniques Based on Combinatorial Optimization for Analyzing Economic Legislation and Its Stress Point Over Time." *Economics Letters* 13:1–9.

Boyles, S. E. 1968. "Estimate of the Number and Size Distribution of Domestic Joint Subsidiaries." *Antitrust Law and Economics Review* 1:81–92.

Breiger, Ronald L., Scott A. Boorman, and Phipps Arabie. 1975. "An Algorithm for Clustering Relational Data, with Applications to Social Network Analysis and Comparison with Multidimensional Scaling." *Journal of Mathematical Psychology* 12:326–383.

Burt, Ronald A. 1980. "Models of Network Structure." *Annual Review of Sociology* 6:79–141.

Cameron, A., and P. Trivedi. 1986. "Econometric Models Based on Count Data: Comparisons and Applications of some Estimators." *Journal of Applied Econometrics* 1.

Granovetter, Mark. 1985. "Economic Action and Social Structure: The Problem of Embeddedness." *American Journal of Sociology* 91:481–510.

Greene, William H. 1985. LIMDEP. Philadelphia: Social Science Data Center.

Hausman, J., B. H. Hall, and Z. Griliches. 1984. "Econometric Models for Count Data with an Application to the Patents—R&D Relationship." *Econometrics* 52:909–938.

Johnson, N. L., and S. Kotz. 1970. *Discrete Distributions*. Boston: Houghton Mifflin.

Maddala, G. S. 1977. *Econometrics*. New York: McGraw-Hill.

Meyer, J. W., and B. Rowan. 1977. "Institutionalized Organizations: Formal Structure as Myth and Ceremony." *American Journal of Sociology* 83:340–363.

Schmittlein, David, and Jinho Kim. 1989. "The Generalized NBD Regression." Mimeographed paper, Department of Marketing, Wharton School, University of Pennsylvania.

Schumpeter, Joseph A. 1934. *The Theory of Economic Development*. Cambridge, MA: Harvard University Press.

Shan, Weijian. 1990. "An Empirical Analysis of Organizational Strategies by Entrepreneurial High-Technology Firms." *Strategic Management Journal* 11:129–139.

Walker, Gordon. 1985. "Network Position and Cognition in a Computer Software Firm." *Administrative Science Quarterly* 30:103–130.

Walker, Gordon, and David Weber. 1984. "A Transaction Cost Approach to Make-or-Buy Decisions." *Administrative Science Quarterly* 29:373–391.

White, Harrison. 1981. "Where Do Markets Come From?" *American Journal of Sociology* 87:517–547.

White, Harrison, Scott A. Boorman, and Ronald L. Breiger. 1976. "Social Structure from Multiple Networks. I. Blockmodels of Roles and Positions." *American Journal of Sociology* 81:730–780.

Williamson, Oliver. 1985. *The Economic Institutions of Capitalism*. New York: The Free Press.

CHAPTER

14

Competitive Cooperation in Biotechnology: Learning Through Networks?

WALTER W. POWELL AND PETER BRANTLEY

The practice of altering genetic structures is as old as the art of breeding crops and animals, and fermentation techniques have been used in beer brewing and bread making for at least eight centuries. But the new biotechnology[1] has created a vastly greater range of possibilities and operates at a very different pace from traditional uses of biological organisms. The science underlying the new biotechnology originated with the efforts of Watson and Crick to describe the double helix in 1953. Twenty years later, Cohen et al. (1973) published their discovery of recombinant DNA methodology (i.e., the techniques to cut and paste DNA and to reproduce the newly created formed DNA in bacteria). DNA sequencing was soon worked out, and in 1974 the first expression of a human gene in bacteria was reported. The cell-fusion formula for producing hybridomas was developed in 1975 by Milstein and Köhler, for which they won a Nobel Prize in 1984. Subsequently, basic research in biotech burgeoned, making it one of the "hottest" areas in contemporary science.

On the commercial side, a young science firm named Cetus decided in the early 1970s to focus its resources on biotechnology. Genentech was founded as a biotechnology firm in 1976. By the early 1980s, dozens of new biotech companies were created annually, due in part to the entrepreneurship of academic scientists and the easy availability of venture-capital funds.[2] By decade's end, the first biotech products (e.g., human insulin, growth hormones, lymphokines, genetically engineered vaccines,

We thank Neil Fligstein, Mark Granovetter, Charles Kadushin, Peter Marsden, Richard Nelson, James Ranger-Moore, and Doug Wholey for helpful suggestions, and Marianne Broome Powell for guidance in understanding the science of biotechnology.

tPA for heart-attack victims, etc.) were on the worldwide market. In every respect, then, biotechnology is a young industry. The history of the ideas behind the research is less than 40 years old, the core technologies are less than 20 years old, and the firms that first moved to commercialize biotechnology are just now entering late adolescence.

It is, however, somewhat inaccurate to speak of biotechnology as an industry. It is rather a set of technologies that may eventually reshape an enormous range of fields: agriculture, hydrocarbon energy, medicine, mining, organic chemicals, pharmaceuticals, and even waste disposal. The breakthroughs in biotechnology are based on three key discoveries, all of which have their roots in the science of molecular biology. Monoclonal antibody (or hybridoma) technology and recombinant DNA (or genetic engineering) technology have existed for more than a decade; protein engineering has emerged more recently as a new core technology.

Antibodies are a major defense mechanism of the immune system. Each monoclonal antibody-producing cell clone has the ability to produce an indefinite number of identical protein molecules, all of which are directed against a single target. The ability to unite an antibody-producing B-cell with an immortal cancer cell is the essence of monoclonal antibody techniques. Genetic engineering is the process of cutting and pasting pieces of DNA, the helical molecules that form the heart of the genetic code, thus allowing new combinations of genetic information to be constructed. Genetic engineering and monoclonal antibody production are very different technologies: the former operates at the level of the gene and the latter at the level of a cell. Protein engineering blurs this neat distinction because it uses the techniques of both to manufacture novel molecules.

Our brief discussion does not do justice to biotechnology's scientific and entrepreneurial origins, but it does highlight the critical role played by an unusual cast of actors—academic scientists, entrepreneurs, and financiers—in the industry's startup. We want to stress two points about biotechnology's early development: (1) the extraordinary manner in which the promise of biotech miracles (e.g., "magic bullets," cures for cancer, etc.) attracted vast sums of money[3] and a good many academic scientists; and (2) the radically destabilizing and decentralizing effects—to both industry and the biomedical establishment—of this young field.

Stephen Carter, a senior vice president for cancer research at Bristol-Myers, has noted the interplay between promise and promotion, and pointed out the gap between fantastic medical and financial expectations and the reality of slow scientific and organizational progress. Observes Carter:

> There were very strong pressures from oncopolitics and oncoeconomics to make biotechnology more miraculous than it really was. By oncopolitics, I mean the need to keep the pump primed for cancer research; by oncoeconomics, the need to finance biotechnology companies. The two are synergistically related (quoted in Teitelman 1989:211, from a 1988 interview).

As the new field took shape, it became evident that not only were its boundaries blurry (i.e., spanning government institutes, universities, and firms in all kinds of industries), but its growth was profoundly reshaping several established domains—among them the pharmaceutical, agriculture, and chemical industries; the bioscience establishment and its heretofore dominant ways of funding research; the opportunity structure for scientists in biomedical research; and ultimately the relationship between universities and research-oriented corporations.

In this chapter we do not pursue the issues of biotechnology politics and financing.[4] As organizational scholars, our questions are more tractable and generalizable. Our concern is whether the speed of change in this new field requires new organizational arrangements and new strategies for survival. From the standpoint of organizational theory, the most interesting questions about a dynamic young industry concern the evolutionary path of organizational development. Do the new upstart firms gradually take on more classical, vertically integrated organizational structures? Does the industry bifurcate into small specialist firms that have carved out distinctive niches and large generalists with diverse research capabilities as well as production and marketing facilities? Or do firms develop fundamentally novel ways of organizing—what we call networks of learning—to keep abreast of fast-changing scientific and marketing developments? Indeed, is there evidence that all three developments— vertical integration, resource partitioning, and extensive use of alliances— are occurring simultaneously?

A WAVE OF CREATIVE DESTRUCTION

Technological innovation is typically an engine of change: scientific breakthroughs reveal entirely new methods, new products are created, and new levels of performance are obtained. Typically, innovation builds on existing know-how; consequently, established firms reap the bulk of the benefits. But in some cases innovation constitutes a radical break from previously dominant technologies. Often such innovations not only reduce the value of existing competencies, but also require new kinds of organizations to exploit the novel developments (Schumpeter 1934; Abernathy and Clark 1985; Tushman and Anderson 1986). Biotechnology is a dramatic case of a competence-destroying innovation because it builds on a scientific basis (immunology and molecular biology) that differs significantly from the knowledge base (organic chemistry and its clinical applications) of the more established, mature pharmaceutical industry.

Biotechnology shares several characteristics with other science-based industries such as computers and semiconductors that have also ushered in a wave of creative destruction. Small entrepreneurial firms and venture capitalists have played a major role in each industry's evolution, and established firms lagged behind during each industry's early stages. But biotechnology has been unique in a number of key respects: the close ties between universities and commercial firms; founders with virtually no prior management or production experience; and a strong reliance on licensing, partnerships, and various alliances to commercialize the new technology. The product-development process in biotechnology is also very research intensive and protracted. It can take from six to nine years to successfully bring a new drug to the market. In contrast, the semiconductor and computer industries have been characterized by rapid, continuous, and nearly exponential improvements on fairly well-understood basic technologies. Finally, the biotech regulatory process (e.g., patent filings, FDA approval) is costly, complex, and slow.

Biotechnology had its origins in the laboratories of universities and research institutes, but it was commercially exploited by small, startup firms (NBFs, or new biotechnology firms). These NBFs, fueled initially by venture-capital money (later by public stock offerings, and still later by equity investments by large firms), were research driven. Biotechnology is a new process technology (i.e., a new method of making substances or the only known way of making them in large quantities), and the people who understood its concepts were scientists. These scientists either left the academy for, or established a dual affiliation with, small private research companies.

Established pharmaceutical, chemical, and agricultural companies were not active during the industry's startup phase. Firms in these industries are relatively mature and established, and their work forces were not trained in biotechnology. Various sources have suggested that these firms feared that they were becoming technologically obsolete.[5] Thus for established companies, biotechnology represented both a threat from upstart NBFs and an opportunity for renewal.

As the biotechnology industry developed in the 1980s, it became clear that the full range of skills (e.g., basic research, applied research, clinical testing procedures, manufacturing, marketing and distribution, and knowledge of and experience with the regulatory process) could not be assembled easily under one roof. The basic science and applied research skills needed to create new products were based in universities, research institutes, and NBFs. But product development required lots of money, extensive clinical trials, and considerable expertise in getting federal regulatory approval.[6] Neither universities nor NBFs are well equipped for these tasks, but the large chemical and pharmaceutical firms most certainly are. On the other hand, established firms were unable to create internally the kind of research environment that fostered innovation and discovery.[7] Nevertheless, large firms were flush with cash and controlled established worldwide marketing channels. Some pharmaceutical companies, especially Japanese firms, were also experienced with large-scale genetic engineering and bioprocess manufacturing. So the various participants in this field have turned to joint ventures, research agreements, minority equity investments, licensing, and various kinds of partnerships to make up for their lack of internal capabilities.

Many analysts have predicted that these lattice-like networks of collaboration would prove transitory (see Pisano et al. 1988), and that a shakeout would eventually lead to industry consolidation. After all, many of these joint agreements are based on a love-hate relationship: the parties need one another, but many participants would much prefer to have the full capabilities at their own disposal. But biotechnology appears to have a most peculiar demography,[8] and it may well be that the extensive pattern of interfirm agreements and university-firm ties have made the industry somewhat immune to more standard demographic processes.

The pattern of entries and exits in biotechnology is atypical indeed. Hundreds of new biotech firms were created over the past decade. Even when the stock market was poor in 1988, 36 new companies opened their doors (Burrill et al. 1989). In a good year, such as 1984, more than three times that number were founded. New companies seem to spawn like mushrooms after a hard rain, attract financing, and begin the process of discovering new drugs, or finding new uses for existing drugs (a surprising new development where products first developed for one disease turn out to be more efficacious with a different disease),[9] or carving out a niche in the diagnostic market. But this healthy founding rate is not accompanied by a comparable death rate. Exits from the industry are strikingly low, all the more so when one realizes that the majority of firms have not yet shown a profit. Nevertheless, investors continue to pour money into the industry—more than $10 billion worth by 1989.

Many analysts have anticipated an inevitable consolidation in biotechnology, and indeed there have been several recent "affiliations." But in general the urge to merge seems muted; indeed, when acquisitions do occur, as in the recent cases of Genentech and Hoffman-LaRoche or Genetics Institute and American Home Products, they are partial (60 percent) acquisitions and the NBFs continue to be independently listed on the stock exchange. Several key factors slow the consolidation process. The abundance of small firms gives large firms ample choice of collaborative partners; the big firms can, in effect, have their pick of the best small firms as partners for particular agreements. Alliances of this sort are vastly cheaper than outright takeovers. Moreover, the diversity of linkages and agreements (the average NBF in our sample has six agreements with outside partners) and their complexity may make mergers quite difficult.[10] Finally, the growing globalization of biotechnology has opened new markets and new partners. Even the smallest U.S. biotech firms are very active in foreign markets. In our view, the industry's diversity and complexity is one of its key strengths. We suspect that biotech innovation is extensive precisely because of the sustained interaction among firms of very different sizes, universities, and research institutes—all with varied capabilities and areas of expertise.[11]

SHIFTING LOCUS OF INNOVATION

Historically, firms have organized their research and development internally, and relied on contract research for only relatively simple types of projects (Mowery 1983; Teece 1988). The reasons why the logical home for R&D was located inside the corporation were varied, ranging from the need for closer integration with production, a concern to minimize transaction costs and opportunism (Williamson 1975), and the unexpected and serendipitous discoveries that stem from tacit knowledge and technological interdependencies (Nelson and Winter 1982). But in the past decade we have seen a pronounced shift away from a strict reliance on internal R&D to a greater emphasis on various forms of externally based collaborative research and development (see Powell 1990:314–318 for an overview of the extensive literature documenting this sea change).

The movement toward stronger involvement in external relationships reflects the fact that the institutional sources of innovation have become much more diverse. Foreign firms (especially German and Japanese corporations), universities, government laboratories, and nonprofit research institutes now play a vital role in developing new forms of knowledge and new kinds of products (Nelson 1990a). To the extent that these innovations do not build on the competencies of established firms, then new technological paradigms are established (Dosi 1988). We believe that biotechnology represents an example of a new technological regime.[12] A key thrust of our research, then, is to explore the notion that biotechnology operates according to a different logic, one in which firms must be expert at both in-house research and cooperative research with external parties (e.g., competitors, university scientists, and research institutes).

We follow the insights of Mowery and Rosenberg (1989:13), who suggest that "basic research should be thought of as a ticket of admission to an information network." They emphasize that basic research done internally and research done with external collaborations should no longer be viewed as substitutes but as complements. Internal R&D is "indispensable" in order to monitor and evaluate research being conducted elsewhere. And collaborative research with external parties is critical to exploit knowledge generated outside the firm. External linkages are thus *both* a means of gaining fast access to knowledge and resources that cannot be secured internally *and* a test of internal expertise and learning capabilities. Collaborative ventures create complex patterns of communication and webs of obligation and dependency (Powell 1990). But by enhancing the diffusion of information and the availability of resources, interorganizational agreements create the possibility for further innovation by bringing together different operating assumptions and new combinations of information.[13]

Agreements with external parties are difficult to set up correctly and to manage well. We suspect that most participants would opt for going it alone were they capable of doing so. But, as we have stressed, few members of the industry have all the relevant skills. So they turn, reluctantly in many cases, to alliances. In our view, successful firms are those who learn most rapidly how to gain from external linkages without creating enemies or behaving opportunistically. Jim Grant, CEO of T-Cell Sciences, has emphasized the delicate balancing act that a small firm faces, the trade-off between giving away too much too early or giving away rights that are too broad, or waiting too long to find a partner and losing out in the R&D race (Peet 1988).[14] Over time, firms get better at striking mutually beneficial agreements and at finding partners with compatible interests and similar time horizons.

We should emphasize, however, that we do not view these young science-based firms as highly calculative strategic actors, scanning market niches they wish to capture and adroitly executing their battle plans. Many of the NBFs lack the relevant managerial expertise to plot the direction of their organizational development carefully; thus they rely on lawyers and venture capitalists for advice. Moreover, they operate in waters that are uncharted, with strong currents that pull them in unfamiliar directions. In fields such as biotech, where knowledge is advancing rapidly, companies have to invest in research in order to know "what to make of the news" (Nelson 1990b; also see Cohen and Levinthal 1989 and Rosenberg 1990). This makes the NBFs active members of the professional research community. Professors take sabbaticals at Genentech and Immunex; postdoctoral fellows move back and forth between universities and NBFs.

The embedding of biotechnology research in this larger scientific community has two consequences that we wish to emphasize. First, commercial firms lose some degree of control over their research agenda. They are tugged and pulled by scientific developments (i.e., new discoveries, techniques, and definitions of important problems; bandwagon effects; and an emerging consensus about what is "doable").[15] Second, technical prowess is the raison d'etre of successful NBFs. As the former president of Cetus (Fildes 1990) suggests, even the rapidly growing companies that are developing their own sales forces and distribution systems remain technologically driven. "Highly productive R&D operations have a nasty habit of running off in every direction at once" (Fildes 1990:67). Basic science research generates many more products than a firm can commercialize internally and often leads in unexpected directions. Alliances are a preferred option to exploit ideas that cannot be given sufficient resources internally.

ALTERNATIVE PERSPECTIVES ON INDUSTRY EVOLUTION

To explore our arguments about the changing locus of innovation, we examine the type and number of interorganizational relationships pursued by new biotechnology firms. Our aim at this stage of our research is to describe the pattern of these relationships and to begin to understand their underlying dynamics. Consequently, a key concern is whether one type of external linkage is a substitute for another type of linkage or complementary to it. If various kinds of agreements are substitutes for one another, this suggests a different interpretation from ours.[16] For example, an ecological argument would suggest that NBFs, faced with competition from large, well-endowed pharmaceutical companies, would pursue a specialist strategy wherein they attempt to exploit a specific market segment. In such situations we would expect that firms would pursue a limited number of agreements with only those partners that contribute to this specialist approach. Or, if NBFs choose to internalize various stages of the production process and resort to external ties only when their internal capability is lacking, a transaction cost argument would contend that over time, successful NBFs would rely less and less on outside parties. The motivation for internalization is clear in Williamson's (1975; 1985) work: when the skills being exchanged are both critical to organizational success and involve a high degree of asset-specificity resulting from learning-by-doing efforts, then internal organization is the preferred mode of governance.

But in our perspective, NBFs are attempting to both develop in-house capabilities and promote external collaboration. External ties should be viewed as complementary; that is, one agreement would serve as a means to enhance a configuration of skills and products that a firm is developing.[17] We argue that firms are pursuing multiple external opportunities and simultaneously building internal expertise in order to stay abreast of the pace of change. Thus we would expect that (1) older firms should not have fewer agreements than younger companies; and (2) external ties should not concentrate exclusively on any one type of agreement (i.e., young firms do not engage only in research partnerships or licensing agreements, nor do older and larger companies restrict themselves to marketing and manufacturing agreements). In short, we argue that external relationships are not restricted to early stages of the life cycle of NBFs, and we contend that different kinds of agreements are complementary rather than substitutable.

DATA AND METHODS

We developed our data base of biotechnology firms through a selection process concentrated on the June 1990 edition of *Bioscan*. This directory, an independent industrial reporting service, lists more than 900 organizations—commercial and nonprofit, U.S. and international, dedicated biotech firms as well as diversified chemical and pharmaceutical corporations. Since our focus is on NBFs, we employed the following criteria for inclusion in our sample: independently owned (NBFs in which no other business, aside from venture-capital firms, has more than a 50% stake), more than 10 employees, a product orientation primarily in therapeutics, diagnostics, or both,[18] and founded in 1987 or earlier. Our selection criteria should be obvious: we chose firms that are viable entities and are larger than a "one-scientist shop." When information in *Bioscan* was incomplete, we consulted the *Genetic Engineering and Biotechnology Related Firms Worldwide Directory* 8th ed. (1990). We also omitted firms that were subsidiaries of larger companies, on the assumption that their choice of partners would be highly constrained. The information gathered for each company relevant to this analysis includes the firm's name, address, product orientation, founding date, and employment figures, including the number of Ph.D.s and M.D.s, if listed. Table 14-1 lists some descriptive characteristics for the 129 firms in our sample.

Since our primary interest concerns the locus of innovation, we gathered data on each agreement listed in the June 1990 *Bioscan* directory. All agreements listed there are in effect at the time of this writing. At this point, we have not augmented the *Bioscan* data with interview data on the importance, duration, or directionality of the agreements (attributes that possess great relevance for our research and could eventually alter the contours of our findings.) Thus for now we treat each agreement as comparable, even though they surely vary in terms of their importance to the respective parties. The agreements are bilateral relationships: in biotech there appears to be little in the way of a group structure (such as the subcontracting networks surrounding large Japanese trading companies or found in industrial districts). Our present sample, which includes 23 firms with zero ties to other organizations, has a total of 765 agreements. The firms with more than the mean number of agreements (six) are presented in Table 14-2.

In addition to firm and agreement data, we also collected information on the organizations that were the partners to each agreement. This sample includes 81 biotechnology firms, of which 27 appear in our primary sample of 129 NBFs in therapeutics or diagnostics. For each partner, we collected the organization's name, and type of organization (such as

Table 14-1

Firm Characteristics

	MEAN	MIN.	MEDIAN	MAX.	VARIANCE	N
Agreements	5.93	0	4	45	65.03	129
Number of employees	127.57	10	60	1775	47267.18	129
Number of Ph.D.s	17.92	1	10	301	1289.69	74
Firm age	8.56	3	8	29	22.44	127
	FREQ.	PERCENT		AVG. EMPS.	AVG. AGE	
Firm Location						
U.S. West Coast	55	42.6		175.51	8.26	
U.S. East Coast	55	42.6		109.20	9.29	
U.S. Middle	19	14.7		42.00	7.26	
Ownership Type						
Private	63	48.8		66.38	7.02	
Public	66	51.2		185.98	10.03	
Product Orientation						
Therapeutics	52	40.3		109.79	8.33	
Diagnostics	22	17.1		108.04	9.32	
Combined	55	42.6		152.20	8.46	

Table 14-2

Firms with More than Mean Number of Agreements, June 1990

NAME OF FIRM	AGREE-MENT COUNT	YEAR FOUNDED	NO. OF EM-PLOYEES	CITY	STATE
Genentech, Inc.	45	76	1775	S. San Francisco	CA
Centocor, Inc.	44	79	572	Malvern	PA
Biogen	40	78	280	Cambridge	MA
Cetus Corp.	36	71	740	Emeryville	CA
Cambridge Bio-science Corp.	26	82	150	Worcester	MA
California Biotech-nology Inc.	24	82	180	Mountain View	CA
Chiron Corp.	21	81	460	Emeryville	CA
ALZA Corp.	18	68	640	Palo Alto	CA
Genetics Institute	17	80	550	Cambridge	MA
Nova Pharma-ceutical Corp.	16	82	174	Baltimore	MD
Genex Corp.	14	77	100	Gaithersburg	MD
T-Cell Science, Inc.	14	83	90	Cambridge	MA
Repligen Corp.	13	81	127	Cambridge	MA
Bio-technology General Corp.	12	80	115	New York	NY
Pharmatec	12	82	16	Alachua	FL
Enzo Biochem, Inc.	11	76	340	New York	NY
Quest BioTech-nology, Inc.	11	86	13	Detroit	MI
Ribi ImmunoChem Research, Inc.	11	81	51	Hamilton	MT
Advanced Mag-netics, Inc.	10	81	65	Cambridge	MA
Amgen Inc.	10	80	700	Thousand Oaks	CA
Collagen Corp.	10	75	390	Palo Alto	CA
Genzyme Corp.	10	81	497	Boston	MA
Collaborative Re-search, Inc.	9	61	99	Bedford	MA
Epitope, Inc.	9	79	80	Beaverton	OR
Immunex Corp.	9	81	315	Seattle	WA
Biotech Research Laboratories	8	73	210	Rockville	MD
CYTOGEN Corp.	8	80	150	Princeton	NJ
Riagnon Corp.	8	86	84	Rockville	MD
Hybritech, Inc.	8	78	800	San Diego	CA
The Liposome Co., Inc.	8	81	71	Princeton	NJ
Cellular Products, Inc.	7	82	22	Buffalo	NY
Creative Biomole-cules, Inc.	7	81	62	Hopkinton	MA
Genetic Therapy, Inc.	7	86	38	Gaithersburg	MD
Immunomedics, Inc.	7	82	45	Warren	NJ
NeoRx Corp.	7	84	120	Seattle	WA
Oncor, Inc.	7	83	26	Gaithersburg	MD

Table 14-2 (Continued)

NAME OF FIRM	AGREE-MENT COUNT	YEAR FOUNDED	NO. OF EM-PLOYEES	CITY	STATE
Senetek plc	7	83	12	St. Louis	MO
Synergen, Inc.	7	81	140	Boulder	CO
XOMA Corp.	7	81	183	Berkeley	CA
IDEC Pharma-ceuticals Corp.	6	86	100	La Jolla	CA
LipoGen, Inc.	6	85	35	Knoxville	TN
Promega Corp.	6	78	105	Madison	WI
Seragen, Inc.	6	79	250	Hopkinton	MA

university, biotechnology firm, research institute, government agency, or type of business). We will soon complete data acquisition for size (in employees, faculty, etc.) and ownership (name, size, location, and primary business of parent) of the partner organizations. A listing of partners in our sample with more than four ties appears in Table 14-3.

The diversity of the partners is remarkable, ranging from federallv funded agencies to international pharmaceutical companies to prominent private U.S. universities. This emphasizes our earlier point that the boundaries of this field are quite broad. Note that the list of partners includes many organizations that in no way compete with one another. This decentralized field appears to have few dominant actors, save for the National Institutes of Health. The large number of ties to the NIH is worth noting, and will have a bearing on our subsequent analyses.

The diversity of partners does not indicate whether individual firms are equally variegated in their choosing, or whether certain types of firms tend to concentrate on particular types of agreements. To try to sort out these issues, we classified agreements into four distinct categories. We followed an implicit "logic of production" in our coding; beginning with research and development, then licensing, and then marketing and production. Our fourth category consists of collaborative ventures that involve multiple stages of the production process.

The first category includes research grants from either corporations or government institutions such as NIH, and R&D agreements with other organizations where no explicit partitioning of marketing rights or other nonresearch obligations takes place. These are essentially pro bono agreements, ostensibly for the mutual scientific benefit of both parties. The second category is comprised of licensing agreements, where one party licenses either a technology or a product from another. Some firms license more broadly than others, in terms of both organizational and geographical scope. A biotech firm may license an integrated pharmaceutical company to market a product, or even an entire class of products, in the world market. Alternatively, a firm might attempt to sign multiple licensing agreements on a single product for smaller segments of the geographical market with many firms. Each such licensing agreement appears as a separate tie in our data base.

Table 14-3

Partners with More than Four Ties to Biotechnology Firms, June 1990

PARTNER NAME	COUNT OF AGREEMENTS
NIH	48
Hoffman-La Roche Inc.	18
E. I. DuPont	12
NCI*	11
Bristol-Myers Squibb Co.	10
CIBA-Geigy, Ltd.	10
Merck & Co., Inc.	9
Mallinckrodt, Inc.	8
Mitsubishi Kasei Corp.	8
SmithKline Beecham plc	8
U.S. Army	8
Baxter International Inc.	7
Boehringer Ingelheim	7
Eastman Kodak Co.	7
Eli Lilly and Co.	7
MIT	7
Pfizer, Inc.	7
Stanford University	7
Abbott Laboratories	6
Behringwerke AG	6
Cetus	6
Daiichi Seiyaku	6
Genentech	6
Harvard University	6
NIAID*	6
Sandoz, Ltd.	6
Burroughs Wellcome	5
Baxter Healthcare Corp.	4
Becton Dickinson & Co.	4
Boehringer Mannheim	4
Erbamont NV	4
Johns Hopkins University	4
Kabi AB	4
Massachusetts General Hospital	4
Memorial Sloan Kettering	4
Organon Teknika Corp.	4
Syntex Corp.	4
Yamanouchi Pharmaceutical Co.	4

*Branches of the National Institutes of Health (NIH)

Marketing agreements, in which another party is granted rights for the marketing, supply, or distribution of a product, constitute the third group. Like licensing agreements, marketing agreements can vary in their exclusivity and expansiveness. Perhaps the most extreme form is exhibited by manufacturing and marketing arrangements in which the second party is allowed to both manufacture and market the product. Marketing agreements are often of shorter duration than licensing arrangements, often for only two or three years (remarkable, as the market impact of traditional therapeutics often lasts at least five years, and that of diagnostics even longer), but they are frequently renewed.

The fourth group consists of joint development agreements. These projects may have disparate outcomes for the participants. In joint development agreements, two or more firms share product development; one firm, usually the one making the largest contribution to amortizing costs, gains concessions for marketing or distribution. As with the other forms of agreements, (save for research grants), the cost to the secondary partner may be cheap or dear. In their most extreme form, biotech companies can become contract research labs for larger integrated companies, much as Battelle and Arthur D. Little were for an earlier era of batch-production industry. In more equitable versions, the development is much closer to a partnership and exploitation is less common. Take the complex relationship between Amgen Inc. and Ortho Pharmaceutical to develop hepatitis-B vaccine, interleukin-2 (IL-2), and erythropoietin (EPO) as an illustration. In this joint development and marketing agreement, Ortho conducts the clinical trials. For hepatitis-B, Ortho has worldwide rights, except for China. For EPO, Amgen has exclusive rights for dialysis use in the United States, Ortho has exclusive rights for nondialysis use in the United States and exclusive rights for the rest of the world except for Japan and China. For IL-2, Ortho has exclusive worldwide rights.

As our example attests, the logic of interorganizational agreements is complex. These arrangements involve neither the explicit criteria associated with arms-length contracting nor the familiar paternalism of hierarchical controls (Powell 1990). Both parties recognize that some gains will result from pooling resources. As a relationship develops, some degree of mutual orientation—knowledge that each partner assumes the other possesses and that is drawn on in communication and problem solving—is established. As Macneil (1985) suggests, the entangling strings of reputation and interdependence become parts of the relationship. Even though the sample of potential partners is large and disparate, the relevant biotech community is tightly knit together through communication networks: news about malfeasance spreads rapidly. Obviously large corporations and powerful research institutes can better withstand questions about their reputation, but individual scientists and small NBFs may be quite vulnerable to charges of opportunism or shirking.

Our sample includes 233 research and development agreements or outright grants; 202 licensing agreements; 168 marketing and supply or distribution agreements; and 162 collaborative agreements, such as development and marketing arrangements or joint ventures. In addition, for each firm possessing at least one tie, we calculated the percentage of its ties falling into each of these four categories. The means of these variables are reported in Table 14-4.

To help us determine whether these different types of agreements are substitutable or complementary, we conducted a principal components factor analysis for those firms with at least one tie. If the different mea-

Table 14-4

Types and Percentages of Ties

	MEAN	MIN.	MEDIAN	MAX.	VARIANCE	N
R&D	1.73	0	0	13	5.70	129
Marketing	1.30	0	0	15	5.81	129
Licensing	1.56	0	0	18	8.17	129
Development & Marketing	1.26	0	0	14	5.47	129
PERCENT						
R&D	35.06	0	25	100	1237.54	106
Marketing	21.21	0	12.2	100	809.83	106
Licensing	24.48	0	20	100	853.76	106
Development & Marketing	17.89	0	11.3	100	522.49	106

Note: Percentages were not calculated for the 23 firms with no external agreements. This allows the sum of the means to approach 100%.

sures are substitutable, then they should load on separate factors. Conversely, if they are complementary, they should load highly on one factor. As Table 14-5 demonstrates, the latter interpretation is supported. The grants, marketing, licensing, and development and marketing variables all load very highly on a single factor. This tends to confirm our view that these different types of agreements are strongly complementary.

Our aim is to ascertain those factors that seem to predispose firms toward the formation of network ties with other organizations, and toward what type of ties in particular. Therefore we conducted regression analysis on the aggregate number of ties and the count of ties appearing in each separate category. In addition, to see if there are different patterns expressed for R&D alliances exclusive of the outright grants provided by NIH, we recalculated the number of R&D alliances by subtracting each firm's count of NIH, NCI (National Cancer Institute), and NIAID (National Institute for Arthritis and Infectious Disease) agreements and incorporated this count as a dependent variable as well.[19]

We anticipate several determinants for the number of ties. Larger firms, as measured by number of employees, should possess more ties

Table 14-5

Factor Analysis of Agreement Variables

UNROTATED FACTOR PATTERN	
	Factor-1
R&D and grants	0.701
Licensing	0.812
Marketing	0.792
Development & marketing	0.873
Eigenvalue	2.539

than smaller firms do. We anticipate that older firms will have gained knowledge about the ins and outs of networking and will be more likely to engage in further agreements, net of their size, than younger ones. Further, public firms, as opposed to private firms which we use as the omitted category, will be more likely to utilize both the knowledge gathering and the symbolic importance of external ties to provide appropriate signals to the relevant financial community. To determine whether there are geographic patterns in network activity, perhaps due to regional agglomeration effects, we included a dummy variable for firms residing in East Coast states and one for those on the West Coast, omitting one for firms falling in the midcontinental hinterland. Finally, we test to see if there are differences among firms with dissimilar product orientations, and whether firms engaging in therapeutic, diagnostic, and diversified strategies have correspondingly divergent network ties, both in terms of the number and type of ties. Diagnostic companies, which tend to be the most specialized, provide our omitted category.

Initial analysis of the joint distributions of firm age, employment, and the number and percentage of ties suggested strong elements of heteroskedasticity. In order to remedy this problem, weighted least squares regressions were used throughout to predict the aggregate number of ties, and ties falling into each category. Our results are displayed in Table 14-6.

Several factors are associated with having a large number of agreements. Employment is significant, although the effect is modest. Publicly owned firms are much more likely to have a large number of ties, and private firms are more likely to accept R&D agreements. Firms that are involved in both diagnostics and therapeutics have a greater number of agreements, particularly R&D agreements when grants from the NIH are subtracted. Finally, younger firms have fewer licensing and more R&D agreements than older firms. What is noteworthy about these models, however, is their homogeneity; we do not find sharply divergent results for different kinds of agreements.

In Table 14-7, we consider regressions on the percentage distribution of ties. By seeing what attributes are associated with choosing one strategy instead of another, we can begin to determine what types of firms pursue one form of agreement to the exclusion of another.

Several features stand out. Again we see the important presence of the NIH. Firms with a high proportion of agreements with the NIH (omitted from the second column) are more likely to be privately owned. In concordance with the findings in Table 14-6, this suggests that it is predominately private firms, safe from the short-run pressures of Wall Street, that embark on research agreements with ambiguous long-range benefits. We also do see some sign of specialization, or a niche strategy: diagnostic firms tend to predominate among the firms with marketing agreements. Once again, however, we do not find strongly divergent results for different kinds of agreements; participation in one form of agreement does not appear to preclude joining in another kind of external relationship.

Table 14-6
Regression Analysis of the Number and Types of Ties (N = 126)

VARIABLE	TOTAL AGREEMENTS		R&D		R&D (w/o NIH)		LICENSING		MARKETING		DEVELOPMENT & MARKETING	
	b	SE (b)	b	SE (b)	b	SE (b)	b	SE (b)	b	SE (b)	b	SE (b)
Employment	0.023**	0.001	0.005**	0.000	0.005**	0.000	0.005**	0.000	0.005**	0.000	0.007**	0.000
Ownership												
Public	3.062**	0.403	0.989**	0.322	0.269	0.150	0.366	0.288	0.776**	0.211	0.943**	0.212
Region												
U.S. West	−1.570**	0.552	−0.697	0.441	−0.224	0.268	−0.668	0.394	0.131	0.289	−0.432	0.290
U.S. East	0.786	0.578	0.760	0.463	−0.041	0.272	0.041	0.413	0.254	0.303	−0.230	0.305
Product mix												
Therap.	0.983	0.542	−0.076	0.434	0.510**	0.167	0.566	0.388	−0.313	0.284	0.684*	0.286
Combined	3.022**	0.560	0.407	0.448	0.617**	0.173	1.170**	0.400	0.467	0.293	0.765*	0.295
Age (years)	−0.013	0.024	−0.056**	0.019	−0.033**	0.010	0.069**	0.017	−0.032*	0.013	−0.080*	0.013
Constant	0.068	0.626	0.886	0.501	0.188	0.271	−0.407	0.447	0.157	0.328	−0.186	0.330
R^2	.95		.62		.67		.75		.78		.87	

Note: $* p < .05$, $** p < .01$

Table 14-7
Regression Analyses of the Percentage Distribution of Ties (N = 104)

VARIABLE	% R&D		% R&D (w/o NIH)		% LICENSING		% MARKETING		% DEVELOPMENT & MARKETING	
	b	SE (b)	b	SE (b)	b	SE (b)	b	SE (b)	b	SE (b)
Employment	-0.011	0.009	0.025	0.005	-0.001	0.010	0.002	0.010	0.013	0.009
Ownership										
Public	-13.477**	4.909	-11.654**	7.062	10.115	5.558	3.554	5.585	4.008	5.244
Region										
U.S. West	0.337	6.208	4.165	14.369	-6.342	7.029	9.057	7.063	-13.313*	6.632
U.S. East	-3.152	5.880	24.019	14.230	7.908	6.658	6.672	6.690	-16.280*	6.282
Product mix										
Therap.	21.533**	6.213	43.884**	8.448	-6.674	7.035	-26.717**	7.069	5.842	6.637
Combined	17.392*	6.674	16.770*	8.409	4.084	7.557	-25.613**	7.593	2.763	7.130
Age (years)	-0.482	0.404	-3.818	0.491	-0.172	0.457	0.844	0.460	-0.460	0.432
Constant	31.598**	6.862	27.772	14.642	14.119	7.769	26.603**	7.807	32.891**	7.330
R^2	.32		.59		.24		.25		.06	

Note: $*p < .05$, $**p < .01$

Table 14-8
Characteristics of Polygamous Firms

	MEAN	MIN.	MEDIAN	MAX.	VARIANCE	N
Agreements	13.47	6	10	45	104.35	43
Employees	255.16	12	127	1775	103986.5	43
Ph.D.s	40.61	2	20	301	4575.78	18
Firm age	10.19	4	9	29	22.87	43

We contend that firms that are most actively involved in interorganizational networks should display agreement patterns different from those of firms that are less connected via formal external ties. We consequently formed a subsample consisting of those firms possessing six ties or more, which we dubbed polygamous firms. We then repeated our analyses using these 43 firms. Let us first comment on the general characteristics of this subsample. As shown in Table 14-8, these firms have an average of 13.5 agreements, are much larger than the mean for the entire sample, and are slightly older. We find these results unsurprising: in our view, larger older firms should have developed more ties and more skill at utilizing these relationships. These larger older NBFs may well be internalizing more activities, *but* they are simultaneously involved in more extensive external ties as well.

In comparison with the full sample, we see in Table 14-9 that polygamous firms have a somewhat smaller percentage of R&D agreements and higher percentages of marketing and development and marketing agreements. What is most remarkable, however, is that the percentage distribution is not markedly different, indicating that each type of tie appears with about the same frequency no matter how polygamous the firm is. To determine if the polygamous firms are biased toward specific types of agreements in a manner that departs from that found for the full sample, we reconducted our regression models. The results are indicated in Tables 14-10 and 14-11.

Table 14-9
Types and Percentages of Ties, Polygamous Firms

	MEAN	MIN.	MEDIAN	MAX.	VARIANCE	N
R&D	3.60	0	3	13	9.24	43
Marketing	3.12	0	2	15	11.44	43
Licensing	3.60	0	2	18	16.96	43
Development & Marketing	3	0	2	14	10.95	43
PERCENT						
R&D	30.12	0	22.2	100	592.16	43
Marketing	22.90	0	18.8	100	445.64	43
Licensing	25.04	0	25	100	486.04	43
Development & Marketing	21.27	0	16.7	100	290.61	43

Table 14-10
Regression Analysis of the Number and Types of Ties (N = 42)

VARIABLE	TOTAL AGREEMENTS		R&D		R&D (w/o NIH)		LICENSING		MARKETING		DEVELOPMENT & MARKETING	
	b	SE (b)	b	SE (b)	b	SE (b)	b	SE (b)	b	SE (b)	b	SE (b)
Employment	0.022**	0.001	0.004**	0.001	0.005**	0.001	0.006**	0.001	0.004**	0.001	0.008**	0.001
Ownership												
Public	2.577	1.331	−1.886	1.069	−0.662	0.505	2.323*	0.968	2.175**	0.795	0.029	0.678
Region												
U.S. West	−3.520*	1.557	0.431	1.250	−1.158	0.768	−4.042**	1.132	0.868	0.930	−0.706	0.793
U.S. East	1.412	1.337	1.677	1.073	−1.590	0.718	−1.779	0.972	0.405	0.799	1.171	0.681
Product mix												
Therap.	0.269	1.570	1.798	1.260	1.892	0.588	0.798	1.141	−4.083**	0.938	1.713*	0.799
Combined	4.617**	1.488	2.902*	1.195	1.165	0.750	2.772*	1.082	−3.023**	0.889	1.918*	0.758
Age (years)	−0.031	0.138	0.195	0.111	−0.068**	0.022	−0.236*	0.100	−0.019	0.083	−0.009	0.070
Constant	2.990	2.049	−0.840	1.645	2.757**	0.773	2.492	1.490	2.758*	1.224	−1.207	1.043
R^2	.93		.48		.68		.67		.68		.85	

*Note: * $p < .05$, ** $p < .01$*

Table 14-11
Regression Analyses of the Percentage Distribution of Ties (N = 42)

VARIABLE	% R&D		% R&D (w/o NIH)		% LICENSING		% MARKETING		% DEVELOPMENT & MARKETING	
	b	SE (b)	b	SE (b)	b	SE (b)	b	SE (b)	b	SE (b)
Employment	-0.011	0.009	0.003	0.006	0.007	0.008	-0.007	0.006	0.011	0.006
Ownership										
Public	-36.498**	10.142	-19.366**	4.581	17.012	8.939	22.526**	6.779	-2.488	6.503
Region										
U.S. West	14.061	11.866	-12.083	6.959	-26.284*	10.458	15.519	7.931	-2.685	7.608
U.S. East	12.100	10.185	-23.949**	6.514	-20.008*	8.977	1.023	6.808	7.299	6.531
Product mix										
Therap.	21.234	11.960	15.295*	6.798	4.527	10.542	-53.347**	7.994	27.416**	7.669
Combined	21.241	11.339	11.083	6.375	14.538	9.994	-50.412**	7.579	14.205	7.271
Age (years)	1.329	1.052	-0.514*	0.198	-1.891*	0.927	-0.073	0.703	0.360	0.675
Constant	22.138	15.613	48.325**	7.006	36.803*	13.761	47.521**	10.436	-4.941	10.011
R^2	.27		.69		.32		.59		.27	

Note: *p <.05, **p < .01

Employment, our proxy for firm size, has a limited effect on number of ties. Although positively associated with the number of ties, its parameters have low magnitudes and it has no effect on the distribution of types of ties. Product diversification, the combination of diagnostics and therapeutics, has a strong positive effect on the number of ties, but less of a relationship to the specific type of tie, with the exception of marketing agreements, which seem to be the preserve of diagnostic firms. We do find upstream and downstream differences when it comes to ownership. Public firms have more marketing and licensing agreements, as well as a smaller percentage of R&D agreements. When the influence of the NIH is removed, this effect recedes somewhat. Nevertheless, we see the familiar developmental pattern with publicly owned firms more likely to be involved in agreements directly related to product commercialization. Finally, age is a weak variable, although older firms seem to accept fewer licensing and R&D agreements, subtracting NIH grants. This suggests that among polygamous biotech companies, long-established firms have learned to court research funds and avoid agreements which lessen control of their profit-making potential.

FURTHER RESEARCH

At this stage of our research, we lack data that enable us to assess the efficacy of the interorganizational agreements in which our sample NBFs are currently engaged. Obviously, the clearest test of our argument would involve documenting the effect of network learning on organizational performance. Assessing the linkage between organizational strategy and performance is always complex, and appropriate data are not readily available, particularly in an industry where few NBFs have shown a profit. We close our paper with a discussion of the various steps we are pursuing to determine the relationship between learning through networks and organizational performance.

Organizational Processes

The descriptive statistics we have presented offer some insight into what kinds of firms are most likely to be involved in multiple formal arrangements. But these data provide little understanding of how NBFs find partners or how particular companies are sought out by larger firms. We also know little about the processes of mutual evaluation and adjustment that occur in the course of interfirm working relationships. Finally, we remain relatively ignorant of the relationships that underlie the traffic back and forth between universities and NBFs. Indeed, our analyses focus entirely on formal agreements; we know that there are extensive informal ties that support the research and development process in this field. As a first step in this direction, we are collecting information on the science advisory boards for the firms in our sample. Initial interviews with scientists who are extensively involved in these consulting relationships suggest, not surprisingly, that formal agreements among universities, research institutes, and NBFs evolve out of preexisting educational and work-related ties.

Conversations with university scientists in molecular biology and cancer research and with scientists and executives at biotech firms convince us that standard questionnaires will not offer much insight into how members of the biotech community search for partners. Instead, detailed personal interviews and participant observations are necessary. We are now exploiting our personal and professional relationships in order to gain access to several NBFs. Our aim is to study firsthand how NBFs develop expertise in this "mating" process. How do NBFs assess the compatibility of partners? Which members of the NBF are involved in the decision to undertake an agreement? How is the performance of an agreement evaluated and by whom? We believe these kinds of questions can be addressed only through sustained personal contact with NBF firms. Our expectation is that most of this kind of expertise is uncodified tacit knowledge, and perhaps has not even been discussed systematically by employees or executives of a NBF. Our goal, then, is to try to explicate through detailed interviews the evolution of the learning function in NBFs—that is, how knowledge is developed about how to do strategic alliances, and where this knowledge resides.

Input Measures

Most of the literature on innovation does not attempt to measure innovation directly. Instead, most researchers employ dependent variables that measure inputs to the innovation process. Two of the most common measures are number of employees engaged in R&D and annual expenditures on R&D. Obviously, data on R&D expenditures are subject to wide variability in reporting because of accounting practices. In addition, privately held firms do not have to report R&D expenditures. Nevertheless, we are in the process of collecting data on R&D expenditures in hopes that this information will offer insight into the productivity of different patterns of R&D funding.

We are more confident about the prospects of collecting data on the number of employees with advanced degrees. Data on educational attainment perform poorly in cross-industry studies of innovation, but they work well as an intraindustry measure (Richard Nelson, personal communication). In some very important respects, the core activities of the NBFs are research, development, and deal making. A measure of the number of employees with advanced degrees engaged in science and development should be a good indicator of innovative effort. If our arguments about learning are to prove compelling, we should find that firms with a higher proportion of Ph.D.s on their staff are involved in more collaborative agreements.[20]

Output Measures

Direct measures of innovative outputs are scarce in the literature on innovation.[21] Patent counts have been used most frequently as proxies for the innovative efforts of firms and industries. They are not without problems, but their limitations are most serious in cross-industry and cross-national studies (Griliches et al. 1987). The intellectual property status of biotechnology patents remains fuzzy, despite a key 1980 Supreme Court decision (*Diamond* v. *Chakrabarty*), which held that new microorganisms can be patented (see Adler 1984). As long as uncertainty remains over the utility and scope of biotech patents, it will not be obvious whether patents protect innovators from imitation.

But there is another side to patents that we believe is much more congruent with the aims of our research. Rather than being viewed as protectors of intellectual property, patents can be seen as "signals" of scientific competence, signals that are particularly relevant to suppliers of capital (obviously a paramount concern for small firms) and to other members of the scientific community (Cohen and Levin 1989; Nelson 1990b). Nelson (1990b) makes this point nicely when he observes that claim staking is not only an effort to establish property rights and attract customers, but equally an attempt to make the financial community happy and to enhance the company's reputation in the science profession. Biotech scientists are major contributors to the scientific literature, and patents are one important form of scientific recognition. Thus our reading of the patent literature and our discussions with molecular biologists convince us that patent filings are a reasonable output measure of scientific performance. We have just begun the tedious process of coding patent filings by the firms in our sample, and we expect that this will serve as a useful indicator of the efficacy of collaborative agreements.

REPRISE

Scholars who lack familiarity with the field of biotechnology may wonder why it has become the object of such intensive study or be puzzled that three chapters on biotechnology are included in this volume when it appears to be such a unique industry. We are obviously convinced that biotechnology is unusually interesting in its own right. The extremely close ties between universities and NBFs raise questions about how university-based norms of openness and free inquiry survive in more proprietary settings. But the playing field for industry has also changed. We argue that commercial success now depends much more on successful and productive collaboration with disparate parties. In this respect, biotechnology is the ideal setting to examine the factors that explain the etiology and durability of interorganizational ventures.

We have offered a rather novel perspective on interfirm collaboration: in industries where the relevant know-how is broadly dispersed, innovation depends on cooperative interaction among different types of organizations. The locus of innovation becomes a network rather than an individual firm. We anticipate that firms with more internal knowledge are more willing to pursue a strategy based on alliances and agreements. We cannot substantiate our conjecture at this point, but we can point out that older firms have not retreated from the practice of engaging in agreements. Moreover, for most firms except the most specialized, agreements of different kinds appear to be complements for one another rather than substitutes, suggesting that firms are continuing to stay involved in external relationships even as they build up internal capabilities.

Much of the current research in network analysis tends to gloss over the content of what it is that is being exchanged. We try to add some texture to network analysis by suggesting that networks are particularly well suited for rapid learning and the flexible deployment of resources. These claims bring our work much closer to the recent burgeoning literature on flexible specialization and industrial districts (Piore and Sabel 1984; Sabel 1989; Herrigel 1990). More broadly, our argument suggests that biotechnology may represent a new kind of industrial order—one in which production depends heavily on the exchange of knowledge and the most critical skill is to develop internal expertise and simultaneously maintain ongoing collaborations with external sources of knowledge and talent.

Finally, research on biotechnology raises fundamental questions about the nature of organizational change. The new kinds of organizational arrangements that have proliferated in biotechnology have been a response to dramatic competence-destroying scientific breakthroughs. Are such fundamental changes in organizational forms possible only when they accompany a wave of technological change? Or will the novelty of biotechnology soon fade, as NBFs evolve into mature corporations and incumbent pharmaceutical and chemical corporations regain their former dominance? Obviously, answers to these questions are premature, but we suspect that considerable insight into the processes of organizational change can be gleaned from close-hand analysis of the ferment in biotechnology.

Notes

1. The Office of Technology Assessment (1984) uses the term "the new biotechnologies" (defined as the use of recombinant DNA, cell fusion, and novel bioprocessing techniques to make or modify products, to improve plants or animals, or to develop microorganisms for specific uses) in order to distinguish recent work in molecular biology from age-old practices of fermentation and selective breeding.
2. Kenney (1986) provides an excellent account of the close links between the science community and the world of venture capital during biotech's heady early days.
3. At this point we lack the relevant insider knowledge to tell the full story of the critical role that funding has played in biotechnology's development.

Venture-capital money helped create this business, Wall Street's initial bullish embrace promoted the industry's early proliferation, and its subsequent bearish rebuff brought about the entry of large pharmaceutical and chemical corporations—notably European and Japanese firms—into the industry's financial picture.

4. The excitement and novelty of biotech has attracted some excellent science reporters. In a crowded field, we have learned a good deal from Angier (1988), Hall (1987) and Teitelman (1989).

5. See "Note on the Biotechnology Industry," S-BP-250, Graduate School of Business, Stanford University, prepared by Coleman, Keating, and Jemison, for an excellent discussion of how technological change threatened established companies. One particularly critical point they make is that new-product introductions have declined precipitously in the pharmaceutical industry. Pisano (1990) found that large pharmaceutical firms with a strong history of internal R&D have not had a greater propensity to pursue biotech projects on their own, suggesting that biotechnology represents a technological discontinuity that robs firms of their historical research capabilities.

6. Many biotechnology companies have stumbled on the path to FDA product approval (see Powell and Brantley 1993). The Cetus Corporation, one of the earliest companies in the field, was dealt a death blow when the Food and Drug Administration, in July 1990, turned down its "flagship" drug, interleukin-2. Cetus eventually merged with its smaller neighbor, Chiron, and in May 1992, after seven years of development and testing, the FDA approved IL-2. More recently, the FDA told Centocor it lacked sufficient data for approval of Centoxin, its core product. Between February and April, 1992, the company lost $1.5 billion in market value. More and more NBFs are hiring experienced pharmaceutical executives to help steer them through turbulent regulatory waters.

7. The reasons why large firms cannot create a hospitable atmosphere for R&D are a matter of considerable debate in the organizational literature (see Williamson 1985). In this case, several factors seem especially relevant. The supply of newly minted Ph.D.s in immunology and molecular biology is limited (Office of Technology Assessment, 1988). Moreover, compensation policies in the NBFs typically include generous stock options (Burrill et al. 1989). Possibly even more important is the intangible issue of atmosphere. NBFs "feel" like science labs, and commonly have close ties to university researchers. Young scientists in NBFs can remain members of their relevant professional community. In large corporate pharmaceutical R&D, the atmosphere of industry replaces that of science.

8. A very good description of these anomalies can be found in "The Money-Guzzling Genius of Biotechnology," The Economist, May 13, 1989, pp. 69–70.

9. Biotech drugs are "biological response modifiers." As such, they typically perform multiple roles, and their unexpected alternative uses can create new areas for research. For example, a number of highly touted drugs, such as alpha interferon and human growth hormone, initially performed poorly with respect to the diseases or conditions they were intended to treat. But subsequent research has revealed many more potential uses, from hepatitis to burn treatment to AIDS. See "The Many Personalities of Gene-Spliced Drugs," Business Week, July 30, 1990, pp. 68–69; and Lawrence Fisher, "The Return of an Ex-Wonder Drug," New York Times, August 16, 1990, pp. C1, C18.

10. The breakup of Cetus, following the FDA's negative ruling on its main product IL-2, is an apt example. Initially, analysts expected Cetus to be a choice takeover target for a large pharmaceutical corporation. But Cetus had such an extensive network of collaborators that it discouraged potential corporate suitors. Eventually, Cetus was chopped up in pieces: its attractive

polymerase chain reactor technology was sold to Hoffman-LaRoche, while its research and development staff and their products were merged into a much smaller NBF, Chiron. The extensive ties that characterize many NBFs render them less attractive as merger targets because so many of the key assets are bound up in agreements with collaborators.

11. In their fascinating analysis of 61 inventions, Jewkes, Sawers, and Stillerman (1969:168) conclude that there may be no optimal size and design for an innovative firm, but rather "an optimum pattern for any industry, such a distribution of firms by size, character, and outlook as to guarantee the most effective gathering together and commercially perfecting of the flow of new ideas."

12. The Office of Technology Assessment (1984:270) reports that biotechnology's utilization of contract research has been without parallel in any commercial sector save perhaps for small defense contractors.

13. See Imai et al. 1985, and Kaneko and Imai 1987 for very useful discussions of the "utility" of networks in supporting learning in Japanese firms.

14. The new drugs with multiple uses mentioned in note 9 provide an apt example. Alpha interferon was initially developed by the NBFs Biogen and Genentech. Both were young, needed cash, and licensed their rights respectively to Schering-Plough and Hoffman-LaRoche. Some ten years later, studies suggest that the pharmaceutical firms have a potent and highly profitable therapeutic drug on their hands. The combination of a firm's life-cycle stage, its need for particular resources, and the complexity of the science, wherein drugs may be only partially understood for years, greatly complicates the choices facing young NBFs.

15. See several fascinating recent studies in the sociology of science on how problems emerge and are defined and how a consensus is constructed as to what research is feasible and what is not: Cambrosia and Keating 1988; Fujimura 1987, 1988; Latour 1987.

16. Theoretical perspectives in organizational analysis are sufficiently new and elastic that they can be refashioned fairly easily. Clearly, we are attempting to pose our networks-of-learning view as a contrast to ecological (Freeman and Barley 1990) and transaction cost arguments. The various approaches, however, are not wholly incompatible. For example, one could argue that NBFs pursue external ties until their learning capabilities are saturated—that is, until their development niches are fully utilized. Similarly, recent work in the transaction cost tradition (Pisano et al. 1988; Pisano 1990; Williamson 1985) recognizes that firms no longer make clear choices between market and hierarchy. Rather, there are various governance mechanisms by which partners with cospecialized assets (Teece 1988) can offer one another credible commitments that they will not behave opportunistically. As an illustration, Tapon (1989) employs a transaction cost analysis framework to explain why large pharmaceutical companies have experienced "organizational failure" in R&D and thus are turning to R&D contracts with outside sources.

17. In very simple terms, imagine that firm A faces a choice of forming an agreement with partner X to pursue a research collaboration, or with partner Y to market a new diagnostic test. If agreements are viewed as substitutes for one another, then the firm would choose only one partner. The choice itself presumably would be dictated by the strategic logic of either specialization or internal integration. In contrast, if agreements are viewed as complementary, then firm A would pursue both agreements, following a strategy that suggests that the gains from one agreement might augment the gains from another.

18. It is relatively easy to classify NBFs on the basis of the primary market that a company serves. The four main market segments that NBFs are found in include diagnostics, therapeutics, agriculture, and instrumentation and supply. Three other very small segments—specialty chemicals, bioremediation

(environmental cleanup) and animal health care—are in very early stages of development. We decided not to include NBFs in instrumentation and supply because their focus on developing research instruments, reagents, and the like makes these firms very distinctive. They are less involved in R&D, do not face costly and complex clinical trials, and do not have close ties to universities. We also omitted agricultural firms. These are companies that focus on plant genetics and the development of microbial pesticides and herbicides. In part because of public opposition and regulatory controls, research in this area is still in its infancy. The regulatory environment for ag-bio is fundamentally different from that of therapeutics and diagnostics. In the latter cases, the risks are ultimately to a single individual who chooses to take a drug or a test, and the benefits are very clear. With ag-bio, the risks are collective. There are possible harmful externalities and the benefits are less obvious.

Our focus is on the most R&D-intensive sectors, where NBF development has been the most pronounced. The human therapeutic market is the most research-intensive segment of the industry and the one for which the greatest promise is held. Therapeutic products address a wide range of diseases and conditions involving the blood system, the immune system, and hormonal balances. These products, which provide therapeutic alternatives where none previously existed or that are superior to existing ones, face a lengthy and costly process of clinical trials to meet government standards for efficacy and safety.

The diagnostic field consists of products used to detect disease conditions (AIDS, cancer), physiological states (pregnancy), or genetic abnormalities. These diagnostic tests are of two types—in vivo and in vitro. In vitro tests are performed in laboratories, usually with blood samples. Because they are used outside the body, in vitro tests are not subject to stringent regulatory review. The subsequently lower costs of development have led to rapid growth in this area. In vivo diagnostics are done in the body itself and basically involve the use of imaging agents. These tests are subject to the same regulatory process as therapeutic products.

19. Both the National Cancer Institute (NCI) and the National Institute for Arthritis and Infectious Diseases (NIAID) are part of the National Institutes of Health. References to the NIH incorporate these bodies. Regressing on the straight count of NIH grants held by each firm would have been problematic, since over the 35 firms possessing at least one agreement, few possessed more than two. Logistic analysis would have prevented the comparability achieved here.
20. Our colleague James Ranger-Moore points out to us, however, that we must separate two potential outcomes. Does having a large staff of Ph.D.s make firms more research focused and more capable of utilizing external knowledge? Or do multiple agreements lead to better performance and therefore generate more money to hire highly educated employees?
21. For an excellent review of the economics literature on innovation, see Cohen and Levin (1989). Basberg (1987) provides a good assessment of the limitations and advantages of patents as a measure of technological innovation.

References

Abernathy, W. J., and K. B. Clark. 1985. "Innovation: Mapping the Winds of Creative Destruction." *Research Policy* 14(1):3–22.

Adler, Reid G. 1984. "Biotechnology as an Intellectual Property." *Science* (April 27): 357–363.

Angier, Natalie. 1988. *Natural Obsessions*. Boston: Houghton Mifflin.

Basberg, Bjorn L. 1987. "Patents and the Measurement of Technological Change: A Survey of the Literature." *Research Policy* 16:131–141.

Bioscan. June 1990. Phoenix: Oryx Press.

Burrill, S. G., with the Ernst & Young High Technology Group. 1989. *Biotech 90: Into the Next Decade.* New York: Mary Ann Liebert.

Cambrosio, A., and P. Keating. 1988. "Going Monoclonal: Art, Science, and Magic in the Day-to-Day Use of Hybridoma Technology." *Social Problems* 35(3):244–260.

Cohen, S., A. Chang, H. Boyer, and R. Helling. 1973. "Construction of Biologically Functional Bacterial Plasmids in Vitro." *Proceedings of the National Academy of Sciences* 70:3240–3244.

Cohen, Wes, and R. C. Levin. 1989. "Empirical Studies of Innovation and Market Structure." In R. Schmalensee and R. D. Willig, eds., *Handbook of Industrial Organization.* New York: Elsevier, pp. 1059–1107.

Cohen, W., and D. Levinthal. 1989. "Innovation and Learning: The Two Faces of R&D." *Economic Journal* 99:569–596.

Dosi, Giovanni. 1988. "Sources, Procedures, and Microeconomic Effects of Innovation." *Journal of Economic Literature* 26(3):1120–1171.

Fildes, Robert A. 1990. "Strategic Challenges in Biotechnology." *California Management Review* 32(3):63–72.

Freeman, John H., and Stephen Barley. 1990. "The Strategic Analysis of Interorganizational Relations in Biotechnology." In R. Loveridge and M. Pitt, eds., *Strategic-Management of Technological Innovation.* New York: Wiley.

Fujimura, Joan. 1987. "Constructing 'Do-able' Problems in Cancer Research." *Social Studies of Science* 17:257–293.

———. 1988. "The Molecular Bandwagon in Cancer Research." *Social Problems* 35(3):261–283.

Genetic Engineering and Biotechnology Related Firms Worldwide Directory. 8th ed. 1990.

Griliches, Zvi, A. Pakes, and B. Hall. 1987. "The Value of Patents As Indicators of Inventive Activity." In P. Dasgupta and P. Stoneman, eds., *Economic Policy and Technological Performance.* New York: Cambridge University Press, pp. 97–124.

Hall, Stephen S. 1987. *Invisible Frontiers.* New York: Atlantic Monthly Press.

Herrigel, Gary B. 1990. *Industrial Organization and the Politics of Industry.* Ph.D. dissertation, MIT, Cambridge, MA.

Imai, Ken-ichi, Ikujiro Nouaka, and Hirotaka Takeuchi. 1985. "Managing the New Product Development Process: How Japanese Companies Learn and Unlearn." In Kim B. Clark et al., eds., *The Uneasy Alliance.* Boston: Harvard Business School Press, pp. 337–375.

Jewkes, John, D. Sawers, and R. Stillerman. 1969. *The Sources of Invention* 2d ed. New York: Norton.

Kaneko, Ikuyo, and Ken-ichi Imai. 1987. "A Network View of the Firm." Paper presented at first Hitotsubashi-Stanford conference.

Kenney, Martin. 1986. *Biotechnology: The University-Industrial Complex.* New Haven: Yale University Press.

Latour, Bruno. 1987. *Science in Action.* Cambridge: Harvard University Press.

Macneil, Ian. 1985. "Relational contract: What we do and do not know." *Northwestern University Law Review* 72(6):854–905.

Mowery, David C. 1983. "The Relationship between Intrafirm and Contractual Forms of Industrial Research in American Manufacturing, 1900–1940." *Explorations in Economic History* 20:351–374.

Mowery, David C., and Nathan Rosenberg. 1989. *Technology and the Pursuit of Economic Growth.* New York: Cambridge University Press.

Nelson, Richard R. 1990a. "U.S. Technological Leadership: Where Did It Come from and Where Did It Go?" *Research Policy* 19:119–132.

———. 1990b. "Capitalism as an Engine of Progress." *Research Policy* 19:165–174.

Nelson, Richard R., and Sidney Winter. 1982. *An Evolutionary Theory of Economic Change.* Cambridge, MA: Harvard University Press.

Office of Technology Assessment. 1984. *Commercial Biotechnology: An International Analysis.* Washington, DC: U.S. Government Printing Office.
———. 1988. *U.S. Investment in Biotechnology.* Washington, DC: U.S. Government Printing Office.
Peet, W. J. 1988. "Technology Alliances: An Interview with James Grant." *McKinsey Quarterly* (Autumn): 58–67.
Piore, Michael, and Charles Sabel. 1984. *The Second Industrial Divide.* New York: Basic Books.
Pisano, Gary. 1988. "Innovation through Markets, Hierarchies, and Joint Ventures: Technology Strategy and Collaborative Arrangements in the Biotechnology Industry." Ph.D. dissertation, University of California, Berkeley.
———. 1990. "The R&D Boundaries of the Firm: An Empirical Analysis." *Administrative Science Quarterly* 35(1):153–176.
Pisano, Gary, W. Shan, and D. Teece. 1988. "Joint Ventures and Collaboration in the Biotechnology Industry." In D. C. Mowery, ed., *International Collaborative Ventures in U.S. Manufacturing.* Cambridge, MA: Ballinger, pp. 183–222.
Powell, Walter W. 1990. "Neither Market Nor Hierarchy: Network Forms of Organization." In L. L. Cummings and B. Staw, eds., *Research in Organizational Behavior.* Greenwich, CT: JAI Press, pp. 295–336.
Powell, Walter W., and Peter Brantley. 1993. "Magic Bullets and Patent Wars: New Product Development and the Evolution of the Biotechnology Industry." In Toshihiro Nishiguchi, ed., *Competitive Product Development.* New York: Oxford University Press.
Rosenberg, Nathan. 1990. "Why Do Firms Do Basic Research (With Their Own Money)?" *Research Policy.* 19:165–174.
Sabel, Charles. 1991. "Flexible specialization and the re-emergence of regional economies." In P. Hirst and J. Zeitlin, eds., *Reversing Industrial Decline?* Oxford, UK: Berg, pp. 17–70.
Schumpeter, Joseph A. 1934. *The Theory of Economic Development.* Vol. XLVI, Harvard Economic Studies. Cambridge, MA: Dept. of Economics, Harvard University.
Tapon, Francis. 1989. "A Transaction Cost Analysis of Innovations in the Organization of Pharmaceutical R&D." *Journal of Economic Behavior and Organization* 12:197–213.
Teece, David. 1988. "Technological Changes and the Nature of the Firm." In G. Dosi, et al., eds., *Technical Change and Economic Theory.* London: Pinter, pp. 256–281.
Teitelman, Robert. 1989. *Gene Dreams: Wall Street, Academia, and the Rise of Biotechnology.* New York: Basic Books.
Tushman, Michael, and Philip Anderson. 1986. "Technological Discontinuities and Organizational Environments." *Administrative Science Quarterly* 31:439–465.
Williamson, Oliver E. 1975. *Markets and Hierarchies: Analysis and Antitrust Implications.* New York: Free Press.
———. 1985. *The Economic Institutions of Capitalism.* New York: Free Press.

NETWORK FORMS OF ORGANIZATIONS

The Network Organization in Theory and Practice

Wayne E. Baker

The *network organization* has become a popular concept in theory and practice. The use of this organizational form has been documented in manufacturing and service firms (see, e.g., Burns and Stalker 1961; Mintzberg 1979; Miles and Snow 1986; Eccles and Crane 1987), and the concept has been promoted by the popular business press (e.g., Guterl 1989) and management consultants (e.g., Nolan, Pollock, and Ware 1988). Prior studies have compiled a useful qualitative base of knowledge about the network organization. In this chapter, I develop the network organization concept with greater theoretical and methodological precision in order to advance the concept in theory and inform the adoption of the network organizational form in practice.

The concept of the network organization may be placed in the context of current debates in organizational theory. Organizational change has "provoked some of the most spirited debates in contemporary organization studies" (Aldrich and Marsden 1988:380). Strategic-choice theorists emphasize the ability of managers to redesign organizations to fit changing tasks and environments. In contrast, population ecologists stress organizational inertia—the inability to change structures and processes once established. In essence, population ecologists view organizational design as a wager on fitness that, once placed, consigns an organization to its fate.

The network organization evades organizational inertia by its very nature. The network form is designed to handle tasks and environments

I am indebted to Cheryl Baker, Selwyn Becker, Ronald Burt, John King, David Krackhardt, Edward Laumann, Mark Shanley, Stanley Wasserman, and members of the Stamer Workshop at Columbia for helpful comments; to Ananth Iyer and Phil Schumm for technical advice and Santosh Nabar for programming assistance; and to the CEO, partners, and the members of the firm for their cooperation and participation in this study.[1]

that demand flexibility and adaptability. A network organization can flexibly construct a unique set of internal and external linkages for each unique project. Unlike a bureaucracy, which is a fixed set of relationships for processing all problems, the network organization molds itself to each problem. Moreover, it adapts itself not by top-management fiat but by the interactions of problems, people, and resources; within the broad confines of corporate strategy, organizational members autonomously work out relationships. This self-adaptability feature led Eccles and Crane (1988) to call the network form a "self-designing" organization. At least in metaphor, the network organization is a market mechanism that allocates people and resources to problems and projects in a decentralized manner. Like a market, efficiency is assumed. For example, in a network organization a novel problem is routed by the shortest path to the right people, while in a hierarchy a novel problem takes long paths by wending its way through channels established for familiar (routine) problems. The intrinsic ability of the network organization to repeatedly redesign itself to accommodate new tasks, unique problems, and changing environments enables such organizations to escape the plight of forms such as bureaucracy, which ossify and become incapable of change.

All known network organizations evolved unplanned or resulted from the redesign of a non-network organization. In this chapter, I study a professional service firm in which the network design was a strategic choice of the founders. The organization, a commercial real estate development firm, began with the network concept as a *conscious* design *prior* to its creation.[2] This provides a rare opportunity to explore the limits and possibilities of the network model where it was implemented in a setting (relatively) uncontaminated by the residues of previous structures, processes, and history. Further, it permits the evaluation of organizational theory put into practice: the network organization as an ideal-type versus real organizational structure.

The presentation is organized in four sections. In section 1, I develop the concept of the network organization in theory. After discussing various conceptions and misconceptions about the network organization, I provide a concrete theoretical definition. In short, it is a social network that is *integrated* across formal boundaries. Interpersonal ties of any type are formed without respect to formal groups or categories. This conceptual definition, as I discuss, is akin to Blau's macrostructual theory of formal differentiation and intergroup relations (e.g., Blau 1977; Blau and Schwartz 1984; Calhoun, Meyer, and Scott 1990) but applied at the organizational level.

In section 2, I describe the data collected on the various networks of relationships among members of the commercial real estate development firm and present a simulation-based method for hypothesis testing. This approach adopts the general logic of blockmodeling (e.g., White, Boorman, and Breiger 1976) but replaces structural equivalence as a basis of subgroup formation with Blau's focus on formal differentiation (cf. Marsden 1981). A priori blockmodels are created, using formal group membership to partition actors into blocks and simulation techniques to compare real a priori blockmodels against the baseline of a theoretical ideal-typical network organization.

In section 3, I analyze a network organization in practice. Specifically, I consider three main questions about the integration of the real estate firm:

1. *Integration of the firm across vertical, horizontal, and spatial boundaries.* I consider the extent to which networks of strong and weak task-related communications are constrained by the formal differentiation of the firm, including hierarchical position (partners, leasing agents, and support staff), market group (retail, industrial, and office real estate), and geographic dispersion (multiple locations).

2. *Integration of "deal makers" across vertical, horizontal, and spatial boundaries.* Integration of the "operating core" (Mintzberg 1979) is critical for a network organization. Here I narrow the analytic focus to consider the integration of the operating core of the real estate firm, the so-called deal makers: senior partners, partners, and leasing agents. The integration of the operating core is examined across three formal dimensions and five types of relations.

3. *Organizational vulnerability due to reliance on the CEO.* The CEO—the founder of the firm—is analyzed as a critical node in the organization. I evaluate the impact of his removal on the relative integration of organizational networks. (This analysis does not consider the extent to which ties lost by removal of the CEO could be replaced by substitute ties formed by other partners or created by a new CEO.)

Concluding remarks are presented in section 4.

1. THE NETWORK ORGANIZATION IN THEORY

Some Clarifications

The concept of a "network organization" suffers from semantic ambiguity, multiple interpretations, and imprecise definitions. Therefore the term must be clarified before we use it further.

1. The network organization is a specific organizational type, but the mere presence of a network of ties is not its distinguishing feature. *All* organizations are networks—patterns of roles and relationships—whether or not they fit the network organization image. Organizational type depends on the particular pattern and characteristics of the network. For example, a network characterized by a rigid hierarchical subdivision of tasks and roles, vertical relationships, and an administrative apparatus separated from production is commonly called a bureaucracy. In contrast, a network characterized by flexibility, decentralized planning and control, and lateral (as opposed to vertical) ties is closer to the network organiza-

tion type. The chief structural characteristic of a network organization is the high degree of integration across formal boundaries.

2.   A network organization is characterized by integration across formal boundaries of *multiple types* of *socially important* relations. Such "thick" network organizations are integrated over many relations—strong and weak task-related communication, informal socializing, advice-giving and advice-getting, promotion decisions, and so on. The thick network concept is consistent with descriptions of known network organizations (see, e.g., Burns and Stalker 1961; Mintzberg 1979; Eccles and Crane 1987). In contrast, management consultants and other practitioners often think of what can be called "thin" network organizations: firms with extensive electronic communication networks (see, e.g., Nolan and Pollock 1986; Nolan, Pollock, and Ware 1988). Though communication technology may help integrate an organization, there is scant consideration of the extent to which the organization is integrated over multiple types of socially important relations.

3.   For a network organization, integration covers *vertical* and *spatial* differentiation as well as *horizontal* differentiation. Considerations of organizational integration are often confined to coordination and interaction between horizontal units such as production, marketing, and research and development. Lawrence and Lorsch's (1967) classic study of differentiation and integration is a case in point. To define and study a network organization, however, the concept of integration must be extended to include interaction across vertical boundaries (hierarchical levels) and across spatial boundaries (multiple geographic locations) as well.

4.   The network organization form is not limited to professional service firms. The task and environmental characteristics that induce integration in professional service firms (see, e.g., Eccles and Crane 1987) also appear in force in other industries—manufacturing (Burns and Stalker 1961), Hollywood feature film making (Baker and Faulkner 1991), book publishing (Powell 1985; Miles and Snow 1986), and aerospace and petrochemicals (Mintzberg 1979)—and induce the emergence of network organizations in these settings as well.

Differentiation and Integration

To advance both theory and practice, it is necessary to move beyond the typical qualitative definitions of a network organization (Eccles and Crane 1987; Mintzberg 1979) and quantify its structural properties. To do so, I examine two key principles of organizational design—*differentiation* and *integration*. Differentiation refers to the formal division of an organization into ranks, functions, departments, work teams, and so on. It includes vertical differentiation such as hierarchical levels, horizontal differentiation such as functional areas, and spatial differentiation such as multiple locations.[3] Integration refers to the degree of coordination (or, in a broader sense, interaction) among organizational units, however differentiated.[4] The critical distinguishing feature of a network organization is a high degree of *integration*. In the ideal-typical network organization, all members are well integrated: formal categories or groups such as formal position, geographic location, and market focus are not significant barriers to interaction. Interpersonal ties of all types—task-related communication, advice, socializing, and so on—are as easily established *between* as *within* formal groups or categories.

Concepts from Blau's macrostructural theory of intergroup relations (e.g., Blau 1977; Blau and Schwartz 1984; Calhoun, Meyer, and Scott 1990) may be used to relate differentiation and integration in an ideal-typical network organization. According to Blau, rates of social interaction between groups (e.g., intermarriage) are a function of "ingroup bias" and "opportunities for contact." Ingroup bias is a preference to associate with similar alters, such as a preference to marry within the same ethnic group. Opportunities for contact refers to differentiation of a population, including *heterogeneity* (division into nominal categories or groups such as race and religion) and *inequality* (differences in income or education, for example, along an interval scale, usually measured as the Gini index). Only heterogeneity is of concern here.

The relationship of formal differentiation and integration in an ideal-typical network organization can now be stated precisely: intergroup relations in a network organization are associated with heterogeneity— opportunities for contact—not with ingroup biases. Interaction in an ideal-typical network organization does not exhibit preferences for ingroup instead of outgroup ties; in other words, formal boundaries do not inhibit relationships. The probability of a tie between members of two different formal groups is a function of the number and relative sizes of formal groups in the organization. (As presented in section 2, this probability is equal to the Gibbs-Martin index of industrial diversification.)

Note that the *reason* for a high degree of integration does not enter into the structural definition of a network organization. A network organization can result naturally from integration-producing forces such as the task and environmental characteristics we will discuss, or from the intentional use of integrating mechanisms—formal liaison positions, multifunctional task forces, role-set composition,[5] formal job rotation, multigroup conferences, facility design, and so on—that act to offset disintegrating forces.

Ingroup and Intergroup Relationships

What induces ingroup ties and intergroup affiliations? For managers, this is more than an academic question. Because many forces act against integration, a network organization may not arise spontaneously and must be intentionally created by the use of integrating mechanisms. (Of course, many forces are outside management control and cannot be altered directly.) The forces that induce or inhibit integration may be classified into three types: task characteristics, organizational characteristics, and environmental factors. I will summarize the three types briefly, focusing particularly on their effects on the integration of organizational networks across formal boundaries.

Task Characteristics The nature of tasks may require interaction across formal boundaries. In investment banks, for example, three task characteristics—the need to process large amounts of information quickly, the production of unique products ("deals"), and the close involvement of customers and suppliers (e.g., law firms) in the production process—create the need for flexible and frequent intergroup ties (Eccles and Crane 1987). The production of unique products, for example, creates regular and frequent cross-group interaction because the mix of experts (e.g., product specialists) and client managers changes from deal to deal. Task characteristics may also necessitate specialization, especially when tasks are nonroutine and require particular knowledge and expertise. Specialization is evident in professional services (such as the proliferation of product specialists in investment banks) and would be expected to reduce integration (but see the potential countervailing effect of heterogeneity discussed in the following section).

Commercial real estate development shares some task characteristics with investment banking, especially the production of unique products and close interaction with clients and suppliers (e.g., law firms, builders, architects, municipal authorities), which should induce integrated organizational networks. However, real estate projects are typically fewer and of longer duration than investment banking deals; such differences should yield less natural integration in real estate firms, compared with the integration of investment banks. These effects, however, could be offset by the use of generalists as integrative devices. Even though real estate development has experienced task specialization and the proliferation of specialists, the firm studied here requires partners and leasing agents to be generalists. As a senior partner put it, "I deal in all aspects of the business. We're not specialists in finance or zoning. I'm well-versed in all aspects of the business; therefore I come in contact with more people in the organization—accounting, property management, and so on." Generalists help to integrate an organization because they have wider and more diverse egocentric networks than do specialists.

It is important to emphasize that integration-inducing task characteristics are found in both service and manufacturing firms. In their landmark study of English and Scottish industrial firms, Burns and Stalker (1961) found "organic" (network) organizations that evolved as responses to task (and environmental) requirements. Hollywood feature films—each a unique and customized product—are made in project-specific network organizations (Baker and Faulkner 1991). Whenever products or projects are unique, require input from various experts, and must be solved creatively, an integrated organization is more effective (see, e.g., Mintzberg 1979)—whether a service is provided or a tangible product is made.

Organizational Characteristics   Many organizational characteristics influence and shape social interaction. As system size increases, for example, the expected number of contacts per person increases at a multiplicative rate, but time and energy constraints eventually dampen the effect (Mayhew and Levinger 1976). But as *group* size increases, the probability of *outgroup* ties decreases (Blau and Schwartz 1984), suggesting that it is increasingly difficult to sustain integration as an organization grows and differentiates. Indeed, the partners of the real estate firm intuitively recognized the potential deleterious effect of size. As one senior partner summarized, "Every time you add a person, it makes life more difficult. Every time we add someone, we are closer to being out of control."

Size also influences integration via its relationship to differentiation. Organizational size is positively associated with the extent of vertical differentiation (more layers), horizontal differentiation (greater division of labor and more functional specialization), and, though the evidence is mixed, with spatial differentiation (more locations) (e.g., Meyer 1972; Mayhew et al. 1972; Blau and Schoenherr 1971). The units formed by differentiation can become loci of ingroup biases, impeding the integration of the organization. For example, as Lawrence and Lorsch (1967) documented in their classic study, members of different departments develop divergent emotional and cognitive orientations that can obstruct the formation of interdepartmental ties. Similarly, geographic separation can permit the emergence of divergent subcultures and decrease the probability of intergroup affiliations. Spatial distance decreases the likelihood of contact (e.g., Blau and Schwartz 1984; Mayhew and Levinger 1976) so that geographic dispersion, which raises the costs of (intergroup) interaction, can decrease outgroup ties and increase ingroup ties. In short, differentiation can create favorable circumstances for the emergence of ingroup biases. These biases can occur for social psychological reasons (the tendency to associate with like others, such as those from the same subculture) and for economizing reasons (the efficient allocation of finite time and energy.[6])

But differentiation can have paradoxical effects. Differentiation means more differences among individuals, which reduce the rate of intergroup ties, but differentiation itself increases the likelihood of intergroup ties because it constrains available choices (Blau and Schwartz 1984:40–42). The opportunity structure created by heterogeneity can increase the chance of intergroup contacts and even overwhelm strong tendencies for ingroup choice. For example, Blau and Schwartz found that heterogeneity promotes intermarriage, despite tendencies for same-group marital choice. Schwartz (1990) found evidence of a similar relationship between heterogeneity and intergroup friendship in elementary schools (though sex heterogeneity could not offset the extreme bias for same-sex friends). Despite common intuition, a well-integrated organization can be created naturally by the formal division of an organization, even in the face of ingroup tendencies.

Other organizational factors that facilitate a well-integrated organization include personnel selection, control systems, facility design, and cultural norms and values. For example, the senior partners of the real estate firm select personnel that "fit" the culture of a network organization (e.g., gregarious generalists, not reclusive specialists). Recruitment is highly selective, involving a lengthy and intensive process of repeated interviews and mandatory participation at social events and recreational activities, and powerful socialization takes place on the job.

An intensified need for frequent communication and interaction across formal boundaries can be created by vague roles and responsibilities (Eccles and Crane 1987), which at the real estate firm is exacerbated by the absence of written policies or objectives, lack of formal strategic planning, and lack of formal performance appraisals. Senior partners play down status distinctions that might discourage intergroup ties. Observed one (senior) partner: "[The CEO] would have to be our senior partner, he has the financial strength. Then the division [also called senior] partners are in charge of each of the three [market groups]. Then we have the junior partners. . . . But generally, *we think of everyone as just partners*" [emphasis mine]. Further, an open office layout—no private offices or even dividers between desks—facilitates interaction by permitting conversations to be overheard and by reducing the costs of interaction.[7]

Finally, organizational form reflects the personal preferences and choices of key decision makers (Andrews 1980). At the real estate firm, the network model reflects the preferences of the CEO and senior partners. The CEO, for example, expressed a clear dislike for formal administration. As he told me, "I'm certainly not complicating my life by becoming an administrator." The network form, which emphasizes decentralized planning, decision making, and control, does not require a traditional (hierarchical) administrator. But the senior partners' preference for a network organization is more than a mere taste for informality; they believe that this form is more efficient and effective internally, as well as a better fit to environmental demands (discussed in next section). For example, it is considered to be cost efficient because it can produce the same as a hierarchically organized firm but with fewer people. The use of generalists reduces costs because project teams can be smaller, outside consultants are required less often, and the firm is not burdened with excessive overhead costs in the form of expensive internal consultants (specialists).[8] Such cost efficiencies helped the firm survive a predicted downturn in the real estate market. Planned integration of deal makers and support staff may offer similar benefits. For example, locating the accounting staff at headquarters and working to create connections between accountants and deal makers ensures quick and accurate transmission of vital information. (As one partner put it, "We want accountability in a personal way—not just pushing the numbers, but pushing the numbers for *someone*.")

Environmental Characteristics   A principal tenet of organizational theory is that structure is related to environment (e.g., Aldrich and Marsden

1988). Organizations that fit their environments will perform better and are more likely to survive than those that do not (Emery and Trist 1965; Wholey and Brittain 1986). Network (or organic) structures are better suited to complex, rapidly changing, and turbulent environments than hierarchical (or mechanistic) structures, which do better in stable, simple, routine environments (Burns and Stalker 1961; Mintzberg 1979; Miles and Snow 1986). For example, investment banks, like many types of professional service firms, use a network design in part because professional services require frequent direct involvement with the environment—customers, competitors, and suppliers (Eccles and Crane 1987). While many organizations buffer their "technological core" from the environment (Thompson 1967), the organization and its environment are closely intermeshed in the production of professional services.

At the real estate firm, many partners believe the network design is a good fit to the dynamic real estate environment, permitting quick and flexible responses to project and market demands. Internal ties among partners, leasing agents, project engineers, accountants, and others easily intermix with externalties to brokers, lawyers, architects, contractors, and municipalities—all of which shift and remix as projects progress through stages of development, new projects come on-line, and other projects are completed. In addition, partners believe that an integrated organization enables the firm to present "one front" to brokers and customers, and to "cross-sell" customers (e.g., marketing the development of industrial warehouse space to a client who had already employed the firm to develop office space).

While a turbulent and complex environment might induce integration, it can also exacerbate ingroup biases. For example, the complexity of a market is simplified by classifying it into types and establishing internal divisions that mirror them. Formal groups in investment banks, for example, reflect market divisions (energy, emerging growth companies, health care, etc.) and products (junk bonds, fixed-income securities, mergers and acquisitions, etc.). The real estate firm in my study has three market foci with internal divisions to match: retail, industrial, and office real estate. Each market group revolves around a unique "focus" of interest (Feld 1981) with specialized task requirements and personnel. Each interacts with a specialized organizational subenvironment, including distinct economic and political conditions and specialized external relationships with customers and suppliers (e.g., architects, contractors). Such differences can engender divergent cognitive and emotional orientations (Lawrence and Lorsch 1967) and impede integration. Indeed, the potential for distinct subcultures is evident in the comment of a leasing agent: "You tend to think like the partner you work with. You respect his values and life style." And the fear of disintegration was reported in several interviews; as a partner claimed, "If we lost [the CEO], I believe that the office and industrial groups would split up since each partner has his own group agenda." Thus the match of internal organizational structure with external market structure can seriously obstruct overall integration.

2. DATA AND METHODS

Data

A multimethod/multistage approach was used to collect qualitative and quantitative data. In the first stage, informal interviews were conducted with all senior partners, most partners and leasing agents, and a small sample of support staff personnel. The interviews provided insights and qualitative data on the administration, culture, and structure of the firm, and perceptions about organizational networks, strengths, and weaknesses.

In the second stage, a network survey instrument was designed, informed by the interviews conducted in the first stage. The questionnaire, with a cover memo from the CEO, was distributed to all members of the firm. The questionnaire was self-administered and mailed directly back to me at the University of Chicago. The original complete personnel list contained 81 names, all of which were included in the instrument. Two support staff had left the firm and were not surveyed. Two new hires responded to the survey, but their responses were excluded because their names were not on the personnel list (and thus not on the instrument). In sum, 77 usable surveys were obtained, yielding a 95% response rate.

The instrument included general background and network questions. Several types of network data were collected. Each respondent was asked to note others with whom he or she had discussions in order to get his or her job done, indicating both the frequency (0–5) and importance (0–5) of such task-related communication. Respondents were also asked about advice getting in difficult business situations ("advice ties"), informal socializing ("social ties"), and discussions about promoting a leasing agent to partner ("promote ties"). Response categories for advice, social, and promote ties were binary.

Ever since Granovetter (1973) proposed the strength-of-weak-ties argument, network theory and research has incorporated the distinction between strong and weak ties. However, as Krackhardt notes in Chapter 8 of this volume, there is considerable ambiguity about what constitutes a strong or weak tie. One may suspect this ambiguity stems from imprecise theory or methods, but in my opinion at least part of the ambiguity about strong and weak ties is a clue that what constitutes strong and weak varies by context.[9] If so, then the search for universal definitions of strong and weak ties is misguided and could lead to invalid classification of ties. Based on my understanding of the real estate firm, coupled with experimentation with alternative definitions, I defined strong and weak ties as follows: For strong ties, I sought a definition that would identify ties of great strength: very frequent and important. All ties with a frequency X importance value of 12 or more were coded as strong. (A histogram revealed a natural break at 12.) To qualify as strong, a respondent had to have reported at least "daily conversations" (frequency code = 4) that were at least "helpful" (importance code = 3), or conversations at least "several times a week" (frequency code = 3) that were at least "very helpful" (importance code = 4). (Thus conversations "several times a week" that were "helpful" would not yield a strong tie.) Weak ties were defined as ties with a frequency of 2 (i.e., ego reported "weekly conversations" with alter). This is the high end of Granovetter's (1973:1371) definition of weak ties as those who interact more than once a year but less than twice a week.[10]

The third stage of research involved presentation of research findings to the assembled senior partners, partners, and some key support staff. All had received a written report (the first version of this paper) prior to the meeting. The final stage was used to (in)validate the results and conclusions and to solicit clarifications, explanations, and speculations about the network organization in theory and practice. All agreed with my major conclusions. Debate focused on the relative importance of findings and possible corrective actions. For example, the lack of integration of (some) leasing agents was viewed as a critical outstanding problem, while many believed the integration of the accounting staff and the rest of the firm had improved since the time of the survey.

A Method for Hypothesis Testing

Introduction The objective of the procedures developed here is to test statistically the extent to which formal organizational dimensions—formal position, geographic location, or market group—are barriers to interpersonal ties. The general null hypothesis is that such formal dimensions are not salient for social interactions; that is, in the ideal-typical network organization, relationships are as easily established between as within formal groups. The alternative hypothesis is that formal groups are significant barriers to interaction. Ingroup biases ("inbreeding") occur within units created by formal differentiation, which are not offset by the effect of heterogeneity or the intentional use of integrating mechanisms.

To evaluate real organizational networks against the theoretical ideal type, I have developed simulation procedures that permit hypothesis testing. The approach uses the general logic of blockmodeling (e.g., White, Boorman, and Breiger 1976) but replaces its technical machinery (such as the algebraic rule of structural equivalence as a basis of subgroup formation) with the focus of Blau and associates on formal differentiation (Blau and Schwartz 1984; Calhoun, Meyer, and Scott 1990). Formal group membership, not structural equivalence, is used to partition nodes into blocks. This produces a priori blockmodels: exogenous information about actor attributes is used to partition a matrix, without reference to the relational data.[11] Other examples of a priori blockmodels include Wasserman and Iacobucci's (1986) study of toy offerings among children in which subjects were blocked according to gender, and the Galaskiewicz et al. (1985) study of corporate board interlocks where firms were blocked according to such company attributes as size and location.

There are, of course, alternatives to the approach used here, such as Holland et al.'s (1983) stochastic a priori blockmodeling methods (see also Fienberg and Wasserman 1981),[12] the application of log-linear models for aggregate choice tables (Marsden 1981; Goodman 1968, 1979), or the use of logistic regression to model dyadic choice as a function of dyad attributes (e.g., Hallinan and Williams 1989).[13] The pros and cons of these methods have been discussed by many; see Baker and Schumm (1991) for a comparison of these methods (and others) for the analysis of organizations as networks. The approach used in the present study was developed for two main reasons: (1) It permits a simple, straightforward, and valid operationalization of the network organization and tests of hypotheses. (2) The simplicity and intuitive nature of the approach improves communication with and between the diverse audiences represented at the Harvard Business School Symposium for which the study was developed and aimed—organizational theorists, network analysts, and nontechnical practitioners and managers. (The statistical results of this study have been corroborated by Log-Linear analysis, available from the author.)

The Method   In the basic blockmodeling approach, one attempts to derive a model of social structure from social network data that is a simpler, reduced representation of the underlying data. This model (called an image) is generated by aggregating nodes into distinct sets (or blocks), using the rule of structural equivalence,[14] and treating each set as internally homogeneous and homogeneous in its relations to every other set. Operationally, a social network with n actors is arrayed as an $n \times n$ matrix with a unique row and corresponding column assigned to each actor. Rows and columns are permuted to cluster structurally equivalent nodes, creating submatrices that are dense or sparse. To form the blockmodel image, a dense submatrix (typically greater than or equal to the overall density of the matrix) is assigned a "1" (oneblock) and a sparse submatrix (less than matrix density) is assigned a "0" (zeroblock). The resulting image is a reduced-form representation of the social network. The validity of the blockmodel is judged on how adequately it represents ("fits") the ties in the original data.

Like the basic approach, I collapse actors into distinct sets and treat them as homogenous within and between, but I use formal group membership as the a priori basis of aggregation. Formal groups are used because I wish to evaluate the extent to which formal dimensions determine the patterns of social networks. Consider, for illustration, the network of "liking" ties among the 14 operators in the famous bank wiring room at Western Electric's Hawthorne Works (Roethlisberger and Dickson 1939; Homans 1950). The original unordered matrix in Figure 15-1(a) is blocked by work unit in the Figure 15-1(b) matrix. Members of a unit work in close proximity (connector units 1 and 2 are located in the front and middle of the room, respectively, with the selector unit in the back).

As can be seen in the blocked matrix and its reduced-form image, liking tends to occur within connector unit 1 and within the selector unit. (The two connector units are also linked, but this interblock tie depends on a single individual, operator 10.)

(a) Original Liking Matrix in Bank Wiring Room

		C1 1	C1 2	C1 3	I 4	S 5	C2 6	C2 7	C2 8	C1 9	C2 10	S 11	S 12	I 13	S 14
C1	1			1	—	—	—	—	—	—	1	1	—	—	—	—
C1	2	1			—	—	—	—	—	—	1	1	1	—	—	—
C1	3	—	—		—	—	—	—	—	—	—	—	—	—	—
I	4	—	—	—		—	—	—	—	—	—	—	—	—	—
S	5	—	—	—	—		—	—	—	—	—	1	1	—	1
C2	6	—	—	—	—	—		—	—	—	—	—	—	—	—
C2	7	—	—	—	—	—	—		—	—	—	—	—	—	—
C2	8	—	—	—	—	—	—	—		—	—	—	—	—	—
C1	9	1	1	—	—	—	—	—	—		1	—	—	1	—
C2	10	1	1	—	—	—	—	—	—	1		—	—	—	—
S	11	—	1	—	—	1	—	—	—	—	—		—	—	1
S	12	—	—	—	—	1	—	—	—	—	—	—		—	1
I	13	—	—	—	—	—	—	—	—	1	—	—	—		—
S	14	—	—	—	—	1	—	—	—	—	—	1	1	—	

(b) Liking Matrix Blocked by Work Unit

		C1 1	C1 3	C1 9	C1 2	C2 10	C2 8	C2 7	C2 6	S 11	S 14	S 5	S 12	I 4	I 13
C1	1		—	1	1	1	—	—	—	—	—	—	—	—	—
C1	3	—		—	—	—	—	—	—	—	—	—	—	—	—
C1	9	1	—		1	1	—	—	—	—	—	—	—	—	1
C1	2	1	—	1		1	—	—	—	1	—	—	—	—	—
C2	10	1	—	1	1		—	—	—	—	—	—	—	—	—
C2	8	—	—	—	—	—		—	—	—	—	—	—	—	—
C2	7	—	—	—	—	—	—		—	—	—	—	—	—	—
C2	6	—	—	—	—	—	—	—		—	—	—	—	—	—
S	11	—	—	—	1	—	—	—	—		1	1	—	—	—
S	14	—	—	—	—	—	—	—	—	1		1	1	—	—
S	5	—	—	—	—	—	—	—	—	1	1		1	—	—
S	12	—	—	—	—	—	—	—	—	—	1	1		—	—
I	4	—	—	—	—	—	—	—	—	—	—	—	—		—
I	13	—	—	1	—	—	—	—	—	—	—	—	—	—	

Image

1	1	0	0	b = .540
1	0	0	0	density = .143
0	0	1	0	Gibbs-Martin = .791
0	0	0	0	% intergroup ties = .385

Note: C1 = connector unit 1, C2 = connector unit 2, S = selector unit, I = inspectors.

Figure 15-1

Network of Liking Ties Among Hawthorne Operators

Beyond visual inspection, the association between liking and work-unit membership is evident in the comparison of the proportion of interblock ties with the Gibbs and Martin (1962) index of industrial diversification. This index, which equals the probability that two randomly selected actors are from different groups, is defined as

$$H = (1 - \Sigma p_k^2),$$

where p = the proportion of actors in category k. (The index is customarily multiplied by $N/(N-1)$ to correct for the possibility of randomly selecting the same person twice.) If the observed proportion of intergroup ties (intergroup ties as a percentage of all ties) is less than the Gibbs-Martin index, then ingroup biases exist. In an ideal-typical network organization, the observed proportion of intergroup ties should equal (or exceed) the Gibbs-Martin index. For liking ties in the bank wiring room, however, only 39% of all ties were between work units, far lower than the probability that two randomly selected operators would be from different units (Gibbs-Martin index = .791). Thus formal heterogeneity in the bank wiring room did not offset ingroup biases. Indeed, if interaction leads to sentiment, as Homans (1950) argued (workers grew to like those with whom they worked), then the formal division of labor in the bank wiring room created "breeding grounds" for ingroup preferences.[15]

How well does the a priori blockmodel of liking in the bank wiring room fit the underlying relational data? Carrington, Heil, and Berkowitz (1980) propose a goodness-of-fit index, b, for blockmodels. For a single matrix,

$$b = \sum_i^c \frac{(o_i - e)^2 s_i}{(et_i)^2 v},$$

where

c = number of defined blocks in the matrix,
o = observed density of the ith block,
e = expected density of each block (matrix density),
s = the size (number of defined elements) of the ith block,
v = size of the matrix (total number of defined elements—for traditional sociomatrices, where the main diagonal elements are undefined because self-selection is not allowed, $v = n(n-1)$, and
t = 1 if $o < e$, and $(1 - e)/e$ otherwise. (This correction makes the function indifferent to relative frequency of zeroblocks or oneblocks.)

Though b is typically applied to matrices blocked by the rule of structural equivalence, b may be calculated to assess the goodness-of-fit for a matrix blocked by any rule, such as formal groups or categories. For example,

$b = .540$ for the blockmodel of liking ties blocked by work-unit membership in Figure 15-1(b). Carrington, Heil, and Berkowitz (1980) do not provide a criterion for evaluating the statistical significance of b (hence the
simulation techniques developed here), but blockmodeling experience
suggests that this value of b is relatively high, indicating a good fit
between the a priori blockmodel formed on the basis of work-unit membership and the underlying relational data.

What blockmodel image would be expected if work-unit membership
and liking were *not* associated? That is, what image would be generated if
operators liked each other without respect to formal groups? In this case,
the submatrices in the blocked matrix would have equal densities,
yielding the following blockmodel image:

$$
\begin{array}{cccc}
1 & 1 & 1 & 1 \\
1 & 1 & 1 & 1 \\
1 & 1 & 1 & 1 \\
1 & 1 & 1 & 1
\end{array}
$$

This image is typically labeled "amorphous" in blockmodeling; it is a perfect reduced-form representation of an ideal-typical network organization.
In this case, the goodness-of-fit measure, b, equals 0, which occurs when
the observed density of each block (o) equals the expected density (e) of
each block. The observed proportion of intergroup ties equals the Gibbs-
Martin index. (Note also that the amorphous model is analogous to the
independence model in log-linear analysis.)

Several graphs would yield the amorphous image of a well-integrated
network. A maximally connected graph, for example, is completely integrated, but it is possible only in a small group or small organization. Due
to bounded rationality and resource constraints, an individual in a large
social system would not be able to have relationships with everyone else.
However, as long as choices are made without respect to formal boundaries, an amorphous image will result. A random process, for example,
would generate a well-integrated network. This does not imply that real
choices are made randomly in a network organization, but that a random
process would generate the equivalent of a real network formed without
respect to formal boundaries.

For hypothesis testing, I use random choice as a baseline generator of
well-integrated networks.[16] To derive the random baseline distribution,
each person in a matrix makes random choices, subject only to the
number of choices the person actually made. Constraining each person to
his or her actual outdegree takes into account real individual differences
in the need or capacity for relating to others, and it ensures that the mean
and standard deviation of each person's random choices are equal to the
mean and standard deviation of the actual choices. (The original matrix
and each random matrix have the same first and second moments.) This
procedure was repeated 100 times for each formal dimension, resulting in
100 independent random matrices and corresponding values of b.[17] The

first two moments of this distribution are then used for hypothesis testing. Using Chebychev's inequality, if the observed b is more than 5 sigmas above the mean, the null hypothesis—that formal boundaries are not barriers to interaction—is rejected.[18]

3. THE NETWORK ORGANIZATION IN PRACTICE

Overall Integration of the Firm

The integration of the commercial real estate development firm as a whole ($n = 77$) was evaluated along three formal dimensions—spatial, horizontal, and vertical differentiation—and two types of relations—strong and weak task-related communication ties. Summary results are reported in Table 15-1, including the density of each observed matrix, the image formed by blocking on a formal dimension (with the order of groups given in the subheading), observed b for the blocked matrix, and the mean, standard deviation, and upper bound (mean + 5 sigmas) of the distribution of b for the 100 random matrices.

Geographic Location Geographic differentiation—the division of the firm into five locations—restricts the formation of strong ties. The observed value of b (.370) is well above the upper bound (.051), which means that the null hypothesis of no differentiation (integration) is rejected. The observed pattern of strong ties is clearly influenced by geographic separation. As shown in the image, strong ties tend to occur within locations (with the exception of reciprocated ties between two satellite offices). Similarly, weak ties are significantly influenced by geographic separation. Weak ties tend to occur within headquarters and the first satellite office, though weak ties interconnect other satellite offices. Overall, geography appears to be a significant barrier to interaction in the firm as a whole.

Market Group Interaction is also differentiated by horizontal divisions, though not as strongly as by geographic separation. The pattern of strong ties, for example, is significantly different from a random matrix of the same ties, indicating that the firm is not well integrated by strong ties across market groups. As shown in the image, strong ties occur within each market group, the accounting group, and other support staff. There are, however, some notable intergroup connections. The industrial and retail groups are interlinked by reciprocated strong ties, and the office and industrial groups each send strong ties to support staff.

The isolation of the accounting group in the strong-tie network might be considered a problem. Indeed, many of those interviewed perceived a lack of integration of the accounting group with the rest of the organization, which was cited as a cause of high turnover and disaffection in the

Table 15-1

Integration of All Members of Firm Across Three Dimensions ($n = 77$)

FORMAL DIMENSION	TYPE OF TIE (density)	IMAGE*	b	RANDOM MATRICES Mean	SD	Upper Bound
Geographic location (headquarters & four satellites)	Strong ties (11.2%)	1 0 0 0 0 0 1 0 1 0 0 0 1 0 0 0 1 0 0 1 0 0 0 0 1	0.370	0.036	0.003	0.051
	Weak ties (6.0%)	1 0 0 0 0 0 1 0 1 0 0 0 0 0 0 0 0 0 0 0 0 0 1 0 0	0.152	0.107	0.005	0.132
Market group (office, industrial, retail, accounting, other support)	Strong ties (11.2%)	1 0 0 0 1 0 1 1 0 1 0 1 1 0 0 0 0 0 1 0 0 0 0 0 1	0.298	0.020	0.004	0.040
	Weak ties (6.0%)	1 0 0 0 0 1 1 1 1 0 1 1 0 1 1 0 1 0 1 0 0 0 0 0 0	0.128	0.069	0.006	0.099
Formal position (partner, leasing agent, accounting, other support)	Strong ties (11.2%)	1 1 1 1 1 0 0 0 0 0 0 1 0 0 0 0	0.084	0.060	0.003	0.075
	Weak ties (6.0%)	1 1 1 1 1 1 1 0 1 0 1 1 0 0 0 0	0.107	0.097	0.005	0.122

*Image cutoff is matrix density.

accounting group. Integration, however, is not always desirable. Monitoring functions such as accounting may require restricted interaction or arm's-length relationships to ensure that objectivity and fairness are not compromised. The formation of strong ties between accountants and deal makers, for example, could create personal loyalties that result in conflicts of interest.

The weak-tie network reveals greater integration of the various market groups, even though the blockmodel structure of weak ties is significantly different from the random baseline. Eight out of eleven oneblocks occur off the main diagonal, indicating extensive intergroup interactions. The retail group in particular plays a large integrative role, sending weak ties to all other groups. The accounting group is integrated by weak ties much more than by strong ties, which may be preferable given the risks of strong ties. The lack of weak-tie integration of other support staff is more than compensated by strong ties sent by the office and industrial groups.

Overall, while the strong- and weak-tie networks reveal considerable differentiation by market group, there are substantial integrative elements in the organization. In particular, the industrial and retail groups play a substantial integrating role; as the union of the strong-tie and weak-tie images shows, both send communication ties to *all* other groups in the firm.

Formal Position   Vertical differentiation creates the lowest barrier to interaction. The observed *b* for the strong-tie network is marginally significant, while the observed *b* for the weak-tie network is not significantly different from a random baseline of the same ties. Partners are the only formal group with strong ingroup ties, but they are also notable integrators, sending strong *and* weak ties to *all* formal levels. Ingroup preference for weak ties is also shown by leasing agents and the accounting group, but both are interconnected with other groups, each playing a moderately integrative role. Overall, the weak-tie matrix blocked by formal position comes the closest to the amorphous image associated with the ideal-typical network organization. This finding is consistent with Granovetter's (1973, 1982) argument that *weak ties* integrate a social system.

Integration of Headquarters

To more closely assess the integration of deal makers and support staff, I focused on the patterns of strong and weak ties within the firm's headquarters office ($n = 48$). This was the company's largest office, and it was staffed with the CEO, the three senior partners, other partners and leasing agents, and numerous support personnel, including most of the accounting group. The 48-person networks were blocked along the formal dimension of position into three groups—accounting staff, deal makers, other support staff. Summary results are provided in Table 15-2.

Strong Ties   Accountants and deal makers at headquarters are not well integrated by strong ties. The observed *b* for strong ties (.339) is much greater than the upper bound (.097), indicating the null hypothesis of no differentiation (integration) is rejected. The image indicates that accountants tend to have strong ties internally and with other support staff, but not with the deal makers. Deal makers tend to have strong ties with one another and with other support staff, but not with the accounting group.

Weak Ties   Accountants and deal makers are integrated by weak ties. The observed *b* for weak ties (.065) is below the upper bound (.068), indicating that the null hypothesis of no differentiation (integration) should *not* be rejected. Deal makers in particular play an integrative role in the weak-tie network, connecting all three formal groups—themselves, the

Table 15-2

Integration of Accounting Staff, Deal Makers, and Other Support Staff
(*n* = 48)

TYPE OF TIE (density)	IMAGE*	*b*	RANDOM MATRICES		
			Mean	SD	Upper Bound
Strong ties (17.9%)	1 0 1 0 1 1 0 0 0	0.339	0.082	0.003	0.097
Weak ties (16.7%)	1 0 0 1 1 1 0 0 0	0.065	0.043	0.005	0.068

*Image cutoff is matrix density.

accounting group, and other support staff. Even though accountants and other support staff do not tend to send weak ties, they are integrated at headquarters by weak ties sent by deal makers.

Integration of Deal Makers

The integration of the twenty deal makers was evaluated along three formal dimensions (geographic location, market group, and position) and five types of tie (strong, weak, advice, social, and promote ties). Summary

Table 15-3

Integration of Deal Makers across Geographic Locations
(two satellite offices and HQ)

TYPE OF TIE (density)	IMAGE*	*b*	RANDOM MATRICES		
			Mean	SD	Upper Bound
Strong ties (28.2%)	1 0 0 0 1 0 0 0 1	0.288	0.061	0.011	0.116
Weak ties (15.8%)	0 0 0 1 0 0 1 1 1	0.141	0.150	0.016	0.229
Advice ties (34.7%)	1 0 0 1 1 1 0 0 1	0.163	0.079	0.007	0.114
Social ties (36.8%)	1 0 0 0 1 0 1 1 1	0.083	0.062	0.008	0.102
Promote ties (14.7%)	1 1 0 0 1 0 0 1 1	0.094	0.095	0.021	0.200

*Image cutoff is matrix density.

Table 15-4

Integration of Deal Makers across Market Groups (office, industrial, retail)

TYPE OF TIE (density)	IMAGE*	b	RANDOM MATRICES		
			Mean	SD	Upper Bound
Strong ties (28.2%)	1 0 0 0 1 0 0 0 1	0.339	0.050	0.013	0.115
Weak ties (15.8%)	0 0 0 1 0 1 1 1 0	0.222	0.080	0.023	0.194
Advice ties (34.7%)	1 0 0 0 1 0 0 0 1	0.136	0.037	0.007	0.072
Social ties (36.8%)	1 0 0 1 1 1 0 0 1	0.161	0.098	0.008	0.138
Promote ties (14.7%)	1 0 0 0 1 0 0 0 1	0.147	0.040	0.020	0.140

*Image cutoff is matrix density.

Table 15-5

Integration of Deal Makers across Formal Positions (senior partners, partners, leasing agents)

TYPE OF TIE (density)	IMAGE*	b	RANDOM MATRICES		
			Mean	SD	Upper Bound
Strong ties (28.2%)	1 1 1 1 0 0 0 0 0	0.120	0.092	0.012	0.152
Weak ties (21.6%)	0 1 1 0 0 0 0 1 1	0.108	0.074	0.024	0.192
Advice ties (34.7%)	1 1 0 1 0 0 0 0 0	0.160	0.093	0.008	0.133
Social ties (36.8%)	1 1 0 1 1 0 0 0 0	0.112	0.085	0.006	0.115
Promote ties (14.7%)	1 1 0 1 1 0 0 0 0	0.319	0.110	0.018	0.200

*Image cutoff is matrix density.

results are provided in Table 15-3 (geographic location), Table 15-4 (market group), and Table 15-5 (position).

Geographic Location The three senior partners, each in charge of a market group, and the CEO are located at the headquarters office. The remaining seventeen deal makers are located at headquarters and two satellite locations that are parts of the office market group. Therefore this analysis evaluates the extent to which office-group deal makers at two satellite offices are integrated with deal makers at headquarters. The geographic separation of offices does impede the establishment of strong ties among deal makers, as it does for the firm as a whole (Table 15-1). With an observed *b* (.288) far above the upper bound (.116), the null hypothesis of integration is clearly rejected. As shown in the image, strong ties tend to occur within geographic locations. This is further corroborated by the multidimensional scaling (MDS) of strong ties (Figure 15-2), which segregated the two satellite locations within the overall office market group. (Boundaries in Figure 15-2 are drawn on the basis of CONCOR partitions, shown in Figure 15-3, with the exception of the "inner circle" of partners.[19])

Unlike strong ties, weak ties are not constrained by location. The pattern of weak ties among deal makers between geographic locations is not

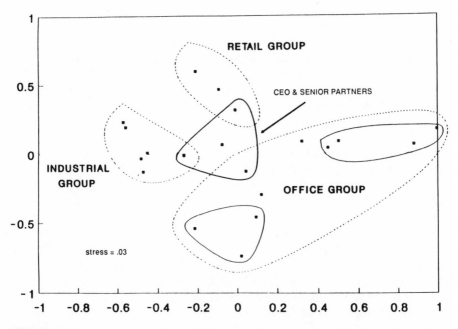

Figure 15-2
MDS Plot of Strong Ties Among Deal Makers

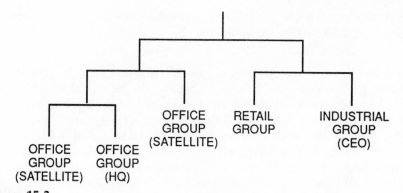

Figure 15-3

CONCOR Tree Diagram for Strong Ties Among Deal Makers

significantly different from the random baseline of a well-integrated net-work. Thus the three locations are integrated by weak ties among deal makers. Recall, however, that the firm as a whole ($n = 77$) is not inte-grated across geographic lines (see Table 15-1).

Advice-getting among deal makers is influenced by location. The null hypothesis of no differentiation is clearly rejected. Advice tends to occur within geographic units. However, the image reveals some integrative ele-ments in the advice network—one satellite office seeks advice from the other satellite and from headquarters (as well as from its own members). In the main, however, advice is sought within each location.

Informal socializing ties integrate deal makers across locations. The observed value of b (.083) is below the upper bound (.102), indicating that the null hypothesis of no differentiation (integration) cannot be rejected for social ties. Similarly, discussions about promoting a leasing agent to partner (promote ties) are not constrained by location.

Market Group   Formal market groups are very strong determinants of all five types of ties among deal makers (Table 15-4). The null hypothesis of integration for strong ties, for example, is clearly rejected, with an observed b of .339 far above the upper bound of .115. The image shows that strong ties do not integrate deal makers across market groups: strong ties occur within, not between, market groups. Weak ties, however, are only marginally shaped by market groups (with an observed b of .222 and upper bound of .194), and the presence of off-diagonal ties in the image indicates that the weak ties tend to bridge market groups, consistent with network theory (Granovetter 1973, 1982).

The strong effect of formal market groups on strong-tie networks is also evident in the MDS plot of strong ties among deal makers (Figure 15-2). The three market groups—retail, industrial, and office—are clearly demarcated. However, the CEO's location in the center of the MDS plot, almost in the middle of the triangle formed by the three senior partners, suggests that an inner circle integrates formal market groups.

The null hypothesis of no differentiation is rejected for both advice ties and promote ties. Like strong ties, their images indicate advice getting and promotion discussions tend to occur within market groups only. Social ties are also differentiated by formal market group—the image shows that members of a market group tend to socialize with one another (but the industrial group also claims social ties with the office and retail groups).

Position   Vertical differentiation—the division into formal ranks—does not appear to be a barrier to strong or weak ties among deal makers (Table 15-5). The null hypothesis of no differentiation for both types of tie cannot be rejected; for both, the observed b falls below its upper bound. Deal makers, like the entire organization (Table 15-1), are integrated across the formal dimension of position.

Position does seem to influence advice getting. The observed b for advice ties (.160) is larger than the upper bound (.133). The image reveals the basic pattern: senior partners seek advice from one another and from other (junior) partners, and partners seek advice from senior partners. Social ties, however, are not influenced by formal position. The observed b for social ties (.112) is less than the upper bound of .115. But the image indicates that informal socializing tends to occur among senior partners and partners and excludes leasing agents. Discussions about promoting a leasing agent to partner (promote ties) are shaped by formal position; these discussions, as indicated by the image, tend to occur among senior partners and partners only.

Structural Criticality of the CEO

The CEO occupies a central cultural[20] and structural position in the organization. As the MDS of strong ties revealed, for example, the CEO was located in the center of the deal-maker network, surrounded by his three senior partners (Figure 15-2). Analysis of point centrality provides further evidence. As shown in Figure 15-4, the CEO is the most central deal maker, whether centrality is measured as "closeness" or "betweenness" (Freeman 1976, 1979) in the strong-tie network.[21] The CEO was not, however, the most central point in the weak-tie network (see Figure 15-5).[22] (Indeed, a junior partner in the office market group was the most central in both closeness and betweenness.) This suggests that the CEO's role in the integrative weak-tie network may not be as critical as in the strong-tie network.

To evaluate the criticality of the CEO's position, I deleted the CEO from the strong-tie and weak-tie networks and reanalyzed them. The resulting matrices report the choices made by the remaining nineteen deal makers. These new matrices were analyzed using the hypothesis-testing

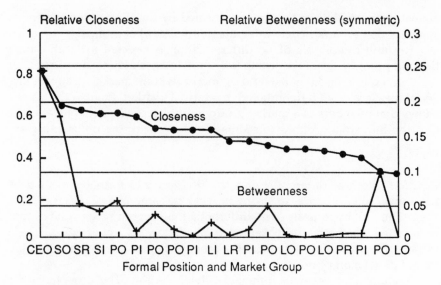

S = senior partner
P = partner
L = leasing agent
O = office
R = retail
I = industrial

Figure 15-4

Centrality of Deal Makers Based on Strong Interactions

procedure outlined in section 2. I then compared the integration networks
with and without the CEO. It is important to note that such comparisons
are based on the assumption that networks are fixed. It is possible, of
course, that ties lost by the removal of the CEO could be replaced by
substitute ties formed by other partners or created by a new CEO. Thus
this analysis assesses the extent to which the removal of the CEO's
relationships causes problems of integration in the *existing* networks.

As I have discussed, formal position was not a significant barrier to
strong-tie and weak-tie interactions in the deal-maker networks. And
removal of the CEO does not cause either network to differentiate.
Indeed, the strong-tie network appears to become slightly *more* integrated
(and the weak-tie network becomes slightly less integrated) without the
CEO. However, the null hypothesis of no differentiation is not rejected
for either network with the CEO removed.

Market groups substantially shape the deal makers' strong-tie network with the CEO present. With the CEO removed, the strong-tie
network remains differentiated, significantly different from random networks. The higher value of b, however, does indicate that strong-tie integration of market groups worsens with the CEO removed. Market groups
also influence the weak-tie network with the CEO present, though the

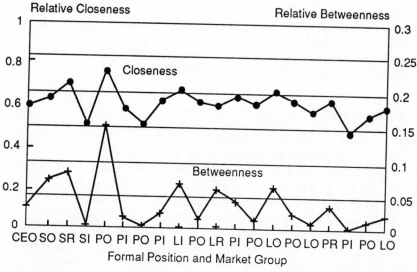

S = senior partner
P = partner
L = leasing agent
O = office
R = retail
I = industrial

Figure 15-5

Centrality of Deal Makers Based on Weak Interactions

observed value of b (.222) is just slightly above the upper bound (.194) of the random distribution (see Table 15-4), indicating that the weak-tie network is almost integrated with the CEO present. Exclusion of the CEO causes the observed value of b to fall below the upper bound, indicating that the weak-tie network becomes integrated once the CEO is eliminated from the deal-maker network.

Finally, there is no discernible difference in the level of integration induced by geographic separation. Both with and without the CEO, location is a significant barrier to strong ties; with and without the CEO, location is not a significant barrier to weak ties. Even without the CEO, geographic locations remain integrated by weak ties.

Overall, deletion of the CEO does not substantially affect organizational networks. With the minor exception of slightly less integration of the strong-tie network across market groups, removal of the CEO does not impair the relative integration of deal makers across the various formal dimensions. Though some partners thought that the loss of the CEO would cause the firm to disintegrate, the CEO's self-perception is consistent with the findings of the network analysis:

> I come to work because I enjoy coming to work. It is part of my life to come and spend several hours with business people in our office and that is really

what motivates me. That may change, but I certainly do not see it
now . . . So, whenever it gets to the point in which it is not as much fun,
then I will probably fade away. But if I were to do that, there is very strong
leadership in the office, primarily [the senior partner of the office group], and
in many respects [the firm] does not need me.

4. CONCLUSION

Organizational design is a solution to problems. As a purposive social
system that directs concerted collective action toward a common goal
(Aldrich and Marsden 1988), an organization must be designed to process
raw materials, people, and information; to do so, it must delineate a division of labor, roles and relationships, coordination mechanisms, and so
on. As an incomplete social system, an organization must be designed to
relate to its environment—suppliers, customers, regulators, competitors,
and the like. Firms with organizational designs that solve such problems
more efficiently or effectively tend to outperform rivals with ill-suited
organizational designs. The multidivisional form, for example, is considered to be a more efficient solution than the traditional unitary form to
problems created by large size and complexity (Armour and Teece 1978;
Chandler 1977; Williamson 1975).

So too with the network organization. As a flexible and self-adapting
organization, it is well suited to unique customized projects, close customer and supplier involvement in the production process, and complex
turbulent environments. These task and environmental characteristics are
often found together in professional services, contributing to the widespread appearance of the network organizational form in financial services, engineering and architectural services, commercial real estate
development, advertising, and management consulting. In the present
case, the real estate firm adopted the network model because it was considered to be cost efficient, suited to tasks and environment, and compatible with the antibureaucratic values of key decision makers. Several
competitors in the same market were organized more hierarchically and
suffered known difficulties in fostering ties across formal boundaries.
Though comparative performance data are not available,[23] senior partners
claimed that the firm was doing well, which was consistent with all out-
ward appearances and reputation in the business community. Most
important, the firm has never laid off an employee, unlike all its competitors, even in the recent downturn in the real estate market. But the
ultimate test of the network design will be the extent to which its self-
designing capabilities will enable it to escape organizational inertia.

Is the real estate firm integrated? I used a strong test to evaluate the
integration of the organization: comparison of real networks against the
network organization as an ideal type. In theory, a network organization
is *integrated* across formal boundaries; interpersonal ties of all types are
formed without respect to vertical, horizontal, or spatial differentiation.
Against this high standard, real organizational networks fared well:

1. For the firm as a whole, spatial differentiation impedes integration by both strong and weak ties, but weak ties integrate the firm across formal groups created by horizontal differentiation, and the firm is integrated by strong and weak ties across formal group boundaries created by vertical differentiation.

2. The networks of deal makers are integrated across formal boundaries created by vertical and spatial differentiation. Formal position is not a barrier to strong ties, weak ties, or informal socializing ties. Further, weak ties, social ties, and promote ties integrate deal makers across the dimension of geography (though strong and advice ties tend to occur within geographic units). Despite integration across vertical and spatial boundaries, horizontal boundaries strongly impede integration, especially for strong, advice, promote, and social ties.

3. The CEO is not a critical node in the deal-maker networks. Even though the CEO occupies a very central position, especially in strong-tie networks, removal of the CEO does not cause existing strong-tie and weak-tie networks in the "operating core" (Mintzberg 1979) of deal makers to become substantially more or less integrated than they already are.

Of the three formal dimensions, horizontal differentiation proved to be the greatest impediment to integration: market groups created the the highest hurdle for intergroup interaction. This may be because the formal dimension of horizontal differentiation is more directly linked to and influenced by the firm's environment than either vertical or spatial differentiation. The internal division of the firm into retail, office, and industrial groups mirrors the external structure of the real estate market. Each market group revolves around a "focus" of interest (Feld 1981) that induces ingroup bias; each market group conducts unique projects and specialized tasks, and engages in specialized external relationships with customers, suppliers (e.g., architects, contractors), and regulatory agencies. Neither natural integrative forces nor intentional integration mechanisms were able to fully overcome barriers created by market groups.

Although the real estate firm is not fully integrated, I conclude that it is moderately well integrated because none of the three dimensions of formal differentiation is a significant barrier to interaction at *two* levels: the firm as a whole and the operating core of deal makers. Lack of integration at one level is compensated by integration at the other. Spatial dispersion is a barrier for the firm as a whole, but deal makers are able to overcome the "friction" of space. Horizontal divisions impede the integration of deal makers, but the firm as a whole is integrated by weak ties across these groups. *Both* levels are well integrated across vertical boundaries. Finally, the relative integration of the real estate firm is evident in an analysis of reachability. As shown in Figure 15-6, more than 95% of all pairs in the firm are "reachable" with more than 65% reachable in paths of two links or less. Figure 15-7 shows comparable percentages for the bank wiring room.[24]

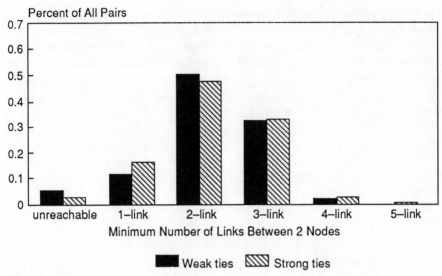

Figure 15-6

Minimum Distances for Strong and Weak Ties, Real Estate Firm

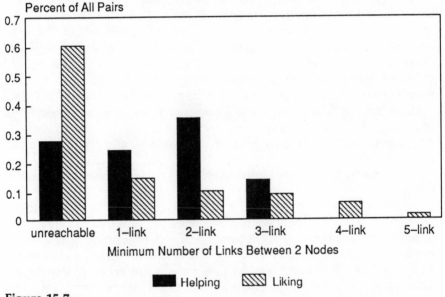

Figure 15-7

Minimum Distances for Helping and Liking Ties, Bank Wiring Room

In general, this study makes contributions to theory, methods, and practice. For theory, a contribution is a precise structural definition of a network organization. A network organization is *integrated* across formal groups created by vertical, horizontal, and spatial differentiation for any type of relation. This structural definition of a network organization can be easily operationalized as an amorphous a priori blockmodel (i.e., when partitions are formed on the basis of formal group membership). For network methods, a contribution is the development of simulation techniques for statistical hypothesis testing that compare the goodness-of-fit (*b*) of real blockmodels against the baseline of the amorphous image. These techniques are generally applicable. They can be used to assess the statistical significance of social networks blocked by formal groups, as in this case, or on bases such as structural equivalence or other attributes. Finally, for practice, the application of the theory and methods to evaluate a real network organization provides insights into specific management questions about the actual integration of the firm. The approach can be used to evaluate any management question that can be posed and operationalized as a particular network pattern.

Notes

1. This chapter is the revision of a paper prepared for the symposium on Networks and Organizations: Theory and Practice, Harvard Business School, August 20–23, 1990. The original symposium paper was presented under the title "Ideal versus Real Structure in an Intentional Network Organization." Versions of the revised paper were presented at the 1991 Sunbelt Social Network Conference (Tampa, Florida) and the Stamer Workshop in Structural Analysis, Department of Sociology, Columbia University (1991). This work was supported by the Graduate School of Business, University of Chicago, and by its William S. Fishman Faculty Research Fund. The paper benefited from the comments of the editors and the symposium participants.
2. The real estate firm used Gore's (n.d.) *lattice organization* as its organizational blueprint. Gore defines the characteristics of the lattice organization as (1) no fixed or assigned authority; (2) direct person-to-person communication; (3) natural leadership defined by skills and experiences; (4) journeyman-apprentice environment; (5) group-imposed discipline; and (6) constant interaction with other members of the organization. (The sixth characteristic is my primary focus in this analysis.)
3. I limit the use of differentiation to the division of a social system into *formal* categories or groups, like Blau and associates (e.g., Blau and Schwartz 1984; Calhoun, Meyer, and Scott 1990), but I fully acknowledge the existence and importance of *informal* differentiation, such as groups formed on the basis of structural equivalence (e.g., White, Boorman, and Brieger 1976), consistent with network theory.
4. In their classic study, Lawrence and Lorsch define integration as "the quality of the state of collaboration that exists among departments [i.e., horizontal differentiation] that are required to achieve unity of effort by the demands of the environment" (1967:11).
5. Role-set composition includes the use of generalists instead of specialists. Generalists, by virtue of multiple roles, have wider and more diverse egocentric networks than specialists, who occupy single roles. Dual-role occupancy, such as the "artistic hyphenate" (screenwriter-director) in Hollywood film making, is another example (Baker and Faulkner 1991).
6. Ingroup biases can also develop when structural differentiation intersects gender stratification. Consider the differentiation of the firm into deal makers and accounting staff. A partner told me that integration of the two groups

was inhibited by the fact that most deal makers are male and most accountants female, but participation in sports (an informal integrating mechanism) was almost exclusively male.

7. Many of the organizational factors that induce integration—careful selection, intensive socialization, unobtrusive social controls (such as the high visibility of the open office), and the lack of written policies and formal systems—also ensure conformity and predictability of behavior. In essence, culture becomes a substitute for formal controls. The use of culture in place of formal controls is not limited to small organizations. Sears, Roebuck & Company, for example, had few written policies and procedures at the corporate level. Instead, the firm relied (in part) on common values bred by internal career ladders and a long tradition of filling senior positions from within, resulting in predictable management behavior (*Harvard Business School* 1985).

8. Real estate generalists were easily switched from development activities in weak markets or products to strong markets or products, or from an inactive stage (e.g., initiation of new developments) to an active stage (e.g., leasing or managing existing properties).

9. Indeed, Krackhardt (this volume) notes that *everyone* at his Silicon Systems is connected by weak ties according to Granovetter's (1973:1371) definition of weak ties as those who interact more than once a year but less than twice a week (the same is true for the real estate firm studied here). However, Granovetter's definition seems quite appropriate to the job-seeking context that originally motivated his weak-tie theory.

10. Ties that fell between strong and weak are considered medium-strength ties and are not considered here because they are so infrequent (89% of all task-related communication ties are either "strong" or "weak").

11. Information other than attribute data can be used to form a priori blockmodels, though attribute data are the most common. Holland et al. (1983), for example, take the CONCOR-derived partitions of the Sampson monastery data as "given" and apply estimation techniques to evaluate the fit of this a priori blockmodel.

12. Wasserman and Anderson (1987) develop methods for stochastic a posteriori blockmodels.

13. The innovative application of log-linear models to study dyad-level properties of a network is yet another alternative (Fienberg and Wasserman 1981; Fienberg et al. 1985), though the application to aggregate choice tables (Marsden 1981) is closer to the objective and purpose of this study.

14. Two actors are structurally equivalent if they have the same relationships to all other actors. That is, a and b are structurally equivalent if and only if $aRc <=> bRc$ and $cRa <=> cRb$ for any c and any relation (e.g., Breiger, Boorman, and Arabie 1975:330).

15. Recall that the operators developed productivity norms (completing "two equipments" per day) that were contrary to organizational goals. Further, the selector unit developed its own deviant subculture; even though its members had the highest dexterity scores, this unit had the lowest productivity in the room and was the worst offender in misrepresenting actual productivity.

16. Random matrices are often generated by randomizing rows and columns (see, e.g., Hubert and Baker 1978). This technique is not appropriate here because actors must remain in their original formal groups; randomizing rows and columns would move actors out of their groups, while randomizing rows and columns within a formal group would have no effect.

17. The simulations for hypothesis testing were conducted with a program I custom designed for this purpose.

18. Chebychev's inequality is $P\{|X - m| > K(sd)\} <= 1/K^2$, where m = the mean and sd = the standard deviation of the distribution (Rohatgi 1976:100). In the present case, I use $K = 5$ in a one-tailed test.

19. As shown in the tree diagram, the CEO—who is not formally associated with any market group—was identified by CONCOR as structurally equivalent with the industrial group.
20. For example, when the CEO as a critical node was discussed during my presentation to the firm (third stage of research), the partners began referring to the CEO as "the node" in the firm.
21. Closeness is typically interpreted as independence from the control of others, and betweenness as control over network resources. (Betweenness is based on the combinatorics of symmetric graphs, so the data were symmetricized for analysis; closeness is based on the original nonsymmetric data.)
22. The weak-tie data were symmetricized for both measures.
23. Comparative performance data are almost impossible to obtain or determine because most commercial real estate firms are privately held and secretive, and properties are held as freestanding units, making it difficult to determine aggregate values).
24. Though the comparison may be tenuous due to important differences in tasks and contexts, reachability in the 77-person real estate firm can be contrasted with the distribution of minimum distances for "helping" and "liking" ties in the 14-person bank wiring room depicted in Figure 15-7. For example, 60% of all pairs are unreachable for liking ties, and almost 30% are unreachable for helping ties. Even though the bank wiring room was one-fifth the size of the real estate firm, it was clearly much more fragmented.

References

Aldrich, Howard E., and Peter Marsden. 1988. "Environments and Organizations." In Neil J. Smelser, ed., *Handbook of Sociology*. Beverly Hills: Sage, pp. 361–392.

Andrews, Kenneth R. 1980. *The Concept of Corporate Strategy*. Homewood, IL: Irwin.

Armour, Henry Ogden, and David J. Teece. 1978."Organizational Structure and Economic Performance: A Test of the Multidivisional Hypothesis." *Bell Journal of Economics* 9:106–122.

Baker, Wayne E., and Robert R. Faulkner. 1991. "Role as Resource in the Hollywood Film Industry." *American Journal of Sociology* 97:279–309.

Baker, Wayne E., and L. Philip Schumm. 1991. "Organizations as Networks: Theory and Methods." Working paper, University of Chicago.

Blau, Peter M. 1977. *Inequality and Heterogeneity*. New York: Free Press.

Blau, Peter M., and Richard A. Schoenherr. 1971. *The Structure of Organizations*. New York: Basic Books.

Blau, Peter M., and Joseph E. Schwartz. 1984. *Crosscutting Social Circles*. New York: Academic Press.

Burns, Tom, and George M. Stalker. 1962. *The Management of Innovation*. London: Tavistock.

Calhoun, Craig, Marshall W. Meyer, and W. Richard Scott. 1990. *Structures of Power and Constraint*. Cambridge: Cambridge University Press.

Carrington, Peter J., Greg H. Heil, and Stephen D. Berkowitz. 1980. "A Goodness-of-Fit Index for Blockmodels." *Social Networks* 2:219–224.

Chandler, Alfred D. 1977. *The Visible Hand: The Managerial Revolution in American Business*. Cambridge, MA: Harvard University Press.

Eccles, Robert G., and Dwight B. Crane. 1987. "Managing Through Networks In Investment Banking." *California Management Review* 30:176–195.

———. 1988. *Doing Deals: Investment Banks at Work*. Boston: Harvard Business School Press.

Emery, F. E., and E. L. Trist. 1965. "The Causal Texture of Organizational Environments." *Human Relations* 18:21–32.

Feld, Scott. 1981. "The Focused Organization of Social Ties." *American Journal of Sociology* 86:1015–1035.

Fienberg, Stephen E., Michael M. Meyer, and Stanley S. Wasserman. 1985. "Statistical Analysis of Multiple Sociometric Relations." *Journal of the American Statistical Association* 80:51–67.

Fienberg, Stephen E., and Stanley S. Wasserman. 1981. "Categorical Data Analysis of Single Sociometric Relations." In Samuel Leinhardt, ed., *Sociological Methodology*. San Francisco: Jossey-Bass, pp. 156–192.

Freeman, Linton. 1976. "A Set of Measures of Centrality Based on Betweenness." *Sociometry* 40:35–41.

———. 1979. "Centrality in Social Networks: I. Conceptual Clarification." *Quality and Quantity* 14:585–592.

Galaskiewicz, Joseph, Stanley Wasserman, B. Rauschenbach, W. Bielefeld, and P. Mullaney. 1985. "The Influence of Corporate Power, Social Status, and Market Position on Corporate Interlocks in a Regional Network." *Social Forces* 64:403–431.

Gibbs, Jack P., and Walter T. Martin. 1962. "Urbanization, Technology, and the Division of Labor." *American Sociological Review* 26:667–677.

Goodman, L.A. 1968. "The Analysis of Cross-Classified Data: Independence, Quasi-independence, and Interaction in Contingency Tables With or Without Missing Cells." *Journal of the American Statistical Association* 63:1091–1131.

———. 1979. "Multiplicative Models for the Analysis of Occupational Mobility Tables and Other Kinds of Cross-Classification Tables." *American Journal of Sociology* 84:804–819.

Gore, W. L. (n.d.) *The Lattice—A Philosophy of Enterprise*. Evanston, IL: W. L. Gore and Associates.

Granovetter, Mark. 1973. "The Strength of Weak Ties." *American Journal of Sociology* 78:1360–1380.

———. 1982. "The Strength of Weak Ties: A Network Theory Revisited." In Peter Marsden and Nan Lin, eds., *Social Structure and Network Analysis*. Beverly Hills: Sage, pp. 105–130.

Guterl, Fred V. 1989. "Goodbye, Old Matrix." *Business Month* (February): 32, 34, 35, 38.

Hallinan, Maureen T., and Richard A. Williams. 1989. "Interracial Friendship Choices in Secondary Schools." *American Sociological Review* 54:67–78.

Harvard Business School. 1985. "Sears, Roebuck & Co. in the '80s: Renewal and Diversification." Teaching Case #9-386-029, Harvard Business School, Boston.

Holland, Paul W., Kathryn Blackmond Laskey, and Samuel Leinhardt. 1983. "Stochastic Blockmodels: First Steps." *Social Networks* 5:109–138.

Hubert, L. J., and F. B. Baker. 1978. "Evaluating the Conformity of Sociometric Measurements." *Psychometrika* 43:31–41.

Lawrence, Paul R., and Jay W. Lorsch. 1967. *Organization and Environment: Managing Differentiation and Integration*. Boston: Harvard Business School Division of Research.

Marsden, Peter V. 1981. "Models and Methods for Characterizing the Structural Parameters of Groups." *Social Networks* 3:1–27.

Mayhew, Bruce H., Roger L. Levinger, J. Miller McPherson, and Thomas F. James. 1972. "System Size and Structural Differentiation in Formal Organizations: A Baseline Generator for Two Major Theoretical Propositions." *American Sociological Review* 37:629–633.

Mayhew, Bruce H., and Roger L. Levinger. 1976. "Size and Density of Interaction in Human Aggregates." *American Journal of Sociology* 82:86–110.

Miles, Raymond E., and Charles C. Snow. 1986. "Organizations: New Concepts for New Forms." *California Management Review* 28:62–73.

Mintzberg, Henry. 1979. *The Structuring of Organizations*. Englewood Cliffs, NJ: Prentice-Hall.

Nolan, Richard L., and Alex J. Pollock. 1986. "Organization and Architecture, or Architecture and Organization." *Stage by Stage* 6:1–10.

Nolan, Richard L., Alex J. Pollock, and James P. Ware. 1988. "Toward the Design of Network Organizations." *Stage by Stage* 8:1–12.

Powell, Walter W. 1985. *Getting into Print*. Chicago: University of Chicago Press.

Rohatgi, V. K. 1976. *An Introduction to Probability Theory and Mathematical Statistics*. New York: Wiley.

Thompson, James D. 1967. *Organizations in Action*. New York: McGraw-Hill.

Wasserman, Stanley, and Carolyn Anderson. 1987. "Stochastic A Posteriori Blockmodels: Construction and Assessment." *Social Networks* 9:1–36.

Wasserman, Stanley, and Dawn Iacobucci. 1986. "Statistical Analysis of Discrete Relational Data." *British Journal of Mathematical and Statistical Psychology* 39:41–64.

White, Harrison C., Scott A. Boorman, and Ronald L. Brieger. 1976. "Social Structure from Multiple Networks, I: Blockmodels of Roles and Positions." *American Journal of Sociology* 81:730–780.

Wholey, Douglas R., and Jack W. Brittain. 1986. "Organizational Ecology: Findings and Implications." *Academy of Management Review* (July): 513–533.

Williamson, Oliver E. 1975. *Markets and Hierarchies*. New York: Free Press

16

Fragments of a Cognitive Theory of Technological Change and Organizational Structure

MICHAEL J. PIORE

This chapter will attempt to clarify and revise several ideas about the relationship between technology, organizational structure, and the economy that Charles Sabel and I used to construct the argument of *The Second Industrial Divide*. The key notions on which I will focus are (1) technological trajectories; (2) the two specific technological trajectories that we term "mass production" and "flexible specialization" in *The Second Industrial Divide*; and (3) the organizational forms associated with these trajectories: *hierarchy* and *network*.

NETWORK THEORY

I begin with some preliminary observations about the kind of network theory toward which I am aiming. The network is increasingly recognized in a variety of social science disciplines as a canonical organizational form, distinct from markets and hierarchies. The dominant approach to explaining this form grows out of neoclassical economic theory. It focuses on the way in which the network resolves certain problems of cooperative behavior among purposive rational actors seeking to maximize their individual economic well-being. And it seeks an understanding of the network that permits a comparison with markets and hierarchies in terms of the effects on individual and collective welfare. This approach is by no means confined to neoclassical economists themselves. It is shared by organizational theorists and sociologists who recognize interdependencies among individuals and a flexibility in individual tastes and preferences that economists themselves assume away, but who nonetheless preserve the basic rational individualistic framework. Ideally, one would also like to understand how networks affect the operation of an economic system when they are embedded within it, but relatively little attention has been devoted to this issue. Because it depends on the other organizational forms with which networks are combined, it is obviously an extremely complex problem.

The argument Sabel and I developed in *The Second Industrial Divide* was built around a distinction between two different approaches to technological change. Organization is a derivative concept. It has become increasingly clear that the organizational form associated with flexible specialization is the *network,* although we have not always used that term. The way we arrived at the issue of organization, through technological change, has led us to a somewhat different approach to understanding the prevalence and efficacy of the network form. We have pursued two theoretical paths in particular. One is essentially epistemological and tends to emphasize the way in which knowledge evolves to generate economic growth. Organizations are distinguished by their perspectives in terms of epistemological (or cognitive) development. The second focus is on the way in which economic institutions are embedded in social structures and seeks to define differences among organizational forms in terms of the social structures with which they are associated. The epistemological and social paths that we have been pursuing are conceptually distinct, although undoubtedly an underlying relationship exists between them. Probably the best way to think about that relationship is in terms of *language* or possibly *culture,* concepts that have both epistemological and social dimensions. However, we have not tried to work out the relationship. Neither the social nor the epistemological theory should in principle conflict with individual welfare maximization. Individuals in our theoretical universe are not irrational, but they may be *a*rational or *pre*rational in the sense that the variables and processes on which the social and the epistemological focus are generally taken as given in—or prior to—the calculations that rational actors in economic theories of organizational structure are presumed to make. Thus the epistemological approach may be thought of as focusing on the *models* of reality in terms of which rational actors calculate gains and losses and the way in which those models evolve over time. Another way of putting this is that it focuses on the presumed relationship between means and ends. The social approach focuses on how the individual *defines* himself or herself; the economist might term this "preference formation," but it is actually the somewhat more complex process of how an actor comes to distinguish between means and ends. Again, language is a good analogy. Can one have economic activity without language? If not, does the particular language of a community have an effect on its economic capacities? Is language then a means to an end—that is, the end of economic welfare? Or is it so fundamental to personal identity that it is ultimately an end in itself? The supposition within which we are working is that these questions do not arise within a rational calculus; to say that language is prior to that calculus, is to push the analysis backward into a theoretical realm in which the very distinction between means and ends does not arise.

This chapter presents ideas associated with the epistemological path. There is not room to discuss both the epistemological and the social approach here. More important, an emphasis on epistemology and cognition flows directly from the idea of a technological trajectory, while the path to theories of social embeddedness is somewhat more circuitous.

TECHNOLOGICAL TRAJECTORY

The concept of a technological trajectory can be located quite precisely in both Marxian and mainstream economic theories, but the terminology implies a certain interpretation of these theories that many who associate themselves with the schools of thought might not accept. In mainstream economics, a technological trajectory is the locus of the mystery surrounding economic growth. I use the term "mystery" because it seems to capture the essence of a story, possibly apocryphal, that I have always thought basic to mainstream growth theory. The story is about Bob Gordon and Simon Kuznets, who were commentators for an American Economic Association panel of papers on economic growth. Simon Kuznets was, of course, the father of national income accounting, and in a sense he invented growth measurement. Bob Gordon is a member of my arrogant generation, and the incident took place at the time when we were at our most arrogant age. Gordon, as the story goes, spoke first, and began by dismissing all the papers with the comment: "The problem of economic growth was solved by Griliches in his article of 19 . . ." In the silence that ensued while the audience waited for him to continue, Kuznets rose from his chair, walked to the podium, gently put his arm around Bob's shoulders and said, "Professor Gordon, you cannot 'solve' the problem of economic growth."

In mainstream theory, the mystery of growth is that an industrial economy is able to generate progressively more output over time with the same resources. This effect is measured by Solow's residual—that, I imagine, is what the Griliches' paper to which Gordon referred "explained." In a crude sense, a technological trajectory is yet another attempt to penetrate that mystery. The criticism is that it, and the various specific trajectories identified in *The Second Industrial Divide*, are basically just new terminologies for the same old thing: they may be nice names, but they leave the mystery unresolved. You can read this chapter as an attempt to respond that criticism.

In one respect the criticism is not well taken. The terminology involves a lot of hand waving, but it invokes at least one substantive proposition: that there is a very specific growth process, so specific that it entrains very definite implications for the institutional structure of the economy. The valid criticism is that Sabel and I assert that relationship without specifying how the institutional structures actually derive from the growth processes. The notion that there is a specific growth process in this sense, however, directly conflicts with a central (albeit implicit) assumption of neoclassical growth theory, which is that the sources of the residual are so various that they have no strong institutional implications: It is this notion of the vast multiplicity of little human actions that is the essence of the idea that growth itself is an impenetrable mystery. However, this view is peculiar to neoclassical growth theory, not universal to mainstream theory as a whole. Indeed, the most recent growth literature in mainstream economics adopts a position much closer to ours.

The school of regulation is not a homogeneous approach to economic analysis either. What Sabel and I found interesting in the regulation approach was the marriage between the neoclassical lessons about an economy as a self-equilibrating system and the Marxist idea of an economy as evolving through history, generating tensions and conflicts that were ultimately disequilibrating and finally resolved through the political process. Defined in this way, as a marriage between neoclassical and Marxian approaches, the notion of a technological trajectory definitely belongs to the Marxian dimension: it is that set of forces that propels the economy through history, causing it to outgrow any particular regulatory framework and enter into crisis.

The idea that something quite specific propels the growth process is, of course, not simply Marxian. It was shared by the classical economists beginning with Adam Smith, and is, as I have already noted, the central tenet of the classical revival at Chicago. In Marx, or at least among Marxists, there are a variety of distinct ideas about what it is that ultimately generates the historical thrust of the system. The major division is between those who see that thrust as rooted in some kind of natural evolution of the technology and those who see it as generated by class conflict. So long as there is only one technological trajectory, however, this distinction does not really matter: in the highly integrated process envisaged by Marx, they both lead to the same set of institutional outcomes. When one postulates, as we have, two trajectories, the outcome is open and the source of these trajectories becomes a central issue. In Marxian terms, a major criticism of *The Second Industrial Divide* is thus the failure to address it. But the flaw in the argument that leads to this reproach is essentially the same as when the argument is viewed from a mainstream perspective: the argument is about the way in which alternative technological trajectories generate particular institutional structures, but we fail to define the trajectories in such a way that the structure can be deduced from them.

Actually, to say that *The Second Industrial Divide* defines a trajectory by the institutions with which it associates is to concede too much. A good deal, in fact, is said about the *trajectory* of mass production independent of its associated institutions. What is said divides roughly into three comments: First, the trajectory of mass production involves the search for growth (or technological innovation) through the process of the division of labor, as exemplified by Adam Smith (1937) in the transition from pin craftsman to pin factory. Second, growth of this kind is argued to have a set of distinct technical characteristics. The critical characteristics, in terms of the institutional structures of the economy, are fourfold: (1) economies of scale within the firm, (2) increasing returns for the economy as a whole, (3) the specialization of productive resources, and (4) the divorce between conception and execution in production.

Third, while we did not specify flexible specialization as a technological trajectory, we did delimit the institutional forms associated with it more sharply than the criticism suggests. The organizational literature at that time—especially, but not only, in economics—distinguished two basic institutional forms: "hierarchies," exemplified by the large, vertically integrated corporation; and "markets," made up of isolated small firms communicating through price signals. We associated flexible specialization with a third institutional structure, one of a series of small (in relationship to the hierarchical corporation) units engaged in intense direct communication and embedded in a dense social network. Because there was relatively little research on this organizational form, we drew primarily on work on industrial districts in central Italy and on old craft communities, generally characterized as "pre-industrial," which in most areas had disappeared. Since we completed *The Second Industrial Divide* in 1984, there has accumulated a much more substantial body of work on what are now termed "network" organizations, and there is an emergent consensus in the management literature that this organizational form is often appropriate not only to organize relationships among small firms but also to structure the relationship among the internal units of large corporate enterprises and between the corporation and its suppliers, customers, and even its external competitors. But the question remains: What is the relationship between this network organization and the characteristics associated with the mass-production trajectory? Is a network responsive to the absence of all of those characteristics, or merely some of them? If a network does not generate growth through the division of labor, how is growth generated?

Before discussing these questions, which are not resolved, it is worth recognizing that what is said about mass production does clarify several issues in the current growth literature. First, it clarifies the relationship between flexible specialization and recent developments in organizational design and manufacturing technology associated with flexibility, to which flexible specialization is frequently linked. A number of the recent developments do not affect any of the basic characteristics of mass production. In particular, they maintain the distinction between conception and execution, they continue to rely on resource specialization, albeit in a somewhat novel way, and they seem to involve both substantial economies of scale and increasing returns. In an earlier study, this difference led to a distinction between flexible specialization and *flexible mass production* (Piore 1991). A given productive operation in the latter produces a gamut of products and is thus not dedicated to a single make and model as in classic mass production. But the variety is limited and the products specified in advance. In flexible specialization, by contrast, the product line is open ended. This distinction also involves certain cognitive differences in the approach to the productive process, but the significance of these differences cannot be deduced from the list of characteristics defining mass production and requires an expanded definition of flexible specialization.

Combining Mass Production and Flexible Specialization

A second point, however, that does emerge from the list of characteristics is the basic difficulty of combining mass production and flexible specialization in a single system. To assert that growth under mass production involves increasing returns is to suggest that alternative trajectory threatens its dynamism.

The idea is that the economy moves down the curve ab over time by increasing output through standardization of products. Smith pointed out that there was another method of production, craft production, that produced specialized goods but with stagnant technology, so that it always had cost a. The result: the consumer is faced with a choice, governed by the price differential between $Pc : Pm(1/q)$, and q grows over time.

The postulate about the emergence of flexible specialization as an alternative growth trajectory is that at some point in the late 1970s a new dynamic of technological change emerges, and Pc begins to fall. As it does so, $Pc - Pm$ declines, and customers are drawn away from mass markets, and q falls. The fall in c, however, itself aggravates the process, raising Pm and further narrowing the price differential.

In analyzing these developments, one can make a further distinction between economies of scale associated with fixed investment in specialized resources and increasing returns associated with the technological development to which the specialization leads. Whether or not the latter is irreversible depends on the precise way in which specialization and technological innovation interact, a point to which we will return shortly. If there is irreversibility, or some irreversibility, then the technological gains may be preserved in smaller units and at least a part of the effects of a declining q are reversed over time as the scale of new plant and equipment is adjusted to the reduced market size. Then mass production will make a resurgence, an effect that we currently seem to be observing. But our characterization of the mass-production trajectory suggests that the resurgence will be temporary; the dynamism of mass production depends on the progressive expansion of q, and once the scale is adjusted, the technology will stagnate.

Flexible Specialization and the Classical Revival

A further observation that one can draw from this characterization of mass production relates to the classical revival at Chicago. The classical revival, as we suggested earlier, has basically accepted the notion that there is a technological trajectory in the sense that we are using the term: that is, a growth process that has substantive implications for the economic structure. But the literature assumes that this process is consistent with a competitive economic structure, and the concern is with modeling that process as a kind of general equilibrium growth. Indeed, the competitive nature of the associated institutional structure is such a fundamental tenet of this literature that it is not even explicitly stated, let alone argued. What makes this curious is that the new Chicago literature draws on exactly the same classical tradition that we use to define mass production. How does this happen? What is the difference? In terms of the list of four defining characteristics, the difference centers around the distinction between increasing returns at the level of the economy and economies of scale at the level of the firm. We have defined mass production in such a way that the two characteristics are inextricably linked: you cannot have the former without the latter. And the Chicago literature assumes that the increasing returns for the economy do not imply economies of scale at the level of the firm. In the Chicago revival literature, increasing returns involve *external economies*. Robert Lucas (1988) even coins the term "external human capital economies" to characterize the growth process. The key question then becomes: are the economies associated with the classical growth process external?

The ideas that such economies are external comes from Marshall. But the Chicago literature does not actually refer to Marshall himself; it tries to make this point instead by reference to Allyn Young (1928). In so doing, it confuses precisely those issues that we are attempting to highlight. The confusion arises because to illustrate his argument, Young uses Adam Smith's pin factory. And in the pin factory example, resources are too specialized to generate "external economies" of scale. Thus Chicago would need to postulate an alternative trajectory in order to sustain its models. It need not as a matter of logic, of course, join the whole debate; it could simply assert that there is a single trajectory with the properties for which it is looking and that Smith and Young were either mistaken about what the pin factory growth process *was* or about its overwhelming importance. But given the extensive literature now developing about network structures, this may be a little harder to do than it was in the past.

Chicago might have gone back to Marshall, instead of Allyn Young, but this would not have solved the problem. There is now a very extensive literature trying to interpret exactly what Marshall observed in the light of contemporary experience. One influential branch of the literature argues that what Marshall observed was essentially akin to the dynamic *industrial districts* that emerged in Italy in the 1970s. Indeed, the very term "industrial district" is taken from Marshall's text (Becattini 1979). But as we have noted, the Italian industrial districts are not markets: the intensity of communication that occurs within them and the social structures in which they are embedded make it very unlikely that they could ever be compatible with a competitive price system. Moreover, there is a real question about the externality of the economies associated with these kinds of network organizations. The research on both the network corporation and the Italian districts suggest that they survive and prosper only if the economies that are external to particular productive units are internalized as parameters in the decisions of some higher-level organization unit—for example, the corporate headquarters in large organizations, and the municipal government, the trade union, and/or a business association in the geographic regions.

My own interpretation of the literature is that Marshall did not observe industrial districts in the sense that contemporary writers in the field of network organization do. I think that Allyn Young's choice of the pin factory example was indeed apt: that what Marshall observed might best be termed a *dispersed hierarchy*, a set of narrowly specialized and hierarchically coordinated productive units. These units operated like the mass-production factory of the functionally divided corporation, but the relationships were organized by contracts rather than by internal rules. His observations call into question much of Oliver Williamson (1986) and Alfred Chandler's (1972) theory of the modern corporation but they are not associated with an independent growth trajectory and the economies of growth are internalized in contracts among these units just as they are in the vertically integrated corporation. Neither reading of Marshall suggests that he was observing a competitive market economy in the sense that we use that term in contemporary economics or that such an economy could sustain growth. To resolve the problem about the relationship between growth and organization form, it appears that one must go back beyond Young and Marshall to the classical economists themselves.

CLASSICAL GROWTH THEORY

Adam Smith

The two key propositions of classical growth theory originate with Adam Smith (1937): growth is produced by the division of labor and the division of labor is limited by the extent of the market. But the classical growth process was actually defined by Adam Smith's *pin factory* example, or rather, the classical growth process is defined by the example of the transition from the master pin maker who made the whole pin to the factory in which "one worker pulls the wire, a second worker cuts the wire, a third worker heads the pin, a fourth points the pin, and so forth" (Smith 1937). There is a certain ambiguity in Smith as to exactly why the division of labor in this sense should enhance productivity. The ambiguity is important, and we will return to it shortly; but the underlying reason is the specialization of productive resources: specially trained workers and specialized tooling. The specialization leads directly to Smith's second proposition, that the division of labor is limited by the extent of the market. Because the resources are specialized, they cannot shift to alternative tasks: the specialization is justified only if labor and capital can be kept employed in the tasks they are specialized to do. This proposition about the extent of the market is an assertion about increasing returns: as the level of output expands, it becomes possible to further divide—hence to further specialize—productive resources. Must these increasing returns be internalized? That is, do increasing returns manifest themselves as economies of scale at the level of the firm? Smith did not seem to see a connection; at least he never identified the conflict between growth and competition that such firm-level economies of scale imply. But modern human capital theory suggests that in the pin factory example the increasing reforms *must* be internalized. The pin factory resources are not just specialized, they are *specific:* they can be used only in the particular pin-making task. By the time we reach the end point of this growth process in Ford's Model-T factory, the resources are specific to the make and model of a particular product. When the model changes, the worker must be retrained and the old equipment scrapped and replaced. Specific investments of this kind will not be made unless the firm can capture the returns. In the pin factory growth process, moreover, the market will *never* support the additional firms that would be required to eliminate the specificity of the investments: in a larger market it will always pay to divide the tasks still further and make the resources still more specific. Increasing returns, economies of scale, and resource specializations are inextricably linked. The Chicago-Marshallian growth process, like flexible specialization, requires a different growth mechanism.

Marglin

The debate about the relationship between the division of labor and productivity growth offers clues for alternative growth mechanisms. Credit for opening, or rather reopening, that debate goes to Stephen Marglin and his 1974 article, "What Do Bosses Do?" Marglin systematically reviews Smith's rationale for the pin factory and adduces evidence that suggests each piece of Smith's argument is either empirically false or quantitatively trivial. Marglin then argues that the division of labor is the product not of efficiency but of class conflict. It is designed to enhance the control of the bosses; it does not contribute to growth. Although it would constitute a considerable digression to engage Marglin's argument fully here, the argument is difficult to sustain. Its chief limitation for our purposes is that it offers no alternative growth theory: either growth is an illusion or, as it is for Kuznets, a mystery. The empirical evidence that Marglin offers suggests that the particular *form* of growth may have been chosen initially because it enhanced the power of the "bosses." For that reason the attempt to alter the growth process may be resisted, but the evidence is consistent with the notion that the growth resulting from the process is real enough. And if in fact one believes that growth to be real, the postulate of an alternative but rejected growth trajectory that we are seeking to sustain here would only strengthen Marglin's assertions about the role of class conflict: the conflict might determine which of several alternative paths was chosen and/or why, once chosen, the commitment was maintained. To invoke class conflict in this way, one need not make growth itself an illusion. But Marglin's criticisms of Smith, while cogent, are not helpful in the construction of a positive theory of growth.

Marx

Much more helpful in this regard are the observations of Karl Marx, not the Marx of class conflict from which Marglin drew his inspiration, but the Marx of technological determinism. Marx's ideas about the efficacy of the division of labor and the enhancement of productivity are, at root, very different from Smith's and much closer to modern theories about cognition. Two of Marx's propositions appear particularly promising in terms of developing the notion of an alternative growth trajectory. One is the distinction he draws between the social division of labor and the detailed division of labor. The second is the relationship he develops between the detailed division of labor and mechanization. Marx makes a third observation about the rise of the factory system that is also extremely suggestive.

The Social Division and the Detailed Division   The distinction between the social division of labor and the detailed division is essentially the distinction between the pin craftsman and the pin header. Marx (1944) suggests that these are two distinct and technologically powerful developments. The pin craftsman—which Smith took as the starting point in the development process—is actually itself a distinct technological development, involving the separation of pin making from the making of other products (like sheep herding, cow tending, cloth making, and the like) which were once all produced together in a self-contained household. The separation contributes to productivity because it isolates an activity with a distinct conceptual core, and by focusing on that core and understanding it better, one will produce better pins, possibly in a more effective way. The isolation of pin heading yields no such advantages, because pin heading is not a conceptually distinct operation; it has no meaning independent of pin making (Marx 1944:390).

Reconceptualization   Indeed, for Marx the contribution of the detailed division of labor was very different. It enabled the production process to assimilate the logic of the machine. In this sense it is virtually the opposite of the social division of labor. One separated out the task of pin heading in order to escape the conceptual apparatus of the pin and think of the task instead in terms of a rationale associated with machinery. Having done so, one is then able to mechanize the task of pin heading. A by-product of this process of technological development is the narrowly trained worker who does the "pin heading" before it is mechanized. This is an extremely important part of the story Marx tells about capitalist development, but it is not central to the issues here.

Reintegration   A third insight into the process of growth is suggested by Marx's (1944) comments on the factory system. For Marx, in contrast to Marglin, the factory system was a real engine of growth. But, Marx cautioned, the growth potential of the factory does not explain its development. The factory itself was created for one series of reasons: to better control a productive process and supervise a labor force that was previously dispersed under the putting out system, to share a common source of power, and so on. Once the separate tasks were brought together under one roof and performed in proximity to one another, people were led to perceive the productive process in new ways, and this changed perception was itself a source of innovation. The new innovations were associated facilitating the *integration* of the district operations. Thus the innovations associated with the factory are different from those associated with mechanization: the latter involves looking at each operation separate from every other operation; the other involves looking at the operations in relation to each other (Marx 1944, especially 414–415).

If one accepts Marx's story about how it is that the division of labor produces growth in mass production, what produces growth under flexible specialization? It seems to me that one can read Marx's comments in at least three different ways. One is as a story about a dominant technology: the shift from handicraft production to machine production. The natural way to extend this story is to postulate a shift in the dominant technology. And surely the new technology on which one would want to focus is information technology—that is, the computer. A second interpretation is that mass production grows out of a focus on the detailed division of labor, and that flexible specialization shifts the focus of technological change backward in the cognitive chain toward the social division of labor. A third reading might focus on the distinction between the fragmentation associated with the detailed division of labor and the integration associated with the factory. Innovation in flexible specialization seems more like the latter than the former.

It would be hard to reject any of these as explanations for contemporary patterns of technological change; indeed, although not precisely in these terms, much of the contemporary literature develops one or another of the three themes. But I am inclined to abstract from Marx a fourth perspective—not necessarily inconsistent with the other three, but more abstract, more general: that technological innovation is a cognitive process and that one needs a cognitive theory to explain it.

The particular cognitive theory on which Marx's own explanation of industrial progress is built is something like the following: Technology is the embodiment of certain concepts or conceptual frameworks in terms of which we think about transforming resources. Each of the frameworks can be thought of as involving a set of abstract principles that tell us how resources can be organized and deployed. The ultimate foundation for technological progress involves the reorganization of our understandings in new, more revealing—hence more powerful—conceptual frameworks.

But in the meantime a second process involves applying the conceptual knowledge we already have to perfect existing technologies and organizations.

The social division of labor involves the organization of production into distinct, conceptually coherent groups of operations. This enables us to perfect the underlying technical know-how involved and apply it in more effective ways. Thus, for example, building and farming are conceptually distinct, and the separation of the two enables us to concentrate better on the development of the concepts appropriate to each. Similarly, within building, carpentry and masonry involve conceptually distinct materials, and for this reason we do better in each when we specialize in them as separate endeavors.

But the organization of knowledge in these ways has certain effects. One is that existing conceptual categories tend to limit the imagination. By directing attention in one way, they block alternative perspectives. In craft pin making, the production process is dominated by the logic of pins on the one hand and the human being on the other. Mechanization involves a different logic. In order to apply that logic, one needs to *separate* pin heading, for example, from the pin. The rationale for the detailed division of labor is thus different from the rationale of the social division. It is to escape one conceptual frame in order to move to another frame.

Finally, any partitioning of the production process into a distinct series of operations creates a problem of reintegration, and this problem arises in both the social division of labor and the detailed division of labor. There are several different ways to understand the issue of integration (or reintegration). One is that it is simply a mechanical by-product of the process of partitioning. Marx's view of the development of the factory, however, implies that integration is more than this: that it is itself a distinct cognitive process. Other clues in the literature suggest this is the case: A study by Persio Arida (1977) shows that innovation in automobile manufacturing oscillated historically between phases in which major improvements involved the perfection of separate operations and phases where improvements derived from achieving a better integration among operations. This pattern is evident in other technologies as well: for a period, IBM focused on perfecting individual machines while Digital's competitive advantage was achieved through *systems*. Audio-stereo technology seems to oscillate between periods where sales promotion focuses on the components individually and periods when the system as a whole is being hyped. Linguist Roman Jakobson (1972) calls the focus on the individual element "metaphor" and the focus on the sequencing of elements "metonomy" and, in studies of child speech development and of stroke-related speech impairment known as aphasia, traces these different operations to separate and distinct parts of the brain.

But while integration appears to be a distinct cognitive process, there are certain dimensions of it that seem basically mechanical. In the detailed division of labor the elements of the production process lose their original cognitive meaning in terms of the product. Indeed, the escape from the cognitive frame of the product is the *purpose* of the detailed division. This loss of independent cognitive meaning is what we mean by the divorce between conception and execution. It therefore leads to both the inflexibility (or rigidity) of task definition and a strictly hierarchical organization in which execution of the individual tasks is subordinated to a higher authority capable of reassimilating them into a cognitive frame wherein they have economic meaning.

In the social division of labor the operations do not necessarily lose their economic meaning. But they might: in a social division of labor, one can further distinguish between a partitioning of operations that maps directly onto the structure of consumption and a partitioning that does not. Examples of the former are such crafts as baking, tailoring, shoemaking, and, indeed, pin making. But the building trades are an example of a partitioning of operations in production that retains cognitive frames but does not map directly onto the structure of consumption: the carpenter, electrician, plumber, mason, and so on. In the first set of crafts, the consumer performs the integration. In the latter case, the integration must be performed prior to consumption in the production process itself. This, I would like to argue, is the definition of flexible specialization. It achieves innovation through the tension between a deepening of understanding within a given cognitive frame and the pull to reintegrate back to a different frame in order to produce a sellable commodity. And it lends itself to a network structure.

This broad story can be reduced to a series of more sharply delimited propositions and summarized as follows:

1.   Economic growth is the product of the division of labor.

2.   The division of labor involves the *partitioning* of economic activity. One needs to understand both the cognitive and the organizational implications of different partitioning principles.

3.   The division of labor has two distinct dimensions: *specialization and integration.*

4.   Cognitively, specialization has two distinct functions:
     a.   The *deepening* of knowledge: the development of a deeper conceptual base—for example, specializing in carpentry as a way of focusing on the properties of wood.
     b.   Reconceptualization: a change in the conceptual frame itself.

5.   Reconceptualization also has two dimensions:
     a.   Transfer: the movement of an element from one conceptual frame to another—for example, the mechanization of pin heading.
     b.   Invention: the creation of a new conceptual frame.

6.   The problem of reintegration is created by a divergence between upstream conceptual categories and downstream conceptual categories, and especially a divergence between the categories in which production is organized and the categories of consumption.

CONCLUSION

What I suggest is that mass production involved growth through the detailed division of labor: growth through reconceptualization and within reconceptualization, primarily transfer. As a result of the transfer, conceptual categories in terms of which the elements of production were performed were distinct from the categories of the final product. This created a problem of reintegration, which led in turn to a hierarchical organization form.

Flexible specialization involves growth through the social division of labor: the *deepening* of knowledge within given conceptual categories. But the partitioning of the productive process is different from the partitioning of the consumption process; hence there is a problem of reintegration similar to the problem in mass production. Network structure facilitates both the deepening and the integration because to better integrate with other conceptual specialties, the specialists are forced to develop their own specialty more fully. The conceptual level of understanding in this form of growth permits horizontal coordination, thus avoiding hierarchy, but the degree of interactions across specialties is too intense to permit a market.

The market organization of the kind that the Chicago school envisages would seem to be more likely when the conceptual structure of production maps directly onto the conceptual structure of consumption. Why this should ever be the case, however, is unclear.

If one understands the process of technological change in terms of the priorities of specialization and integration, it may be that what we think of as networks are a natural form of organization and that markets and hierarchies are two extremes. The market extreme involves no integration at all. The hierarchical organization involves completely rigid integration. This implies, however, that there is a continuum of intermediate cases, depending on how much scope is given to specialization and how much to integration. In other words, there are many different kinds of networks; what we think of as a network is an organization where the two cognitive moments, integration and specialization, are in relative balance. Or, to use Granovetter's (1973) terms and translate a cognitive into a social theory, weak ties and strong ties are balanced.

References

Arida, Persio. 1977. "Cycles of Innovation in Automobile Assembly," Unpublished paper, MIT, Cambridge, MA.

Becattini, Giacomo. 1987. "Introduzione: Il distretto industriale marshalliano; cronaca di un retrovamento." In G. Becattini, ed., *Mercato E. Forze Locali: Il Distvetto Industriale*. Bologna: il Mulino.

Bellandi, M. 1982. "Il distretto industriale in Alfred Marshall." *L'Industria* 3:186–199.

Chandler, A. D. 1977. *The Visible Hand: the Managerial Revolution in American Business*. Cambridge, MA: Belknap Press.

Dei Ottati, Gaby. 1986. "Distretto industriale, problemi della transazioni e Mercado communitario: prime considerazioni." *Economie e Politice Industriale* 51:93–121.

Granovetter, M. S. 1973. "The Strength of Weak Ties." *American Journal of Sociology* 78(6):1360–1380.

Jakobson, Roman. 1972. *Child Language. Aphasia and Phonological Universals.* The Hague-Paris: Mouton.

Lucas, Robert E. 1988. "On the Mechanics of Economic Development." *Journal of Monetary Economics* 22:3–42.

Marglin, Stephen. 1974. "What do bosses do? The origins and functions of hierarchy in capitalist production." *The Review of Radical Political Economy,* Part I.

Marshall, Alfred. 1975a. *The Pure Theory of Domestic Value.* In J. Whitaker and J. King, eds., *Early Economic Writings of Alfred Marshall, 1867–1890.* New York: The Free Press.

———. 1975b. *Industry and Trade, 1919.* In J. Whitaker and J. King, eds., *Early Economic Writings of Alfred Marshall, 1867–1890.* New York: The Free Press.

———. [1890] 1961. *Principles of Economics.* New York: Macmillan.

Marx, Karl. 1944. *Capital.* New York: Modern Library.

Piore, Michael J. 1990. "Work, Labor, Action: Work Experience in a System of Flexible Production." In *Industrial Districts and Interfirm Cooperation in Italy.* Geneva: International Institute for Labor Studies.

———. 1991. "Corporate Reform in American Manufacturing and the Challenge to Economic Theory." In *Collected Essays on Management for the 1990s.* Oxford University Press.

Piore, Michael J., and Charles Sabel. 1984. *The Second Industrial Divide.* New York: Basic Books.

Romer, Paul M. 1986. "Increasing Returns and Long Run Growth." *Journal of Political Economy* 94(5):1002–1038.

Smith, A. 1937. *An Inquiry Into the Nature and Causes of the Wealth of Nations.* New York: Modern Library.

Solow, R. 1956. "A Contribution to the Theory of Economic Growth." *Quarterly Journal of Economics.* 70(1) (Feb.): 65–94.

———. 1957. "Technical Change and the Aggregate Production Function." *Review of Economics and Statistics* 39(3) (Aug.): 312–320.

Williamson, O. E. 1986. *Economic Organization: Firms, Markets, and Policy Control.* New York: New York University Press.

Young, Allyn A. 1928. "Increasing Returns and Economic Progress." *The Economic Journal* 38:527–542. Reprinted in Kenneth J. Arrow, et al., eds., *Readings in Welfare Economics.* London: Allen and Unwin, 1969, pp. 228–241.

Small-Firm Networks

CHARLES PERROW

It is clear that the past fifteen years have seen dramatic changes in the form of economic organizations in North America, Europe, and Japan, generally a move towards decentralized structures and loose alliances.[1] I will briefly characterize this change in section I. In section II, I will review three explanations for it, and argue in section III that none of them have provided fully satisfactory accounts for the changes. One of the new forms to emerge, *nondependent subcontracting*, is discussed in section IV. The most interesting form, *networks of small firms*, will be the focus of the rest of the chapter. It is the least significant form in terms of economic output—on a worldwide basis the output of small-firm networks (SFNs) is probably trivial—but I will argue in section V that while it is small and fairly new, it is a diverse and possibly durable economic phenomenon that deserves attention, and in section VI that conventional economic theories and even leftist theories fail with this form. It is significant in three respects that I want to deal with: in section VII, the potentials for what I call the "production of trust," a generally neglected and always unspecified factor of production; in section VIII, the welfare implications, such as effects on the distribution of wealth and power in society, which should be the final referent in all we do, I believe. Section IX reviews the fundamental question of whether it is size or networks that is important, and concludes that one must have both small size and networking to realize the advantages. Section X discusses the third significance of SFNs, that they reverse a 150-year trend toward the absorption of society by large organizations, an absorption that I believe has weakened civil society.

I. THE INTEGRATED FIRM, M FIRM, AND THE DEVOLUTION

Figure 17-1 pictures the integrated firm (IF). It buys out as many of its competitors as it can and integrates backward and forward to control as much as it can of the "throughput" (Chandler 1977) from raw materials to

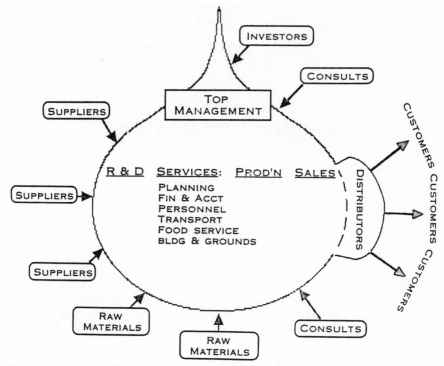

Figure 17-1

Integrated Firm Model

final consumer. It absorbs the sources of uncertainty in its environment and in the process reduces the number of autonomous organizations. I have listed a few business and financial service functions to remind us that these also might have been performed by independent organizations before the integration took place. The IF deals with consultants and suppliers, of course, but in order to control transaction costs and throughput coordination it prefers to make rather than to buy, according to theory. (The onion shape in Figure 17-1 indicates the post-1945 swelling of middle levels and relative decline of the hourly work force.)

Figure 17-2 pictures some of the other forms of economic organizations we should consider. It is shaped like an American football rather than a continuum because in between the two extremes (the integrated firm and the SFN) are a variety of possibilities. Uniting a few integrated firms in different products or in related industries produces the *multidivisional firm*, and uniting a multidivisional with some integrated firms, possibly including some with highly dependent subcontractors, or sweatshops, produces the *conglomerate*. If the state owns conglomerates, we have command economies; if they are in private hands, we have advanced capitalism.

That is roughly an account of United States economic history from,

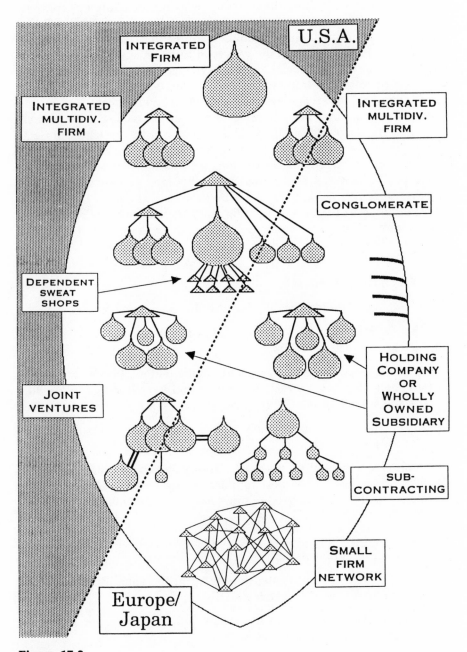

Figure 17-2

Other Forms of Economic Organizations

say, 1850 to 1970 or so. Most of the firms of industrial America are still at the integrated production end of the football; the large and powerful ones have become multidivisional (and multinational, of course) or conglomerate firms. But supposedly in response to competition from abroad, U.S. firms have been devolving, downsizing, delaying, breaking up, spinning off, and combining in joint ventures. The two forms in Figure 17-2 that indicate joint ventures, and the holding company or wholly owned subsidiary, only feebly represent the variety of forms involved in this change. (See Powell 1990 and Sabel 1991 for a broader look.) These forms have been widespread in Europe and Japan at least since the 1960s, but my impression is that they are less evident in the United States.

More radical forms are illustrated by the subcontracting and the small-firm network diagrams in Figure 17-2. These will be discussed in detail shortly, but for the present suffice it to say that the subcontracting model involves a greater degree of devolution, with perhaps 70% of the components produced by independent firms that are generally under 100 employees in size, while the small-firm network is the most radical form, with nothing but small firms of under, say, 10 or 25 persons producing a large variety of goods and services, almost everything except extractive goods and basic industrial output.

II. WHY THE CHANGE?

Three arguments provide reasons for the change:

1. The *flexible production* school, optimistic about the efficiencies of deconcentration, cite such things as

- a flexible response to changing and fragmented markets because small suppliers have more direct information and have it more quickly than the specialized units of large bureaucracy;

- small units have more widely skilled personnel who can be redeployed more quickly;

- information technology reduces transaction delays and costs when firm A searches for the best supplier among firms B, C, and D, thus offsetting the advantage large firms have from centralized purchasing or in-house suppliers;

- technological changes make the production of small runs and changes in products more feasible;

- effort is more directly related to reward in the small firm, and there are more chances of ownership status;

- nonspecialized tasks in smaller organizations reduce the separation between conception and execution.

(While I have emphasized the role of size in this list theoretically, there is nothing preventing the large bureaucracy from restructuring itself to realize most of the gains of the list.) The grand outlines of this school are best represented by Charles Sabel, Michael Piore, and Jonathan Zeitlin in the various references to their work in the bibliography.

2.   Less sanguine are the critics of capitalism who cite *capitalist failure*, the externalization of social costs to smaller units. In particular they cite harder work, longer hours, less pay, no union protection, and the absorption of risk by the small firm. (See, for example, Murray 1983 and 1987; Hyman 1988; Smith 1989; Pollert 1988; Sakai 1990; Wood 1988; and for an ambivalent effort to come to terms with flexible specialization by the Left, Thompson 1989.) Ironically for capitalism's critics, as bad as big organizations are, big organizations are better than small ones if capitalism reigns. They have better labor practices, internal labor markets, more social services, and there is even evidence from the United States that large bureaucratic firms promote more cognitive complexity among employees than do small firms.[2] Though I have not seen it discussed, I would anticipate a "self-exploitation" argument here as well: the fetish of consumption drives people to work long hours in order to accumulate and spend.

An additional anticapitalist explanation, independent of the preceding claims about exploitation, asserts that the deconcentration in the United States could be explained by the collapse of U.S. industrial hegemony; rather than buying up cheap industrial property to integrate further vertically and horizontally, the giants are getting rid of their own and speculating with the proceeds. Here the U.S. response is different from other countries'; having acquired hegemony through market control and monopsony, when faced with superior quality and more efficient production from other countries, the U.S. firms can only sell off units and trade with the proceeds. But there is a worldwide decline of profits and intensification of competition, according to this branch of the "capitalism's failure" argument, and it affects the Japanese and European firms that have emphasized flexibility and quality. They are externalizing social costs through contracting out, thus contributing to the changes in organizational forms.

3.   The third explanation could be called the *organizational failure* analysis. Along with the first explanation (flexible production), it emphasizes flexibility and speed, but it has fewer of the first's social concerns with broad upskilling, independency, and what we have not discussed yet: fostering cooperation through networks. Instead, the third argument has more organizational efficiency concerns that might be associated with management schools, even with "agency theory" (see Perrow, 1986a and 1986b for a critique of agency theory). Here, big firms have gotten too big; internal vested interests create a small-numbers bargaining position that top management cannot cope with; these vested interests create inflexibilities and inefficiencies when markets are fragmenting and technologies changing.[3]

There are two variants of interest, one structural and one entrepreneurial. As an example of the first, Swedish organizational theorist Bengt

Stymne argues that management is whipped at both ends of the labor market by a "rigid wage structure" that prevents rewarding the specialized people much in demand (management experts, software experts, engineers, etc.) so they leave to form their own companies. At the other end, the rigid wage structure overpays unskilled workers for such jobs as cleaning, transport, and copying, so outside firms offer cleaning services at lower prices (Stymne 1989). The second variant cites the stifling of initiative for true entrepreneurs in large firms; they break free and start their own. (That they hope to make *their* firms large and thus stifling never receives comment.)

The cause of the organizational failure in either version of this third view is rather vague—bureaucracy, or "interests." The structuralist, Stymne, implies a surprising inability of those at the top of large, previously successful organizations to have either the wit to foresee or the power to control the development of internal interests; they appear unable to find structural alternatives. This view strongly bounds the rationality of management and may verge on a "culture of the firm" explanation of failure. It is not clear why big organizations can reward top management so fully but not reward software experts, even in Sweden with its "wage solidarity" policy. Nor is it clear why big organizations got into the practice of overpaying the unskilled so extensively that they can't cut their wages but have to fire the lot and rehire them as workers for a separate firm. Presumably, the very high rate of unionization in Sweden may explain why cleaners are paid well in big firms but paid much less by small contractors, but it is not clear why the wage structure is inflexible for software experts (and not for top management) in Sweden's case, nor why unions could have much impact in the United States with only 17% of the work force unionized. In any case, Stymne's (1989) thesis about bipolar wage failures deserves testing and fits in with the general organizational failure picture painted by those who favor entrepreneurship.

Most who cite organizational failure as the explanation of deconcentration seem to be entrepreneurial consultants who favor entrepreneurship and seek out the evidence for drive, hard work, creativity, and risk taking, and discuss the entrepreneur's social marginality and family and minority ethnic ties. This is the small-business literature that I find least useful because it rarely conceptualizes networks per se but talks mostly about the importance of "networking" as a personal attribute, and rarely deals with such variables as input and output dependencies, distribution of wealth, hierarchy, and authority structure. However, there is a related but different cultural argument that may be more important. It stresses the difference between entrepreneurial and proletarian cultures; cites the importance of regions with small farmers and small craftsmen who have business experience and value autonomy above high wages and income security (e.g., Amin 1989; Brusco 1982, 1986); and acknowledges the role of national cultures—for example, the Irish culture, which allegedly does not favor entrepreneurial styles (O'Farrell 1986).

III. INADEQUACIES OF THE EXPLANATIONS

All three of these explanations—flexible production, capitalism's crisis, and organizational failure—have their merits. But I am still puzzled by the deconcentration of U.S. firms that is said to be going on: I should think they would have the wit to capture the profit stream of suppliers and distributors, and enlarge that stream because of increased market control that would come from vertical integration. And they certainly could continue their historical role of buying out the best of the entrepreneurs after the niche is discovered and made profitable.

The best explanation, but still unsatisfactory, may lie in one part of the anticapitalist view. It may be that the business climate in the United States is too unpromising in the long term to avoid decentralization; reasons include low-productivity growth, firm debt, an insufficiently skilled work force, and risk-averse investors and banks that no longer can afford a long-term perspective if too many favor a short-term one. Under these circumstances where firms cannot control the rate of product change and technological change, markets are more likely to fragment, and above-normal returns from oligopoly and the associated mass production of low-quality goods are no longer available. The profits of some units may fall below those of the entire firm, and they will be sold off, even at the expense of losing some market control; lending institutions, resistant to lending for production because of its low returns, may make it harder for the firm to raise money, forcing the firm to sell some of its assets; and union or government regulations may be avoided by divesting.

But I am still puzzled by these arguments. True, one sells off low-return units because total return is less important than the rate of return, and poorly performing investments can be redeployed. But the less profitable ones have to be sold at a loss. Since buyers also have alternatives for investing their capital, why buy low-profit businesses? If it is good enough for someone to buy, why sell? And when one's organization is smaller, it will have less political power and less market power. A second problem with the explanation concerns experience and "fit." Firms sell off incompatible units or ones they have little experience in running. Both are important, of course, but firms are selling off units they have had experience in running; they will lose that experiential investment. If their experience is inadequate, we should recall that throughout the history of capitalism firms have found it quite easy to purchase experience; they pay for it and get it from those who have it. According to economic arguments, if any good—including experience—is in very short supply, the demand will rise quickly and the supply will rise to meet the demand.

Regarding compatibility with the main line of products, years of successful growth of diversified and divisionalized firms supposedly has taught us the value of synergy, cross-subsidization, hedges against particular market declines, and balanced investments. I do not think these arguments rebut those who see a failure of capitalism.

Putting the foregoing problems aside, if the pessimistic "capitalism's failure" argument can stand, it can be combined with parts of the optimistic "flexible production" argument. Big firms must downsize in order to even survive because the competition is such that attributes associated with small size—flexibility and product development and quality and speed—are what matter most. It is not vested interests and bureaucratic red tape that matter, but (1) small size and (2) the advantages of at least some degree of networking among autonomous firms. This will be the central thrust of the chapter.

Before I explore the evidence for the virtues of small size and networking, I should indicate still another puzzlement: to be efficient, the big firm does not need to spin off or sell off parts of itself and become smaller, as so many say it must; each time it does so it loses some of the profit stream. Most of the advantages of flexible specialization can be achieved by the judicious restructuring of the big firm: flattening the overall hierarchy by creating many more subunits and giving them considerable autonomy. Furthermore, the firm then keeps the ultimate prize, the contribution to overall profit that the effort of each unit brings. If the firm creates a subsidiary, it must give up part of the profits to the head, who takes the risks; a joint venture works similarly. If the head of the unit is salaried, the firm takes the profits. If downsizing means loss of profit opportunities, why has it happened?

Only yesterday we were told by economists that the success of the multidivisional firm and of large firms in general rested in their ability to innovate and provide for a bewildering variety of styles and models; diversification was the appropriate hedge and source of innovative ideas; economies of scale appeared to have no upper bounds, since the bigger the firm, the more power it would have in the capital market, the more cross-subsidization it could do; and the technological changes permitting flexible and decentralized short-product-run production should be even more available to big rich firms, permitting flexible mass production. With all these advantages plus their market power and their political power, the need to restructure should be minimal.

Why would big firms wish to avoid the restructuring that is said to go on? Two simple reasons come to mind: If the restructuring means subsidiaries, a premium must be paid to the head of the subsidiary that comes out of the return to the owners and head of the firm. If the restructuring means selling off units and contracting out, or joint ventures, again the profit that has to go to these other units to make them viable capitalist units is lost to the original firm. After all, one of the main advantages of integrated production was that the profit streams of all the independent organizations could be appropriated by buying them up or driving them out of business by producing the goods or services yourself. Why would firms now distribute profits to heads of subsidiaries (*some* premium must be paid for assuming that risk and extra effort) and to contractors?

One factor that has changed substantially might account for the new competition, since such things as better quality, more variety, and rapid styling changes have always been sought: new technologies allow multipurpose machines and equipment and rapid data processing. This undoubtedly facilitates decentralized production. But it also makes it just as possible to have highly flexible *centralized* production with attendant economies of scale in terms of research and development, personnel allocation, and so on. The technological tide should raise the level of both big and small firms; the big firms should be able to benefit sufficiently to avoid the need to spin off, sell off, contract out, and joint venture. But technological change may still favor small firms in the sense that it puts them closer to technological parity with the big firms; both benefit, but the small firms benefit more.

In any case, IP is a way to capture returns while allowing for market and firm growth. It is effective for owners if (1) markets are controlled sufficiently to *control* the rate of product and technological change (it is not necessary to suppress it); (2) the market is stable for other reasons such as oligopoly, near saturation, technological stability, or government regulation; or, though this is less frequent, (3) small firms are unable to evade governmental laws and regulations and thus cannot outperform large firms. Conditions 1 and 2 permit the economies of scale that come from mass production and the possibility of lowering the quality of goods and services in order to increase returns. Mass production is not only the result of market control, but also encourages a firm to seek market control because of the cost of capital tied up in mass production; market control makes it easier to keep investments working. Once a market breaks up into pieces that require different types of activities, such as frequent changes in production lines, producing non-formula motion picture films (Storper 1989), or generating new financial services, IP firms will be threatened by new firms offering the new goods or services. To these we will finally turn.

IV. NONDEPENDENT SUBCONTRACTING

The subcontracting form in Figure 17-2 is a distinct new form that grew fast in Japan from the 1960s on; it may also be well represented in Europe, but I am unsure about that. I will refer to it as the *nondependent subcontracting model*. Here the firm has a first line of subcontractors (perhaps 300 is the most that can be managed even by a big auto firm), which in turn have second and third lines of subcontractors, most of them quite small. In some elaborate examples the second and third tiers would have more than one customer; that is, the subcontractor would sell to two or three or more primary firms. Conceivably, the prime contractors could also have other customers. Note that the picture of the subcontracting model is a picture of an integrated firm except for the fact that all of these firms are independent; we lack the all-important line drawn around the firms indicating ownership and retention of profits and responsibility for losses. (Again, some might have other customers, just as units within the IF might sell some of their services outside.) Retaining their own profits, instead of passing them on to headquarters, may be the most important difference between the subcontracting and the IF models. (But that again raises the question of why the parent firm does not just buy up the subcontractors and appropriate their profits. The most pleasant hypothesis is that the owners would not work as hard if they were employees, and the employees themselves would not work as hard for the big corporation as they did for the original owner of the small firm.)

The Japanese favor this form. In general, Japan has a higher proportion of small firms than the United States, though this gross figure can be misleading. More to the point, while General Motors (like most large European auto firms) makes 50% of the car, the average auto firm in Japan makes only 30% of the car. While GM deals directly with 3,500 parts suppliers, the Japanese firm deals directly with between 100 and 300 component suppliers, who in turn deal with about 5,000 subcontractors arranged in tiers (Best 1991:163).

Subcontractors in Japan are no longer dependent on the big organizations they sell to. In 30 years, subcontractors have gone from the highly dependent positions typical of the United States to quite independent or mutually dependent positions. In Japan, according to Nishigushi (1990), the figure for the following measures went from about 20% of subcontractors in all industry in 1950 to about 80% in 1980:

- joint determination of prices

- design input

- sharing of production information between firm and contractor

- contracts for large modules rather than single items

- payment within 2 months rather than 9 or 12 months

The figure went from about 60% of the wage rate in the big firms to 80% or more. In 1982, subcontractors had an average of 6.5 parent companies, according to figures assembled by Best (1991:161–163).

There is a quite depressing side to the Japanese miracle in terms of driving labor (Sakai 1990; Dohse, Jurgens, and Malsch 1985) and the exploitation of women, but it is not essential to the *form*, could be eliminated, and Best and others appear to believe it has been mitigated to some extent.

V. SMALL-FIRM NETWORKS

Finally, there is the SFN. Imagine breaking up the integrated firm into units with an average of 10 employees each. For example, instead of 2,000 employees in one firm, there would be 200 firms of 10 employees each. Figure 17-3 captures the essentials of this form. It is new to this half of the twentieth century, but was evident in the nineteenth century, as Sabel and Zeitlin (1985) and Best (1991) have argued.[4]

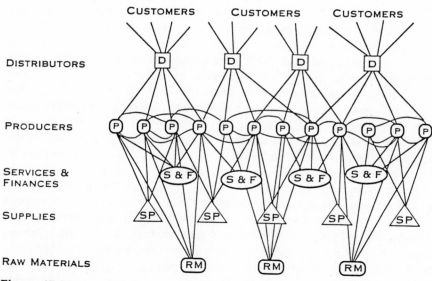

Figure 17-3
Small-Firm Networks

The firms are usually very small—say 10 people. They interact with one another, sharing information, equipment, personnel, and orders, even as they compete with one another. They are supplied by a smaller number of business service firms (business surveys, technical training, personnel administration, transport, research and development, etc.) and financial service firms. There are, of course, suppliers of equipment, energy, consumables, and so on, as well as raw material suppliers. Finally, while producers may do their own marketing and distribution, it is more common for there to be a fair number of quite small distributors, which is especially striking because SFNs typically export most of their output.

The small firms are surrounded by an infrastructure that is essential for their survival and for their economies of network scale: local and regional government provides roads, cheap land, educational services, and even financing; trade associations provide economic information, training, financing, and marketing services; and both of these along with unions monitor unfair business and labor practices.[5] Unfortunately, the issue of economies of scale that attach to a network of firms has received almost no development since it was first discussed in 1919 by Marshall (1919:283–288). One assumes that while shared investments in equipment may be involved, most of the economies come from shared information and efficient allocation of labor or human resources.

SFNs do not exist in heavy industry or extractive industry, and in final assembly for large goods such as autos we have the nondependent subcontracting form rather than a true SFN. SFNs are said to exist in clothing, food, light machinery, metal working, electronics and small- to medium-sized electronic goods, ceramics, furniture, auto components, motorcycles, small engines, machine tools, robots, textile and packaging machinery, mining equipment, industrial filters, and agricultural machinery. But it is not clear from the literature that in all cases *networks* of small firms are involved, though networks exist in most.

There is a tendency to dismiss the importance of SFNs by tarring them with the brush of small firms in general, which are held to be exploitative, or limiting them to consumer products from Northern Italy or even simply to textile firms in Prato and to speak of these as sweatshops. But clearly this is not the case. Small firms are ubiquitous in all countries, and generally are havens for low wages, dependency, and exploitation, but I am referring exclusively to *networks* of small firms with ties to one another and to multiple customers and suppliers. While there is some evidence of exploitation (often self-exploitation through 10- or 11-hour work days) in textile firms in Prato and Modena in Northern Italy, the literature almost always stresses the prosperity of the firms and the locality, and the skills of the work force, when these economic issues are discussed.

Amin (1989), for example, finds wages high in "industrial districts," which is another term for SFNs, and discredits the low-wage and exploitation thesis. Capecchi (1989) speaks at one point of "widespread" exploitation without giving details, but also notes the following about Emilia-Romagna: child labor declined, day-care centers expanded (12% of children under 3 in day care in Bologna, 0.3% in Naples); there was a sizeable decrease in birthrate and in the proportion of "housewives"; an increase in educational level with females surpassing males in high school and university studies; a rising demand for instruction in physical exercise, nutrition, and so on; one of the lowest unemployment rates in Italy; and growing demand for personal and household services. Taplin (1989) notes that employment relations are largely nonadversarial in his study of textile industry in Prato, Italy, but subcontractors setting up small workshops can impose long hours and poor benefits. Mark Lazerson, in an earlier draft of his 1991 manuscript, offered evidence of long hours and dangerous conditions for some young women in the knitting industry of Modena, but also noted the prosperity of the region. One should also note the failure of exploited workers to seek work in nearby textile factories with better wages and benefits.

We have excellent empirical evidence from Italian social scientists and others on their reality and success in Northern Italy.[6] The next best documented case is that of a mountain town in Japan, producing machine tools (Friedman 1988). Less detailed evidence, but at least some, comes from Germany, Denmark, perhaps Sweden, and France.[7] Outside of Madrid there is an emerging, struggling case in electronics (Benton 1986). There is a debate about the character of Silicon Valley in the United States, but if we count it, it is about the only SFN I know of in the United States (Florida and Kenney 1990; Saxenian 1991).[8] No evidence of SFNs appears in Britain (as distinct from small firms; for the growth of these, see Keeble and Wever 1986; for the failure of flexible specialization, see Hirst and

Zeitlin 1989) or Ireland. So SFNs are not, as many continue to think, limited to textiles or other soft consumer goods from Northern Italy.

Though Figure 17-3 does not faithfully reproduce this, an essential point is that any focal organization has multiple upstream and downstream ties. Figure 17-4 makes the basic point. I think Burt (1983) has done the most to explicate and empirically demonstrate this, but Pfeffer and Salancik (1978) have a cogent discussion in connection with the resource dependency model, and the strategy is as old as capitalism. If you stand at the narrow waist, you can play several customers, or suppliers, off against each other; they are forced to trade with you—or with your nominal competitor. If you stand in the broad waist of the SFN, however, your customers have choices; so do your suppliers, and so do you. A lot of potential power that is concentrated in the capitalist ideal is dissipated in the SFN.[9]

This is a *structural* basis for cooperation, I should point out. A firm has no option but to avoid deception and exploitation; if it deceives or exploits, another firm will get the business. The antitrust legislation in the United States was initially intended to create this structural condition but failed to do so for many reasons. But a multiple-tie network may exist not because of the essentially *negative* reason that it forestalls maximizing self-interest with guile, but for the *positive* reason that it provides for the flexibility of the sector or industry, stimulates innovation, and maximizes sectorwide problem solving. The returns come first to the sector, or the local industry, and the health of any single firm is known to be dependent on the collectivity of competitive firms.

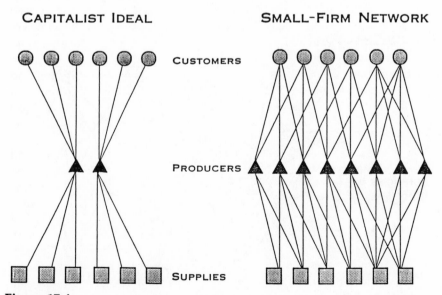

Figure 17-4
Dependency and Independency in Networks

These positive reasons may account for the appearance of the highly successful subcontracting model in Japan. It seems to gain the benefits of multiple ties without actually having multiple ties at all levels. In Figure 17-5 we see a SFN existing up to the level of the producers, but above that is a structure that would permit the creation of highly dependent relations at the subassembly level and in its ties with final assembly in the parent firm. The fact that the parent does not appear to exploit the subassembly independent firms, nor do they exploit their strategic advantage over the producers, suggests that this aspect of trust can be produced without the structural condition of Figure 17-4—the broad waist. There is other evidence—for example, in German firms—of the dominant firm insisting that its subcontractors do no more than one-third of their business with the dominant firm, thus voluntarily giving up *strategic* power over

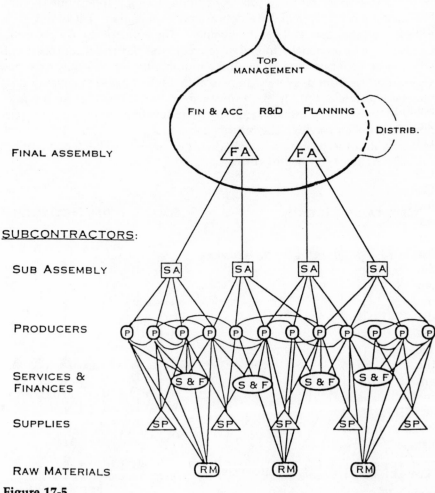

Figure 17-5
Subcontracting Model

suppliers in order to ensure the viability and health of those suppliers. This, of course, is just the opposite of the strategy used by the integrated firm (which controls its suppliers to the extent of absorbing them) and contradicts the arguments of transaction costs analysis.

There are other reasons why networks of small firms do not become "Chandlerized" and end up as one integrated firm. It is not that the members are less greedy or competitive than our industrial ancestors and their present offspring in the United States; it is because competition requires continual innovation in methods and products. This requires the full use and commitment of employees, a condition best achieved by reducing the gap between *conception* and *execution*, the gap introduced by Taylorism. Though the large firm is not incapable of reducing this (see Sabel 1991, on the Moebius Strip firm), the small firm does it more as a matter of course. Thus the small firm can react more quickly and fruitfully to change in technology and markets. This has been the consistent explanation for small firm networks since the initial work of Brusco, Sabel, Piore, and Zeitlin.

VI. EXPLAINING SMALL-FIRM NETWORKS

Small as the phenomenon of SFNs is, it is theoretically implausible and violates established theories of industrialization of both the Right and the Left.

On the Right we should have only integrated production and the multidivisional firm, according to the magnificent synthesis of Alfred DuPont Chandler. He emphasizes that *technology* made it possible to greatly increase the size of vertically integrated firms and permit economies of *scale;* that vertical integration and technology permitted *efficient* throughput coordination from raw material to consumer outlet; and that *bureaucracy* made it possible to exquisitely control the mass of employees and the diversity of processes and products. We can include Oliver Williamson here, with his emphasis on making sure that you won't be cheated in your transactions, which is solved by buying out your suppliers and distributors and settling disputes autocratically instead of by bargaining. (See the critique of the markets and hierarchies approach in Lazerson 1988.) But we have the problem of accounting for the apparent decline of the multidivisional (M) form and the large integrated production form; and if that is exaggerated, we have the problem of the appearance of so many SFNs around the world.

The problem with the account of the Right is the quite negligible role it assigns to *trust* and *cooperation,* or what is called "other regarding behavior," in economic affairs, and the dominant role it assigns to the maximization of individual self-interest. We cannot account for SFNs *solely* on the basis of varied and rapidly changing markets and the new technologies that allow decentralized production. Otherwise, the big firms would find it profitable to simply decentralize and reward a multitude of small divisions for their flexibility, but retain the "profit stream." They are trying this, of course. In fact, some on the Left feel they will displace SFNs as they spin off wholly owned subsidiaries. The Left argues this way because it has a *power*, rather than an efficiency explanation for the rise of integrated production and the M form. Market power and political power account for the rise. While I share this, I feel that the Left also is burdened with an assumption that no longer applies.

The problem with the Left, then, is its view that under capitalism and the capitalist state change can come only from the *organization of the proletariat*, the workers. The only organizational change of much concern for the Left is reorganization of the *labor process* to eliminate exploitation and de-skilling. The Left says little about firm size, interfirm networks, marketing techniques, product redesign, trade associations, competition, efficiencies, and the infrastructure that makes networks viable.

But those who created the SFNs were not often alienated proletarians, but usually farmers, shopkeepers, and artisans; and instead of the organization of the proletarians, we find trade associations that facilitate commercial and industrial interactions. In some cases, especially in Northern Italy, unions are important, but as regulators of labor conditions in small firms, as providers of business services, and as supporters of such things as autonomous work groups (Herman 1990)—an effort that fell on very rich soil as the small firms already had strong inducements in that direction. No worker fight against de-skilling was needed; the production techniques and the changing market made skills necessary.

Now the Left is correct that exploitation of labor is always a problem, especially in small organizations. But *networks* of small organizations supported and regulated by a revitalized local government, by trade associations of the small producers, and in some cases by unions, have managed to limit exploitation greatly in these regions, a job made easier by the regions' low unemployment levels and remarkable prosperity.

Thus powerful theories of both the Right and Left need to be questioned. Both have neglected the economic power of three things that help account for the success of SFNs: economies of scale through networks (still insufficiently theorized); trust and cooperation coexisting with competition; and welfare effects that increase the efficiency of the region and industry. These may be as important as varied markets and new technologies.

VII. THE PRODUCTION OF TRUST

Let me elaborate on the "production of trust" in SFNs. The production of trust is difficult to demonstrate and even to illustrate. As Sabel notes in a remarkable essay (1991), trust seems to be found only retrospectively, never created intentionally. I wish to argue that trust is generated by structures or contexts; these can be deliberately created, encouraging trust, even if trust itself cannot be deliberately created.

Here are some characteristics—all distinctive of SFNs—that are more likely to generate trusting than self-interest-maximizing behavior in a group of firms:

- Sharing and discussing information on markets, technologies, pay scales, and profits of firms.

- Sufficient similarity in processes and techniques among firms so that one can understand and judge each other's behavior. (It's the difference between saying "I don't know how to make it, so I *have* to trust you," and saying "I know how to make it, so I *can* trust you.")

- Experience of getting helped by another firm. (In fact, one should design incomplete organizations, so they have to ask or borrow.)

- Long-term relationships, but possibly quite intermittent contacts.

- Little difference among firms by size, power, or strategic position.

- Rotation of leadership is required to represent a collection of firms.

- Similar financial rewards to the firms and the employees within them.

- Firms *collectively* experience the economic advantages of increased sales and profit margins.

- An awareness of a bounded community of fate generated by trade or professional associations, municipal service groups, unions, and the like.

Where these conditions exist, the possibility of trust is increased.

Now elites have long known this, and ruling classes show many of these characteristics without the trust extending to those they rule. Employees of large firms generate *some* trust through unions, but it is small compared to elite cohesion and trust. One gets trust between owners and employees, and between owners in competing firms, when firms are small and networked. SFNs maximize the possibility for these conditions; the integrated production model does not, and the nondependent subcontracting model does so only partially.

VIII. WELFARE FUNCTIONS

Big organizations did not invent *all* the curses of our times, but they certainly had a lot to do with the centralization of power and authority in modern societies. The larger the organization, the more power and authority at the top to hire and fire, develop or enfeeble workers, relocate, influence politicians, influence elections, pollute, eliminate competitors, invest money, buy supplies from you or someone else, discriminate ethnically and sexually, and to corrupt. The bigger they are, the more power is generated, and the more concentrated it becomes.

If we take two furniture factories employing 5,000 people each, a total of 10,000, and arrange them into 1,000 small firms of 10 each, most producing furniture but some marketing it and others delivering it, buying materials, doing the accounts, counseling employees, and so on—all things done in the IP model *within* the firm—think of the dispersion of power and authority. And don't dismiss this example as farfetched: the average firm size for the very prosperous furniture industry of the Lombardy province in Italy is fewer than five (Kozul 1991; Best 1991).

Another thing that big organizations have not invented but have certainly perfected is *hierarchy:* rights and privileges and authority and status are clearly defined and differentiated by rank or level in the organization, and movement from one rank to another is guarded by formal criteria. The big furniture firm will have a dozen major grades and many minor ones. It is a fine control device, as well as a rationalizer. But the small firm will have two, perhaps three grades, and movement up and down them will be easy. A study of Japanese blue- to white-collar movement found it very high in small firms, and low in very big ones (Friedman 1988). In Italy, people move back and forth from owner to worker to owner as demand and styles change.

That takes care of two of the four horsemen of bureaucracy, *centralization* and *hierarchy*. The other two are *formalization* and *standardization;* these permit repetitive, high-volume production. Fortunately for small firms, formalization and standardization are minimized, simply because high-volume production is not a characteristic of the product markets these firms service. Thus the four dreadnoughts of bureaucracy dissolve when the large firm does, and neither are they reproduced in SFNs nor do the networks find alternative ways to amass and concentrate power.

Another consequence of moving from integrated production to a network of small firms is that the *distribution of wealth* in society is affected, and thus are the spending patterns. The heads of 1,000 firms related to furniture production will receive a great deal less in salary and benefits than the two heads of the two large firms. I support any development that will make the distribution of wealth more even without significantly changing the total amount, and if it can be done without taking taxes from the rich each year to provide inefficient programs for the poor—a politically expensive effort—all the better. Furthermore, one of the problems of uneven development and uneven economies associated with multidivisional and giant firms is that locally generated wealth is spent or invested nonlocally; it is taken from the city, province, region, or nation and sent elsewhere, enriching elsewhere and concentrating the wealth of the elsewhere. The wider distribution of wealth reduces this. None of the 1,000 owners is likely to make shopping trips from Northern Italy to Paris and New York, and they will use their village banks.

Finally, a network of small firms appears to be associated with strong *local* government institutions. This appears to foster a more responsive educational system, more distributive policies regarding land use and city planning, a wider range of social services including child care, and perhaps more political involvement of the citizens. These are particularly well discussed by Aydalot (1986) and Capecchi (1989). The networks of firms and families also generate their own welfare functions in policing labor exploitation, lending money and equipment, and providing informal apprenticeships.

One of the most striking documentations of this comes from a comparison of two U.S. fishing towns, New Bedford and Gloucester (Doeringer, Moss, and Terkla 1986). In one, the fishing fleet was dominated by boats owned by capitalists who hired captains and crews; in the other, most of the fleet was owned by the individual captains, and family and friends and relatives made up the crew. The latter made longer-term investments in new equipment and methods, shared work instead of using layoffs in slack time, and, when forced to reduce ranks, laid off the oldest, who did not have growing families, rather than the youngest or first hired. When business picked up, they responded more quickly, benefiting the community.

IX. SIZE OR TIES

In thinking about the consequences of SFNs—the production of trust, minimizing the centralization of power and authority, reducing hierarchy, standardization and formalization, and distributing wealth and reducing uneven development—I am at a loss to specify which of these stems from the "small" and which from the "networks" in the notion of SFNs. Clearly, size is very important, and it is the most convenient way to discuss bureaucracy, but small by itself is hardly beautiful. All of these propositions about consequences of *size* become unstable without *ties*— networks. The small firms clustered about one or two mass marketers in the shoe industry in Alicante as described by Benton (1986, 1989) are not networked, and they compete fiercely and savagely for the few crumbs that the big corporations hand out. There is so little wealth generated among them that its distribution is insignificant; secrecy and distrust reign, as does the exploitation of workers and family members.

Perhaps it is not size per se, then, that has welfare functions for society, but the network. Yet a network of large firms is familiar to us in cartels, trusts, and interlocking directorates, and in the United States such networks are associated with concentrated power and predatory business practices toward small firms and consumers. Networks per se, then, can have few welfare functions for society. An elite that generates trust among its members can be powerful and exploitive. The networks of large firms in Europe and Japan may not be as predatory as those in the United States, but I doubt they generate few if any welfare functions on their own, or welcome the state apparatus that requires it of them. Clearly, both characteristics are needed—small units need to network to produce a good or service to which they all contribute.

(Note that I avoid discussion of SFNs as a phenomenon of entrepreneurship. That formulation suggests the primacy of motivation and the individual characteristics of leaders. While those factors are certainly important, I prefer a more structural approach: what are conditions under which an area is able to shape or give reign to motivations and leadership characteristics favorable to SFNs?)

Phrased this way, in terms of small size and dense networks of firms with complementary skills and functions, and emphasizing the importance of the public and quasi-public infrastructure, the notion of successful small-firm networks confronts directly the received theory and wisdom that the multidivisional firm, with its assumed economies of scale and of throughput, is economizing and efficient, and that autonomy is required for the pursuit of self-interest.

X. THE RETURN OF CIVIL SOCIETY?

My work on SFNs is a part of a larger project (Perrow 1986a:49–52; 1991). It traces the development of the IP firm from the 1820s in the United States. The firm restructured our social landscape and generated externalities that spawned public and nonprofit organizations, which, copying the bureaucratic form of the IP firm, generated further externalities. I argue that wittingly, but mostly unwittingly, the big organizations, public and private, in their role of employers, increasingly performed more and more of societal functions such as socialization, providing occasions for social interactions and handling personal crises, recreation, cultural productions, skill acquisition, and whatever else you wish to ascribe to "society." The units that once performed these functions were either weakened or made dependent on the big employing organization: families, neighborhoods, schools, independent local governments, small and local guilds, and business and trade associations. Less and less existed outside the large employing organization or the flock of wholly dependent small firms clustering about them. In effect, society was being absorbed by the big organizations. I am not referring to a welfare-state *government* providing services, but the employer presenting society to his or her employees.

The possibility of SFNs is the possibility of a massive disengorgement from the big organizations, a spewing out of functions over delimited spaces where they are taken up by small independent organizations. These are linked together with a sense of a community of fate, rather than a link based on sharing the goals of the owners and top executives of a big organization. Figure 17-6 gives you a bit of an idea of all the opportunities for independent organizations falling out of the big corporation; and the same can be done for other big employers, such as big government, big school districts, big unions, and big centralized church bodies. If there are economies afforded by trust, networks, and the limitation of social externalities—that is, if trust is an alternative way of seeking to

SOME PRODUCTION STAGES   BUSINESS FUNCTIONS

Retail distribution   Transportation
Wholesale distribution   Food service
Final assembly   Legal services
Final production   Accounting
Initial production   Advertising
Raw materials processing   Research & development
Raw materials extraction   Purchasing
                                                    Training
                                                    Business travel services

CORPORATE SERVICES

Medical & dental   Retirement counseling
Fitness facilities   Career counseling
Sports programs   Legal services
Off-site recreational activities   Drug & alcohol abuse
Vacation planning, sites   programs
Child care   Psychological counseling

Figure 17-6

Activities That Could Be Performed by Separate Organizations

reduce transaction costs, if networks are a way of achieving economics of scale, and if we can use community institutions as an alternative to externalizing social costs—then there is no need for one organization to do all the things in Figure 17-6; indeed, it is a waste. More important, the fully integrated firm in the figure signifies the erosion of *civil society*, that precious area outside the big organizations, public and private, an area with a minimum of either market-driven behavior, or of hierarchy.

Notes

1. The change is celebrated in the more popular management literature, such as the good stories Kanter (1989) tells, or the boxes and arrows and injunctions to "strategize" in Morton 1991; analyzed and worried over in compendiums such as the MIT study edited by Kochan and Useem, *Transforming Organizations* (1992); and imaginatively explored by Powell (1990) and Sabel (1991). Sabel's "Moebius Strip" is perhaps the most intriguing discussion of the variety of variables involved, but the evidence is anecdotal and largely European/Japanese. Good anecdotes and analysis of downsizing in Silicon Valley are found in Saxenian (1991a). I have yet to find any definitive statistics of downsizing. Sengenberger et al. (1990) indicate downsizing in all industrial nations, but the figures are too general to allow much interpretation. Badaracco (1988) has weak empirical evidence for deconcentration and joint ventures and gives some case examples.
2. Melvin Kohn and Carmi Schooler's work (1983, Ch. 2) shows that men who work in bureaucratic organizations, blue and white collar, are more likely than those in nonbureaucratic organizations to value change and to have cognitive complexity and flexibility, open mindedness, personal responsibility, and self-direction. They emphasize the protection that large permanent

bureaucratic organizations provide rather than the attributes of size per se, but it is still a warning about the dynamics of small organizations in the United States.

3. There is a rueful acknowledgment of these organizational failures in Oliver Williamson's work (1975, 1985), but it hardly encumbers his transaction cost analysis. Similarly, in his very last pages, Chandler (1977) jolts one out of the somnolence of ever-increasing production figures with a plaintive query about the costs of giganticism. Neither acknowledgments deflect their authors' relentless efficiency arguments.

4. The classic piece comparing "flexible production" through small firms (what I refer to as small-firm networks or SFNs) in the nineteenth and the late twentieth century is Sabel and Zeitlin (1985). For a good account of the Springfield Armory as an SFN—or more accurately, a network of small firms serving a final assembler, as in the nondependent subcontractor model—see Best (1991:29–45). A striking comparison of the putting-out system in the eighteenth and nineteenth centuries with SFNs in the Modena knitwear industry today is found in Lazerson (1991).

5. The literature on the infrastructure is now substantial, and it is one of two things that sharply distinguish *networks* of small firms from clusters of small firms about a dominant buyer. (The other is the minimal and very competitive contacts among small firms where they are dependent on a few big customers.) See Brusco (1982), one of the first articles, as well as Brusco (1986), Brusco and Righi (1989), Herrigel (1988), Piore and Sabel (1984), Sabel (1989), and Trigilia (1986). Best (1991) provides some of the most detailed discussion of infrastructure in Northern Italy, with excellent accounts of business services and financing. Excellent details on computer clones and the box making and packaging machinery industries can be found in Capecchi (1989). A detailed account of the role of unions in very small firms can be found in Herman (1990).

6. In addition to those already cited, see the dissertation by Kozul (1991), which contrasts the booming SFN furniture industry in Northern Italy with the failing furniture industry in Yugoslavia.

7. For several of these countries see the general discussions in Sabel (1989), Piore and Sabel (1984), and Best (1991). For France, see Lorenz (1988). For mechanical engineering and machine tools in Germany, see all three Herrigel citations. The Swedish example, the area around Vaxjo, is discussed in Johannisson (1990), but from the point of view of the entrepreneur rather than of the relations among firms. It appears that there is no common product in this burst of small-firm industry in a thoroughly agricultural region of Sweden, but there is considerable sharing of entrepreneurial ideas and perhaps resources. This may be true of Jutland, too, but the information is scanty.

8. See Sabel (1990), "Studied Trust . . . ," for one optimistic U.S. study in progress; see Saxenian (1991a) for a network description of Silicon Valley. But the account that Florida and Kenney (1990: Ch. 5, 6, 7) give of the rapacious, shortsighted, individual-self-interest-maximizing firms in Silicon Valley is very depressing, even if Saxenian is correct that the trusting network, while limited to the small firms, is still important. Christopherson and Storper (1989) and Storper (1989) find evidence of flexible specialization in the motion picture industry. The New England fishing example is discussed in section VIII.

9. The matter, of course, is always more complicated, as DeFillippi (1991) notes in his dissertation on the subcontracting practices of three U.S. aerospace firms. Lyons, Krachenberg, and Henke (1990) and Kamath and Liker (1990) point out that dependent suppliers are more likely to receive technical assistance from their customers because of the customers' dependency on limited

suppliers. This is not always the case, however, and depends on the complexity of the product, its fit with the supplier's product, length of the relationship, and so on.

References

Amin, Ash. 1989. "A Model of the Small Firm in Italy." In Edward Goodman et al., *Small Firms and Industrial Districts in Italy*. New York: Routledge, pp. 111–121.

Amin, Ash, and Kevin Robins. 1989. "Industrial Districts and Regional Development Limits and Possibilities." Working paper, University of Newcastle upon Tyne, England.

Aydalot, Philippe. 1986. "The Location of New Firm Creation: The French Case." In D. Keeble and E. Wever, eds., *New Firms and Regional Development in Europe*. London: Croom Helm, pp. 105–123.

Badaracco, Joseph L. Jr. 1988. "Changing Forms of the Corporation." In J. R. Meyer and J. M. Gustafson, eds., *The U.S. Business Corporation*. Cambridge, MA: Ballinger, pp. 57–91.

Benton, Lauren A. 1986. "The Role of the Informal Sector in Economic Development: Industrial Restructuring in Spain." Ph.D. dissertation, Department of Anthropology and History, Johns Hopkins University, Baltimore, MD.

———. 1989. "Homework and Industrial Development: Gender Roles and Restructuring in the Spanish Shoe Industry." *World Development* 17(2):255–266.

Best, Michael. 1991. *The New Competition*. Cambridge: Harvard University Press.

Brusco, Sebastiano. 1982. "The Emilian Model: Productive Decentralization and Social Integration." *Cambridge Journal of Economics* 3:167–184.

———. 1986. "Small Firms and Industrial Districts: The Experience of Italy." In D. Keeble and E. Wever, eds., *New Firms and Regional Development in Europe*. London: Croom Helm.

Brusco, Sebastiano, and Ezio Righi. 1989. "Local Government, Industrial Policy and Social Consensus: The Case of Modena (Italy)." *Economy and Society* 18(4):405–424.

Burt, Ronald. 1983. *Corporate Profits and Corporation*. New York: Academic Press.

Capecchi, Vittorio. 1989. "The Informal Economy and the Development of Flexible Specialization in Emilia-Romagna." In Alejandro Portes, Manuel Castells, and Lauren A. Benton, *The Informal Economy: Studies in Advanced and Less Developed Countries*. Baltimore: Johns Hopkins University Press, pp. 189–215.

Chandler, Alfred. D. Jr. 1977. *The Visible Hand*. Cambridge, MA: Harvard University Press.

Christopherson, Susan, and Michael Storper. 1989. "The Effects of Flexible Specialization on Industrial Politics and the Labor Market: The Motion Picture Industry." *Industrial and Labor Relations Review* 42(3):331–347.

DeFillippi, Robert John. 1991. "Supplier-Customer Collaboration in Commercial and Military Aerospace Projects: A Comparative Case Study." Unpublished dissertation, Yale University School of Organization and Management.

Doeringer, Peter B., Philip I. Moss, and David G. Terkla. 1986. "Capitalism and Kinship: Do Institutions Matter in the Labor Market?" *Industrial and Labor Relations Review* 40(1):48–60.

Dohse, Knuth, Ulrich Jurgens, and Thomas Malsch. 1985. "From 'Fordism' to 'Toyotism'? The Social Organization of the Labor Process in the Japanese Automobile Industry." *Politics and Society* 14(2):115–146.

Florida, Richard, and Martin Kenney. 1990. *The Breakthrough Illusion: Corporate America's Failure to Move from Innovation to Mass Production.* New York: Basic Books.

Friedman, David. 1988. *The Misunderstood Miracle.* Ithaca, NY: Cornell University Press.

Herman, Bruce G. 1990. "Economic Development and Industrial Relations in a Small Firm Economy: The Experience of Metal Workers in Emilia-Romagna, Italy." Paper presented at the Conference on Economic Restructuring, Princeton, NJ, October 5–6.

Herrigel, Gary B. 1988. "The Political Embeddedness of Small and Medium-Sized Firm Networks in Baden Wurttemberg: A Challenge From Above?" Paper delivered at the Workshop on Interfirm Innovation Dynamics, Stuttgart, Germany, October 3–4.

———. 1989. "Industrial Order and The Politics of Industrial Change: Mechanical Engineering in the Federal Republic of Germany." In Peter J. Katzenstein, ed., *Industry and Politics in West Germany: Toward the Third Republic.* Ithaca, NY: Cornell University Press.

———. ND. "Industrial Order in the Machine Tool Industry: A Comparison of the United States and Germany." Conference paper at Social Science Research Council.

Heydebrand, Wolf V. 1989. "New Organizational Forms." *Work and Occupations* 16(3):323–357.

Hirst, Paul, and Jonathan Zeitlin. 1989. "Flexible Specialisation and the Competitive Failure of UK Manufacturing." *Political Quarterly* 60(2):164–178.

Hyman, Richard. 1988. "Flexible Specialisation: Miracle of Myth?" In R. Hyman and W. Streeck, eds., *New Technology and Industrial Relations,* pp. 48–60.

Johannisson, Bengt. 1990. "Organizing for Local Economic Development." Working paper, Vaxjo University, Sweden.

Kamath, Rajan R., and Jeffrey K. Liker. 1990. "Supplier Dependence and Innovation: A Contingency Model of Suppliers' Innovative Activities." *Journal of Engineering and Technology Management* 7:111–127.

Kanter, Rosabeth Moss. 1989. *Teaching Elephants to Dance: The Postentrepreneurial Revolution in Strategy Management and Careers.* New York: Simon and Schuster.

Keeble, David, and Egbert Wever. 1986. *New Firms and Regional Development in Europe.* London: Croom Helm, Ch. 1, pp. 1–34.

Kochan, Thomas, and Michael Useem, eds. 1992. *Transforming Organizations.* New York: Oxford University Press.

Kohn, Melvin, and Carmi Schooler. 1983. *Work and Personality.* Norwood, NJ: Ablex.

Kozul, Zeljka. 1991. "Innovation and Industrial Organization: A Comparative Study of the Dynamics of the Italian and Yugoslav Furniture Industry." Working paper, Faculty of Economics and Politics, Jesus College, Cambridge, England.

Lazerson, Mark. 1988. "Organizational Growth of Small Firms: An Outcome of Markets and Hierarchies?" *American Sociological Review* 53:330–342.

———. 1991. "A New Phoenix: Putting-Out in the Modena Knitwear Industry." Working paper, Department of Sociology, SUNY Stony Brook.

Lorenz, Edward H. 1988. "Neither Friends Nor Strangers: Informal Networks of Subcontracting in French Industry." In Diego Gambetta, ed., *Trust: Making and Breaking Cooperative Relations.* Oxford: Blackwell, pp. 194–210.

Lyons, Thomas, A. Richard Krackenberg, and John Henke. 1990. "Mixed Motive Marriages: What's Next for Buyer-Supplier Relations." *Sloan Management Review* 31:29–36.

Marshall, Alfred. 1919. *Industry and Trade.* London: Macmillan, pp. 283–288.

Morton, Michael S. Scott, ed. 1991. *The Corporation of the 1990s: Information,*

Technology, and Organizational Transformation. New York: Oxford University Press.

Murray, Fergus. 1983. "The Decentralization of Production: The Decline of the Mass-Collective Worker?" *Capital and Class* 19:74–99.

———. 1987. "Flexible Specialization in the 'Third Italy.'" *Capital and Class* 33:84–95.

Nishiguchi, Toshihiro. 1993. *Strategic Industrial Sourcing: The Japanese Advantage* (working title), New York: Oxford University Press.

O'Farrell, Patrick. 1986. "The Nature of the New Firms in Ireland: Empirical Evidence and Policy Implications." In D. Keeble and E. Wever, eds., *New Firms and Regional Development in Europe.* London: Croom Helm, pp. 151–183.

Perrow, Charles. 1986a. *Complex Organizations: A Critical Essay,* 3d ed. New York: Random House.

———. 1986b. "Economic Theories of Organizations." *Theory and Society* 15:11–45.

———. 1991. "A Society of Organizations." *Theory and Society* 20:725–762.

Pfeffer, Jeffrey, and Gerald Salancik. 1978. *The External Control of Organizations.* New York: Harper and Row.

Piore, Michael, and Charles Sabel. 1984. *The Second Industrial Divide.* New York: Basic Books.

Pollert, Anna. 1991. "The Orthodoxy of Flexibility." In Anna Pollert, ed., *Farewell to Flexibility.* London: Blackwell.

———. 1988. "The 'Flexible Firm': Fixation or Fact?" *Work, Employment, and Society* 2(3):281–316.

Powell, Walter W. 1990. "Neither Market Nor Hierarchy: Network Forms of Organization." *Research in Organizational Behavior* 12:295–336.

Sabel, Charles. 1989. "Flexible Specialisation and the Reemergence of Regional Economies." In P. Hirst and J. Zeitlin, eds., *Reversing Industrial Decline.* New York: St. Martin's, pp. 17–70.

———. 1991. "Moebius-Strip Organizations and Open Labor Markets: Some Consequences of the Reintegration of Conception and Execution in a Volatile Economy." In J. Coleman and P. Bourdieu, eds., *Social Theory for a Changing Society.* Boulder, CO: Westview Press.

———. 1990. "Studied Trust: Building New Forms of Cooperation in a Volatile Economy." Paper presented at MIT, August 7.

Sabel, Charles, and Jonathan Zeitlin. 1985. "Historical Alternatives to Mass Production: Politics, Markets and Technology in Nineteenth Century Industrialisation." *Past and Present* 108:133–175.

Sakai, Kuniyasu. 1990. "The Feudal World of Japanese Manufacturing." *Harvard Business Review* 68 (Nov/Dec):38–49.

Saxenian, AnnaLee. 1991a. "The Origins and Dynamics of Production Networks in Silicon Valley." *Research Policy,* Special Issue on Networks of Innovators.

———. 1991b. "Response to Richard Florida and Martin Kenney 'Silicon Valley and Route 128 Won't Save Us.'" *California Management Review* 33:136–142.

Sengenberger, Werner, Gary Loveman, and Michael Piore, eds. 1990. *The Reemergence of Small Enterprise: Industrials Restructuring in Industrialized Economies.* Geneva: International Labor Organization.

Smith, Chris. 1989. "Flexible Specialisation, Automation, and Mass Production." *Work, Employment and Society* 3(2):203–220.

Storper, Michael. 1989. "The Transition to Flexible Specialisation in the U.S. Film Industry: External Economies, the Division of Labour, and the Crossing of Industrial Divides." *Cambridge Journal of Economics* 13:273–305.

Stymne, Bengt. 1989. *Information Technology and Competence Formation in the Swedish Service Sector: An Analysis of Retail Strategy and Development of the Finance Sector.* Stockholm: The Economic Research Institute, Stockholm School of Economics.

Taplin, Ian M. 1989. "Segmentation and the Organisation of Work in the Italian Apparel Industry." *Social Science Quarterly* 70(2):408–424.

Thompson, Grahme. 1989. "Flexible Specialisation, Industrial Districts, Regional Economies: Strategies for Socialists?" *Economy and Society* 18(4):527–545.

Trigilia, Carlo. 1986. "Small-firm Development and Political Subcultures in Italy." *European Sociological Review* 2(3):161–175.

Williamson, Oliver E. 1975. *Markets and Hierarchies.* New York: The Free Press.

———. 1985. *The Economic Institution of Capitalism.* New York: The Free Press.

Wood, Stephen. 1988. "Between Fordism and Flexibility? The U.S. Car Industry." In Richard Hyman and Wolfgang Streeck, eds., *New Technology and Industrial Relations.* Oxford and New York: Basil Blackwell, pp. 101–117.

On the Limits of a Firm-Based Theory to Explain Business Networks: The Western Bias of Neoclassical Economics

NICOLE WOOLSEY BIGGART
AND
GARY G. HAMILTON

INTRODUCTION

The leading business success story of the last two decades cannot be disputed: the tremendous growth and economic development of the East Asian economies. During the fifteen-year period from 1965 to 1980, Japan and the newly industrialized countries (NICs) of South Korea, Taiwan, Hong Kong, and Singapore grew at an average annual rate of 8.8% At the same time, the U.S. economy grew 2.9%. In the period from 1980 to 1985, a time of world recession, Japan grew 3.8%, while the Asian NICs "slowed" to 6.6%. The comparable figure for all industrial market economies for that five-year period was 2.5%.

Both the popular and the scholarly press have lauded the economic development of Asia using such hyperbole as "miracle" and "astounding" to describe nations whose economies were little more than rubble after World War II and the Korean War. Observers have marveled at the ability of countries with poor resources not only to grow, but also to become world-class competitors in the most advanced industrial sectors, including automobiles, steel, shipbuilding, electronics, and pharmaceuticals.

It is no small irony that precisely those countries that Westerners have marveled at have come under severe attack for their patterns of economic development and international trade practices. Analysts and trade negotiators describe Japan and her neighbors as being "unfair" in bilateral trading relations, and suffering "imperfections" that "distort" their domestic economies. These criticisms are most often leveled at the dense networks of ties between firms in Asia, ties that look like cartels to Westerners. Network ties link major industrial firms into groups, such as Sumitomo in Japan and Samsung in Korea, as well as the myriad small manufacturers in the Taiwanese economy.

Why the paradox? Why should Asian economies that have been extraordinarily successful by every economic measure at the same time be described as unprincipled and distorted? Is it merely a reflection of Westerners' sense of fair play or perhaps even their own inadequacy in the face of vigorous economic competition? Or is it a fundamental misunderstanding of the patterns of Asian capitalism?

While it is no doubt frightening to have one's economic well-being challenged by other nations' competitive success, we do not believe that this is the primary reason for the strong American critique of Asian economies. For example, the United States has had substantial trade deficits with its second-largest trading partner, Canada, for years with little public outcry. The recent heavy investment by the Japanese in the United States has met with far more invective than has U.S. investment by the British or the Dutch, two economies that have higher levels of American investment than Japan does.

We believe, rather, that the response to Asian capitalism as unfair and distorted is primarily the result of ethnocentrism, a Western-based view of the proper organization and functioning of a market economy. American economic thinking is largely grounded in the neoclassical economic tradition. This perspective views competition between autonomous economic actors, both individual capitalists and firms acting as fictive individuals, as a necessity of mature capitalism. In numerous ways the United States has institutionalized competitive individualism in its market structure. Asian economies, in contrast, are organized through networks of economic actors that are believed to be natural and appropriate to economic development. Likewise, Asian nations have institutionalized policies and practices that flow from a network vision of correct market relations.

We argue two points in this chapter. First, Western academic and popular conceptualizations of Asia, particularly those based on the neoclassical model, are biased portrayals of Asian economic dynamics. A Western perspective leads analysts to conclude that Asia's network capitalism rests on market imperfections, and therefore that the vibrant capitalism of the region has been artificially induced and maintained. Second, and more important, the successful network structure of Asian capitalism reveals the neoclassical model to be not a general theory of capitalism, but rather an ethnocentric model developed from Western experience and applicable only to Western economies. We will not argue that neoclassical economics is wrong, merely that its utility is limited to settings where its institutional assumptions are in force.

MARKETS ARE NOT ALL ALIKE

The neoclassical economic paradigm conceives of ideal conditions for perfect competition: a large number of firms making substitutable products so that buyers have no reason to prefer one firm's output over another, independent and dispersed firms, and complete knowledge of all offers to buy and sell (Stigler 1968).

This model of competitive economic relations conceives of actors as isolated units. Capitalists, both buyers and sellers, ideally are independent and mindless of one another and indifferent as to the parties from whom they buy or to whom they sell. Price is the only criterion for a transaction. This is an asocial conceptualization of economic action (Abolafia and Biggart 1990) in the sense that it believes meaningful social relations are unimportant to competitive outcomes under idealized conditions. Where social relations are recognized to occur, they are viewed pejoratively and called "friction." Social relations in a market can lead only to such anticompetitive practices as price-fixing, restriction of output, and other forms of collusion. Keeping economic actors apart is a crucial condition of capitalism in the neoclassical view.

Western markets, particularly the Anglo-American economies, attempt to approximate tenets of the neoclassical paradigm at the level of both firms and individuals. Laws, including corporate and employment regulations, stress individual rights and obligations. Contracts, for example, bind only on the parties involved and not on their families or communities. Employers for the most part hire, promote, and otherwise reward workers based on their personal efforts. Seniority, to many Americans, does not seem a just way of determining pay or promotion. Affirmative action laws similarly express a belief that employment decisions should be made regardless of social characteristics or connections; it is individual competence and effort that should be the basis of selection.

Americans are fearful of hiring spouses, blood relatives, and even friends into the same company. Many firms have antinepotism rules to limit the effects of personal relations in the workplace, effects assumed to be detrimental. Employers may require disclosure of stock ownership and other ties, even through relatives, to outside firms. Disclosure guards against favoritism in awarding contracts, something most Americans think is wrong.

An individualistic institutional structure exists at the corporate level as well. State regulatory agencies, such as the Federal Trade Commission, prevent firms from colluding with each other. Strong antitrust laws enforced by the Attorney General limit monopoly power and the formation of cartels, except under very unusual situations (such as public utilities, where there exists what economists call a "natural" monopoly). The role of the U.S. government in the economy is largely a regulatory one. Government does not have a coordinated planning role, and does not have a strategic management plan for the United States's place in the world economy. Its primary function is to maintain competitive—that is, autonomous—conditions between economic actors.

At both the level of individuals and the level of corporations, people in the United States act to maintain an "open" market in which independent buyers, sellers, and workers can pursue their own interests in arm's-length transactions. In the United States "open" means free from social relations between individuals and firms.

Markets Conditions in Asia

The free market conditions Westerners think are crucial technical requisites for a successful capitalist economy are frequently not in evidence in Asia. In fact, they are often not even presumed to be necessary. Asian economies espouse different institutional logics from Western economies, ones rooted in connectedness and relationships: Asians believe that social relations between economic actors do not impede market functioning, but rather promote it. Just as Western economies have institutionalized ways of maintaining autonomy between actors, Asian economies are rooted in institutions that encourage and maintain ties.

For example, the crucial economic actor in Asian societies is typically not the individual, but rather the network in which the individual is embedded. In major Japanese firms, cohorts are often hired, compensated, and promoted, with individual performance differences having little import until late in a career (Clark 1979). Korean firms encourage workers to nominate their friends and relatives for vacant jobs; Koreans believe that social relations exert pressure on workers to perform well and to work hard for fear of embarrassing their nominators. The major source of venture capital in Taiwan, a country noted for its economy of small-scale entrepreneurial concerns, is friends and relatives (Biggs 1988). Impersonal sources of funds, such as banks and unknown investors, are far less important in Taiwan than in Western societies. In all three countries, buyers favor suppliers with whom they have an established relation, rather than the least-cost supplier. They routinely violate the neoclassical expectation that price is the critical factor in purchase decisions.

Although relationships are manifest in multiple ways at the interpersonal level in Asian business, they are seen dramatically and most importantly in business networks between Asian firms. It is impossible to underestimate the importance of business networks—sometimes called enterprise or business groups—to the development of Asian capitalism. The Japanese economy is dominated by *kigyo shudan*, modern-day descendants of pre–World War II *zaibatsu*, family-controlled conglomerates. Kigyo shudan are networks of firms in unrelated businesses that are joined together, no longer by family ties, but by central banks or trading companies. Michael Gerlach (1992) has recently argued that these intermarket networks constitute a form of capitalism that he calls "alliance capitalism." Many of the largest firms in Japan are members of these major business networks: Mitsubishi, Mitsui, Sumitomo, Fuji, Dai-Ichi, and Sanwa. Other forms of networks link Japanese businesses: for example, a major manufacturer and its affiliated subcontractors (e.g., the Toyota "independent group"), and small neighborhood retailers *(gai)* that may invest together (Orru, Hamilton, and Suzuki 1989).

The South Korean economy is dominated by networks that on the surface resemble Japan's, but in fact have substantial differences (Amsden 1989; Whitley 1990; Kim 1991; Biggart 1990; Orru, Biggart, and Hamilton 1991; Hamilton and Biggart 1988). South Korean *chaebol* are networks of firms owned and controlled by a single person or family and organized through a central staff, which may be a holding company or "mother" firm. By far the most powerful actors in the Korean economy are the major chaebol networks, which include Samsung, Hyundai, Lucky-Goldstar, Daewoo.

The Japanese and Korean economies are ruled by networks of medium-sized to very large firms. Networks are important in Taiwan, too, but they link smaller numbers of smaller firms (Numazaki 1986; Hamilton and Kao 1990; Hamilton and Biggart 1988). The leading economic actor in Taiwan, although occupying a less central position than the kigyo shudan or chaebol, is the family firm and family-owned conglomerates, which are called *jituanqiye*. Chinese business networks are usually based on family and friendship ties between owners and partners who often cross-invest in businesses, hold multiple positions throughout the network, and act as suppliers or upstream producers to downstream firms.

What the American economy works so studiously to prevent—connections between individuals, links between firms—Asian economies accept as appropriate and inevitable. Moreover, Asian nations have institutionalized networks and built economic policies around the presence and presumption of social relations among market actors.

EXPLAINING DIFFERENCES

With the extraordinary success of Asian economies, both business people and scholars have attended to the apparent differences between Asian and Western business practices. Analysts hope to understand the differences in order to explain success, to project patterns of growth, and to predict likely competitive outcomes of Asian economic practices. There are diverse explanations for Asian economic differences from the West, but three types of theories are most influential: development theories, culture theories, and market imperfection theories.

Development Theory

Development theories are concerned with the factors that aid or impede economies in their presumed march toward industrialization. In their earliest form, "modernization" theories assumed a linear progression that all nations passed through on the path toward development into a modern capitalist economy, epitomized by the United States and industrialized Europe. There was the presumption that stages of development were more or less alike and that at some unspecified future moment there would be a convergence, with all market economies having similar market institutions—for example, a capitalist class, a freely accessible money and banking system, a rational orientation toward economic matters.

More recent versions of modernization theory argue that learning is possible; countries can skip stages by observing and emulating more advanced nations, or by having "modern" economic practices imposed on them through colonial subjugation, for example, or as a precondition for development loans. Alice Amsden's *Asia's Next Giant: South Korea and Late Industrialization* (1989) is in this genre, arguing that South Korea was able to rapidly industrialize, leapfrogging early development stages, by appropriating technologies and processes formulated by more advanced nations.[1]

Alternatively, another set of development theories, conventionally labeled "dependency" theories, argues that the more-developed industrial economies are systemically linked to and impede the development of the less-developed economies (Evans and Stephens 1988). Powerful advanced nations maintain the dependency of less-developed economies by enforcing, for example, unfavorable trading relations or lending policies. A web of political relations shapes nations' differential possibilities for advancement.

There are a number of criticisms of development theories (Evans and Stephens 1988). It is increasingly clear, for example, that there is no convergence toward a single model of capitalism as exemplified by the West. It is also equally apparent that the world economy is neither a monolithic economic system nor easily divided into core and peripheral areas (Gereffi and Hamilton 1990). Moreover, Asia's differences, as well as those of some other industrializing nations, are not disappearing as they become more developed (Orru, Biggart, and Hamilton 1991). While it is certainly true that nations can learn from more-developed economies, the learning thesis is not especially useful because it cannot predict which countries can or will learn, or indeed which models they will choose to emulate. For example, both Taiwan and South Korea were colonies of Japan, and both received substantial economic aid and policy directives from the United States. Neither economy looks very much like the United States or Japan, although Korea has adopted some elements of Japanese industrial organization.

One branch of development economics, the endogenous growth models, does ask why differences in the fact and rate of economic growth and well-being persist over time. Neoclassical economic models predict that capital, both labor and financial, flows to the most efficient locales, eventually limiting nation-state differences. In fact, there is great diversity in per capita economic well-being and national growth rates, and the differences endure. Endogenous growth models posit that variations are attributable to differences in trade policies and human capital differences—that is, the differential investment in learning by various labor forces. Labor forces are not all the same in their approach to hard work, learning, and productivity. Endogenous growth models go beyond an earlier individualistic approach to human capital, which focused on the returns on investment in learning by individuals, to posit that there are social returns or effects, at the level of groups such as families and firms, to the acquisition of new skills and orientations by labor. It seems to us that this perspective is important in raising the unit of observation from the individual to the group, showing the cumulative effects of individual economic decisions (for example, to invest in school rather than to take a low-skilled job). By focusing on effects, however, endogenous growth models do not seek answers as to why observably different patterns are pursued in different locales, whether they be trade policies or human capital decisions. R. E. Lucas, for example, dismisses the possibility of identifying the social impulse for human capital acquisition: "We can no more directly measure the amount of human capital a society has, or the rate at which it is growing, than we can measure the degree to which a society is imbued with the Protestant Ethic" (1988:35).

Culture Theory

Culture theories do precisely what the endogenous growth models leave aside: attempt to account for the differential bases for economic action and organization. They are popular in journalistic accounts of Asian management practice, but also have academic standing (e.g., Berger and Hsiao 1988). Culture—the beliefs, values, symbols—of a society is understood to be the basis for economic practices and institutions. For example, the Japanese penchant for involving all members of a firm in decision making is seen to be an expression of a belief in the importance of consensus and harmony (*wa*) (Alston 1986). In contrast, the American CEO is expected to make independent decisions, probably after consulting subordinates, but ultimately to take individual responsibility. The two sets of decision-making practices, common in their respective economies, are explained by culture theory as respective expressions of the cultural values of communitarianism and individualism.

Cultural explanations have much truth in them; clearly, a preference for groupness or individualism will be reflected in commercial practices. Culture, though, is a problematic basis for comparative analysis (Hamilton and Biggart 1988: S69–S74). American culture, even if one could define it, cannot explain the differences in business practice one encounters in the United States. Is IBM's strong hierarchical management style the "true" organizational expression of American culture? Or is Apple Computer's decentralized and team-based system the "real" exemplar of American ideals? When comparing Japan with the West, which Western practices form the basis of comparison? Culture theories, by building up from rich and diverse data in a single society, make generalizations—and hence comparisons—difficult.

Market Imperfection Theory

Market imperfection theory is based on the logic of neoclassical economics and is the most important explanation of Asian distinctiveness. Under perfectly competitive market conditions, optimal firm size is a function of the demand for and the economies of scale to produce a product (Stigler 1968:1). When markets are not fully competitive, that is, when they suffer from constraints, then firm size is influenced by the constraints as well as by production and demand requirements. For example, when there is no market, as in a socialist command economy, then decrees by the state will influence the size and structure of the firm. Although economists recognize that a fully competitive market is an ideal condition that does not exist anywhere in reality, they use this conception of the ideal market and the optimal firm as a model against which to assess real conditions. They can then compare actual markets and firms to see how well they conform to the ideal. Deviations are either more or less "perfect."

This conceptualization of the perfect market, with its conditions of autonomy and impersonality and its resultant "optimal" firms, was developed as a means to understand the structure and functioning of Western societies, primarily the British and American economies. Economists, however, do not regard this model as an abstract, ethnocentric representation of these economies, but rather as a general model of capitalism that can be applied worldwide.

According to neoclassical theory there are only two forms of economic organization: markets and firms (also called hierarchies). Economists have difficulty applying this model of markets and firms to Asia with its developed interfirm networks (Aoki 1984, 1990; Goto 1982). Networks are neither independent market actors, nor hierarchically governed firms. Nonetheless, Western economists attempt to interpret Asian economic organization in terms of this dualistic neoclassical conceptualization. Alfred Chandler, for example, describes the Japanese zaibatsu, the historical precursor to the kigyo shudan, as an "organization comparable to the M-form," or multidivisional firm that originated in the United States (1982:22). Nathaniel Leff (1976, 1978) writes that Asian firms, as well as firms in other non-Western societies, actually constitute a single firm organized on a "group principle." "The group is a multicompany firm which transacts in different markets but which does so under common entrepreneurial and financial control" (Leff 1978:664). Others endorse the idea that despite some differences, the Asian business group is the functional equivalent of the Western firm. Like Western firms, some groups are large and monopolistic while others are small or operate in competitive markets in which the group principle allows economies of scale without actually expanding the size of firms.

Several Japanese economists (Aoki 1984; Goto 1982) have slightly qualified this view. Knowing Japan well, they argue that Japanese business groups are neither firms nor markets, but constitute an intermediate phenomenon that exists between the two. They argue that Japanese business groups do not operate like a single firm. They have neither a single set of owners, nor a tightly integrated system of financial controls. They are not independent, competitive firms, nor do they constitute a single megafirm. They are networks, according to Goto (1982), that buffer and channel market forces.

Despite some disagreement about how to categorize Asian business groups, economists do concur on how to explain their presence. Virtually all use a theory of market imperfections that to neoclassical economists seems self-evident. States Leff:

> The group pattern of industrial organization is readily understood as a micro-economic response to well-known conditions of market failure in the less-developed countries. In fact, the emergence of the group as an institutional mode might well have been predicted on the basis of familiar theory and a knowledge of the environment in these countries (1978:666).

Chandler (1982) explains the differences between the Japanese zaibatsu and the M-form American and European conglomerates by citing "unde-veloped" capital markets in Japan. Even Goto explains Japanese business group networks the same way:

> The group is an institutional device designed to cope with market failure as well as internal organizational failure. Under certain circumstances, trans-actions within a group of firms are more efficient than transactions through the market or transactions through the internal organization of the firm (1982:69).

More recently, but using the same logic, Jorgensen, Hapsi, and Kiggundu (1986) argue that in developing countries, a category in which they place Japan, market imperfections occur in the course of "striving for self-sufficiency" and the absence of an adequate "density of market trans-actions" (424). In promoting a "rational," risk-controlling policy for indus-trialization, governments promote such market "distortions" as tariffs to protect infant industries, exchange controls to create price advantages, and administrative hierarchies to coordinate resource allocation and other forms of market imperfections (426). They note four common "aberra-tions" in developing economies: the entrepreneurial family firm, the industrial cluster, the multinational corporation subsidiary, and the state-owned enterprise (427–432). All four of these so-called aberrations are common in Asian economies, even the most developed, and are not dis-appearing.

There are other variants of the market imperfections thesis. Political economists emphasize the importance of the "developmental state" in creating systemic distortions, both in the economy and in the society, that allow for concentrated capital accumulation and rapid development. Such theorists thus create a link between market imperfection and development theories. American trade negotiators likewise argue that Japan has created "structural impediments" to "free" trade that prevent American access to Japanese markets; most notable of the alleged impediments are business groups that limit competition. Although they focus more on political factors that create distortions, the logic of both political economists and trade negotiators is much the same as the market-imperfections thesis: Asian economies deviate from the Western ideal and therefore suffer imperfections.

We believe that market imperfection theories, like developmental and cultural theories, do not explain the Asian "difference" very well. The neoclassical paradigm is a framework that assumes one fundamental "perfect" economy against which real economies can be gauged. Although it does not exist anywhere in reality, the model is an approximation of the market economies that developed during Western industrialization. It is not a theory of Asian capitalism but a theory of Western capitalism applied to Asia, and its logic is akin to the logic of Henry Higgins' question in *My Fair Lady:* "Why can't a woman be more like a man?" Answers to a question so framed can only detail the ways in which a woman deviates from a man; they cannot lead to discovery of what a woman is. A market imperfection theory can describe the ways in which Asian capitalism deviates from the neoclassical ideal, but it cannot discover the principles of Asian capitalism.

Evidence of the economic vitality of Asia leads us to advance two points. First, a model of Asian capitalism based on Asia's institutional foundations is overdue. It stretches credibility to describe Japan, the world's second-largest economy, as "imperfect" or "deviant," even for analytic purposes. Second, the poor fit of the neoclassical model to the Asian case, suggests to us not an imperfect economy, but rather an inappropriate theory. Asia calls into question the presumption that this model is a general theory of capitalism. We will argue that the neoclassical model is more suited to the institutional arena that it was developed to explain: England and the United States. In fact, neoclassical economics rests on an institutional theory of firm autonomy that displays great power in explaining Western economic dynamics. It is not, however, a general theory of capitalism.

THE DEVELOPMENT OF MARKETS IN THE WEST

The neoclassical model is based on a central idea: the autonomy of economic actors, both individuals and firms, who seek their self-interest in economic matters. Actors go into the marketplace and, mindless of all social and moral considerations, rationally calculate exchanges based only on price. This portrait of economic actors as individuated, asocial, and rational is the useful fiction that economists have drawn to provide a parsimonious behaviorist model of economic action. While few economists would argue that any real person acts exactly this way, it is assumed that this is the ideal that most people, at least in the aggregate, approximate.

Homo economicus is a generic individual distinguished not by sex, ethnicity, religion, age, or any other social characteristic. The presumption is that any person, in any place, at any time would behave more or less the same way—that is, as a rational individual. In building on this central idea, neoclassical economics assumes that social relations and characteristics do not make significant differences in economic choice. To the extent that these assumptions have a universal reality, they support claims that the neoclassical paradigm is a general theory of capitalism.

Recently, a number of scholars have attempted to question tenets of the neoclassical paradigm. For example, the individual decision-making studies of psychologists Tversky and Kahneman (1974) suggest that people are not the hyperrational actors assumed by the model. Economic sociologist Amitai Etzioni (1988) has marshaled substantial evidence that people consider moral as well as economic factors in making economic choices. Anthropologist Richard Shweder's (1986) anthropological studies of a community in India demonstrate that economic rationality is based on substantive beliefs, not abstract calculus. Similarly, Mark Granovetter has argued that the economy is embedded in social relationships and is not the aggregate activity of isolated individuals (1985). Our own studies (Hamilton and Biggart 1988; Orru, Biggart, and Hamilton 1991) have suggested, as we do in this chapter, that Asian economic action is based on different principles of social action, principles developed through the historical experience of Asian nations.

While these and other studies question crucial elements of the neoclassical model, particularly as they apply to non-Western locales, it remains clear that the model does describe in important ways the aggregate dynamics of Western economies, especially those of the United States.

We believe that it is possible to reconcile the power of the neoclassical paradigm in understanding much of the West, with its limitations in explaining microeconomic phenomena, especially in non-Western settings: The neoclassical model assumes and tacitly incorporates many of the features of the Western societies it was developed to explain. Its "ideal-typical" premises aptly characterize the institutional setting in which Anglo-American capitalism developed.[2]

The Institutional Foundations of Western Markets

The rise of markets in Western Europe followed what Barrington Moore (1966) called the "routes" that Western nations took in moving from feudalism to modernity. At the first of the period, sometime before the thirteenth century, markets were embedded in an *oikos* economy dominated by aristocratic households. A market city either comprised a part of the manor and was actually owned by the lords of the land (Koebner 1964), or existed as a free city, characterized by Weber (1968:1212–1236) as a "non-legitimate" enclave located at the margin of a manorial economy. Although it varied from region to region, the feudal economy was embedded in the political structure of Western Europe, and when that structure began to change decisively with the rise of absolutism, market economies also began to change.

Absolutism gradually moved the organizing locus of the economy from manors to cities, particularly national cities such as London and Paris that were dominated by kings. Mercantilism followed an economic policy designed to fill royal treasuries, which were used mainly to pay for navies and land armies needed to defend or expand territory. When European kings had difficulty gaining revenues from territory owned by their fellow aristocrats, they tried to compensate by creating royal companies, such as the East India Company, designed to generate royal surplus from overseas adventures. Mercantilistic policies created national urban-centered, consumer-oriented economies. Urban-centered consumption in turn fostered an integrated marketing system linking urban, rural, and overseas areas and nurtured rural industries that produced raw resources and handicraft items for urban consumption (Jones 1987). Although commercial markets were certainly growing and prospering, the mercantilistic economy rested on royal institutions, including the kings' courts and the kings' companies.

The revolutionary period, starting in the last half of the eighteenth century, entirely changed the institutional structure of Western economies and accelerated the growth of "free market" capitalism. Social scientists have described the changes from a mercantilistic to a free market economy as a "great transformation" (Polanyi 1957). The phrase is somewhat hyperbolic for economic activity but quite accurate for the institutional change that occurred after these revolutions, a period in which all the major economic institutions that we associate with capitalism first developed.

The change in government from absolutism to democracy marked a pivotal switch from an institutional environment based on centralized public spheres to one dispersed through decentralized private spheres. With great insight, Michel Foucault (1979) has described this shift in connection with the institutions for criminal justice, but an even larger and more profound shift occurred in the regulation and conduct of the economic activity. Isomorphic with the shift in other institutional spheres, the shift in the economic sphere in Western Europe and the United States moved from centrally instituted economies through royal banks, companies, courts, market taxes—all institutions against which Adam Smith (1991) inveighed in his *Wealth of Nations*—to a "self-regulating" economy. The economic counterpart of Bentham's Panopitcon that so intrigued Foucault (1979) was the commodity and equity markets created in the same period as circular Panopitcon prisons. Both institutional structures embodied the principles of self-regulation: in the circular market pit, where all buyers and all sellers exchange simultaneously, everyone sees everything.

The Institutionalization of Firm Autonomy

Underlying self-regulation in markets, as in prisons, was the notion of the autonomy of individual units. In the criminal justice system, as in society in general, rested the presumption that every individual was distinct and responsible for his or her own actions. The same principles applied in the economy: every firm was distinct and responsible for its own actions.

This belief in individual autonomy, as applied to both people and their businesses, arose out of an intellectual tradition that is characteristically Western. The strands of this tradition can be traced to antiquity, particularly to the Roman legal system, which had decisive effects on modern Western European state structure, citizenship, commercial law, and to Christianity, which conceptualized each individual as a distinct soul-bearing entity. Despite the many strands, however, the institutionalization of individual autonomy did not occur until after absolutism gave way to democracy.

The cornerstone of self-regulating markets based on firm autonomy came from the Enlightenment philosophers' reconceptualization of private property. In Western Europe, with the enactment of the constitutional state based on natural laws, ownership and control of property were not so much an economic issue as a political issue with economic implications. Property rights became a crucial principle in the articulation of democracy, an idea used by citizens to claim rights over jurisdictions that formerly had been held by absolutist monarchs. The writings of eighteenth-century philosophers, such as John Locke and slightly later Adam Smith, are rife with the notion of private property and its implications for individual political control vis-à-vis an authoritarian state. Therefore, when constitutional states were enacted, the right to property was embodied in individualism, in the very conception of what an individual was.

The idea of individual autonomy in a society is the principle of nineteenth-century democracy, and the idea of firm autonomy in the economy is the principle of self-regulating markets in a democratic society. These ideas were not only abstract philosophies, but also working principles gradually instituted throughout society to conform to changing social and economic conditions. Such abstract ideas have a very technical dimension when they are used to order everyday reality.

The legal assignment of private property rights requires a clear delineation of who claims ownership and what is owned. When non-state businesses in the West were subsumed under the legal definition of private property, business firms became in principle separate, distinct, and independent. They became conceptualized as a person—as autonomous, legally indivisible units that could form contractual links with people and with other firms. The clearest demonstration of this occurred in the United States, where under the Fourteenth Amendment corporations were held to be a person and could not be "deprived of life, liberty, or property" without due process.

In the early nineteenth century, when businesses were small and individually or family owned, firms were equated with property and due process applied to their owners, and not to the firms as separate entities. With the growth of American capitalism and large firms with multiple owners, the firm itself took on the status of an individual. The test case in the U.S. Supreme Court in 1882 was a conflict between a California county and the Southern Pacific Railway Company. The issue was who owed taxes to the government. The Court upheld the idea, already established, that "incorporation" created a unified entity—literally, a body—that had an existence over and above the parts that made it up.

This legal formulation had far-reaching effects on the development of Western business practices. Importantly, the law required the individuation of firms. Each firm was conceptualized as a corporate body, a single entity distinct from all others. Business practices conformed to this principle, not because it was efficient or necessary, but because it was the law and deeply rooted in Western political and social ideas. The principle of individual corporateness established an institutional environment that formed a basis for Western capitalism's organizational structure and dynamics.

As legislated by most Western countries, and independently by states in the United States, laws of incorporation require firm autonomy, require the specification of ownership and corporate assets. National and state laws of taxation demand accounting procedures that delineate ownership and income. Capital markets assume that firms are autonomous: the loan provisions of the banking system, the equity provisions of the stock markets, the insurance provisions of industry all have institutionalized the principle of firm autonomy. Antitrust legislation, in working to prevent cartels and monopolies, provides sanctions to sustain autonomous corporations.

Firm autonomy has been institutionalized in many ways. A part of this process has been to work out legally and procedurally modes of legitimate interfirm linkages. That firms are really autonomous from all other firms or that individuals are entirely independent of one another is, of course, a fiction. But it is a fiction that was created historically as a means to specify institutionally the interrelation among people in the creation of a democratic political order. The fiction of autonomy became true, with time, for firms as well as for people. Interrelationships between businesses and people in the West are specified in legal terms, through contracts—that is, through autonomous entities exercising their free will to make agreements. Firm autonomy and personal autonomy are not independent of the institutions that reinforce such autonomy.

Therefore, to see firm autonomy as a universal element of capitalism, as something inherent to it in all time and all places, is really a misreading of history and of economies. It is a profoundly ethnocentric point of view.

THE DEVELOPMENT OF MARKETS IN ASIA

It is incorrect to think that Asian economies "matured" only after being exposed to Western capitalism. While it is certainly the case that they changed considerably after the nineteenth century opening of Chinese and Japanese economies, it is not the case that the respective economies were undeveloped before the nineteenth century. The dazzling innovation in, and virtual explosion of, Western societies and economies after the seventeenth century has obscured the fact that Asian societies were economically quite advanced and quite complex. Although neither was heading toward industrial capitalism, both Japanese and Chinese economies were quite dynamic and quite old. They had been mature for a long time.

The organization of these economies, like the organization of society, rested on principles quite different from those found in the West. The great historian of Chinese science, Joseph Needham, has clarified these differences by contrasting Chinese "associative thinking" with what he calls the Western "billiard ball" conception of reality. Westerners, he says, see their world in terms of "rational" cause and effect: like billiard balls bouncing off each other, one motion causes another motion, which causes another motion in turn. Had he written later, he might have called this the "rational choice" model of human behavior: reduced to individual units, causative, and lawlike.

According to Needham (1956:279–291), a Chinese world-view is completely unlike a Western one. Although highly developed and more advanced than Western science until the seventeenth and eighteenth centuries, Chinese science did not rest on correlations based on cause and effect, on first principles, or on lawlike assertions. Instead, Chinese science rests on a conception of order. In the Chinese thinking, order rests on a stable relationship among things. There is order in a family when all the relationships in a family are obeyed; there is order in a country when all the reciprocal relationships between subjects and rulers are fulfilled; there is order in the universe when mankind fulfills its relationship with heaven and earth. Needham (1956:286) compares this Chinese notion of order to a dance that has no beginning and no ending and in which all partners dance in time to the music: "an extremely and precisely ordered universe, in which things 'fitted' so exactly that you could not insert a hair between them." Everything causes everything else. Therefore, what is essential in life is not the individual cause and effect, but the order in the group as a whole.

In Asian societies the principle informing human behavior is not for people to obey the law, whether God's laws or natural laws or economic laws. Instead it is for people to create order by obeying the requirements of human relationships as these are manifest in a situational context. The person in Asia is always embedded in ongoing relationships and is not an abstract entity that exists outside society, not even for purposes of rational calculation.

Just as individualism is institutionalized in the Western societies, social relationships are institutionalized in Asian societies. Legal codes in Asia, as many have argued, are in fact codifications of morality embedded in social relationships. For instance, the Tang Dynasty legal codes, which influenced Japan's legal codes and were passed down more or less intact through all the remaining dynasties in China, made unfilial behavior to one's parents one of the "Ten Abominations," and a crime punishable by death. Other relationships, such as those outlined in the *wulun* (five relationships: parent/child, emperor/subject, husband/wife, older sibling/younger sibling, and friend), were upheld in the magistrate's courts as well as in quasi-legal settings such as the lineage, village, and merchant associations. Because everyone has a responsibility for order in a group, failure to uphold one's responsibility in a relationship could lead not only to personal punishment, but also to the punishment of others in one's group. In this way mutual surveillance has come to be an essential part of the institutionalization of social relationships in East Asian societies. The Western concept of an individual's "right to privacy" has no meaning in an Eastern setting.

The eminent Chinese sociologist Fei Xiaotong (1992) shows that this relational logic produces a society that rests on social networks. Every person is a part of multiple networks: family, friends, neighbors, co-workers—the list goes on and on. Each person is not an independent, self-willed actor, but rather is responsible simultaneously for the order within multiple networks; Fei shows that network ties are ranked, with family ties taking precedence over more distant kinship ties, which in turn may (or may not, depending on the context) have priority over ties with other types of people. Fei also shows that every institutional sphere, including the economy, is based on a structure of networks of relationships.

The Institutional Foundations of Asian Markets

Using these insights, we can show that network organization is an institutional feature of Asian capitalism. These networks precede the modern era. For instance, in China during the Ming and Qing Dynasties (extending from the sixteenth to the twentieth centuries), commercial activities and handicraft industries were highly developed with a level of production and a volume of movement exceeding all other locations in the world until the eighteenth century. This level of complexity was achieved without support from the state, even in such matters as maintaining a currency, establishing weights and measures, and creating commercial laws. In short, creating order within the worlds of merchants and artisans was not a function undertaken by the imperial state, but one that remained in the hands of those actually engaged in business.

Through *huiguan*, associations of fellow regionals, merchants and artisans themselves established and enforced economic standards that created predictability and continuity in the marketplace (Hamilton 1985). Huiguan were literally meeting halls, places where people from the same native place would congregate. As a number of researchers have shown (Fewsmith 1983; Golas 1977; Hamilton 1979; and Skinner 1977) all the main merchant groups in late imperial China were out-of-towners organized through huiguan. Within the huiguan, people with common origins were pledged to a moral relationship *(tongxiang guanxi)* that generated sufficient trustworthiness for them to monopolize an area or areas of business for themselves. They would set and enforce standards for the trade as well as moral standards for fellow regionals in the trade.

Although the regional associations mediated the trading relationships, the actual firms engaged in business were always family firms. The family firms, through their ties with other firms, often owned by fellow regionals, stretched beyond any one locale. In fact, through using native place ties as the medium of organization, merchants were able to monopolize commerce in a commodity for an entire region, as the Swatow merchants did for the sugar trade for all of China. The success of the overseas Chinese in Southeast Asia in the nineteenth century was organizationally based on regional networks.

In the premodern era, Japanese merchants were organized quite differently from the Chinese merchants. Japanese merchants were organized as members of city-based guilds. Unlike Chinese firms, which would come and go, Japanese merchant and artisan firms were members of stable communities of firms, each one of which would be passed from father to eldest son or to a surrogate for him. Whereas Chinese firms would often be dissolved at the death of the owner because of partible inheritance, many Japanese firms continued intact for generations. Moreover, as members of stable networks of urban-based firms, Japanese merchants often developed long-term creditor-debtor relationships with members of the samurai class.

In the modern era, the same general network configurations persist both in overseas Chinese communities, including Taiwan, Hong Kong, and Southeast Asia, and in modern Japan. Continually changing patrilineal networks of small firms that connect near and distant kin, and frequently friends, into production-and-supply networks characterize modern Chinese economies. Likewise, relatively stable business networks of large firms dominate the modern Japanese economy. Neither Asian social sphere has ever had a legacy of autonomous firms comparable to those of the West, nor are they likely to develop. Recent scholarship confirms that the institutional environments that support associative network relationships remain strong in Asia at the interpersonal, business, and state levels.

CONCLUSION: THE NEOCLASSICAL PARADIGM AS AN INSTITUTIONAL THEORY

The fundamental assumptions of neoclassical economics include the idea that economic actors are rational and autonomous, and that they seek their self-interest independent of social relations or characteristics. Even a brief examination of the history of Western Europe demonstrates that these characteristics of individuals, to the extent that they are true now, were not always evident. In feudal society, people were not autonomous but were bound by traditional ties of fealty and homage. In absolutist Europe, people belonged to the "body politic" that was personified by

Networks and Organizations

the king himself (Kantorowicz 1957). Kings "embodied" nations, so that individuals within those jurisdictions were presumed to have no ultimate autonomy. Only after the institutionalization of the constitutional states in the West did an order arise in which the building blocks of societies and economies—people and firms—became rationally and systematically individuated.

The factors that neoclassical economics assumes are universal traits of the human condition are, in fact, part of the development of the modern West. Western institutions are embodiments of beliefs in individual autonomy and economic rationality. Now institutionalized, these principles are reproduced by individuals and firms who go about acting "rationally" and "autonomously." Neoclassical economics captures, at least at some level, institutional characteristics of American and European societies, and it would be surprising if this theory did not work well in explaining important aspects of Western economic activity. Nonetheless, this paradigm cannot sustain a claim to universal status. It fits poorly the Asian economies that do not have the same institutional heritage. Asian societies have never had a Western-style legal system that treated each person as a separate entity, equal to all others. Asia has had no salvationist religion from which to derive a principle of individual rights. Individuals are not the basic social, economic, or political units in Asia. Rather, networks of people linked together through differentially categorized social relationships form the building blocks of Asian social orders and derive from Asia's institutional history. Individuals play roles in these networks, to be sure, but it is the networks that have stability. The presence of networks—of kin, of friends, of fellow regionals—is institutionalized in business and other social practices.

Persuasive explanations for the success of Asian business will ultimately come from an institutional analysis of Asian societies and the economies that are embedded in them. Explanations will not come— indeed, cannot come—from an attempt to apply a theory rooted in Western experience to an alien institutional arena. That can only result in explaining Asia as "imperfect" and "distorted."

Notes

1. Earlier versions of this theory include Marion Levy (1972) and the very sophisticated treatment of Ronald Dore (1973) as applied to Japan.

2. This point requires a short digression into what the methods of what Milton Friedman calls "positive economics." Friedman (1953) makes it clear that not even those economists who believe fully in the utility of models of perfect competition would argue for the universality and the validity of these theories. Friedman argues for the utility of economic models, but at the same time says that they are not valid or universal in an absolute sense. In this regard, economic models resemble Weberian ideal types more than they resemble natural laws. Economic models represent a slice of reality from which a few causal factors or processes are reformulated at a more abstract plane and are made more precise and internally logical. The model is then applied back to the same or like contexts from which the main elements have been abstracted in order to see how well the model predicts the actual

behavior. "The ideal types," says Friedman (1953:36), "are not intended to be descriptive; they are designed to isolate the features that are crucial for a particular problem." In this role economic models, logically, neither make a truth claim nor require an assumption of universality. The model merely has to meet the test of usefulness.

References

Abolafia, Mitchel, and Nicole Woolsey Biggart. 1990. "Competition and Markets." In Amitai Etzioni and Paul Lawrence, eds., *Perspectives on Socio-Economics*. Armonk, NY: M. E. Sharpe.

Alston, Jon. 1986. *The American Samurai*. Berlin: De Gruyter.

Amsden, Alice. 1989. *Asia's Next Giant: South Korea and Late Industrialization*. New York: Oxford University Press.

Aoki, Masahiko. 1984. *The Economic Analysis of the Japanese Firm*. Amsterdam: North-Holland.

———. 1990. "Toward an Economic Model of the Japanese Firm." *Journal of Economic Literature* 28:1–27.

Berger, Peter L., and Hsin-Huang Michael Hsiao, eds. 1988. *In Search of an East Asian Development Model*. New Brunswick, NJ: Transaction Books.

Biggart, Nicole Woolsey. 1990. "Institutionalized Patrimonialism in Korean Business." In Craig Calhoun, ed., *Comparative Social Research* 12. Greenwich, CT: JAI Press, pp. 113–133.

Biggs, Tyler S. 1988. "Financing the Emergence of Small and Medium Enterprises in Taiwan: Financial Mobilization and the Flow of Domestic Credit to the Private Sector." Working paper.

Chandler, Alfred D., and H. Daems. 1980. *Managerial Hierarchies: Comparative Perspectives on the Rise of the Modern Industrial Enterprise*. Cambridge, MA: Harvard University Press.

Clark, Rodney. 1979. *The Japanese Company*. New Haven: Yale University Press.

Dore, Ronald. 1973. *British Factory—Japanese Factory: The Origins of National Diversity in Industrial Relations*. Berkeley: University of California Press.

Etzioni, Amitai. 1988. *The Moral Dimension: Toward a New Economics*. New York: Free Press.

Evans, Peter B., and John D. Stephens. 1988. "Development and the World Economy." In Neil J. Smelser, ed., *Handbook of Sociology*. Newbury Park, CA: Sage, pp. 739–773.

Fei, Xiaotong. 1992. *Up From the Soil: The Foundations of Chinese Society*. Gary G. Hamilton and Wang Zheng (trans.). Berkeley: University of California Press.

Fewsmith, Joseph. 1983. "From Guild to Interest Group: The Transformation of Public and Private in Late Qing China." *Comparative Studies in Society and History* 25:617–640.

Foucault, Michel. 1979. *Discipline and Punish: The Birth of the Prison*. New York: Vintage.

Friedman, Milton. 1953. *Essays in Positive Economics*. Chicago: University of Chicago Press.

Gereffi, Gary, and Gary G. Hamilton. 1990. "Modes of Incorporation in an Industrial World: The Social Economy of Global Capitalism." Unpublished paper presented at the American Sociological Association meetings, Washington, DC, August.

Gerlach, Michael. 1992. *Alliance Capitalism: The Social Organization of Japanese Business*. Berkeley: University of California Press.

Golas, Peter J. 1977. "Early Ch'ing Guilds." In G. William Skinner, ed., *The City in Late Imperial China*. Stanford: Stanford University Press, pp. 555–580.

Goto, Akira. 1982. "Business Groups in a Market Economy." *European Economic Review* 19:53–70.

Granovetter, Mark. 1985. "Economic Action and Social Structure." *American Journal of Sociology* 91:393–426.

Hamilton, Gary G., and Nicole Woolsey Biggart. 1988. "Market, Culture, and Authority: A Comparative Analysis of Management and Organization in the Far East." *American Journal of Sociology* 94 (Supplement): S52–S94.

Hamilton, Gary G., and Cheng-shu Kao. 1990. "The Institutional Foundations of Chinese Business: The Family Firm in Taiwan." *Comparative Social Research* 12:95–112.

Jones, Eric L. 1987. *The European Miracle*. Cambridge: Cambridge University Press.

Jorgensen, Jan J., Taieb Hafsi, and Moses N. Kiggundu. 1986. "Towards a Market Imperfections Theory of Organizational Structure in Developing Countries." *Journal of Management Studies* 24(4):419–442.

Kantorowicz, Ernst. 1957. *The King's Two Bodies*. Princeton: Princeton University Press.

Kim, Eun Mee. 1991. "The Industrial Organization and Growth of the Korean Chaebol: Integrating Development and Organizational Theories." In Gary G. Hamilton, ed., *Business Networks and Economic Development in East and Southeast Asia*. Hong Kong: Centre of Asian Studies.

Koebner, R. 1964. "German Towns and Slav Markets." In Sylvia L Thupp, ed., *Change in Medieval Society*. New York: Appleton-Century-Crofts.

Leff, Nathaniel. 1976. "Capital Markets in the Less Developed Countries: The Group Principle." In Ronald I. McKinnon, ed., *Money and Finance in Economic Growth and Development: Essays in Honor of Edward S. Shaw*. New York: M. Decker, pp. 97–122.

———. 1978. "Industrial Organization and Entrepreneurship in the Developing Countries: The Economic Groups." *Economic Development and Cultural Change* 26(4):661–675.

Levy, Marion. 1972. *Modernization: Latecomers and Survivors*. New York: Basic Books.

Lucas, R. E. 1988. "On the Mechanics of Economic Development." *Journal of Monetary Economics* 22:3–42.

Moore, Barrington. 1966. *Social Origins of Dictatorship and Democracy: Lord and Peasant in the Making of the Modern World*. Boston: Beacon Press.

Needham, Joseph. 1956. *The Grand Titration*. Toronto: Toronto University Press.

Numazaki, Ichiro. 1986. "Networks of Taiwan Big Business." *Modern China* 12:487–534.

Orru, Marco, Nicole Woolsey Biggart, and Gary G. Hamilton. 1991. "Organizational Isomorphism in East Asia." In Walter W. Powell and Paul DiMaggio, eds., *The New Institutionalism in Organizational Analysis*. Chicago: University of Chicago Press.

Orru, Marco, Gary G. Hamilton, and Mariko Suzuki. 1989. "Patterns of Inter-Firm Control in Japanese Business." *Organization Studies* 10(4):549–574.

Polanyi, Karl. 1957. *The Great Transformation*. Boston: Beacon Press.

Schweder, Richard. 1986. "Divergent Rationalities." In R. W. Fiske and R. A. Schweder, eds., *Metatheory in the Social Sciences: Pluralisms and Subjectivities*. Chicago: Chicago University Press.

Skinner, William F. 1977. *The City in Late Imperial China*. Stanford: Stanford University Press.

Smith, Adam. 1991. *The Wealth of Nations*. New York: Knopf.

Stigler, George. 1968. *The Organization of Industry*. Homewood, IL: Irwin.

Tversky, Amos, and Daniel Kahneman. 1974 "Judgement Under Uncertainty: Heuristics and Biases." *Science* 185:1124–1131.

Weber, Max. 1968. *Economy and Society*. Berkeley: University of California Press.

Whitley, Richard D. 1990. "Eastern Asian Enterprise Structures and the Comparative Analysis of Forms of Business Organization." *Organization Studies*. 11:47–74.

19

The Organization of Business Networks in the United States and Japan

MICHAEL L. GERLACH
AND
JAMES R. LINCOLN

This chapter presents a research agenda for bringing structural analysis to bear on the study of interfirm business networks in the world's two largest market economies, the United States and Japan. Structural analysis refers to the process of "studying directly how patterns of ties allocate resources in a social system" (Wellman and Berkowitz 1987) and is part of a growing trend in the social sciences toward seeking explanation, not in the intrinsic properties of social units, but in the networks of structural relations in which they are embedded. We argue that networks among financial, commercial, and industrial firms in an economy determine significant features of that economy's overall organization and its resulting performance. Thus the theories and methods of network sociology have much to offer in the study of comparative economic organization. In order for this potential to be reached, however, certain steps are required:

1. Significant efforts must be made to collect and codify pertinent network-level data.

2. To allow for valid cross-national comparisons, the coding and measurement operations in each country must be coordinated and adjustments made to control for systematic measurement biases and ensure conceptual equivalence.

3. The formal quantitative portions of the network study must be backed by an intimate familiarity with the social and institutional context of the economies in question in order to render the results intelligible.

The research program described here does, we believe, satisfy these requirements. Included in the large-scale data bases that we have created are information on firms' top-ten shareholders, the amounts of these hold-ings, and the identity and company affiliations of all outside directors. These data have been systematically coded for a series of key years for the 200 largest industrial firms and 50 largest financial institutions in both the United States and Japan. For Japan, information on companies' top-ten creditors, the amounts of their borrowings, and the identities of their leading trading partners are also coded. (These data are not available from published sources for U.S. firms.) Brief company histories, including name changes and major restructurings, have been written for each com-pany in the sample. *Moody's* provided this information for the 250 U.S. firms, while *Kaisha Nenkan* provided the same information for the 250 Jap-anese firms. For the Japanese sample, affiliations with industrial group-ings were coded based on listings in two publications, *Industrial Groupings in Japan* and *Keiretsu no Kenkyū*.

The result is a corporate network data base that we believe represents a substantial improvement in several respects over those used in previous interfirm network studies. First, it is explicitly comparative. Identical net-work measures have been taken from both Japan and the United States, allowing for direct comparisons of network structures between the two countries while minimizing systematic measurement errors. Second, the data base is longitudinal. Two of the network measures coded so far (equity and bank capital connections) are observed over the period from 1964 to 1986, in most cases on a biannual basis. Third, the data base includes a broader range of network variables than have previous network data sets. We have coded not only directorship interlocks for U.S. and Japanese firms, but also equity interlocks. In addition, for the Japanese networks (for which data sets on interfirm relationships are more thorough than in the United States) we have coded information on firms' banking relationships and their leading trading partners. These data on the "multiplexity" of intercorporate ties permit analyses of the compara-tive structure of and relationships among network types within each country. A summary of the network variables included in the data base at present is provided in Appendix A.

Present data-collection efforts are focused on two areas. First, we are expanding the network portion of the data base by adding observations from multiple time periods on the other two network measures (inter-locking directorships and leading trading partners). The result will be a longitudinal data base across four key network measures—equity, loaned capital, directorships, and leading trading partners—that will permit studies of networks as they develop over time. Second, we are in the process of coding data on such corporate-level attributes as internal organizational form, diversification strategy, and financial performance.

Finally, the quantitative analyses that rely on these data will be rein-forced by each investigator's extensive research experience in both the United States and Japan using archival, survey, and ethnographic methods.

JAPAN'S NETWORK ECONOMY

The Japanese economy is of enormous importance to the United States and to the world, serving as a major trading partner, as a model of rapid development (especially for the newly industrializing countries of East Asia), as a competitive challenger in frontier industries, and now as the world's largest net creditor nation. It has successfully overcome three major hurdles during the postwar period—first from the devastation of the war, second from the oil shocks of the 1970s, and third from the doubling of the value of the yen since 1985—and it is now rapidly moving its operations overseas through foreign direct investment. An important reason for this remarkable dynamism, we believe, lies in the distinctive institutional characteristics of Japanese industrial organization. These include not only the micro-level internal organizational practices and labor-management relations of the Japanese firm and the macro-level processes of government-business interactions, but also the meso-level structures of relationships among firms themselves.

Central to this level of analysis is what Dore (1986) calls "organized capitalism" and Gerlach (1987; 1992a) refers to as "alliance capitalism." The essence of alliance capitalism is the strategic forging of long-term intercorporate relationships across a broad spectrum of markets: with banks and insurance companies in the capital market, with *sōgō shōsha* (general trading companies) in primary goods markets, with subcontractors in component parts markets, and with competitors in new technology development. These networks of relations are most evident when they become institutionalized into identifiable *keiretsu*, or industrial groupings. The keiretsu are of two distinct, though overlapping, types. The vertical keiretsu organize suppliers and distribution outlets hierarchically beneath a large, industry-specific manufacturing concern. Toyota Motor's chain of upstream component suppliers is a well-known example of this form of vertical interfirm organization. These large manufacturers in turn are often clustered within groupings involving trading companies and large banks and insurance companies. These large clusterings, which we term "inter-market keiretsu" (Gerlach 1992a), provide for their members reliable sources of loan capital and a stable core of long-term shareholders. Moreover, like the vertical keiretsu, they establish a partially internalized market in intermediate products.

A basic schematic of linkages within and between the vertical and the intermarket keiretsu is shown in Figure 19-1. Since our study focuses on networks of relationships among large firms, intermarket keiretsu-type linkages (e.g., between industrial firms and their financial affiliates) are especially well represented. The network data base also includes a substantial number of parent-company/satellite-company linkages, making possible the study of vertical keiretsu-type supplier ties. Among the 200 Japanese industrials, 57 are subordinate affiliates of larger manufacturers also within the sample (i.e., where the industrial parent company holds an equity position in excess of 10%). Thus it will be possible using our network sample to study several different kinds of interfirm ties, both horizontal and vertical.

The prevalence of network organization in the Japanese economy poses a formidable challenge to Western economic theories that view hierarchical organization (government or corporate) and atomized markets as the polar twin mechanisms through which transactions in an advanced economy take place. On the one hand, the Japanese economy appears to make less use of bureaucratic structures in the organization of production and exchange than does the American economy. Japanese firms are on average smaller, more specialized to particular industries, less vertically

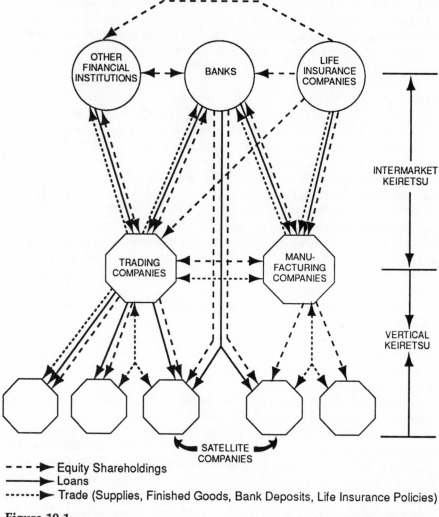

Figure 19-1

Debt, Equity, and Trade Linkages in the Vertical and Intermarket Keiretsu

Source: Gerlach (1992a, p. 5)

integrated, and far less likely to pursue growth and diversification strategies through merger and acquisition (Clark 1979). Yet the alternative to formal hierarchy in Japan is not impersonal arm's-length markets, but informal networks based on trust and long-term "relational contracting" (Baker 1984; Dore 1986; Gerlach 1992). Like the myriad other ties that thread through the Japanese economy, they have an enduring, obligatory, and cooperative character that economic models of efficient markets fail to capture.

Ronald Dore (1983), for example, refers to the singular importance in Japanese market organization of *goodwill*, or "the sentiments of friendship and the sense of diffuse personal obligation which accrue between individuals engaged in recurring contractual economic exchange" (460). As a result, he continues, it is tangible relationships rather than impersonal market processes that explain Japanese industrial organization:

> The Japanese, in spite of what their political leaders say at summit conferences about the glories of free enterprise in the Free World, and in spite of the fact that a British publisher with a new book about Adam Smith can expect to sell half the edition in Japan, have never really caught up with Adam Smith. They have never managed actually to bring themselves to believe in the invisible hand" (470).

The network forms prevalent in the Japanese economy may provide an explanation for the competitive vitality of Japan and at the same time reveal structural weaknesses in Western economies. Rapidly gaining ground as a critique of U.S. economic organization is the claim that antitrust and banking regulation has ruled out many of the network mechanisms that provide flexible coordination and efficient economic action in Japan (Jorde and Teece 1989). American regulatory and tax policy, on the other hand, has been much more supportive than Japan's of wholesale takeovers and mergers that may impose, often in inefficient ways, centralized control on a diverse array of business units and activities. More flexibility in building interfirm networks while preserving the independence and distinct cultures of individual corporate entities might allow the United States to capture some of the elusive organizing economies that the Japanese appear to enjoy.

We do not, however, intend by this that network models are at present appropriate only to Japan while the extremes of market and bureaucratic organization govern the economy of the United States. Interfirm networks may not be as expansive or as central to economic organization in the United States as in Japan, but they clearly perform an important and growing role. Interlocking directorate research has documented the communication and control functions of this form of network integration at the top of large corporations (Mintz and Schwartz 1985; Pfeffer and Salancik 1978). Moreover, network forms appear to be proliferating as corporate downsizing and streamlining, often in response to competitive challenges from Japan and Europe, have encouraged joint ventures, subcontracting, industry consortia such as Sematech, and other cooperative arrangements among firms. Finally, new manufacturing technologies and production systems have led to stronger bonds and closer working relationships between manufacturers and subcontractors (Schonberger 1982, Ch. 7). Many of these changes are being recognized by business scholars who in growing numbers are writing of the emergence of network forms of organization in Europe and the United States (Piore and Sabel 1984; Miles and Snow 1987; Powell 1987; Johanson and Mattsson 1987; Eccles and Crane 1987). The Japanese economy, where network forms are already well developed, provides a significant comparative frame of reference for this discussion.

SUBSTANTIVE RESEARCH QUESTIONS

Our research program may be divided into three sets of substantive issues, each of significant theoretical and practical interest. These are (1) an empirical mapping of patterns within overall interfirm networks; (2) delineation of relationships between interfirm network organization and firm-level structure and strategy, including the prevalence of the multidivisional organizational form and processes of corporate diversification; and (3) measurement of the effects of network position and structure on corporate performance outcomes.

1. Network Structure in the United States and Japan

The first priority is an empirical mapping of broad interfirm network patterns in the two economies. Previous studies of business network structure in the United States have stressed either specific relations of resource dependency (Pfeffer and Salancik 1978; Pennings 1980) or general relations of class cohesion (Palmer 1983; Useem 1984). Rarely have researchers placed U.S. networks in a comparative context (but see Scott 1986; Stokman, Ziegler, and Scott 1985). This has limited their usefulness for understanding the impact of network forms on overall social structure and economic performance. Clearly, there are reasons to believe that such forms vary markedly between the United States and Japan, with major consequences for the economic organization of each country. These considerations lead to several testable hypotheses.

> Proposition 1a. *Interorganizational network "density" is greater in Japan than in the United States.*

Japanese industrial organization has been characterized as "a thick and complex skein of relations matched in no other industrial country" (Caves and Uekusa 1976:59). This is particularly apparent in the case of equity networks. Cross-shareholdings in the Japanese economy represent a major institutional device for building stable linkages among firms that do business together and defending against unfriendly takeovers. Basic summary statistics from the network data base support this view. Figure

19-2 compares the levels of overall network density in intercorporate shareholding networks in Japan and the United States. Among the largest 200 industrials and 50 financial institutions in each country, the proportion of top-ten equity ties between companies actually constituted was more than twice as high in Japan than in the United States during the period in which the data overlap (1980–1984).[1] In addition, we find that density of top-ten equity ties among large companies in Japan increased by about 25% during the 1970s, indicating an increasing consolidation of leading stockholding positions among large industrial and financial institutions, before stabilizing in the 1980s.

On the other hand, as Ueda (1989) has documented, the overall density of interlocking directorates is lower in the Japanese than in the U.S. economy. There appear to be several reasons for this. One is the far smaller number of outside directors on Japanese boards. Yet this is a bit misleading. The practice by large Japanese companies of "dispatching" directors to affiliated companies and subcontractors serves much the same function, but does not represent a directorate interlock in the conventional sense. That is, the large firm will transfer an employee to a management

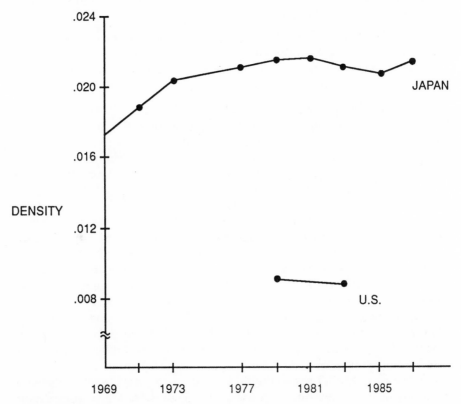

Figure 19-2
Density of Equity Interlocks, Japan and the United States

position in the new company and a seat on its board. The officer is a full-time employee of the second firm and thus an inside director, but a strong bond to the parent company is nonetheless preserved. Our data coding and analysis of directorate ties allow for such cases by noting prior management (and board) positions held by each director in our sample of firms.

However, there are other reasons to expect lower density of directorate interlocking in Japan, particularly among large companies. First, the *shachō-kai*, or presidents' council, in the intermarket corporate groups in some ways functions as an overarching board, although under normal conditions it does not as a body take action to intervene in the affairs of member firms. Second, as we suggested previously, exchange (or dispatching) of directors tends chiefly to be a *vertical linkage* device. That is, it enables a large firm to monitor and control the actions of satellite subcontractors and other *kogaisha* ("child" companies) and *kanren gaisha* ("related" companies). Given the alternative forms of linkage available for this purpose, it is less commonly a means of managing relations among the large-firm members of an intermarket group (e.g., between group banks and industrial firms). As we show later, however, the directorate interlocks that do exist among large Japanese firms are highly concentrated within such groups.

> Proposition 1b. *Financial institutions will have dominant (central) positions in interfirm networks in both the United States and Japan. However, whereas institutional banks are important in the United States, large commercial banks will prove more important in Japan.*

Advocates of the finance-capitalism model of the U.S. economy have emphasized the asymmetric character of interfirm networks, particularly the central role of financial institutions (Kotz 1978; Mintz and Schwartz 1985). However, there are reasons to believe that financial institutions are even more dominant in Japan than in the United States. Japan has but 13 major commercial banks, known as "city" banks. Restrictions on bank ownership over companies are much weaker in Japan than in the United States (where the Glass-Steagall Act prohibits the linking of equity ownership by banks to their commercial loan business) as are restrictions on domestic expansion (due to interstate banking laws in the United States). As a result of these and other factors, Japan's banking industry is far more concentrated than that in the United States, and commercial banks are likely to be even more central in Japanese networks than they are in the United States. The comparatively important role of stock markets in allocating capital in the United States, in contrast, suggests that institutional investors, such as pension and trust funds, and investment banks will be more central in U.S. networks.

Table 19-1 shows the ownership breakdown for the United States and Japanese firms in the sample for the period 1980–1984. Given the extraordinary size of Japanese commercial banks, we were somewhat surprised to find that they represented a smaller proportion of intercorporate ownership in Japan than in the United States. While the 22 commercial

Table 19-1

Sending of Equity Ties by Institutional Type, 1980–84

TYPE OF INSTITUTION	JAPAN	UNITED STATES
Commercial Banks (J = 22; US = 29)	38%	83%
Trust Banks (J = 6)	17	—
Other Banks (J = 3)	12	—
Nonlife Insurance Companies (J = 10; US = 9)	13	6
Securities Companies (J = 4; US = 4)	1	0
Sogo Banks/Savings and Loans (J = 5; US = 4)	0	0
Miscellaneous Financial Institutions (US = 4)	—	0
Financial Subtotal	81%	89%
Industrial Companies (J = 199; US = 200)	19%	11%
Total	100%	100%

banks in the Japanese sample (including second-tier regional banks) constituted 38% of the equity linkages within the 250 × 250 matrix, the 29 commercial banks in the American sample controlled 83%. Note, however, that this is a proportion of total intercorporate ties, not an absolute number. Given the higher overall densities in Japan, this works out to approximately the same number of equity ties sent on average by each commercial bank in both countries. On the other hand, industrial firms appear to be relatively more actively involved in intercorporate ownership networks in Japan than in the United States, especially when the higher overall intercorporate densities are considered. This may reflect the taking of partial equity positions in affiliated suppliers and distributors as a substitute for full-scale integration. The big differences in Japanese stock ownership, therefore, appear to be the smaller role of shareholding by noncorporate institutions and the more varied pattern of shareholding by corporate institutions.

We conclude from this that there is general support for the "finance capitalism" argument of financial centrality when viewed in terms of equity ownership. Commercial banks and other financial institutions do hold the largest overall equity positions in Japan's leading corporations (not to mention serving as companies' leading creditors in the loan capital market). The picture is complicated somewhat, however, by two other considerations. First, industrial corporations play a more important ownership role in Japanese than in American stockmarkets. Second, shareholding relationships are more likely to be reciprocal in Japan, suggesting that corporate control is exercised less hierarchically than it is in the United States.

Proposition 1c. *Overall network structures are more stable in Japan than in the United States.*

The longitudinal nature of our data set permits an assessment of a number of issues pertaining to change and stability in Japanese and U.S. corporate networks. A first prediction is that greater stability is characteristic of Japanese interfirm networks. There are several reasons to expect this. First, in general we believe that network linkages are a more important mechanism of coordination among companies in the Japanese than in the U.S. economy. The boards of companies affiliated with a common keiretsu draw their outside directors almost exclusively from other member firms. Moreover, the strong lifetime loyalties that bind top Japanese managers to their companies render elite theories of the upper-class cohesion function of interlocking directorates less compelling than in the United States.

Research on interlocking directorates in the American economy has indicated that highly stable ties (i.e., those that are reconstituted on the departure of a director) are particularly indicative of interfirm coordination and have a significant bearing on company performance (Palmer 1983; Richardson 1987). There is no reason to presume that such results are limited to the case of interlocking directorates. Our data will permit, for both the United States and Japan, an assessment of "broken" equity interlocks. Here, departures from positions as leading shareholders are equated with the breaking of an interfirm connection. Moreover, for Japan, similar analyses of change and stability can be made of trading and credit relations. Our perspective opens new data to a variety of methods and theoretical issues not generally associated with research on corporate control.

Preliminary analyses of the durability of interorganizational relationships utilizing equity networks strongly support the stability hypothesis. Whereas in the United States 77% of the leading equity positions were broken between 1980 and 1984 (i.e., under 25% of the top-ten shareholders remained the same throughout this four-year period), only 18% of the equity interlocks were broken in Japan during the same period. The view that Japanese companies enjoy long-term shareholders while American firms do not is strongly supported here. Moreover, the trend in Japan from 1969 to 1986 was toward increasing shareholder stability, contrasting sharply with the frequently depicted image of radical change in Japanese business relationships often found in the media and other writings on Japan.

We are also able to assess with the Japanese data base the stability of banking relationships over this same period of time. Figure 19-3 compares the proportion of top-ten borrowing ties broken for two different sets of Japanese companies. One set is made up of those companies that sit on a presidents' council in one of Japan's six major business groupings ("alliance") and the other of firms that do not ("independent"). These results suggest two things: (1) that the recent move away from bank borrowings

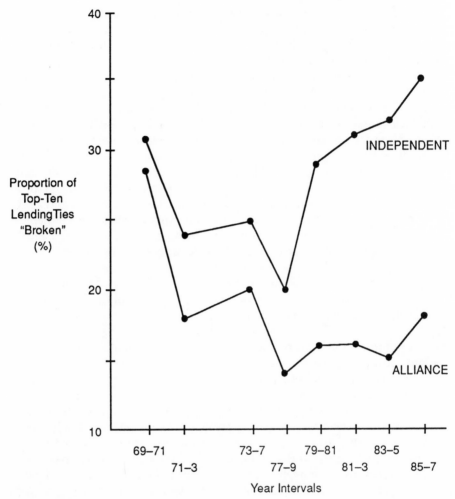

Figure 19-3
"Broken" Banking Ties, Alliance v. Independent

as a source of capital in Japan has come primarily from independent firms, and (2) that banking relationships overall tend to be somewhat more fluid than shareholding relationships.

> Proposition 1d. *Ownership and control relations (shareholding and director-ship interlocks) exhibit greater reciprocity in Japan than in the United States.*

Reciprocal shareholding and directorship exchanges are common patterns among Japanese business firms, and serve as means of protecting managers from hostile outsiders (Nakatani 1984; Gerlach 1987). They are apt to be far less common in the United States due to the lack of coherent intercorporate alliances around which to organize and to their uncertain legality under antitrust laws of reciprocity where partners also do business together. We find some support for this hypothesis in our shareholding data. Among the intercorporate equity interlocks in Japan, 7% are reciprocated in 1980, while this figure is only 1% in the United States in 1980 and declines to less than ½% by 1984.

Still, the reciprocity figure for Japan is less than we expected. One possibility we tested is that mainly very large Japanese companies reciprocate ties. Our sample of the 200 industrial firms includes 57 firms that are satellites (kogaisha or kanren gaisha) of a major parent manufacturer. These firms are unlikely to send reciprocated ties since theirs are primarily subordinate relationships. To test this prediction, we analyzed reciprocated ties solely among the 40 largest industrials and 20 largest financial institutions. When we limit intercorporate interlocks to these 60 companies, reciprocity rates for 1980 more than double, increasing from 7% to 18%. Company size, therefore, appears to be an important determinant of companies' position in equity networks in Japan, just as it has been in previous research on directorship interlocks in the United States.

Proposition 1e. *Equity and directorship interlocks are more likely to be linked to other business relationships in Japan than in the United States; that is, interfirm networks are more multiplex in Japan.*

A number of important sociological and economic theories of organization (resource dependence, transaction-costs economics, and agency theory) view the taking of equity or board positions in other companies as means of managing dependency and gaining control over critical banking and trading relationships (Pfeffer and Salancik 1978). Given the permanence and reciprocity of trade and financial dependencies among Japanese companies within an enterprise group, we expect cross-shareholding and board interlocking networks to follow closely the contours of banking and trading relations. Relatively strong securities regulations in the United States limit the methods by which shareholders can control firms, as does the so-called Wall Street Rule among large investors (i.e., expressing dissatisfaction with company performance by selling shares rather than exercising voice). Japanese firms, not so encumbered, will be more likely to reinforce and manage their financial and trade transactions by surrounding them with reciprocal ownership and control relations.

In network terminology, the hypothesis is that intercorporate bonds tend toward greater multiplexity in the Japanese economy (Scott 1986). Given the absence of firm-level data on banking and trade ties, we can only determine whether the U.S. networks are multiplex with respect to cross-shareholdings and directorate interlocks. The Japanese data permit a stronger assessment of the extent of multiplexity, as data are available for all four network ties. (Lincoln, Gerlach, and Takahashi 1992)

The evidence we have supports the prediction of a high degree of multiplexity in Japan. For Japanese firms that dispatched one or more directors to another firm, there was a 51% probability that it also held a top-ten equity position in the same firm. For the American firms, this

Table 19-2

Multiplexity and Director Interlocks, 1980

INTERLOCK(S)		JAPAN	UNITED STATES
Directors only	=	37.4%	96.9%
Directors + equity	=	10.0	3.1
Directors + debt	=	3.2	
Directors + trade	=	8.9	
Directors + equity + debt	=	26.1	
Directors + equity + trade	=	14.1	
Directors + equity + debt + trade	=	0.3	
Total	=	100%	100%

probability was only 3%, indicating a seventeen-fold difference along this multiplexity dimension.

For the Japanese data, we are also able to discern other forms of multiplexity, including overlaps between directorship and debt and trade positions. Table 19-2 shows the extent to which directorship shareholdings are associated with three types of ties. In nearly two-thirds of all cases where a director comes from outside the company, we are able to detect simultaneous relationships in at least one other network; in 40% of the cases these relationships came in two other networks. Equity overlaps were especially common. Overall, the sender of a director was also a leading shareholder in 51% of the cases, a top-ten lender in 30% of the cases, and a leading trading partner in 33% of the cases.

Proposition 1f. *Overall network structures in Japan are significantly more likely than those in the United States to be organized around coherent cliques or alliances that persist over time.*

In the United States, clustered interest groups of firms have proved notoriously difficult to detect and are also unstable. As Useem (1980:51) has put it, "the precise location of clique boundaries is elusive and highly sensitive to the methodology employed." The primary clusters detected in American interlocking directorate research appear to be regionally based (Mintz and Schwartz 1985; Scott 1986). Interest group structures are far more coherent in Japan, where durable keiretsu groupings organize relationships among large financial institutions, trading companies, and major industrial producers, while industrial concerns form their own affiliated supplier networks, strategic alliances, and industry-wide consortia.

Addressing the comparative strength of network clique structures requires the systematic coding of network data across several network types. Interlocking directorships have been the predominant form of linkage in U.S. studies, but patterns of equity ties, banking connections, and trading relations are also important in delineating overall network structure. This study examines a broader range of network measures than has previous research, including not only directorship interlocks, but equity cross-holdings and (for Japanese firms) banking and trading relations. To the extent that cohesive, persistent cliques exist, such data, collected over a series of periods, should identify them.

In Japan, of course, "cliques" are clearly evident in the form of keiretsu groupings, the membership of which can be obtained readily from sources such as *Keiretsu no Kenkyū*. To what extent, however, do these nominal groupings correspond to real bounded clusters in the network of interorganizational relationships? To answer this question, it is not sufficient to examine network ties solely among the predefined "group" firms—the practice of nearly all prior researchers of business groups in Japan and other East Asian countries. The existence of connections among these firms may be an artifact of high overall levels of density in interfirm networks rather than an indication of truly differentiated clusters of firms. (In other words, any random subsample of firms would show similarly high levels of connection.) The approach we advocate and follow in this study, is to code network data systematically for *all* large corporations and to derive patterns *empirically* (see Gerlach 1992b).

This is not to say that categories of membership defined by the business community and other commonsense classifications are not important. They represent hypotheses as to where boundaries in the Japanese corporate network fall. A preliminary test of one such hypothesis is provided in Table 19-3, which links an a priori classification of groups— namely, participation in a presidents' council of one of Japan's six big groups—with classification-neutral network data. This table shows the extent to which shares of group companies are held by firms in the same group (underlined, along the diagonal), by firms in one of the other major groups, and by independent firms not in one of these six groups. In the cases of all six groups, we find that a far larger portion of shares are held by other firms within the same group than by firms in any of the other groups. In some cases (the ex-zaibatsu groupings of Mitsui, Mitsubishi, and Sumitomo), the firms in the same group own more shares even than the firms in the much larger category of independents. Although the results are not reported here, similar tables from earlier and later years for the equity networks show that internalization of shareholding within groups has remained stable, and in several groups has even increased over time. In addition, similar results have been found for directorship, debt, and trade networks (see Gerlach 1992a, Chapter 4).

It is evident, therefore, that coherent and durable cliques of firms do exist in Japan, and that empirical network data can be used to verify their existence. But clique identification is only a portion of what network analysis is capable of offering. To the extent that clusters in the Japanese interfirm network conform to the boundaries of known alliances, for example, we have a number of expectations concerning their roles and locations in the network. In general, we predict that the internal cohesion of enterprise cliques is inversely related to their centrality in (thus connectedness to) the corporate network as a whole. Specifically, the old zaibatsu groups (Mitsui, Mitsubishi, Sumitomo) should appear as very tightly knit cliques with generally sparse links to other alliances and independent companies. The newer, bank-centered groups (Fuji, Sanwa, Dai-

Table 19-3

Internalization of Equity Shareholdings, 1986

ISSUING CO. AFFILIATION	SHAREHOLDING COMPANY AFFILIATION					
	Mitsui (15)	Mitsubishi (15)	Sumitomo (13)	Fuji (17)	Sanwa (19)	DKB (22)
Mitsui	51.4	2.3	2.1	0.7	4.3	2.3
Mitsubishi	1.6	63.4	0.8	4.0	4.7	4.3
Sumitomo	1.5	2.2	63.9	3.7	3.9	2.8
Fuji	0.0	1.5	2.2	38.1	4.8	4.4
Sanwa	10.0	8.8	9.1	11.1	28.0	10.2
DKB	1.3	3.1	0.1	10.4	12.8	31.6

Note: The numbers represent the percentage of corporate shares held by other companies, based on group affiliation. Underlined figures along the diagonal are intragroup shareholdings.

Source: Gerlach (1992a, p. 126).

Ichi Kangyo) should prove less tightly bound internally but more centrally positioned in the overall network space. Most central of all will be the independent firms (e.g., Nippon Steel, Matsushita Electric) linked to actors across the network, including both other independent firms and group firms. Among firms affiliated through vertical keiretsu we expect in general to find parent firms more central in the overall network than their satellite as the latter rely on the parent companies for access to bank capital and to other business relationships.

2. Networks, Structure, and Strategy

The remainder of the chapter lays out our arguments relating network patterns in the United States and Japan to the structure, strategy, and performance of individual firms. This work lies farther ahead, however, and we cannot yet bring any evidence directly to bear on our hypotheses.

The second substantive area in our research agenda links business network structure to corporate organizational form and strategy. Williamson (1985), Chandler (1977), and others have emphasized the role of internal organization and formal hierarchy as functional alternatives to impersonal market contracting, which under various conditions (uncertainty, asset specificity, frequency of transaction) give rise to greater economic efficiency. We and others have further argued that interfirm networks represent yet another structure for managing economic transactions and thus substitute for both pure-type internal organization and pure-type market relationships. This reasoning implies several propositions regarding the impact of network embedding on a firm's structure and competitive strategy. Supplemented by firm-level data on assets, sales, and profitability; employment size; internal organizational form; and market position, the network data included in this study will allow us to address this issue through intra- and intercountry comparisons.

Proposition 2a. *Japanese firms are more likely to rely on interfirm networks to coordinate exchange than are U.S. firms. As a result, the average size of the Japanese firm (measured by number of employees and holding constant company sales) will be smaller than for a comparable U.S. firm.*

Japanese firms appear to depend far more heavily than U.S. firms on closely related supply and distribution firms. Toyota Motors is perhaps an extreme example of this. Toyota produces over two-thirds as many automobiles as General Motors with only one-tenth the number of employees. A significant reason is that much of the added value in a Japanese car comes from quasi-integrated subcontractors who perform the basic assembly operations that in the United States are often carried out in-house. This practice appears to permit Japanese firms to keep the size of their core staff smaller and to utilize suppliers as external buffers.

Unfortunately, despite its intuitive appeal, this is not an easy hypothesis to test, for the causality between firm size and network linkage is complex. For reasons of rising visibility, scope of operations, and capacity to dominate their environments, firms accumulate external linkages as they grow in size (Pfeffer and Salancik 1978). Interlocking directorate research has consistently documented the tendency for large firms to have more interlocks (Mintz and Schwartz 1985). Furthermore, as our focus is on ties among large companies, we miss many of the subcontract relations that link a major manufacturer such as Toyota to the numerous satellite suppliers that surround it. Even so, given the longitudinal data at our disposal, it is feasible to model antecedent shifts in a firm's network position and centrality on its size and growth (see, e.g., Richardson 1987).

Proposition 2b. *Companies with strong and dense linkages to other firms (as in keiretsu membership) will be less likely to adopt M-form structures. As a result, the M-form will be less widely adopted in Japan than in the United States, and with weaker performance consequences.*

The rise of the multidivisional form (M-form) organizational structure introduces market-like incentives into the corporation and appears to permit the relatively rapid growth of firms (Chandler 1962; Williamson 1975). The M-form has been far less widely adopted in Japan (Yoshihara et al. 1981), and with apparently little effect on corporate performance (Cable and Yasuki 1985). One possibility is that the role of the M-form as an "internal capital market" (Williamson 1975) is supplanted in Japan by networks of relations between financial institutions, especially large city banks, and large industrial users of capital (Dore 1987). A recent investigation using U.S. data (Palmer, Jennings, and Zhou 1988) has produced some evidence of an inverse relation between corporate interlocks and M-form adoption over the period from 1962 through 1968. It may be that the process of substituting interfirm network ties for internal organization operates similarly in both economies, but the greater density and integration of Japanese corporate networks produces the lower rate of M-form adoption overall. Furthermore, the overall greater density of Japanese interfirm networks combined with the nature of Japanese capital and labor markets will likely attenuate the efficiency advantages of the M-form that some studies have shown to exist for U.S. firms (Armour and Teece 1979).

We will follow standard procedures for classifying multidivisional and functional organizational forms, as discussed in Chandler (1962) and Rumelt (1974). Information for U.S. firms will be coded primarily from companies' annual reports, Moody's manuals, and 10-K forms filed with the Securities and Exchange Commission. Where firm identities and time periods overlap, these classifications will be tested against those provided in the Chandler and Rumelt studies. The comparable information for Japanese firms will be derived from organizational charts housed in several research centers in Japan, including the Nihon Seisan-Sei Honbu Seisan-Sei Kenkyū-Jo and the Kigyō Kenkyū-Kai Soshiki-Zu Kōkan Center. For information on Japanese organizational structures unavailable through these sources, we will use the Diamond *Kaisha Shokuin-Roku*. The resulting classifications will be checked against those provided in Yoshihara et al. (1981).

Proposition 2c. *Dense interfirm linkages also serve as functional substitutes for firm-level diversification. As a result, Japanese firms will be less diversified than U.S. firms (holding constant firm size and extent of adoption of the M-form), and will be less likely to diversify into unrelated areas.*

If external linkages to banks and other key actors are strategies for stabilizing the firm's environment in Japan, as several writers have suggested (Nakatani 1984; Gerlach 1992a; Lincoln, Gerlach and Takashi 1992), then interfirm networks may replace conglomerate diversification as a means of risk reduction (Pfeffer and Salancik 1978; Thompson 1967). The resulting tendency of Japanese firms to focus on their own core industries (Clark 1979) may be reinforced by characteristics of Japanese labor and corporate control markets. The prevalence and strength of internal labor markets in Japan have permitted Japanese firms to invest heavily in firm- and industry-specific human capital. This human capital is typically deployed in related rather than in unrelated business activities in order to maximize the transferability of skills. Moreover, the inability to lay workers off except under extreme conditions requires strategies of carefully controlled expansion in order to minimize the dangers of future redundancy. The relatively low level of merger and acquisition activity in Japan also makes strategic movement into new businesses more difficult for Japanese than for U.S. firms, for expansion plans must be negotiated through mutual agreement rather than by aggressive takeover.

For classifying diversification strategies, we will again rely on Rumelt (1974), whose major categories have been used successfully in a variety of later studies (e.g., Christensen and Montgomery 1981; Bettis and Mahajan 1985; Hoskisson 1987). Data on U.S. companies' businesses will be coded primarily based on information provided incorporate annual reports, corporate security prospectuses, and Moody's industrials. For the Japanese companies, business-line information is provided both in the *Japan Com-*

pany Handbook and in company security reports, copies of which are available in the Tokyo Securities Library. Classification of diversification strategies will be checked against those provided in Rumelt (1974) for U.S. firms, and Yoshihara et al. (1981), for Japanese firms.

3. Network Influences on Corporate Performance

Our third substantive focus is on the determinants of corporate performance in the United States and Japan, with particular attention to network-level variables. The effects of interorganizational structures on corporate and aggregate economic performance have been largely overlooked in both the theoretical and the empirical literature. The structure-conduct-performance paradigm in industrial organization (Scherer 1980) tends to ignore specific patterns of relationships in its emphasis on aggregate industry measures of concentration and theories of price leadership. Within organizational sociology, in contrast, one finds numerous elaborate investigations of the structure of intercorporate relations but little theoretical or empirical attention to performance outcomes (Mintz and Schwartz 1985; for an exception, see Burt 1983).

A key strength of the proposed data base is the range of interfirm *and* firm-level explanatory variables to be included. While our interest centers on the effects of network properties, we will be able to build well-specified causal models containing controls for numerous variables known to affect corporate performance: financial structure, diffusion of ownership, age, industry, market position, and internal structure. Such a full set of controls not only allows unbiased estimates of network effects, but also affords a comparison of the relative predictive power of network versus firm-level attributes on corporate performance outcomes.

> Proposition 3a. *Network affiliation and centrality will have positive net effects on corporate performance, as measured by rates of profitability and sales growth and share price appreciation. Also, given the greater structuring and stability of Japanese business networks, these effects should be more pronounced in Japan than in the United States.*

This hypothesis follows from much of our previous discussion and from the general assumption that Japanese business networks are a factor in the adaptiveness and efficiency of individual firms, industries, and the economy as a whole. Moreover, it is consistent with a transaction-costs interpretation of the role of enterprise groups and networks: that they spread risk and absorb uncertainty, diminish incentives for opportunism, and allocate information and resources in ways that avert both bureaucratic and market failures. However, the evidence to date has not been clearly supportive of the proposition that network affiliation has positive consequences for the performance of Japanese firms. Previous statistical analyses of the profitability and growth rates of Japanese firms have turned up negative effects of keiretsu membership, at least in the post-1960 period (Caves and Uekusa 1976; Nakatani 1984). These findings appear consistent with the speculative suggestion of some observers of Japanese business that the truly innovative, high-performing Japanese firms are the entrepreneurial independents such as Honda or Sony rather than the stodgier old-line companies that make up the traditional zaibatsu groups (Abegglen and Stalk 1975). On the other hand, Nakatani's influential analysis also revealed that keiretsu affiliates exhibit lower sales and profits variance than more independent firms. This raises the possibility that enterprise groupings buffer individual firms from market pressures to short-term profit maximize, giving them the latitude to pursue collectively a strategy of slow but stable growth.

Other recent evidence has also suggested that the impact of alliance membership on corporate performance and success is conditioned on the stage of development of the Japanese economy as well as stage in the life cycle of individual firms (Roehl 1989). When firms are small and growth is rapid, the advantages of network affiliation appear greatest, for the group provides economies of scale in production and distribution, quick access to capital and sourcing, and diversifies the risk of new investment. Large firms in periods of slow growth are more likely to see the group as a liability, for they have less need of the group's resource-aggregating capacity, and they themselves may have to bear the burden of subsidizing the weaker and smaller members of the network. Such interactions with network membership in the determination of firm-level outcomes can be assessed with our data, although the time limits on our panel obviously constrains our ability to test hypotheses regarding periodization of the network-performance relationship.

Finally, it seems clear that the implications of group affiliation for corporate performance depend upon the market or industry in which a firm operates. Japanese banks and trading companies have traditionally benefited from the stable demand for their services that group affiliation guarantees. Moreover, as banks are typically central players in such networks, they enjoy a special degree of control and access to information. Likewise, high-tech manufacturers find support within the group for their risky ventures and rapid capital turnover. On the other hand, established industrial firms with large market shares and an abundance of capital are apt to find the constraints of group membership onerous and the resources and protection inessential.

The problem with both the Nakatani and Caves and Uekusa analyses is that the enterprise groups they consider are generally the oldest, most established alliances, whose famous names and clear boundaries make them easily identifiable. These well-known keiretsu are not necessarily representative of the clusters that segment the modern Japanese economy, and generalizations from the relative performance of their affiliated companies are hazardous at best. A major part of the rationale for our network analytic approach to these issues is that, in tracing the shifting and permeable boundaries that follow clusters in the network, we are not limited by the available taxonomies of named enterprise groups. We consider a variety of corporate performance measures, including several measures of profitability (e.g., return on assets, return on shareholder equity), profit variance (a measure of investment risk), sales growth and variance (if managerial goals are paramount), and stock-market price. Since results often vary considerably by the performance measure employed, we will be including each of these measures in the study. These are all available for the 250 U.S. firms from the Standard and Poor's COMPUSTAT tape, a copy of which is available at Berkeley. The comparable data base for Japanese firms is put out by Nihon Keizai Shimbun, the mounted tape form of which is best organized for longitudinal studies of corporate performance.

Analyzing Network Effects on Firm-Level Outcomes

A number of analytic strategies can be applied to the evaluation of network effects on corporate structure, strategy, and performance. These are grouped as follows:

1. Centrality Effects For each type of relation, the location of a firm within the network of intercorporate ties can be assessed by a centrality measure, indexing the overall access (in terms of distance, number, and strength of relations) of that firm to others and others to it. A large number of centrality measures have been proposed in the literature. While we intend to experiment with alternative indices, we expect to make particular use of the network "prestige" index: $P_i = \Sigma_j R_{ij} P_j$, where the prestige of node i is a sum of the relations (R_{ij}; e.g., proximities) directed toward i by the J nodes in the network, each relation weighted by the initiating node's own prestige (P_j). Laumann, Knoke, and Kim (1985:9) have recently used P_i to index advantageous location within an interorganizational network of information exchanges.

As centrality indices are defined for individual firms, it is a straightforward matter to model corporate organizational form, strategy, and performance (profitability, market share, growth rates) as functions of network centrality and other relevant firm and industry-level explanatory variables.

2. Cluster Effects The analysis we envision of the influence of network clusters (cliques and positions) on company structure, strategy, and performance is simple enough. Moreover, it follows the lines of recent investigations of formal enterprise groups in the Japanese economy (Gerlach 1992; Nakatani 1984; Roehl 1989). Dummy variables can be coded for $K - 1$ of a set of K clusters and added to the right-hand side of an appropriately specified regression model for each firm-level outcome variable. Our primary interest here is in testing the hypothesis that network affiliation boosts profitability and growth when alliances are defined not in terms of conventional zaibatsu groupings, but in terms of network boundaries that may or may not coincide with those of traditional named groups. Following indications from other current research that the association between firm performance and group affiliation depends on the type of group classification used (Gerlach 1992; Kotabe 1989), we plan a series of analyses in which alternative a priori group classifications, as well as taxonomies derived from network analysis, are placed in competition for explanatory power.

CONCLUSIONS

While the Japanese and U.S. economies are each nominally capitalist, they appear to differ dramatically in the structural relationships through which that capitalism is manifest. There is strong support for the characterization of Japan's as a network economy (Lincoln 1990) that relies to an extraordinary degree on a dense web of social bonds and obligations to manage and coordinate transactions. Previous comparative studies of the United States and Japan have focused on the micro-level question of differences in companies' internal structures and personnel practices or the macro issue of contrasting roles played by the state in industrial development. Systematic comparative studies at the meso-level of intercorporate relationships are generally not to be found.

It is interesting to note that the network character of Japanese industrial organization is also apparent in other East Asian economies, including Korea through its zaibatsu-like *chaebol*, and Taiwan through its own distinctive form of extended family groupings (Hamilton and Biggart 1988). The remarkable growth rates of these economies demand a better understanding of how interfirm linkages shape corporate and overall economic performance. Network theories and methods, when teamed with comparative network data on intercorporate ties and close substantive familiarity with the institutions of each society, should prove powerful tools in advancing our understanding of such network economies and their competitive advantages relative to United States.

APPENDIX 19-1:
METHODS OF DATA ANALYSIS

We have broad experience with quantitative network analytic techniques (Lincoln 1982; 1984; 1985; Lincoln and Miller 1979; Schrader, Lincoln, and Hoffman 1989), and envision a number of strategies for analyzing the Japanese and U.S. corporate network data. As outlined, our analyses have two general focuses: (1) mapping the structure of interfirm networks in the United States and Japan; (2) evaluating the effects of network properties and network position on the firm and industry-level outcomes of structure, strategy, and performance. The specific techniques we consider are, for the most part, familiar to network analysts. Many are available from such standard network software packages as STRUCTURE and UCINET. Others involve procedures we ourselves have developed in previous network research (Lincoln 1984; Lincoln and Miller 1979). They are grouped as follows:

1. *Descriptive Network Statistics.* A useful first approach to ascertaining patterns in network data is to examine distributions and summary statistics on a variety of network variables. These include measures of indegree (number of incoming ties), outdegree (number of outgoing ties), density, connectivity, multiplexity, the prevalence of asymmetric, mutual, and null dyads, and similar indices (cf. Stokman, Ziegler, and Scott 1985).

    A number of interesting comparisons can be made from the distributions and central tendencies of such network variables. First, this information serves our interest in contrasting the overall texture and form of the U.S. corporate network with the Japanese corporate network. We expect to find, for example, a greater level of density, connectivity, and reciprocity in the Japanese nets, but also more indications of clustering and hierarchy following the lines of the keiretsu structure of the Japanese economy.

    Although our intention is to apply network analysis to the task of revealing the boundaries of enterprise groupings in Japan and the United States, another useful line of inquiry, at least in Japan, is to take the boundaries of named groups as givens, and perform separate network analyses within each. The network configurations of individual groups can then be compared. Groups may be quantitatively scored in terms of such internal network properties as density, connectivity, reciprocity, and so on (see, e.g., Schrader, Lincoln, and Hoffman 1989). This would facilitate a multivariate assessment of the antecedents (age; diversification; horizontal, bank-centered group vs. vertical, subcontract group) and consequents (profitability, growth) of the network properties of Japanese enterprise groups.

2. *Measurement and Analysis of Dyadic Ties.* Dyads and dyadic relations are the elemental units of network structure. Our concerns here are with the operationalization of a network tie between a pair of firms and with the modeling of that relation as a function of baseline stochastic generators (indegrees, outdegrees, reciprocity; cf. Wasserman 1980) and causally interesting covariates.

    a. *Measuring Dyadic Relations.* The content of the specific network ties we wish to study (directorate interlocks, cross-shareholding, trading partners, debt relations) is fixed by the nature of large economic organizations in the United States and Japan and by our research design. However, the same initial datum on a relation— for example, the presence or absence of an interlock—can lend itself to a variety of transformations that measure quite distinct aspects of the relation. Initial binary (1, 0) measures are often converted in network analyses to *proximity* measures (e.g., the graph-theoretic *path distance*) that convey information on the length and number of paths in the network through which a pair of nodes is connected (Alba 1982). By taking into account such indirect relations, proximity indices circumvent to some degree the criticism that dyad-level models are insensitive to the embeddedness of pairs in larger networks. Another virtue of proximity transformations is that in modeling the relation in a dyad analysis, the dependent variable has a more statistically tractable, quantitative form. That is not a crucial consideration for us, as the relational variables we consider (number of interlocks, shares held, etc.) already have a quantitative metric, and, in any case, statistical models for qualitative outcomes are readily available.

b. *Dyad Analysis.* Much of our analysis of interfirm relations in the United States and Japan, then, will make use of dyad analysis, modeling ties and flows between pairs of firms as a function of other relations between the pair as well as attributes of the individual parties (Laumann, Marsden, and Galaskiewicz 1977).

   A number of the questions raised in our study may be rigorously addressed in this way: the extent of multiplexity and reciprocity in interfirm networks; how common or divergent keiretsu membership shapes strength and type of tie; the influences of firm size, industry, ownership and control (private vs. public; management vs. stockholder). A key virtue of the dyad-analytic models discussed by Lincoln (1984; 1985) is that they maintain a clear distinction between *main effects* of nodal attributes (those increasing the density of a firm's network relations across the board) and *interaction* effects (affecting relations only with particular types of alters). Such models take the form

$$E_{ij} = \beta E_{ji} + d'X_i + f'X_j + GX_iX_j' + e_{ij},$$

where E_{ij} = the equity (e.g., percent of shares) in firm j owned by firm i; $X_i = aK \times 1$ column vector of K variables describing firm "i"; X_j is the same $K \times 1$ column vector of variables describing firm "j"; e_{ij} is the stochastic error term for the "ij"th dyad; β, $d'(1 \times K)$, $f'(1 \times K)$, and $G(K \times K)$ are regression coefficients to be estimated. An identical equation can be written for E_{ji}, reversing the i and j subscripts. E_{ij} and E_{ji} are thus shown to be simultaneously determined endogenous variables and β measures the reciprocity effect.

   Moreover, two important theoretical frameworks in the study of internal organization and interorganizational networks may best be tested via a dyad-level analysis. *Resource dependence* theory from sociology and Williamson's *transaction-cost* paradigm in

economics make predictions about the likelihood and strength of
bonds of cooptation and control between a pair of firms. Both
stress the role of bilateral dependence and uncertainty in
motivating organizations to manage the relationship by building
stable ties—even to the point of full internalization through
merger or acquisition. Again, the dyad-level models reviewed by
Lincoln (1984; 1985), we submit, are particularly useful for teasing
evidence on resource dependencies from a statistical model estimated over dyads.

We intend to use this and similar dyadic modeling strategies
on the U.S.-Japan intercorporate data (see Lincoln, Gerlach, and
Takashi 1992). However, as our research design calls for the analysis
of *panel* data on U.S. and Japanese corporate networks, these
models require modification to exploit the dynamic character of
these data. We are not aware of a versatile yet rigorous methodology
for analyzing longitudinal network data. Tuma and Hallinan (1979)
have applied an ad hoc regression procedure to panel data on children's friendships. Their methods can be faulted on statistical
grounds (Lincoln 1984), but they are simple and versatile. The
efforts of Holland and Leinhardt (1977) and Wasserman (1980;
Galaskiewicz and Wasserman 1981) to adapt Markov models to
the study of network change, are statistically elegant but computa-
tionally cumbersome and do not easily accommodate covariates.
A more fruitful approach to the dynamic analysis of binary tie
data for dyads may be the application of event-history models.
Two of our colleagues in the Berkeley Business School, Glenn
Carroll and Trond Petersen, are highly skilled in the use of such
models, and we have been discussing applications to longitudinal
network data with them. Of course, where we have quantitative
relational measures (total number of firm *A*'s shares held by firm
B), the usual methods of panel regression are appropriate, con-
founded only by the usual problem of dyad nonindependence.

c. *Cluster Analysis.* An alternative to dyad analysis—and one which
some scholars feel is better suited to uncovering the macrostructural properties of a network—is an empirical clustering strategy.
In our current work with these data, we are using network clustering algorithms (available in such network software packages as
UCINET and STRUCTURE) to identify empirically the boundaries
of enterprise groupings. We can assess the extent to which such
clusters correspond to the usual nominal classifications of Japanese keiretsu.

When the clustering algorithm is applied to raw tie data or
proximity measures, we have what is commonly known as *clique
detection*, the emergent groupings (cliques) consisting of actors
with close, dense, and frequent bonds to one another. Industrial
groups in the Japanese economy, we argue, are corporate cliques

in this sense: sets of firms in complementary industries that maintain stable, reciprocal bonds with one another (White 1981). Clique detection is thus the appropriate strategy for ferreting out the groupings in the Japanese corporate economy. Following the interesting but highly preliminary work by Scott (1986), the primary hypothesis to be tested is whether the established, named enterprise groups correspond to the clusters that a clique analysis of corporate interlock, equity cross-holding, debt-holding, and trading partner relations reveals.

Our hypotheses regarding the network locations and the internal clustering of various known keiretsu (e.g., Mitsui vs. Mitsubishi) can be addressed with the kind of spatial representations derived from multidimensional scaling that has been the hallmark of Laumann's approach to network analysis (e.g., Laumann, Knoke, and Kim 1985; see also Lincoln and Miller 1979; Lincoln 1982). By rotating axes in the space or drawing "fault lines" through the plotted points (nodes), these methods are also useful for giving a sense of the substantive dimensions underlying boundaries and locations in a network.

Clustering organizations according to the similarity of their ties to third parties (the structural equivalence criterion) identifies jointly occupied *positions* in a network of intercorporate ties. The position (block) is linked to other positions in distinct ways, and occupancy of a position by a firm signals the pattern of relations it would be expected to have with other firms. Industries thus constitute a position in this sense within a network of market transactions, as do the dual economy classifications of core-periphery (Baron and Bielby 1984). Scott (1986) has used the CONCOR algorithm to test the financial hegemony hypothesis that banks, insurance companies, and other financial institutions play a central and controlling role in corporate interlock networks. He finds the clearest support for this hypothesis in the case of Britain. In the United States regional boundaries tended to differentiate the hegemonic group, and in Japan the evidence for a single hegemonic control position was obscured by the patterns produced by group affiliations (see also Gerlach 1992b).

A judicious use of both clustering strategies—blocking into structurally equivalent positions and clique detection—should give us a clear picture of how individual firms fit into a matrix of cliques and positions, and how the underlying criteria and the strength of clique and position boundaries differ between the United States and Japan.

c. *Network Regression Models.* Finally, and perhaps most interesting of the alternative strategies for evaluating network influences on firm performance, we plan to use network regression models, the necessary computer software for which we already possess. These models, first proposed by economic geographers for controlling nonindependence biases in spatial data, have in recent years seen wide application in sociology and anthropology. They represent a highly promising approach to our hypotheses regarding network influences on corporate internal organization, performance, and other outcomes. Consider a model of the form:

$$x_1 = \Sigma_k r_k W x_k + \Sigma_{k+1} \beta_k x_k + e$$

Where x_k is an $N \times 1$ vector of observations on the kth variable defined for a population of N firms; W is an $N \times N$ matrix of network relations among the N firms, $\{w_{ij}\}$ (where $i=1, \ldots N$; $j=1, \ldots N$; $w_{ii} = w_{jj} = 0$); e is an $N \times 1$ vector of stochastic error terms; and the $\{r_k\}$ and $\{\beta_k\}$ are regression coefficients to be estimated, preferably with a maximum likelihood procedure (Doreian 1982), although serviceable alternatives are available (Burt 1987). For an individual firm, i, $W x_k$ can be written as $\Sigma_j w_{ij} x_{jk}$, and is thus seen to be a weighted average of the x_k-values of the $N - 1$ other nodes in the network.

Applied to the problem of accounting for corporate outcome variables in a network of intercorporate ties, this model says that firm i's, say, performance (x_{i1}) depends not only on its own intrinsic attributes ($x_{i2} - x_{iK}$; e.g., technology, level of investment, organization) but on the aggregated performance and other attributes of the firms with which it is linked in the network. Note that $W x_1$ is the analogue to a lagged endogenous variable in a time-series model, and r_1 thus measures network autoregression in the $\{x_{i1}\}$. As Erbring and Young (1979) have noted, the network regression model is an elegant approach to the study of "contextual effects." In the usual contextual model (see, e.g., Lincoln and Zeitz 1980), $w_{ij} = 0$ when nodes i and j are members of different groups. When i and j are in the same group, $w_{ij} = 1/N_m$, where N_m is the size of the mth group. In the network model, however, the $\{w_{ij}\}$ can be any kind of relation (normed so that each row sum equals 1) between nodes i and j.

A significant effect, r_1, of the network autoregression term, $W x_1$, would signify the existence of interdependencies among the performances of firms linked into a common network, and the greater the linkage the greater is the extent to which each firm's success depends on that of others. The notion of a network autoregression effect relating some structure or behavior of a single company to those of firms with which it is linked is strongly reminiscent of White's structuralist theory of markets as transacting cliques of firms to which production volume and quality depends not on an aggregated set of independent responses to consumer demand, but on each taking its cues from and modeling its production on the behavior of others (White 1981).

Note

1. Equity relationships are treated asymmetrically, with incoming and outgoing ties coded separately. Note that the number of ties actually constituted is truncated by the fact that only the top-ten shareholder relationships are coded. Were smaller, non-top-ten equity holdings also to be coded, the overall densities in both countries would, of course, increase.

References

Abegglen, James C., and George Stalk. 1985. *Kaisha: The Japanese Corporation.* New York: Basic Books.

Alba, Richard D. 1982. "Taking stock of network analysis: a decade's results." In Samuel B. Bacharach, ed., *Research in the Sociology of Organizations,* Vol. 1. Greenwich, CT: JAI Press, pp. 39–74.

Armour, Henry, and David Teece. 1979. "Organizational structure and economic performance." *Bell Journal of Economics* 10:106–122.

Baker, Wayne E. 1984. "Social structure of a securities market." *American Journal of Sociology* 89:775–811.

Baron, James N., and William T. Bielby. 1984. "The organization of work in a segmented economy." *American Sociological Review* 49:454–473.

Bettis, Richard A., and Vijay Mahajan. 1985. "Risk/return performance of diversified firms." *Management Science* 31:785–799.

Breiger, Ronald. 1976. "Career attributes and network structure: a blockmodel study of a bio-medical research specialty." *American Sociological Review* 41:117–135.

Burt, Ronald S. 1980. "Models of network structure." *Annual Review of Sociology* 6:79–141.

———. 1983. *Corporate Profits and Cooptation: Networks of Market Constraints and Directorate Ties in the American Economy.* New York: Academic Press.

———. 1987. "Social contagion and innovation: cohesion versus structural equivalence." *American Journal of Sociology* 92:1287–1335.

Cable, John, and Hirohiko Yasuki. 1985. "Internal organization, business groups, and corporate performance: an empirical test of the multidivisional hypothesis in Japan." *International Journal of Industrial Organization* 3:401–420.

Caves, Richard, and Masu Uekusa. 1976. *Industrial Organization in Japan.* Washington, DC: The Brookings Institution.

Chandler, Alfred D. 1962. *Strategy and Structure.* Cambridge, MA: MIT Press.

———. 1977. *The Visible Hand.* Cambridge, MA: Harvard University Press.

Christensen, H. Kurt, and Cynthia A. Montgomery. 1981. "Corporate economic performance: diversification strategy versus market structure." *Strategic Management Journal* 2:327–343.

Clark, Rodney C. 1979. *The Japanese Company.* New Haven: Yale University Press.

Coase, Ronald H. 1937. "The nature of the firm." In George J. Stigler and Kenneth E. Boulding, eds., *Readings in Price Theory.* Homewood, IL: Irwin, pp. 386–405.

DiMaggio, Paul. 1987. "Structural analysis of organizational fields: a blockmodel approach." In Barry M. Staw and L. L. Cummings, eds., *Research in Organizational Behavior,* Volume 10. Greenwich, CT: JAI Press.

Dore, Ronald. 1986. *Flexible Rigidities.* Stanford: Stanford University Press.

———. 1987. *Taking Japan Seriously.* Stanford: Stanford University Press.

Doreian, Patrick. 1982. "Maximum likelihood methods for linear models: spatial effects and spatial disturbance terms." *Sociological Methods and Research* 3:243–270.

Eccles, Robert G., and Dwight Crane. 1987. "Managing through networks in investment banking." *California Management Review* 30:176–195.

Erbring, Lutz, and Alice A. Young. 1979. "Contextual effects as endogenous feedback." *Sociological Methods and Research* 7:396–430.

Fligstein, Neil. 1985. "The spread of the multidivisional form among large firms, 1919–1979." *American Sociological Review* 50:377–391.

Galaskiewicz, Joseph, and Stanley S. Wasserman. 1981. "A dynamic study of change in a regional corporate network." *American Sociological Review* 46:475–484.

Gerlach, Michael L. 1987. "Business alliances and the strategy of the Japanese firm." *California Management Review* 30:126–142.

———. 1992a. *Alliance Capitalism: The Social Organization of Japanese Business.* Berkeley: University of California Press.

———. 1992b. "The Japanese corporate network: A blockmodel analysis." *Administrative Science Quarterly*, 37:105–139.

Hall, Marshall, and Leonard Weiss. 1967. "Firm size and profitability." *The Review of Economics and Statistics* 59:310–331.

Hamilton, Gary G., and Nicole Woolsey Biggart. 1988. "Market, culture, and authority: a comparative analysis of management and organization in the Far East." *American Journal of Sociology* 94 (Supplement): S52–S95.

Holland, Paul W., and Samuel Leinhardt. 1977. "A dynamic model for social networks." *Journal of Mathematical Sociology* 5:5–20.

Hoskisson, Robert E. 1987. "Multidivisional structure and performance: the contingency of diversification strategy." *Academy of Management Journal* 30:625–644.

Imai, Kenichi. 1988a. "Network industrial organization in Japan (First Part)." *Gestion 2000* 2:19–31.

———. 1988b. "Network industrial organization in Japan (Second Part)." *Gestion 2000* 2:19–31.

Imai, Kenichi, Ikujiro Nonaka, and Hirotaka Takeuchi. 1985. "Managing new product development: how Japanese companies learn and unlearn." In Kim B. Clark, Robert H. Hayes, and Christopher Lorenz, eds., *The Uneasy Alliance.* Boston: Harvard Business School Press, pp. 337–376.

Johanson, Jan, and Lars-Gunnar Mattsson. 1987. "Interorganizational relations in industrial systems: a network approach compared with the transaction-cost approach." *International Studies of Management and Organization* 17:34–48.

Jorde, Thomas M., and David J. Teece. 1987. "Using antitrust's 'state action doctrine' to promote beneficial collaboration and cooperation among California firms: an exploration." Berkeley Business School Working Paper Series.

Kagono, Tadao, Ikujiro Nonaka, Kiyonori Sakakibara, and Akihoro Okumura. 1985. *Strategic vs. Evolutionary Management: A U.S.-Japan Comparison.* Amsterdam: Elsevier North-Holland.

Kotabe, Masaaki. 1989. "How cooperative are member companies in the Japanese industrial group?" Paper presented to the Association of Japanese Business Studies, San Francisco.

Kotz, David M. 1978. *Bank Control of Large Corporations in the United States.* Berkeley: University of California Press.

Laumann, Edward O., David Knoke, and Yong-Hak Kim. 1985. "An organizational approach to state policy formation: a comparative study of energy and health domains." *American Sociological Review* 50:1–19.

Laumann, Edward O., Peter V. Marsden, and Joseph Galaskiewicz. 1977. "Community elite influence structures: extension of a network approach." *American Journal of Sociology* 83:594–632.

Lincoln, James R. 1982. "Intra- (and inter-) organizational networks." In Samuel B. Bacharach, ed., *Research in the Sociology of Organizations*, Vol. 1. Greenwich, CT: JAI Press, pp. 1–38.

———. 1984. "Analyzing relations in dyads: problems, models, and an application to interorganizational research." *Sociological Methods and Research* 13:45–76.

————. 1990. "Japanese organization and organization theory." In Barry M. Staw and L. L. Cummings, eds., *Research in Organizational Behavior*, Vol. 12. Greenwich, CT: JAI Press.

Lincoln, James R., and Kerry McBride. 1985. "Resources, homophily, and dependence: organizational attributes and asymmetric ties in human resource networks." *Social Science Research* 14:1–30.

Lincoln, James R., Michael L. Gerlach, and Peggy Takahashi. 1992. "*Keiretsu* networks in the Japanese economy: A dyad analysis of intercorporate ties." *American Sociological Review*, 57(5): (forthcoming).

Lincoln, James R., and Jon Miller. 1979. "Work and friendship ties in organizations: a comparative analysis of relational networks." *Administrative Science Quarterly* 24:181–199.

Lincoln, James R., and Gerald Zeitz. 1980. "Organizational properties from aggregate data: separating individual and structural effects." *American Sociological Review* 45:391–409.

Lorrain, Francois, and Harrison C. White. 1971. "Structural equivalence of individuals in social networks." *Journal of Mathematical Sociology* 1:49–80.

Miles, Raymond E., and Charles C. Snow. 1987. "Organizations: new concepts for new forms." *California Management Review* 28:62–73.

Mintz, Beth, and Michael Schwartz. 1985. *The Power Structure of American Business*. Chicago: University of Chicago Press.

Nakatani, Iwao. 1984. "The economic role of financial corporate grouping." In Masahiko Aoki, ed., *The Economic Analysis of the Japanese Firm*. Amsterdam: North-Holland, pp. 227–258.

Palmer, Donald. 1983. "Broken ties: interlocking directorates and intercorporate coordination." *Administrative Science Quarterly* 28:40–55.

Palmer, Donald, P. Devereaux Jennings, and Xueguang Zhou. 1988. "From corporate strategies to institutional prescriptions: adoption of the multidivisional form, 1962–1968." Unpublished paper, Graduate School of Business, Stanford University.

Pascale, Richard T. 1984. "Perspectives on strategy: the real story behind Honda's success." In Glenn Carroll and David Vogel, eds., *Strategy and Organization: A West Coast Perspective*. Boston: Pitman, pp. 38–63.

Pfeffer, Jeffrey, and Gerald R. Salancik. 1978. *The External Control of Organizations*. New York: Harper & Row.

Piore, Michael J., and Charles F. Sabel. 1984. *The Second Industrial Divide: Possibilities for Prosperity*. New York: Basic Books.

Powell, Walter W. 1987. "Hybrid organizational arrangements." *California Management Review* 30:67–87.

Richardson, R. Jack. 1987. "Directorship interlocks and corporate profitability." *Administrative Science Quarterly* 32:367–386.

Roehl, Thomas. 1989. "Japanese industrial groupings: a strategic response to rapid industrial growth." Paper presented to the Association of Japanese Business Studies, San Francisco.

Rumelt, Richard P. 1974. *Strategy, Structure, and Economic Performance*. Boston: Harvard Business School.

Scherer, Frederic M. 1980. *Industrial Market Structure and Economic Performance*, 2d ed. Chicago: Rand McNally.

Schonberger, Richard J. 1982. *Japanese Manufacturing Techniques*. New York: Free Press.

Schrader, Charles B., James R. Lincoln, and Alan Hoffman. 1989. "The network structures of organizations: effects of task contingencies and distributional form." *Human Relations* 42:43–66.

Scott, John. 1986. *Capitalist Property and Financial Power*. Brighton, England: Wheatsheaf Books.

Stokman, Frans N., Rolf Ziegler, and John Scott. 1985. *Networks of Corporate Power*. Cambridge, England: Polity Press.

Tuma, Nancy B., and Maureen T. Hallinan. 1979. "The effects of sex, race, and achievements on schoolchildren's friendships." *Social Forces* 57:1265–1285.

Ueda, Yoshiaki. 1989. "Similarities of the corporate network structure in Japan and the U.S." *Ryutsu-Kagaku Daigaku-Ronshu* 2:49–61.

Useem, Michael. 1984. *The Inner Circle.* New York: Oxford University Press.

Wasserman, Stanley S. 1980. "A stochastic model for directed graphs with transition rates determined by reciprocity." In Karl F. Schuessler, ed., *Sociological Methodology.* San Francisco: Jossey-Bass, pp. 392–412.

Wellman, Barry, and S. D. Berkowitz. 1987. "Introduction: studying social structures." In Barry Wellman and S. D. Berkowitz, eds., *Social Structures: A Network Approach.* Cambridge: Cambridge University Press, pp. 1–15.

White, Harrison C. 1987. "Where do markets come from?" *American Journal of Sociology* 87:517–547.

Williamson, Oliver E. 1975. *Markets and Hierarchies: Analysis and Antitrust Implications.* New York: Free Press.

———. 1985. *The Economic Institutions of Capitalism.* New York: Free Press.

Yoshihara, Hideki, Akimitsu Sakuma, Hiroyuki Itami, and Tadao Kagono. 1981. *Nihon Kigyoo no Tayo-ka Senryaku: Keiei Shigen Approach* (The Diversification Strategy of Japanese Firms: A Managerial Resource Approach). Tokyo: Nihon Keizai Shinbun-Sha.

Making Network Research Relevant to Practice

ROSABETH MOSS KANTER
AND
ROBERT G. ECCLES

The papers in this volume represent some of the best contemporary academic research on networks. As a body, they summarize much of what we already know about networks and point in a number of exciting new directions. Theoretical developments, substantive applications, and methodological advances are all inevitable and we look forward to them.

However, it is safe to say that most of this anticipated work will be by and for academics. While we obviously have no objections to this, it is important to emphasize that there is another important audience, which is managers who are interested in using network concepts to create effective organizations. Attending the conference were a number of practitioners who both learned and contributed a great deal to the small and large group discussions. Our belief that managers would find the ideas in the papers of interest was the reason practitioners were invited, and this belief was confirmed by what actually happened.

Yet a gulf remains in bringing what we already know about networks to bear on practice. This gulf goes beyond the obvious and often-cited problem of dense academic jargon that makes much writing about networks virtually inaccessible to managers. While important, this problem is easy to solve in a variety of ways.

More fundamentally, the gulf is based on differences in perspective, which is vividly illustrated in differences in language. Whereas academics typically talk about "networks" or "network organizations," it is much more common for managers to talk about "networking." In contrast to academics, who are interested in *understanding* the noun and adjective, are the managers, who are interested in *using* the verb. Academics want to identify characteristics, properties, and consequences of networks.

Managers want to create networks for themselves and their organizations in order to improve the effectiveness of both. Thus popular writing in the self-help literature on management is filled with advice on how to develop and benefit from an old boys' or old girls' network. The recognized importance of networks in everyday managerial life (and life in general for that matter) is nicely captured in the phrase, "It's not what you know but who you know."

Such colloquial use of the network concept is a far cry from the theoretical and methodological sophistication displayed in the papers in this volume. More significantly, contained within every single chapter in this book are some important implications for managers. While we could list what we see them to be, as a practical matter there is little reason to do so. Anyone reading this book will be able to identify the implications for practice that are relevant to him or her.

What we will do instead is briefly discuss four key issues that we believe academics need to be conscious of when conducting their research: network data, network characteristics, network organization, and network building. By increasing their awareness of these four issues from the perspective of managers, we believe that academics will increase the extent to which the practical implications of their research can be made useful to managers. We also believe that rather than representing a sacrifice of theoretical and methodological sophistication, doing so will actually require more of each. An appreciation for practice is good for theory and method.

NETWORK DATA

The data managers and academics have about networks are of very different kinds. Managers are concerned about their place in a variety of networks based on different types of ties. Managers are quite aware of the people with whom they have ties, what comprises these ties, how these ties are changing in strength and other ways, and how these ties compare with one another. The nuances and subtleties that are contained in this network perspective of a manager's world are rich and evocative in their detail.

These data are also very egocentric. While the manager has a very good idea of the ties he or she has with others, he or she has at best a rough idea of these others' networks. Thus a manager may know that someone is especially well-connected and may even know many of these connections, but he or she will not know all of them. Nor will the manager have a complete picture of the connections among connections.

A manager's network data are also asymmetric to some degree. Projections by the manager of how the tie is perceived by the other party— including whether or not the other even sees the tie as existing—do not match perfectly with the perceptions of the others. This is true whether the tie is defined in absolute (e.g., is a friend of) or relative (e.g., is one of the top three sources of information) terms. Social ties depend upon perceptions and evaluations, and while there are pressures that push in the direction of similarity, asymmetry of various kinds and to varying degrees is common.

Network data collected by researchers directly captures these asymmetries. By soliciting the perceptions of each party about his or her tie to the other, it is then easy to compare them. Whether differences in perception are regarded as important is to some extent dependent upon the problem being studied. In general, however, these asymmetries are ignored and some decision rule is used to determine how the data should be coded, such as both parties must identity the tie or just one has to. This is necessary in order to analyze the characteristics of the network in question. However, elimination of this ambiguity also eliminates what for the manager is a very central question: the relative importance of a tie to the other, since imbalances are the source of power and dependency.

The network data of researchers present a more nearly complete "objective" or "outside" view than that of managers since the data capture the ties of and between others that a manager can only estimate. It is for this reason we describe it as more nearly complete, although it is often more incomplete as well, since limits are often put on the number of ties that are recorded for each person. While we do not wish to accord a superior ontological status to researcher data that aggregates the perceptions of many people, it does provide a view different from that of an individual manager. As with asymmetry, differences between perceived networks and actual networks (defined in terms of the perceptions of many) can be ignored or explored. While academics tend to do the former in order to pursue their analytical ends, managers are especially interested in identifying and filling in these gaps. Knowing the network ties of others can be a very practical and useful piece of information.

The greater completeness of researcher data is obtained by sacrificing much of the subtlety, nuance, and change in network ties that individuals are aware of. Subtlety and nuance are lost due to the difficulty of capturing and using such data as the varying elemental composition of ties and gradations of intensity. Change is lost because the data collection necessarily takes place at a certain point in time. Even when multiple assessments are made, they are taken as snapshots. These data do not capture changes in ties, or even the directions of these changes, such as whether a tie is becoming more or less intense. But for managers, the direction and realization of these changes is as important, and often more so, than what the network structure is at an arbitrarily fixed point in time.

In making these comparisons between managers' and researchers' network descriptions, we do not mean to imply that one is better or worse. All that we want to do is to make the differences explicit and to raise two points. The first is that more attention should be paid to comparing the two. This requires an ability to make the description of each more available to the other, which is our second point. Most current methodologies used by researchers to collect data are fairly time-consuming and represent a noticeable intervention in the organization in which the data are collected. At the same time, they do not lend themselves to measuring subtlety, nuance, or change.

Methods need to be developed to more easily give managers a more complete view of a network, such as collecting data via networked personal computers, when such a system exists. When data collection of the gross structural characteristics has been made easier, it will then be possible to find ways to capture more detail on a basis closer to real time. As academics develop a better appreciation of what kind of network data are of interest to managers and develop tools for providing these data, then managers will be able to make a more rigorous and precise use of the network concepts that these tools represent.

NETWORK CHARACTERISTICS

A great deal of research has been devoted to developing measures of the important structural characteristics of networks. Much of this work has focused on identifying measures that capture some key aspect of a complicated network structure or of a node in the structure. Typically, these characteristics are obtained by computations that can be very complex—at least relative to the abilities of most managers who are not trained in this methodology. There are also problems of getting the data used to compute these measures in the first place, as already discussed.

But assuming that some progress is made in improving both the type and the ease with which data on networks are collected, two very large opportunities exist for making academic research on networks more useful to managers. The first is to develop very user-friendly software that will enable managers to assess the characteristics of the networks of which they are a part. Such software would have to be accompanied by explanations of the measures used to define particular network characteristics. But because so much fine work has already been done in this domain, it is simply a matter of making the measures and concepts behind them accessible to managers.

The second opportunity, which to some extent depends upon the first being accomplished, is to better understand what it is that managers want to know about networks. For some questions, measures and methodologies may already exist. For others, new ones will have to be developed. In either case, we can safely predict that managers will be interested in the relationships between network characteristics and various kinds of outcomes. And again, for some of these questions substantial research already conducted will be relevant, and it is simply a matter of making managers aware of it.

What are some of the obvious relationships that are of interest to managers? One is what network characteristics best facilitate the efficient and effective flow of information. A common complaint among managers is that their organizations perform poorly in this regard and experience has shown that information technology provides only a partial solution, and can even make matters worse. Another obvious—although no doubt difficult-to-demonstrate—matter of general interest is the relationship between various network characteristics and profitability. This topic can be explored at different levels of analysis from small business units to entire companies. A third area worth exploring is the relationship between various network characteristics and such perceptual variables as job satisfaction, sense of participation, felt autonomy, and experienced efficacy.

These general topics can be explored in a number of particular situations. Certain network characteristics may prove to be especially effective for fostering the kind of communication necessary among the members of a large sales and service team that calls on large multinational customers. Some types of product development networks will prove to be better than others at reducing the length of the product development cycle. Top management committees with a certain network structure will be better at articulating and implementing a firm's strategy than those with a different structure.

Which relationships will turn out to be of greatest interest to managers and which ones will most lend themselves to better understanding through network concepts and techniques remains to be seen. At this stage the best thing to do is to more aggressively determine what kinds of questions related to networks are of interest to managers. Those that can be addressed through research already conducted should be and the others will provide interesting avenues for future research that will have a high probability of being relevant to managers.

NETWORK ORGANIZATION

So far, we have used the term "network" as an attribute of any organization to describe the pattern of ties that exist, defined by hierarchical reporting relationships, task interdependencies, information sharing, and so forth. Many of the articles in this volume are about the network properties that can be identified in any organization or set of interorganizational relationships. But the term "network" is also used to refer to a particular *type* of organization (as is the case for other articles in this volume), often by contrasting this type with a hierarchical or market form of organization. Although the precise definition of the so-called "network organization" varies from person to person, in general, it is regarded as having many felicitous properties—flexibility, responsiveness, adaptability, extensive cross-functional collaboration, rapid and effective decision making, highly committed employees, and so on—not found to the same degree in alternative organizational forms.

We see no reason to engage in a debate over whether a network is a property of any organization, as just discussed in terms of network characteristics, or a type of a particular kind of organization. But we do think it is important to understand better how managers use the term when referring to it as a type and what they are trying to accomplish in doing so. We see this as complementary rather than contradictory to better understanding relationships between network characteristics and outcomes.

Managers often talk about creating a "network organization" when they are trying to change the way the present organization is functioning. The "network organization" is offered as a model that is superior to the existing "bureaucratic functional hierarchy" and is intended to improve the organization's capabilities in certain regards by overcoming problems that are perceived as inhibiting its effectiveness. The desired attributes of the new organization—for example, decentralized decision making, better customer service, more attention to quality, or tighter cross-functional integration—are typically used to describe the characteristics of the "network organization."

However one chooses to define the network organization, there are two important questions where academic research can make an important contribution to managers. The first is to provide insight into how one *creates* a network organization. Undoubtedly, examples can be found where this stated intention becomes a reality for everybody in the organization when they agree that, indeed, it has been transformed from a hierarchical to a network organization. In other cases, people become cynical and regard all of the talk about a network organization as only that, with little real change having occurred. Understanding these differences in outcomes is a very important contribution academics can make to managers, especially those for whom the "network organization" is an important part of their managerial rhetoric defined in its most positive sense. Addressing this issue requires the recognition that perceptions and opinions about whether or not a network organization has been created are data as valid as measures that assess the degree to which certain attributes of the network organization actually exist.

The second issue is closely related to the first and demonstrates the complementarity between network as a characteristic and network as a type: Are there distinct differences in the network characteristics of those organizations agreed to being "network organizations" by their members compared to those characteristics in those organizations not perceived as being so? For example, a reasonable hypothesis is that organizations having many meaningful ties that cross hierarchical levels and functional boundaries will be perceived as being network organizations, whereas those having few such ties will not. These characteristics can then be related to outcomes to see if there really are differences in performance between network and non-network organizations, as is believed by many people today.

NETWORK BUILDING

In discussing network data, we noted that most of the methods and concepts used by academics to study networks have a static, snapshot quality to them. Their focus is largely on structural characteristics of the network being studied, with little attention paid to how these networks were constructed by their members and how these members are using them. But it is from this action perspective that managers derive their interest in networks. The kind of knowledge that can be made available through studying network characteristics and the network organization needs to be supplemented with knowledge about how to build and use networks.

The best way to acquire this kind of knowledge is to study individual managers who have been successful in doing so. Through interviews and surveys, especially conducted over time, of these managers and the people they work with, it will be possible to identify network building strategies that exemplify the active "networking" activity that managers engage in in order to get things done. For managers, networks are both something that sets the context for the actions they wish to take—thereby providing resources and constraints—as well as things that can be manipulated in order to provide more resources and fewer constraints. Learning about how managers themselves come to understand the nature of the networks they are involved in and how they then seek to alter and use them for their own purposes will add a more active, process view of networks to the structural view that currently predominates. In doing this research, it is important to recognize that virtually every person in the network is seeking to shape and use it for his or her own purposes. The constantly evolving network they construct is a result of these struggles for control that are playing off of and responding to one another. As such, pressures are always coming from one person or another to make it more responsive to his or her own ends. Structure is thus seen as a representation at a particular point in time of an underlying process made up of these struggles for control. By explicitly studying these struggles for control in and of networks, academics have an opportunity to better understand the nature of networks in a way that will be of great theoretical and practical relevance. We believe that if academics accept this challenge, the result will be the reinvigoration of an important domain of social theory that has already contributed much to our understanding of organizations and promises to contribute a great deal more.

CONTRIBUTORS

WAYNE E. BAKER is Associate Professor of Business Policy and Sociology at the Graduate School of Business, University of Chicago. He teaches organizational behavior, networks, and business policy in the school's MBA and Executive MBA programs. His research interests include network theory and methods, organizations, interorganizational relations, economic sociology, markets, and innovative management practices.

STEPHEN R. BARLEY received his Ph.D. in Organization Studies from the Massachusetts Institute of Technology in 1984. He is Director of the Program on Technology and Work and an Associate Professor of Organizational Behavior in the School of Industrial and Labor Relations at Cornell University. Professor Barley's research focuses on the impact of microelectronic technologies in the workplace and on the scientific, technical, and professional workforce. His current research includes field research on new technical occupations and a study of strategic alliances in biotechnology. His most recent papers have appeared in *Administrative Science Quarterly, Organization Science,* and *Research in Organizational Behavior.* He has recently edited a special volume of *Research in the Sociology of Organizations* with Dr. Pamela Tolbert, entitled *Professions and Organizations.*

NICOLE WOOLSEY BIGGART has appointments at the Graduate School of Management and Department of Sociology at the University of California at Davis. Her interests include economic sociology, the intersection of organization and culture, and the institutional analysis of East Asian business. She is the author of *Charismatic Capitalism: Direct Selling Organizations in America* (Chicago: University of Chicago Press, 1989). She is currently conducting a study of the leisure industry in the United States.

PETER BRANTLEY is a Ph.D. candidate in Sociology at the University of Arizona. He is studying the responses of established pharmaceutical companies to the opportunities and threats posed by biotechnology.

DANIEL J. BRASS is Associate Professor of Organizational Behavior in the Smeal College of Business Administration at The Pennsylvania State University. He received both the M.A. in labor and industrial relations and his Ph.D. in organizational behavior from the University of Illinois, Urbana-Champaign. His research focuses on the relationship of power and social networks to technology, organizational design, and individual jobs, behaviors, attitudes, and demographics. He recently studied the effects of a change in technology on the social network patterns and power relationships in an organization.

MARLENE E. BURKHARDT is Assistant Professor of Management at the Wharton School of the University of Pennsylvania. She has published in *Administrative Science Quarterly* and Academy of Management publications. Her research interests include a longitudinal examination of changes in technology, structure, and power, and how social network structure affects the attitudes and behaviors of organizational members.

RONALD S. BURT is Professor of Sociology and Business at Columbia University. His research and consulting most related to this volume concern the connection between performance and personal contact networks within corporate hierarchies, management teams, and customer market segments. His most recent book is *Structural Holes* (Cambridge: Harvard University Press, 1992), which expands the ideas described in his contribution to this volume.

PAUL DIMAGGIO, Professor of Sociology at Princeton University, has written extensively about organizational theory and the sociology of culture. He is author of *Managers of the Arts* and (with Francie Ostrower) of *Race, Ethnicity, and Participation in the Arts,* and editor of *The New Institutionalism in Organizational Analysis* (with Walter W. Powell), *Nonprofit Enterprise in the Arts,* and *Structures of Capital: The Social Organization of the Economy* (with Sharon Zukin). He is currently writing on the social organization of the arts in the United States from 1860 through the present.

VICTOR DOHERTY is a cultural anthropologist whose primary research interests have been the transfer of technology in underdeveloped communities. Recently he has focused on transferring computer technologies in corporations and has published several articles on technology transfer.

ROBERT G. ECCLES is a Professor of Business Administration and Chairman of the Organizational Behavior/Human Resource Management Department at the Harvard Business School. Most recently he has been teaching the required first-year M.B.A. course, "Information, Organization, and Control." His latest book *Beyond the Hype: Rediscovering the Essence of Management* (with Nitin Nohria and James D. Berkley) was published by Harvard Business School Press in 1992.

JOHN FREEMAN is the Charles H. Dyson Professor of Management at the S.C. Johnson Graduate School of Management and Professor of Sociology at Cornell University. He is also the editor of the *Administrative Science Quarterly.* He is best known for his research on the population ecology of organizations, which applies natural selection logic to the explanation of variation in organizations. Freeman recently coauthored *Organizational Ecology* with Michael T. Hannan (Cambridge: Harvard University Press, 1989).

MICHAEL L. GERLACH is Assistant Professor at the Haas School of Business, University of California at Berkeley. His current research focuses on the comparative organization of business networks in Japan and the United States. Recent publications include *Alliance Capitalism: The Social Organization of Japanese Business* (Berkeley: University of California Press, 1992); "Twilight of the *Kieretsu?* A Critical Assessment" (*Journal of Japanese Studies,* Winter 1992); and "The Japanese Corporate Network: A Blockmodel Analysis" (*Administrative Science Quarterly,* March 1992). He received his Ph.D. in organizational behavior from Yale University.

MARK GRANOVETTER is Professor and Chair of Sociology at the State University of New York at Stony Brook. He is the author of *Getting a Job: A Study of Contacts and Careers* and of a series of articles on social networks and economic sociology. He is currently at work on a book entitled *Society and Economy: The Social Construction of Economic Institutions.*

GARY G. HAMILTON is a Professor of Sociology and the Director of the International Program on East Asian Business and Development at the University of California at Davis. He is the author of many articles on historical and comparative perspectives on Chinese society and economics. Many of these articles have been translated and published in *Zhonggua shehui yu jingji* (Taipei: Lien-ching, 1990). His most recent book (with Wang Zheng) is an introduction to and translation of Fei Xiaotong's *Xiangtu Zhonggui,* entitled *From the Soil: The Foundation of Chinese Society* (Berkeley: University of California Press, 1992). He received a Fulbright Hay award to teach for the 1984–85 academic year at Tunghai University in Taichung, Taiwan. He is the recipient of many honors, including a UC Davis Distinguished Teaching Award, Guggenheim Fellowship, and grants from the National Science Foundation, Ford Foundation, and Chiang Ching-kuo Foundation.

CAROL HEIMER is Associate Professor of Sociology at Northwestern University and Research Fellow at the American Bar Foundation. She received a Ph.D. in sociology from the University of Chicago in 1981. Major publications include *Reactive Risk and Rational Action* (Berkeley: University of California Press, 1985), "Social Structure, Psychology and the Estimation of Risk," (*Annual Review of Sociology,* 1988), and a forthcoming paper on how families get information when they have babies in neonatal intensive care units. She is currently writing two books on responsibility, one a theoretical piece and the second a study of who takes responsibility for graduates of neonatal intensive care units.

RALPH C. HYBELS is a Ph.D. candidate in organizational behavior at the New York State School of Industrial and Labor Relations, Cornell University. His dissertation research focuses on applying structural models to interorganizational networks in the field of biotechnology. He is also exploring the effects of interoccupational dynamics on the strategic management of science-based firms.

HERMINIA IBARRA is Assistant Professor at Harvard University Graduate School of Business Administration. Her current research interests include managerial networks, informal networks of women and minorities in organizations, and organizational innovation. She received her Ph.D. and M.A. degrees in Organizational Behavior from Yale University.

ROSABETH MOSS KANTER holds the Class of 1960 Chair as Professor of Business Administration at the Harvard Business School, serving also as Editor of the

Harvard Business Review from 1989 through 1992, adding the responsibilities of vice Chair of HBS Publishing in 1992. Her books include *The Challenge of Organizational Change*, 1992; *When Giants Learn to Dance*, 1989; and *The Change Masters*, 1983.

BRUCE KOGUT is an Associate Professor of Management at the Wharton School of the University of Pennsylvania. He has published articles on joint ventures such as options, foreign direct investment for the sourcing of technology, and international strategy. His current research is on the knowledge of the firm and historical patterns in country competition.

DAVID KRACKHARDT is Associate Professor of Organizations and Public Policy at the Heinz School of Public Policy and Management, Carnegie-Mellon University. He is best known for his work in social network analysis, especially as it applies to organizations. His publications appear in a variety of journals in the areas of psychology, sociology, anthropology, management, and statistical methodology. His current research focuses on the dimensions of hierarchy in informal organizations and their effects on organizational performance.

JAMES R. LINCOLN is Professor in the Haas School of Business and an affiliated faculty member in the Department of Sociology at the University of California at Berkeley. He is the author of *Culture, Control, and Commitment: A Study of Work Organization and Work Attitudes in the U.S. and Japan* (New York: Cambridge University Press, 1990), as well as numerous articles on Japanese management and labor topics. He currently is collaborating with Michael Gerlach on a study of business networks in the Japanese economy.

JAMES L. MCKENNEY is the John G. McLean Professor of Business Administration at Harvard University, Graduate School of Business Administration. His research relating to this volume concerns how the functioning of electronic networks improves the information processing of coherent working groups and how management action can improve the effectiveness of electronic networks. His most recent book, (with James Cash and Warren McFarlan), which includes the results of this work, is *Corporate Information Systems Management* (Homewood, IL: Richard D. Irwin, 1992).

NITIN NOHRIA is an Assistant Professor of Business Administration and Control. His research and teaching interests are primarily in the area of organization structure and change. He has recently written a book in collaboration with Robert G. Eccles and James D. Berkley called *Beyond the Hype: Rediscovering the Essence of Management* (Boston: Harvard Business School Press, 1992).

CHARLES PERROW is an organizational theorist concerned with present competitiveness issues, the role of large organizations in shaping the United States from 1820 to the present, and with the theory of "normal accidents" in high-risk systems. He teaches in the Sociology Department and the School of Organization and Management at Yale University.

MICHAEL J. PIORE is David W. Skinner Professor of Economics and Management at Massachusetts Institute of Technology. His work has focused upon the social embeddedness of economic activity. Most recently, he has been engaged in a series of studies of the institutional transformation of the American economy.

WALTER W. POWELL is Professor of Sociology at the University of Arizona and editor of *Contemporary Sociology*. His most recent book is *The New Institutionalism in Organization Analysis*, co-edited with Paul DiMaggio.

WEIJAN SHAN is an Assistant Professor of Management at the Wharton School of the University of Pennsylvania. His research interests and publications are in the areas of international competition and cooperation, particularly in the commercialization of high technologies.

GORDON WALKER is Adjunct Associate Professor of Management at the School of Organization and Management, Yale University. His research focuses on problems of business strategy, vertical integration, and interfirm coordination of technology-based relationships. He has written numerous articles on strategy and organization. Professor Walker received his Ph.D. from the Wharton School, University of Pennsylvania, and was previously Associate Professor at the Sloan School at MIT and at the Wharton School.

HARRISON WHITE is the author of the forthcoming *Identity and Control: A Structural Theory of Social Action* (Princeton, NJ: Princeton University Press, 1992), and of books on vacancy chains, on the rise of the French Impressionists, and on role structure models, as well as of articles on topics ranging from social networks and industrial markets to social mobility. Currently, he chairs the Department of Sociology and is Director of the Center for the Social Sciences at Columbia University.

MICHAEL H. ZACK is an Assistant Professor of MIS at Northeastern University, College of Business Administration. He received his DBA from Harvard Business School. His current research interests focus on information technologies used to support communication and information exchange among individuals and organizations.

Index

Aalto Scientific Ltd., 320
Abbott, Andrew, 102, 108
Abegglen, James C., 509
Abernathy, W. J., 368
Abolafia, Mitchel, 473
Ackerman, Rose, 40–41
Action: embeddedness and its effects on economic, 32–37; managerial, 165–169; mobilizing, 296–297; over- and undersocialized conceptions of, in sociology and economics, 28–32; theory of, 13–14
Adler, Reid G., 388
Advanced Genetic Sciences, 335
Agency, 95–96; and delegation, 96–97, 99; how to manage, 101–104
Agnew, Jean-Christophe, 95
Agriculture, Department of, 320
Akerlof, George, 41
Alba, R. D., 179, 513
Albright-Knox Gallery (Buffalo), 127
Alderfer, C., 180
Aldrich, H. E., 262, 397, 404–405, 422
Aldrich, William, 125
Alford, Robert R., 100, 109–110
Allen, T. J., 299
Alliances, strategic, 11–12
Alston, John, 477
Ambiguity, negotiating uncertainty and, 295–296
American Association of Museums, 129
American Economic Association, 432
American Federation of Arts, 129
American Home Products, 370
American Research and Development Corporation (ARDC), 252, 253, 255

American Sociological Meetings, 92n
Amgen Inc., 335, 378
Amin, Ash, 450, 456
Amsden, Alice, 475, 476
Anderson, Perry, 101
Anderson, Philip, 368
Andrews, Kenneth R., 404
Anheier, Helmut K., 133, 137
Aoki, Masahiko, 478
Apple Computer, 477
Applegate, Lynda, 291
Arabie, Phipps, 355, 357
Arendt, Hannah, 14
Arensberg, Conrad, 28
Arida, Persio, 441
Armour, Henry, 422, 507
Arrow, Kenneth, 36, 41, 257
Arthur, Brian, 50–51
Arthur D. Little, 378
Ashford, Douglas E., 110
Asia: development of markets in, 484–487; economic differences between the West and, 475–480; market conditions in, 474–475. See also Japan
Asilomar Conference, 315
AT&T, 221, 348n
Atomization, in social thought, 26–28
Attanucci, Jane, 159
Autonomy: cohesion vs., 178–180; institutionalization of firm, 482–484; structural, 82–83
Aydalot, Philippe, 463

Bacharach, S. B., 170, 184
Back, Kurt, 36, 66
Bair, James, 265

Baker, Cheryl, 397n
Baker, Wayne, 13, 36, 241, 288, 349,
    397, 400, 402, 408, 495
Barkey, Karen, 77
Barley, Stephen R., 5, 11, 132, 184,
    311, 319, 337
Barnard, Chester I., 131, 262, 363
Barnes, J. A., 3
Barney, J. B., 168
Baron, James N., 515
Barr, Alfred H., Jr., 124, 125, 130
Baruch, Bernard, 101
Battelle, 378
Baumol, William, 48
Bazerman, Max H., 242
BCS (Boston Computer Society), 245,
    255
Bearman, Peter, 92n
Becattini, Giacomo, 436
Becker, Gary, 32, 33–34
Becker, Howard, 93
Becker, Selwyn, 397n
Beckman Instruments, 320
Belanger, Michael, 244–245
Bell, Daniel, 288
Benhabib, Seyla, 154
Beniger, James R., 291
Ben-Porath, Yoram, 44
Bentham, Jeremy, 29
Benton, Lauren A., 456, 464
Berelson, Bernard, 60, 235
Berg, Paul, 314
Berger, Peter, 25, 33, 477
Berkman, Lisa F., 61
Berkowitz, S. D., 93, 288, 410–411, 491
Berman, Harold J., 108
Best, Michael, 2, 454, 462
Bettis, Richard A., 507
Bielby, William T., 515
Biggart, Nicole Woolsey, 13, 471, 473,
    475, 476, 477, 481, 511
Biggs, Tyler S., 474
Biogen, 320, 335
Bioscan, 319, 354, 355, 375
Biotechnology, 343–344, 366–368, 388–
    389; alternative perspectives on
    industry evolution in, 372–375; and
    centrality in network of strategic
    alliances, 328–332; community, his-
    tory of, 314–319; ecological findings,
    322–324; firms, data and methods
    for study of, 375–385; further
    research in, 385–388; and microelec-
    tronics, 316–317; by nationality,
    325–328; and niche and alliance pat-

terns, 332–338; and niche and
    market orientation, 338–343; shifting
    locus of innovation in, 370–372;
    strategic alliances in, 317–319; study,
    319–322; as wave of creative destruc-
    tion, 368–370. See also New
    biotechnology firms (NBFs)
Biotechnology Investments Ltd., 320
Biotechnology Review Associates, 320
Birch, David, 254
Blau, J. R., 177
Blau, Peter M., 7, 132, 179, 180, 398,
    401, 402, 407
Bliss, Lilly, 123–124
Bodin, Jean, 95, 99, 100–101, 103, 105
Boeker, Warren, 350
Boje, David M., 312
Bolt, Beranek and Newman, 320
Bonacich, Phillip, 129, 193, 195, 200
Boorman, Scott A., 93, 120, 256, 355,
    357, 398, 407
Bott, Elizabeth, 93
Bougon, M. G., 264
Bourdieu, Pierre, 122, 127
Bowles, Samuel, 31
Boxman, Ed A. W., 61
Boyd, John P., 104
Boyer, Herbert, 314, 315
Boyles, S. E., 352
Bradach, J., 92n, 289
Brady, Robert A., 110
Brantley, Peter, 12, 366
Brass, Daniel J., 9, 172, 173, 191, 194,
    199, 200, 211, 213
Breiger, Ronald L., 120, 131, 191, 277,
    355, 357, 398, 407
Brimm, M., 167, 172, 174, 175
Bristol Meyers, 367
British Medical Research Council, 314
British Petroleum, 303
Brittain, Jack W., 316, 405
Brokerage, 6
Brown, Ernest Phelps, 30
Brown, Roger, 42
Brusco, Sebastiano, 450, 459
Bureaucracy, universalism and, 146–
    148
Burkhardt, Marlene E., 9, 191, 199, 213
Burns, Tom, 12, 168, 169, 174, 290,
    397, 400, 402, 405
Burrill, G. Steven, 318, 370
Burt, Ronald S., 3, 6, 7, 10, 14, 57, 60,
    64, 66, 71, 78, 82, 84, 122, 129, 166,
    170, 179, 180, 195, 288, 312, 328, 332,
    397n, 457, 508, 516

Business ventures, creating new, 241–244

Byrne, D., 219

Cable, John, 506
CALCOPT, 357
Calgene, 335
Calhoun, Craig, 398, 401, 407
California, University of: at Davis, 320; at San Francisco, 314, 315
California Biotechnology, 335
Cambridge Technology, Inc., 320
Camic, Charles, 29
Campbell, Karen E., 60
Capecchi, Vittorio, 456, 463
Capitalist failure, 449
Carleton, Willard T., 318
Carnegie Corporation of New York, 130
Carrington, Peter J., 410–411
Carroll, Glenn, 514
Carter, Stephen, 367
Case, T., 178, 182
Case study(ies), 99; as probe, 100–101
Cash, James I., 291
Caves, Richard, 496, 508, 509
Centocor, 320, 335
Centrality, 191–193, 194; betweenness measures of, 195, 202, 223–224; closeness measures of, 195, 202; and communication network, 198; degree measures of, 194, 201, 223; and friendship network, 198; measures of, 195–196, 205–207, 211–212; and network connections, 198–200, 212–213; in network of strategic alliances, biotechnology and, 328–332; and units of reference, 196–197, 207–209, 210–211; and work-flow network, 197–198
Centralization, 462; measures of, 7–8; specialization and, 97–98
CEO, structural criticality of, 419–422
Cetus, 320, 335, 366
Chandler, Alfred, 98, 101, 104, 109, 422, 437, 445, 459, 478, 479, 505, 506, 507
Cherry, Colin, 292
Chicago Art Institute, 127
Child, John, 288, 290, 291
Chiron, 335
Christensen, H. Kurt, 507
Christie, B., 297
Cicourel, Aaron V., 98
City of Hope (hospital), 320

Clark, K. B., 368
Clark, Rodney, 474, 495, 507
Clark, Stephen, 127
Classical growth theory, 437–442
Classical revival, flexible specialization and, 435–437
Clegg, Stewart, 100
Cohen, Michael D., 104, 122, 136
Cohen, Stanley, 314, 315, 366
Cohen, Wes, 372, 388
Cohesion, 6, 65–66, 67; vs. autonomy, 178–180
Colander, David, 46
Cole, Robert, 31
Coleman, James S., 60, 168, 195
Collaborative Research, 335
Collins, Randall, 122, 127, 292
Columbia, Stamer Workshop at, 397n
Comaroff, John L., 150
Communication network, 198
Compaq Computer Corporation, 301
Complementarity, similarity vs., 180–181
Compton, Carl Taylor, 252–253
CONCOR, 357
Conglomerate, 446
Connecticut Venture Capital Group, 245
Contexts, institutions as, 104–108
Control, 94–95; in networks, 92–94; and organizing networks, 124; propositions to regain or enhance, 99–101; and tertius gaudens, 75–79
Cook, Karen S., 122, 192, 193, 194, 198–199
Cooperation: firm attributes as determinants of interfirm, 352–353; network structure and, 350–351
Corey, E. Raymond, 103
Cornell Supercomputer Center, 311n
Corning Glass, 320
Coser, Rose Laub, 76
Cote, Marcel, 257
Counteragency, 103–104
Crane, Dwight B., 131, 175, 182, 289, 301, 397, 398, 400, 402, 404, 405, 496
Crawford, Albert M., 296
Crick, Francis H. C., 366
Crozier, Michel, 103, 173, 236
Cuff, Robert D., 101
Culnan, Mary J., 301
Culturalism, pitfalls of, 47–51
Culture, problem of, 119–123
Culture theory, 477
Cyert, Richard, 122

Daems, Herman, 109
Daewoo, 475
Daft, R. L., 263, 265, 295–296
Dai-Ichi Kangyo, 474, 504–505
Dalton, Melville, 131, 134, 136, 167, 171, 175
Data General, 253
Dauber, Ken, 92n
David, Paul, 50, 51
Davis, James A., 217, 235
Davis, Stanley, 104
Dayton, P. W., 217
De Graaf, Nan D., 60
De Graaf, Paul M., 61
Delaney, John, 93, 256
Delbecq, A. L., 174, 177
Delegation, agency and, 96–97, 99
Development theory, 475–477
Dialog, 255
Diamond exchange, 44
Dickson, W. J., 1, 131, 173, 408
Differentiation, and integration, 400–401
Digital Equipment Corporation (DEC), 253, 254, 297, 301, 441
Dill, William R., 5
DiMaggio, Paul, 5, 10, 14, 105, 118, 120, 123, 176, 180, 249
Dix, G., 107–108
Doeringer, Peter B., 463
Doherty, Victor S., 262
Dohse, Knuth, 454
Dominant coalition, 202–203
Donnellon, Anne, 293
Dore, Ronald, 135, 493, 495, 506
Doreian, Patrick, 516
Dorfman, Nancy S., 253, 257
Dosi, Giovanni, 371
Drucker, Peter, 289, 290
Dubinskas, Frank A., 316
Duesenberry, James, 30
Dumaine, Brian, 290, 291
Dumin, Mary, 60
Duncan, R., 169, 177
Du Pont, 314
Durkheim, Emile, 26
Dutton, William, 291

East India Company, 482
Eccles, Robert G., 3, 15, 92n, 109, 126, 131, 143n, 175, 182, 288, 289, 290, 301, 397, 398, 400, 402, 404, 405, 496, 521
Economic institutions, social construction of, 47–51

Economist, 300
Effectiveness, 69–70
Efficiency, 67–68
Eisenberg, R. M., 166, 167
Electronically mediated exchange, 304–305; face-to-face and, in network organization, 299–303; vs. face-to-face interaction, 292–299; implications of, 303–304
Electronic mail (EM), comparison of face-to-face communication and, 262–264; conclusions, 283–285; data, 269–271; data analysis, 271–283; research objectives and propositions, 264–267; study, 267–269
Electronic networks, 290–292
Elster, Jon, 49, 298
Embeddedness, 26–28; and its effects on economic action, 32–37; and its effects on trust and malfeasance, 38–47; and new industries, 350
Emerson, Richard M., 193, 196, 211
Emery, F. E., 405
Ensel, Walter M., 60, 217
Entrepreneurs, 79; and measurement implications, 81–82; opportunity and motivation of, 80–81
Environmental characteristics, and ingroup and intergroup relationships, 404–405
Equivalence, 6; structural, 65, 66–67
Erbring, Lutz, 516
Erickson, E., 217
Erickson, Fred, 131
Ertman, Tom, 92n
Espeland, Wendy, 143n, 148
Etiology, and dynamics of networks, 15
Etzioni, Amitai, 173, 481
Evan, William M., 5
Evans, Peggy, 118n
Evans, Peter, 104, 476

Face-to-face interaction, see Electronically mediated exchange; Electronic mail
Faulkner, Robert R., 241, 400, 402
Fayol, H. G., 263
Federal Street SBIC, 253
Federal Trade Commission, 313, 473
Feld, Scott, 251, 405, 424
Fennema, Meindert, 312
Fernandez, Roberto, 92n
Festinger, Leon, 36, 66, 72
Fewsmith, Joseph, 486
Fields, Debbie, 300

Fienberg, Stephen E., 408
Fildes, Robert A., 372
Findley, Carter D., 104
Fine, Gary, 31, 256
Firestone, W. A., 174
First National Bank of Boston, 253
Fischer, Claude S., 60, 64, 219–220
Flap, Hendrik D., 60, 61
Flexible production, 448–449
Flexible specialization, 434–435; and classical revival, 435–437; combining mass production and, 435
Fligstein, Neil, 105, 366n
Florida, Richard L., 253–254, 456
Fluidity, stability vs., 181–182
Flusser, David, 106
Fombrun, Charles, 166, 167, 172, 173, 176, 191, 197, 199
Food and Drug Administration (FDA), 148, 320
Ford Motor Co., 438
Forester, Tom, 289
Formal/informal dichotomy, rethinking, 131–137
Formalization, 462
Formal networks, 93–94
Fortune, 290, 303
Foschi, Martha, 126
Foster, C. C., 93
Foucault, Michel, 482
Fred Hutchins Cancer Research Center, 320
Freeman, John, 123, 311, 316, 319, 324, 328, 337
Freeman, Linton, 192, 194, 195, 198, 201–202, 223, 419
Friedell, Morris, 104
Friedkin, Noah E., 196, 217, 256
Friedkin, R., 109
Friedman, David, 456, 462
Friedman, Milton, 48
Friendship network, 198
Friesen, P., 171
Fuji, 474, 504–505
Fulk, Janet, 291
Functionalism, pitfalls of, 47–51

Galaskiewicz, Joseph, 167, 181, 191, 312, 407–408, 513, 514
Galbraith, Jay, 291
Gandossy, Robert, 45
Garfinkel, Harold, 122, 293
Gargiulo, Martin, 92n
Gartrell, C. David, 36
Gaudet, Hazel, 60

Geertz, Clifford, 43, 243
Geertz, Hildred, 243
Geneen, Harold, 303
Genentech, 315, 320, 335, 337, 366, 370, 372
General Motors, 173, 174–175, 454, 506
Genetics Institute, 335, 370
Genex, 335
Genzyme, 335
Gereffi, Gary, 476
Gerlach, Michael L., 13, 474, 491, 493, 495, 501, 504, 507, 510, 511
Gibbs, Jack P., 410
Giddens, Anthony, 122
Gilligan, Carol, 144–145, 159
Gillmore, Mary R., 198
Gintis, Herbert, 31
Glass-Steagall Act, 498
Goffman, Erving, 255, 293, 294
Gogel, Robert, 312
Golas, Peter J., 486
Goldman Sachs, 129
Gomes-Casseres, Benjamin, 313
Goodman, L. A., 408
Goodyear, A. Conger, 124, 125, 127
Gordon, Bob, 432
Goto, Akira, 478–479
Gould, Roger, 92n
Gouldner, Alvin W., 134
Granovetter, Mark S., 13, 25, 37, 60, 72, 74, 75, 93, 96, 144, 179, 216, 217–219, 221, 224, 237–238, 240, 251, 256, 304–305, 350, 366n, 406, 407, 414, 418, 443, 481
Grant, Jim, 371–372
Grant, R. M., 106
Greenwald, P., 217
Griliches, Zvi, 388
Gronn, P. C., 293
Groppa, Richard, 296–297
Guggenheim, Solomon, 126
Guterl, Fred V., 397

Hackman, J. R., 171, 173, 175, 263, 264, 292, 297
Hafner, Katie, 298
Hahn, Frank, 36
Hallinan, Maureen T., 408, 514
Hambrecht and Quist, 320
Hamilton, Gary G., 13, 471, 475, 476, 477, 481, 486, 511
Han, Shin-Kap, 92n
Hannah, Leslie, 105
Hannan, Michael T., 123, 324
Hafsi, Taieb, 479

Harrigan, Kathyrn Rudie, 313
Harvard University, 124, 129, 134
Hauptman, O., 305
Hawley, Amos H., 316
Hawley, Ellis W., 109
Hedlund, Gunnar, 289
Heider, Fritz, 217, 218–219, 234, 235
Heil, Greg H., 410–411
Heimer, Carol A., 105, 143, 147, 156,
   159, 295
Held, Virginia, 159
Hempel, Carl, 49
Herman, Bruce G., 460
Herrigel, Gary B., 389
Heterogeneity, 401
Heydebrand, W. V., 289
Hickson, David J., 193
Hierarchy, 462
Hiltz, Roxanne S., 289
Hintze, Otto, 100–101, 109
Hirsch, Paul, 45
Hirschman, Albert, 27, 29, 38
Hirst, Paul, 456–457
Hobbes, Thomas, 27, 29, 31, 38, 39, 45
Hoffman, Alan N., 167, 170, 511, 512
Hoffman-La Roche, 337, 370
Holbeck, J., 169, 177
Holland, Paul W., 408, 514
Homans, George C., 66, 72, 408, 410
Honda, 509
Horton, Robert B., 303
Hoskisson, Robert E., 507
Howard, Ted, 317
Hsiao, Hsin-Huang Michael, 477
Hubbell, Charles H., 195
Huber, George P., 288
Hume, David, 29
Hurlbert, Jeanne S., 60, 66
Hybels, Ralph C., 311
Hyman, Richard, 449
Hyundai, 475

Iacobucci, Dawn, 407
Ibarra, Herminia, 5, 10, 165
IBM, 158, 221, 441, 477
Identity, 294–295
Immunex, 372
Imperial Chemical Industries, 104
Inco Securities Corporation, 320
Industrial Groupings in Japan, 492
Inequality, 401
Information, 61–62; access, timing,
   and referrals, 62–63; and benefit-rich
   networks, 63–65; technology, 290–
   292; and tertius gaudens, 78–79

INSNA conference (1990), 237
Institutions: as contexts, 104–108;
   social construction of economic, 47–
   51
Integrated firm (IF), 445–448
Integrated Genetics, 335
Integration: of deal makers, 415–419;
   differentiation and, 400–401; of firm,
   overall, 412–414; of headquarters,
   414–415
Interpretive aspects, 98–99
Intraorganizational networks, formal
   roles, attributes and structuration of,
   131–137
Iyer, Ananth, 397n

Jacques, E., 100
Jakobson, Roman, 441
Japan: analyzing network effects on
   firm-level outcomes in U.S. and,
   510–511; network economy of, 493–
   496; network influences on corporate
   performance in U.S. and, 508–510;
   networks, structure, and strategy in
   U.S. and, 505–508; network struc-
   ture in U.S. and, 496–505. See also
   Asia
Jelineck, M., 166, 175, 185
Jennings, P. Devereaux, 506
Jensen, Michael C., 96
Johanson, Jan, 496
Johnson, John M., 150
Johnson, N. L., 358
Jones, Eric L., 482
Jorde, Thomas M., 495
Jorgensen, Jan J., 479
Jurgens, Ulrich, 454

Kadushin, Charles, 166, 167, 172, 174,
   175, 366n
Kahneman, Daniel, 481
Kaisha Nenkan, 492
Kanter, Rosabeth Moss, 10, 15, 131,
   134, 135, 137, 147, 157, 165, 171, 174,
   176, 178, 180, 181, 521
Kantorowicz, Ernst, 488
Kao, Cheng-shu, 475
Kaplan, R. E., 178, 181, 182
Katz, Donald R., 101, 104
Katz, Elihu, 36
Keeble, David, 456
Keen, Peter G. W., 291
Keiretsu no Kenkyu, 492, 504
Keller, M., 173, 175
Kellett, J. R., 105

Kenney, Martin, 253–254, 456
Keys, B., 178, 182
Kidder, Tracy, 297
Kieretsu, Japanese, 12
Kiesler, Sara, 291, 292, 293, 295, 296, 297, 298
Kiggundu, Moses N., 479
Kim, Eun Mee, 475
Kim, Yong-Hak, 510, 515
Kincaid, D. L., 181
King, John, 288n, 298, 397n
Kinney, Martin, 317
Kirshenman, Joleen, 147
Kleinman, Sherryl, 31, 256
Kleinrock, Leonard, 93
Knoke, David, 312, 313, 510, 515
Kochen, Manfred, 93
Kodak, 320
Koebner, R., 481
Koenig, Thomas, 312
Kogut, Bruce, 12, 348
Kohler, Georges, 314, 366
Konsynski, Benn R., 291
Kotabe, Masaaki, 511
Kotter, J. P., 165, 178, 183, 262, 263, 297
Kotz, David M., 498
Kotz, S., 358
Kozul, Zeljka, 462
Krackhardt, David, 11, 118n, 129, 167, 170, 173, 175, 191, 211, 216, 218, 220, 221, 222, 236, 237, 397n, 406
Kreps, David M., 240
Kriedte, Peter, 96
Krimsky, Sheldon, 315
Kurke, L. B., 262
Kuznets, Simon, 432, 438

Lachmann, Richard, 92n
Larsen, Judith K., 252–253, 257, 316
Laumann, E. O., 4, 180, 191, 312, 397n, 510, 513, 515
Lawler, E. J., 170, 184
Lawrence, Paul, 104, 168, 400, 403, 405
Lazarsfeld, Paul, 36, 60, 235
Lazear, Edward, 40
Lazega, Emmanuel, 118n
Lazerson, Mark, 456, 459
Leff, Nathaniel, 478, 479
Legitimacy, and organizing networks, 124, 128–129
Leibenstein, Harvey, 32, 33–34
Leidner, Robin L., 147
Leifer, Eric M., 92n, 96, 110
Leinhardt, Samuel, 514

Lengel, R. H., 263, 265, 295–296
Levin, R. C., 388
Levinger, Roger L., 403
Levinthal, D., 372
Levitt, Paul R., 355
Lewis, Michael, 136
Lie, John, 92n
Lin, Nan, 60, 217
Lincoln, James R., 4, 13, 165, 167, 170, 180, 288, 491, 511, 512, 513, 514, 515, 516
Locke, John, 38, 483
London Stock Exchange, 300
Lorentz, Elizabeth, 3
Lorsch, Jay W., 168, 400, 403, 405
Lucas, Robert E., 436, 477
Luckmann, Thomas, 25, 33
Lucky-Goldstar, 475
Lyon, David, 305

Macaulay, Stewart, 155
McCaskey, M. B., 262
McClelland, David C., 79, 82
McCloskey, Donald, 48
McDonald's, 147
McKenney, James L., 262, 263, 266, 296
Macneil, Ian R., 96, 378
McPhee, W. N., 235
MacPherson, C. P., 95
McPherson, J. M., 132, 180
McPherson, Michael, 38, 40, 41
Mahajan, Vijay, 507
Malfeasance, embeddedness and its effects on, 38–47
Malone, Thomas W., 289, 291
Malsch, Thomas, 454
Mansbridge, Jane J., 143n, 159, 160
Manufacturers Hanover Trust, 297
March, James G., 104, 122, 136, 263, 266
Marglin, Stephen, 438–439, 440
Mariolis, Peter, 312
Market(s): conditions in Asia, 474–475; development of, in Asia, 484–487; development of, in the West, 480–484; imperfection theory, 478–480
Markoff, John, 298
Markus, M. Lynne, 301
Marsden, Peter V., 60, 64, 66, 122, 132, 180, 193, 194, 288, 312, 366n, 397, 398, 404–405, 408, 422, 513
Marshall, Alfred, 30, 436, 437, 455
Martin, J., 174
Martin, Walter T., 410
Marvin, Carolyn, 305

Marx, Karl, 30, 433, 439–441
Massachusetts General Hospital, 320
Massachusetts High Technology
    Council (MHTC), 255
Mass production: flexible, 434; and
    flexible specialization, combining,
    435
Masten, Scott E., 313
Matsushita Electric, 505
Mattsson, Lars-Gunnar, 496
Matza, David, 45
Mayhew, Bruce H., 403
Mechanic, David, 198
Meckling, W. H., 96
Meehan, James W., 313
Menger, Karl, 30
Merton, Robert K., 49, 76, 136
Methodological advances, 15
Metropolitan Museum of Art, 126, 129,
    134
Meyer, J. W., 122, 137, 353
Meyer, Marshall W., 398, 401, 407
Meyerson, D., 174
Miles, Raymond E., 288, 290, 397, 400,
    405, 496
Mill, John Stuart, 29, 30
Miller, D., 171
Miller, J., 180
Miller, Jon, 511, 512, 515
Miller, Roger, 257
Mills, Quinn, 289
Milo Manufacturing, 134
Milstein, Cesar, 314, 366
Mintz, Beth, 312, 495, 498, 503, 506,
    508
Mintzberg, Henry, 262, 335, 397, 399,
    400, 402, 405, 423
Missionary outreach, 106–108
MIT, 252, 253, 254, 255, 320; Enterprise
    Forum, 255
Mitchell, J. C., 166, 288
Mitnick, B. M., 105
Mitsubishi, 474, 504
Mitsui, 474, 504
Mizruchi, Mark S., 312
Molecular Genetics, 335
Monge, P. R., 166, 167
Monsanto, 320
Montgomery, Cynthia A., 507
Moody's, 492
Moore, Barrington, 481
Moore, James Ranger, 366n
Moote, A. Lloyd, 101–102, 103
Morris, C. G., 292
Moss, Philip I., 463

Mowery, David C., 371
Mrs. Fields Cookies, 300
Multidivisional firm, 446
Murnighan, J. Keith, 194, 200, 211
Murphree, Carol, 311n
Murray, Fergus, 449
Museum of Modern Art (MOMA, New
    York), 10–11, 123–130

Nabar, Santosh, 397n
Nadel, S. F., 119–123, 127
Nadler, D. A., 267
Nagel, Ernest, 49
Najemy, John M., 98
Nakatani, Iwao, 501, 507, 508, 509, 510
NASDAQ, 300
National Institutes of Health, see NIH
National Labor Relations Board
    (NLRB), 225–227
National Science Foundation, 311n
NCI (National Cancer Institute), 379
Neckerman, Kathryn M., 147
Needham, Joseph, 485
Nelson, Reed E., 7, 132, 133, 137
Nelson, Richard, 48, 366n, 371, 372,
    387, 388
Neoclassical paradigm, as institutional
    theory, 487–488
Network(s): building, 526–527; charac-
    teristics, 524–525; control in, 92–94;
    data, 522–524; economy, Japan's,
    493–496; forms of organization, 169–
    177; vs. networking, 521–522, 527;
    strategies, 178–184; structure, in
    U.S. and Japan, 496–505; structure
    and cooperation, 350–351; theory,
    430–432
Networking Institute, The (TNI), 255
Network organization, 397–399, 422–
    425, 525–526; data and methods,
    406–412; in practice, 412–422; in
    theory, 399–405
Network perspective: agenda for
    further developing, 13–16; gains
    from adopting, 8–13; studying
    organizations from, 4–8
New biotechnology firms (NBFs),
    study of history of cooperation
    among, 349–353; conclusion, 363–
    364; discussion, 361–363; negative
    binomial regression, 358;
    operationalization of network struc-
    ture, 355–358; research design, 353–
    355; results, 359–360. See also
    Biotechnology

Newcomb, J. M., 217
New Competition, 2, 12–13
Newell, A., 277
Newman, John Henry, 106
NIAID (National Institute for Arthritis and Infectious Disease), 379
NIH (National Institutes of Health), 320, 376, 379, 381, 385
Nippon Steel, 505
Nitzan, Shmuel, 40
Nohria, Nitin, 1, 11, 118n, 125, 126, 132, 143n, 240, 288, 290
Nolan, R. L., 169, 171, 174, 183, 185, 289, 300, 397, 400
Nondependent subcontracting model, 453–454
Noneconomic motives, in social thought, 26–28
North, Douglass, 28
North Carolina Biotechnology Center, The, 320
Numazaki, Ichiro, 475
Nyce, Edward H., 296–297
Nystrom, H., 181

Oakey, Ray, 316
O'Farrell, Patrick, 450
Office of Technology Assessment, 316, 318
Okun, Arthur, 37, 40, 41
Olsen, Kenneth, 253
Olson, Mancur, 46
128 Venture Group, 240–259; search and, 247–251, 257
OPM leasing fraud, 45
Opportunity, and social capital, 57–61
Organizational characteristics, and ingroup and intergroup relationships, 403–404
Organizational failure, 449–450
Organizing efforts, 10–11
Organizing networks, 123–131
Orru, Marco, 475, 476, 481
Ortho Pharmaceutical, 378
Orton, J. D., 171–172, 174, 177, 181
Oryx Press, Inc., 319, 354
Ouchi, William, 47

Padgett, John F., 92n, 105, 110
Pakes, Ariel, 40
Palmer, Donald, 496, 500, 506
Pappi, Franz U., 191, 312
Pareto, Vilfredo, 27
Parsons, Talcott, 28, 29, 38, 119, 120, 122, 143, 144, 146, 149, 152, 153, 168

Particularism: and biography and trust, 157; in career development, 155–156; disinterested, 153; legislating universalism vs., 148–154; and organizational networks, 157–158; in organizations, reasons for importance of, 154–157; in relations with customers and clients, 154–155; and responsibility and relationships, 159–160; self-interested, 153; universalism and, 143–146
Pearson, Harry, 28
Peet, W. J., 372
Peltz, D. C., 181
Pennsylvania, University of, Wharton School of, 348n
Perrow, Charles, 13, 136, 267, 445, 449, 464
Petersen, Trond, 514
Pettigrew, A., 104, 168, 170, 178, 179
Pfeffer, Jeffrey, 16, 100, 172, 193, 196, 198, 212, 213, 457, 495, 496, 502, 506, 507
Pierce, J. L., 174, 177
Piore, Michael J., 31, 240, 258, 290, 389, 430, 434, 449, 459, 496
Pisano, Gary, 370
Polanyi, Karl, 28, 482
Pollert, Anna, 449
Pollock, A. J., 169, 171, 174, 181, 183, 397, 400
Pool, I. de Sola, 218, 305
Poole, M. S., 168, 184
Porter, L., 266
Porter, Michael, 5–6
Poster, Mark, 296, 297
Powell, Marianne Broome, 366n
Powell, Walter W., 5, 12–13, 96, 105, 109, 123, 134, 165, 169, 174, 176, 180, 288, 366, 371, 378, 400, 448, 496
Power, 191–193; and influence in organizations, 9–10; measures of, 202; of others, 200, 203, 209–210; theoretical discussion of, 193–194
Prisoners' Dilemma, 42–43
Process, management as, 94–99
Prominence, 6
Propositions, to regain or enhance control, 99–101, 105–106
Pugh, D. S., 7

Quantum, 303
QWERTY typewriter keyboard, 50

Ragin, Charles, 93
Raider, Holly, 92n
Range, 6
Ranson, S., 167, 168, 184
Rapoport, A., 93
Rate of return, and structural holes, 81–82
Rawls, John, 27
Reagan, Ronald, 313
Recombinant DNA Advisory Committee (RAC), 315
Recruitment in interorganizational anarchies, 123–131
Reder, Melvin, 37
Reiss, Marvin M., 92n
Relationships, ingroup and intergroup, 401–405
Reliability, bases for determining, 125–127
Rhee, Jae Soon, 92n
Ricardo, David, 30
Rice, Faye, 303
Rice, Ronald E., 265
Richardson, R. Jack, 500, 506
Rifkin, Jeremy, 317
Robbins, Lionel, 32–33
Roberts, Edward B., 253
Roberts, K. H., 266
Roberts, Simon, 150
Robustness, 297–299
Rockefeller, Abby Aldrich, 123–124, 125
Rockefeller, John D., Jr., 123
Rockhardt, John F., 289, 291
Roehl, Thomas, 509, 510
Roethlisberger, Fritz J., 1, 3, 131, 173, 408
Rogers, David L., 312, 313
Rogers, E. M., 181, 252–253, 256, 257, 316
Romanelli, E., 185
Romo, Frank P., 133, 137
Rosen, Lawrence, 243
Rosenberg, Nathan, 371, 372
Route 128, 240, 241, 243, 244, 245, 258; social structure of, 251–256
Rowan, Brian, 122, 137, 353
Ruddick, Sara, 159
Rules: bureaucratic, 146–147, 148; making particularistic, 148–154; universalistic, 144, 145, 147, 148
Rumelt, Richard P., 507, 508

Sabel, Charles, 34, 240, 258, 290, 389, 430, 431, 432, 433, 448, 449, 454, 459, 460, 496

Sachs, Paul, 124, 129–130
Sakai, Kuniyasu, 449, 454
Salancik, Gerald, 100, 172, 193, 212, 457, 495, 496, 502, 506, 507
Sampson, S. F., 133
Samsung, 475
Samuelson, Paul, 27, 30
Sanwa, 475, 504–505
Sarason, Seymour B., 3
Saxenian, AnnaLee, 255, 456
SBANE (Small Business Association of New England), 245, 255
SBIC, 253
Schachter, Stanley, 36, 66
Schegloff, Emanuel A., 293
Schelling, Thomas C., 93
Scherer, Frederic M., 508
Schering-Plough, 320
Schlenker, B., 295
Schoenherr, Richard A., 403
Schoeps, Hans-Joachim, 106
Schonberger, Richard J., 496
Schoonhoven, C. B., 166, 175, 185
Schotter, Andrew, 48
Schrader, Charles B., 167, 170, 171, 176, 511, 512
Schumm, L. Philip, 397n, 408
Schumpeter, Joseph A., 79, 350, 352, 368
Schurmann, F., 104
Schwartz, Joseph E., 398, 401, 403, 407
Schwartz, Michael, 105, 312, 495, 498, 503, 506, 508
Scott, John, 496, 502, 503, 512, 515
Scott, W. Richard, 143n, 398, 401, 407
Sears, 101
Seashore, Stanley, 36
Securities and Exchange Commission (SEC), 43, 46, 313, 329, 507
Segal, Alan F., 106
Selznick, Philip, 130
Sen, Amartya, 14
Shan, Weijian, 348, 352
Shanley, Mark, 397n
Shapiro, Susan, 40, 43, 46
Shatin, D., 181
Shaw, Marvin E., 191
Shell Oil, 320
Shils, Edward A., 144, 146, 149, 153
Short, J., 297
Shultz, Jeffrey, 131
Shweder, Richard, 481
Similarity, vs. complementarity, 180–181
Simirenko, Alex, 104

Simmel, Georg, 39, 76, 77, 251
Simon, H. A., 122, 263, 266, 277
Skinner, William F., 486
Small-firm networks (SFNs), 454–459, 463–465; consequences of, 462–463; explaining, 459–460; production of trust in, 460–462
Smith, Adam, 27, 28, 29, 30, 46, 433, 435, 437–438, 439, 482, 483
Smith, Charles W., 96
Smith, Chris, 449
Smith-Lovin, Lynn, 132, 180
Snow, Charles C., 288, 290, 397, 400, 405, 496
Snyder, Edward A., 313
Social capital, opportunity and, 57–61
Social network, defined, 4, 164
Solomon, Jolie, 297
Solow, R., 432
Sondak, Harris, 242
Sony, 509
Soong, Roland, 93
Southern Pacific Railway Company, 484
Specialization, and centralization, 97–98
Spence, A. M., 243
Sproull, Lee, 291, 293, 295, 296, 297
Stability, vs. fluidity, 181–182
Stalk, George, 509
Stalker, G. M., 12, 168, 169, 174, 290, 397, 400, 402, 405
Standardization, 462
Stanford University, 314, 315, 320
Stephens, John D., 476
Stephenson, Karen, 195
Stern, Robert N., 175, 218, 236
Stevenson, W. B., 167
Stigler, George, 86, 244, 473, 478
Stinchcombe, Arthur L., 49, 105, 143n, 152, 155, 179
Stokman, Frans N., 496, 512
Stone, Rosanne A., 297–298
Storper, Michael, 453
Story, Ronald, 134
Strategy(ies): individual, 165–169, 177–184; network, 178–184; structure and, 168
Strauss, G., 181
Structural alignments, 165–169; defining network context for action, 171–172; in hierarchical systems, 172–175; in integrative systems, 175–177
Structural autonomy, 82–83

Structural holes, 65; and efficient-effective network, 67–72; empirical indicators of, 65–67; qualities of, 83–87; rate of return and, 81–82; and weak ties, 72–75
Structure: prescribed and emergent, 166–168; and strategy, 168
Stymne, Bengt, 449–450
Suleiman, Ezra N., 103
Sullivan, Mary, 124
Sumitomo, 474, 504
Supreme Court, U.S., 484
Suzuki, Mariko, 475
Swanson, Guy, 315
Swart, Koenraad W., 102
Swedburg, Richard, 57n
Sykes, Gresham, 45
Syme, S. Leonard, 61

Talmud, Ilan, 92n
Tandem Computers, 296
Taplin, Ian M., 456
Task characteristics, and ingroup and intergroup relationships, 402
Tazelaar, F., 60
T-Cell Sciences, 371
Technological trajectory, 432–437
Teece, David, 371, 422, 495, 507
Teitelman, Robert, 315, 317, 318, 337
Tennessee Valley Authority, 130
Terkla, David G., 463
Tertius gaudens: control and, 75–79; defined, 76
Theissen, Gerd, 107
Thoenig, J. C., 103
Thomas, Robert, 28
Thompson, Grahme, 449
Thompson, James D., 198, 405
Thorelli, H. B., 288
Tichy, N. M., 166, 167, 172, 173, 175, 176, 197, 266
Ties: different types of, and their implications, 14; networks of strong, 221–223; and *philos*, 218–220; psychology of strong, 217; strength of strong, 217–218; structural holes and weak, 72–75
Tilly, Charles, 46, 152–153
Tomkins, Calvin, 134
Torhoff, Murray, 289
Touraine, Alain, 288
Toyota Motor, 475, 493, 506
Trevino, L. K., 265, 295, 299–300
Trist, E. L., 405
Trust, embeddedness and its effects on, 38–47

Tuchman, Gaye, 277
Tuma, Nancy B., 514
Tushman, M. L., 172, 185, 197, 267, 368
Tversky, Amos, 481

Ueda, Yoshiaki, 497
Uekusa, Masu, 496, 508, 509
Uncertainty and ambiguity, negotiating, 295–296
Unionization attempt, 225–237
Universalism: and bureaucracy, 146–148; legislating, vs. particularism, 148–154; and particularism, 143–146
Useem, Michael, 26, 496, 503
Useem, P., 244

Vancil, Richard F., 101, 109
Van De Ven, A. H., 168, 184
Van Rossem, Ronan, 92n
Vaughn, John C., 60, 217

Walker, Gordon, 267, 348
Walras, Léon, 30
Walton, R. E., 171, 173, 175, 180, 263, 264, 291, 300
Ware, J. P., 169, 171, 174, 183, 185, 397, 400
War Production Board (WWI), 101
Warren, Roland L., 5
Wasserman, Stanley, 312, 397n, 407, 408, 512, 514
Watson, James D., 366
Wealth, distribution of, 463
Weber, Max, 32, 33, 79, 134, 146, 481
Webster, Murray, Jr., 126
Weick, K., 148, 171–172, 174, 177, 181, 263, 264, 265, 267, 284
Welfare functions, 462–463
Wellman, Barry, 14, 93, 170, 288, 491
West, development of markets in, 480–484
Western Electric, Hawthorne Works of, 408

Westinghouse, 314
Wever, Egbert, 456
Whetten, David A., 312
White, Harrison C., 2, 7, 8, 10, 14, 92, 96, 110, 120, 121, 127, 133, 137, 143n, 267, 277, 350, 355, 398, 407, 515, 516
Whitehead Institute, The, 320
Whitley, Richard D., 475
Whitney, Gertrude Vanderbilt, 126
Wholey, Douglas R., 366n, 405
Wiginton, J. C., 265
Wilensky, H. L., 174
Williams, E., 297
Williams, Richard A., 408
Williamson, Oliver, 28, 38, 39, 40, 100, 371, 373, 422, 437, 459, 505, 506, 513
Winter, Sidney, 48, 371
Wood, Stephen, 449
Work-flow network, 197–198
Wrong, Dennis, 28–29, 30

Xiaotong, Fei, 486

Yamagishi, Toshio, 198–200
Yancey, W., 217
Yasuda, Yuki, 92n
Yasuki, Hirohiko, 506
Yoshihara, Hideki, 506, 507, 508
Young, Alice A., 516
Young, Allyn, 436, 437
Yoxen, Edward, 315

Zack, Michael H., 262, 263
Zald, Mayer, 92n, 94–95
Zaltman, G., 169, 174, 177
Zeitlin, Jonathan, 449, 454, 456–457, 459
Zeitz, Gerald, 516
Zelen, Marvin, 195
Zhou, Xueguang, 506
Ziegler, Rolf, 496, 512
Zuboff, Shoshana, 291
Zucker, Lynne, 40, 122